Exemplary Comparison
from Homer to Petrarch

Exemplary Comparison

from Homer to Petrarch

Olive Sayce

Emeritus Fellow and Tutor of
Somerville College, Oxford

D. S. BREWER

First published 2008
D. S. Brewer, Cambridge

ISBN 978–1–84384–099–2

D. S. Brewer is an imprint of Boydell & Brewer Ltd
PO Box 9, Woodbridge, Suffolk IP12 3DF, UK
and of Boydell & Brewer Inc,
668 Mt Hope Avenue, Rochester, NY 14620, USA
website: www.boydellandbrewer.com

A CIP catalogue record for this book is available
from the British Library

This publication is printed on acid-free paper

Printed in Great Britain by
Antony Rowe Ltd, Chippenham, Wiltshire

For Michael Hawcroft

Contents

Acknowledgements   viii

The Texts   ix

Abbreviated References   x

Abbreviations of Poets' Names   xii

Introduction   1

1   Homer: The *Iliad* and the *Odyssey*   9

2   Virgil: The *Aeneid*   29

3   Latin Poets from Catullus to Ovid   38

4   Latin Poets from Antiquity to the Middle Ages   84

5   The Troubadour Poets   141

6   The Trouvère Poets   199

7   The German Poets   238

8   The Sicilian and Italian Poets   288

Conclusion   343

Bibliography   356

Glossary of Technical Terms   375

Index of Poets and Works   378

Index of Proper Names   380

General Index   408

Acknowledgements

In preparing this book I have incurred many debts, first and foremost to Michael Hawcroft, who read and commented on the drafts of all the chapters as they took shape. I dedicate the book to him as a sign of my gratitude for his long-standing friendship and generous scholarship. My next most considerable personal and scholarly debt is to John Waś for his expertise and willing help in so many areas, from the interpretation and translation of classical Greek and Latin and medieval Latin texts, to technical problems of layout and typesetting.

I have benefited greatly from the specialist knowledge and help of other colleagues, in particular, Tony Hunt, Peter Hainsworth, Valerio Lucchesi, and Russell Goulbourne. I am particularly indebted to the resources of the Taylorian and Bodleian libraries and their librarians past and present. My family and many friends, among them in particular Robin Jacoby, have continued to encourage and support me throughout. To them all I express my heartfelt thanks. The scholarly example of my husband, Richard Sayce, remained a constant inspiration.

Finally, I wish to acknowledge the award of a grant from a fund set up in Somerville College by a legacy under the will of Rose Graham (1875–1963), a distinguished medieval historian, 'to assist the publication of contributions to learning by members of the College'. For this I am doubly indebted – not only to the college, but also to the generous and enlightened intentions of the donor.

Oxford, November 2007   OLIVE SAYCE

The Texts

Since the classical and post-classical texts in chapters 1–4 are mainly intended as background to illustrate general developments in the use of exemplary comparisons, the original classical texts in chapters 1–3 are taken from editions in the Loeb Classical Library (Harvard University Press). In the post-classical texts in chapter 4, the Loeb editions of Statius, *Silvae*, the *Minor Latin Poets* and [Cicero], *Rhetorica ad Herennium* are likewise cited, but in most cases an abbreviated reference is given at the head of each text to the standard individual or collected edition. In the vernacular poets, the first line of the poem from which the extract is taken (or an abbreviated form of it), an indication of the type of poem, an abbreviated reference to the standard bibliography in the case of troubadour and trouvère poems, and an abbreviated reference to the edition used, is placed at the head of the entry. For abbreviations of individual and collected editions, see the relevant section of the Bibliography. The Index of Poets and Works gives page references to all textual examples cited.

The translations

Even where the texts are taken from editions with facing translations, these are always omitted. All the translations are my own.

Numbering

Exemplary comparisons are numbered in bold. In order to avoid confusion between poem and stanza numbering, arabic numbers are normally used for poems, and roman numerals for stanzas, or sections in a *leich* (even if this differs from the numbering of the edition adopted). The only exceptions are Marner **1–3**, in which the edition of Strauch/Brackert uses roman numerals to group together all stanzas in the same form, either in a polystrophic poem (as in **1**), or in longer series of didactic stanzas (as in **2** and **3**), and arabic numerals for individual stanzas. Here, exceptionally, the roman numerals are retained for the series, but in order to avoid confusion between stanza and line numbering, roman numerals are used for stanzas, as elsewhere.

Other graphic conventions

Textual omissions in the main verse texts and their translation are indicated by [. . .].

Passages in speech are enclosed in double quotation marks in both text and translation.

Abbreviated References

Aen.	Virgil, *Aeneid*
Am.	Ovid, *Amores*
Append. Tibull.	*Appendix Tibulliana*
Archiv	*Archiv für das Studium der neueren Sprachen und Literaturen*
Ars Am.	Ovid, *Ars Amatoria*
ATB	Altdeutsche Textbibliothek
Carm. Cant.	*Carmina Cantabrigiensia*
CB	*Carmina Burana*
CFMA	Classiques Français du Moyen Age
D	preceding numbering of troubadour poems, see Distilo, *Per le concordanze*, p. 360
DVjs	*Deutsche Vierteljahresschrift für Literaturwissenschaft und Geistesgeschichte*
Epist.	Horace, *Epistles*
Epod.	Horace, *Epodes*
Ex Ponto	Ovid, *Ex Ponto*
GAG	Göppinger Arbeiten zur Germanistik
Her.	Ovid, *Heroides*
Il.	Homer, *Iliad*
KLD	see Kraus, *Liederdichter*, p. 370
L.	refers to Lachmann's numbering of the poems of Walther von der Vogelweide
'Laus Pis.'	'Laus Pisonis'
Loeb	Loeb Classical Library
Mar. Am.	*Il Mare Amoroso*
Mem. Bol.	*Memoriali Bolognesi*
Met.	Ovid, *Metamorphoses*
MF	*Des Minnesangs Frühling*
MGH AA	*Monumenta Germaniae Historica, Auctores Antiquissimi*
MGH Poetae	*Monumenta Germaniae Historica, Poetae latini medii Aevi*
MGH Scriptores	*Monumenta Germaniae Historica, Scriptores rerum Germanicarum in usum scholarum separatim editi*
MHG	Middle High German
MJ	*Mittellateinisches Jahrbuch*
MLP	*Minor Latin Poets*
MLat.	Medieval Latin
MS J	see *Die Jenaer Handschrift*, ed. Holz/Saran/Bernouilli
MTU	Münchener Texte und Untersuchungen zur deutschen Literatur des Mittelalters
OBMLatV	*Oxford Book of Medieval Latin Verse*

Oc.	Occitan, from the designation *langue d'oc*
Od.	Homer, *Odyssey*
Odes	Horace, *Odes*
OF	Old French
OP	Old Provençal
PC	preceding numbering of troubadour poems, see Pillet/Carstens, *Bibliographie*, p. 360
PLM	*Poetae latini minores*
Pr. *Trist.*	Prose *Tristan*
Purg.	Dante, *Purgatorio*
R	preceding the numbering of OF poems, see Raynaud, *Bibliographie*; Spanke, *Raynauds Bibliographie*; Linker, *Bibliography*, pp. 364 f.
Rem. Am.	Ovid, *Remedia Amoris*
RLR	*Revue des Langues Romanes*
Sat.	Horace, *Satires*
SATF	Société des Anciens Textes Français
Silv.	Statius, *Silvae*
SM	*Studi Medievali*
SM[1]	*Die Schweizer Minnesänger*, ed. Bartsch
SM[2]	*Die Schweizer Minnesänger*, ed. Schiendorfer
TLF	Textes Littéraires Français
Trist.	Ovid, *Tristia*
VL[2]	*Verfasserlexikon*[2]
ZfdP	*Zeitschrift für deutsche Philologie*
ZRP	*Zeitschrift für romanische Philologie*

Abbreviations of Poets' Names

Ad. Halle	Adam de la Halle
Aim. Bel.	Aimeric de Belenoi
Aim. Peg.	Aimeric de Peguilhan
Alb. Mass.	Alberto di Massa di Maremma
Alexander	Der wilde Alexander
'Amico'	'Amico di Dante'
Andr. Contr.	Andrieu Contredit d'Arras
Arn. Dan.	Arnaut Daniel
Arn. Mar.	Arnaut de Mareuil
Azalais	Azalais d'Altier
Baudri	Baudri de Bourgueil
Benzo	Benzo of Alba
Bernger	Bernger von Horheim
Bern. Vent.	Bernart de Ventadorn
Bertr. Born	Bertran de Born
Binduccio	Binduccio da Firenze
Blondel	Blondel de Nesle
Botenlouben	Otto von Botenlouben
Calvo	Bonifacio Calvo
Catull.	Catullus
Cerverí	Cerverí de Girona
Chiaro	Chiaro Davanzati
Chrétien	Chrétien de Troyes
Cino	Cino da Pistoia
Claud.	Claudian
Comte Bret.	Le Comte de Bretagne
Comt. Dia	La Comtessa de Dia
Couci	Le Chastelain de Couci
D. Maiano	Dante da Maiano
Daude Prad.	Daude de Pradas
Donzella	La Compiuta Donzella
Duch. Lorr.	La Duchesse de Lorraine
Einh.	Einhard
El. Barj.	Elias de Barjols
El. Cair.	Elias Cairel
Ermold.	Ermoldus Nigellus
Eustache	Eustache le Peintre
Falq. Rom.	Falquet de Romans
Fil. Mess.	Filippo da Messina

Folq. Mars.	Folquet de Marseille
Gace	Gace Brulé
Gar. Apch.	Garin d'Apchier
Gauc. Faid.	Gaucelm Faidit
Gaut. Darg.	Gautier de Dargies
G. Vins.	Geoffroi de Vinsauf
Giac. Lent.	Giacomo da Lentini
Giac. Pugl.	Giacomino Pugliese
Gille Vin.	Gille le Vinier
Giov. Arezzo	Giovanni d'Arezzo
Girald.	Giraldus Cambrensis
Gliers	Der von Gliers
Gottsch.	Gottschalk
Guido Col.	Guido delle Colonne
Guil. Ad.	Guilhem Adémar
Guil. A. Novella	Guillem Augier Novella
Guil. Berg.	Guillem de Berguedà
Guil. Ferr.	Guillaume de Ferrières
Guil. Magr.	Guillem Magret
Guil. R. Giron.	Guilhem Raimon de Gironela
Guil. Tor	Guilhem de la Tor
Guiot	Guiot de Provins
Guir. Born.	Guiraut de Bornelh
Guir. Cal.	Guiraut de Calanso
Guir. Ros	Guiraudo lo Ros
Guir. Sal.	Guiraut de Salinhac
Guittone	Guittone d'Arezzo
Gutenburg	Ulrich von Gutenburg
Hausen	Friedrich von Hausen
Hil.	Hilarius of Orléans
Hild.	Hildebert of Le Mans
Hor.	Horace
J. Mostacci	Jacopo Mostacci
J. Neuv.	Jean de Neuville
Jord. Bon.	Jordan Bonel
Lapo	Lapo Gianni
Liechtenstein	Ulrich von Liechtenstein
M. Torr.	Maestro Torrigiano di Firenze
Marc.	Marcabru
M. Vend.	Matthieu de Vendôme
Moniot	Moniot d'Arras
Morungen	Heinrich von Morungen
Ov.	Ovid
Paul. Diac.	Paulus Diaconus
Paul. Mars.	Paulet de Marselha

Peire Alv.	Peire d'Alvernha
Peire Card.	Peire Cardenal
P. R. Tolosa	Peire Raimon de Tolosa
Peire Vid.	Peire Vidal
Perr. Ang.	Perrin d'Angicourt
Petr. Gramm.	Petrus Grammaticus
Pier Vign.	Pier della Vigna
Pons Capd.	Pons de Capduelh
Primas	Hugh Primas
Prisc.	Priscian
Prop.	Propertius
Raim. Jord.	Raimon Jordan
Raim. Mir.	Raimon de Miraval
Raimb. Or.	Raimbaut d'Orange
Raimb. Vaq.	Raimbaut de Vaqueiras
R. Filippi	Rustico Filippi
R. Soiss.	Raoul de Soissons
Re Giov.	Re Giovanni
Rich. Fourn.	Richard de Fournival
Rig. Berb.	Rigaut de Berbezilh
Rin. Aq.	Rinaldo d'Aquino
Sed.	Sedulius Scottus
Serlo	Serlo of Wilton
Sid.	Sidonius Apollinaris
Stat.	Statius
T. Faenza	Tomaso da Faenza
Theod.	Theodulf of Orléans
Thib. Bl.	Thibaut de Blaison
Thib. Ch.	Thibaut de Champagne
Tibull.	Tibullus
Uc Bac.	Uc de la Bacalaria
Uc Pena	Uc de Pena
Veldeke	Heinrich von Veldeke
Venant.	Venantius Fortunatus
Verg.	Virgil (the abbreviation is derived from Vergilius, the correct Latin form of the name)
Wil. Corb.	Wilart de Corbie
Wolfram	Wolfram von Eschenbach
Zorzi	Bartolomeo Zorzi
Zweter	Reinmar von Zweter

Introduction

The book is an attempt to examine the significance, function, and placing of comparisons and identifications with an exemplary figure, primarily in the main branches of the Western European vernacular lyric up to the end of the fourteenth century, i.e. the troubadour lyric of Southern France (including also Catalan and Italian poets who write in the *langue d'oc*), the trouvère lyric of Northern France, the German lyric, and the Sicilian and Italian lyric. These branches are all interrelated, in that the trouvère lyric, the German lyric, and the Sicilian and Italian lyric are all to a greater or lesser extent influenced either directly or indirectly by the troubadour lyric. Thus among the first attested exemplary comparisons in the medieval German lyric are those which are directly based on Romance models, suggesting that this was an unfamiliar stylistic feature in the indigenous lyric and one borrowed, along with much else, from Romance poets.

In order to set exemplary comparisons and identifications in the medieval vernacular lyric in context, it is necessary firstly and more generally to consider their antecedents in the classical tradition of simile, as it was initially established in the works of Homer and at first mediated indirectly to the West through Virgil and other Latin authors. The tradition continues not only in narrative poetry, but also in all types of classical and post-classical Latin verse. Due allowance must of course be made for differences between narrative and other poetic genres as the context in which the examples are set, but none the less, reference to the general tradition is instructive as background to a closer study of exemplary comparisons and identifications in the medieval vernacular lyric.

The arrangement of the material, and of poets and poems within chapters, is largely in chronological order, in so far as this can be ascertained,[1] but in order to keep the two epic poets together, chapter 1 treats Homer (7th century BC?) and chapter 2 Virgil (70–19 BC), even though Virgil is of later date than some of the poets in the following chapter. There follow in chapter 3 Latin poets from Catullus (c. 84–c. 54 BC) to Ovid (43 BC–AD 17?), and in chapter 4 Latin poets from Antiquity to the Middle Ages, including named and identifiable poets from Statius (c. AD 45–96) to Giraldus Cambrensis (c. 1146–1220). The Romance and German material is arranged in the order of the first

---

[1] Much of the dating is uncertain, particularly in the case of anonymously transmitted items; see also actual or putative dating given in individual chapters.

attestations of the vernacular lyric in each language. This shows clearly the chronological primacy of the troubadour lyric, which influenced all the other branches in turn, and explains why the Sicilian and Italian lyric does not follow immediately after the troubadour and trouvère lyric in the sequence. Thus chapter 5 treats the troubadour lyric from Marcabru (fl. c. 1130–1148) to poets of the last decades of the 13th century; chapter 6 the trouvère lyric from Chrétien de Troyes (fl. c. 1160–c. 1185?) to poets of the last decades of the 13th century; chapter 7 the German poets from Friedrich von Hausen (attested 1171–1190) to Frauenlob (d. 1318), and chapter 8 the Sicilian and Italian poets, from c. 1230–1250 to Petrarch (1304–1374).

An exemplary comparison is an explicit comparison or contrast with a specific named or otherwise clearly identifiable figure from myth, the Bible, history and historical legend, or literary tradition, which serves as an exemplar against which another figure and its emotions, actions, or appearance is measured.[2] The main subject of the comparison may be either the poet himself, speaking in the first person, or a figure referred to indirectly in the third person, or, less frequently, one addressed in the second person in apostrophe. There are examples of this latter type in Homer, Propertius, Horace, Ovid, and the medieval Latin poets. In the vernacular love lyric in Oc., OF, and German they are very rare, because the main emphasis is on the poet's protestations that his love equals or outdoes that of famous exemplars, i.e. the comparison refers to the first-person speaker. In the Sicilian and Italian lyric, in which the theme of the lady's beauty and perfection becomes more prominent, there is a corresponding increase in comparison in apostrophe. In addition it is necessary to take into account those instances in which a comparison or contrast is implied without the use of explicit linguistic markers, and merely conveyed implicitly by means of textual juxtaposition. On occasion the comparison may be expressed in hypothetical terms. Related to comparison proper is exemplary parallel, in which an exemplary character or story is introduced to furnish a textual parallel.

Closely related to exemplary comparison are those instances in which the degree of similarity to an exemplar is such that it is expressed as identity, as when the author of CB 61 addresses his beloved as *Blanziflŏr et Helena, Venus generosa*. From a solely technical and grammatical point of view, identification with an exemplar and transfer of name represents a sub-category of the rhetorical figure of *antonomasia*, literally 'naming with a new name',[3] but the-

---

[2] Not usually included are those instances in which a generalized category of mankind, e.g. 'the man who', or the representative of a specific type, e.g. 'a bad debtor' in reference to Love, serves as exemplar – but see Folquet de Marseille 1.39 f. n.

[3] *Antonomasia* includes the use of a common name in place of a proper name or vice versa; the substitution of an epithet for a proper name; the substitution of a descriptive phrase for a proper name (this is closely related to the figure of periphrasis).

matically it is of major importance, in that it fulfils functions closely similar to those of exemplary comparison, primarily the expression of praise or blame. Identifications with an exemplar are therefore treated as a distinct category, which must be considered in conjunction with exemplary comparisons.

A particular type of identification attested in the religious lyric, which is semantically quite distinct from that described above,[4] is that deriving from typology, which interprets events and persons of the Old Testament as types and prefigurations of those of the New. Thus Christ may be interpreted as the second Adam, the Virgin as a second Eve. See for instance Der Marner **3**, in which Mary is apostrophized as the throne of Solomon, Judith, Esther, Jael, and Abigail. In such instances, the second manifestation of the type surpasses and outshines the first, which merely prefigures and foreshadows it, i.e. this differs fundamentally from the transfer of the name of an exemplary figure, and with it of the qualities attaching to it, to a new subject, which is the type of identification found in the secular lyric.

Exemplary comparisons are primarily expressed by means of the stylistic figure of simile, which appears to be an archetypal feature of world literature, found from the earliest times in narrative, dramatic, didactic, biblical and lyric texts alike. Simile is based on the perception and expression of similarity between two apparently dissimilar items and no doubt reposes on the analogical working of the human mind, seeking to establish relationships between disparate phenomena. Simile makes the perceived connection explicit by means of linguistic markers expressing similarity, such as 'like', 'as', and those indicating a comparison of degree, such as 'equal to', 'greater than', 'lesser than'. Identification is closely related to simile, and may be expressed by the use of the verb 'to be' or other syntactical means in order to posit identity between two subjects. The linguistic markers cited above represent only a small sample of the wide range of lexical, morphological and syntactical features which may be employed to express explicit comparison, contrast, or identity. Simile in general has many functions. It may serve as embellishment, elaboration or enhancement of the theme. The re-use of well-known similes, exemplary or other, also establishes links with the mainstream of literary tradition and thereby affirms both the continuing validity of that tradition and its power to confer authority on a later work. This can be seen very clearly in the re-working of Homeric similes in Virgil, and of Homeric and Virgilian similes in poets such as Dante and Milton.

In the course of the period surveyed, there are considerable developments in the presentation of comparisons and identifications, and in the range of exemplary figures cited. In the *Iliad*, all the comparisons, apart from that

---

[4] Formally, however, it may be expressed by the same grammatical markers as identification proper.

with an attribute of the Gorgon/Medusa, are with divine figures or their attributes, and most refer to a male subject. In the *Odyssey*, most of the comparisons refer to a female subject and are once more with deities, but there are additional figures of legend: the daughter of Pandareos (Aëdon), the daughter of Tyndareus (Clytemnestra), and the Centaur Eurytion. In the *Iliad*, ten of the comparisons occur in the narrative and two in speech; in the *Odyssey* there are six comparisons in the narrative and four in speech. In the *Iliad*, exemplary similes may be linked with others of non-exemplary type to form a sequence. There are no instances of identification with an exemplar in either the *Iliad* or the *Odyssey*. There is one implied comparison in the *Odyssey*, but none in the *Iliad*. In the *Aeneid*, there are seven non-divine exemplary figures, and one implied comparison. There are four examples of identification, all in speech: these examples and the hypothetical comparison by Turnus of himself with Achilles, also in speech (expressing for the first time the motif of outdoing the exemplar, albeit in hypothetical form) present the subjective viewpoint of the speaker, as opposed to that of the narrator.

The evidence in Catullus suggests that in classical Latin verse genres other than epic, exemplary comparisons were established from an early date. Explicit comparisons with divine figures are now very rare, but there are comparisons with divine attributes, and there is a further increase in non-divine exemplars, including a few from history or historical legend. There are many allusions to narrative details associated with the exemplars and to characters and stories which furnish parallels to them. Comparisons and identifications are associated with themes of love, lament, praise and imprecation, and poetic boasts. There is a wide variety of voice and person, including first-person presentation, and there are examples of speech in dialogue in Horace and Ovid. The motif of outdoing the exemplar is attested in Horace, Propertius and Ovid, but comparisons of likeness remain the dominant type.

The later and medieval Latin poets represent a much broader chronological and geographical span than the classical poets, and there is a correspondingly wider range of types of poem and themes, including panegyric, epithalamium, epitaph and funeral lament, confession and prayer, and particularly in the Ripoll and *Carmina Burana* collections, love and the praise of beauty. There is in consequence a much more extensive repertoire of exemplars, with the addition of figures from the Bible, the Church, history and historical legend, and the authorial canon. Some poets refer exclusively to figures of classical literature and legend, a feature which persists in much of later love poetry, but combinations of figures from different spheres is common. There are a few comparisons or identifications with divinities, and comparisons with divine attributes still persist. Particularly in panegyric, the combination of attributes of different exemplars is frequent. As in the classical poets, comparison may be textually linked with implied comparisons with exemplary figures in specific narrative episodes. There is considerable syntactical and stylistic variety in the presentation of examples, and there are instances of the combination of comparison and identification. The incidence of rhyme in later examples reinforces the emphasis on names placed in final position. There is a continuing increase in the motif of surpassing the exemplar.

In the troubadour lyric, the majority of exemplary comparisons are associated with the theme of the poet's love for a perfect lady, and a first-person authorial stance therefore predominates. Exemplars may be drawn from classical literature and legend, mostly via medieval adaptations, and with a restriction to better known figures, the Bible, history, and historical legend, but there is a new group of figures derived from the *chanson de geste*, Arthurian and other romances, the Tristan legend and other medieval stories, and combinations of figures from different spheres are frequent. There are no comparisons with deities. Exemplary comparisons are also found in conjunction with the didactic motif of Love's illustrious victims such as Solomon, and with themes of lament, panegyric, and chivalric and crusading exploits. Identifications are rare. Most examples occur in the *canso*, but there are instances also in a range of other structural types, including *descort*, *salut*, *tenso*, *partimen*, *sirventes*, and *planh*. There are a few brief references to narrative motifs or episodes associated with the exemplar. Exceptions to first-person presentation in the *canso* are rare, and there is frequent apostrophe, particularly in address to the lady; third-person formulations tend to occur in objective genres such as *sirventes* and *planh*. There is very little direct speech, except in the fictive dialogues of *tenso* and *partimen*. For the first time, there are more comparisons expressing superiority, rather than likeness, to the exemplar.

The trouvère lyric coincides in most of the above respects with the troubadour lyric, which was its model: most comparisons are presented from a first-person authorial standpoint and there are similar combinations of voice and person, but apostrophe is less frequent. However, overall there is a considerable degree of simplification and restriction. Although two trouvère poets are added to the repertoire of exemplary lovers, a narrower range of exemplars is cited, with a further concentration on better known names; there are fewer instances of comparisons in poems other than the *chançon*; there is an almost exclusive association with the theme of love; there is less variety of stylistic and syntactical presentation; in many later examples it seems as if exemplary comparisons are viewed merely as a convenient device for providing a rhyme. There is a further increase in the motif of outdoing the exemplar.

In the German lyric, there is a double tradition, that of polystrophic love poetry, decisively influenced by Romance traditions, and that of didactic poetry, in which the basic unit is predominantly a weightier single stanza

within a series in the same metrical form. Exemplary comparisons and identifications occur in both types, in the love lyric chiefly in the isostrophic *Minnelied*, the equivalent of the Romance *canso*, and in the heterostrophic *leich*,
the equivalent of Romance *descort*. The instances in the didactic lyric occur
in association with themes of panegyric, exhortation, censure, and warning,
and also with the theme of love, either with or without specific reference to
the poet himself: some of the latter type are more like general *exempla*. Some
features are more akin to the medieval Latin than to the Romance lyric: the
higher number of identifications, of comparisons with attributes of the exemplar, and of detailed reference to narrative situations. Unusually, there are
a few comparisons with goddesses. The exemplary figures are drawn from the
same main areas as in the Romance lyric, with the addition of a few German
authorial names. The prestige of Romance literature is such that there are
very few figures from indigenous traditions. The form of some of the names
ultimately derived from Romance sources indicates that they are taken from
German adaptations of French material. In the love poetry, a first-person authorial stance predominates, with varying combinations of voice and person,
as in the Romance lyric, but in the didactic lyric there is a higher proportion
of third-person presentation. There are a roughly equal number of explicit
comparisons of likeness and of superiority, but if implied comparisons are
included, there are slightly more of the former type, which runs counter to
developments in the Romance lyric.

The use of exemplary comparisons in the Sicilian and Italian lyric was
probably at first derived indirectly from knowledge of the troubadour lyric,
which was its model. There is, however, a restriction to the better known
figures, and there are very few exemplars from the *chanson de geste* or the
original Arthurian romances, but several from later continuations and adaptations. In the main, there is a restriction to the theme of love, and praise of
the lady's beauty, previously relatively rare, becomes more common; a few
examples relate to the theme of poetic skill. There are several instances of
comparison with attributes of the exemplar. There are few narrative allusions.
Petrarch differs from all the other poets, in that he refers only to classical and a
few historical figures, and disregards medieval exemplars altogether; he is also
unique in his distinctive adaptation of the stylistic figure of identification and
in the grammatical means he uses to express it. In other poets, identification
is rare. Examples of comparison occur mainly in the *sonetto*, an adaptation
of the *canzone* strophe, in the *canzone* itself, and in a few instances in the
heterostrophic *discordo*. As in the troubadour lyric, a first-person authorial
stance predominates, with varying combinations of voice and person, and
frequent apostrophe of the lady. Comparisons expressing superiority to the
exemplar predominate, as in the troubadour and trouvère lyric.

The placing of exemplary comparisons and identifications is usually significant. In Homer and Virgil, placing of the exemplary comparisons is determined by the demands of the narrative: they serve to enhance the status of the main characters, to focus attention on a stage in the action or a character newly introduced, or to emphasize a key theme, such as the constancy of Penelope in the *Odyssey*, or the love-induced frenzy of Dido in the *Aeneid*. In the poets from Catullus to Ovid, examples may be placed at or near the beginning, or less often at or near the end, of a poem or book. In the post-classical Latin poets, there appear to be fewer examples of deliberate placing in longer poems, but it is common in shorter poems. Initial placing is rare, but there are several examples of central or near-central, and of final or near-final placing.

In the vernacular lyric in Romance and German, comparisons may be placed to coincide with the main structural divisions of stanza and poem. They may form the main focus of a stanza in *canso*, *chançon*, *canzone*, or *Lied*, or of a section in *descort*, *discordo* or *leich*, or of a *tornada* or *envoi*; they may be placed at the beginning, centre, or end of stanza or section, in octave or sestet in the *sonetto*, or at the beginning or end of the poem. There are some differences between the individual branches of the lyric in respect of such placing: in the troubadour and Sicilian and Italian lyric, there is a tendency towards final placing in both structural unit and poem; in the trouvère lyric there are fewer instances in which a comparison forms the main focus of a stanza or unit, and the tendency towards final placing in the stanza is less marked; in the German lyric, central placing is rare. In all the poets, including the epic poets, names of exemplars may be placed in a prominent position at the beginning or the end of lines, or both, and in the later examples predominantly in rhyme. In the troubadour, German, and Sicilian and Italian (but not the trouvère) lyric, there are instances of rhyme between names; in the troubadour lyric, names may be placed in isolated rhyme, rhyming only from stanza to stanza, thus singling them out further; in the Sicilian and Italian lyric, grammatical and punning rhyme with names is common.

In all the poets, exemplary figures may be designated by proper name, but in the classical and post-classical poets there is considerable variety of alternative types of naming.[5] The following main types occur: patronymics, e.g. *Alcides* (Hercules); alternative names, e.g. *Liber* (Bacchus); topographical adjectives, e.g. *Gnosia* 'the Cretan' (Ariadne); common nouns for proper names, e.g. *matrem* (Clytemnestra), in grammatical association with the name *Orestes*; periphrasis indicating patrilineal or matrilineal descent; periphrasis alluding to actions or events associated with the exemplary figure, which makes its identity clear. There may also be combinations of different types, e.g. proper name, alternative name, or common noun + patronymic or topographical adjective. In addition, in the classical epic, proper names or alterna-

---

[5] See n. 3 above on the rhetorical device of *antonomasia*.

tive names may be reinforced by descriptive adjectives, e.g. *sanguineus Mavors* in Virgil. By contrast in the vernacular poets, there is a very restricted range of alternative designations. There are a few examples of the following types: alternative names, e.g. *il Sole* and *Phebo* beside *Apollo* in Petrarch; periphrasis, in which the context or association with another name makes the reference clear, e.g. *sel qe pres Tir* (Alexander); *la bell' a cui servi Tristans* (Iseut); common nouns for proper nouns, e.g. *ein kint* (Narcissus). It is noteworthy that of all the vernacular poets, Petrarch has the highest number of alternative designations; this is partly to be explained by the strong element of classical influence in his work, but also by his unique identification of Laura with Daphne, in which examples of periphrasis or periphrastic allusion permit the possibility of reference to either or both figures.

1

Homer: The *Iliad* and the *Odyssey*

Similes of all kinds may be used in Homer to embellish the narrative and lend weight to the characters, to emphasize a particular stage in the action or a key theme, and to introduce an element of comment and interpretation which permits events and characters to be viewed from a different angle. The fact that the dominant part of complex similes, that which contains the actual comparison (the *comparatio*), is usually expressed verbally by the timeless present or aorist, in contrast to the subject of the comparison, i.e. that to which the comparison is applied (the *comparandum*), which as part of the narrative is associated with the historic past, lends a generalizing and universal perspective to the work. There is a considerable difference between the *Iliad* and the *Odyssey*, both in the incidence of similes in general, and also in the nature and structure of exemplary comparisons in particular, which is in part explained by the different subject-matter of the two works.[1]

The *Iliad*

Similes are one of the great glories of the *Iliad*. They are very numerous, frequently extended, and at high points in the action may appear in contiguous clusters. They are varied alike in content and linguistic expression, drawing on a wide range of elemental and natural phenomena and of human activities and experience. They frequently contain dramatic images of the sea, storm, and fire, or of predators attacking their prey. They are dynamic, rather than merely descriptive, conveying visual and acoustic phenomena, and actions and processes. The abundance of similes adds a futher dimension to the narrative: they depict as background to the work a universe with all the specificity of the real world; they create a pause in the descriptions of the horrors of warfare and form a contrast to them – that this is one of their functions is suggested by the relative paucity of similes in the *Odyssey*. The dynamic nature of most of the similes in the *Iliad* no doubt explains why there are very few exemplary comparisons among them and why most of the latter are very brief, since the

---

[1] Homer's dates are unknown. The works attributed to him can perhaps be assigned, with great uncertainty, to the seventh century BC. In each work only the exemplary comparisons proper are numbered, either singly, if they are distinct, or in groups, if the same phrase is repeated.

comparison of one figure with another tends to be predominantly descriptive and static in nature.

There are two main types of personal comparison in the *Iliad*: firstly those which liken the characters to an unspecified god or to the gods in general, and secondly comparisons with one named god in particular, and in one case (VIII. 349 – see *Il.* 2) with a non-divine mythological figure. Only those of the latter type are exemplary comparisons proper, but they are closely related to the former type, being merely a more precise rendering of the general comparisons with divine beings, made specific by the addition of a proper name.

The personal comparisons, general and exemplary, are cast in adjectival, adverbial, verbal, and participial constructions. The general comparisons occur in conjunction with forms of the substantive θεός 'god', or the feminine form θεά, or of the substantivized adjective ἀθάνατος 'immortal'. The constructions may contain the adjectives ἀτάλαντος, 'equal to', ἐναλίγκιος 'like', ἐπιείκελος 'like', ἴσος 'equal to', the adverb ὥς 'as', or forms of the defective verb ἔοικα 'resemble'. They express likeness to the gods in general, for example: I. 265 "Θησέα τ' Αἰγεΐδην, ἐπιείκελον ἀθανάτοισιν" ("and Theseus, son of Aegeus, like the immortals"); III. 230 "'Ιδομενεὺς δ' ἑτέρωθεν ἐνὶ Κρήτεσσι θεὸς ὥς | ἔστηκ'" ("and Idomeneus stands opposite among the Cretans, like a god"); XXIV. 486 "μνῆσαι πατρὸς σοῖο, θεοῖς ἐπιείκελ' Ἀχιλλεῦ, | τηλίκου ὥς περ ἐγών, ὀλοῷ ἐπὶ γήραος οὐδῷ" ("remember your father, Achilles like unto the gods, of age equal to mine, on the grievous threshold of old age"). Sometimes the comparison is made more specific by reference to a particular divine attribute: XVII. 477 "Πάτροκλος, θεόφιν μήστωρ ἀτάλαντος" ("Patroclus, equal to the gods as counsellor"); XIX. 250 Ταλθύβιος δὲ θεῷ ἐναλίγκιος αὐδήν (and Talthybius, like a god in voice); XXIV. 629 ἦ τοι Δαρδανίδης Πρίαμος θαύμαζ' Ἀχιλῆα, | ὅσσος ἔην οἷός τε· θεοῖσι γὰρ ἄντα ἐῴκει (then indeed Priam the son of Dardanus marvelled at Achilles, how tall he was and of what nature, for he was like the gods to look upon). There are four instances in which female figures are compared to goddesses: the most significant example is that referring to Helen. As she approaches the Trojan elders sitting on the walls of Troy, they marvel at her beauty: III. 156 "οὐ νέμεσις Τρῶας καὶ ἐϋκνήμιδας Ἀχαιοὺς | τοιῇδ' ἀμφὶ γυναικὶ πολὺν χρόνον ἄλγεα πάσχειν· | αἰνῶς ἀθανάτῃσι θεῇς εἰς ὦπα ἔοικεν" ("it is no cause for just anger that the Trojans and well-greaved Achaeans should for such a woman long suffer ills; she is marvellously like the immortal goddesses to look upon"). There are three shorter descriptions: VIII. 305 καλὴ Καστιάνειρα δέμας ἐϊκυῖα θεῇσι (beautiful Castianeira, in form resembling the goddesses); XI. 638 and XIX. 286 (of Hecamede and Briseis respectively) γυνὴ ἐϊκυῖα θεῇσιν (a woman resembling the goddesses).

As in the *Odyssey*, there are also many epithets, usually of compound formation, expressing general likeness to the divine, such as ἀντίθεος 'godlike', θεοείκελος 'godlike', θεοειδής 'of divine form', θεῖος 'divine', ἰσόθεος 'equal to the gods', for example: I. 264 *"ἀντίθεον Πολύφημον"* ("godlike Polyphemus") – see also *Od.* 9; I. 131 *"θεοείκελ' Ἀχιλλεῦ"* ("godlike Achilles"); II. 623 Πολύξεινος θεοειδής (Polyxeinos of divine form); II. 335 Ὀδυσσῆος θείοιο (of divine Odysseus); II. 565 Εὐρύαλος . . . ἰσόθεος φώς (Euryalus . . . a man equal to the gods). The adjective δῖος appears largely to have lost its original etymological sense of 'divine' and is used extremely widely, not solely of persons, as a general laudatory epithet in the sense of 'pre-eminent', 'supreme', 'excellent', and has therefore not been included in the above group. In addition, there are semantically related compound adjectives, not, however, themselves comparative in nature, which reinforce the idea of the proximity of the heroes to the gods: ἀρηΐφιλος 'dear to Ares', διογενής 'sprung from Zeus', διΐφιλος 'dear to Zeus', for example: III. 52 *"ἀρηΐφιλον Μενέλαον"* ("Menelaus dear to Ares"); IV. 489 Αἴας διογενής (Aias sprung from Zeus); VIII. 493 Ἕκτωρ . . . διΐφιλος (Hector . . . dear to Zeus).

Exemplary comparisons

The exemplary comparisons proper, with the exception of *Il.* **4**, are very brief, unlike most of the other similes in the work (in *Il.* **1** the exemplary comparison is contained only in the last two and a half lines of the passage). They refer predominantly to the male figures, who are most often likened to Ares, also referred to by the epithet Ἐννάλιος, 'the warlike', derived from the name Ἐννώ, the goddess of war.

Iliad **1**

> τοὺς δ᾽, ὥς τ᾽ αἰπόλια πλατέ᾽ αἰγῶν αἰπόλοι ἄνδρες   II. 474
> ῥεῖα διακρίνωσιν, ἐπεί κε νομῷ μιγέωσιν,
> ὣς τοὺς ἡγεμόνες διεκόσμεον ἔνθα καὶ ἔνθα
> ὑσμίνηνδ᾽ ἰέναι, μετὰ δὲ κρείων Ἀγαμέμνων,
> ὄμματα καὶ κεφαλὴν ἴκελος Διὶ τερπικεραύνῳ,
> Ἄρεϊ δὲ ζώνην, στέρνον δὲ Ποσειδάωνι.   479

[And just as goatherds easily separate the widely scattered flocks of goats, when they mingle in the pasture, so their leaders marshalled them on this side and that to enter into the battle, and among them lord Agamemnon, his eyes and head like Zeus who delights in thunder, his waist like Ares, and his breast like Poseidon.]

This passage describes the marshalling of the Achaean hosts. The exemplary comparison at the end is syntactically linked to the preceding simile and forms part of a sequence of similes.

Iliad 2

"Έκτωρ δ' ἀμφιπεριστρώφα καλλίτριχας ἵππους,   VIII. 348
Γοργοῦς ὄμματ' ἔχων ἠδὲ βροτολοιγοῦ Ἄρηος.

[Hector turned his fair-maned horses this way and that, possessing the eyes of the Gorgon or man-destroying Ares.]

The slaying of Euphorbus by Menelaus:

Iliad 3

αἵματί οἱ δεύοντο κόμαι Χαρίτεσσιν ὁμοῖαι   XVII. 51
πλοχμοί θ', οἳ χρυσῷ τε καὶ ἀργύρῳ ἐσφήκωντο.

[With blood his hair was drenched, hair like that of the Graces, and his locks that were braided with gold and silver.]

The exemplary comparison is immediately followed by two similes relating to Euphorbus.

Iliad 4

ὣς ἄρ' ἔφαν, Αἴας δὲ κορύσσετο νώροπι χαλκῷ·   VII. 206
αὐτὰρ ἐπεὶ δὴ πάντα περὶ χροῒ ἕσσατο τεύχεα,
σεύατ' ἔπειθ' οἷός τε πελώριος ἔρχεται Ἄρης,
ὅς τ' εἶσιν πόλεμόνδε μετ' ἀνέρας, οὕς τε Κρονίων
θυμοβόρου ἔριδος μένεϊ ξυνέηκε μάχεσθαι.   210
τοῖος ἄρ' Αἴας ὦρτο πελώριος, ἕρκος Ἀχαιῶν.
μειδιόων βλοσυροῖσι προσώπασι.

[Thus, then, they spoke and Aias armed himself in gleaming bronze, but when he had clothed his body in all his armour, he then sped in the same manner as huge Ares goes forth when he enters into battle among men whom the son of Cronos [Zeus] has brought together to fight in the fury of soul-devouring strife. In like manner huge Aias sprang forth, the bulwark of the Achaeans, with a smile on his grim face.]

Iliad 5

μαίνετο δ' ὡς ὅτ' Ἄρης ἐγχέσπαλος ἢ ὀλοὸν πῦρ   XV. 605
οὔρεσι μαίνηται, βαθέης ἐν τάρφεσιν ὕλης.

[And he [Hector] raged as when Ares, wielder of the spear [rages], or as when destructive fire rages among the mountains in the thickets of a deep wood.]

Iliad 6

6a   τῶν αὖθ' ἡγεμόνευε Μέγης ἀτάλαντος Ἄρηϊ.   II. 627
[And their leader was Meges, equal to Ares.]

Cf. the same phrase describing Meges in XV. 302.

6b   ἔνθα Πυλαιμένεα ἑλέτην ἀτάλαντον Ἄρηϊ.   V. 576
[Then they slew Pylaemenes, equal to Ares.]

6c   Αἰνείας τε καὶ Ἰδομενεύς, ἀτάλαντοι Ἄρηϊ.   XIII. 500
[Aeneas and Idomeneus, equal to Ares.]

Iliad 7

Μηριόνης τ᾽ ἀτάλαντος Ἐνυαλίῳ ἀνδρειφόντῃ.   II. 651
[Meriones, equal to Enyalius, slayer of men.]

Cf. also the identical description of Meriones in VII. 166, VIII. 264, XVII. 259.

Iliad 8

Πάτροκλος δὲ Τρωσὶ κακὰ φρονέων ἐνόρουσε.   XVI. 783
τρὶς μὲν ἔπειτ᾽ ἐπόρουσε θοῷ ἀτάλαντος Ἄρηϊ,
σμερδαλέα ἰάχων, τρὶς δ᾽ ἐννέα φῶτας ἔπεφνεν.
[Patroclus fell upon the Trojans with evil intent; three times he then fell upon them, equal to swift Ares, shouting a terrible cry, and three times he slew nine men.]

In VIII. 215 and XVII. 72 the phrase θοῷ ἀτάλαντος Ἄρηϊ 'equal to swift Ares', as in 784, is used of Hector, in XIII. 295, 328, 528 of Meriones, in XVII. 536 of Automedon.

Iliad 9

ὣς ὥρμαινε μένων, ὁ δέ οἱ σχεδὸν ἦλθεν Ἀχιλλεὺς   XXII. 131
ἶσος Ἐνυαλίῳ, κορυθάϊκι πτολεμιστῇ.
[So he [Hector] pondered as he stood his ground, and near to him came Achilles, equal to Enyalius, the helmet-shaking warrior.]

The greatest heroes are likened to Zeus in their gift of counsel:

Iliad 10

10a   ""Ἕκτορ, υἱὲ Πριάμοιο, Διὶ μῆτιν ἀτάλαντε,   VII. 47
ἦ ῥά νύ μοί τι πίθοιο; κασίγνητος δέ τοί εἰμι."
["Hector, son of Priam, equal to Zeus in counsel, will you now be persuaded by me? For I am your brother."]

10b   τῶν μὲν Ὀδυσσεὺς ἦρχε Διὶ μῆτιν ἀτάλαντος.   II. 636
[Odysseus was their leader, equal to Zeus in counsel.]

Cf. the same phrase referring to Odysseus in II. 169, 407 and X. 137.

There are only three exemplary comparisons whose subject is a female figure. Achilles scornfully rejects the offer of Agamemnon's daughter in marriage:

Iliad 11

> "κούρην δ' οὐ γαμέω Ἀγαμέμνονος Ἀτρεΐδαο,   IX. 388
> οὐδ' εἰ χρυσείῃ Ἀφροδίτῃ κάλλος ἐρίζοι,
> ἔργα δ' Ἀθηναίῃ γλαυκώπιδι ἰσοφαρίζοι·
> οὐδέ μιν ὣς γαμέω."

["And the daughter of Agamemnon, son of Atreus I will not marry, even though she were to vie in beauty with golden Aphrodite, and were in handiwork to equal flashing-eyed Athena; not even so will I marry her."]

Iliad 12

12a   Βρισηῒς . . . ἰκέλη χρυσέῃ Ἀφροδίτῃ.   XIX. 282

[Briseis . . . like golden Aphrodite.]

This is followed in XIX. 286 by the general comparison of Briseis with goddesses.

12b   Κασσάνδρη, ἰκέλη χρυσέῃ Ἀφροδίτῃ.   XXIV. 699

[Cassandra, like golden Aphrodite.]

The 'Iliad': conclusion

All the comparisons cited in *Il.* 1–12 are explicit similes proper, expressing likeness to, or equality with, the exemplar, and there are no identifications. Of the general comparisons with the divine cited as examples, several occur in speech: the speaker in I. 265 is Nestor, in III. 230 Helen, and in XVII. 477 Automedon; in III. 156 ff. the Trojan leaders are addressing each other. In some instances, as in XXIV. 486 (in which Priam is the speaker), the comparison with the divine is a formula of eulogistic and persuasive address. The placing in speech may permit the characters and the action to be viewed from a different perspective, as for instance when the elders of Troy judge that Helen's divine beauty is such that it represents a valid justification for the war. In the comparisons with a particular divine or mythological figure, on the other hand, most instances occur in the narrative, with the exception of the short passage in the speech of Helenus (*Il.* **10a**), and the speech of Achilles (*Il.* **11**). *Il.* **10a** is the only example in which direct address in the second person occurs in conjunction with the comparison itself. The relative infrequency of comparisons in speech perhaps suggests that similes of whatever kind, exemplary and other, were felt to be predominantly a narrative device.

 Il. 1–3 compare attributes of the heroes with those of divine or fabled exemplars, Zeus, Ares, and Poseidon in *Il.* **1** (thus stressing the supreme heroic status of Agamemnon), Ares and the Gorgon/Medusa in *Il.* **2**, the Graces in *Il.* **3**. This type of comparison of specific attributes becomes common later, usually, however, in positive descriptions of beauty, as in *Il.* **3**. In *Il.* **4–10** it is the heroes themselves, and in *Il.* **11** and **12** the female figures, who are compared to a divine exemplar: in *Il.* **4, 5, 6a–c,** and **8** to Ares, in *Il.* **7** and **9** to Ares under his other name of Enyalius; in *Il.* **10a** Hector, and in **10b** Odysseus is compared to Zeus in counsel; in *Il.* **11** there is a hypothetical comparison to Aphrodite and Athena; in *Il.* **12a** Briseis, and in **12b** Cassandra is compared to Aphrodite. Apart from the instances in which the epithet Enyalius 'the warlike' replaces the name of Ares, the figures, exemplary and other, are designated by proper name, with the addition of a phrase indicating patrilineal descent to the name in *Il.* **10a** and *Il.* **11.** Zeus is referred to solely by patronymic in *Il.* **4;** the daughter of Agamemnon is anonymous in *Il.* **11.** The name of an exemplary figure is frequently reinforced by the addition of a descriptive epithet, e.g. 'man-destroying Ares' *Il.* **2,** 'golden Aphrodite' *Il.* **11, 12a, 12b;** less frequently a descriptive phrase occurs, e.g. 'huge Aias, the bulwark of the Achaeans' *Il.* **4.** The proper names themselves are frequently placed in prominent position, at the beginning, or more often at the end of verse lines. At the beginning of the line: *Il.* 2. 348; *Il.* 7. 651; *Il.* 8. 783; *Il.* **10a.** 47; at the end of the line: *Il.* 1. 477, 479; *Il.* 2. 349; *Il.* 4. 208; *Il.* **6a, 6b, 6c;** *Il.* 8. 784; *Il.* 9. 131; names at both the beginning and the end of the line: *Il.* **12a** and **12b.**

The syntactical structure of most of the exemplary comparisons proper is very simple and uniform, the main exceptions being *Il.* **4, 5** and **11.** The basic type consists of a phrase made up of an adjective expressing likeness, in conjunction with a dependent substantival phrase in the dative case. Of this type are *Il.* **3, 6a, 6b, 6c, 7, 8, 9, 12a** and **12b.** In *Il.* **1** and **10** this basic type is supplemented by the addition of accusatives of respect which particularize the description, in **1** ὄμματα καὶ κεφαλὴν . . . ζώνην . . . στέρνον, in **10a** and **10b** μῆτιν. In *Il.* **2** the idea of comparison is expressed by the participle ἔχων 'having', in conjunction with a direct object linked to a genitive; this is a structural type found in other similes in the *Iliad*, which are, however, not exemplary in nature, e.g. XVI. 751 f. and XXI. 251 f. (see also ἔχε in *Od.* 1). In *Il.* **11** the comparison is expressed in a hypothetical conditional clause with the optative forms ἐρίζοι and ἰσοφαρίζοι, which express a potentially active sense. All the examples, with the exception of *Il.* **4, 5** and **11,** can therefore be said to consist of descriptive phrases, which are static in nature. In *Il.* **4, 5** and **11** on the other hand, the verbal element lends the comparison an active sense, and this is reflected in *Il.* **4** and **5** in the structure.

Il. **4** has the structural pattern of most of the extended similes in the *Iliad*, which consist of two syntactically and semantically corresponding halves, introduced by paired words, here the pronoun οἷος and the demonstrative τοῖος respectively. The reason for this choice of structure and its relatively greater length is no doubt the fact that this example is more akin to the dominant pattern of similes in the *Iliad*, in that it expresses action and movement (see p. 9). The repetition of the proper name Αἴας and of the adjective πελώριος in each half of the simile, and the morphological and semantic parallelism between the verb forms σεύατ’ and ὦρτο is a characteristic feature of this type of simile in the rest of the work. *Il.* **5** is somewhat similar, but on a much-reduced scale: it has two paired syntactical units, the second introduced by the adverb + conjunction ὡς ὅτ’, and the paired verbs μαίνετο and μαίνηται. As in *Il.* **4**, this bipartite structure, making it more akin to the dominant type of simile, is no doubt suggested by the active nature of the comparison itself, perhaps also by the introduction of the second comparative element ἢ ὀλοὸν πῦρ, which is of a lexical type frequently found in other active similes in the *Iliad* – see for instance II. 455, in one of the similes preceding the exemplary comparison in *Il.* **1**: ἠύτε πῦρ ἀΐδηλον ἐπιφλέγει ἄσπετον ὕλην (as consuming fire sets alight a boundless forest). Overall, however, the syntactical structures of the exemplary comparisons, apart from that in *Il.* **4**, are in no way complex, unlike those of most other similes in the work.

In three instances the exemplary comparisons occur in close proximity to other similes. In *Il.* **5**, the exemplary comparison with Ares is syntactically linked to the image of the consuming fire. *Il.* **1** is set within a sequence of similes which serve to emphasize an important turning-point in the action, the marshalling of the Achaean hosts. The series begins at II. 455 and is concluded at II. 483; II. 455–8: as consuming fire sets alight a boundless forest on mountain peaks and the glare is seen from afar, so the dazzling gleam of their armour ascended to heaven as they marched forth; II. 459–68: as countless flocks of birds fly with loud cries over the Asian meadow, so as they marched forth, the earth resounded beneath the tread of men and horses; they were as numberless as leaves and flowers in their season; II. 469–73: as swarms of flies buzz round the milk-pails in the farmstead in spring, even so numberless were the Achaeans, eager to rend the Trojans asunder; II. 474 to the first half of 477: as goatherds easily separate their flocks, so the leaders marshalled the hosts; there follows in the last half of 477 and 478 f. the exemplary comparison of the attributes of Agamemnon with those of Zeus, Ares and Poseidon, which is syntactically linked to the preceding simile; II. 480–3: even as a bull stands out among the herd, so Zeus made Agamemnon pre-eminent among the warriors. The exemplary comparison in *Il.* **1** is thus enclosed within two similes, and syntactically linked to the first of them; it forms part of a larger sequence of similes devoted to the praise of the Achaeans and of Agamemnon. *Il.* **3** refers to the slaying of Euphorbus by Menelaus. It is immediately followed by two similes: XVII. 53–60: as a flourishing sapling is uprooted in a storm, so Menelaus slew Euphorbus and stripped him of his armour; XVII. 61–9: as a mountain lion seizes a heifer from the herd and the fearful herdsmen are powerless to attack him, so none of the Trojans dared confront Menelaus.

The *Odyssey*

In the *Odyssey* there are overall fewer similes than in the *Iliad*, and among them only a relatively small number of exemplary comparisons. These are, however, more complex and varied in structure than those in the *Iliad*. There are, as in the *Iliad*, a considerable number of shorter syntactical constructions expressing likeness. Among these are many formulations which compare the chief protagonists in a general non-specific way with gods, as in the description of Telemachus (II. 5): βῆ δ᾽ ἴμεν ἐκ θαλάμοιο θεῷ ἐναλίγκιος ἄντην (he went forth from his chamber like a god to look upon). There are also, as in the *Iliad*, many epithets, usually of compound structure, which in themselves indicate likeness to the gods, such as ἀντίθεος 'godlike', θεοειδής 'of divine form', θεοείκελος 'godlike', θεῖος 'divine', ἰσόθεος 'equal to the gods'.[2]

Of the six instances[3] of positive exemplary comparisons in the work relating to female figures, four are relatively brief and only two are more elaborate. There is one negative example cited as a contrast to Penelope. The subjects of the positive comparisons are Hermione, Helen, Nausicaa, and Penelope. In five of the six instances a comparison is made with a named goddess, and in the other, Penelope compares herself to an unnamed figure of myth who is, however, clearly identifiable from the name of her father and the details of her story.

Hermione, the daughter of Helen, is compared to Aphrodite:

Odyssey 1

> Ἑλένῃ δὲ θεοὶ γόνον οὐκέτ᾽ ἔφαινον,   IV. 12
> ἐπεὶ δὴ τὸ πρῶτον ἐγείνατο παῖδ᾽ ἐρατεινήν,
> Ἑρμιόνην, ἣ εἶδος ἔχε χρυσέης Ἀφροδίτης.

[For the gods did not grant Helen further offspring, after she had first borne her beautiful child Hermione, who had the form of golden Aphrodite.]

Helen herself is likened to Artemis:

Odyssey 2

> ἐκ δ᾽ Ἑλένη θαλάμοιο θυώδεος ὑψορόφοιο   IV. 121
> ἤλυθεν Ἀρτέμιδι χρυσηλακάτῳ εἰκυῖα.

[Helen came out of her fragrant, high-roofed chamber, resembling Artemis of the golden arrows.]

---

[2] The f. form of ἀντίθεος occurs in speech in XI. 117 and XIII. 378 referring to Penelope. For δῖος, see under *Il.* above. See also διογενής 'born of Zeus', applied to Odysseus, usually in a formula of address, e.g. XVIII. 312; XXII. 164; XXIV. 542.

[3] XVII. 36 f. and XIX. 53 f. have an identical formulation in the phrase describing Penelope and have therefore been counted as one instance.

After Odysseus has been shipwrecked on the island ruled over by Alcinous, the theme of the divine beauty of the king's daughter Nausicaa is first introduced in a general way:

> βῆ δ' ἴμεν ἐς θάλαμον πολυδαίδαλον, ᾧ ἔνι κούρη   VI. 15
> κοιμᾶτ' ἀθανάτῃσι φυὴν καὶ εἶδος ὁμοίη,
> Ναυσικάα, θυγάτηρ μεγαλήτορος Ἀλκινόοιο.

> [She [Athena] went to a richly fashioned chamber in which slept a maiden like the immortal goddesses in form and appearance, Nausicaa, the daughter of great-hearted Alcinous.]

This paves the way for the two exemplary comparisons proper relating to Nausicaa, the first in the narrative, the second in speech:

Odyssey 3

> οἵη δ' Ἄρτεμις εἶσι κατ' οὔρεα ἰοχέαιρα,   VI. 102
> ἢ κατὰ Τηΰγετον περιμήκετον ἢ Ἐρύμανθον,
> τερπομένη κάπροισι καὶ ὠκείῃς ἐλάφοισι·
> τῇ δέ θ' ἅμα νύμφαι, κοῦραι Διὸς αἰγιόχοιο,   105
> ἀγρονόμοι παίζουσι, γέγηθε δέ τε φρένα Λητώ·
> πασάων δ' ὑπὲρ ἥ γε κάρη ἔχει ἠδὲ μέτωπα,
> ῥεῖά τ' ἀριγνώτη πέλεται, καλαὶ δέ τε πᾶσαι·
> ὣς ἥ γ' ἀμφιπόλοισι μετέπρεπε παρθένος ἀδμής.

> [As Artemis, delighting in arrows, roves over the mountains, along lofty Taygetus or Erymanthus, rejoicing in the pursuit of boars and swift deer, and with her the wood-nymphs, the daughters of Zeus who bears the aegis, sport, and Leto is glad at heart – high above them all she holds her head and brow and may easily be known, though all are fair – so she among her handmaidens was pre-eminent, the unmarried girl.]

See Verg. **1**.

When Odysseus then encounters Nausicaa with her handmaidens on the shore, he addresses her, comparing her to a goddess:

Odyssey 4

> "γουνοῦμαί σε, ἄνασσα· θεός νύ τις, ἦ βροτός ἐσσι;   VI. 149
> εἰ μέν τις θεός ἐσσι, τοὶ οὐρανὸν εὐρὺν ἔχουσιν,
> Ἀρτέμιδί σε ἐγώ γε, Διὸς κούρῃ μεγάλοιο,
> εἶδός τε μέγεθός τε φυήν τ' ἄγχιστα ἐίσκω."

> ["I beseech you, O queen, are you a goddess or are you mortal? If you are a goddess, one of those who hold broad heaven, to Artemis, the daughter of great Zeus, I liken you most nearly in beauty, stature, and form."]

As Nausicaa stands in her father's palace, watching and marvelling at Odysseus, she is described as possessing beauty given by the gods (VIII. 457

Ναυσικάα δὲ θεῶν ἄπο κάλλος ἔχουσα); she bids him farewell, exhorting him to remember her on his return home because he owes his life to her, to which Odysseus replies that for that reason he will always pray to her as to a god:

> "τῷ κέν τοι καὶ κεῖθι θεῷ ὣς εὐχετοώμην   VIII. 467
> αἰεὶ ἤματα πάντα· σὺ γάρ μ' ἐβιώσαο, κούρη."

["Then I will always pray to you there as to a god all my days, for you, maiden, have given me life."]

Of the positive exemplary comparisons attaching to Penelope, one occurs in the narrative at XVII. 36 f. and is repeated at XIX. 53 f., the other in speech:

Odyssey 5

> ἡ δ' ἴεν ἐκ θαλάμοιο περίφρων Πηνελόπεια,   XVII. 36
> Ἀρτέμιδι ἰκέλη ἠὲ χρυσέῃ Ἀφροδίτῃ.

[Then from her chamber came wise Penelope, like Artemis or golden Aphrodite.]

In book XIX, in a speech to the apparent stranger, who is really Odysseus in disguise, Penelope begins with a reference to the approach of night, a time of rest for others, but for her one of continuing sorrow. The comparison proper begins at line 518, when she likens herself to the daughter of Pandareos (Aëdon), who having mistakenly killed her own son Itylus, was turned into a nightingale, constantly grieving. So she too is prey to conflicting emotions, uncertain whether she should go with one of the wooers, or stay, remaining faithful to her absent husband:

Odyssey 6

> "αὐτὰρ ἐμοὶ καὶ πένθος ἀμέτρητον πόρε δαίμων·   XIX. 512
> ἤματα μὲν γὰρ τέρπομ' ὀδυρομένη, γοόωσα,
> ἔς τ' ἐμὰ ἔργ' ὁρόωσα καὶ ἀμφιπόλων ἐνὶ οἴκῳ·
> αὐτὰρ ἐπὴν νὺξ ἔλθῃ, ἕλῃσί τε κοῖτος ἅπαντας,   515
> κεῖμαι ἐνὶ λέκτρῳ, πυκιναὶ δέ μοι ἀμφ' ἀδινὸν κῆρ
> ὀξεῖαι μελεδῶνες ὀδυρομένην ἐρέθουσιν.
> ὡς δ' ὅτε Πανδαρέου κούρη, χλωρηῒς ἀηδών
> καλὸν ἀείδῃσιν ἔαρος νέον ἱσταμένοιο,
> δενδρέων ἐν πετάλοισι καθεζομένη πυκινοῖσιν,   520
> ἥ τε θαμὰ τρωπῶσα χέει πολυηχέα φωνήν,
> παῖδ' ὀλοφυρομένη Ἴτυλον φίλον, ὅν ποτε χαλκῷ
> κτεῖνε δι' ἀφραδίας, κοῦρον Ζήθοιο ἄνακτος,
> ὣς καὶ ἐμοὶ δίχα θυμὸς ὀρώρεται ἔνθα καὶ ἔνθα,
> ἠὲ μένω παρὰ παιδὶ καὶ ἔμπεδα πάντα φυλάσσω,   525
> κτῆσιν ἐμήν, δμῷάς τε καὶ ὑψερεφὲς μέγα δῶμα,
> εὐνήν τ' αἰδομένη πόσιος δήμοιό τε φῆμιν,

ἢ ἤδη ἅμ' ἕπωμαι Ἀχαιῶν ὅς τις ἄριστος
μνᾶται ἐνὶ μεγάροισι, πορὼν ἀπερείσια ἕδνα."

["But to me a god has given immeasurable grief, for by day I find joy in mourning and lamenting, while attending to my household tasks and those of the women in the house, but when night comes and sleep lays hold of all, I lie on my bed and sharp cares, crowding close about my throbbing heart, afflict me as I mourn. As when the daughter of Pandareos, the olive-green nightingale, sings sweetly when spring has newly come, perched among the thick foliage, and with frequent trilling notes pours out her melodious voice, lamenting for her child, dear Itylus, the son of king Zethus, whom once she had unwittingly slain with the sword: even so my heart is torn this way and that in uncertainty, whether I should remain with my child and guard everything securely, my possessions, my slaves, and the great high-roofed house, respecting the bed of my husband and the voice of the people, or whether I should now follow whoever is the best of the Achaeans who woos me in the hall, offering bridal gifts past counting."]

In this instance a comparison with a goddess would not be appropriate, since Penelope is referring to herself. The name of the mythological figure is omitted, because it is clear from the context and coincides with the designation of the nightingale (ἀηδών). There is a related simile, not, however of the same exemplary nature, in Penelope's prayer to Artemis in XX. 61 ff. She wishes that she might die and be borne to the underworld, as were the two orphan daughters of Pandareos, carried off by the Harpies to Hades:[4]

"Ἄρτεμι, πότνα θεά, θύγατερ Διός, αἴθε μοι ἤδη   XX. 61
ἰὸν ἐνὶ στήθεσσι βαλοῦσ' ἐκ θυμὸν ἕλοιο
αὐτίκα νῦν, ἢ ἔπειτα μ' ἀναρπάξασα θύελλα
οἴχοιτο προφέρουσα κατ' ἠερόεντα κέλευθα,
ἐν προχοῇς δὲ βάλοι ἀψορρόου Ὠκεανοῖο,   65
ὡς δ' ὅτε Πανδαρέου κούρας ἀνέλοντο θύελλαι."

["Artemis, revered goddess, daughter of Zeus, O that now, fixing an arrow in my breast, you might straightway take away my life, or that a storm wind, catching me up, might bear me away over the dark ways and cast me up at the mouth of backward-flowing Oceanus, as when storm winds took up the daughters of Pandareos."]

This is followed in lines 67–78 by an account of the daughters' fate, and in line 79 by a resumption of the prayer:

---

[4] The orphan daughters are elsewhere named as Cleothera and Merope. It is not certain whether XIX. 518 and XX. 66 refer to the same figure of Pandareos, or to two different figures, the identity of name having prompted the inclusion of the story, but the significant factor is the tragic fate of all the daughters, as a parallel to that of Penelope herself.

"ὣς ἔμ᾽ ἀϊστώσειαν Ὀλύμπια δώματ᾽ ἔχοντες,   79
ἠέ μ᾽ ἐϋπλόκαμος βάλοι Ἄρτεμις, ὄφρ᾽ Ὀδυσῆα
ὀσσομένη καὶ γαῖαν ὕπο στυγερὴν ἀφικοίμην,
μηδέ τι χείρονος ἀνδρὸς ἐϋφραίνοιμι νόημα."

["Even so might those who have dwellings on Olympus blot me from sight, or fair-tressed Artemis strike me, so that with Odysseus before my eyes I might pass beneath the hateful earth and never at all gladden the heart of a lesser man."]

This example, although cast in part in the form of a simile, interrupted by a narrative digression within the speech, is an instance rather of an exemplary mythological story, of a kind found elsewhere in both the *Odyssey* and the *Iliad* and frequent in the Latin poets.

There is one example of a negative exemplary comparison used to throw into relief the unblemished reputation of Penelope. This occurs after the wooers have been killed and their spirits led by Hermes to the underworld, where the shade of Agamemnon questions them, seeking to know the reason for their presence. In his reply Amphimedon recounts the events of their wooing of Penelope, her constant resistance, and the final outcome, thus summing up in brief the whole of the story as it relates to Penelope. This prompts Agamemnon, in a speech at first addressed in an admiring exclamation to the absent Odysseus (an instance of apostrophe), but then continuing in the third person, to praise the faithfulness of Penelope, which will live on in song, explicitly contrasting it with the evil deeds of Clytemnestra:

Odyssey 7

"ὄλβιε Λαέρταο πάϊ, πολυμήχαν᾽ Ὀδυσσεῦ,   XXIV. 192
ἦ ἄρα σὺν μεγάλῃ ἀρετῇ ἐκτήσω ἄκοιτιν.
ὡς ἀγαθαὶ φρένες ἦσαν ἀμύμονι Πηνελοπείῃ,
κούρῃ Ἰκαρίου· ὡς εὖ μέμνητ᾽ Ὀδυσῆος,   195
ἀνδρὸς κουριδίου· τῷ οἱ κλέος οὔ ποτ᾽ ὀλεῖται
ἧς ἀρετῆς, τεύξουσι δ᾽ ἐπιχθονίοισιν ἀοιδὴν
ἀθάνατοι χαρίεσσαν ἐχέφρονι Πηνελοπείῃ,
οὐχ ὡς Τυνδαρέου κούρη κακὰ μήσατο ἔργα,
κουρίδιον κτείνασα πόσιν, στυγερὴ δέ τ᾽ ἀοιδὴ   200
ἔσσετ᾽ ἐπ᾽ ἀνθρώπους, χαλεπὴν δέ τε φῆμιν ὀπάσσει
θηλυτέρῃσι γυναιξί, καὶ ἥ κ᾽ εὐεργὸς ἔῃσιν."

["Happy son of Laertes, Odysseus of many devices, truly you won a wife full of great excellence. Such good understanding had blameless Penelope, daughter of Icarius; so mindful she was of Odysseus, her wedded husband. Therefore the fame of her virtue will never perish, and the immortals will make among those on earth a pleasing song of wise Penelope. Not in this manner did the daughter of Tyndareus (Clytemnestra) devise evil deeds, slaying her wedded husband; and she will be a hateful song among men and she will bring grievous repute upon all the female sex, even the woman who acts rightly."]

Although general comparisons of the male protagonists with gods are extremely common, there appear to be only two brief examples of a comparison of a male figure with a named god and one mythological comparison. In the description of the contests of strength on the island ruled over by Alcinous, Euryalos is compared to Ares:

Odyssey 8

ἂν δὲ καὶ Εὐρύαλος, βροτολοιγῷ ἶσος Ἄρηϊ.   VIII. 115

[... and also Euryalus, equal to man-destroying Ares.]

When the minstrel sings of the exploits of Odysseus at Troy, he describes him in a similar phrase:

Odyssey 9

ἄλλον δ᾽ ἄλλη ἄειδε πόλιν κεραϊζέμεν αἰπήν,   VIII. 516
αὐτὰρ ᾽Οδυσσῆα προτὶ δώματα Δηϊφόβοιο
βήμεναι, ἠΰτ᾽ Ἄρηα σὺν ἀντιθέῳ Μενελάῳ.

[Of the others he sang how in different ways they laid waste the lofty city, but of Odysseus how he went like Ares to the house of Deiphobus, together with godlike Menelaus.]

There is one instance of an exemplary comparison of Odysseus with a figure of myth which is of a negative kind and which is rendered in part implicitly. When Odysseus returns to his home in the disguise of a beggar and offers to try to string the bow in the test which is to decide the fate of the wooers, he is harshly rebuked by Antinous, who accuses him of being foolishly emboldened by wine. It was wine which caused the downfall of the Centaur Eurytion. This part of the comparison between Odysseus and the Centaur is implied solely by lexical, semantic, and syntactic juxtaposition and is not explicitly expressed by means of linking words:

Odyssey 10

"οἶνός σε τρώει μελιηδής, ὅς τε καὶ ἄλλους   XXI. 293
βλάπτει, ὃς ἄν μιν χανδὸν ἕλῃ μηδ᾽ αἴσιμα πίνῃ.
οἶνος καὶ Κένταυρον, ἀγακλυτὸν Εὐρυτίωνα,
ἄασ᾽ ἐνὶ μεγάρῳ μεγαθύμου Πειριθόοιο,
ἐς Λαπίθας ἐλθόνθ᾽."

["It is honey-sweet wine which overpowers you, wine that impairs the sense of others too, if anyone snatches it up greedily and drinks without moderation. Wine led astray even the Centaur, renowned Eurytion, in the hall of great-hearted Pirithous, when he went to the Lapiths."]

The lexical, semantic, and syntactic parallelism between οἶνός σε τρώει μελιηδής and οἶνος καὶ Κένταυρον . . . ἄασ' implies a derogatory comparison between Odysseus and the Centaur.

There follows in ll. 297–304 of the speech an account of the battle of the Lapiths and Centaurs and the maiming of Eurytion, at the end of which Antinous returns to the theme of wine-induced folly and makes an explicit link with the fate awaiting Odysseus if he persists:

> "ὣς καὶ σοὶ μέγα πῆμα πιφαύσκομαι, αἴ κε τὸ τόξον   XXI. 305
> ἐντανύσῃς· οὐ γάρ τευ ἐπητύος ἀντιβολήσεις
> ἡμετέρῳ ἐνὶ δήμῳ, ἄφαρ δέ σε νηΐ μελαίνῃ
> εἰς Ἔχετον βασιλῆα, βροτῶν δηλήμονα πάντων,
> πέμψομεν· ἔνθεν δ' οὔ τι σαώσεαι· ἀλλὰ ἔκηλος
> πῖνέ τε, μηδ' ἐρίδαινε μετ' ἀνδράσι κουροτέροισιν."   310

[“Likewise I declare great misery for you if you string the bow, for you will meet with no kindness among our people, but we will send you straightway in a black ship to king Echetus, the destroyer of all men, from whom you will not escape with your life; come then, drink in peace and do not vie with younger men.”]

There is here a double comparison: the first part is on the one hand complete in itself, and is on the other linked both to the narrative account and to the second comparison. The second part is more closely linked to the preceding section of narrative, since it is this which recounts the downfall of the Centaur, thus permitting the introduction of the fate awaiting Odysseus. The comparisons, implicit and explicit, serve here as an ironic commentary on the action, since the hearer or reader is aware that it is Antinous himself who will perish and Odysseus who will exact vengeance upon him.

The 'Odyssey': conclusion

As in the *Iliad*, the exemplary comparisons in the *Odyssey* are similes proper, and there are no identifications. Of the ten exemplary comparisons, six occur in the narrative (*Od.* 1, 2, 3, 5, 8, 9) and four in speech (*Od.* 4, 6, 7, 10). Of those in speech, *Od.* 4 combines the first person with direct address in the second person; *Od.* 6 contains first-person forms; *Od.* 10 includes second-person address. The examples in speech are rendered more immediate and graphic, particularly where the present tense occurs, as in *Od.* 4. In six of the examples (*Od.* 1, 2, 4, 5, 8, 9) the actual comparison is contained in static descriptive phrases; only in *Od.* 3, 6, 7 and 10 is there a greater active element. Most of the comparisons are with divine beings: Artemis (*Od.* 2, 3, 4, 5), Aphrodite (*Od.* 1, 5), Ares (*Od.* 8, 9). In *Od.* 1, as in *Il.* 1, 2 and 3, the comparison is not with the figure itself, but with one of its attributes; *Od.* 4 is similar to *Il.* 10a and b in that comparison with a divine figure is particularized with reference to specific attributes. Three comparisons are with figures of legend: Eurytion (*Od.* 10), the daughter of Pandareos (*Od.* 6), the daughter of Tyndareus (*Od.* 7) – apart from these two examples, designation of the figures is by proper name. As in the *Iliad*, proper names may occur in conjunction with an indication of descent (e.g. *Od*. **4**. 151) or with a descriptive epithet (e.g *Od*. **3**. 102). As in the *Iliad*, the proper names may be placed in prominent position: at the beginning of the line in *Od*. **1**. 12; *Od*. **4**. 151; at the end in *Od*. **5**. 36, 37; *Od*. **7**. 192, 194, 195, 198; *Od*. **8**. 115; *Od*. **9**. 518, 519; *Od*. **10**. 295, 296; at both the beginning and the end in *Od*. **1**. 14; *Od*. **5**. 37.

Seven of the comparisons have a female figure as their subject, and only three refer to a male figure, but the very frequent adjectival and other constructions expressing general likeness to the divine are applied almost without exception to the male characters of the work. The only extended comparisons refer to Nausicaa (*Od*. **3**), Penelope (*Od*. **6** and **7**), and Odysseus (*Od*. **10**). Only in *Od*. **6** is the speaker herself, Penelope, the subject of the comparison. *Od*. **3** forms part of a group of passages praising the divine beauty of Nausicaa. This theme is first introduced in the general comparison with goddesses near the beginning of book VI; it continues in the extended comparison with Artemis, unusual in that this contains precise topographical names; the comparison with Artemis is repeated in Odysseus' address to Nausicaa in *Od*. **4**. The likening of Nausicaa to divine beings recurs in book VIII. 457 ff. with the description of her beauty as a gift from the gods, and Odysseus' promise to pray to her as a god on his return home. The function of the comparisons and the passages related to them is therefore in this instance thematic, serving to emphasize a key theme.

The two extended comparisons referring to Penelope stress her unswerving constancy to Odysseus. The first (*Od*. **6**) sets out graphically in her own words the extent of her grief and her mental conflict. It occurs at a significant point in the action when, unrecognized by her, Odysseus has in fact already returned in disguise and it therefore sums up and stresses her suffering just before she is due to be reunited with him. Her distress and the wish for death, expressed in the prayer to Artemis in XX. 61 ff., stand in ironic contrast with the actual situation, which is already revealed to the hearer or reader, but is as yet unknown to her. The second extended comparison of which Penelope is the subject (*Od*. **7**) once more stresses the theme of her constancy, in stark contrast with the perfidy of Clytemnestra, but now against the background of the resolution of the conflict, after the wooers have been vanquished and Odysseus and Penelope reunited. There is, however, an extra dimension, in that this passage is spoken by the shade of Agamemnon in the underworld and lends the authority of a great hero to the praise of Penelope. Like the passages relating to Nausicaa, these two comparisons have a thematic function. The comparison made by Antinous between the downfall of the Centaur (*Od*. **10**) and the fate to be predicted for Odysseus if he persists in what Antinous interprets as wine-induced folly is, like *Od*. **6**, a clear instance of ironical contrast with the real situation. At the same time it allows a narrative digression within the speech, recounting the battle of the Lapiths and Centaurs; this interrupts the two parts of the simile, the first part containing an implicit comparison, conveyed only by textual juxtaposition, the second a comparison made explicit by linguistic means.

The exemplary comparisons of the *Odyssey* are syntactically and structurally more varied than those in the *Iliad*, in which the majority of examples are brief and uniform in structure. The basic type of phrase made up of an adjective expressing likeness, together with a dependent substantival phrase in the dative case, found in *Il.* **3**, **6a–c**, **7**, **8**, **9**, occurs in *Od.* **2**, **5** and **8**. *Od.* **1**, with the verb ἔχε + direct object linked to a genitive of the proper name, denoting the possession of a divine attribute, is similar to *Il.* **2**. In *Od.* **4** the idea of likeness is expressed by means of the first-person verb form ἐίσκω with a dative object, with the addition of a particularizing accusative of respect, as in *Il.* **1** and **10a** and **b**; in *Od.* **9** likeness is conveyed by means of the adverbial phrase ἠΰτ' Ἄρηα; neither of these constructions is paralleled in the exemplary comparisons of the *Iliad*.

There remain the more complex examples *Od.* **3**, **6**, **7**, and **10**. *Od.* **3** has the characteristic bipartite structure of Homeric similes, with two corresponding parts, each introduced by a comparative word, in this instance the relative pronominal form οἵη in the first line and the adverb ὥς in the final line. There is lexical and morphological correspondence between ἥ γε in l. 107, referring to Artemis, and ἥ γ' in l. 109, referring to Nausicaa, and semantic correspondence between πασάων δ' ὑπὲρ . . . κάρη ἔχει ἠδὲ μέτωπα, | ῥεῖά τ' ἀριγνώτη πέλεται and ὥς . . . ἀμφιπόλοισι μετέπρεπε – just as Artemis stands out among the nymphs, so Nausicaa is pre-eminent among her handmaidens.

Od. **6** is an unusual example, in that the comparison is strictly between the first part of the speech, which is outside the simile proper, and the first part of the simile itself, i.e. between Penelope's description of her unremitting sorrow in ll. 512–17 and the lasting grief of Aëdon in ll. 518–23. The second part of the simile, describing the mental conflict resulting from Penelope's sorrow, is less closely related to the first than is customary. The simile itself has the usual bipartite structure, in this instance with two nearly symmetrical corresponding halves, introduced by the conjunction ὡς in l. 518, and the adverb ὥς in l. 524. There appear to be no linguistic correspondences between the two halves of the simile proper, but there are morphological and semantic links between ὀδυρομένη in l. 513 and ὀδυρομένην in l. 517 in the first part of the speech and ὀλοφυρομένη in l. 522 within the first part of the simile itself. *Od.* **6** is moreover very closely linked to Penelope's prayer to Artemis in XX. 61 ff.: just as in XIX. 512 ff. she likens her grief to that of Aëdon, daughter of Pandareos, so in the prayer she expresses the wish to suffer the fate of the orphan daughters of Pandareos. Even if the identical name in the two passages does not designate the same figure, it reinforces the textual connection between them.

Od. 7 is unusual, in that the second part of the passage forms a negative contrast to that which precedes it. There is, however, once more a bipartite division, ll. 192–8 referring positively to Penelope, ll. 199–202 negatively to Clytemnestra, but the two parts are not linked by paired comparative words as is customary and only by οὐχ ὡς in l. 199 at the beginning of the second part, no doubt because the introduction of the negative element disrupts the usual parallel structure (ὡς in ll. 194 f. has here a different syntactic function, that of qualifying and emphasizing ἀγαθαὶ φρένες and εὖ μέμνητ᾽ respectively).

Od. 10 is a complex example. It is bipartite, but the two parts are separated by a narrative section within the speech. There is in the first part of the speech an implicit derogatory comparison of Odysseus with the Centaur, expressed by juxtaposition and lexical, semantic, and syntactic parallelism, but without linking words. This prompts Antinous to recount the battle of the Centaurs and Lapiths, from which he deduces the warning prediction that Odysseus will suffer a similar fate. This is then explicitly linked to the account of the battle and also to the previous negative comparison in lines 293–7 by the phrase ὡς καὶ σοὶ μέγα πῆμα πιφαύσκομαι in line 305. There is thus a double comparison, the first implicit, that of Odysseus with the Centaur, led astray by wine to folly, and the second explicit, that of the fate of Odysseus with the maiming of the Centaur. Both passages are linked between themselves and also with the narrative passage in the speech, but the link is closest between the second part of the comparison and the narrative account of the battle.

The *Iliad* and the *Odyssey* Compared

All the exemplary comparisons in both the *Iliad* and the *Odyssey* are similes proper, and there are no identifications. In the *Iliad*, general comparisons of the characters, chiefly the heroes, with divine figures, or epithets expressing their close affinity with the gods, are extremely common. Exemplary comparisons with a particular divine, or in one instance (*Il.* 2) a mythological, figure represent simply a variation on the above feature, rendered precise by the addition of a proper name. There are only three examples which refer to a female figure, *Il.* 11 and the two instances in *Il.* 12, which are identical apart from the proper name. In *Il.* 1, 2, and 3 a comparison is made, not with the divine or mythological figure itself but with one of its physical attributes, and in the examples under *Il.* 10 with the gift of counsel possessed by Zeus. Most examples are very brief and simple in structure, the majority being variations on the same basic syntactic pattern, and most are descriptive and static in nature. The only examples which have the bipartite structure with two halves linked by linguistic correspondences, which is characteristic of similes elsewhere in the work, are *Il.* **4**, and to a greatly reduced extent *Il.* **5**. They are also dynamic, and not merely descriptive, with verbs expressing action, which no doubt explains the choice of this particular structure. Whereas many of the constructions expressing general comparisons with the divine are in speech, most of the exemplary comparisons proper are in the narrative. In three instances exemplary comparisons occur in close proximity to other similes: in *Il.* **5** the comparison with Ares is linked with the image of fire; *Il.* **3** is followed by two related similes also relating to Euphorbus; *Il.* **1** is set in a sequence of similes, is enclosed within two of them, and is syntactically linked to the one which precedes it. In every instance the exemplary comparisons have the function of enhancing the status of the character referred to; this is even the case in the hypothetical construction in *Il.* **11**, in which the potential comparison with Aphrodite and Athene only serves to emphasize the value of the prize which Achilles is rejecting.

In the *Odyssey*, as in the *Iliad*, there are many general comparisons of the characters with the divine, expressed in similar constructions. In the exemplary comparisons proper, *Il.* **10a**, *Od.* **4**, and *Od.* **10** are alike, in that the comparison (explicit in *Il.* **10a** and *Od.* **4**, implied by textual juxtaposition in *Od.* **10**) is formulated in apostrophe and refers to the person addressed (there is, however no parallel instance of implied comparison in the *Iliad*). *Od.* **1** is similar to *Il.* **2**, and *Od.* **4** to *Il.* **1** and **10a** and **b** in respect of the comparison with attributes of the exemplary figure. In the main, however, there are very considerable differences between the two works. Most comparisons in the *Odyssey* are applied to female figures; *Od.* **6**, **7**, and **10** refer to figures of legend in extended passages, whereas the one mythological reference in *Il.* **2** amounts only to one short phrase; the important examples *Od.* **4**, **6**, **7**, and **10** are in speech and are thereby rendered more immediate, and *Od.* **4** and **7** are lent greater authority by the fact that Odysseus and the shade of Agamemnon respectively are the speakers. Most examples are structurally and syntactically more complex than those in the *Iliad*, the simple structural type represented in eight out of twelve examples in the *Iliad* being paralleled in only three out of ten examples in the *Odyssey*. The function of the exemplary comparisons in the *Odyssey* is more varied, in keeping with the greater element of complexity which several of them display. However, in spite of this greater variety and complexity, six out of ten examples in the *Odyssey* are descriptive in nature, like most of those in the *Iliad*, and only four have an active element.

Od. **3**, **6**, **7**, and **10** have the bipartite structure characteristic of extended similes in the *Iliad*, but *Od.* **7** lacks an introductory comparative word in the first half, and the two parts of *Od.* **10** are separated by a narrative passage. There are instances of greater integration between exemplary comparisons and the rest of the text, something not found in the *Iliad* (except to the extent that *Il.* **1**, **3**, and **5** are associated with other similes of non-exemplary type). *Od.* **3** is the centrepiece of a series of passages describing the divine beauty of Nausicaa, which begin when Athene plans that Odysseus should encounter her, and conclude when Odysseus bids her farewell. In *Od.* **6** the first part of the simile is closer thematically to the preceding part of Penelope's speech than to the second part of the simile itself. In addition, *Od.* **6** has close links with the simile and exemplary story contained in Penelope's prayer to Artemis. In *Od.* **10** the second part of the simile is more closely linked to the narrative account which precedes it in the speech of Antinous than to the first part of the comparison. Whereas in the *Iliad* the exemplary comparisons appear chiefly to serve the purpose of enhancing the status of the characters, certain of those in the *Odyssey* have in addition the function of stressing a key theme, such as the constancy of Penelope in *Od.* **6** and **7**, or of providing an ironic contrast to the events of the narrative, as in *Od.* **6** and **10**.

The exemplary comparisons of the *Iliad* are considerably less frequent and of lesser significance than the very abundant similes of non-exemplary kind in the work. Their association with other similes in *Il.* **1**, **3**, and **5** perhaps confirms their subordinate position. Their structure is mostly simple and of uniform type and their function is limited. In the *Odyssey*, where there are overall fewer similes of all kinds, they are much more prominent. There is greater complexity in their structure, function, and integration into the text. The increased mythological element permits a greater wealth of allusion to other tales, both within the comparison itself, as in *Od.* **6**, **7**, and **10**, and in the exemplary stories linked to *Od.* **6** and **10**. The *Odyssey* therefore seems to represent a distinct advance in the use and elaboration of exemplary comparisons, which paves the way for further developments in Latin and later poets.

2

Virgil: The *Aeneid*

There is in the *Aeneid* of Virgil,[1] as in Homer, more particularly in the *Iliad*, a very great abundance of similes, and many of them are indeed based on Homeric models. The general range of their subject-matter is very similar to that in Homer, with images derived from the natural and animal world, the heavens, elemental phenomena, and human pursuits. As in Homer, the similes are mostly extended, active and dynamic in nature, and bipartite in structure.

There is one instance of a general comparison with attributes of a god: I. 588 *restitit Aeneas claraque in luce refulsit,* | *os umerosque deo similis* (Aeneas stood forth and was resplendent in the clear light, like a god in face and shoulders). This passage is associated with another simile in the lines which follow: this beauty had been bestowed on him by his mother, beauty such as that which the hand gives to ivory, or when silver or Parian marble is set in gold. When Juno fashions a likeness of Aeneas to send into battle to confound the enemy, his head is described as *divus* 'godlike': X. 638 *Dardaniis ornat telis, clipeumque iubasque* | *divini adsimulat capitis* (she adorns it with Dardanian weapons, and simulates the shield and the plumes on his godlike head). So too in XI. 657 Camilla is described as *dia Camilla* (see Verg. **5**). These rare examples are in marked contrast to the profusion of general comparisons of the heroes with the divine in Homer.

Exemplary comparisons

As Aeneas stands marvelling at the depictions of the Trojan war in the temple, Dido appears:

Virgil **1**

Haec dum Dardanio Aeneae miranda videntur,	*Aeneid* I. 494
dum stupet obtutuque haeret defixus in uno,	
regina ad templum, forma pulcherrima Dido,	
incessit, magna iuvenum stipante caterva.	
qualis in Eurotae ripis aut per iuga Cynthi	
exercet Diana choros, quam mille secutae	
hinc atque hinc glomerantur Oreades; illa pharetram	500
fert umero gradiensque deas supereminet omnis;	
Latonae tacitum pertemptant gaudia pectus:	

---

[1] Virgil lived from 70 to 19 BC. The *Aeneid* was written during the last ten years of his life.

talis erat Dido, talem se laeta ferebat
per medios, instans operi regnisque futuris.

[While these marvels are seen by Dardanian Aeneas, while he is amazed
and stands transfixed, engrossed in one act of contemplation, the queen,
Dido, advanced towards the temple, most beautiful in appearance, with a
large company of youths thronging around her. As on the banks of Eurotas
or along the heights of Cynthus Diana guides her bands of dancers and in
her train there gather on all sides a thousand Oreads; she bears a quiver on
her shoulder and as she progresses she rises high above all the goddesses;
joys pervade Latona's silent breast – such was Dido, so she moved rejoicing
through their midst, urging on the work of her emerging kingdom.]

This example is based on *Od.* VI. 102 ff. (see *Od.* **3**), which compares Nausicaa
to Artemis. It shares with it: the basic comparison to Artemis/Diana; expressions denoting movement, in *Od.* **3** εἶσι κατ᾽ οὔρεα, in *Aen.* **1** *incessit, per
iuga Cynthi exercet . . . choros, secutae, gradiensque, se . . . ferebat*; the precise
topographical names; the allusion to the accompanying band of mountain
nymphs; the rejoicing of Leto/Latona; the pre-eminence of Artemis/Diana,
which is matched by that of Nausicaa and Dido respectively – there is close
semantic and partial morphological correspondence between μετέπρεπε in
Od. **3** and *supereminet* in Verg. **1**. In both works the comparison occurs in the
narrative.

Virgil **2**

ipse ante alios pulcherrimus omnis	*Aeneid* IV. 141
infert se socium Aeneas atque agmina iungit.	
qualis ubi hibernam Lyciam Xanthique fluenta	
deserit ac Delum maternam invisit Apollo	
instauratque choros, mixtique altaria circum	145
Cretesque Dryopesque fremunt pictique Agathyrsi;	
ipse iugis Cynthi graditur mollique fluentem	
fronde premit crinem fingens atque implicat auro,	
tela sonant umeris: haud illo segnior ibat	
Aeneas, tantum egregio decus enitet ore.	150

[Aeneas himself, most beautiful beyond all others, advances to join her and
unites his train with hers. As when Apollo abandons wintry Lycia and the
streams of Xanthus and visits his maternal Delos; he renews the dances
and mingling round his altars Cretans, Dryopes, and painted Agathyrsi
give voice; he himself treads the heights of Cynthus, and with soft foliage
adorns and fashions his flowing locks, intertwining them with the gold;
the arrows rattle on his shoulders – so no less ardently than he progressed
Aeneas, such grace shines forth from his illustrious face.]

Although separated from Verg. **1** by Aeneas' long recital of the events of
the Trojan war in books II and III, this passage is a pendant to it. Just as

Dido resembles Diana, so Aeneas resembles Apollo: thus Dido and Aeneas are thereby shown to be both of equal status and equally matched to each other.

Virgil 3

agit ipse furentem   *Aeneid* IV. 465
in somnis ferus Aeneas; semperque relinqui
sola sibi, semper longam incomitata videtur
ire viam et Tyrios deserta quaerere terra;
Eumenidum veluti demens videt agmina Pentheus,
et solem geminum et duplices se ostendere Thebas,   470
aut Agamemnonius scaenis agitatus Orestes
armatam facibus matrem et serpentibus atris
cum fugit, ultricesque sedent in limine Dirae.

[In her sleep fierce Aeneas himself pursues her in her frenzy, and she seems
ever to be left solitary, ever following a long road, companionless, seeking
Tyre in a waste land; even as mad Pentheus sees the band of the Eumenides,
and a double sun and twofold Thebes appearing before him, or as when
Agamemnon's son Orestes, driven across the stage, flees from his mother,
who is armed with brands and black serpents, and on the threshold sit the
avenging Furies.]

468 *Tyrios*, lit. 'the Tyrians', by metonymy for 'Tyre'; see *Colchos* Ov. **12**.157 n.

The references in IV. 469–73 are to drama, as *scaenis* in 471 makes clear: in the *Bacchae* of Euripides the Theban king Pentheus is driven mad by Bacchus because he had scorned his rites; in the *Eumenides* of Aeschylus the ghost of Clytemnestra incites the Furies against Orestes, who had killed her to avenge the murder of Agamemnon. This passage is textually linked to others describing the madness caused in Dido by love, from the first moment when, at the command of Venus, Cupid assumes the form of Ascanius to ensnare her.[2] It has particular parallels in two other similes: when first inflamed by love, Dido wanders in a frenzy through the city, like a hind stricken by an arrow (IV. 65–73); when she learns of Aeneas' impending departure, she rages through the city like a wild Bacchante (IV. 300–3).

Aeneas performs great feats in the battle against Turnus:

Virgil 4

Aegaeon qualis, centum cui bracchia dicunt   *Aeneid* X. 565
centenasque manus, quinquaginta oribus ignem
pectoribusque arsisse, Iovis cum fulmina contra
tot paribus streperet clipeis, tot stringeret ensis:

---

[2] I. 657 ff.; cf. with reference to Dido the participle *furens* 'frenzied' I. 659; IV. 65, 69; V. 6; the noun *furor* 'frenzy', 'madness' IV. 91, 101, 501, 697.

> sic toto Aeneas desaevit in aequore victor,
> ut semel intepuit mucro.   570
>
> [Like Aegaeon, who they say had a hundred arms and a hundred hands
> and fire burning from fifty mouths and breasts, when against Jove's thun-
> derbolts he clashed with as many like shields and drew as many swords –
> so Aeneas rages victorious over the whole plain, when once his sword grew
> warm.]

The reference is to the monstrous giant Aegaeon/Briareos, as in the *Iliad* I.
402 ff. (see also Primas **1**.77).

Virgil **5**

> At medias inter caedes exsultat Amazon,   *Aeneid* XI. 648
> unum exserta latus pugnae, pharetrata Camilla,
> et nunc lenta manu spargens hastilia denset,   650
> nunc validam dextra rapit indefessa bipennem;
> aureus ex umero sonat arcus et arma Dianae.
> illa etiam, si quando in tergum pulsa recessit,
> spicula converso fugientia dirigit arcu.
> at circum lectae comites, Larinaque virgo   655
> Tullaque et aeratam quatiens Tarpeia securim,
> Italides, quas ipsa decus sibi dia Camilla
> delegit pacisque bonas bellique ministras:
> quales Threiciae cum flumina Thermodontis
> pulsant et pictis bellantur Amazones armis,   660
> seu circum Hippolyten seu cum se Martia curru
> Penthesilea refert, magnoque ululante tumultu
> feminea exsultant lunatis agmina peltis.
>
> [But in the midst of the slaughter, an Amazon, one breast bared for battle,
> bearing a quiver, Camilla rages, and now from her hand she scatters tough
> javelins thick and fast, now her unwearied hand snatches a strong battle-
> axe; the golden bow and the shafts of Diana clang from her shoulder. And
> even if, driven back, she withdraws, she turns her bow and aims arrows as
> she flees. But around her are her chosen comrades, the maiden Larina, and
> Tulla, and Tarpeia, brandishing an axe of bronze, daughters of Italy, whom
> godlike Camilla herself chose as her adornment, good attendants in both
> peace and war. Such are the Thracian Amazons, when they march over the
> streams of Thermodon and wage war in decorated armour, whether round
> Hippolyte, or when Penthesilea, child of Mars, returns in her chariot and
> amid loud tumult of cries the female army exults with crescent shields.]

This example is unlike the previous instances in that it contains both general and particular comparisons: that of Camilla and her attendants with
Amazons in general, and by implication that of Camilla herself with individual named Amazons. In XI. 648 *Amazon* stands in apposition to *Camilla* in

the following line and identifies Camilla as an Amazon-like figure (for this type of compressed comparison see the examples under Verg. **8** and **9**). The passage beginning with *quales* in XI. 659 refers to *lectae comites* and *ministras*: Camilla's followers are likened to the Thracian Amazons surrounding Hippolyte or Penthesilea, but this implicitly compares Camilla herself to the figures of Hippolyte and Penthesilea, around whom they gather.

Virgil **6**

Turnus ut Aenean cedentem ex agmine vidit *Aeneid* XII. 324
turbatosque duces, subita spe fervidus ardet;
poscit equos atque arma simul saltuque superbus
emicat in currum et manibus molitur habenas.
multa virum volitans dat fortia corpora Leto,
semineces volvit multos aut agmina curru
proterit aut raptas fugientibus ingerit hastas. 330
qualis apud gelidi cum flumina concitus Hebri
sanguineus Mavors clipeo intonat atque furentis
bella movens immittit equos; illi aequore aperto
ante Notos Zephyrumque volant, gemit ultima pulsu
Thraca pedum circumque atrae Formidinis ora 335
Iraeque Insidiaeque, dei comitatus, aguntur:
talis equos alacer media inter proelia Turnus
fumantis sudore quatit, miserabile caesis
hostibus insultans.

[Turnus, when he saw Aeneas withdrawing fom the ranks, and the captains in confusion, burns hot with sudden hope. He calls for horses and arms, and at the same time with a bound leaps proudly into his chariot and controls the reins with his hands. As he flies along, he consigns many strong bodies of men to oblivion, rolls many half-dead men over, or crushes the ranks with his car, or seizing spears, thrusts them at those fleeing. As when by the streams of icy Hebrus, aroused, bloody Mavors thunders with his shield and, inciting war, gives rein to his frenzied steeds; they fly over the open plain swifter than the South wind and the West wind, and furthest Thrace groans with the beat of their hooves, and on all sides figures of black Terror, Anger and Ambush, companions of the god, are driven on – even so in the midst of the battle Turnus eagerly goads his horses, steaming with sweat, leaping upon the enemy, miserably slain.]

Passages in speech

There is a group of short passages in speech which express comparison or identification with a named exemplar. Closest to an exemplary comparison proper is Turnus' boast, expressed in a hypothetical construction, that he will vanquish Aeneas, even if he surpasses Achilles:

Virgil **7**

> "ibo animis contra, vel magnum praestet Achillem   *Aeneid* XI. 438
> factaque Volcani manibus paria induat arma
> ille licet."
>
> ["I will confront him boldly, even though he may surpass great Achilles or
> don like armour, fashioned by the hands of Vulcan."]

For a similar hypothetical construction see *Iliad* **11**.

A further development is represented by instances in which comparison
is replaced by identification with a named figure, the name alone conferring
like status. The Sibyl's prophecy describes Turnus:

Virgil **8a**

> "alius Latio iam partus Achilles,   *Aeneid* VI. 89
> natus et ipse dea."
>
> ["Another Achilles now brought forth in Latium, and likewise born of a
> goddess."]

Turnus was the son of a sea-nymph, described in *Aen.* X.76 as *diva Venilia*,
whereas Achilles was the son of the sea-goddess Thetis. There may also be the
implication that Turnus is the equal of Aeneas, born of Venus, and frequently
addressed in the phrase *nate dea*, e.g. *Aen.* I. 582.

Turnus boasts to Pandarus that he is the equal of Achilles:

Virgil **8b**

> "hic etiam inventum Priamo narrabis Achillem."   *Aeneid* IX. 742
>
> ["You shall relate to Priam that here too another Achilles has been
> found."][3]

By contrast, identification with Paris has a negative function. Thus Iarbas,
a suitor rejected by Dido, refers dismissively to Aeneas:

Virgil **9a**

> "et nunc ille Paris cum semiviro comitatu,   *Aeneid* IV. 215
> Maeonia mentum mitra crinemque madentem
> subnixus, rapto potitur."
>
> ["And now that Paris with his unmanly train, a Maeonian headband prop-
> ping up his chin and oiled locks, takes possession of the spoil."]

---

[3] Cf. also Verg., *Eclogue* IV. 34 *alter erit tum Tiphys, et altera quae vehat Argo | delectos
heroas; erunt etiam altera bella | atque iterum ad Troiam magnus mittetur Achilles* (then
there shall be a second Tiphys, and a second Argo to carry chosen heroes; there shall be
also a second war and once more a great Achilles shall be sent to Troy).

Juno predicts the evils of the coming war: just as Hecuba dreamt that she would give birth in Paris to a firebrand, so Venus has given birth in Aeneas to a second Paris, spreading fire and destruction:

Virgil **9b**

"nec face tantum   *Aeneid* VII. 319
Cisseis praegnas ignis enixa iugalis,
quin idem Veneri partus suus et Paris alter,
funestaeque iterum recidiva in Pergama taedae."

["Nor did the daughter of Cisseus alone, pregnant with a firebrand, bring forth nuptial flames, indeed Venus has the like in her offspring, a second Paris, once again a marriage torch bringing destruction to Troy restored."]

These examples represent a compressed and implicit form of exemplary comparison, in which a proper name, with all its associations, is transferred to another subject. The second bearer of the name is thereby not merely compared to, but identified with, the first. The relationship of the second figure to the first is expressed by the addition of qualifiers: **8a**. 89 *alius . . . Achilles*; **8b**. 742 *hic etiam . . . Achillem*; **9a**. 215 *ille Paris*; **9b**. 321 *Paris alter*.

Conclusion

Verg. **1–6** are straightforward similes, expressing likeness to the exemplar, of the kind found in Homer. Verg. **8a**, **8b**, **9a** and **9b** introduce the theme of identification with the exemplar, and Verg. **7** expresses, albeit in hypothetical form, the motif of outdoing the exemplar – neither of these types is found in Homer, but both become common in later poets. In contrast to Homer, there are hardly any general comparisons with gods in the *Aeneid* and only three comparisons with named divinities; there are no comparisons with divine or mythological attributes. There are six straightforward exemplary comparisons: Dido is compared positively with Diana in Verg. **1** and negatively in her madness with Pentheus and Orestes in Verg. **3**; Aeneas is compared with Apollo in Verg. **2** and with Agaeon in **4**; Turnus is compared with Mars in Verg. **6**. Verg. **5** is a combination of the general and the particular in the comparison of Camilla and her followers with Amazons, and by implication, of Camilla with Hippolyte and Penthesilea. As in the *Iliad*, all these examples occur in the narrative.[4] The short examples in speech (Verg. **7**, **8a** and **8b**, and **9a** and **9b**), which have some links with exemplary comparisons, are more subjective, representing the viewpoint of the speaker; Verg. **7** contains a first-person formulation, **8b** the second person of direct address. Verg. **7**, cast in hypothetical form, is closest to an exemplary comparison proper. The examples in Verg. **8a** and **8b** and **9a** and **9b** express comparison by positing

---

[4] By contrast *Odyssey* **4**, **6**, **7** and **10** contain extended comparisons in speech.

identity with a named figure, positively with reference to Achilles, negatively with reference to Paris. If these examples of identification with heroes are included, there is overall a greatly increased proportion of comparisons with non-divine figures. Thus whereas there is only one such reference in the exemplary comparisons of the *Iliad* and three in those of the *Odyssey*, there are in the examples of the *Aeneid* a total of seven non-divine exemplary characters cited: Pentheus, Orestes, Agaeon, Hippolyte, Penthesilea, Achilles, and Paris. These are all referred to by proper name, with the addition of the adjective *Agamemnonius* indicating patrilineal descent in conjunction with *Orestes* in Verg. **3**, and of the epithet *Martia*, lit. 'belonging to Mars', in conjunction with *Penthesilea* in Verg. **5**. As in Homer, the proper names may be placed in prominent position: at the beginning of the line in Verg. **1**. 502; **2**. 150; **4**. 565; **5**. 662; **6**. 324; at the end of the line in **1**. 496; **2**. 144; **3**. 469, 471; **5**. 649, 652, 657; **6**. 337; **7**. 438; **8a**. 89; **8b**. 742.

All the main examples, Verg. **1–6**, contain a high proportion of verb forms expressing action and movement, in line with the dynamic nature of other similes in the work: **1** *incessit, exercet … choros, secutae, gradiensque, se … ferebat*; **2** *infert se, iungit, deserit, invisit, instauratque, fremunt, graditur, premit, implicat, sonant, ibat*; **3** *agit, ire, quaerere, agitatus, fugit*; **4** *arsisse, streperet, stringeret, desaevit, intepuit*; **5** *exsultat, spargens, denset, rapit, sonat, pulsa recessit, spicula fugientia dirigit, quatiens, pulsant, bellantur, se . . . refert*; **6** *cedentem, turbatosque, ardet, emicat, volitans, dat, volvit, proterit, fugientibus, ingerit, concitus, intonat, furentis, movens, immittit, volant, gemit, aguntur, quatit, insultans*. This is in marked contrast to Homer, where most exemplary comparisons in the *Iliad*, and the majority in the *Odyssey*, are descriptive and static in nature. Even those instances in the *Odyssey* which are not purely descriptive, i.e. *Od*. **3**, **6**, **7**, and **10**, have a lower proportion of verbs expressing action and movement. Thus *Od*. **3**, on which Verg. **1** is modelled, has only one verb form expressing movement, as against five in Verg. **1**.

All the main examples are bipartite in structure, with the two parts of the comparison joined by linking words: in Verg. **1** and **6** the pronominal adjective *qualis* corresponds to the demonstrative *talis*; in **2** *qualis* is paired with the comparative phrase *haud illo segnior*; in **4** *qualis* is paired with the adverb *sic*; **5** has *quales* without a matching word; **3** links the two parts of the comparison with the adverb *veluti*.

Verg. **1** and **2** are clearly a matching pair of comparisons referring to Dido and Aeneas respectively, in spite of the long narrative digression in the text which separates them. Verg. **1** is closely modelled on *Od*. **3** and like the latter serves to focus attention on a character newly introduced into the narrative; it includes similar precise topographical names, a feature not paralleled in other *Odyssey* examples, but found also in Verg. **2**, **5**, and **6**. Verg. **3** is textually linked to other passages containing the key words *furens* or *furor* and in particular to two other related similes describing Dido's love-induced frenzy. The function of the narrative examples seems to be primarily that of enhancing the status of the main characters in Verg. **1**, **2**, **4**, **5**, and **6**; in addition Verg. **1** focuses attention on a character newly introduced, and like Verg. **2**, **3**, **4**, **5**, and **6** emphasizes a key stage in the action; in Verg. **3** the comparison with figures of myth as they are represented in drama emphasizes Dido's unhappy plight and the theme of the frenzy caused by love. The function of the examples in speech in Verg. **7** and Verg. **8a** and **8b** is also that of enhancement, whereas those in Verg. **9a** and **9b** are used by the speakers to denigrate Aeneas.

3

Latin Poets from Catullus to Ovid

In contradistinction to Homer and Virgil, the Latin poets examined in this chapter, Catullus, Tibullus, Propertius, Horace and Ovid,[1] utilize a much wider range of voice and person, frequently adopting a first-person stance, so that the exemplary comparisons and identifications in their work may be presented from a perspective differing from that in epic narrative. In order to assess the significance of specific comparison or identification with an exemplar, it is necessary also to examine the extent to which each poet makes general reference to the characters and stories of myth in his work.

Catullus

Catullus, the earliest of this group of poets, makes considerable use of exemplary comparisons, and particularly in poem 68 (see Catull. **2–4**) they form a very significant element in the development and structure of the text. By comparison with Homer and Virgil, there is a very marked increase in the number of non-divine figures cited in the comparisons and the one example of identification (Catull. **7**).

In a poem addressed to Hortalus, accompanying the promised translation of a poem by Callimachus, Catullus cites his grief at the death of his brother as the reason for the delay in completing it. In the following lines he addresses his brother directly:

Catullus **1**

> numquam ego te *potero posthac audire loquentem,*   65. 9
>   *numquam ego te,* vita frater amabilior,
> aspiciam posthac? at certe semper amabo,
>   semper maesta tua carmina morte canam,
> qualia sub densis ramorum concinit umbris
>   Daulias absumpti fata gemens Ityli.   14

[Shall I never hereafter be able to hear your voice, never see you again hereafter, brother dearer than life? But certainly I shall always love you, always sing songs rendered sad by your death, such as under the dense shadows of the branches the Daulian bird sings, lamenting the fate of Itylus lost.]

14 *Daulias* 'the Daulian' denotes the nightingale.

---

[1] Some of the dates are uncertain: Catullus c. 84–c. 54 BC; Tibullus 48?–19 BC; Propertius c. 54–48 BC?–after 16 BC?; Horace 65–8 BC; Ovid 43 BC–AD 17?

The reference is to the story of Procne of Daulis, married to Tereus, who raped her sister Philomela and cut out her tongue. In revenge Procne served up the flesh of their son Itys to Tereus (here the name of Itys has been replaced by that of Itylus, who belongs in a different story, also with a character transformed into a nightingale – see Homer, *Od.* 6). Catullus clearly knew the rarer version in which it is Procne who is turned into a nightingale (as in Ovid, *Heroides* XV. 153 f.), but in other versions it is Philomela who becomes a nightingale, and Procne a swallow.

   Catull. **2**, **3** and **4** in poem 68 form part of a complex sequence of associated themes and similes and must be considered together in the context of the whole poem. The first example is preceded by a group of similes: 68. 51–6 Venus formerly caused me to burn as hot as the Trinacrian rock or the springs of Thermopylae; ll. 57–66 as a cooling stream flows down from a mountain top over the parched earth, or as a favouring breeze comes to a storm-tossed sailor, so Allius came to my aid:

Catullus 2

is clausum lato patefecit limite campum,	68. 67
isque domum nobis isque dedit dominam,	
ad quam communes exerceremus amores.	
quo mea se molli candida diva pede	70
intulit et trito fulgentem in limine plantam	
innixa arguta constituit solea;	
coniugis ut quondam flagrans advenit amore	
Protesilaëam Laodamia domum	
inceptam frustra, nondum cum sanguine sacro	75
hostia caelestis pacificasset eros.	

[He opened up a fenced field with a broad path, he gave me a house and my mistress, a house where we might enjoy our shared loves. Thither my fair goddess came with soft step, and set her shining foot on the worn threshold, stepping with a tap of her sandal, even as once, burning with love, Laodamia came to the house of her husband Protesilaus, a house begun in vain, since not yet had a sacrificial victim with its sacred blood appeased the lords of heaven.]

   68 *dominam*: perhaps 'its mistress'.

It was perhaps the motif of the house which initially prompted the comparison with Laodamia. Already in the *Iliad* (II. 701), the house of Protesilaus is described as 'half-complete' (ἡμιτελής), which later gave rise to the interpretation that the omission of sacrificial rites was the cause of the death of Protesilaus in the Trojan war. Thus the repetition of the word *domum*, applying in the first instance to the house procured by Allius for the encounter, and in the second to the house of Protesilaus, and the morphological and semantic correspondence between *intulit*, with the poet's mistress as subject, and *advenit*, with Laodamia as subject, serve to bind the two halves of the comparison together. There is, however, a latent ironic contrast between the coming of Laodamia as a bride to her husband's house and the coming of the poet's mistress to a house procured for a secret tryst.

In 68. 77 f. the poet prays never to undertake anything against the will of the gods. This leads on in ll. 79–90 to the consequence of the omitted sacrifice, Laodamia's separation from Protesilaus in the early days of marriage, his death, and a lament for the slaughter in the Trojan war; ll. 91–100 my brother too died in Troy and is buried in a hated alien land; ll.101–4 to this land the youth of Greece hastened to avenge the abduction of Helen by Paris; ll. 105–7 your fate, Laodamia, was caused by these events. This is followed by three further similes relating to Laodamia's love of Protesilaus: ll. 107–17 you were swept into an abyss of love deeper than the gulf of Pheneus; ll. 119–24 not so dear to an aged parent is a grandchild born late to his only daughter, securing the family inheritance. The third simile is specifically linked to a further comparison between the poet's mistress and Laodamia:

Catullus **3**

> nec tantum niveo gavisast ulla columbo   68. 125
>   compar, quae multo dicitur improbius
> oscula mordenti semper decerpere rostro,
>   quam quae praecipue multivolast mulier.
> sed tu horum magnos vicisti sola furores,
>   ut semel es flavo conciliata viro.   130
> aut nihil aut paulo cui tum concedere digna
>   lux mea se nostrum contulit in gremium,
> quam circumcursans hinc illinc saepe Cupido
>   fulgebat crocina candidus in tunica.

> [Nor did any dove delight so much in her snowy mate, the dove which is said ever to snatch kisses with bites of her bill more wantonly than any woman who exceeds others in intensity of desire. But you alone surpassed the great passion of these when once you were united with your golden-haired husband. Worthy to yield to her in nothing or in but little, she who is my light came to my breast, and often circling round her, flying hither and thither, Cupid shone bright in saffron tunic.]

Earlier Laodamia had been described as *flagrans . . . amore* when coming as a bride to her husband's house (see Catull. **2** above), and as too soon bereft of the physical union of marriage: 81 *ante . . . | quam veniens una atque altera rursus hiemps | noctibus in longis avidum saturasset amorem* (before the coming of one and then a second winter with its long nights might satisfy her eager love). The two similes in ll. 107–24 are appropriate to this love within the marriage bond; although that in ll. 107–17 expresses overwhelming emotion, it is not overtly sexual, and that in ll. 119–24 is neutral and familial in nature. There is, however, a distinct shift in the third simile (see Catull. **3** above). The description of the billing and cooing of the doves, in particular the negative comparative adverb *improbius* in l. 126 and *mordenti . . . rostro* in l. 127, indicate lasciviousness, an idea strengthened by both the adjectival and the verbal component in *multivolast* in l. 128, which suggest excessive desire. This comparison is perhaps not wholly appropriate to Laodamia as she has been portrayed so far, and there appears to be a contrast between the more positive phrases referring to her love, *avidum . . . amorem* in l. 83 and *tuus altus amor* in l. 117, and the more negative phrase *sed tu horum magnos vicisti sola furores* in l. 129. The comparison, and in particular the compound verb *multivolast* is, however, as it were by anticipation, no doubt entirely appropriate to the poet's mistress, and therefore forms a transition to ll. 131–34. The actual grammatical and semantic link between these lines and ll. 125–30 is established by the somewhat ambiguous phrase *aut nihil aut paulo cui tum concedere digna*, which has been interpreted in two radically opposed senses, either as meaning 'to whom she is worthy to yield in nothing or only in little', i.e. 'she is worthy, or almost so, to be compared with her', or conversely 'to whom she is not at all or only barely worthy to yield', i.e. 'she is not really worthy to be compared with her'. In the light of the whole poem and of the particular context, it is much more likely that the former interpretation is correct. The line must be seen in relation both to what precedes and to what follows. Firstly, it probably refers back, particularly in *nihil . . . cui concedere digna*, to ll. 125–30: in respect of the love just described, the poet's mistress in no way yields to Laodamia. This positive interpretation is confirmed by ll. 132–4: when she comes to the poet's arms, Cupid attends her, which perhaps suggests an implicit comparison with Venus herself, the epitome of love and beauty. Secondly, however, by the addition of the restrictive phrase *aut paulo*, Catullus at the same time concedes that his mistress does not altogether equal Laodamia, thus preparing the way for the revelation of her infidelity in the immediately following passage. He has in part lessened the difference between the two figures by linking Laodamia in the simile of the doves with love of a more overtly sensual kind, that which characterizes his mistress, but now for the first time he admits his mistress's infidelity and implies a comparison of their relationship with that between Juno and Jove:

Catullus **4**

> quae tamen etsi uno non est contenta Catullo,   68. 135
>   rara verecundae furta feremus erae,
> ne nimium simus stultorum more molesti.
>   saepe etiam Iuno, maxima caelicolum,
> coniugis in culpa flagrantem contudit iram,
>   noscens omnivoli plurima furta Iovis.   140
> atque nec divis homines componier aequumst.

[Yet though she is not content with Catullus alone, I will bear the rare stolen loves of my discreet mistress, lest I be over-tiresome after the fashion of fools. Even Juno, the greatest of heavenly dwellers, has often checked her burning anger at her husband's guilt, when learning of the many stolen loves of all-willing Jove; but it is not just for men to be compared to gods.]

The passage beginning at l. 138 is linked solely by its placing and by *etiam* to that which precedes it, but its final line clearly indicates that Catullus recognizes that he was by implication suggesting a comparison of himself with the wronged Juno, and of his mistress with the erring Jove, something which he then retracts as inappropriate. The adjective *omnivoli* referring to Jove in l. 140 echoes *multivolast* in l. 128. It is significant that it is only at this late stage in the poem that the infidelity of the poet's mistress is revealed. Moreover, the admission is followed by the poet's explicit statement in ll. 143–6: after all, she did not come to me, led to the house by her father (i.e. as a bride), but snatched the delights she bestowed on me from her husband. This not only refers back, particularly in the phrase *nec . . . venit . . . domum* in ll. 143 f., to the theme of Laodamia coming as a bride to the house of Protesilaus, which occurs in Catull. **2**, but now makes fully explicit the difference between his mistress and Laodamia which is only partly implicit in the comparisons. However, the balance is redressed by a return to the initial theme of the poet's enduring love, and the poem concludes with the lines: 159–60 *et longe ante omnes mihi quae me carior ipsost | lux mea, qua viva vivere dulce mihist* (and far above all, she who is my light and dearer to me than my own self, whose life alone makes it sweet for me to live).

The following examples occur in a poem celebrating the marriage of Junia and Manlius:

Catullus **5**

    namque Iunia Manlio,   61. 16
    qualis Idalium colens
    venit ad Phrygium Venus
    iudicem, bona cum bona
       nubet alite virgo.   20

[For now shall Junia be married to Manlius, Junia like Venus who dwells in Idalium, when she came to the Phrygian judge, a good maiden with a good omen.]

18 f. *ad Phrygium . . . iudicem*: a reference to the judgement of Paris (see Prop. **6**.13 n.).

This is followed later in the poem by a wish for the offspring of the union:

Catullus **6**

> talis illius a bona   61. 219
> matre laus genus approbet,
> qualis unica ab optima
> matre Telemacho manet
>   fama Penelopeo.

[May such praise, deriving from his virtuous mother, approve his descent, as for Telemachus, son of Penelope, remains unsurpassed the renown deriving from his noble mother.]

There is one poem which alludes to the convention of identification with a named exemplar. The poet describes his vain search for Camerius and the impossibility of finding him, even were he to possess the form of fabled beings or their attributes:

Catullus **7**

> non custos si fingar ille Cretum,   55. 14
> non Ladas ego pinnipesve Perseus,
> non si Pegaseo ferar volatu,
> non Rhesi niveae citaeque bigae.

[Not if I were fashioned in the form of that Cretan guardian, nor if I were Ladas or wing-footed Perseus, not if I were borne with the flight of Pegasus, or (like) the snowy swift steeds of Rhesus.]

14 *custos ... ille Cretum*: the Minotaur, guardian of the labyrinth.   15 *Ladas*: the runner of Alexander the Great.   17 *Rhesi*: Rhesus, a Thracian king, robbed of his horses before Troy.

Mythological allusions are here used with humorous exaggeration in a negative hypothetical construction to express potential identification with characters of legend. It shows that Catullus was aware of the convention, which he adapts to his own purposes. It is an early, albeit atypical, example of one particular type of mythological reference.

The structure of Catull. 1 is very straightforward, the two parts of the comparison being linked syntactically by *qualia* and by the correspondence between *canam* in the first part and *concinit* in the second. That of Catull. 2, although of greater length, is also simple, falling into two asymmetrical narrative sections, linked by *ut*, by the repetition of *domum*, and the two corresponding verbs *intulit* and *advenit*. The progression of thought in the interlinked similes in Catull. 3 is much more complex and this is reflected in the syntactical structure and the varying ways in which comparison is expressed: *nec tantum ... quam, vicisti, aut nihil aut paulo cui tum concedere digna*. In Catull. 4 comparison is implied solely by means of textual juxtaposition and *etiam*. In Catull. 5 comparison is conveyed by *qualis*, and in Catull. 6 by *talis ... qualis*.

In Catull. **7** potential identification with an exemplar is conveyed by the verb *fingar* in l. 14, with a verb understood also in the following line.

There is elsewhere in the poems of Catullus relatively little mythological reference, except in poems 64 and 66. In poem 64 the subject is the marriage of Peleus and Thetis, from which Achilles was to be born; on the marriage bed is a coverlet depicting the story of Theseus and Ariadne, which the poet recounts at length. Poem 66 relates the story of the lock of Berenice. In 64 and 66 the stories are self-contained and are not used to cite mythological parallels of the kind found in the other poets.

Catullus: conclusion

There is thus in the poetry of Catullus one reference in Catull. **7** to the conventions of identification with an exemplar and five explicit exemplary comparisons expressing likeness or equality: that with Procne in Catull. **1**; two interconnected exemplary comparisons of the poet's mistress with Laodamia in Catull. **2** and **3**; a comparison with Venus in Catull. **5**; comparisons with Penelope and Telemachus in Catull. **6**; there is an implicit exemplary comparison of the relation between the poet and his mistress with that between Juno and Jove in Catull. **4**. The comparison in Catull. **2** is more neutral, because the main emphasis lies on the coming of the poet's mistress to the house procured by Allius, just as Laodamia came as a bride to the house of Protesilaus – indeed this shared motif of the house as the place of meeting may well have determined the choice of this particular mythological story in the first place. There is, however, already in this first example a latent contrast between the nature of the two encounters and between the poet's mistress and Laodamia. This becomes clearer in the course of the poem, in which Laodamia is portrayed as an exemplar of profound love and fidelity within marriage. This paves the way for the poet's admission in Catull. **3** that his mistress falls short of Laodamia, if only in little, but he partly minimizes the effect of this by stressing more strongly the sensual nature of Laodamia's love in the simile to which the comparison is attached, thus depicting her as more closely akin to his mistress. It is only after this point in the poem that the poet reveals his mistress's infidelity, which leads to the implied comparison with Juno and Jove in Catull. **4**, conveyed by means of textual juxtaposition and *etiam*, and hastily retracted as inappropriate. This is followed by a further revelation of the full extent of the difference between Laodamia and the poet's mistress, in that she is not only unfaithful to Catullus, but also to her husband, but the poem none the less ends on a declaration of unconditional love. The poem is thus a highly complex one, combining a variety of themes and perspectives and a mixture of voices: first-person confession, third-person narrative and direct address.

It is noteworthy that two of the poems in which the most substantial exemplary comparisons occur, nos. 65 and 68, are in elegiac couplets. This metre, made up of a hexameter followed by a pentameter, has affinities with the hexameter of epic verse, which perhaps suggests that in the lyric, exemplary comparisons were initially associated with weightier metres akin to those of epic, and indeed that the conventions of exemplary comparison themselves were probably drawn from epic narrative. The exemplary comparisons in Catullus are skilfully woven into the fabric of the text in such a way that they mirror the development of the themes. It is thus clear that even at this early stage the tradition of using mythological comparisons in non-epic poetry must already have been well established, enabling Catullus to make highly sophisticated use of it.

Tibullus

There is very little mythological reference in the extant poems of Tibullus. There is one exemplary comparison proper and one parallel exemplary story.[2]

The poet attempts to banish the pains of love with wine and another woman, but Venus intervenes, bidding him remember his mistress, and deserts him in his love-making:

Tibullus 1

> tunc me discedens devotum femina dixit,   I. 5. 41
>   a pudet, et narrat scire nefanda meam.
> non facit hoc verbis, facie tenerisque lacertis
>   devovet et flavis nostra puella comis.
> talis ad Haemonium Nereis Pelea quondam   45
>   vecta est frenato caerula pisce Thetis.

[Then, departing, the woman declared me bewitched – oh shame! – and spreads it abroad that my mistress is versed in black arts. She does not do this by means of words, my girl bewitches me with her face, her soft arms and her golden hair. Such was the Nereid, sea-blue Thetis, when she was formerly borne on her bridled fish to Peleus of Haemonia.]

The comparison is conveyed solely by *talis* in line 45 and is active, rather than descriptive, similar in that respect to the dominant type of epic simile (for dynamic similes in Homer and Virgil see pp. 9 f., 27, 29, 36).

Tibullus laments that his mistress is absent in the country:

---

[2] The appendices to the *Corpus Tibullianum* contain a poem, certainly however not by Tibullus, which praises Messalla as surpassing Nestor and Ulysses. This kind of exemplary comparison is common in panegyric and the poem has therefore been placed together with other examples of the type in chapter 4.

Tibullus **2**

> o ego, dum aspicerem dominam, quam fortiter illic   II. 3. 5
>   versarem valido pingue bidente solum
> agricolaeque modo curvum sectarer aratrum,
>   dum subigunt steriles arva serenda boves!
> nec quererer quod sol graciles exureret artus,
>   laederet et teneras pussula rupta manus.   10
> pavit et Admeti tauros formosus Apollo;
>   nec cithara intonsae profueruntve comae,
> nec potuit curas sanare salubribus herbis:
>   quidquid erat medicae vicerat artis amor.

[Oh, if I could only look upon my mistress, how vigorously there would I turn the fertile soil with my strong hoe and follow the curved plough like a husbandman, while the barren oxen broke up the clods for sowing! Nor would I complain that the sun burnt my slender limbs or that broken blisters hurt my delicate hands. Beautiful Apollo too fed the bulls of Admetus; nor were his cithara and his flowing locks of any avail, nor could he cure his ills with health-giving herbs. Love had triumphed over every remedy of the healing art.]

11 The reference is to Jove's banishment of Apollo from heaven, making him serve Admetus as herdsman. In a later version of the story, that adopted by Tibullus, Apollo's servitude is associated with subjection to love, which provides the link with the poet himself.   12 *intonsae*: lit. 'unshorn'.

There is no explicit comparison with Apollo, but the poet cites the story in justification of his desire to till the fields to be near his mistress. Ll. 5–10 are syntactically linked to ll. 11–14 by *et* in l. 11 and by the parallels between ll. 9 f. and 11 respectively: just as there is a contrast between the present appearance of the poet and that of the sunburnt and blistered husbandman which he wishes to become, so there is a contrast between the beauty of Apollo and his state of subjection both to Admetus and to love; ll. 12–14 furthermore imply that the poet's subjection to love is a parallel to that of Apollo. This is an instance of the use of an exemplary story to lend credence to the poet's depiction of his emotional state. The comparison with the story of Apollo is conveyed implicitly by means of textual juxtaposition, reinforced by one specific syntactic link.

Propertius

There is a vast array of mythological references in the poems of Propertius, which frequently take the form of parallel exemplary stories of the kind found in Tibull. **2**. There are, however, also explicit exemplary comparisons, cast in a wide range of syntactical constructions containing adjectives, demonstratives, adverbs, conjunctions and verbs expressing a comparative sense, and also instances in which comparison or contrast is replaced by identification with an exemplary figure (see Prop. **8**, **9** and **11a**). The comparisons also include instances which express superiority to the exemplar (see Prop. **3**; **4**; **6**. 13 f.; **7**; **11b**). Exemplary stories and exemplary comparisons often appear together in the same poem, either separately or linked together.

Propertius 1

> Qualis Thesea iacuit cedente carina   I. 3. 1
>   languida desertis Gnosia litoribus;
> qualis et accubuit primo Cepheia somno
>   libera iam duris cotibus Andromede;
> nec minus assiduis Edonis fessa choreis   5
>   qualis in herboso concidit Apidano:
> talis visa mihi mollem spirare quietem
>   Cynthia non certis nixa caput manibus,
> ebria cum multo traherem vestigia Baccho,
>   et quaterent sera nocte facem pueri.   10

[As the Cretan maid lay languishing on the deserted shore, as the ship of Theseus was departing; and as Andromeda, child of Cepheus, lay down in her first sleep, now free from the hard rock; as the Thracian Bacchante, no less wearied by the unremitting dance, fell prostrate on the grassy banks of Apidanus, so Cynthia seemed to me to breathe gentle rest, her head supported on her slackened hands, as I dragged my footsteps, drunk from much wine, and the slaves were shaking their torches at an advanced hour of the night.]

   2 *Gnosia*: Ariadne; see *Gnosida* Ov. **11**.

The comparison is placed in a prominent position at the beginning of the poem, and clearly signalled as such by the opening pronominal adjective *qualis*, repeated in ll. 3 and 6, which has its counterpart in the demonstrative *talis* in l. 7, referring to Cynthia. It is followed a few lines later by another exemplary comparison, this time applied by the poet to himself:

Propertius 2

> non tamen ausus eram dominae turbare quietem,   I. 3. 17
>   expertae metuens iurgia saevitiae;
> sed sic intentis haerebam fixus ocellis,
>   Argus ut ignotis cornibus Inachidos.

[Yet I had not dared to disturb my mistress's rest, fearing the rebukes of her fierce temper, (often) experienced, but remained with my eyes fixed intently on her, even as Argus (fixed his gaze) upon the unfamiliar horns of the daughter of Inachus.]

   20 Io, daughter of Inachus, king of Argos, was loved by Jupiter and changed through fear of Juno into a heifer (Ov., *Met.* I. 611); Juno demanded her from Jupiter and set the many-eyed Argus to guard her. There is thus also an im-

plicit comparison of Cynthia with Io, as equally worthy to be loved by Jupiter, and equally needing to be guarded.

Propertius **3**

> tu licet Antiopae formam Nycteidos, et tu   I. 4. 5
>   Spartanae referas laudibus Hermionae,
> et quascumque tulit formosi temporis aetas:
>   Cynthia non illas nomen habere sinat:
> nedum, si levibus fuerit collata figuris,
>   inferior duro iudice turpis eat.   10

> [You may recount in your praises the beauty of Antiopa, daughter of Nyc-
> teus, and of Spartan Hermione and all those whom the age of beauty
> bore: Cynthia would not allow them to possess renown; still less, if she
> were compared with minor figures, would she emerge as unpleasing, lower
> in the estimation of a harsh judge.]

Here the negative paraphrase *non illas nomen habere sinat*, with a verb in the subjunctive, is semantically equivalent to a positive assertion in the indicative, i.e. 'Cynthia surpasses them'. The idea of comparison is continued in the past participle *collata*, and that of outdoing is expressed negatively in a further paraphrase *nedum . . . inferior . . . turpis eat*.

In I. 13. 13 ff. the poet describes how he was witness to the passionate embraces of Gallus and his mistress and cites exemplary parallels:

Propertius **4**

> non sic Haemonio Salmonida mixtus Enipeo   I. 13. 21
>   Taenarius facili pressit amore deus,
> nec sic caelestem flagrans amor Herculis Heben
>   sensit in Oetaeis gaudia prima iugis.

> [Not thus did the Taenarian god, united with Haemonian Enipeus, em-
> brace the child of Salmoneus in consenting love. Not thus did the burning
> love of Hercules for divine Hebe experience its first delights on the heights
> of Oeta.]

21 f. Neptune (*Taenarius . . . deus*) assumed the form of the river-god Enipeus in order to ravish Tyro, daughter of Salmoneus.

These references are followed by an explicit comparison applied to the mistress of Gallus:

> nec mirum, cum sit Iove digna et proxima Ledae   I. 13. 29
>   et Ledae partu gratior, una tribus;
> illa sit Inachiis et blandior heroinis,
>   illa suis verbis cogat amare Iovem.

> [It is no wonder, since she is worthy of Jove and almost equal to Leda, and

more pleasing than the offspring of Leda, of herself alone surpassing all
three; she would prove more charming than all the Grecian heroines; by
her words she would force Jove to love her.]

30 *tribus* i.e. Helen, Castor, and Pollux.

Here comparison is expressed explicitly by the comparative adjectives *gratior*
and *blandior* and in the phrase *proxima Ledae*, but in addition the formulation *Iove digna et proxima Ledae* implies that if Gallus' mistress is worthy of
Jove and similar to Leda, she is being implicitly compared to all Jove's other
mortal loves, perhaps also in *Iove digna* to Juno herself.

Propertius 5

> est tibi non infra speciem, non nomine dispar,   I. 20. 5
>   Theiodamanteo proximus ardor Hylae.
>
> [You have an object of love not inferior in beauty, not unequal in repute,
> most like Hylas, child of Theodamas.]

The comparison is expressed negatively in the first line, positively in the
second. The poem is addressed to Gallus, warning him to guard his love. The
reference is to Hylas, a beautiful youth loved by Hercules, snatched away by the
nymphs and sought by Hercules in vain. This story is recounted in ll. 15–50
of the poem and is followed by the concluding warning: 51 *his, o Galle, tuos
monitus servabis amores* (warned by these happenings, O Gallus, you shall keep
your love secure). As in Prop. 4, an exemplary comparison occurs together with
an exemplary story, which in this instance, however, is of a cautionary nature.

Propertius 6

> fulva coma est longaeque manus, et maxima toto   II. 2. 5
>   corpore, et incedit vel Iove digna soror,
> aut cum Dulichias Pallas spatiatur ad aras,
>   Gorgonis anguiferae pectus operta comis;
> qualis et Ischomache Lapithae genus heroine,
>   Centauris medio grata rapina mero;   10
> Mercurio et sacris fertur Boebeidos undis
>   virgineum Brimo composuisse latus.
> cedite, iam, divae, quas pastor viderat olim
>   Idaeis tunicas ponere verticibus!
>
> [Her hair is golden and her hands long and slender, her whole figure stately,
> and she moves as a worthy sister to Jove, or as when Pallas proceeds to the
> Dulichian altars, her breast covered by the locks of the snake-wreathed
> Gorgon. Like Ischomache, heroic child of the Lapiths, a welcome prize
> carried off by Centaurs in the midst of the feast; and (like) Brimo, said
> to have laid down her virgin side by Mercury beside the sacred waters of
> Boebeis. Yield now, ye goddesses, whom the shepherd formerly saw lay
> aside your garments on the heights of Ida.]

6 *incedit vel Iove digna soror*: this probably refers to Juno, who was both
Jupiter's sister and wife; see e.g. Ov., *Met.* III.265 f., in which Juno, angered
that Semele had conceived a child by Jove, refers to herself as *regina, Iovisque |
et soror et coniunx, certe soror* (queen, both sister and wife of Jove – certainly
sister).   8 Pallas bore the head of the Gorgon, killed by Perseus, on her
shield.   13 *pastor*: Paris, the son of Priam and Hecuba, who had dreamt
that she would bring forth a firebrand, destroying the city (see Verg. **9b**.320).
Paris was therefore entrusted at birth to a shepherd, who reared him as his
own child, and whose sheep he pastured on mount Ida.   Lines 13 f. refer
to the judgement of Paris, when he decided the contest between Juno, Pallas
and Venus for the golden apple, inscribed 'for the fairest'. Bribed by a promise
of Helen, he decided in favour of Venus.

The phrase in l. 6 indicates likeness to the bearing of Juno; this is echoed in
aut cum Dulichias Pallas spatiatur ad aras in l. 8, in which *aut*, linked to *vel* in
the previous line, and the verb *spatiatur*, corresponding to *incedit*, bind the
two lines together syntactically and imply an equivalent comparison with the
bearing of Pallas. The expression of the comparison through the periphrasis
replacing the proper name in l. 6, the use of the adjective *digna* instead of
a more explicit comparative marker and the verbs of movement[3] make the
comparison with Juno and Pallas less direct, but that it is intended as such,
although mediated indirectly, is suggested also by the corresponding comparison with the paired figures of Ischomache and Brimo in the following lines.
Comparison with Ischomache is conveyed explicitly by *qualis* in l. 9, and that
with Brimo implicitly by means of textual juxtaposition in ll. 11 f. The imperative *cedite* in l. 13 is once more a varying expression of comparison: the
goddesses must yield because Cynthia outshines them.

Propertius 7

> Quid fles abducta gravius Briseide? quid fles   II. 20. 1
>   anxia captiva tristius Andromacha?
> quidve mea de fraude deos, insana, fatigas?
>   quid quereris nostram sic cecidisse fidem?
> non tam nocturna volucris funesta querela   5
>   Attica Cecropiis obstrepit in foliis,
> nec tantum Niobe bis sex ad busta superba
>   sollicito lacrimas defluit a Sipylo.

[Why do you weep more bitterly than Briseis torn away (from Achilles)?
Why do you, distressed, weep more sadly than captive Andromacha? Or
why, mad girl, do you tire the gods with my treachery? Why do you complain that my loyalty has sunk so low? Not so intensely does the nocturnal

---

[3] For verbs of movement in exemplary comparisons referring to a female subject, see *Od.* 3;
Verg. 1; Catull. 2; Tibull. 1; Ov. 1. The examples closest to Prop. 6 are *Od.* 3 and Verg. 1, in
which an explicit comparison is made with Artemis/Diana.

bird of Attica pour forth her mournful lament amidst Cecropian foliage, not so abundantly does proud Niobe by twice six tombs pour down tears from sorrowing Sipylus.]

5 f. refers to the story of Procne (see Catull. **1**. 14 n.).　　　7 f. Niobe's twelve children were killed by Apollo and Artemis, because she had boasted, on account of her many children, of being at least equal to their mother Leto, who bore two only. She was turned into a stone transported to the top of Mount Sipylus, which was perpetually wet with her tears.

The poet boasts that he is inexhaustible in love:

Propertius 8

> Iuppiter Alcmenae geminas requieverat Arctos,　　　　　　II. 22. 25
> 　　et caelum noctu bis sine rege fuit;
> nec tamen idcirco languens ad fulmina venit:
> 　　nullus amor vires eripit ipse suas.
> quid, cum e complexu Briseidos iret Achilles?
> 　　num fugere minus Thessala tela Phryges?　　　　　　30
> quid, ferus Andromachae lecto cum surgeret Hector?
> 　　bella Mycenaeae non timuere rates?
> ille vel hic, classes poterant vel perdere muros:
> 　　hic ego Pelides, hic ferus Hector ego.

[Jupiter for Alcmena's sake stayed the twin constellation of the Bear, and heaven was twice by night without its ruler, yet not on that account did he return faint to his thunderbolts. No love robs itself of its own strength. How then, when Achilles came from Briseis' embrace? Did the Phrygians any less flee the Thessalian shafts? How then, when fierce Hector rose from Andromache's bed? Did not the Mycenean vessels fear the battle? The one or the other of these could destroy fleets or walls: in this I am the son of Peleus, in this I am fierce Hector.]

The first part of this passage contains exemplary parallels with Jupiter, Achilles and Hector without linking or comparative words, but in the last line the poet claims not similarity, but identity with Achilles and Hector, in that he shares their salient characteristic: as they are undaunted in warfare, so he is undaunted in love. This is a further development of the exemplary comparison, found also in the *Aeneid* (see Verg. **8a**, **8b**, **9a** and **9b**). Syntactically it is a reduction of a comparative formulation, stripped of comparative markers.

Propertius 9

> miles depositis annosus secubat armis,　　　　　　II. 25. 5
> 　　grandaevique negant ducere aratra boves,
> putris et in vacua requiescit navis harena,
> 　　et vetus in templo bellica parma vacat:

at me ab amore tuo deducet nulla senectus,
    sive ego Tithonus sive ego Nestor ero.

[The aged soldier sleeps alone, his weapons laid aside; oxen of great age
refuse to draw the plough; the decaying ship rests on the empty sands, and
the ancient shield of war hangs idle in the temple: but from love of you old
age shall never divide me, even if I become Tithonus, or I become Nestor.]

10 Tithonus, granted immortality, but not eternal youth, by his consort Aurora, lived into great old age. Nestor, aged counsellor of the Greeks in the
Trojan war, famed for his wisdom, lived through three generations (see Propertius II. 13. 46).

As in Prop. **8**, the poet does not simply compare himself with Tithonus and
Nestor: since they symbolize old age, he imagines himself becoming one of
them, were he himself to grow old.

Propertius **10**

Vidi te in somnis fracta, mea vita, carina   II. 26. 1
    Ionio lassas ducere rore manus,
et quaecumque in me fueras mentita fateri,
    nec iam umore graves tollere posse comas,
qualem purpureis agitatam fluctibus Hellen,   5
    aurea quam molli tergore vexit ovis.

[I saw you in dreams, my life, your vessel shipwrecked, moving your weary
hands through the Ionian waters, and confessing all your falsehoods towards me, unable to lift your hair, heavy with water, like Helle, tossed on
the purple waves, whom the golden ram bore on its soft back.]

5 f. Helle escaped from her stepmother Ino on the back of a ram with golden
fleece and was drowned.

The poet urges Postumus not to doubt his wife's constancy when he is
absent at war:

Propertius **11a**

Postumus alter erit miranda coniuge Vlixes.   III. 12. 23

[Postumus will be another Ulysses with a wife to marvel at.]

This is followed in ll. 24–37 by an account of the adventures of Ulysses and
his return to his faithful wife, and the poem concludes with the line:

Propertius **11b**

vincit Penelopes Aelia Galla fidem.   III. 12. 38

[Aelia Galla surpasses the fidelity of Penelope.]

Two different types of comparison are here combined: Postumus will be a
second Ulysses, and Aelia Galla even more faithful than Penelope.

Propertius: conclusion

There is a very considerable increase in the range of mythological figures cited in the exemplary comparisons and identifications of Propertius, by comparison with earlier poets. There are only two divine figures, Juno and Pallas in Prop. **6** (see **6. 6** n.): the comparison is with the gait and bearing of Juno and Pallas, but this example seems closer to an exemplary comparison than to a comparison with specific divine physical attributes of the kind found in Ov. **4**, **5** and **15**, particularly since it is linked to the comparison with paired mythological figures in the following lines. It probably indicates that it was no longer felt appropriate to make too direct a comparison with deities. The phrase *Iove digna* in Prop. **4** may imply a comparison with Juno. The following non-divine figures occur: Gnosia (Ariadne), Andromeda (Prop. **1**); Argus, Inachis (=Io) (Prop. **2**); Antiopa, Hermione (Prop. **3**), Leda and her three children, Helen, Castor and Pollux (Prop. **4**); Hylas (Prop. **5**); Ischomache, Brimo (Prop. **6**); Briseis, Andromache, the Attic bird (Procne), Niobe (Prop. **7**); Pelides (Achilles), Hector (Prop. **8**); Tithonus, Nestor (Prop. **9**); Helle (Prop. **10**); Ulysses (Prop. **11a**), Penelope (Prop. **11b**); Penelope is also referred to indirectly in Prop. **11a** in the paraphrase *miranda coniuge*.

One of the most striking features of the exemplary comparisons and identifications in Propertius is the very varied range of syntactic constructions in which they are formulated. Comparative markers of usual type are: the pronominal adjective *qualis* in conjunction with the demonstrative *talis* in **1**, *qualis* in **6**, *qualem* in **10**; the adverb *sic* together with the conjunction *ut* in **2**; the comparative adjectives *inferior* in **3**, *gratior* and *blandior* in **4**; the comparative adverbs *gravius* and *tristius* in **7**; the phrases introduced by the negative adverbial syntagmas *non tam* and *nec tantum* in **7**. In addition, the following features are used to convey comparison: the positive adjective *digna* in **4** and **6** and the superlative adjectives *proxima* in **4** and *proximus* in **5**; the negative periphrastic phrases in **3** and the exemplary parallels in **8**; a conditional clause with the perfect subjunctive of a verb indicating comparison in *si fuerit collata in* **3**; the constructions with the negative adverb *infra* and the negative adjective *impar* in **5**; the imperative *cedite* in **6** and the indicative *vincit* in **11b**. A further development is represented by the combination of a proper name with forms of the verb 'to be' in **9** and **11a**; in **9**, in conjunction with the first person, it expresses the poet's identification with an exemplary figure; in **11a**, in conjunction with the adjective *alter* and the third person, it indicates a second manifestation of an exemplar; **8** is similar to **9**, except that a verb is lacking, but the repetition of the pronoun *ego* makes the first-person identification clear. Syntactically these examples lacking comparative markers represent a reduction of comparisons of the usual type. There are a number of verb forms expressing action and movement: **1** *accubuit, concidit*;

6 *incedit, spatiatur, composuisse;* **7** *fles, fatigas, quereris, obstrepit, defluit;* **10** *ducere . . . manus, tollere, agitatam, vexit;* **11b** *vincit.* The comparisons and identifications may all be said to have a basic laudatory or elevatory function, but illustrate specific individual variations in its expression: in Prop. **2**, **8**, and **9** the poet praises himself; Prop. **1**, **2**, and **7** raise the mundane to a higher level; Prop. **10** serves to veil criticism by setting the scene in a dream vision.

The examples of Prop. **4**, **5**, **8**, and **11a** and **11b** show how exemplary comparisons or identifications may be combined with parallel mythological characters and stories in the structure of a poem. In Prop. **4**, the preceding theme of the passionate love of Gallus is linked to that of the loves of Neptune and Tyro, Hercules and Hebe in ll. 21–4 by the negative adverbial formulation *non sic* in l. 21; this is then followed by the statement that the love of Gallus and his mistress surpasses that of all previous lovers, which in turn forms a transition to the exemplary comparison in ll. 29–32, in which, like *non sic* in l. 21, *nec mirum* in the first line establishes a link with what precedes.

In I. 20 (see Prop. **5**), the poem begins with a warning to Gallus to guard his love: heedlessness may lead to disaster, as Ascanius could tell you. This reference to the river, on whose banks the abduction of Hylas by nymphs took place, is followed by the brief exemplary comparison in which Hylas is named (Prop. **5**), and by warnings to avoid like places where nymphs may lie in wait. A considerable part of the poem is then taken up by the story itself, followed by a concluding warning. There is in this instance no explicit linguistic link of the kind found in the previous example, but the theme of warning binds the whole together. The exemplary comparison is in this case subordinate to the parallel mythological story which takes up most of the poem.

In Prop. **8**, the passage begins with nine lines of exemplary parallels. Ll. 25–7, referring to Jupiter, take the form of declarative statements, followed in l. 28 by an aphoristic pronouncement summming up the conclusion to be drawn from them. Ll. 29 f. and 31 f., referring to Achilles and Hector respectively, consist entirely of four rhetorical questions: the choice of this particular stylistic device serves to confirm the validity of the poet's reasoning. L. 33 sums up the strengths of the two heroes with whom the poet is about to identify himself. In the final line *hic* 'in this respect' refers back metaphorically to the heroic exploits just described and *ferus* repeats the epithet applied to Hector in l. 31. The connection between the mythological parallels in ll. 25–33 and the poet's identification of himself with Achilles and Hector is conveyed largely by textual juxtaposition, but *hic*, the proper names, and *ferus* establish a link with what precedes. In III. 12. 23 ff. (see Prop. **11a**), Postumus setting off for war, leaving a faithful wife behind, is identified with Ulysses. This forms a transition to the story of the voyages of Ulysses and his return to his wife and home, which in turn permits the comparison of Aelia Galla with the constant Penelope in Prop. **11b**.

These examples show how subtle and varied the textual links between parallel mythological stories and explicit exemplary comparisons may be. There are many other instances of such stories which are used as exemplification, justification or warning. There are so many of these that it is impossible to deal with them individually. Those closest to explicit exemplary comparisons are linked to the surrounding text by adverbial formulations such as *non sic* (as in Prop. 4.21), or introduced by the noun *testis* 'witness'. Of the first type is I. 2. 1 ff., in which the poet urges Cynthia not to resort to artificial aids to beauty, and in a passage introduced by *non sic* in l. 15 cites Phoebe, Hilaira, the daughter of Euenus (Harpessa) and Hippodamia as positive examples to be followed. In I. 15 the poet laments Cynthia's fickleness, introducing the contrary *exempla* of Calypso, Hypsipyle, Alphesiboea and Evadne with *at non sic* in l. 9 and *nec sic* in l. 17. In II. 6 the poem begins with *Non ita*: the courtesans Lais, Thais and Phryne were not so besieged as Cynthia; to illustrate his own jealousy the poet cites the envious feuds giving rise to the Trojan war and the battle of the Centaurs, following this with the question *cur exempla petam Graium?* (why should I seek examples among the Greeks?); in answer he cites the abduction of the Sabines, returning to the theme of Cynthia's infidelity with the contrary Greek examples of Alcestis and Penelope, who remained true. In II. 14 the poem likewise begins with *Non ita*, followed by three examples of *nec sic*: neither Agamemnon nor Ulysses, nor Electra or Ariadne experienced such joy as I experienced last night. In II. 21 the poet taunts Cynthia with her lover's infidelity in taking a wife: 11 *Colchida sic hospes quondam decepit Iason* | . . . *sic a Dulichio iuvene est elusa Calypso* (thus the stranger Jason once deceived the maid of Colchis . . . thus was Calypso tricked by the Dulichian youth). In II. 18 a textual link is established by two statements beginning with the conjunction *at* 'but', 'yet', which enclose the exemplary story. The poet begins by asking 'what if I were old?' and cites the example of Tithonus: II. 18. 7 *at non Tithoni spernens Aurora senectam* | *desertum Eoa passa iacere domo est* (yet Aurora did not despise the old age of Tithonus and did not suffer him to lie abandoned in the abode of the east). At the conclusion of the story the poet compares his own fate with that of Tithonus: 19 *at tu etiam iuvenem odisti me, perfida, cum sis* | *ipsa anus haud longa curva futura die* (yet you hate me even when I am young, faithless one, though you yourself will be a bent old woman on no far distant day).

In other instances, *testis* 'witness' at the beginning of a line serves to introduce parallel characters or stories which serve as corroboration of what precedes. Thus in II. 13. 51 ff. the poet predicts that when he is dead, Cynthia will sometimes mourn him, since it is right to continue to love those no longer living; *testis* at the head of l. 53 then introduces the story of the death of Adonis and the consequent grief of Venus. In III. 15. 1 ff. the poet urges his mistress to abandon her jealousy of Lycinna, citing the warning example of Dirce (11 *testis erit Dirce* . . .), who, driven mad by her frenzied jealousy of Antiopa, brought disaster upon herself. In III. 19. 11 ff. he counters Cynthia's accusation that men are more lustful than women by citing a list of contrary examples of women led astray by passion: Pasiphae, Tyro, Myrrha, Medea, Clytemnestra and Scylla. The first two of these are introduced by *testis*, the others occur in varying syntactical constructions, but it is clear that all are intended to bear witness to the poet's defence.

Furthest removed from exemplary comparisons are those instances in which there is no textual link between a parallel story or character and the rest of the poem, but in which the placing of the mythological elements clearly indicates what they are intended to illustrate. A few examples must suffice: I. 19. 5 ff.: even when I am dead, I will not forget you; Protesilaus returned from Hades as a shade, longing to see his wife and former home; II. 24. 41 ff.: many have loved you but have been faithless; Theseus was untrue to Ariadne, Demophoon to Phyllis, Jason to Medea; III. 11. 1 ff.: why marvel that I submit to a woman? Medea, Penthesilea, Omphale, Semiramis and Cleopatra exercised power over men and events.[4]

There is thus a very widespread and varied use of mythological reference in the poems of Propertius, ranging from explicit exemplary comparisons and identification with named exemplars, to parallel stories which may be either syntactically linked to the text, or incorporated into it without overt linguistic markers. This thematic and stylistic variety is matched by an equally wide range of lexical and syntactical features, including comparison referring to the person addressed in apostrophe in Prop. **7** and **10**, and a great diversity of expressive function, embracing exemplification, emphasis, praise, justification, corroboration, or warning.

Horace

Most of the exemplary comparisons in Horace occur in the *Odes*, with one example in *Epodes* no. XVII (see below, Horace 7).

The poet asks Lydia why she is leading Sybaris astray:

Horace 1

> quid latet, ut marinae   *Odes* I. 8. 13
>   filium dicunt Thetidis sub lacrimosa Troiae
> funera, ne virilis
>   cultus in caedem et Lycias proriperet catervas?

[Why does he lie hidden, as they say the son of sea-born Thetis did before

---

[4] See also Propertius II. 1. 57–64; II. 3. 45–54; II. 9. 1–16; II. 15. 11–16; II. 28. 15–24; II. 32. 29–40; III. 2. 1–8; III. 13. 47–58.

the tearful destruction of Troy, lest manly attire should drag him forth to slaughter and the Lycian bands?]

13 ff. Achilles is said to have been disguised as a girl by his father Peleus or his mother Thetis, in order to prevent his death in the Trojan war. This verse forms the conclusion of the poem.

The poet describes how after death his fame will be immortal, as he ascends to heaven as a swan (a frequent image of the poet):

Horace 2

iam Daedaleo notior Icaro   *Odes* II. 20. 13
visam gementis litora Bosphori
   Syrtesque Gaetulas canorus
      ales Hyperboreosque campos.

[Soon, more renowned than Icarus, sprung from Daedalus, a singing bird, I shall visit the shores of the moaning Bosphorus, the Gaetulian Syrtes and the Hyperborean plains.]

This simple type of comparison, expressed in a single phrase containing a comparative adjective, is found also in *Odes* III. 12. 8 in the description of Hebrus as *eques ipso melior Bellerophonte* (a rider better than Bellerophon himself).

Horace 3

"Donec gratus eram tibi   *Odes* III. 9. 1
   nec quisquam potior bracchia candidae
cervici iuvenis dabat,
   Persarum vigui rege beatior."

"donec non alia magis   5
   arsisti neque erat Lydia post Chloen,
multi Lydia nominis
   Romana vigui clarior Ilia."

["While I was dear to you and no more favoured youth clasped his arms around your white neck, I lived happier than the king of Persia." "While you were not more aflame for another, and Lydia did not come after Chloe, I, Lydia, in my great renown, lived more illustrious than Roman Ilia."]

4 *Persarum ... rege*: cf. *Odes* II. 12. 21 *dives Achaemenes* 'wealthy Achaemenes' (ancestor of the Persian kings); in both instances the king of Persia symbolizes the possession of fabulous wealth, to which love is to be preferred.   8 *Ilia*: the mother of Romulus and Remus.

The poet pleads with Lyce to show mercy:

Horace **4**

ingratam Veneri pone superbiam,   *Odes* III. 10. 9
ne currente retro funis eat rota:
non te Penelopen difficilem procis
    Tyrrhenus genuit parens.

[Lay aside your haughtiness, hateful to Venus, lest the rope run back when
the wheel turns. You are no Penelope unyielding to suitors, whom a Tyrrhenian parent has engendered.]

10 The image is that of a device such as a windlass running out of control.

This an example of negated identification with an exemplar.

Horace **5**

Herculis ritu modo dictus, o plebs,   *Odes* III. 14. 1
morte venalem petiisse laurum
Caesar Hispana repetit penates
    victor ab ora.

[Caesar, just lately said after the manner of Hercules, o people, to have
sought the laurel bought with death, seeks again his household gods, (returning) as victor from the Spanish shore.]

3 *Caesar*, i.e. Octavian, also known as Augustus.

The placing of the proper name in initial position immediately establishes the
comparison of Caesar with Hercules, but since Caesar returns alive as victor,
it is implied that he thereby surpasses Hercules.

To Pyrrhus: beware of your rival for the love of the beautiful youth
Nearchus:

Horace **6**

interim, dum tu celeres sagittas   *Odes* III. 20. 9
promis, haec dentes acuit timendos,
arbiter pugnae posuisse nudo
    sub pede palmam

fertur et leni recreare vento
sparsum odoratis umerum capillis,
qualis aut Nireus fuit aut aquosa   15
    raptus ab Ida.

[Meanwhile, as you are drawing your swift arrows and she is sharpening
her redoutable teeth, the arbiter of the battle is said to have trampled the
palm beneath his bare foot and in the gentle breeze to be refreshing his
shoulders covered with his perfumed locks, such as was Nireus or he who
was carried off from watery Ida.]

15 Nireus, according to Homer, *Il.* II. 673, the handsomest man among the

Greeks.   15 f. *aquosa | raptus ab Ida*: Ganymede, on account of his beauty carried off to heaven to be Jupiter's cup-bearer.

Epodes no. XVII begins with a plea to the sorceress Canidia, to whom the whole Epode is addressed, to revoke her magic spells. This is followed in ll. 8–18 by examples of those moved to pity: Achilles took pity on Telephus (who was cured by the spear which had wounded him), and allowed Priam to retrieve the body of Hector from within the Greek camp; Circe restored the followers of Ulysses to their human form. Ll. 19–29 describe the poet's torments and are followed by two linked similes:

Horace 7

> "quid amplius vis? o mare et terra, ardeo,   *Epodes* XVII. 30
> quantum neque atro delibutus Hercules
> Nessi cruore, nec Sicana fervida
>   virens in Aetna flamma."

["What more do you desire? oh sea and earth! I burn, as (did) neither Hercules, smeared with the black blood of Nessus, nor the live Sicilian flame in fiery Aetna."]

32 f. *nec Sicana fervida . . .*: probably a reference to the torments of the giant Typhoeus, struck by Jove's thunderbolt and buried under Aetna.

In her reply, the sorceress rejects the poet's plea for mercy, condemning him to continuing torment, because he had revealed and mocked orgiastic rites, citing in ll. 65–9 Tantalus, Prometheus, and Sisyphus as instances of those who vainly longed for release from suffering. The poem thus combines the exemplary comparison with mythological parallels cited in justification by each protagonist in the debate.

Horace: conclusion

The number of exemplary comparisons in Horace is surprisingly small, and is no doubt in part explained by the use in the *Odes* and *Epodes* of metrical forms with relatively short lines and in the *Odes* of short stanza forms, in which it is more difficult to accommodate them, whereas general mythological reference may be more dispersed throughout the poem (see below). Among the comparisons, Hor. **2**, **3** and **7** express the theme of outdoing the exemplar. The syntax is straightforward, expressing comparison by use of the following: the conjunction *ut* in **1**; the comparative adjectives *notior* in **2**, and *beatior* and *clarior* in **3** (and *melior* in III. 12. 8 – see under Hor. **2**); the substantival ablative *ritu* 'after the manner of' in **5**; the pronominal adjective *qualis* in **6**; the adverb *quantum* in **7**. The name of Ganymede is lacking in **6**. 15 f., but his identity is made clear by the paraphrase. The comparisons in Hor. **3** are placed in the first two verses of the poem (and the comparative adjectives *beatior* and *clarior* are matched in similes of non-exemplary type in the final verse of the poem by *pulchrior . . . levior . . . iracundior*); the comparison in Hor. **5** is placed at the beginning of the poem, that in Hor. **1** at the end. The comparisons in Hor. **3**, referring to the two first-person speakers respectively, and those in Hor. **4** and **6** are set in apostrophe, but only the negated identification in Hor. **4**, addressed to Lyce, refers to the person addressed.

By contrast with the relatively small number and the brevity of the comparisons, there is considerable reference to parallel exemplary characters and stories, again mostly in the *Odes* (see also the examples cited under Hor. **7** above). These serve the purpose of illustrating general didactic themes, pointing a warning or reinforcing panegyric, and in one instance an imprecation. To the first category belongs *Odes* I. 3, which begins with a prayer to the gods to preserve Virgil, setting out for Greece: men showed daring in first embarking on the unknown dangers of the sea and venture even on what is forbidden; Prometheus brought fire to men, Daedalus attempted flight on wings denied to humans, Hercules burst through Acheron. *Odes* III. 4. 42 ff. illustrates how force is punished when not tempered by wisdom: the Titans – Typhoeus, Mimas, Porphyrion, Rhoetus and Enceladus – were struck down by Jove's thunderbolt; a second list in ll. 69 ff. of those punished for impious deeds – Gyas, Orion, Tityos, Pirithous – is introduced in the phrase *testis mearum . . . sententiarum* (witness to my judgements) (cf. the similar instances with *testis* in Propertius). In *Epistles* I. 2 the poet tells Lollius Maximus that he has been rereading Homer, who teaches what is beautiful and useful and their opposites, and cites Ulysses as example: 17 *rursus, quid virtus et quid sapientia possit,* | *utile proposuit nobis exemplar Ulixen* (again, of the power of worth and wisdom he has set before us an instructive exemplar in Ulysses). A frequent theme is the inevitability of death: *Odes* I. 28. 7 ff.: death befell Tantalus, Tithonus, Minos and Euphorbus; *Odes* II. 16. 25 ff.: rejoice in the present – Achilles in his glory was snatched away to an early death, Tithonus lived long, but died wasted by old age; *Odes* IV. 7. 25: *infernis neque enim tenebris Diana pudicum* | *liberat Hippolytum,* | *nec Lethaea valet Theseus abrumpere caro* | *vincula Pirithoo* (for Diana is unable to release chaste Hippolytus from the infernal darkness, nor has Theseus the power to break the Lethean chains of his dear Pirithous). Closely related to this theme is the vanity of riches: *Odes* II. 18. 33 ff.: no gold could bribe the ferryman to allow Prometheus, Tantalus or Pelops to return from the underworld; *Satires* I. 1. 68 (of the miser's greed) *Tantalus a labris sitiens fugientia captat* | *flumina – quid rides? mutato nomine de te* | *fabula narratur* (Tantalus athirst catches at the streams which fly from his lips – why do you laugh? if the name is changed, the story is told of you).

A few of the examples are associated with the theme of love. In *Odes* II. 4, the poet encourages Xanthias not to feel shame that he loves a slave: Briseis was loved by Achilles, Tecmessa by Ajax, and Chryseis by Agamemnon. In *Odes*

IV. 11 the poet warns Phyllis against seeking out Telephus, who is above her in status: 25 *terret ambustus Phaëthon avaras | spes, et exemplum grave praebet ales | Pegasus terrenum equitem gravatus | Bellerophontem, | semper ut te digna sequare et ultra | quam licet sperare nefas putando disparem vites* (scorched Phaethon inspires fear, deterring from inordinate hopes, and winged Pegasus, who refused to bear his earthly rider Bellerophon, affords the weighty lesson, always to follow what is fitting for you, and thinking it wrong to hope for what is beyond that permitted, to avoid an unequal partner).

Two poems in particular celebrate the power of poetry to confer immortality: *Odes* IV. 8. 22 ff.: the Muses do not permit the fame of victorious Caesar, Romulus, Aeacus, Hercules, Castor, Pollux and Bacchus to perish; *Odes* IV. 9. 13 ff.: it is only poetry which has preserved the memory of the love of Helen and Paris and the deeds of the heroes of the Trojan war – those who came before them are consigned to eternal darkness.

Exemplary characters are particularly appropriate to panegyric (see also Hor. 5). In *Odes* I. 12, in praise of Augustus, the poet begins by asking the Muse what god or hero is worthy to be celebrated and responds by singing the praises first of Jove, then of Pallas, Bacchus, Diana, Phoebus, Hercules, Castor and Pollux, followed by those of Romulus and other great Roman heroes, amongst whom the Julian constellation shines supreme. The praises thus culminate in this final reference to the Julian lineage, which forms a transition to the celebration of Caesar which is the climax of the poem. His exalted status is now made explicit: he rules under Jove's protection and is second only to Jove himself in power. In *Epistles* II. 1. 5 ff. (addressed to Caesar) the poet cites Romulus, Bacchus, Castor, Pollux and Hercules as having achieved full renown only after death: you, Caesar, are celebrated in your lifetime. In one instance a mythological reference serves to reinforce an imprecation: in *Epodes* X the poet wishes that Mevius, embarking on a sea voyage, may meet with storms and shipwreck such as befell the Greek fleet: 11 *quietiore nec feratur aequore | quam Graia victorum manus, | cum Pallas usto vertit iram ab Ilio | in impiam Aiacis ratem* (and on no gentler sea may he be borne, than was the host of the victorious Greeks, when Pallas turned her wrath from Ilium destroyed by fire against the impious bark of Ajax).[5]

Many of the references to parallel characters and stories are not linked syntactically to the text of the poem in which they occur, their significance being made clear by their placing – this is the case, for instance, in *Epodes* XVII, in the passages beginning at ll. 8 and 65 which introduce the mythological characters (see above under Hor. 7). In other instances there are explicit syntactic and lexical links of the type found in the examples above, e.g. *Odes*

---

[5] For further examples of exemplary characters or stories see *Odes* I. 6. 5 ff.; I. 16. 5 ff.; I. 18. 7 ff.; II. 9. 13 ff.; III. 3. 9 ff.; III. 7. 13 ff.; III. 11. 25 ff.; III. 16. 1 ff.; III. 27. 25 ff.; IV. 4. 61 ff.; *Satires* I. 7. 12 ff.; II. 1. 26 f.; *Epistles* I. 18. 41 ff.

III. 4. 69 *testis*; *Odes* IV. 7. 25 *neque enim . . . nec*; *Odes* IV. 11. 25 *terret . . .
et exemplum grave praebet*; *Epistles* I. 2. 18 *utile . . . exemplar*; *Epodes* X. 11
quietiore nec feratur aequore . . . quam.

Ovid

Characters and stories from myth are everywhere present in the works of Ovid,
and three in particular – the *Metamorphoses*, the *Heroides*, and the vitupera-
tive *Ibis* – testify to his encyclopaedic knowledge of classical mythology. The
Metamorphoses is a vast compendium, in which stories are embedded within
stories, all welded together by ingenious narrative links to form a harmonious
whole. The *Heroides* is a series of fictive letters, purportedly written by fabled
lovers: I–XV are ascribed to women, whereas XVI–XXI are paired letters, e.g.
XVI Paris to Helen, XVII Helen to Paris. The *Ibis* uses myth in very concentrated form in a series of linked curses. However, not only in these, but in
all his works, Ovid makes abundant use of mythological reference. There are
firstly many instances of specific comparison or identification with a mythological figure or its attributes, the majority of which have a laudatory and
emphatic function. Secondly, there is more general reference to the characters
and stories of myth. This is used to provide instructive *exempla*, which act as
illustration and justification of the poet's argument or serve to reinforce an
injunction or a warning. Both types of mythological reference may occur in
close conjunction in passages containing comparisons or identifications with
an exemplar, as in Ov. **6, 7**, and **11**. Alternatively, the connection between the
two types of reference may be less close, as in Ov. **2** and **3**.

The works on love have been grouped together on account of their similar
subject-matter, followed by the *Heroides* and *Metamorphoses* and the remaining major works, with the exception of the *Fasti*, which contains little of
relevance to the present subject. Most instances of exemplary comparisons
are cited, except that it is possible to give only a representative sample from
the *Ibis* (see prefatory note to Ov. **17**), and for reasons of space the selection
from the *Tristia* and *Ex Ponto* is not exhaustive, since it was largely the works
on love and the *Heroides* and *Metamorphoses* which were influential later.

Amores

Ovid **1**

> Aestus erat, mediamque dies exegerat horam;   *Amores* I. 5. 1
>   adposui medio membra levanda toro.
> [. . .]
> ecce, Corinna venit, tunica velata recincta,   9
>   candida dividua colla tegente coma –

qualiter in thalamos famosa Semiramis isse
  dicitur, et multis Lais amata viris.

[It was sultry and the day had passed the meridian; I laid my limbs to rest them on the middle of my couch. [. . .] Lo! Corinna comes, draped in a girdled tunic, with her divided hair covering her white neck, just as famed Semiramis is said to have come to the bridal chamber, and Lais loved of many men.]

11 *Semiramis*: queen of Assyria.   12 *Lais*: a Corinthian courtesan.

The poet repents of having struck his mistress in anger:

Ovid 2

ergo ego digestos potui laniare capillos?   *Amores* I. 7. 11
  nec dominam motae dedecuere comae.
sic formosa fuit. talem Schoeneida dicam
  Maenalias arcu sollicitasse feras,
talis periuri promissaque velaque Thesei   15
  flevit praecipites Cressa tulisse Notos;
sic, nisi vittatis quod erat Cassandra capillis,
  procubuit templo, casta Minerva, tuo.

[Did I, then, have the right to rend her ordered hair? and yet her disarrayed locks did not ill become my mistress. She was beautiful thus. Such, I might say, was the daughter of Schoeneus, as she harried the Maenalian beasts with her bow; such the Cretan maid as she wept that the headlong South winds had borne away the sails and promises of perjured Theseus; thus was Cassandra – except that her hair was bound in fillets – when she sank down at your shrine, chaste Minerva.]

13 *Schoeneida*: Atalanta.   16 *Cressa*: Ariadne.

This passage is preceded in ll. 7–10 by references to Ajax and Orestes, couched in rhetorical questions: were they too not driven by frenzy in the pursuit of vengeance and made to suffer for their impious deeds? It is followed later in the poem by the poet's comparison of his action with that of Diomedes in wounding Venus (Homer, *Il.* V. 330 ff.):

pessima Tydides scelerum monimenta reliquit.   31
  ille deam primus perculit – alter ego.

[The son of Tydeus left the most vile memorial of his crimes. He was the first to strike a goddess – I am the second.]

31 f. See also Ov. **9**; 32 implies a comparison with Venus.

The positive exemplary comparisons in 13 ff. are thus preceded and followed by negative mythological *exempla* which furnish a parallel to the poet's temerity in striking his mistress.

Ovid 3

> Qualis ab Eurota Phrygiis avecta carinis   *Amores* I. 10. 1
>   coniugibus belli causa duobus erat,
> qualis erat Lede, quam plumis abditus albis
>   callidus in falsa lusit adulter ave,
> qualis Amymone siccis erravit in agris,   5
>   cum premeret summi verticis urna comas,
> talis eras; aquilamque in te taurumque timebam,
>   et quidquid magno de Iove fecit amor.

[Such as was she carried off from the Eurotas in Phrygian vessels to be a cause of war to two husbands; such as was Leda, whom the cunning lover deceived in the guise of a bird covered with white plumage; such as was Amymone when she wandered through parched fields, as the urn pressed on the hair of the crown of her head – such were you. I feared the eagle and the bull on your account and whatever form love made great Jove take.]

1 f. refers to Helen.   3 f. Jupiter seduced Leda in the guise of a swan (*Met.* VI. 109).   5 f. Sent by her father to fetch water, Amymone was seduced by Neptune.   7 Jove assumed the form of an eagle to carry Ganymede to heaven (Ov., *Met.* X. 155 ff.); in the form of a bull he abducted Europa (*Met.* II. 847 ff.).

There follows a passage in which the poet declares that he has now abandoned such fear and love because his mistress demands gifts. After a condemnation of the evils of cupidity, he cites in ll. 49–52 Tarpeia and Eriphyle as examples of those who brought disaster upon themselves by seeking reward: Tarpeia demanded in recompense for her betrayal of the citadel to the Sabines what they wore on their left arms, i.e. their armlets, but was instead crushed under the weight of their shields, worn on the same arm; Eriphyle betrayed her husband for a necklace and was slain by her son.

In the following two instances comparisons are made with specific divine attributes. In the first the poet laments the cutting of his mistress's long hair:

Ovid 4

> Formosae periere comae – quas vellet Apollo,   *Amores* I. 14. 31
>   quas vellet capiti Bacchus inesse suo!
> illis contulerim, quas quondam nuda Dione
>   pingitur umenti sustinuisse manu.

[The beautiful tresses have gone – such as Apollo might desire, such as Bacchus might desire for their own heads! With them I could compare those which the naked Dione is depicted as holding up of old with dripping hand.]

31 f. See Ov. **15**.   33 *Dione*: the name of the mother of Venus, but also, as here, of Venus herself.   34 *umenti ... manu*: a reference to an alternative version of the birth of Venus, in which she is not the child of Jupiter and

Dione, but rises from the waves, wringing out her tresses, hence her Greek epithet Anadyomene 'she who emerges'.

There is an illuminating comment on such descriptions in *Amores* II. 4. Having first stated that he is susceptible to all kinds of beauty, the poet indicates that he can always find a parallel in myth for its different manifestations:

> seu pendent nivea pulli cervice capilli,   *Amores* II. 4. 41
>   Leda fuit nigra conspicienda coma;
> seu flavent, placuit croceis Aurora capillis.
>   omnibus historiis se meus aptat amor.

> [If dark locks hang on a snowy neck – Leda was fair to behold with black hair; if they are blond – Aurora was pleasing with golden locks. To all the old tales my love can adapt itself.]

In the second similar instance, the poet describes how, as they sit at the races, the falling cloak reveals the lady's figure:

Ovid 5

> talia Milanion Atalantes crura fugacis   *Amores* III. 2. 29
>   optavit manibus sustinuisse suis.
> talia pinguntur succinctae crura Dianae
>   cum sequitur fortes, fortior ipsa, feras.

> [Such were the limbs of swift Atalanta that Milanion longed to support with his hands; such are depicted the limbs of girded Diana as she pursues powerful wild beasts, herself more powerful.]

As the procession of gods is carried past before the race, Venus seems to nod in answer to the poet's prayer:

> quod dea promisit, promittas ipsa, rogamus;   59
>   pace loquar Veneris, tu dea maior eris.

> [What the goddess has promised, promise yourself, I beg; with Venus' permission let me say, you will be the greater goddess.]

Ars Amatoria

There are two striking passages in which the poet praises his own skill, the first at the beginning of book I, the second at the end of book II:

Ovid 6

> Arte citae veloque rates remoque moventur,   *Ars Amatoria* I. 3
>   Arte leves currus; arte regendus amor.
> Curribus Automedon lentisque erat aptus habenis,   5
>   Tiphys in Haemonia puppe magister erat:
> Me Venus artificem tenero praefecit Amori:
>   Tiphys et Automedon dicar Amoris ego.

[By skill swift ships are propelled by sail and oar, by skill light chariots; by skill must Love be guided. To chariots and pliant reins Automedon was suited, Tiphys was the helmsman of the Haemonian ship: me has Venus set over tender Love as master of the art; I shall be called the Tiphys and Automedon of Love.]

This example neatly combines the citation of mythological parallels with the poet's identification of himself with them. It is followed by a passage describing how the Centaur Chiron subdued and taught Achilles, which concludes with the lines:

Aeacidae Chiron, ego sum praeceptor Amoris: 17
  Saevus uterque puer, natus uterque dea.

[Chiron was the teacher of Aeacides, I am the teacher of Love: each boy is unruly, and each born of a goddess.]

Ovid **7**

Quantus apud Danaos Podalirius arte medendi,   *Ars Amatoria* II. 735
  Aeacides dextra, pectore Nestor erat,
Quantus erat Calchas extis, Telamonius armis,
  Automedon curru, tantus amator ego.
Me vatem celebrate, viri, mihi dicite laudes,
  Cantetur toto nomen in orbe meum.   740
Arma dedi vobis: dederat Vulcanus Achilli;
  Vincite muneribus, vicit ut ille, datis.

[As great as was Podalirius among the Greeks in the art of healing, or Aeacides in strength of hand, Nestor in understanding, as great as was Calchas in interpreting the entrails, or Telamon's son in arms, or Automedon in the chariot, so great a lover am I. Celebrate me, the poet, o men, speak my praises, let my name be sung in the whole world. I have given you armour – Vulcan gave armour to Achilles – conquer as he conquered, by means of the gift.]

736 *Aeacides*: Achilles.   *Nestor*: see Prop. **9**. 10 n.   737 *Telamonius*: Ajax.

In this instance a mythological parallel, that of Vulcan's gift to Achilles, is combined with a series of explicit comparisons of the poet with exemplary figures. See the reference to Podalirius in Ov. **10**.

Ovid **8**

Nominibus mollire licet mala: fusca vocetur,   *Ars Amatoria* II. 657
  Nigrior Illyrica cui pice sanguis erit;
Si paeta est, Veneris similis: si flava, Minervae;
  Sit gracilis, macie quae male viva sua est.   660

[With names it is possible to soften defects: let her be called dark, whose blood is blacker than Illyrian pitch; if she has a cast in her eye, similar to Venus, if yellow-haired, to Minerva; let her be slender whose life is imperilled by her thinness.]

659 *paeta*: an occasional epithet of Venus, perhaps with the sense '(prettily) glancing' (?). 660 *macie quae male viva sua est*: lit. 'who is barely alive on account of her thinness'.

Remedia Amoris

This work is extremely rich in mythological reference, but there appear to be no exemplary comparisons and only two instances of identification with a named exemplar, the first negative, the second positive.

Ovid 9

> Legerat huius Amor titulum nomenque libelli   *Remedia Amoris* 1
>   "Bella mihi video, bella parantur" ait.
> "Parce tuum vatem sceleris damnare, Cupido,
>   Tradita qui toties te duce signa tuli.
> Non ego Tydides, a quo tua saucia mater   5
>   In liquidum rediit aethera Martis equis."

[Love read the title and the name of this book: "Wars", he said, "wars are preparing for me, I see." "Refrain from condemning your poet for a crime, Cupid, I who have so often under your command borne the standards you committed to me. I am no Tydides, from whom your mother returned wounded to the pure air of heaven borne by the horses of Mars".]

Here the poet disclaims any intention to attack Love and therefore disavows identification with Diomedes, whose action in striking Venus he cites as exemplary parallel in Ov. **2**. 31 f.

Ovid 10

> Haeserat in quadam nuper mea cura puella: *Remedia Amoris* 311
>   Conveniens animo non erat illa meo:
> Curabar propriis aeger Podalirius herbis,
>   et, fateor, medicus turpiter aeger eram.

[Lately my attention was fixed on a certain girl: she was not willing to comply with my wishes. I treated myself with my own herbs, a sick Podalirius, and I confess I was a shamefully sick physician.]

For the physician Podalirius see under Ov. **7**.

Heroides

Sappho to Phaon:

Ovid 11

> Est in te facies, sunt apti lusibus anni –   *Heroides* XV. 21
>   o facies oculis insidiosa meis!

sume fidem et pharetram – fies manifestus Apollo,
    accedant capiti cornua – Bacchus eris:
et Phoebus Daphnen, et Gnosida Bacchus amavit,   25
    nec norat lyricos illa vel illa modos;
at mihi Pegasides blandissima carmina dictant,
    iam canitur toto nomen in orbe meum.
[...]
tu mihi Leucadia potes esse salubrior unda,   187
    et forma et meritis tu mihi Phoebus eris.

[You have beauty and your years are suited to pleasures – o beauty that ensnares my eyes! Take up the lyre and quiver – you will be Apollo manifest; let horns be set upon your head – you will be Bacchus. Phoebus loved Daphne and Bacchus loved the Gnosian maid, and neither of these knew the lyric modes, but for me the daughters of Pegasus dictate most pleasing songs, my name is already sung in the whole world. [...] You can be more restorative to me than the Leucadian wave, and in beauty and deserts you will be to me Phoebus.]

25 f. *Gnosida*: Cretan, i.e. Ariadne (see *Gnosia* Prop. **1**). Sappho implies that as a lyric poet she is more worthy of love than either Daphne or Ariadne. 27 *Pegasides*, i.e. the Muses.   187 Sappho is said to have leapt into the sea from a cliff on the island of Leucadia.

Leander to Hero:

Ovid **12**

est aliud lumen, multo mihi certius istis,   *Heroides* XVIII. 155
    non errat tenebris quo duce noster amor;
hoc ego dum spectem, Colchos et in ultima Ponti,
    quaque viam fecit Thessala pinus, eam,
et iuvenem possim superare Palaemona nando
    miraque quem subito reddidit herba deum.   160

[There is another light, far more fixed to me than these, and when it guides me through the darkness, my love cannot stray from its course; while I fix my gaze on it, I could go to Colchis or the furthermost parts of Pontus and where the ship of Thessalian pine took its way, and I could outdo the young Palaemon in swimming and him whom the marvellous herb suddenly made a god.]

157 *Colchos*: lit. 'the Colchians', by metonymy for Colchis (see *Tyrios* Verg. **3.** 468 n.)   158 *Thessala pinus*: the *Argo*, ship of Jason.   159 f. Palaemon and Glaucus (to whom 160 refers) were changed into marine deities.

Acontius to Cydippe:

Ovid 13

> tu facis hoc oculique tui, quibus ignea cedunt   *Heroides* XX. 55
>   sidera, qui flammae causa fuere meae;
> hoc faciunt flavi crines et eburnea cervix,
>   quaeque, precor, veniant in mea colla manus,
> et decor et vultus sine rusticitate pudentes,
>   et Thetidis qualis vix rear esse pedes.   60

[You are the cause of this, and your eyes to which the fiery stars yield in brightness, which were the occasion of my burning love. This is caused by your golden hair and your ivory throat and the hands which I pray may clasp my neck, and your grace and your features, modest yet not unrefined, and feet which I think those of Thetis could scarcely equal.]

Cydippe to Acontius:

Ovid 14

> verba quid exultas tua si mihi verba dederunt,   *Heroides* XXI. 121
>   sumque parum prudens capta puella dolis?
> Cydippen pomum, pomum Schoeneida cepit;
>   tu nunc Hippomenes scilicet alter eris.

[Why do you exult if your words deceived me, and I a girl with too little wisdom was captured by your wiles? An apple caught Cydippe, an apple caught the daughter of Schoeneus – you will now truly be a second Hippomenes.]

123 *Schoeneida*: see Ov. **2**. 13 n.

Acontius gave Cydippe an apple on which was written 'I swear by Diana to marry Acontius'; by reading it aloud she was bound by the oath. Atalanta lost the race by stopping to pick up the golden apple dropped by Hippomenes. The comparison with Atalanta in line 123, conveyed solely by the two juxtaposed phrases linked by the same verb, prepares for the identification of Acontius with Hippomenes in the final line.

Metamorphoses

Narcissus gazes at his reflection:

Ovid 15

> spectat humi positus geminum, sua lumina, sidus   *Metamorphoses* III. 420
> et dignos Baccho, dignos et Apolline crines
> inpubesque genas et eburnea colla decusque
> oris et in niveo mixtum candore ruborem,
> cunctaque miratur, quibus est mirabilis ipse.

[Prostrate on the ground he gazes at his own eyes, twin stars, and his hair, worthy of Bacchus, and worthy of Apollo, his youthful cheeks, his ivory

neck, the beauty of his face, the red mixed with snowy white, and all these
he admires, for which he himself is admired.]

421 See Ov. **4**.

Orpheus turns to look back at Eurydice, causing her to return to Hades:

Ovid **16a**

Non aliter stupuit gemina nece coniugis Orpheus,   *Metamorphoses* X. 64
quam tria qui timidus, medio portante catenas,
colla canis vidit, quem non pavor ante reliquit,
quam natura prior saxo per corpus oborto,
quique in se crimen traxit voluitque videri
Olenos esse nocens, tuque o confisa figurae
infelix Lethaea tuae, iunctissima quondam   70
pectora, nunc lapides, quos umida sustinet Ide.

[No less stunned was Orpheus by his wife's double death than the fright-
ened man who saw the three heads of the dog, with chains on the middle
neck, whose fear only left him when his former nature departed and the
stone had spread throughout his body, or no less than Olenos who took
a crime upon himself and was willing to appear guilty, and you, unhappy Lethaea, (arrogantly) confident of your beauty, once two forms
most closely joined in embrace, now stones which watery Ida holds.]

65–71 The story of the unknown man turned to stone at the sight of Cerberus
and that of Olenos and Lethaea appear only to be attested here.

Ovid **16b**

Met. XV. 547 ff. This example, difficult to detach syntactically from the
lengthy story of Cipus which is appended to it, and very similar to **16a**, is
therefore merely summarized: the nymphs were amazed when Egeria was
turned into a spring, and Hippolytus, here designated as *Amazone natus*,
was no less amazed (553 *haud aliter stupuit*) than the Tyrrhenian peasant
when he saw a clod of earth turn into the Etruscan god Tages, or Romulus
when he saw his spear putting forth leaves, or Cipus when he saw horns
springing from his head.

These two examples represent a reversal of the standard pattern of exemplary comparisons, in that Orpheus and Hippolytus normally belong to the
category of figures themselves cited as exemplars, with whom others are compared. It was no doubt difficult to find suitable exemplary figures with which
to compare them in their turn, and it is perhaps for that reason possible that
Ovid invented the two otherwise unknown stories in Ov. **16a** above.

Ibis

This work, directed at an unnamed enemy, uses comparison with mythological figures as a medium of vituperation. Ll. 251–636 are a sustained series of

imprecations, wishing on the enemy and his family every conceivable evil fate attested in myth. As a concentrated catalogue of mythological characters and stories, the work is a *tour de force*. Here it is possible to cite only an illustrative sample from the beginning of the list of imprecations:

Ovid **17**

> Neve sine exemplis aevi cruciere prioris,   *Ibis* 251
>   sint tua Troianis non leviora malis,
> Quantaque clavigeri Poeantius Herculis heres,
>   tanta venenato vulnera crure geras.
> Nec levius doleas, quam qui bibit ubera cervae,   255
>   armatique tulit vulnus, inermis opem;
> Quique ab equo praeceps in Aleïa decidit arva,
>   exitio facies cui sua paene fuit.

> [And that you may not be tormented without the examples of a former age, may your ills be no lighter than those of Troy, may you endure such wounds as the son of Poeas, the heir of club-wielding Hercules, bore in his poisoned leg, nor may you suffer less grievously than the one who drank from the hind's udders, received a wound from an armed man and aid from one unarmed, or than him who fell headlong from his horse into the Aleian fields, whose face was almost his destruction.]

253 *Poeantius*: Philoctetes.   255 f. The reference is to Telephus; the armed man is Achilles, the unarmed man the healer Machaon.   257 f. refers to Bellerophon.

Tristia and *Ex Ponto*

To his wife, from exile:

Ovid **18**

> nec probitate tua prior est aut Hectoris uxor,   *Tristia* I. 6. 19
>   aut comes extincto Laodamia viro.
> tu si Maeonium vatem sortita fuisses,
>   Penelopes esset fama secunda tuae.

> [In goodness neither Hector's wife is superior to you, nor Laodamia, companion of her slain husband. If you had been allotted the Maeonian bard, Penelope's fame would be second to yours.]

19 *Hectoris uxor*: Andromache.   21 *Maeonium vatem*: Homer.

Ovid **19**

> non equidem dubito, quin haec et cetera fiant,   *Tristia* IV. 3. 27
>   detque tuus maesti signa doloris amor,
> nec cruciere minus, quam cum Thebana cruentum
>   Hectora Thessalico vidit ab axe rapi.

[I do not indeed doubt that this and other things occur, and that your love gives signs of sad grief, that you are tormented no less than the Theban princess, when she saw blood-stained Hector dragged by the Thessalian chariot.]

29 *Thebana*: Andromache.   30 *Thessalico . . . ab axe*: by the chariot of Achilles.

On his wife's birthday:

Ovid **20**

> haec ergo lux est, quae si non orta fuisset,   *Tristia* V. 5. 41
>   nulla fuit misero festa videnda mihi.
> edidit haec mores illis heroisin aequos,
>   quis erat Eëtion Icariusque pater.

[This then is the day – had it not risen, there would have been no festal anniversary to be seen by me in my misery. This brought forth a nature equalling those famed heroines whose fathers were Eëtion and Icarius.]

44 Eëtion and Icarius were the fathers of Andromache and Penelope respectively.

To Rufinus:

Ovid **21**

> utque Machaoniis Poeantius artibus heros   *Ex Ponto* I. 3. 5
>   lenito medicam vulnere sensit opem,
> sic ego mente iacens et acerbo saucius ictu
>   admonitu coepi fortior esse tuo,
> et iam deficiens sic ad tua verba revixi,
>   ut solet infuso vena redire mero.

[As the Poeantian hero through the skills of Machaon felt in his assuaged wound the healing aid, so I, prostrate in mind and wounded by a bitter blow, began to grow stronger through your admonition; already on the point of failing, I was as much restored to life by your words as the pulse is wont to recover when wine is administered.]

5 *Poeantius . . . heros*: see Ov. **17**. 253 n.

Ovid: conclusion

Of the above examples, Ov. **1–3, 7, 12, 16a, 16b** contain comparisons with exemplary figures and Ov. **14** includes an implicit comparison between Cydippe and Atalanta. Ov. **4, 5, 8, 13, 15** are comparisons with attributes. Ov. **6, 9, 10, 11, 14** contain identification with an exemplar. Ov. **5.**60, **12, 13.**60 and **18** express the motif of outdoing the exemplar. Comparison with named figures is expressed syntactically by the following means: **1** *qualiter*; **2** *talem, talis, sic*; **3** *qualis* (3×) . . . *talis*; **7** *quantus* (2×) . . . *tantus*; **12** *iuvenem possim superare*

Palaemona nando . . .; **16a** *non aliter . . . quam*; **16b** *haud aliter . . . quam*; **17** *non leviora, quantaque . . . tanta, nec levius . . . quam* (and many other similar examples in the rest of *Ibis*); **18** *nec prior est; esset fama secunda tuae*; **19** *nec minus . . . quam*; **20** *mores illis heroisin aequos*; **21** *utque . . . sic, sic . . . ut*. In **14**. 123 comparison is expressed solely by the juxtaposition of two parallel phrases with a single verb, without a comparative word. Comparison with attributes is expressed as follows: in **4** with two subjunctive relative clauses indicating a wish, and a relative clause prefaced by *illis contulerim*; in **5** by *talia . . . talia*; in **8** by *similis*; in **13** with *qualis*; in **15** with *dignos Baccho, dignos et Apolline crines*. Identification with an exemplar is usually expressed by means of the name in conjunction with a verb: **6** *Tiphys . . . dicar*; **10** *curabar . . . aeger Podalirius*; **11** *fies . . . Apollo*; *Bacchus eris*; *Phoebus eris*; **14** *Hippomenes . . . alter . . . eris*; only in the negative example in **9** *non ego Tydides* is a verb lacking (for a similar example see Prop. **8**).

Apart from proper names of the usual type, the figures of myth are designated by patronymics or other indications of parental descent in *Schoeneida* in **2** and **14**, *Aeacides* and *Telamonius* in **7**, *Tydides* in **9**, *Poeantius* in **17** and *Poeantius . . . heros* in **21** (see also *Pegasides* in **11**); by the parental name in **20** (referring to Andromache and Penelope); by substantivized topographical adjectives in *Cressa* in **2**, *Gnosida* in **11** and *Thebana* in **19** (see also *Thessala pinus* of the ship of Jason in **12** and *Thessalico . . . ab axe* of the chariot of Achilles in **19**); by periphrasis in **3** (of Helen), **12** (of Glaucus) and **17** (of Telephus and Bellerophon); by the substantivized past participle *armatique* (of Achilles) and the substantivized adjective *inermis* (of Machaon) in **17**.

The function of the passages cited is basically laudatory, whether they express comparison or identification with an exemplar, or comparison with individual attributes, but some examples are more complex. In Ov. **2** there is also an element of self-justification – in spite of the poet's blows, Cynthia's beauty is unimpaired; in Ov. **8** praise becomes mendacious flattery; in Ov. **11** Sappho praises not only Phaon but herself as poet, and as therefore superior to Daphne and Ariadne; Ov. **19** stresses also the extreme intensity of grief; the poetic boasts in Ov. **6** and **7** are certainly in part humorous; the negative disclaimer in Ov. **9** is indirect self-praise. Identification with Podalirius in Ov. **10**, unlike that in Ov. **7**, marks a contrast between the poet and the exemplar; that with Hippomenes in Ov. **14** expresses censure, and the many examples of comparison in the *Ibis*, including those in Ov. **17**, are used for purposes of vituperation. Ov. **16a** and **16b** are unusual, in that they reverse the usual pattern of comparison by making Orpheus and Hippolytus not the exemplars, but the main subjects to which the comparison refers. Ov. **1**, **3**, **6**, **9**, and **21** are given prominence by being placed in initial or near-initial position; Ov. **7** is at the end of a book.

As throughout in the works of Ovid, there is considerable variety of voice and person even within the limited confines of exemplary comparison, identification and exemplary parallel.[6] In particular, the letter form in the *Heroides*, *Tristia*, and *Ex Ponto* dictates a predominantly first-person voice but also apostrophe of the intended recipient. The exemplary comparisons in Ov. **1**, **5**, **8**, and **15** are in the third person. Ov. **2** combines predominanly third-person reference with the first-person *dicam* and the apostrophe *sic ... Cassandra ... | procubuit templo, casta Minerva, tuo.* Ov. **7** combines third- and first-person in a series of explicit comparisons applied to the poet himself. In Ov. **9**, the poet's disclaimer that he is no Tydides is addressed in apostrophe to Cupid. Leander speaks in the first-person singular in Ov. **12**, but introduces a first-person plural in *noster amor.* Ov. **14** combines first and second person with a third-person reference by Cydippe to herself in l. 123. Ov. **16a** combines third-person enumeration with second-person singular apostrophe in *tuque o confisa figurae | infelix Lethaea tuae*; in Ov. **20** third-person reference is combined with the first-person pronoun *mihi*; Ov. **21** combines first person with apostrophe. There are several instances in which a first-person voice is associated with comparison or identification referring to the subject addressed in apostrophe: Ov. **3**; Ov. **11**. 21 ff., 187 f.; Ov. **13**; Ov. **14**. 124; Ov. **18**; Ov. **19**. The curses addressed to an enemy in the *Ibis*, of which Ov. **17** gives a sample, are couched in a series of apostrophes.

By contrast with the use of myth in exemplary comparisons and identifications with an exemplar, general mythological references in Ovid have a more varied function. Myth may provide a warning example, often signalled by the word *exemplum* itself. Thus the story of Cephalus and Procris in *Ars Am.* III. 687 ff. is prefaced in ll. 685 f. by the admonition: *nec cito credideris: quantum cito credere laedat, | exemplum vobis non leve Procris erit* (nor be quick to believe: how much harm quick belief can do, Procris will be to you an example not lacking in weight). While resting on the hunt, Cephalus is wont to summon cooling breezes with the words "*mobilis aura, veni*" ("wandering breeze, come"), which when conveyed to Procris are taken by her to be an invocation of the name of Aura. Convinced of his infidelity, she hides in a grove to entrap Cephalus, but when she hears the now unambiguous words "*zephyri molles auraque*" *dixit* "*ades*" ("soft zephyrs and gentle breeze", he said, "come"), she starts forth, but he, thinking her to be a wild beast, kills her. In *Rem. Am.* the example of the self-inflicted death of Phyllis after her abandonment by Demoophon is cited as a warning to lovers against nursing grief in solitude: 607 *Phyllidis exemplo nimium secreta timeto, | laese vir a domina, laesa puella viro* (by the example of Phyllis fear too much seclusion, lover injured by your mistress, girl injured by your lover). Likewise in *Met.* IX. 454–6 Byblis serves as a warning to pursue love only within lawful bounds: *Byblis in exemplo est, ut ament concessa puellae, | Byblis Apollinei correpta cupidine fratris; | non soror*

---

[6] Only the formulation of actual examples is considered, disregarding the surrounding context.

ut fratrem, nec qua debebat, amabat (Byblis is a warning that girls should love what is permitted, Byblis, seized by desire for her brother, the descendant of Apollo; she did not love him as a sister loves a brother, nor in the way she should).

Mythological parallels may be used to support entreaty or persuasion. In *Am.* II. 17. 11 ff. the poet pleads with Corinna not to scorn him, even if he is beneath her: the nymph Calypso loved Ulysses, Thetis was united with Peleus, Egeria with Numa and Vulcan with Venus. In *Ars Am.* I. 440 ff. he urges lovers to employ earnest pleas: Achilles was moved by Priam's plea to give up the body of Hector, and the gods when angry are swayed by prayer. In *Her.* IV. 93 ff. Phaedra attempts to persuade Hippolytus to abandon the chase in favour of love, as did Cephalus in consorting with Aurora, Adonis with Venus, and the son of Oeneus with Atalanta: 101 *nos quoque iam primum turba numeremur in ista* (let us too now for the first time be numbered in that company).

In *Am.* II. 12. 17 ff. the poet draws parallels with his own victory in the warfare of love, outwitting a husband's guard: in other wars too, a woman was the cause and the prize fought over, as in the abduction of Helen, the attempted abduction of Hippodamia in the battle of the Lapiths and Centaurs, or the contest of the Trojans and Latinus for the sake of Lavinia. This example shows how exactly Ovid matches myth to the situation, since in each case a rival does battle with a husband or intended husband.

The exemplary figures may be cited in related groups. Thus in *Ars Am.* I. 269 f. the poet asserts that women are easily caught, like birds in a snare, since they are more prone than men to excessive desire. There follow as proof in ll. 283–342 the examples of Byblis, Myrrha, Pasiphaë, Aerope, Scylla, Creusa and Medea, and of Nisus, Agamemnon, Phoenix, Hippolytus and Phineus as male victims of women's lust. In *Rem. Am.* 55 ff. the poet boasts that had they had the benefit of his advice, many women could have been saved from their fate: Phyllis would not have died, Dido would not have seen Aeneas sail away, Medea would not have killed her children, Tereus would not have committed a crime against Philomela, Pasiphaë not loved the bull; Phaedra would not have indulged in shameful love, Helen would not have been abducted, and Scylla would not have betrayed her father. In *Rem. Am.* 400 ff. the poet advises the lover to have two mistresses, in order to moderate the sufferings of love, and cites a list of examples in which a second love ousted the first: Minos, Paspihaë and Procris; Phineus, Cleopatra and Idaea; Alcmaeon, Alphesiboea and Callirrhoe; Paris, Oenone and Helen; Tereus, Procne and Philomela. He concludes the list by asking, certainly with tongue in cheek: 461 *quid moror exemplis, quorum me turba fatigat?* (why do I dwell on examples, whose number wearies me?), but a few lines later gives the further example of Agamemnon, who, when forced to give up Chryseis, demanded Briseis from Achilles in return. The poet's advice is summed up in the exhortation: 485 *ergo adsume*

novas auctore Agamemnone flammas, | *ut tuus in bivio distineatur amor* (there-
fore take on a new attachment after the manner of Agamemnon, so that at
the parting of the ways your love may be divided).

These examples show that Ovid had a vast body of mythological knowledge at his disposal, and that it came naturally to him to quote it, adapting it
to the argument of the moment. Perhaps the most striking example of all in
this respect is the letter to his wife in *Ex Ponto* III. I, in which he urges her to
plead with the wife of Augustus for his release from exile. He first sets before
her noble examples of conjugal fidelity to follow: Alcestis, should she have
to offer her life in exchange for his; Penelope, if it should prove necessary to
repel importunate suitors; Laodamia, who followed her husband to the grave
(see Ov. **18** above), or Euadne, who threw herself on her husband's pyre. He
then retracts these harsh injunctions, however, by stating that death is in no
way needful if she will but approach Caesar's wife boldly. She, who has the
form of Venus and the character of Juno,[7] is not to be feared, since she is no
Procne, Medea, Danaid, Clytemnestra, Scylla, Circe or Medusa: there is none
more illustrious in the whole universe, save only Caesar himself. This passage
thus combines different types of mythological parallel, the citation of positive
models, and the rejection of negative exemplars, together with a description
of Caesar's wife as possessing the attributes of divinities. Such a display of
learning and the flattery of Caesar and Caesar's wife certainly suggest that the
letter was not destined for the eyes of the poet's wife alone and was intended
to show him and his cause in the most favourable light.

Whereas the function of the exemplary comparisons and identifications
with an exemplar is largely laudatory, or on occasion the expression of contrast
or censure, or in the unique case of the *Ibis* that of vituperation, the general
mythological parallels in Ovid, those not cast in the form of comparison or
identification, have more varied functions. They may be used to cite positive
or warning examples, to reinforce entreaty and persuasion, to exemplify the
poet's own situation, to illustrate advice, to justify assertions and to lend the
authority of tradition to the poet's pronouncements.

Catullus to Ovid: Conclusion

If exemplary comparisons, identification with an exemplar, and parallel mythological stories are all taken into account, it is clear that the Latin poets from
Catullus to Ovid were able to draw on a vast repertoire of mythological knowledge, and that it provided a useful thematic and stylistic resource. Most of the

---

[7] III. I. 117 *quae Veneris formam, mores Iunonis habendo* | *sola est caelesti digna reperta toro* (who
possessing the form of Venus and the character of Juno has alone been found worthy of the
divine couch). The semi-divine status of the imperial consort no doubt explains the choice
of formulation. Descriptions of this kind are common later in panegyric of royal personages.

examples cited in the poets are exemplary comparisons: among these, the motif of outdoing the exemplar occurs in Prop. **3, 4, 6**. 13 f., **7**, and **11b**; Hor. **2, 3**, and **7**; Ov. **5**. 60, **12, 13**, and **18**. Identification with an exemplar is found in Catull. **7** (in atypical form); Prop. **8, 9**, and **11a**, and in Ov. **6, 10, 11**, and **14**. In Hor. **4** and Ov. **9** identity with an exemplary figure is negated; in Ov. **14** it is used to express censure. Comparison with attributes occurs in Ov. **4, 5, 8, 13, 15**.

There are fewest instances of mythological reference in Tibullus. The evidence in Catullus shows, however, that conventions of exemplary comparisons and identification with an exemplar were already well established in verse genres at an early date. Particularly in poem 68 (see Catull. **2, 3** and **4**) Catullus is able to make extremely skilful use of exemplary comparisons in the structure and development of the poem. There is a vast array of mythological reference in the work of Propertius, taking the form both of exemplary comparisons and identifications on the one hand, and of parallel mythological stories on the other. Both types of reference are combined in the textual context in which Prop. **4, 5, 11a** and **11b** are set and within the example itself in Prop. **8**. There is a particularly wide range of lexical and syntactic features in the exemplary comparisons of Propertius and also considerable variety in the way in which he incorporates parallel exemplary stories into the text, either explicitly by means of lexical and syntactic links, or implicitly by juxtaposition. The number of exemplary comparisons in Horace is meagre, but there are many exemplary stories, particularly in the *Odes*. Ovid's work contains an encyclopaedic compendium of mythological knowledge which he adapts with consummate skill to different contexts: there are many instances of exemplary comparisons or identification with an exemplar, several comparisons with attributes, and many parallel mythological figures and stories which are used to furnish instructive *exempla*. As in Propertius, both types of reference occur together in Ov. **6, 7**, and **11**. The *Ibis* is unique in its use of a wealth of mythological parallels in a catalogue of vituperation. The earliest evidence in Catullus and the negative evidence of Horace suggest that exemplary comparisons were particularly associated with weighty metrical forms made up of long lines, more akin to those of epic, which could more easily accommodate them.

In the explicit comparisons and identifications the exemplary mythological figures are referred to in the following ways: (i) by proper name or adjective derived from a proper name; (ii) by patronymic or other indication of descent (sometimes in conjunction with a proper name); (iii) by topographical designation (sometimes in conjunction with a proper name); (iv) by a circumlocution; (v) by a general designation replacing a proper name (*antonomasia*):[8]

(i) Proper names or derivations from proper names: *Ityli* (Catull. **1**); *Protesilaëam* (adj.) . . . *domum, Laodamia* (Catull. **2**); *Venus* (Catull. **5**); *Ladas*,

---

[8] For a definition of *antonomasia*, see Introduction, n. 3.

Perseus, Pegaseo . . . volatu (Catull. **7**); *Thesea* (adj.) . . . *carina* (Prop. **1**); *Argus* (Prop. **2**); *Iove, Ledae* (Prop. **4**); *Pallas, Ischomache, Brimo* (Prop. **6**); *Briseide, Andromacha, Niobe* (Prop. **7**); *Briseidos, Hector* (Prop. **8**); *Tithonus, Nestor* (Prop. **9**); *Hellen* (Prop. **10**); *Vlixes* (Prop. **11a**); *Penelopes* (Prop. **11b**); *Penelopen* (Hor. **4**); *Herculis* (Hor. **5**); *Nireus* (Hor. **6**); *Hercules* (Hor. **7**); *Semiramis, Lais* (Ov. **1**); *Thesei, Cassandra* (Ov. **2**); *Lede, Amymone* (Ov. **3**); *Apollo, Bacchus, Dione* (Ov. **4**); *Milanion, Atalantes, Dianae* (Ov. **5**); *Automedon, Tiphys* (Ov. **6**); *Podalirius, Nestor, Calchas, Automedon, Achilli* (Ov. **7**); *Veneris, Minervae* (Ov. **8**); *Podalirius* (Ov. **10**); *Apollo, Bacchus* (Ov. **11**); *Palaemona* (Ov. **12**); *Thetidis* (Ov. **13**); *Cydippen, Hippomenes* (Ov. **14**); *Baccho, Apolline* (Ov. **15**); *Orpheus, Olenos, Lethaea* (Ov. **16a**); *Romulus, Cipus* (Ov. **16b**); *Hectoris, Laodamia, Penelopes* (Ov. **18**); *Hectora* (Ov. **19**).

(ii) Patronymics or other indications of descent: *Inachidos* (Io, Prop. **2**); *Pelides* (Achilles, Prop. **8**); *Schoeneida* (Atalanta, Ov. **2** and **14**); *Aeacides* (Achilles, Ov. **7**), *Telamonius* (Ajax, Ov. **7**); *Tydides* (Diomedes, Ov. **9**); *Poeantius Herculis heres* (Philoctetes, Ov. **17**); *Poeantius . . . heros* (Philoctetes, Ov. **21**); patronymics or other indications of descent in conjunction with a proper name: *Nereis . . . Thetis* (Tibull. **1**); *Cepheia . . . Andromede* (Prop. **1**); *Antiopae . . . Nycteidos* (Prop. **3**); *Theiodamanteo . . . Hylae* (Prop. **5**); *Daedaleo . . . Icaro* (Hor. **2**); cf. also *Telemacho . . . Penelopeo* (Catull. **6**), with an adjective derived from the maternal name.

(iii) Topographical designations: *Daulias* (Procne, Catull. **1**); *Gnosia* (Ariadne, Prop. **1**); *Cressa* (Ariadne, Ov. **2**); *Gnosida* (Ariadne, Ov. **11**); *Thebana* (Andromache, Ov. **19**). Topographical designations in conjunction with a proper name: *Haemonium . . . Pelea* (Tibull. **1**); *Romana . . . Ilia* (Hor. **3**); *Spartanae . . . Hermionae* Prop. **3**.

(iv) Circumlocutions: *Phrygium . . . iudicem* (Paris, Catull. **5**); *custos . . . ille Cretum* (the Minotaur, Catull. **7**); *Ledae partu gratior, una tribus* (Helen, Castor and Pollux, Prop. **4**); *Iove . . . soror* (Juno, Prop. **6**); *nocturna volucris . . . Attica* (Procne, Prop. **7**); *filium . . . Thetidis* (Achilles, Hor. **1**); *aut aquosa | raptus ab Ida* (Ganymede, Hor. **6**); *qualis ab Eurota Phrygiis avecta carinis | coniugibus belli causa duobus erat* (Helen, Ov. **3**); *miraque quem subito reddidit herba deum* (Glaucus, Ov. **12**); *Amazone natus* (Hippolytus, Ov. **16b**); *qui bibit ubera cervae, | armatique tulit vulnus, inermis opem* (Telephus, Achilles, Machaon, Ov. **17**); *quique ab equo praeceps in Aleïa dicidit arva, | exitio facies cui sua paene fuit* (Bellerophon, Ov. **17**); *Hectoris uxor* (Andromache, Ov. **18**); *illis heroisin aequos, | quis erat Eëtion Icariusque pater* (Andromache and Penelope, Ov. **20**); *Sicana fervida | virens in Aetna flamma* (Hor. **7**) is probably a reference to the torments of Typhoeus.

(v) General designations replacing a proper name (examples of *antonomasia*): *flavo . . . viro* (Protesilaus, Catull. **3**); *miranda coniuge* (Penelope, Prop. **11a**); *coniugis* (Eurydice, Ov. **16a**).

The circumlocutions in Hor. **6**, Ov. **3, 12**, and **17** identify the figure by means of narrative details which give the gist of the story. In the implied comparisons, there are the proper names *Iuno, Iovis* (Catull. **4**); *Apollo* (Tibull. **2**); *Phoebus, Daphnen, Bacchus* (Ov. **11**), and the topographical designation *Gnosida* (Ariadne, Ov. **11**). The patronymics and other indications of descent, the topographical designations and above all the circumlocutions show how well known the stories were to an educated audience, so that an indirect reference could suffice. In this fairly wide selection of figures from myth, several are referred to more than once, among the female figures: Andromache, Ariadne, Atalanta, Helen, Penelope, Pallas/Minerva, Procne, Laodamia, Leda, Thetis; among the male figures: Achilles, Apollo and Bacchus, Automedon, Hector, Hercules, Nestor, Philoctetes, Podalirius. All the above exemplary figures, with the possible exception of *Ladas*, the fabled runner of Alexander the Great in Catull. **7**, and *Lais*, the name of a Corinthian courtesan in Ov. **1**, are mythical. Even those perhaps considered as historical – *Ilia* in Hor. **3**, *Semiramis* in Ov. **1**, *Romulus* and *Cipus* in Ov. **16b** – are in fact legendary.

In contrast to Homer and Virgil, there are very few comparisons with divine beings. There is one comparison of Junia with Venus in Catull. **5**. In Tibull. **2** the poet does not compare himself with Apollo, but cites the story of Apollo tending the flocks of Admetus in justification of his own desire to undertake rural tasks in order to be near his mistress. In Prop. **6** the comparison with Juno and Pallas is conveyed by the adjective *digna* and the verbs *incedit* and *spatiatur*, which places the emphasis on the gait and bearing of the goddesses, rather than on the figures themselves, thus rendering the comparison less direct. In Prop. **8** the poet cites Jupiter, Achilles and Hector as proof of the assertion that love does not exhaust its own strength, but it is significant that he identifies himself in extent of love solely with the last two of the three figures. Indeed that comparisons with gods were felt to be impious is clearly indicated by the hasty retraction of an implied comparison with Jove and Juno in Catull. **4** (*q.v.*). The divine attributes which form the basis of comparison and praise are: hair that Apollo or Bacchus would desire, and like that of Venus rising from the waves (Ov. **4**); limbs resembling those of Diana (Ov. **5**); hair worthy of Bacchus and Apollo (Ov. **15**); in Ov. **8** (*q.v.*) comparisons with the glance of Venus and the hair of Minerva are recommended to disguise defects.[9]

There is considerable lexical, morphological and semantic variety in the expression of comparison. The following forms occur: the pronominal adjective *qualis* Catull. **1**, Prop. **6, 10**, Hor. **6**, Ov. **13**; the demonstrative *talis* Tibull. **1**, Ov. **2, 5**; *qualis . . . talis* Prop. **1**, Ov. **3**; the adjectives *quantus . . . tantus* Ov. **7, 17**; the adverbs *qualiter* Ov. **1**; *quantum* Hor. **7**; *sic* Ov. **2. 17**; the conjunction *ut* Catull. **2**, Hor. **1**; adverb + conjunction *sic . . . ut* Prop. **2**; *utque . . . sic* Ov. **21**.

[9] See also n. 7.

Positive forms of adjectives: *digna* Catull. **3**, Prop. **4**, **6**; *dignos* Ov. **15**; *similis* Ov. **8**; *secunda* Ov. **18**; *aequos* Ov. **20**. Comparative adjectives: *inferior* Prop. **3**; *gratior, blandior* Prop. **4**; *notior* Hor. **2**; *beatior, clarior* Hor. **3**; *leviora* Ov. **17**; *prior* Ov. **18**. Superlative adjectives: *proxima* Prop. **4**; *proximus* Prop. **5**. Comparative adverbs: *gravius, tristius* Prop. **7**; *levius* Ov. **17**. In *Herculis ritu* in Hor. **5**, the ablative *ritu* 'after the manner of' expresses the idea of similarity. Negative constructions, usually adverbial in nature: *nec tantum* Catull. **3**; *nec minus* Prop. **1**, Ov. **19**; *non infra speciem, non nomine dispar* Prop. **5**; *non tam . . . nec tantum* Prop. **7**; *non aliter* Ov. **16a**; *haud aliter* Ov. **16b**. By contrast, in those examples in which a comparison is implied, but not explicitly formulated, the lexical and syntactical links are much less specific. Thus in Catull. **4** the implicit comparison with Juno and Jove is linked to what precedes it only by the adverb *etiam* in the phrase *saepe etiam Iuno*; in Tibull. **2** the parallel between the poet and Apollo is conveyed solely by the conjunction *et* in the line *pavit et Admeti tauros formosus Apollo*. In Ov. **11** the comparison with Daphne and Ariadne is likewise first conveyed neutrally by *et* in the line *et Phoebus Daphnen, et Gnosida Bacchus amavit*, but the constructions introduced by the negative conjunction *nec* and the restrictive conjunction *at* in the following lines express an implicit contrast between Sappho and Daphne and Ariadne, loved by Apollo and Bacchus respectively. The example in Ov. **14** *Cydippen pomum, pomum Schoeneida cepit* is unusual, in that the comparison between the fate of the two figures is conveyed solely by the juxtaposition of the two corresponding phrases which are linked by their syntactical structure and by a single verb which is relevant to each.[10]

There are several constructions in which verbs express the sense of likeness or outdoing: Catull. **3** *sed tu horum magnos vicisti sola furores | . . . aut nihil aut paulo cui tum concedere digna*; Prop. **3** *Cynthia non illas nomen habere sinat: | nedum, si levibus fuerit collata figuris, | inferior duro iudice turpis eat*; Prop. **6** *cedite, iam, divae . . .*; Prop. **11b** *vincit Penelopes Aelia Galla fidem*; Ov. **4** *illis contulerim, quas quondam nuda Dione | pingitur umenti sustinisse manu;* Ov. **12** *et iuvenem possim superare Palaemona nando;* Ov. **13** *oculique tui, quibus ignea cedunt | sidera.*

Some of the comparisons contain verb forms expressing movement and are active, rather than merely descriptive: Catull. **2** *quo mea se molli candida diva pede | intulit . . . coniugis ut quondam flagrans advenit amore | Protesilaëam Laodamia domum*; Tibull. **1** *talis ad Haemonium Nereis Pelea quondam | vecta est frenato caerula pisce Thetis*; Prop. **6** *et incedit vel Iove digna soror, | aut cum Dulichias Pallas spatiatur ad aras*; Hor. **2** *iam Daedaleo notior Icaro | visam gementis litora Bosphori*; Hor. **6** *qualis aut Nireus fuit aut aquosa | raptus ab*

---

[10] There is also considerable lexical and syntactic variety in the way in which parallel mythological stories not cast in the form of comparison are linked to the text. See under Prop., Hor. and Ov.

Ida; Ov. **1** *ecce, Corinna venit . . . qualiter in thalamos famosa Semiramis isse* |
dicitur; Ov. **3** *qualis ab Eurota Phrygiis avecta carinis* | *. . . qualis Amymone siccis
erravit in agris*. This feature is undoubtedly influenced by the active nature of
many epic similes.

Identification with an exemplar is usually conveyed verbally: Catull. **7** *non
custos si fingar ille Cretum*; Prop. **9** *sive ego Tithonus sive ego Nestor ero*; Prop.
11a *Postumus alter erit miranda coniuge Vlixes*; Ov. **6** *Tiphys et Automedon
dicar Amoris ego*; Ov. **10** *curabar propriis aeger Podalirius herbis*; Ov. **11** *fies
manifestus Apollo . . . Bacchus eris . . . tu mihi Phoebus eris*; Ov. **14** *tu nunc Hippomenes scilicet alter eris*; a form of the verb 'to be' is lacking, but understood
in Prop. **8** *hic ego Pelides, hic ferus Hector ego* and Ov. **9** *non ego Tydides*.

There is considerable variety of person and voice, except that in the examples from Tibullus there is no instance of apostrophe. The first-person
voice, often emphasized by the introduction of the pronoun *ego*, is particularly prominent in certain examples: thus in Tibull. **2** 5–9 the opening phrase
o ego and the first-person potential subjunctives *aspicerem, versarem, sectarer,
quererer* serve to stress the intensity of the poet's desires. The use of the first
person is also striking in examples of identification with an exemplar, as in
Prop. **9**. 9 f. *at me ab amore tuo deducet nulla senectus,* | *sive ego Tithonus sive
ego Nestor ero*, and in Ov. **6**. 7 f. *me Venus artificem tenero praefecit Amori:* |
Tiphys et Automedon dicar Amoris ego. It is particularly appropriate to boasts
of poetic fame, as in Ov. **7**. 738 f. *. . . . tantus amator ego.* | *me vatem celebrate,
viri, mihi dicite laudes,* | *cantetur toto nomen in orbe meum*, and in Sappho's
words in Ov. **11**. 27 f. *at mihi Pegasides blandissima carmina dictant,* | *iam
canitur toto nomen in orbe meum*. In all these examples the proliferation of
first-person pronominal forms and their initial or final placing is emphatic.

In the use of apostrophe there is a wide range of person addressed: the
poet's dead brother, Catull. **1**; Laodamia, Catull. **3**; the poet's audience or
another poet, Prop. **3**; Gallus, Prop. **5**; Minerva, Ov. **2**; goddesses, Prop. **6**; the
mistress, Hor. **3**. 1–4 (in dialogue); Hor. **4**; Prop. **7**; **10**; Ov. **3**; the Roman
people in *o plebs*, Hor. **5**; Pyrrhus, Hor. **6**; the sorceress Canidia, Hor. **7**; *viri*,
Ov. **7** (see above); Cupid, Ov. **9**; Lethaea, Ov. **16a**; the unnamed enemy, Ov.
17; the recipients of the fictive letters of the *Heroides*, Ov. **11**, **13**, and **14**, and
those of the real letters – the poet's wife, Ov. **18** and **19**, Rufinus, Ov. **21**.[11]

The placing of examples is often significant. They may occur at or near the
beginning of poems or books, or less often at or near the end. Thus Prop. **1**,
7, and **10**; Hor. **5** and Ov. **3** are placed in initial position; Tibull. **2**; Prop. **3, 5,
6**, and **9**; Ov. **1, 6, 9**, and **21** are near the beginning of poems or books. Prop.
11b; Hor. **1** and **6**. 15 f. are at the end of a poem; Ov. **7** at the end of a book;

---

[11] For instances in which comparison or identification refers to the person addressed in apostrophe, see under Prop., Hor. and Ov.

Prop. **4** occurs towards the end of the poem. Proper names are also placed in significant positions, either at the beginning or end of verse lines, and in two instances in both. Thus Catull. **1**. 14 begins with *Daulias* and ends with *Ityli*; Prop. **2**. 20 has *Argus* at the beginning and *Inachidos* at the end. Initial placing in the line; Catull. **2** *Protesilaëam*; Prop. **1**, **3** *Cynthia*; Hor. **2** *Icaro*; Hor. **5** *Herculis*; Ov. **6** *Tiphys* (2×); Ov. **7**. 736 *Aeacides*, 738 *Automedon*; Ov. **14** *Cydippen*; Ov. **16a** *Olenos*; Ov. **18** *Penelopes*; Ov. **19** *Hectora*. Final placing: Catull. **4** *Iovis*; Tibull. **1** *Thetis*; Tibull. **2** *Apollo*; Prop. **1**. 4 *Andromede*, 9 *Baccho*; Prop. **3** *Hermionae*; Prop. **4**. 29 *Ledae*, 32 *Iovem*; Prop. **5** *Hylae*; Prop. **7** *Andromacha*; Prop. **8**. 29 *Achilles*, 31 *Hector*; Prop. **10** *Hellen*; Prop. **11a** *Vlixes*; Hor. **3** *Ilia*; Hor. **7** *Hercules*; Ov. **2** *Thesei*; Ov. **4**. 31 *Apollo*, 33 *Dione*; Ov. **5** *Dianae*; Ov. **7** *Achilli*; Ov. **8** *Minervae*; Ov. **11** *Apollo*; Ov. **16a** *Orpheus*.

The general function of the exemplary comparisons and identifications with a mythological exemplar is that of embellishment and emphasis, and apart from a few exceptions is largely laudatory. Their range of function is more restricted in this respect than that of parallel mythological stories which may also be cited to illustrate general didactic themes and to reinforce advice, warning, or entreaty (see under the individual poets). The comparisons and identifications are in the main used to lend weight to the praise of beauty or excellence: the likening of Augustus to Hercules in Hor. **5** is of a type which was to become very common later in princely panegyric. They serve to give embodiment to abstractions and lend the authority of established tradition to the poet's pronouncements. They raise the mundane to a higher level: thus in Prop. **1**, Cynthia asleep is like Ariadne on the desert shore, Andromeda freed from the rock, or a Bacchante exhausted by the dance, and the poet watches her as intently as Argus watched over Io. In Prop. **7**, her tears and grief exceed those of Briseis, Andromache, Procne and Niobe. As in this instance, comparisons are frequently used to exemplify intense emotion. In Catull. **1** the poet's mourning songs for his brother are like those of Procne lamenting for Itylus (for the substitution of this name for that of Itys, see the note, *ibid.*). In Hor. **7** the poet describes his burning torments as greater than those of Hercules in the poisoned shirt of Nessus or than the eternal flame of Aetna. In Ov. **19** the grief caused to the poet's wife by his sufferings is said to equal that of Andromache when she saw Hector dragged by Achilles' chariot. In Ov. **12** Leander's love is such that he boasts of outdoing the marine deities Palaemon and Glaucus in swimming. There are a few negative examples. In Ov. **14** Cydippe uses the analogy of Atalanta and Hippomenes to censure Acontius for tricking her with the apple. In Hor. **4** the poet attempts to persuade Lyce to abandon her resistance, since she is no Penelope; in Ov. **17** (and the rest of the poem) a string of comparisons with ill-fated figures of myth serves the purpose of vituperation.

There are many complex examples. In Prop. **10** the poet recounts his dream of his mistress shipwrecked: the comparison with Helle borne across the sea on the ram's back is laudatory in nature, but he imagines his mistress as she struggles against the waves repenting of all her past falsehoods towards him – the imaginary dream setting and the comparison with Helle moderate the poet's criticism of her faithlessness. Ov. **21** expresses submissive gratitude and flattery of Rufinus by likening him to the healer Machaon, but at the same time the poet compares himself to the corresponding figure of Philoctetes, one of much greater renown. There is no doubt an element of humour in the poetic boasts in Ov. **6** and **7**, and irony in the likening of Sybaris in Hor. **1** to Achilles hiding from the combat, and the comparison of the handsome perfumed youth in Hor. **6** to Nireus or Ganymede – such uses of the convention of exemplary comparisons show how firmly the tradition was established, in that it could be exaggerated for ironic or humorous effect. In poem 68, the interlinked comparisons Catull. **2**, **3**, and **4** are an integral part of the structure of the poem and mirror its thematic development – the ironic contrast between the poet's mistress and Laodamia, already implicit in the outwardly wholly laudatory comparison of Catull. **2**, is made partly explicit in Catull. **3**, in which the poet concedes that she does not match Laodamia in every respect, and is then fully revealed in the implicit comparison with Jove's infidelities towards Juno in Catull. **4**.

4

Latin Poets from Antiquity to the Middle Ages

From Antiquity onwards the Latin language remained in use as a supranational medium in Western, and later also in parts of Eastern, Europe as the language of education and all higher learning, of the Church, of law and administration, and as the vehicle of written texts of all kinds, including poetic texts. The tradition of exemplary comparisons and identifications attested in the classical Latin authors is transmitted to later Latin poets in the period stretching from Antiquity to the Middle Ages and beyond. The repertory of exemplars no longer consists solely of mythological characters, though these are still frequent, but may be expanded by the introduction of historical and biblical figures and the names of classical authors, often with combinations of figures from all these different spheres, but the basic principle prompting their use, that of lending weight to praise or blame, remains the same. The period from Antiquity to the Middle Ages is a vast one. It is difficult to draw a clear dividing line between the different phases of post-classical Latin language and literature, and to say where late Antiquity ends and the Middle Ages begin, a subject which has prompted considerable scholarly debate. Moreover, for the purposes of the present study any attempt at chronological division is of lesser importance, since the tradition of exemplary comparison and identification is a continuous one. Therefore no attempt has been made to draw a chronological distinction, which would be largely artificial. That part of the Latin tradition which is of particular relevance to the main flowering of the vernacular European lyric in the twelfth and thirteenth centuries stretches roughly from Antiquity up to the thirteenth century. Therefore selected Latin examples from this period, arranged in rough chronological order, have been chosen to illustrate the different types of context in which exemplary comparisons and identifications may occur. The concern with the vernacular lyric as prime focus has also necessitated the exclusion of a large body of other Latin literature: post-Virgilian epic, the bulk of Christian verse, and prose of all kinds, including prose panegyric, which follows the same principles as panegyric in verse but whose inclusion would have swollen the already unwieldy material unduly. The representative sample chosen includes examples both from individual poets up to the end of the thirteenth century, and from collections such as the *Carmina Cantabrigiensia*, the Ripoll lyrics and the *Carmina Burana*.[1]

---

[1] The 11th-century MS of *Carm. Cant.* includes poems referring to German emperors of the 10th and 11th centuries. The Ripoll lyrics are a 12th-century addition to a 10th-century

The contexts in which the examples are chiefly attested are: panegyric, epithalamium, funeral lament and epitaph, religious poetry, occasional poems and, particularly in the later period, love poems and descriptions of beauty. The latter types of description occur not only in the poets themselves, but in theoretical treatises on the art of poetry, such as those by Matthieu de Vendôme and Geoffroi de Vinsauf.

Exemplary Comparisons and Identifications

The following panegyric of Valerius Messalla Corvinus (64 BC–AD 8), soldier, orator and statesman, opens the fourth book of the *Corpus Tibullianum*, but is not considered to be by Tibullus himself. It was therefore not included under Tibullus in the previous chapter, particularly since it has affinities with later examples of verse panegyric:

Appendix Tibulliana 1

> nam seu diversi fremat inconstantia vulgi,   Tränkle VII   45
> non alius sedare queat; seu iudicis ira
> sit placanda, tuis poterit mitescere verbis.
> non Pylos aut Ithace tantos genuisse feruntur
> Nestora vel parvae magnum decus urbis Vlixem,
> vixerit ille senex quamvis, dum terna per orbem   50
> saecula fertilibus Titan decurreret horis,
> ille per ignotas audax erraverit urbes,
> qua maris extremis tellus includitur undis.

> [For whether the fickleness of the warring crowd is in uproar, none other than you can appease it; whether the anger of a judge must be assuaged, he will grow calm in response to your words. Neither Pylos nor Ithaca can be said to have brought forth any so great in Nestor or in Ulysses, the great adornment of a humble city, though that old man lived while Titan ran his course for three generations over the earth with his fertile seasons, and the other boldly roamed through unknown cities where the land is bounded by Ocean's furthermost waves.]

49 *Nestora . . . Vlixem*: for Nestor and Ulysses in association with eloquence see 'Laus Pis.' 1. 61, 64 and nn.; for Ulysses, cf. Archipoeta 1.1.

There follows in ll. 54–80 an account of the adventures of Ulysses, which concludes with the line: 81 *sit labor illius, tua dum facundia, maior* (he may be greater in labours, but you are greater in eloquence).

MS. The MS of the *Carmina Burana* (CB) dates from the first half of the 13th century but includes earlier material. The only relevant example in the Arundel collection occurs also in the *Carmina Burana* and has been included under the CB examples (see CB 4).

The following anonymous panegyric probably celebrates Gaius Calpurnius Piso, conspirator in the plot against Nero in AD 65. He is praised for his political and judicial oratory:

'Laus Pisonis' **1**

Minor Latin Poets I, p. 298

> nam tu, sive libet pariter cum grandine nimbos   57
> densaque vibrata iaculari fulmina lingua,
> seu iuvat adstrictas in nodum cogere voces
> et dare subtili vivacia verba catenae,   60
> vim Laertiadae, brevitatem vincis Atridae;
> dulcia seu mavis liquidoque fluentia cursu
> verba nec incluso sed aperto pingere flore,
> inclita Nestorei cedit tibi gratia mellis.

[But whether it pleases you to hurl rain storms together with hail and frequent thunderbolts with your lashing tongue, or whether it is your pleasure to compress compact expressions into one point and to lend vigorous words to the elegant sequence, you surpass the force of the son of Laertes (Ulysses), the brevity of the son of Atreus (Menelaus); or whether you prefer to adorn sweet eloquent words in their flowing course, not with an enclosed but with an open flower of style, the renowned grace of Nestor's honeyed speech yields to you.]

60 *catenae*: lit. 'chain'.   61 *Laertiadae . . . Atridae*: *Il.* III.221–3 praises the forceful eloquence of Odysseus, III.213–15 the brevity of Menelaus.   64 *Nestorei . . . mellis*: lit. 'of Nestorian honey'; in *Il.* I.249 Nestor's speech is described as sweeter than honey. See also *Append. Tibull.* **1.**49 n.

Statius (*c.* AD 45–96)

In an exchange between Cupid and Venus in the *Epithalamium in Stellam et Violentillam*, Cupid reports that he has vanquished the noble youth Stella at the command of Venus, who praises the bride:

Statius **1**

1a   "mihi dulcis imago   *Silvae* I. ii   112
> prosiluit. celsae procul aspice frontis honores
> suggestumque comae. Latias metire quid ultra
> emineat matres: quantum Latonia nymphas   115
> virgo premit quantumque egomet Nereidas exsto.
> [. . .]
> hanc si Thessalicos vidisses, Phoebe, per agros   130
> erraret secura Daphne; si in litore Naxi
> Theseum iuxta foret haec conspecta cubile,
> Gnosida desertam profugus liquisset et Euhan.
> quod nisi me longis placasset Iuno querelis,

falsus huic pennas et cornua sumeret aethrae 135
rector, in hanc vero cecidisset Iuppiter auro."

["She has grown as my sweet image. Observe from afar the beauty of her lofty forehead and the piling high of her hair. Measure by how far she rises above Roman women: by as much as the Latonian maid (Diana) overshadows the nymphs, and as I stand out above the Nereids. [. . .] If you, Phoebus, had seen her, over the Thessalian fields Daphne would have wandered secure. If on the shore of Naxos she had been seen near the couch of Theseus, Euhan (Bacchus) too, fleeing, would have left the Cretan maid abandoned. Indeed, if Juno had not appeased me with her long complaints, the false lord of heaven for her sake would have taken on plumage and horns, upon her would Jupiter have descended in the form of gold."]

130 *Phoebe*: Apollo; Apollo's pursuit of Daphne, cf. Ov., *Met.* I.452 ff. 132 f. *Theseum iuxta . . . cubile,* | *Gnosida*: Ariadne (cf. *Cressa* Sid. 5.6); *Euhan* (Bacchus): a ref. to Theseus' abandonment of Ariadne on Naxos after she had helped him escape from the labyrinth, and the subsequent love of Bacchus for her; cf. Ov., *Met.* VIII.172 ff. 135 f. The reference is to Jove's disguises as swan, bull and golden shower to seduce Leda, Europa and Danae, with whom the bride is therefore implicitly compared. The listing of the disguises is derived from Ovid, *Met.* VI.103 ff. See also Sid. 5.89 f.; Baudri 2a.21 f.; Hilarius 1b; CB 4; G. Vins. 2.

The bridegroom rejoices at the coming of the bride:

1b   Amyclaeis minus exultavit harenis 213
pastor ad Idaeas Helena veniente carinas;
Thessala nec talem viderunt Pelea Tempe, 215
cum Thetin Haemoniis Chiron accedere terris
erecto prospexit equo.

[On the sands of Amyclae the shepherd was less exultant when Helen came to the ships of Ida; Thessalian Tempe did not see Peleus thus (joyful) when Chiron, rearing high on his horse's body, looked out and saw Thetis approaching Haemonian lands.]

214 *pastor*: Paris (see Prop. 6.13 n.).

In a veiled description of the wedding night (ll. 241 ff.), there is a further comparison of the bride with Ilia (mother of Romulus and Remus), Lavinia and Claudia, who proved her virginity by causing a ship stuck fast to move:

1c   sic victa sopore doloso 242
Martia fluminea posuit latus Ilia ripa;
non talis niveos tinxit Lavinia vultus,
cum Turno spectante rubet; non Claudia talis 245
respexit populos mota iam virgo carina.

[Thus overcome by a treacherous sleep Ilia, bride of Mars, lay down on the river bank; not thus did Lavinia tinge her snowy cheeks, when she blushed beneath the gaze of Turnus; not thus did Claudia look back at the crowd when the ship had moved, now (proved) a virgin.]

243 ff. *Ilia, Lavinia, Claudia*: these names, perhaps considered to be historical, belong rather to legend; see also n. 12.

The poet pleads with his wife to return with him from Rome to Naples, his birthplace:

Statius 2

> heu ubi nota fides totque explorata per usus,   *Silvae* III.v   44
> qua veteres Latias Graias heroidas aequas?
> isset ad Iliacas – quid enim deterret amantes? –
> Penelope gavisa domos, si passus Ulixes;
> questa est Aegiale, questa est Meliboea relinqui,
> et quam – quam saevi! – fecerunt maenada planctus.
> nec minor his tu nosse fidem vitamque maritis   50
> dedere.

[Alas, where is that well-known loyalty, put to the test on so many occasions, in which you equal ancient Roman and Greek heroines? Penelope would have gone rejoicing to Trojan habitations – for what can deter those who love? – if Ulysses had permitted it; Aegiale lamented, Meliboea lamented to be deserted, as did she also whom her plaints – how wild! – made of her a frenzied maenad. You are no less able than these to devote your loyalty and your life to a husband.]

48 *Aegiale*: abandoned by Diomedes. *Meliboea*, lit. 'the Meliboean' (identification uncertain).   49 Laodamia, whose husband Protesilaus was killed in the Trojan war (see Catull. 2.74).   50 *maritis*: the pl., inappropriate to the sg. grammatical subject *tu*, has no doubt arisen by attraction to the pl. *his*, referring to the several heroines listed and their devotion to their husbands.

Claudian (fl. c. 390–405)

In a panegyric on Probinus and Olybrius, consuls in 395, Claudian compares the emperor Theodosius, victorious against the enemies of Rome, with Mars:

Claudian 1

> haud procul exacto laetus certamine victor   *MGH, AA* X, p. 7   113
> caespite gramineo consederat arbore fultus
> acclines humeros; dominum gavisa coronat   115
> terra suum, surguntque toris maioribus herbae.
> sudor adhuc per membra calet creberque recurrit
> halitus et placidi radiant in casside vultus:
> qualis letifera populatus caede Gelonos
> procubat horrendus Getico Gradivus in arvo;   120

exuvias Bellona levat, Bellona tepentes
pulvere solvit equos, immensaque cornus in hastam
porrigitur tremulisque ferit splendoribus Hebrum.

[Not far off the victor, rejoicing in the battle accomplished, was seated
on a grassy field, supported by a tree, against which his shoulders rested;
earth, rejoicing, crowns her lord and verdure springs up on swelling banks.
The sweat is still warm on his limbs, his breath comes quick and his calm
features are reflected in his helmet. Just as Gradivus (Mars), when he
has devastated the Geloni with death-bringing slaughter, rests, a dreaded
figure, on the Getic plain: Bellona lifts off his armour, Bellona loosens
his steeds, warm in their coating of dust; an immense cornel branch is
stretched forth to form his spear and strikes the Hebrus with quivering
splendour.]

121 *Bellona*: the goddess of war.

Panegyric on the fourth consulship of the emperor Honorius in 398:

Claudian 2

quis decor, incedis quotiens clipeatus et auro	*MGH, AA* X, p. 169	523
squameus et rutilus cristis et casside maior!		
sic, cum Threicia primum sudaret in hasta,		525
flumina laverunt puerum Rhodopeia Martem.		
quae vires iaculis vel, cum Gortynia tendis		
spicula, quam felix arcus certique petitor		
vulneris et iussum mentiri nescius ictum!		
scis, quo more Cydon, qua dirigat arte sagittas		530
Armenius, refugo quae sit fiducia Partho.		
sic Amphioniae pulcher sudore palaestrae		
Alcides pharetras Dircaeaque tela solebat		
praetemptare feris olim domitura Gigantes		
et pacem latura polo, semperque cruentus		535
ibat et Alcmenae praedam referebat ovanti.		
caeruleus tali prostratus Apolline Python		
implicuit fractis moritura volumina silvis.		

[With what grace you are wont to advance, in shield and gold-scaled
armour, radiant in your plumes and made taller by the helmet! Thus was
the young Mars when first he toiled and sweated, wielding the Thracian
spear, and the waters of Rhodope bathed him. With what strength you hurl
the javelin or when you shoot the Cretan arrows, how surely the bow seeks
out the certain wound and never fails to strike the appointed blow. You
know in what manner the Cretan, with what skill the Armenian directs his
arrows, what brings assurance to the fleeing Parthian. Thus the descendant
of Alceus (Hercules), fair with the sweat of the Theban wrestling-ground,
was wont to try out his quivers and his Boeotian arrows on wild beasts,
later destined to subdue the Giants and bring peace to heaven, and was

always stained with blood, as he brought back spoils to Alcmena who rejoiced. Thus was Apollo when the dark Python slain by him in its dying throes wound its coils round shattered forests.]

524 *squameus* lit. 'scaly', as of fishes and reptiles.   537 *Python*: seeking to found an oracular shrine at Delphi, Apollo killed the monstrous serpent Python, guardian of an earlier shrine; see also Sid. 1.153.

Prefatory verses to the epithalamium in honour of the marriage of the emperor Honorius in 398:

Claudian 3

3a	Princeps corusco sidere pulchrior,	MGH, AA X, pp. 119 f. 1
	Parthis sagittas tendere certior,	
	eques Gelonis imperiosior,	
	quae digna mentis laus erit arduae?	
	quae digna formae laus erit igneae?	5
	te Leda mallet quam dare Castorem;	
	praefert Achilli te proprio Thetis;	
	victum fatetur Delos Apollinem;	
	credit minorem Lydia Liberum.	
	[...]	
	Venus reversum spernit Adonidem,	16
	damnat reductum Cynthia Virbium.	
	[...]	
	tu si nivalis per iuga Caucasi	31
	saevas petisses pulcher Amazonas,	
	peltata pugnas desereret cohors	
	sexu recepto; patris et inmemor	
	inter frementes Hippolyte tubas	35
	strictam securim languida poneret	
	et seminudo pectore cingulum	
	forti negatum solveret Herculi,	
	bellumque solus conficeret decor.	

[Prince, fairer than a bright star, more sure at shooting arrows than the Parthians, rider more powerful than the Geloni, what praise is worthy of your elevated mind, what praise is worthy of your resplendent form? Leda would prefer to bear you rather than Castor; Thetis places you before her own Achilles; Delos declares Apollo vanquished; Lydia thinks Liber (Bacchus) inferior to you. [. . .] Venus spurns Adonis returned to life, Cynthia (Diana) rejects Virbius restored. [...] If over the heights of snowy Caucasus you in your beauty had sought out the fierce Amazons, the armed band would have abandoned the fight, their sex once more acknowledged, and unmindful of her father, Hippolyte amid the resounding trumpets would weakly lay down her drawn battle-axe and with half-bared breast would loose the girdle which she denied to strong Hercules. Your beauty alone would end the combat.]

17 *Virbium*: Hippolytus, restored from death as the minor god Virbius.

In the epithalamium itself there is an exchange between Cupid and Venus, and Venus addresses the bride (*AA* X, p. 136):

3b   Aurorae vincis digitos umerosque Dianae.   270

[You surpass in beauty the fingers of Aurora and the shoulders of Diana.]

Claudian 4

In sepulchrum speciosae   *MGH, AA* X, p. 292

Pulchris stare diu Parcarum lege negatur.   1
   Magna repente ruunt; summa cadunt subito.
Hic formosa iacet, Veneris sortita figuram
   Egregiumque decus invidiam meruit.

[*On the tomb of a beautiful woman*: To the beautiful to live long is denied by the law of the Fates. What is great falls suddenly into decay; what is supreme perishes without warning. Here lies a beautiful woman: allotted the beauty and surpassing loveliness of Venus, she earned envy.]

Sidonius Apollinaris (c. 430–c. 479)

Panegyric of Anthemius: the poet praises the emperor's youthful skill at hunting, which exceeds that of Achilles and Apollo:

Sidonius 1

conde Pelethronios, alacer puer et venator,   *MGH, AA* VIII, p. 177   149
Aeacida, titulos, quamquam subiecta magistri
terga premens et ob hoc securus lustra pererrans
tu potius regereris equo. non principe nostro
spicula direxit melius Pythona superstans
Paean, cum vacua turbatus paene pharetra
figeret innumeris numerosa volumina telis.   155

[Hide your Pelethronian honours, eager youth and huntsman, descendant of Aeacus (Achilles); although seated on your master's submissive back and therefore roaming safely through the haunts of beasts, it was rather you who were controlled by your steed. Paean (Apollo) did not aim his shafts better than our prince, when standing over Python, distressed that his quiver was almost empty, he pierced its numerous coils with innumerable arrows.]

149 f. *Pelethronios . . . titulos*: the adj. refers to a region of Thessaly inhabited by the Lapiths and Centaurs; it is used here by association with the Centaur Chiron, the tutor of Achilles (cf. *magistri*).   153 *Pythona*; see Claud.

2.537 n.   154 *Paean* (lit. 'healer'): Apollo was the god of divination and prophecy, the arts and archery, and the patron of medicine.

In the panegyric on Maiorianus, praise of the emperor's achievements is emphasized by being put in the mouth of his enemy, the wife of Aëtius, who has ambitions for the advancement of her own son. In her address to Aëtius she first lists the exemplary figures whom Maiorianus outstrips in their individual skills:[2]

Sidonius 2

2a   "libeat decernere caestu: *MGH, AA* VIII, pp. 191 ff.   160
          cessit Eryx Siculus
          [...]
          qui vigor in pedibus! frustra sibi natus Ophelte   164
          Sicaniam tribuit palmam, plantasque superbas
          haud ita per siccam Nemeen citus extulit Arcas
          [...]
                    vitam tum si tibi fata dedissent,   181
          Maioriane ferox, vetuisses Castora frenos,
          Pollucem caestus, Alconem spicula nosse,
          Bellerophonteis insultaturus opimis.
          si clipeum capiat, vincit Telamone creatum
          [...]
          segnius insertae trepidans pro fasce Camillae   189
          excussit telum Metabus, nec turbine tanto
          stridula Pelidae per Troilon exiit ornus;
          nec sic heroum tardantem busta Creontem
          Atticus Aegides rupit Marathonide quercu;
          nec sic intortum violatae Phoebados ultrix
          in Danaos fulmen iecit   195
          [...]
          parva loquor. quid quod, quotiens tibi bella geruntur,   198
          discipulus, non miles adest? et fingit alumnum:
          aemulus econtra spectat. quod viceris odit
          et quos vincis amat. totus dormitat ad istum
          magnus Alexander, patris quem gloria torsit."

["If it pleases him to decide the contest in boxing, Sicilian Eryx has yielded his supremacy [...] What power of foot! In vain did the son of Opheltes (Euryalus) claim for himself the Sicilian prize, nor did the swift Arcadian (Parthenopaeus) thus lift his proud feet speeding over dry Nemea [...] If fate had granted you to live then, bold Maiorianus, you would have denied Castor mastery of the bridle, Pollux that of boxing, Alcon that of

---

[2] The whole passage (ll. 151–97) is very dense, the allusions to the exemplary figures being interspersed with details of the exploits attaching to them. Only the main sections are given here.

the arrow, and you would have mocked Bellerophon's spoils. If he takes up the shield, he excels the offspring of Telamon (Ajax) [. . .] More feebly did Metabus propel his spear, fearful for the bundle enfolding Camilla, nor with such whirling force did the whistling ashen shaft of the son of Peleus (Achilles) strike through Troilus, nor thus did the Athenian, son of Aegeus (Theseus), crush Creon, as he delayed the heroes' burial, with the Marathonian oak, nor thus did the avenger of the wronged votary of Phoebus launch the hurled thunderbolt against the Greeks [. . .] I speak of trifles. How is it that whenever you wage war, he is at your side as learner, not as soldier? – and he feigns to be a pupil, whereas on the contrary he looks upon you as a rival. He hates the fact that you have conquered and loves those you vanquish. By comparison with him, Alexander the Great, to whom his father's glory was a torment, is a complete sluggard."]

189 f. Driven into exile, Metabus took with him his infant daughter Camilla, and when crossing a river, fastened her to his spear which he hurled safely to the opposite bank.   194 *violatae Phoebados ultrix*: Pallas Athena avenged the violation of Cassandra by Aias, son of Oïleus, by hurling a thunderbolt against the returning Greek ships.   200 ff.: probably a reference to quarrels concerning the succession between Alexander and his father Philip of Macedon.

On his campaigns, Maiorianus slaughters a barbarian wedding-party:

2b   "non sic Pholoetica monstra   230
atque Pelethronios Lapithas Semeleius Euhan
miscuit, Haemonias dum flammant orgia matres
et Venerem Martemque cient" . . .

["Not with such force did Euhan (Bacchus), son of Semele, embroil the monsters of Pholoe and the Pelethronian Lapiths, when his orgies inflamed the Thessalian women and incited love and war" . . .]

The panegyric of Avitus contains Rome's appeal to Jupiter, lamenting the lack of a great ruler and listing those of the past:

Sidonius **3**

                                                      MGH, AA VIII, pp. 206 ff.

3a   "Traianum nescio si quis   116
aequiperet, ni fors iterum tu, Gallia, mittas
qui vincat."

["I do not know whether any can equal Trajan, unless perchance, Gaul, you might once again send forth one who could surpass him."]

116 *Traianum*: Trajan, Roman Emperor AD 98–117, renowned for his justice and benevolence; cf. Prisc. 1.49; Venant. 1.82.

Jupiter commends Avitus as a worthy successor. In youth, unarmed, he had killed a wolf with a stone:

3b   "sic meus Alcides, Nemeae dum saltibus errat,   183
           occurrit monstro vacuus, non robora portans,
           non pharetras; stetit ira fremens atque hoste propinquo
           consuluit solos virtus decepta lacertos."

["In the same manner my Alcides (Hercules), as he roamed the mountain
valleys of Nemea, confronted the monster empty-handed, bearing neither
club nor quiver; he stood his ground, roaring with rage, and with the
enemy at hand his brave spirit, caught off guard, sought help from his
strong arms alone."]

183 f. *errat, occurrit* are historic present forms.

On his return from the hunt Avitus resembled Hippolytus:

3c   "sic Pandioniis castae Tritonidos arvis   198
           Hippolytus roseo sudum radiabat ab ore."

["Thus in the Pandionian fields of chaste Tritonis, Hippolytus radiated
brightness from his rosy face."]

198 *Tritonidos*, gen. of *Tritonis* 'belonging to lake Triton', an appellation of
Pallas Athena.

He spurns the proffered friendship of the barbarian Theoderic:

3d   "rigidum sic, Pyrrhe, videbas   226
           Fabricium, ingestas animo cum divite fugit
           pauper opes, regem temnens, dum supplice censu
           pignus amicitiae vili mendicat ab auro."

["Just as immovable, Pyrrhus, you saw Fabricius, when, a poor man of rich
spirit, he shunned the wealth pressed upon him, spurning the king when,
making his substance the suppliant, he begged a pledge of friendship with
base gold."]

229 *mendicat*: a historic present (see **3b**.183 f. n.).

He avenges the death of his slaughtered servant like Achilles avenging Patroclus (272 ff.), and when presented with the insignia of office, resembles
Hercules taking the burden of the world from Atlas:

3e   "haud alio quondam vultu Tirynthius heros   581
           pondera suscepit caeli simul atque novercae
           cum Libyca se rupe gigas subduceret et cum
           tutior Herculeo sedisset machina dorso."

["With the same look the Tirynthian hero (Hercules) once took up the
burden at once of his stepmother and of the heavens, when the giant
withdrew from the Libyan rock and the vault of heaven had sunk down
more securely on the back of Hercules."]

582 *novercae*: the hatred of his stepmother Juno was the prime cause of
Hercules' labours.   583 *gigas*: Atlas.

In *Ad Consentium*, Sidonius praises the father of Consentius as equalling or surpassing all Greek and Roman authors, scholars, philosophers, orators and statesmen. The list begins (l. 101 ff.) by citing Thales, Cleobulus, Periander, Bias, Pittacus, Solon, Chilon, Aratus, Euclid and Chrysippus. After Chrysippus there occurs a comparison with figures of Greek myth:

Sidonius **4**

4a hic cum Amphioniae studebat arti   *MGH, AA* VIII, pp. 250 ff.   120
plectro, pollice, voce tibiaque,
Thrax vates, deus Arcas atque Phoebus
omni carmine post erant et ipsas
Musas non ita musicas putares.

[When he devoted himself to the art of Amphion, in plectrum, thumb, voice and flute, the Thracian bard (Orpheus), the Arcadian god (Pan), and Phoebus (Apollo) were inferior to him in every kind of song and you might not consider the Muses themselves to be as musical.]

120 *Amphioniae ... arti*: Amphion, son of Jupiter and Antiope, renowned for his playing on the lyre, the magical power of which caused the stones of the walls of Thebes to fit themselves into place.

After this passage the list continues, citing Sophocles, Euripides, Menander, Herodotus, Homer, Demosthenes, and among the Romans, Cicero, Livy, Virgil, Terence, Plautus, Varro, Crispus, Tacitus, Arbiter, Ovid, Seneca, Martial, Lucan. Sidonius concludes the catalogue, which is eloquent testimony to his own learning, as follows:

4b quid multos varii stili retexam?   167
arguti, teneri, graves, dicaces,
si Consentius affuit, latebant.

[Why should I rehearse the names of many with diverse styles? – the precise, the delicate, the weighty, the witty – if Consentius appeared, they were obscured.]

167: for comparisons with classical authors see in particular Petr. Gramm. **1**; Paul. Diac. **1**; Einh. (?) **1**; Sed. **3**; Baudri **2b**.

In a dialogue with Venus in the *Epithalamium Ruricio et Iberiae dictum*, Cupid first lists the heroines of old who would have been vanquished by love for Ruricius:

Sidonius **5**

"esset si praesens aetas, impenderet illi   *MGH, AA* VIII, p. 229   65
Lemnias imperium, Cressa stamen labyrinthi,
Alceste vitam, Circe herbas, poma Calypso,
Scylla comas, Atalanta pedes, Medea furores,
Hippodame ceras, cygno Iove nata coronam;

huic Dido in ferrum, simul in suspendia Phyllis,   70
Euadne in flammas et Sestias isset in undas."
His haec illa refert: "Gaudemus, nate, rebellem
quod vincis laudasque virum: sed forma puellae est,
quam si spectasset quondam Stheneboeius heros,
non pro contemptu domuisset monstra Chimaerae;   75
Thermodontiaca vel qui genetrice superbus
sprevit Gnosiacae temeraria vota novercae,
hac visa occiderat, fateor, sed crimine vero;
et si iudicio forsan mihi quarta fuisset,
me quoque Rhoetea damnasset pastor in Ida.   80
[...]
te quoque multimodis ambisset, Hiberia, ludis   86
axe Pelops, cursu Hippomenes luctaque Achelous,
Aeneas bellis, spectatus Gorgone Perseus;
nec minor haec species, totiens cui Iuppiter esset
Delia, taurus, olor, satyrus, draco, fulmen et aurum."   90

["If it were at the present time, the maid of Lemnos (queen Hypsipyle)
would have freely bestowed on him her sovereignty, the Cretan maid the
thread of the labyrinth, Alcestis her life, Circe her herbs, Calypso the
apples, Scylla the hair, Atalanta her (swift) feet, Medea her mad fury,
Hippodamia the wax, Jove's swan-born daughter (Helen) the crown; for
him Dido would have hastened upon the sword and Phyllis to the noose,
Evadne into the flames, the maid of Sestos into the waves." To this she
replies: "We rejoice, O son, that you vanquish and praise the recalcitrant
hero, but the maiden's beauty is such that if in former times the hero
loved by Sthenoboea had seen her, he would not, because he had scorned
her, have (had to) overcome the monster of Chimaera; or he, proud son
of an Amazon mother, who spurned the rash entreaties of his Cretan
stepmother, having seen her would indeed have been struck down, but on
a true charge; and if perchance she was a fourth with me in the contest,
the shepherd on Rhoetean Ida would have pronounced his verdict against
me also. [...] And for you, Hiberia, would have contended in all manner
of exploits Pelops in the chariot, Hippomenes in the race and Achelous in
wrestling, Aeneas in wars, Perseus who endured the gaze of the Gorgon.
No less is this beauty for which Jupiter would so often have become the
Delian goddess (Diana), bull, swan, satyr, serpent, thunder and gold."]

66 *Cressa*: Ariadne; cf. *Gnosida* Stat. **1a**.133.   67 *Alceste*: sacrificed herself for her husband Admetus.   *Circe*: a sorceress on the island of Aeaea;
Odysseus is given a herb by Hermes to counter her magic potions (*Od.*
10.210 ff.).   *poma Calypso*: Calypso is not associated with apples, but in
Homer, *Od.* VII.245, she is said to be the daughter of the Titan Atlas. According to Ov. *Met.* IV. 637 f. Atlas had a garden with a golden tree producing
golden fruit, which may explain the reference here.   68 *Scylla*: daughter
of Nisus, who for love of Minos cut off the lock of hair on which his father's

life depended.   *Atalanta*: ran more swiftly than all her suitors in the race to win her hand, until Hippomenes succeeded by means of a trick.   69 *Hippodame*: Hippodamia, daughter of Oenomaus, who caused wax to be inserted into the axles of her father's chariot, enabling Pelops to win the race.   *cygno Iove nata*: Helen, daughter of Leda and Jupiter in the guise of swan (see 90 n.), crowned Menelaus with a garland as her chosen suitor.   70 *Dido*: fell on Aeneas' sword when he deserted her.   *Phyllis*: hanged herself when Demophoon failed to return at the appointed time.   71 *Euadne*: threw herself on her husband's funeral pyre.   *Sestias*: Hero. When Leander drowned, she threw herself into the sea.   74 *Stheneboeius heros*: Bellerophon, loved by Stheneboea, wife of Proteus. When he spurned her, he was sent at her instigation with a calumnious letter to Iobates, requesting the latter to kill him, but was instead set the task of slaying the Chimaera.   76 ff. Hippolytus, son of the Amazon Hippolyte, resisted his stepmother Phaedra, but, falsely accused by her, was cursed by his father Theseus and torn to pieces by his own horses. 80 *pastor*: Paris. The reference is to the judgement of Paris, who decided the contest of beauty in favour of Venus (see Prop. **6**.13 f. n.).   87 f. These lines suggest that the bride surpasses those for whom the heroes named contended, i.e. Hippodamia (Pelops), Atalanta (Hippomenes), Deianira (Achelous), Lavinia (Aeneas), and Andromeda (Perseus).   90 The reference is to the disguises adopted by Jupiter in the seduction of Callisto (Diana), Europa (bull), Leda (swan), Antiope (satyr), Semele (thunder) and Danae (gold). The disguise as serpent is usually associated with Proserpina, as in Ov., *Met.* VI.114, but in the epithalamium of Polemius and Araneola (*AA* VIII, p. 238,175 f.), Sidonius explicitly associates it with Mnemosyne, which is perhaps also intended here (in *Met.* VI.114 the disguise in the seduction of Mnemosyne is, as is usual, that of shepherd). For all these figures, except Callisto and Semele, see Ov., *Met.* VI.103 ff.; for Semele, *ibid.* III.259 ff. For Callisto, see Ov., *Met.* II.417 ff. See also Stat. **1a**.135 f. n.; G.Vins. **2**.613 ff. n.

Priscian (*early 6th century*)

In praise of the emperor Anastasius:

Priscian **1**

est iustus, sapiens, castus fortisque piusque,	*PLM* V, p. 266	42
est clemens, stabilis, moderatus, mitis, honestus,		
et, loquar ut breviter quod sentio corde sub imo,		
possidet hic veterum quidquid laudatur in ullo:		45
Antoninum huius pietas, sapientia Marcum,		
et mitem Nervam lenissima pectora vincunt,		
promeruitque Titus non tantum mente benigna;		
gloria magnanimi Traiani cesserit isti [...]		

[He is just, wise, virtuous and strong and dutiful; he is clement, steadfast, moderate, gentle, honourable, and that I may briefly speak what I feel in the depth of my heart, he possesses whatever is praised in those of old: his *pietas* surpasses Antoninus, his wisdom Marcus and his most mild disposition gentle Nerva; Titus was not so meritorious on account of his benevolent spirit, the fame of magnanimous Trajan would yield to him [...]]]

46 *Marcum*: Marcus Aurelius, the philosopher-emperor; cf. Einh. (?) **1**.73; Serlo **1**.16; Serlo **2**.13.   49 *Traiani*: cf. Sid. **3a**.116 n.

Venantius Fortunatus (*b. c. 535–540, d. c. 600*)

In praise of king Charibert:

Venantius **1**

quod tam mirifico floret patientia cultu,   MGH, AA 4.1, p. 133   77
   est tibi Daviticae mansuetudo vitae.
iustitiae rector, venerandi iuris amator,
   iudicium sapiens de Salomone trahis,   80
tu melior fidei merito: nam principis ampli
   Traiani ingenium de pietate refers.
quid repetam maturum animum, qui tempore nostro
   antiqui Fabii de gravitate places?

[Since you have an abundance of patience, so admirably cultivated, the gentleness of the life of David is yours. Guide of justice, lover of venerable law, you derive your wise judgement from Solomon, though superior through the merit of faith, for you reproduce anew the character of the renowned prince Trajan through your *pietas*. What need to refer again to your mature spirit, who in our time are pleasing with the *gravitas* of Fabius of old?]

78 *Daviticae . . . vitae*: David is frequently cited as an ideal exemplar of kingship; cf. Theod. **1**.30; Poeta Saxo **1**.661; Anon. **1**.7.3; *Carm. Cant.* **1**.4a.5 f.; Archipoeta **1**.6.2.   80 *Salomone*: in association with David, as here, also in Theod. **1**.29 f.   82 *Traiani*: cf. Sid. **3a**.116 n.

In praise of St Martin of Galicia (c. 520–80), who converted the Arian Christians of Galicia to Catholic orthodoxy. He became bishop of Dumio and later archbishop of Braga:

Venantius **2**

Martino servata novo, Gallicia, plaude: MGH, AA 4.1, p. 104   17
   sortis apostolicae vir tuus iste fuit
qui virtute Petrum praebet tibi, dogmate Paulum,
   hinc Iacobi tribuens, inde Iohannis opem.
[...]
Heliae meritis alter redit imber aristis,   25
   munera roris habens, ne premat arva sitis.

[Saved by a new Martin, applaud, Galicia. This man of yours was allotted an apostolic destiny, he who represents to you Peter in virtue, Paul in doctrine, showing the strength of James on the one hand, of John on the other [. . .] By the merits of Elijah new rain comes again upon the crops, bearing the blessings of dew, that drought may not bear down upon the fields.]

17 *Martino novo*: the reference is to the earlier St. Martin, bishop of Tours (d. 397), as exemplar; cf. Archipoeta **1.6.3**.   19 *Petrum . . . Paulum*: see G. Vins. **1.12**.   20 *Iohannis*: cf. G. Vins. **1.11**.   25 cf. 1 Kgs. 18:1–2, 41.

Epithalamium on the marriage of king Sigibert and queen Brunhild:

Venantius **3**

> mox ubi conspexit telo superante Cupido   *MGH, AA* 4.1, pp. 124 ff.   47
> virginea mitem torreri lampade regem,
> laetus ait Veneri: "mater, mea bella peregi:
> pectore flagranti mihi vincitur alter Achilles."
> [. . .]
> incipit inde Venus laudes memorare puellae: 99
> "o virgo miranda mihi, placitura iugali,
> clarior aetheria, Brunichildis, lampade fulgens,
> lumina gemmarum superasti lumine vultus,
> altera nata Venus, regno dotata decoris,
> nullaque Nereidum de gurgite talis Hibero
> Oceani sub fonte natat, non ulla Napaea   105
> pulchrior, ipsa suas subdunt tibi flumina nymphas."

[As soon as Cupid, his conquering dart striking home, saw the gentle king set aflame by the maiden's radiance, rejoicing, he said to Venus: "Mother, I have finished my wars: with heart on fire, a second Achilles is vanquished by me." [. . .] Thereupon Venus begins to recount the praises of the maiden: "O maiden, a marvel to me, about to delight your husband, shining more brightly, Brunhild, than the lamp of heaven, you have surpassed the light of jewels with the light of your countenance, born a second Venus, endowed with the sovereignty of beauty; no such Nereid of the Western sea swims beneath the waters of Ocean, nor is any wood-nymph more beautiful, the streams themselves make their nymphs subject to you."]

102 *altera nata Venus*: see Venant. **4.8**.

Venantius **4**

> *Epitaphium Eusebiae*
> nobilis Eusebiae furibundi sorte sepulchri   *MGH, AA* 4.1, p. 100   5
>   hic, obscure lapis, fulgida membra tegis.
> cuius in ingenio seu formae corpore pulchro
>   arte Minerva fuit, victa decore Venus.

docta tenens calamos, apices quoque figere filo,
　　quod tibi charta valet hoc sibi tela fuit.　　　　　　　　　　　　10

[*Epitaph for Eusebia*: Through the destiny of the cruel tomb, here, dark
stone, you cover the radiant limbs of noble Eusebia. By her ability and the
beauty of her form, Minerva was surpassed in skill, Venus in grace. Versed
in holding the reed and also in fixing outlines with the thread (?), what a
sheet of paper is to you, a web was to her.]

5 *furibundi sepulchri*: lit. 'of the furious/raging tomb'.　　　　8 *Minerva*: the
goddess of all the arts and sciences, and also of crafts such as weaving.
9 *calamos*: *calamus* 'reed' is applied also to objects made from reed. The
weaver's reed (see *OED s.v.*), originally made of strips of reed, later of metal,
was used to separate the threads of the warp; see Ov., *Met.* VI.55 *stamen secer-
nit harundo* (the reed separates the warp), in which *harundo* is synonymous
with *calamus*. There is probably also a punning reference to *calamus* in the
sense of pen, in association with *charta* in l. 10, i.e. she was as skilled in using *calamos* ('the weaver's reed'), as you in using *calamos* ('pens').　　*apices
quoque figere filo* lit. 'to fix the points with the thread'; *apex* denotes 'point',
'head', but is also used to signify the form or outline of a written character.
The plural *apices* may therefore refer to the forms or outlines of the weaving
design, perhaps with a punning reference, similar to that in *calamos*, to the
forms of letters, a sense appropriate to *charta*.

Petrus Grammaticus and Paulus Diaconus

An exchange of verse epistles in the 780s between Petrus Grammaticus (Peter
of Pisa) and Paulus Diaconus (d. 802). Whereas Petr. Gramm. 5.1–3 is cast
in the form of identification with an exemplar, Paul. Diac. 4.1–3 is expressed
syntactically as simile:

Petrus Grammaticus **1**

　　　　　　　　　　　　　　　　　　　MGH, Poetae I, XI, p. 48

　　Greca cerneris Homerus, Latina Vergilius,　　　　　　　　　　5　1
　　in Hebrea quoque Philo, Tertullus in artibus,
　　Flaccus crederis in metris, Tibullus in eloquio.

　　[In Greek you are acknowledged as a Homer, in Latin a Virgil, and in
　　Hebrew a Philo, Tertullus in the arts; you are held to be a Flaccus in metre,
　　Tibullus in eloquence.]

5.1 ff.: see Paul Diac. **1**.4.1 ff., and for comparisons with classical authors Sid.
4b.167 n.　　　　5.3 *Flaccus*: Horace (Horatius Flaccus).

In a poem of reply, Paulus Diaconus repeats this hyperbolic praise only to
reject it:

Paulus Diaconus 1

MGH, Poetae I, XII, p. 49

> Dicor similis Homero, Flacco et Vergilio,   4   1
> similor Tertullo sive Philoni Memphitico,
> tibi quoque, Veronensis o Tibulle, conferor.

> Peream, si quenquam horum imitari cupio,   5   1
> avia qui sunt sequuti pergentes per invium;
> potius sed istos ego conparabo canibus!

> [I am said to be similar to Homer, Flaccus and Virgil, I am likened to
> Tertullus or Philo of Memphis, to you too, O Tibullus of Verona, am
> I compared. May I perish if I desire to imitate any of them, who have
> pursued byways, proceeding into trackless wastes. Rather on the contrary
> will I compare them to dogs!]

4.3 *Veronensis*: there appears to be no evidence linking Tibullus with Verona
(the birthplace of Catullus).   5.2 f. *avia . . . invium*: it is implied that
pagan authors have strayed from the straight path of truth.

The following three examples are in praise of Charlemagne (d. 814):

Theodulf of Orléans (*c. 760–821*)

Theodulf 1

MGH, Poetae I, XXV, p. 484

> nomine reddis avum, Salomonem stemmate sensus,   29
> viribus et David, sive Ioseph specie.

> [In name you recall your grandfather, Solomon in noble heritage of under-
> standing, and in strength David, in beauty of appearance Joseph.]

29 *Salomonem*: cf. Venant. 1.80 n.; *stemma* 'garland', metaphorically 'lineage',
'descent'.   30 *David*: see Venant. 1.78 n.

Einhard (?) (*c. 770–840*)

Einhard (?) 1

MGH, Poetae I, p. 368

> summus apex regum, summus quoque in orbe sophista   70
> exstat et orator, facundo famine pollens;
> inclita nam superat praeclari dicta Catonis,
> vincit et eloquii magnum dulcedine Marcum,
> atque suis dictis facundus cedit Homerus,
> et priscos superat dialectica in arte magistros.   75

> [The greatest crown of kings and also the greatest sage in the world, he
> is distinguished too as orator, powerful in eloquent expression, for he
> outdoes the renowned sayings of illustrious Cato and vanquishes great

Marcus in the sweetness of his eloquence; to his sayings also eloquent Homer yields and he surpasses the masters of old in the art of dialectic.]

72 *dicta Catonis*: this appears to be a reference to the *Disticha* (or *Dicta*) *Catonis*, a collection of moral maxims of uncertain date and authorship, associated with the name of Cato the Censor (234–149 BC), known for his stern morality. The work was later adapted to Christian teaching and was very widely known throughout the Middle Ages. The choice of Cato as moral exemplar may be derived, as here, from knowledge of the *Disticha*, but is probably mainly based directly on the reputation of the historical figure, as in Poeta Saxo 1.V.656; Benzo 1.10; Baudri 2b.28 f.; Serlo 1.15; M. Vend. 1.62.   73 *Marcum*: Marcus Aurelius; see Prisc. 1.46 n.   74 *Homerus*: see Sid. 4b.167 n.

Poeta Saxo (*c. 890*)

Poeta Saxo 1

MGH, Poetae IV.1, p. 70

non Decii, non Scipiadę, non ipse Camillus,   V   655
    non Cato, non Caesar maior eo fuerat;
non Pompeius huic merito vel gens Fabiorum
    pręfertur pariter mortua pro patria.
terrea forsan eis fuerit par gloria; sed nunc
    caelestis Carolus culmen honoris habet.   660
illic Daviticae pollet virtutis honore
    cum Constantino atque Theodosio.

[Not the Decii, not the Scipios, not Camillus himself, not Cato, not Caesar were greater than he. Not Pompey nor likewise the race of the Fabians who died for their fatherland can be ranked above him in merit. His earthly glory may have equalled theirs, but now Charlemagne in celestial realms occupies the height of honour. There he possesses in abundance the honour accorded to the valour of David, together with Constantine and Theodosius.]

655 ff.: Charlemagne surpasses all eminent pagan figures, and is likened only to David and the Christian emperors Constantine and Theodosius.   656 *Cato*: see Einh. (?) 1.72 n.   660 *caelestis*: in opposition to *terrea*, the adj. suggests a) dwelling in heaven, as opposed to on earth, and b) the semi-divine nature of Charlemagne.   661 *Daviticae . . . virtutis*: see Venant. 1.78 n.

Gottschalk (*c. 803–c. 869*)

In a poem of penitent confession and prayer (c. 825), Gottschalk identifies himself as a sinner with the biblical exemplars of the Prodigal Son[3] and Lazarus,[4] restored through Christ's mercy from death to life.

---

[3] Luke 15:11 ff. There is a similar use of the parable of the Prodigal Son in Baudri 1.
[4] John 11:1 ff.

Gottschalk 1

MGH, *Poetae* VI, p. 92

1a   Ego, pater, ille tuus   prodigus sum filius,   29 1
abs te procul exul factus,   qui fui diutius
meretricibus coniunctus   et consumptis omnibus

Quae tu bonis es largitus;   panis miser indigus   30 1
effectus fui subulcus,   saturari cupidus
siliquis, sed dedit nullus,   quae dabantur suibus.

[I, Father, am that prodigal son of yours, rendered an exile far from you, who have long associated with whores, wasting all the good things you freely dispensed; wretched, in want of bread, I became a swineherd, eager to be satisfied with the husks that were given to the swine, but no one gave me any.]

29.3 *consumptis omnibus*: Luke 15:14 *Et postquam omnia consummasset . . .*
30.2 f. Luke 15:15 f. *Et misit illum in villam suam ut pasceret porcos. Et cupiebat implere ventrem suum de siliquis, quas porci manducabant: et nemo illi dabat.*

Verses 37–42 recount the return of the Prodigal Son, to which are appended in verses 43–7 prayers for like mercy, immediately followed by the example of Lazarus, who in spite of his sins was restored from the grave to life at Christ's command. As Lazarus was unbound from the grave clothes, so the poet is released from the bonds of sin by Christ's merciful response to his prayer of penitence:

1b   Benedictus sit excelsus   genitor et genitus,   56 1
spiritus necnon et sanctus,   predulcis paraclitus,
per quem suus est secundus   suscitatus Lazarus.

[Blessed be the most high begetter and his begotten son, and the Holy Spirit, the sweet Paraclete, through whom His second Lazarus has been reawakened to life.]

Ermoldus Nigellus (first attested 823)

In praise of Charles, the young son of Louis the Pious:

Ermoldus 1

MGH, *Poetae* II, p. 73

hunc puerile decus hinc inde frequentat et ambit,   IV 531
   hunc patris virtus, nomen et ornat avi,
qualis Apollo micat gradiens per culmina Deli,
   Latonae matri gaudia magna ferens.

[Boyish perfection attends and encompasses him on every side; the virtue of his father, the name of his grandfather adorn him, as Apollo is resplendent as he moves over the heights of Delos, bringing great joy to Latona his mother.]

533 f. The comparison, set in a hunting scene in which the boy has been allowed to kill a doe, is modelled on the comparison in *Aeneid* IV.143 ff. of Aeneas with Apollo, as he takes part in the hunt with Dido (see Verg. **2**).]

In praise of Pippin, son of Louis the Pious:

Ermoldus **2**

MGH, Poetae II, p. 86

pulcher es aspectu, vultu pulcherrimus extas,	27
atque oculis paribus lumina digna geris.	
vertice de summo plantam ut veniatur ad imam,	
in toto macula corpore nulla manet;	30
et tibi lingua sagax, prudens verbum, inclita vox est,	
sensus adest facilis, mensque benigna satis –	
si Veneris soboles, Priami si filius adsit,	
Hector et Aeneas cedet uterque tibi.	
regibus antiquis quicquid cecinere poetae,	35
tu, Pippine meus, omnia solus habes.	

[You are beautiful in appearance, you are pre-eminent as most beautiful of face and in your evenly set eyes there is a noble light. From the crown of your head to the soles of your feet there is no blemish in your person. You also possess a wise tongue, prudent words, a distinguished voice; to these is added a ready intelligence and a suitably benevolent disposition. If the offspring of Venus, if the son of Priam were here among us, Hector and Aeneas would each yield to you. Whatever qualities poets celebrated in kings of former times, you, my Pippin, of yourself alone possess them all.]

Sedulius Scottus (fl. c. 850–859)

On the birth of Charles, son of the emperor Lothar:

Sedulius **1**

MGH, Poetae III, XXIII, p. 189

hic novus est Karolus Karoli de semine magni:	5
omnes laetemur, hic novus est Karolus.	

[This child is a new Charles, of the seed of Charles the Great: let us all rejoice, this child is a new Charles.]

5 f. i.e. not long after his lifetime, Charlemagne has become a new historical exemplar (see also Sed. **2**).

On Karolus Calvus (Charles the Bald), son of Louis the Pious:

Sedulius **2**

MGH, Poetae III, XXVIII, p. 194

splendida progenies Karoli de semine magni,	51
pacifer ut Salemon regia sceptra tenens.	

Caesaris es magni Ludewici florida virga,
  proles Isaac ceu benedicta micas:
Abrahae similis Karolus perfulserat orbem,   55
  filius Isaac sic Ludewicus erat,
tertius es veluti Iacob benedictus et heres
  Isaac patris celsithronique ducis.

[Splendid progeny of the seed of Charles the Great, peaceably like Solomon
wielding the royal sceptre. You are the flowering stem of the great emperor
Louis, you shine forth like the consecrated scion of Isaac: like Abraham,
Charles illumined the globe; in the same way his son Louis was Abraham's
son Isaac; you are the third, like Jacob, blessed, and heir of Isaac, father
and high-throned ruler.]

52 *Salemon*: see Venant. **1.80** n.   55 *Karolus*: see Sed. **1.5** f. n.

In a dialogue between the poet and the Muse, the poet begins by ques-
tioning the Muse: who has invested you with the poet's mantle and crown
and caused you to rejoice? In her reply the Muse praises Gunther, bishop of
Cologne (850–63):

Sedulius 3

                                          MGH, Poetae III, LXXV, p. 225

"Inveni magnum – fateor tibi, Tyrsis – Homerum,   5
  inveni Musas organicosque tropos:
dextera praepollens Gunthari praesulis almi
  his ornamentis me decoravit ovans.

Me docuit dulces Musarum farier odas:
  doctior is Phebo Musica flabra sonat.   10
cuius in aspectu nihil est crinitus Apollo:
  glorifica vatem, quem, bone Christe, patrem."

["I have found – I confess to you, Thyrsis – great Homer, I have found the
Muses and melodious songs. The powerful right hand of Gunther, the
gracious bishop, has amid rejoicing embellished me with these adorn-
ments. He has taught me to speak sweet songs of the Muses: more skilled
than Phoebus, he breathes forth sounds of music. In his presence long-
haired Apollo is naught: glorify the poet, dear Christ, who is father of his
flock."]

5 *Tyrsis*: Thyrsis, the name of a shepherd in Virgil, *Ecl.* 7, used as a designation
of the poet.   *Homerum*: see Sid. **4b**.167 n.   10 *flabra*: lit. 'winds', 'breezes'.

On the accession in 888 of Odo to the kingdom of the Franks:

MLat. Anon. 1

        Sis deo dignus ut Abel,   *MGH, Poetae* IV.1, p. 138   3   1
        sis fidelis ut Samuel,
        sic iudices ut Daniel

et credas ut Natanael.

[. . .]

Monarcha sis ut Iulius,   7   1
set deo dignus melius,
ut Davit, rex mitissimus,
et Iudas, victor optimus.

Ut Alexander Maximus   8   1
pugnator sis aptissimus,
tibique sit contrarius
ceu fugiens Pompegius.

[May you be worthy in the eyes of God like Abel, may you be faithful like
Samuel, may you judge like Daniel, and may you believe like Nathaniel.
[. . .] May you be a monarch like Julius, but more worthy in the eyes of
God, like David, a most clement king, and like Judas, a supreme victor.
Like Alexander the Great may you be a most ready fighter and may your
opponent be like Pompey put to flight.]

4.1–6.4 In the omitted verses the further OT characters *Enohc, Sadoc, Iacob, Iob, Abraam, Balaam, Geroboam, Ioatam, Salomon, Samson, Absalon,
Gedeon* are each associated with a particular quality to be emulated by Odo.
7.1 f. Caesar, as a pagan, is on that account less worthy.   7.3 *Davit*: see
Venant. **1**.78 n. *Iudas*: Judas Maccabaeus, renowned as victor (1 Mach.3.1 ff.).
8.1 *Alexander Maximus*: frequently cited as exemplifying supreme military
skill; cf. Archipoeta **1**.6.1; Serlo **2**.13 f.   8.4 Pompey was put to flight by
Caesar in 48 BC.

On the coronation of the Emperor Conrad II in 1027:

Carmina Cantabrigiensia **1**

Quem providentia   *Carm. Cant.* ed. Strecker 3   4a   1
Dei preclara predestinavit
et elegit,
regere gentes strennue   5
Davidis exemplo
Messieque triumpho.

[Whom the illustrious providence of God has predestined and elected to
rule the peoples powerfully after the example of David and the triumph
of the Messiah.]

6 *Davidis exemplo*: see Venant. **1**.78 n.   7 *Messieque triumpho*: in typological interpretation David is the type of the expected Messiah, foreshadowing
Christ. The emperor is thus elected to rule after the example of David and
that of Christ which supersedes it.

Benzo of Alba (bishop of Alba before 1059, d. post 1085)

In a poem of eight verses at the end of book VI of *Ad Heinricum IV imperatorem libri VII* (a *prosimetrum*), Benzo praises the supremacy of the emperor Heinrich IV (1056–1106):

Benzo 1

> Tantus es, o cesar, quantus et orbis,   Seyffert, p. 574   1
> cis mare vel citra tu leo fortis.
> presso namque tua calce dracone
> victor habes palmam cum Scipione.
>
> Ille quidem Penos exsuperavit,   5
> sed tua Romuleos dextra fugavit;
> ille palaciola fregit Elisse,
> tu Romę muros Iulius ipse.
>
> Transcendens Fabios et Cicerones,
> cunctos Fabricios atque Catones,   10
> das populis iura cum Salomone;
> nam mel ab utroque funditur hore.
>
> Reges christicolas atque profanos
> et Theodosios, Iustinianos
> et magnos Karolos atque Pipinos –   15
> altius ut dicam – atque Sabinos:
>
> Transilis hos sensu, viribus, armis
> de cęlo missus, non homo carnis.
> te quoque regna tremunt, cesar amande;
> temet ubique deus ambulat ante.   20

[You, O Caesar, are as great as the world; on this side of the sea and on the other you are a strong lion, for since the serpent has been crushed under your heel, as victor you share the palm with Scipio. He, however, overcame the Carthaginians, but you have put the descendants of Romulus to flight with your right hand; he laid low Elissa's small palace, you, a very Julius, the walls of Rome. Transcending those such as Fabius and Cicero, all the Fabricii and the Catos, you give your people laws in company with Solomon, for honey flows from either mouth. Christian and pagan kings and those such as Theodosius and Justinian and such as the great Charles and Pippin – that I may utter higher praise – and also the Sabines: these you surpass in intellect, strength and arms, a man sent from heaven, not of human flesh. Kingdoms tremble before you, Caesar, worthy to be loved. God walks before you wherever you go.]

7 *Elisse*: 'of Elissa', a designation of Dido, queen of Carthage.   In 9 and 14 f. the generalizing plural of names has singular meaning, indicating 'belonging to the type of'. In 10 and 16 the names are true plurals, in *Catones* 10 probably designating the two famous bearers of the name, the earlier Cato

(the Censor) and the younger (see also Einh. (?) 1.72 n.).   11 *Salomone*:
see Venant. 1.80 n.

Baudri de Bourgueil (1046–1130)

Baudri 1

ne me despicias: ego sum tibi filius ille,   Hilbert 122   114
qui pavi porcos in longinqua regione.
tota paternarum michi reddita portio rerum,
quam te dante, pater, et me poscente recepi,
in meretricales periit dispersa tabernas.
ecce, pater, redeo nec debeo filius esse,
qui, quod contuleras, deformiter omne voravi.   120
fac me servorum conservum, quaeso, tuorum.
[...]
nemo redit vacuus qui te devotus adivit.   124

[Do not despise me, I am that son of yours who fed the swine in a far-off region. The whole portion of paternal goods bestowed on me, which I as supplicant received from you, Father, as giver, is wasted, dissipated in taverns, the haunt of prostitutes. Behold, Father, I return and am not worthy to be your son, I who have wantonly squandered everything which you had granted. Make me a fellow servant among your servants, I beg. [...] None returns empty-handed who has approached you with faith.]

114 ff. See Gottschalk 1. As in the latter, there are correspondences with the text of the Vulgate.   115 ff. Luke 15:13 [...] *peregre profectus est in regionem longinquam, et ibi dissipavit substantiam suam vivendo luxuriose.*   119 Luke 15: 21 *iam non sum dignus vocari filius tuus.*   121 Luke 15:19 *fac me sicut unum de mercenariis tuis.*

There then follows in substantiation of the statement in l. 124 a series of biblical *exempla* of healing: Peter's wife's mother, the daughter of the woman of Canaan, the centurion's servant, the blind man, the daughter of Jairus, the woman cured of an issue of blood.

In support of his pure and blameless love for Constantia and in praise of her beauty, virtue and talents, the poet cites positive parallels from myth, in ll. 91 ff. rejecting unworthy negative examples:

Baudri 2a

Ad Dominam Constantiam   Hilbert 200

pluris es ipsa michi Paridi quam filia Ledae   19
    quamque Venus Marti, quam dea Iuno Iovi.
nec tanti *Dafnes*, neque tanti constitit Io,
    pro quibus aurum et bos Iupiter ipse fuit.
vates ad Stygias querulus cum tenderet undas,

non habuit pluris Orpheus Euridicen.   24
[...]
nec lascivus amor, nec amor petulantis amoris   49
    pro te subvertit corque iecurque meum,
in te sed nostrum movit tua littera sensum
    et penitus iunxit me tua Musa tibi.
denique tanta tuae vivit facundia lingue,
    ut possis credi sisque Sibilla michi.   54
[...]
ipsa Iovem summum posses deducere celo,   67
    de Iove si verax fabula Greca foret,
in quascumque velis se formas effigiasset,
    si tua te seclis tempora prestiterint.
[...]
virtutum gradiamur iter, gradiamur ad astra,   113
    gentiles etiam sic properare monent.
si mea vivere vis, vives mea, vive Diana;
    Alcidem volo vel Bellorofonta sequi.

[*To the lady Constantia*: You yourself are more to me than the daughter of Leda to Paris, than Venus to Mars, than the goddess Juno to Jove. Not of such worth was *Danae* or Io, for whom Jupiter himself became gold and bull. As the bard took his course, lamenting, over the Stygian waves, Orpheus did not hold Eurydice more dear. [. . .] No lascivious love or desire of wanton love overturns my heart and soul on your account, but your missive draws my feelings towards you, and your Muse has united me inwardly with you. Indeed, such is the lively eloquence of your language that you may be accounted and are a Sibyl to me. [. . .] You yourself would be able to bring great Jove down from heaven – if the Greek myth concerning Jove should be true – in whatsoever forms you might wish that he should clothe himself, if your lifetime had coincided with former ages. [. . .] Let us pursue the path of virtue, let us strive towards the stars, the pagans themselves exhort us thus to hasten onwards. If you will live as my own, live as mine, live as Diana; I will follow the descendant of Alceus and Bellerophon.]

21 f. *Dafnes ... aurum*: the form of the name is probably the result of scribal corruption; the reference should properly be to Danae, seduced by Jove in a shower of gold, see Ov., *Met.* VI.113. In l. 21 Jove's disguise as bull belongs to the story of Europa, not to that of Io: it was Io herself who was changed into a heifer (Ov., *Met.* I.610 f.), which may explain the confusion. For Jove's disguises see also Stat. **1a**.135 f. n.; Prop. 2.20 n.; G. Vins. **2**.616.   54 *Sibilla*: see also Baudri no. 153.13 (in praise of the nun Emma) *nobis, Emma, refers lingua sensuque Sibillam* (to us, Emma, you represent the Sibyl in language and sense) and the epitaph, no. 213.6. The Sibyl is here an exemplar of know-

ledge and wisdom.[5]   116 *Alcidem*: Hercules. The reference here is to the story, going back to the Greek sophist Procidus, of Hercules at the crossroads, choosing the steep and rugged path of virtue as opposed to the easy path of pleasure.   *Bellerofonta*: Bellephoron virtuously resisted the adulterous advances of Stheneboea (see Sid. **5**.74 n.) and accomplished the extreme tests of valour imposed on him as a result of her calumny.]

In her reply Constantia praises the poet's learning and poetic skill:

Baudri **2b**

> hunc si Roma sibi quondam meruisset alumnum,   Hilbert 201   27
>   iste Cato rigidus, Tullius iste foret.
> hunc facerent verba Ciceronem, facta Catonem,
>   multos iste valet solus Aristoteles.   30
> iste videtur et est et dicitur alter Homerus:
>   o quanta versus commoditate canit.
> hystorias Grecas et earum mystica novit,
>   atque, quid hec aut hec fabula significet.

[If Rome had in former times gained this man as her son, he would be stern Cato, he would be Tullius. His words would make him Cicero, his deeds Cato, he alone would be equivalent to many Aristotles. He appears, and is, and is accounted a second Homer. Oh with what harmony he sings his verses. He knows Greek tales and their mysteries and what this or that myth signifies.]

28 ff. For comparisons with classical authors see Sid. **4b**.167 n.   28 *Cato*, 29 *Catonem*: see Einh. (?)**1**.72 n.   *Tullius*: one of the names of Cicero (Marcus Tullius Cicero); cf. Archipoeta **1**.5.1; M. Vend. **1**.52.61.

On the death of Burchard, a soldier:

Baudri **3**

> Si quis Achilleos mirando recenseat actus,   Hilbert 57   1
>   actus Burchardi pluris habens recolat.
> corporis aut animi nulli virtute secundus,
>   viveret ipse diu, Iulius alter erat.

[If anyone surveys with wonder the deeds of Achilles, let him call to mind the deeds of Burchard, estimating them more highly. In excellence of body and mind second to none, had he lived longer, he would have been another Julius.]

---

[5] See also Hildebert *Ad M⟨urielem⟩ litteratam* (ed. Scott, p. 17), in which the learned addressee is described as a Sibyl: 1 *Tempora prisca decem se iactavere sibillis, … unius ingenio praesentia secula gaudent* (Antiquity boasted of ten Sibyls, … the present time rejoices in the talents of one alone).

Hilarius of Orléans (*probably b. c. 1075, d. after 1145*)

Hilarius wrote several poems in praise of a beautiful youth, after the manner of a Greek *paidikon*, alluding to the exemplar of Ganymede, snatched up to the heavens by Jove in the form of an eagle to be his cupbearer (Ovid, *Met.* X.155 ff.). The name *Ganimedes* occurs in **1a**, but is lacking in **1b** and **1c**.[6]

Hilarius **1a**

> Crede michi: si redirent prisca Iovis secula,   Bulst/Bulst–Thiele IX   21
> Ganimedes iam non foret ipsius vernacula,
> sed tu raptus in supernis, grata luce pocula,
> gratiora quidem nocte Iovi dares oscula.

> [Believe me, if the former ages of Jove were to return, Ganymede would not now be his cupbearer, but you, snatched up to the realms above, would by day give Jove goblets for his pleasure, but by night kisses yet more pleasing.]

This poem, like no. XIII, has the title *Ad puerum Anglicum*; ll. 27 f. in the final verse play on the virtual identity between two adjectives: let those who mistakenly call you *Anglicum* ('English') insert an *e* and call you *Angelicum* ('angelic').

Hilarius **1b**

> Si nunc certe regnaret Iupiter,   Bulst/Bulst–Thiele X   29
> pro puella bos factus turpiter,
> avis foret *pro te* similiter,
> aput illum ut fores iugiter.

> [Assuredly, if Jupiter now reigned, he who stooped low to become a bull for a girl's sake would be a bird for your sake likewise, so that you might be with him continually.]

> 30 *bos*: Jove adopted the form of a bull to carry off Europa; see Stat. **1a**.135 f. n.
> 31 *avis*: a reference to Jove's disguise as eagle in the abduction of Ganymede.

Hilarius **1c**

> Nam et rector superorum,   Bulst/Bulst–Thiele XIII   17
> raptor olim puerorum,
> si nunc esset, tam decorum
> ad celestem ferret torum.

---

[6] For Ganymede as a negative exemplar see Baudri, Hilbert, no. 3, an admonitory poem addressed to a young man: 24 *laudo, Iovis quoniam Ganimedes esse refutas,* | *et precor et laudo ne corrumparis amando* (I praise, since you resist being Jove's Ganymede, and pray and praise, that you may not be corrupted by loving), and Hilbert, no. 77, in a poem urging Gérard of Loudun to enter the monastery: 95 *per multos aedes discurrit adhuc Ganimedes,* | *multus homo lasciuus adhuc vult Iuppiter esse* (Ganymede roves still through many houses and many a lascivious man still wishes to be Jupiter).

Aula tandem in superna   21
satis promptus ad alterna
nunc in toro, nunc pincerna
Iovi fores gratus verna.

[For also the ruler of those above, formerly the abductor of boys, if he
were present now would bear such a beautiful youth to his celestial couch.
Then in halls above, quick to serve by turns in either, now in his couch,
now as cupbearer, you would be to Jove a pleasing slave.]

Hugh Primas (c. 1093–1160)

The poet describes the occasion when, requesting the payment of money owed
to him, he is chased down the stairs:

Primas 1

Si non esset talus velox,   McDonough 15   41
Primas esset velut Pelox,
set, qui sedet super celos,
cui cantant dulce melox
   beatorum anime,   45
non concessit ius insano,
homocide, Daciano,
quod noceret veterano;
alioquin (vera cano)
perissem celerrime.   50
[...]
Proclamabam: "Heus! Heus!   73
miserere mei deus!",
dum instaret hostis meus.   75
eram enim ut Zacheus:
ipse velut Briareus
aut Herodes Galileus
   sive Dionisius [...]   79

[If he had not been so swift of foot, Primas would have been like Pelops,
but He who sits above the heavens, to whom the souls of the blessed sing
a sweet melody, did not grant the madman, the murderer, the Dacian, the
right to harm the aged man. Otherwise – I speak the truth – I would have
most swiftly perished. [...] I cried "Alas, Alas, may God have mercy on
me", as my enemy pressed close upon me. I was like Zacchaeus, he like
Briareus or Herod of Galilee or Dionysius [...].]

42 *Pelox*, i.e. Pelops, served up in his childhood as food for the gods by his
father Tantalus, but recalled to life by Jupiter.   47 *Daciano*: a mem-
ber of the warlike Dacii.   76 *Zacheus*: described in Luke 19:3 as small
of stature.   77 *Briareus*: a hundred-handed giant, otherwise known as

Agaeon, as in Verg. **4.**   78 f. *Herodes Galileus* | *siue Dionisius*: examples
of cruel tyrants.

The Archipoeta (fl. c. 1159–1165)

The poet praises his patron Reinald von Dassel, chancellor of the emperor
Frederick I, and entreats his help:

Archipoeta **1**

> Ulixe facundior   Tulliane loqueris,   Watenphul/Krefeld VII   5   1
> columba simplicior   nulli fraudes ingeris,
> serpente callidior   a nullo deciperis.
>
> Alexandro forcior   inimicos conteris,   6   1
> David mansuetior   a cunctis diligeris,
> Martinoque largior   das, quod iuste peteris.
>
> [. . .]
>
> Poeta conposuit   racionem rithmicam,   11   1
> †atyrus inposuit   melodiam musicam,
> unde bene meruit   mantellum et tunicam.

> [More eloquent than Ulysses, you speak in Ciceronian manner, more
> harmless than the dove, you practise deceit against none, wiser than the
> serpent, you are deceived by none. More powerful than Alexander, you
> destroy your enemies, more clement than David, you are loved by all,
> and more bountiful than Martin, you give what is rightfully requested of
> you. [. . .] The poet has composed a rhythmical poem; [∗∗∗] has fitted to
> it a musical accompaniment; therefore he has well deserved a cloak and
> tunic.]

5.1 *Ulixe*: see *Append Tibull.* **1.**49 n.; Archipoeta IV. 33 *Archicancellarie, spes et
vita mea,* | *in quo mens est Nestoris et vox Vlixea.   Tulliane*: cf. Einh. (?) **1.**73 n.;
for *Tullius* designating Cicero see Baudri **2b.**28 n.   **5.**2 f. Matt. 10:16.
6.2 *David*: cf. Venant. **1.**78 n.   **6.**3 *Martinoque largior*: St. Martin repu-
tedly gave half his cloak to a beggar; cf. Venant. **2.**17 n.   **11.**2 †*atyrus*: none
of the conjectures suggested is satisfactory (see Watenphul/Krefeld, p. 127).

In an appeal to his patron to restore him to favour, the poet identifies himself with Jonah, at God's command swallowed by the whale in punishment,
but released by His mercy, thus implicitly comparing his patron with God:

Archipoeta **2**

> Nomen vatis vel personam   Watenphul/Krefeld II   17
> manifeste non exponam;
> sed quem fuga fecit Ionam,
> per figuram satis bonam   20
> Ione nomen ei ponam.

Lacrimarum fluit rivus
quas effundo fugitivus
intra cetum semivivus,
tuus quondam adoptivus;   25
[. . .]

Ecce Ionas tuus plorat,   45
culpam suam non ignorat,
pro qua cetus eum vorat:
veniam vult et implorat,
ut a peste, qua laborat
solvas eum, quem honorat   50
tremit, colit et adorat.

Si remittas hunc reatum
et si ceto des mandatum,
cetus, cuius os est latum
more suo dans hiatum   55
vomet vatem decalvatum
et ad portum destinatum
feret fame tenuatum,
ut sit rursus vates vatum
scribens opus tibi gratum.   60

[The name of the poet and his identity I shall not set forth explicitly, but him whom flight has made a Jonah, to him will I give the name of Jonah, by means of an apt enough figure. A stream of tears flows, which I, a fugitive, shed, half alive in the whale, your erstwhile adoptive son. [. . .] Behold your Jonah weeps, he is not unaware of his guilt, on account of which the whale swallows him. He seeks and implores pardon, that you may release him from the tribulation under which he labours – you whom he honours, before whom he trembles, whom he venerates and supplicates. If you release this miscreant, and if you give the whale the command, the whale, whose mouth is broad, will, as is his custom, opening it wide, vomit forth the poet rendered bald and bear him to the appointed haven, weakened as he is by hunger, so that once again he may be the poet of poets, composing a work pleasing to you.]

There are precise correspondences with the Vulgate text of the Biblical story. 19 *fuga*, 23 *fugitivus* (and 31 *fugam petens fuga rui*): Jonah 1:3 *Et surrexit Ionas, ut fugeret in Tharsis a facie Domini.*   20 *per figuram*: an allusion to typological interpretation, according to which OT figures prefigure those of the NT.   22 f., 45 ff.: Jonah 2:2 f. *Clamavi de tribulatione mea ad Dominum,| Et exaudivit me.*   47: Jonah 2:1 *Et praeparavit Dominus piscem grandem ut deglutiret Ionam.*   50 f. *honorat| tremit, colit et adorat*: these verbs are appropriate to religious veneration, and together with l. 53 implicitly compare the poet's patron with God.   53 ff.: Jonah 2:1 *Et dixit Dominus pisci; et*

evomuit Ionam in aridam.   59 *vates vatum*: perhaps an allusion to the
name Archipoeta.

Serlo of Wilton (*d. 1181*)

In praise of king Louis VII (*Regi Francorum minimus sic Serlo suorum*). Clotho
spins the threads of the king's fate:

Serlo **1**

> ex filis illis virtutem format Achillis,   Öberg 16   11
>   format Priamidem Pirithoique fidem.
> reddit Sanxsoni similem, reddit Ciceroni,
>   reddit Theside viribus, ore, fide.
> cor probat ornatum Salomon, mores Cato, fatum   15
>   Marcus, conatum fortis inopsque datum.

[From those threads she fashions the courage of Achilles, she fashions
Priam's son and the faithfulness of Pirithous, she makes him like Samson,
like Cicero, makes him like the son of Theseus in strength, appearance,
trustworthiness. Solomon approves his illustrious spirit, Cato his moral
character, Marcus his eloquence, the strong his endeavour, the needy his
munificence.]

12 *Priamidem*: Hector; cf. Ermold. 2.34.   14 *Theside*: Hippolytus.   15 *Salomon*: see Venant. 1.80 n.   *Cato*: see Einh. (?) 1.72 n.   16 *Marcus*: Marcus
Aurelius; cf. Prisc. 1.46 n.

On the death of Robert, count of Gloucester, d. 1147:

Serlo **2**

> Plangite Robertum, miles, Glovernia, vates,   Öberg 15   11
>   morte ducem, comitem, philosophumque premi.
> miles, Alexandrum, plex, Marcum, clere, Maronem.
>   flete simul cassi robore, iure, stilo.
> [...]
> Mens Salomonis ei, non crimen; posse Neronis,   25
>   non mens, non Paridis dedecus, imo decor.
> os Paridem, non mens, non etas Nestora sed mens
>   fecit eum, iuvenem forma, sophia senem.

[Weep, soldier, Gloucester, poet, for Robert, leader, count, philosopher,
a prey to death. Soldier, lament Alexander, people Marcus, clergy Maro.
Mourn, deprived at once of his strength, his justice, his writings. [...] His
was Solomon's mind, not his fault, Nero's power, not his mind; not the
dishonour of Paris, but his beauty. His face made him Paris, not his mind,
not his age Nestor, but his mind; his appearance made him a youth, his
wisdom an old man.]

13 *Alexandrum*: see MLat. Anon. 1.8.1 f. n.   *Marcum*: see 1.16 n.   *Maronem*:

Virgil (P. Vergilius Maro).   25 *Salomonis*: see Serlo 1.15 n.   27 *Nestora*: see Prop. 7.10 n.

MLat. Anon. 2 (from a late 12th-century MS)

Werner, *Beiträge* 206 (see also *id.* 164)

Epitaphium

Forma refert Paridem, manus Hectora, sensus Ulixem: 1
    in tribus iste tribus non tulit esse minor.

[*Epitaph*: His form recalls Paris, his valour Hector, his intellect Ulysses: in these three attributes he did not submit to be less than these three.]

Twelfth- and Thirteenth-Century Collections

The Ripoll Lyrics

Ripoll 1

fore suum   Latzke 3   37
crinem tuum
Venus ipsa cuperet,
si videret,   40
et doleret,
suum quod exuperet.

[Venus herself would wish that your hair might be hers, if she were to see it and grieve that it surpassed her own.]

Ripoll 2

dic mihi, flameolum valet exornare capillos,   Latzke 11   9
    quos Febi crinis vincere non poterit?

[Tell me, has a flame-coloured veil the power to adorn the tresses which the hair of Phoebus could certainly not outdo?]

9 *flameolum*: lit. 'a small flame-coloured wedding veil'. For the *flammeum* as part of the bride's attire, see Catullus 61.8 and 115. These lines imply that the splendour of the hair outshines that of the veil. See also Ripoll 5, part of the same poem.

Ripoll 3

huius crinis   Latzke 14   19
non affinis
terrenorum crinibus
nobis deam   22
Cithaream
representat omnibus.

[Her hair, not akin to the hair of mortals, shows forth to us all an image of the Cytherean goddess.]

22 f. *deam Cithaream*: Venus, so called because the island of Cythera was a centre of her cult; cf. CB **1.3.2**; CB **5.2.8**.

The motif of hair which a god would desire (Ripoll **1**), or equal to that of a god (Ripoll **2, 3**) is derived from Ovid – see Ov. **4** and **15**.

Ripoll **4**

> Conqueror et doleo de te, mea dulcis amica.   Latzke 9   1
> quod prohibet facies: nimis exigis esse pudica.
> fac placeas Veneri, Veneris vel desine formam.
> me doctore potes Veneris cito discere normam.
>
> [I am vanquished and afflicted on your account, my sweet love. What your beauty forbids, you demand too insistently to be chaste. Act that you may be pleasing to Venus, or put off the appearance of Venus. With me as teacher you can quickly learn the precepts of Venus.]

These lines form the first verse of an alternating dialogue between *amicus* and *amica*. 2 f. Latzke, p. 180 cites Ovid, *Heroides* XVI. 289 f. (Paris to Helen): *aut faciem mutes aut sis non dura, necesse est;* | *lis est cum forma magna pudicitiae* (either you must needs change your appearance or not be obdurate: there is great strife between chastity and beauty).

Ripoll **5**

> non tibi sunt similes per se Venus atque Diana   Latzke 11   21
> sed si iungantur, sunt tibi consimiles.
> arte tua superas Venerem, candore Dianam:
> arte Diana valet, candor inest Veneri.
> ergo tui forma superat quodcumque videtur,   25
> cum nihil est usquam, quod tibi sit simile.
>
> [Venus and Diana separately are not similar to you, but if they are combined, they are entirely similar to you. In your perfection you surpass Venus, in your purity Diana: Diana is endowed with perfection, purity resides in Venus. Therefore your beauty surpasses whatsoever exists, since there is nothing anywhere which is similar to you.]

21 *Venerem*: cf. **4.3** f.   25 *videtur*: lit. 'is seen'.

In this example Venus represents beauty of appearance, Diana purity and chastity.[7] Since the qualities of the two divine figures are combined in the subject of the panegyric, each goddess is therefore said to have acquired the predominant attribute of the other (l. 24). See also Ripoll **2**, which is part of the same poem.

---

[7] But see Ripoll 20.5, in which a girl is addressed as *formosior ipsa Diana* ('more lovely than Diana herself').

The Carmina Burana[8]

The basic corpus of the *Carmina Burana* contains didactic, religious and satirical poems, together with a large group of love poems. It is noteworthy that identifications with an exemplary figure occur in all the different types of poem, whereas exemplary comparisons are found only among the love poems.

There are several brief instances of identification, in which the name of an exemplary figure confers the nature of the latter on the person to whom it is assigned: *Codrus* (after Juvenal, *Satires*, III. 203) for an impoverished poet in CB 1.6.4 and 19.5.8; *Dalida* (Delilah) for a treacherous woman in 31.3.1 and 8.6; *Panphile* in CB 29.4, after Pamphilus, the name of a young lover in Terence's plays *Hecyra* and *Andria*; in a poem by Walter of Châtillon, the Roman cardinals are described (41.25.4) as *Petrus foris, intus Nero* (Peter without, Nero within); in CB 8.2.6, 9.4.1, and 10.29 ff. the name *Symon* (after *Act. Apost.* 8:18–20) is given to priests who sell the sacraments (in CB 9.1.1 ff. they are implicitly compared to Judas). In two poems, the object of the poet's love is given the name of Thisbe (*Tispes* CB 68.5.1, *Tysben* 70.1.5); in 84.4.1 the poet refers to himself as *Tantalus*, frustrated but determined not to let the fulfilment of love elude his grasp; in 92.31.3 *Ganimedes* stands for an attendant page, after Ganymede, cupbearer to the gods (see Hilarius **1a–c**). There is one clear instance of a biblical figure cited as *exemplum*: Lazarus, restored to new life through the power of Christ should serve as example to truly repentant sinners (CB 49.12.1 f.).

Carmina Burana **1**

> Dum alumpnus Palladis   Vollmann 56   3   1
>   Cytharee scolam
> introissem, inter multas
>   bene cultas
>   uidi unam solam   5
> facie   Tyndaride
>   ac Veneri secundam,
> plenam elegantie
>   et magis pudibundam.
> [...]
> Parce, puer, puero!   5   1
> faue, Venus, tenero,
>   ignem mouens,
>   ignem fouens,
> ne mori sit, quod uixero,   5
>   nec sit Daphnes Phebo!

---

[8] In CB **1**, **4** and **6a** the refrain has been omitted as not relevant to the exemplary comparison.

quid me ipsum dedo?
olim tyro Palladis
    nunc tuo iuri cedo.

[When, as a pupil of Pallas, I had entered the school of the Cytherean, I saw among many elegant girls one alone in appearance second only to the daughter of Tyndareus and Venus, full of grace and more chaste. [. . .] Youthful god, spare a youth! Be favourable, Venus, to one of tender age, kindling and tending a fire, that my life henceforth may not be death, nor she be Daphne to Phoebus! Why do I surrender myself? Once a recruit of Pallas, now I yield to your law.]

3.1, 5.8 *Palladis*: Pallas/Minerva, here cited as the goddess of learning. 3.2 *Cytharee*: here a substantivized adjective; see Ripoll **3**.22 f. n.   3.6 *Tyndaride*: Helen; cf. CB **2**.6.4; **6a**.5.1; **6d**. 9.6.   3.7 *Veneri*: MS *ueneriſ* (which Vollmann adopts). For the comparison with Venus cf. CB 84.2.3 *cev Dyone nata | Veneris legata* (like the daughter of Dione (mother of Venus), an ambassador of Venus).   5.6 *Daphnes*: pursued by Apollo, Daphne begged her father Peneus, a river-god, to help her escape him, and was turned into a laurel (Ov., *Met.* I.452 ff.).

In 3.6 f. there is an explicit comparison, expressed by *secundam*; in the negative wish in 5.6 the girl and the poet are hypothetically identified with Daphne and Apollo respectively.

Carmina Burana 2

O decora super ora	Vollmann 61	5a	1
belli Absalonis,			
et non talis, ut mortalis			
sis conditionis!			
[. . .]			
Tuum prestolor nuntium;		6	1
dele merorem conscium,			
mundani decus iubaris,			
o uerecunda Tindaris!			
Apollo mire uinctus est		7a	1
Peneide respecta,			
sic meus amor tinctus est			
re ueteri deiecta.			
[. . .]			
Miranda de Priamide		7c	1
rememorantur gesta,			
qui militauit floride;			
sic ualent mea festa.			

[O fair one, surpassing beautiful Absalom and not such as to seem to be of human kind. [. . .] I await your messenger. Put an end to the grief made known to you, height of earthly radiance, O chaste Tyndaris. Apollo was strangely fettered when he gazed at the daughter of Peneus. So my love has been washed clean, former things cast away. [. . .] Marvellous deeds are recalled of the son of Priam, who accomplished splendid feats of arms; my celebrations are worth as much.]

5a.2 *belli Absalonis*: see 2 Sam. 14: 25.   6.4 *Tindaris*: Helen; see CB 1.3.6 n.
7a.2 *Peneide*: Daphne; see CB 1.5.6 n.   7c.1 *Priamide*: the form of the name was no doubt suggested by the need for a rhyme in *-ide*. Both Paris and Hector were sons of Priam, but *gesta* and the verb *militavit* suggest that Hector is here indicated, unless a reference to the warfare of love is intended. The obscurity of the following line makes interpretation uncertain.

There is an instance of identification in 6.4, and comparison in the other examples, expressed in 5a.1 by *super*, in 7a.3 and 7c.4 by *sic*.

Carmina Burana 3

"Aue formosissima,   gemma preciosa,   Vollmann 77   8   1
aue decus uirginum,   uirgo gloriosa,
aue lumen luminum,   aue mundi rosa,
Blanziflŏr et Helena,   Venus generosa!"

[. . .]

Visus tuus splendidus   erat et amenus,   14   1
tamquam aer lucidus   nitens et serenus.
unde dixi sepius: "Deus, deus meus,
estne illa Helena,   uel est dea Venus?"

["Hail, most beautiful one, precious jewel, hail, ornament of maidens, glorious maiden! Hail, light of lights, hail, rose of the world, Blancheflor and Helen, noble Venus!" [. . .] Your countenance was radiant and charming, shining and serene like the bright air. Therefore I said repeatedly: "O God, dear God, is she Helen or is she the goddess Venus?".]

8.3 *lumen*: MS *mundi*.   8.4 *Blanziflŏr*: the heroine of the OF *Floire et Blancheflor*. See Index of Proper Names, *s.v.*

Carmina Burana 4

O, si forte Iupiter   hanc uideat   Vollmann 83 (=Arundel 8.7)   5   1
timeo, ne pariter   incaleat
     et ad fraudes redeat,
  siue Dane pluens *aurum*
     ymbre dulci mulceat,   5
  uel Evropes intret thaurum,
     uel *Ledheo* gaudeat
        rursus in olore.

[O, if perchance Jupiter were to see her, I fear he would be equally inflamed and would revert to his deceptions, whether, sending down a golden shower upon Danae, he would caress her with gentle rain, or would enter into the bull of Europa, or again take his pleasure in the form of Leda's swan.]

5.1 ff. This passage follows after two verses describing the naked Flora. For the deception by Jupiter of Danae, Europa and Leda (with whom Flora is implicitly compared), see Stat. **1a**.135 f. n.   5.4 *aurum* (confirmed by the Arundel MS): CB MS *antrum* 'cave' (adopted by Vollmann).   5.6 *uel*: MS *ne*.   5.70 *uel Ledheo gaudeat*: MS *uel et hec congaudeat*; Arundel MS *vel ledeo canderat*.

Carmina Burana **5**

Delium flagrantem,   Vollmann 109 2 1
procantem,   anhelantem
Daphne respuit,   rennuit
puduit   amplexari.
michi refragari   5
nittitur,   que petitur,
subuertitur   spes mea,
quia Cytharea,
lese partis rea,
cedit in contrarium.

[As the Delian was aflame, pleading, panting in pursuit, Daphne repulsed and rejected him, drawing back in shame from embraces. She whom I entreat strives to resist me. My hope is ruined because the Cytherean, guilty of a change of allegiance, has turned against me.]

1 *Delium*: Apollo (Delos was his birthplace); cf. CB 65.3b.7, in which the poet describes himself as *Delio liberior* (freer than Apollo). For the story of Apollo and Daphne see CB **1**.5.6 n.   8 *Cytharea*: see Ripoll **3**.22 f. n.

There are a number of short examples, here grouped together, in most of which there is a comparison or identification with Helen, either with or without mention of Paris:

Carmina Burana **6a**

Virgo, par Tindaride,   Vollmann 103 5 1
tuo faue Paridi!

[Maiden, equal to the daughter of Tyndareus, look favourably on your Paris.]

1 *Tindaride*: see CB **1**.3.6 n. and **6d** below.

Carmina Burana **6b**

cuius laus est singularis   Vollmann 111 3 1
pro qua non curasset Paris
Helene consortium.

[She is uniquely worthy of praise: Paris would not have sought the society of Helen in preference to her.]

Carmina Burana 6c

"si tu esses Helena,   uellem esse Paris!"   Vollmann 142   3   3

["If you were Helen, I would wish to be Paris."]

Carmina Burana 6d

que uix potest corrigi,   Vollmann 163   9   5
    ut Tyndaris sit illa.

[She barely admits of any improvement in order to be the daughter of Tyndareus.]

  6 *Tyndaris*: see **6a**.1 n.

There is one comparison with an unspecified historical figure:

Carmina Burana 6e

prestantior omni creatura   Vollmann 78   2   5
placet plus Francie regina.

[Surpassing every creature, she is more pleasing than the queen of France.][9]

There is one implied comparison with the loves of Jove:

Carmina Burana 6f

me Corinna,   Ioue digna,   nexuit   Vollmann 103   8   7
suis frenis   et abenis   domuit.

[Corinna, worthy of Jove, has bound me with her bridle and curbed me with her reins.]

  7 *Ioue digna*: see Prop. **4**; Sid. **5**.89 n.

There are short examples in which the poet compares or identifies himself with exemplary figures:

Carmina Burana 7a

nunquam tanti cordis fuit Priiupiter,   Vollmann 61   2b   1
de spe Venerea opinor iugiter.

[Jupiter (?) was never in such a state of emotion; my thoughts turn constantly to the hope of love's fulfilment.]

---

[9] The queen of France is cited in the Romance lyric as an ideal or unattainable object of love, usually with reference to the lost tale of the tragic love of Andrieu for the queen of France (see R. Jordan **2**.24 and n.); see also Guinizzelli 11.13 (Contini II, p. 473) *ben mi rasembra reina di Franza* (she seems to me most like the queen of France).

Carmina Burana **7b**

            set Alcide fortior   Vollmann 63   4a   1
            aggredior
pugnam contra Venerem.

[But stronger than the descendant of Alceus (Hercules), I take up the fight against Venus.]

1 *Alcide*: cf. Claud. **2**.533 n.

Carmina Burana **7c**

finem uelis   dare telis!   tunc in celis   Vollmann 103   4b   1
      Iouis fungar solio,
      Platone doctior,
      Sampsone fortior,
      Augusto dicior.

[Put an end to your darts! Then in the heavens I shall occupy the throne of Jove, more learned than Plato, stronger than Samson, more prosperous than Augustus.]

This versicle immediately precedes the plea in CB **6a** above.

Carmina Burana **7d**

si me dignetur, quam desidero,   Vollmann 116   2   1
felicitate Iouem suppero.

[If she whom I desire deigns to favour me, I shall be superior to Jove in felicity.]

Carmina Burana **7e**

simus iussu Cypridis   Vollmann 143   3   5
gloriantes   et letantes
pares esse Paridis!

[Let us at the command of the Cyprian rejoice and be glad to be the equals of Paris.]

5 *Cypridis*: of Venus, because the island of Cypris (Cyprus) was a centre of her cult; see Girald. **1**.15.

Carmina Burana **7f**

tamen cano,   sed de uano   Vollmann 147   2   1
      statu Veneris,
cuius Paris   et scolaris
      sum cum ceteris.

[Yet I sing, but of the vacillating nature of Venus, whose Paris and pupil I am with the rest.]

Carmina Burana 7g

> liber ego liberum   me iactito,   Vollmann 178   4   1
> casto fore similem   Ypolito.

[Free, I boast of being free, like chaste Hippolytus.]

There is one German stanza among those added to Latin poems which contains a series of comparisons with exemplars of beauty:

Carmina Burana 8

> Si ist schôner den uro Dido was,   Vollmann 155a   1
> si ist schôner denne vrowe Helena,
> si ist schôner denne vrowe Pallas,
> si ist schôner denne vrowe Ecuba,
> si ist ist minnechlicher denne vrowe Isabel   5
> und urôlicher denne Gaudile;
> > mines hercen chle
> ist tugunde richer denne Baldine.

> [She is more beautiful than lady Dido was, she is more beautiful than lady
> Helen, she is more beautiful than lady Pallas, she is more beautiful than
> lady Hecuba, she is more lovely than lady Isabel and more joyful than
> Gaudile; my heart's clover is richer in excellent qualities than Baldine.]

CB 155a is appended to the third stanza of CB Latin 155 and was composed in
order to imitate the form of CB 155. It is included here because of its metrical
and textual links with 155 and because it stands outside the mainstream of the
German lyric. The first two stanzas of CB 155 describe a figure of ideal beauty
in terms appropriate to Venus. The third stanza lists those whose help the poet
must entreat: Jove, Hercules, Juno, Pallas, Helen, Venus. The names *Helena* and
Pallas have been taken from this Latin stanza, but set in a new context, that of
a series of exemplary comparisons in which the names *Dido* and *Ecuba* have
been added, the latter for reasons of rhyme. This accumulation of classical
names would not be customary in the German lyric, and the Romance names
Isabel, Gaudile and *Baldine* suggest that the author is a Romance, probably an
Italian, speaker with a rudimentary command of German.[10] It is noteworthy
that of the exemplary comparisons in Latin poems applied to female figures
only CB **6e** above expresses comparison by means of a comparative adjective
(*prestantior*), corresponding to *schôner* in CB 155a.

Giraldus Cambrensis (*c. 1146–1220*)

The poet observes a girl bathing in a spring:

---

[10] See Sayce, *Plurilingualism in the Carmina Burana*, pp. 46 ff.

Giraldus **1**

> nuda sedet, niveusque nitor radiosus in undis   *OBMLat.* V 248   13
>   fulget, et umbrosum non sinit esse locum.
> non aliter Cypris, non luderet ipsa Diana,   15
>   non Naïs sacri fontis amoena colens,
> surgit ut Eois cum sol emergit ab undis,
>   ut premit astra dies, sic premit illa diem.

[Naked, she sits, and a snowy radiance shines bright in the water, permitting no shade in the place. Most like the Cyprian or Diana herself at play, or a Naiad dwelling in the fair surroundings of a sacred spring, she comes forth, as when the sun rises from the Eastern waves; as day eclipses the stars, so she eclipses the day.]

15 *Cypris*: see CB **7e**.3.5 n.

The Poetic Theorists

The medieval poetic theorists give sample positive or negative descriptions of persons which often incorporate identification or comparison with exemplary figures. Thus a long description of Ulysses in the *Ars Versificatoria* of Matthieu de Vendôme (probably composed before 1175) concludes with a series of identifications with authorial, historical and mythical figures:

Matthieu de Vendôme

Matthieu de Vendôme **1**

> Tullius eloquio, conflictu Cesar, Adrastus   Munari iii, p. 73   52.61
>   consilio, Nestor mente, rigore Cato.

[A Cicero in eloquence, a Caesar in conflict, Adrastus in counsel, Nestor in intellect, in moral rigour Cato.]

61 *Tullius*: see Baudri **2b**.28 n. *Cato*: see Einh. (?) **1**.72 n.   *Adrastus*: king of Argos, one of the Seven against Thebes.   62 *Nestor*: see Serlo **2**.27 n. *Cato*: see Einh. (?). **1**.72 n.

This is followed by a similar passage in the negative description of Davus (the name given to a slave in the comedies of Plautus and Terence):

Matthieu de Vendôme **2**

> forma Tersites, ad fraudes Argus, ad equum   Munari, iii, p. 74   53.7
>   Tyresias, Verres crimine, fraude Synon.[11]

---

[11] See also the positive example of this type given by G. de Vinsauf (Faral, p. 251): 1775 *es Cato mente,* | *Tullius ore, Paris facie, Pirrusque vigore* (you are Cato in intellect, Tullius in speech, Paris in appearance, and Pyrrhus in vigour).

[In appearance Thersites, in respect of trickery Argus, in respect of fairness Tiresias, Verres in crime, in treachery Sinon.]

7 *Tersites*: an ugly and scurrilous figure in Homer.   *Argus*: a monster with eyes all over his body, who was yet tricked by Mercury into relaxing his guard over Io, after she had been changed into a heifer by Jove (Ov. *Met.* I. 625 ff.). 8 *Tyresias*: decided a dispute between Jove and Juno in favour of the former (Ovid, *Met.* III. 316 ff.) and was struck blind by Juno for his championship of Jove.   *Verres*: a notorious governor of Sicily, known through the speeches of Cicero.   *Synon*: Sinon, a pretended deserter from the Greeks, who tricked the Trojans into admitting the wooden horse within their walls (Verg., *Aen.* II.79, 195, 259).

Geoffroi de Vinsauf

Geoffroi de Vinsauf prefaces his *Poetria Nova* (c. 1208–1213) with a dedication to pope Innocent III (d. 1216), in which he compares him in respect of individual attributes to Apostles, and places him above other authorities of the Church on account of his mastery of language:

Geoffroi de Vinsauf **1**

Egregius sanguis te confert Bartholomaeo,	Faral p. 197 10
Mite cor Andreae, pretiosa juventa Johanni,	
Firma fides Petro, perfecta scientia Paulo,	
Ista simul nulli. Superest de dotibus una,	
Quam nulli fas est attingere: gratia linguae.	
Augustine, tace! Leo papa, quiesce! Johannes,	15
Desine! Gregori, subsiste! Quid eloquar omnes?	

[Your illustrious blood likens you to Bartholomew, your gentle heart to Andrew, your precious youth to John, your firm faith to Peter, your excellent learning to Paul, these things together to none of these. There is one further gift, which it is permitted to none to approach: the elegance of language. Augustine, fall silent! pope Leo, abstain! John, desist! Gregory, refrain! Why need I speak of them all?]

11 *Johanni*: cf.Venant. 2.20.   12 *Petro ... Paulo*: cf.Venant. 2.19.   13 *ista simul nulli*: i.e. none of those named possesses all these attributes together. 15 f. *Leo* and *Gregori* designate popes, *Augustine* a Doctor of the Church; it is therefore likely that *Johannes* here refers to John of Damascus, also a Doctor of the Church.

In his sample description of a beautiful woman in the same work (Faral, pp. 214 ff.) Geoffroi begins with an enumeration of physical features, proceeding as is usual from the head downwards, then adds a description of rich clothing and finally a whole range of mythological figures whom the subject may be said to outdo:

Geoffroi de Vinsauf **2**

Si Jupiter illis   Faral p. 216   613

Temporibus vidisset eam, nec in Amphitrione
Luderet Alcmenam; nec sumeret ora Dianae,   615
Ut te fraudaret, Calixto, flore; nec Yo
Nube, nec Antiopam satyro, nec Agenore natam
Tauro, Mnemosyne nec te pastore, vel igne
Asopo genitam, vel te Deonis in angue,
Vel Ledam cygno, vel Danem falleret auro.   620
Hanc unam coleret omnesque videret in una.

[If Jupiter in those times had seen her, he would not in the guise of Amphitryon deceive Alcmene, nor would he assume the appearance of Diana, that he might trick you, Callisto, out of your virginity; nor would he deceive Io in a cloud, nor Antiopa as a satyr, nor the daughter of Agenor as a bull, nor you, Mnemosyne, as a shepherd, or in the form of fire the daughter of Asopus, or you, daughter of Deo, as a snake, or Leda as a swan, or Danae in (a shower of) gold. He would cultivate this one alone and would see them all in one.]

613 ff. All the victims of Jove's disguises here cited occur together in Ovid, *Met.* VI. 103 ff., with the exception of Io (*Met.* I. 588 ff.) and Callisto (*Met.* II. 417 ff.). See also Stat. **1a**.135 f. n.   616 *Yo*: cf. Baudri **2a**.21. n.   617 *Agenore natam*: Europa.   618 *Mnemosyne*: MS *Messione*.   619 *Asopo* (MS *Ansepho*) *genitam*: Aegina.   *Deionis*: Proserpina.

Conclusion

This chapter covers a particularly wide chronological span and includes an extensive range of poetic texts containing exemplary comparisons and identifications – panegyric, epithalamium, religious poetry, epitaph, occasional compositions, and love poetry. The poets no longer draw solely on classical myth and legend, but also on history,[12] including the history of the Church, the Bible, and the names of representative authorial figures such as Homer and Cicero which constitute an established literary canon. However, in the earlier examples cited, those from the *Appendix Tibulliana*, the 'Laus Pisonis', and the poems of Statius and Claudian, the exemplary figures are still derived solely from classical legend and literature. This feature may survive throughout the whole period, depending on the type of poem. Thus like the epithalamia Statius **1** and Claudian **3**, the later examples of the genre, Sidonius **5** and Venantius **3** continue this tradition of solely mythological and legendary

---

[12] Like the few seemingly historical examples in the earlier classical poets, the names *Ilia*, *Lavinia* and *Claudia* in Stat. **1c**, and *Aeneas* in Ermold. **2**, are treated as belonging to legend and literature rather than to history and are included under figures of myth.

reference, as does also much of later love poetry. There is a much greater variety in types of comparison and identification than in the Classical poets, and in particular a very considerable increase in instances of comparison which express superiority to the exemplar, which make up almost half the total of the examples discussed.

From Sidonius onwards, verifiable historical figures may be cited as exemplars and from Venantius Fortunatus on, figures derived from the Bible or the Church. In a specific poem, poets may use solely one type of reference, as in the examples above, or in the panegyric in Priscian **1**, which refers solely to historical figures, or Sedulius **2**, which contains solely biblical exemplars. On the other hand, combination of different types is very common. Thus Sidonius **3** combines comparison of Avitus with Hercules, Hippolytus (and in the omitted lines 272 ff. also with Achilles), with allusions to the Roman figures of Trajan and Fabricius; in Sidonius **4** the father of Consentius is said to excel all Greek and Roman authors, scholars, philosophers, orators and statesmen, but in music to outdo Orpheus, Pan and Apollo. Combinations of historical and biblical exemplars are also common. Thus Anon. **1** cites a long list of OT characters as models of kingship, but includes also Julius Caesar and Alexander the Great, and Benzo of Alba combines pagan and Christian, including Carolingian, rulers with Solomon.

The mythological figures most frequently cited as exemplars (in rough order of frequency) are Venus, Helen, Apollo and Achilles, followed by Hercules, Paris and Diana, followed by Danae, Nestor, Hippolytus and Ulysses (see Index of Proper Names). Whereas in Homer most comparisons are with named divinities, this is much rarer in Virgil and infrequent in the poets from Catullus to Ovid, except in an indirect example such as Prop. **6**.6, and in comparisons, not with the divinity itself, but with one of its attributes. In the poets included in this chapter there are a few direct comparisons or identifications with divinities, such as that with Mars in Claud. **1** and **2**; with Apollo in Claud. **2** and **3**, Sid. **1** and **4a**, Ermold. **1** (borrowed from Virgil) and Sed. **3**; with Venus in Stat. **1a**, Venant. **3** and CB **3**, or with Venus and Diana together in Girald. **1**. As in the earlier poets, however, comparison with divine aspects or attributes is frequent, as in Claud. **3b**.270, Claud. **4**, Venant. **4**, Ripoll **1–4** and CB **1**; in Ripoll **5** attributes of Venus and Diana are combined.

The designation of mythological exemplars

As in the poets from Catullus to Ovid, the mythological exemplars may be designated in different ways:[13]

---

[13] In order to make the range of exemplars clear, non-exemplary uses of the same name, and names of figures associated with exemplars in the same context are not included in the following lists: see e.g. in Stat. **1a** *Phoebe*; *Theseum*; *Euhan*; *Iuppiter, Iuno*. The Index of Proper Names lists all occurrences of names.

(i) By proper name: *Nestora*; *Vlixem, Append. Tibull.*; *Nestorei* (adj.) . . . *mellis* Laus Pis. **1**. *Daphne* Stat. **1a**; *Helena*; *Thetin* Stat. **1b**; *Ilia*; *Lavinia*; *Claudia* Stat. **1c** (for the three pseudo-historical names see also n. 12). *Penelope*; *Aegiale* Stat. **2**. *Martem*; *Apolline* Claud. **2**. *Castorem*; *Achilli*; *Apollinem*; *Adonidem*; *Herculi*; *Aurorae*; *Dianae* Claud. **3a**. *Veneris* Claud. **4**. *Eryx*; *Castora*; *Pollucem*; *Alconem*; *Bellerophonteis* (adj.) . . . *opimis*; *Metabus* Sid. **2a**. *Hippolytus* Sid. **3c**; *Herculeo* (adj.) . . . *dorso* Sid. **3e**. *Alceste*; *Circe*; *Calypso*; *Scylla*; *Atalanta*; *Medea*; *Hippodame*; *Dido*; *Phyllis*; *Euadne* Sid. **5**. *Achilles*; *Venus* Venant. **3**. *Minerva*; *Venus* Venant. **4**. *Apollo* Ermold. **1**. *Hector*; *Aeneas* Ermold. **2**. *Apollo* Sed. **3**. *Venus*; *Iuno*; *Dafnes* (see n.); *Io*; *Euridicen*; *Sibilla*; *Diana*; *Bellerofonta* Baudri **2a**. *Achilleos* (adj.) . . . *actus* Baudri **3**. *Ganimedes* Hilarius **1a**. *Pelox*; *Briareus* Primas **1**. *Ulixe* Archipoeta **1**. *Achillis*; *Pirithoique* Serlo **1**. *Paridis*; *Paridem*; *Nestora* Serlo **2**. *Paridem*; *Hectora*; *Ulixem* Anon. **2**. *Venus* Ripoll **1**. *Veneris* Ripoll **4**. *Venus*; *Diana* Ripoll **5**. *Veneri*; *Daphnes* CB **1**. *Apollo* CB **2**. *Helena*;[14] *Venus* CB **3**. *Dane*; *Evropes*; *Ledheo* (adj.) CB **4**. *Daphne* CB **5**. *Paridi* CB **6a**. *Helene* CB **6b**. *Helena*; *Paris* CB **6c**. *Priiupiter* CB **7a**. *Iouis* CB **7c**. *Iouem* CB **7d**. *Paridis* CB **7e**. *Paris* CB **7f**. *Ypolito* CB **7g**. *Dido*; *Helena*; *Pallas*; *Ecuba* CB **8**.[15] *Diana* Girald. **1**. *Nestor* M. Vend. **1**. *Tersites*; *Argus*; *Tyresias*; *Synon* M. Vend. **2**. *Alcmenam*; *Calixto*; *Yo*; *Antiopam*; *Mnemosyne*; *Ledam*; *Danem* G. Vins. **2**.

(ii) By alternative name: *Gradivus* Claud. **1**. *Liberum*; *Virbium* Claud. **3a**. *Paean* Sid. **1**. *Euhan* Sid. **2b**. *Phoebus* Sid. **4a**. *Phebo* Sed. **3**. *Febi* Ripoll **2**. *Phebi* CB **1**.

(iii) By patronymic or indication of descent: *Laertiadae*; *Atridae* 'Laus Pis.' **1**. *Alcides* Claud. **2**. *Aeacida* Sid. **1**. *natus Ophelte*; *Telamone creatum*; *Pelidae*; *Aegides* Stat. **2a**; *Semeleius* (*Euhan*) Sid. **2b**. *Alcides* Sid. **3b**. *cygno Iove nata* Sid. **5**. *filia Ledae*; *Alcidem* Baudri **2a**. *Priamidem*; *Theside* Serlo **1**. *Tyndaride* CB **1**. *Tindaris*; *Peneide*; *Priamide* CB **2**. *Tindaride* CB **6a**. *Tyndaris* CB **6d**. *Alcide* CB **7b**. *Agenore natam*; *Asopo genitam*; *Deionis* G. Vins. **2**.

(iv) By topographical designation: *Latonia*; *Gnosida* Stat. **1a**. *Meliboea* Stat. **2**. *Arcas* Sid. **2a**. *Tirynthius heros* Sid. **3e**. *Thrax vates*; *deus Arcas* Sid. **4a**. *Lemnias*; *Cressa*; *Sestias* Sid. **5**. *deam Cithaream* Ripoll **3**. *Delium*; *Cytharea* CB **5**. *Cypridis* CB **7e**. *Cypris* Girald. **1**.

In addition to named mythical exemplars, there are also indirect references. Thus the circumlocution in Stat. **2**.49 *et quam . . . fecerunt maenada planctus* designates Laodamia. When Venus declares in Stat. **1a**.112 f. that the bride has grown in her own image, or in Sid. **5**.79 f. that Paris would have pronounced judgement in favour of Hiberia instead of herself, it is implied that she is the exemplar against which the bride is to be measured. In Stat.

[14] Coupled with the name *Blanziflŏr*, derived from OF romance.
[15] This German stanza also contains the Romance names *Isabel, Gaudile, Baldine*.

1a.135 f. the reference to Jove's disguises in *pennas ... cornua ... auro* indirectly indicates Leda, Europa, and Danae as those whom the bride surpasses, just as in Sid. **5**.90 the enumeration *Delia, taurus, olor, satyrus, draco, fulmen et aurum* indirectly refers to Callisto, Europa, Leda, Antiopa, Proserpina (or perhaps incorrectly Mnemosyne, see **5**.90 n.), Semele and Danae as exemplars. In Sid. **5**.65 ff. Cupid's listing of Hypsipyle, Ariadne, Alcestis, Circe, Calypso, Scylla, Atalanta, Medea, Hippodamia, Helen, Dido, Phyllis, Euadne and Hero as those who would submit to love for Ruricius implies that the bridegroom surpasses the heroes with whom they were associated, i.e. Jason, Theseus, Admetus, Ulysses, Minos, Hippomenes, Menelaus, Aeneas, Demophoon, Capaneus and Leander; similarly when Venus replies by citing in ll. 86 ff. Pelops, Hippomenes, Achelous, Aeneas and Perseus as those who would have contended for Hiberia's favour, she implies that the bride surpasses Hippodamia, Atalanta, Deanira, Lavinia and Andromeda respectively. In Sidonius **2** the context makes it clear that *violatae Phoebados ultrix* (l. 194) refers to Pallas Athena as exemplar. In Hilarius **1b** and **1c** the general context and *auis* in **1b** make the reference to Ganymede clear. This type of indirect reference occurs only among the examples derived from classical myth and legend.

Classical authors and historical figures[16] cited as exemplars often occur together and are therefore not listed separately: *magnus Alexander* Sid. **2a**. *Traianum* Sid. **3a**; *Fabricium* Sid. **3d**. *Antoninum*; *Marcum*; *Nervam*; *Titus*; *Traiani* Prisc. **1**. *Traiani*; *Fabii* Venant. **1**. *Homerus*; *Vergilius*; *Philo*; *Tertullus*; *Flaccus*; *Tibullus* Petr. Gramm. **1**. *Homero*; *Flacco*; *Vergilio*; *Tertullo*; *Philoni*; *Tibulle* Paul. Diac. **1**. *Catonis*; *Marcum*; *Homerus* Einh.(?) **1**. *Decii*; *Scipiadę*; *Camillus*; *Cato*; *Caesar*; *Pompeius*; *gens Fabiorum*; *Constantino*; *Theodosio* Poeta Saxo **1**. *Karolus* Sed. **1** (see **1.5** n.). *Homerum* Sed. **3**. *Iulius*; *Alexander Maximus* MLat. Anon. **1**. *Scipione*; *Iulius*; *Fabios*; *Cicerones*; *Fabricios*; *Catones*; *Theodosios*; *Iustinianos*; *Karolos*; *Pipinos*; *Sabinos* Benzo **1**. *Cato*; *Tullius*; *Ciceronem*; *Catonem*; *Aristoteles*; *Homerus* Baudri **2b**. *Iulius* Baudri **3**. *Daciano*; *Herodes Galileus*; *Dionisius* Primas **1**. *Tulliane* (adv.); *Alexandro* Archipoeta **1**. *Ciceroni*; *Cato*; *Marcus* Serlo **1**. *Alexandrum*; *Marcum*; *Maronem*; *Neronis* Serlo **2**. *Platone*; *Augusto* CB **7c**. *Tullius*; *Cesar*; *Adrastus*; *Cato* M. Vend. **1**. *Verres* M. Vend. **2**. For the catalogue of authors and authorities in Sid. **4** see *ad loc.* and for *Francie regina* in CB **6e** see n. 9.

The following biblical names[17] occur: *Daviticae* (adj.) ... *vitae*; *Salomone* Venant. **1**. *Petrum*; *Paulum*; *Iacobi*; *Iohannis*; *Heliae* Venant. **2**. *Salomonem*; *David*; *Ioseph* Theod. **1**. *Daviticae ... virtutis* Poeta Saxo **1**. *Lazarus* Gottsch. **1**. *Salemon*; *Isaac*; *Abrahae*; *Iacob* Sed. **2**. *Abel*; *Samuel*; *Daniel*; *Natanael*;

---

[16] See n. 12.

[17] Female biblical names are rare, but see e.g. Walahfrid Strabo (*MGH, Poetae* ii, pp. 375 f.), in which Judith, wife of Louis the Pious, is identified with Rachel, and her name stated to be not inappropriate, since she resembles the Apocryphal Judith in virtue and religion.

Davit; *Iudas* MLat. Anon. **1** – for other OT figures in this poem see also *ibid.* 4.1 ff. n. *Davidis*; *Messieque, Carm. Cant.* **1**. *Salomone* Benzo **1**. *Zacheus* Primas **1**. *David* Archipoeta **1**. *Ionam*; *Ionas* Archipoeta **2**. *Sanxsoni*; *Salomon* Serlo **1**. *Salomonis* Serlo **2**. *Absalonis* CB **2**. *Sampsone* CB **7c**. See also the designations of the Prodigal Son: *ille tuus prodigus . . . filius* Gottsch. **1**; *ego sum tibi filius ille, qui paui porcos* . . . Baudri **1**. St. Martin is referred to in *Martino* Venant. **2** (see l. 17 n.) and *Martinoque* Archipoeta **1**. G. Vins. **1** combines the biblical names *Bartholomaeo*; *Andreae*; *Johanni*; *Petro*; *Paulo* with those of the ecclesiastical authorities *Augustine*; *Leo papa*; *Johannes*; *Gregori*.

As in the classical poets, names may be placed in a prominent position, at the beginning or end of lines, or in both positions. Beginning of the line: Claud. **2**. 533 *Alcides*. Sid. **1**.150 *Aeacida*; 154 *Paean*. Sid. **2a**.183 *Pollucem*; 184 *Bellerophonteis* (adj.); 193 *Atticus Aegides*; 202 *magnus Alexander*. Sid. **3c**.199 *Hippolytus*; **3d**.227 *Fabricium*. Sid. **5**.66 *Lemnias*; 68 *Scylla*; 69 *Hippodame*; 71 *Euadne*. Venant **1**.82 *Traiani*. Venant. **2**.17 *Martino*; 25 *Heliae*. Petr. Gramm. **1**.5.4 *Flaccus*. Ermold. **2**.34 *Hector et Aeneas*. Sed. **2**.55 *Abrahae*; 58 *Isaac*. *Carm. Cant.* **1**. 6 *Davidis*; *Messieque*. Baudri **2a**.116 *Alcidem*. Hil. **1a** *Ganimedes*. Hil. **1c**. 24 *Iovi*. Archipoeta **1**.5.1 *Ulixe*; 6.1 *Alexandro*, 2 *David*; 3 *Martinoque*. Serlo **1**.16 *Marcus*. CB **2**.7a.1 *Apollo*. CB **3** *Blanziflŏr*. CB **5**.1 *Delium*; 3 *Daphne*. CB **6b**.3 *Helene*. CB **7c**.2 *Iovis*; 3 *Platone*; 4 *Sampsone*; 5 *Augusto*. M. Vend. **1**.61 *Tullius*. M. Vend. **2** *Tyresias*. G. Vins. **1**.15 *Augustine*. G. Vins. **2**.619 *Asopo genitam*.

End of the line (exs. in rhyme are underlined): 'Laus Pis.' **1**.61 *Atridae*. Claud. **2**.526 *Martem*. Claud. **3a**.6 *Castorem*; 8 *Apollinem*; 9 *Liberum*; 16 *Adonidem*; 17 *Virbium*. Sid. **2a**.164 *natus Ophelte*; 166 *Arcas*; 185 *Telamone creatum*; Sid. **2b**.231 *Euhan*. Sid. **3e**.581 *Tirynthius heros*. Sid. **4a**.122 *Phoebus*. Sid. **5**.70 *Phyllis*; 87 *Achelous*. Prisc. **1**.46 *Marcum*. Venant. **2**.19 *Paulum*. Venant. **3**.50 *Achilles*. Venant. **4**.8 *Venus*. Petr. Gramm. **1**.5.1 *Vergilius*. Paul. Diac. **1**.4.1 *Vergilio*; 2 *Philoni Memphitico*. Einh. (?)**1**.72 *Catonis*; 73 *Marcum*; 74 *Homerus*. Poeta Saxo **1**.655 *Camillus*; 657 *Fabiorum*; 662 *Theodosio*. Gottsch. **1**. 56.3 <u>*Lazarus*</u>. Sed. **1** *Karolus*. Sed. **3**.5 *Homerum*; 11 *Apollo*. MLat. Anon. **1**.3.1 <u>*Abel*</u>; 2 <u>*Samuel*</u>; 3 <u>*Daniel*</u>; 4 <u>*Natanael*</u>; 7.1 *Iulius*; 8.1 <u>*Alexander Maximus*</u>. Benzo **1**.4 <u>*Scipione*</u>; 9 <u>*Cicerones*</u>; 10 <u>*Catones*</u>; 11 <u>*Salomone*</u>; 14 <u>*Iustinianos*</u>; 15 <u>*Pipinos*</u>; 16 <u>*Sabinos*</u>. Baudri **2a**.19 *filia Ledae*; 21 *Io*; 24 *Euridicen*; 115 *Diana*. Baudri **2b**.29 *Catonem*; 30 *Aristoteles*; 31 *Homerus*. Primas **1**.42 <u>*Pelox*</u>; 47 <u>*Daciano*</u>; 76 <u>*Zacheus*</u>; 77 <u>*Briareus*</u>; 78 <u>*Herodes Galileus*</u>; 79 <u>*Dionisius*</u>. Archipoeta **2**.19 <u>*Ionam*</u>. Serlo **1**.11 *Achillis*; 13 *Ciceroni*. Serlo **2**.13 *Maronem*; 25 *Neronis*. MLat. Anon. **2**.1 *Ulixem*. Ripoll **3**. 22 f. *deam* | *Cithaream*. Ripoll **5**.21 *Diana*; 23 *Dianam*; 24 *Veneri*. CB **1**.3.6 <u>*Tyndaride*</u>; 5.6 <u>*Phebo*</u>. CB **2**.5.2 <u>*Absalonis*</u>; 6.4 <u>*Tindaris*</u>. 7c.1 <u>*Priamide*</u>. CB **3**.14.4 <u>*Venus*</u>. CB **6a**.1 <u>*Tindaride*</u>; 2 <u>*Paridi*</u>. CB **6b**.2 <u>*Paris*</u>. CB **6c** <u>*Paris*</u>. CB **7b**.3 <u>*Venerem*</u>. CB **7e**.3.7 <u>*Paridis*</u>. CB **7g**.4.2 <u>*Ypolito*</u>. Girald. **1**.15 *Diana*. M. Vend. **1**.61 *Adrastus*,

62 *Cato.* M. Vend. **2.53.8** *Synon.* G. Vins. **1**.10 *Bartholomeo*; 11 *Johanni*; 13 *Paulo*; 15 *Johannes.* G. Vins. **2**.616 *Yo*; 617 *Agenore natam.* See also the names in rhyme in the German stanza CB **8**.2 *Helena*; 3 *Pallas*; 4 *Ecuba*; 5 *Isabel*; 6 *Gaudile*; 8 *Baldine.* The underlined examples show that names may be a useful resource in rhyme.

Names both at the beginning and end of the line: *Append. Tibull.* **1**.49 *Nestora . . . Vlixem.* Stat. **1a**.133 *Gnosida . . . Euhan.* Stat. **2**.47 *Penelope . . . Ulixes.* Sid. **4a**.122 *Thrax vates . . . Phoebus.* Sid. **5**. 67 *Alceste . . . Calypso*; 88 *Aeneas . . . Perseus.* Prisc. **1**.46 *Antoninum . . . Marcum.*

The majority of the examples included in this chapter are explicit comparisons, whether of similarity to, or superiority to, the exemplar, with a considerable increase in the latter category. Syntactically straightforward instances such as the following are rare: see e.g. in comparisons of similarity, *qualis Apollo micat gradiens per culmina Deli* Ermold. **1**.533; *non aliter Cypris, non luderet ipsa Diana* Girald. **1**.15; in comparisons of superiority or outdoing, *non Decii, non Scipiadę, non ipse Camillus, | non Cato, non Caesar maior eo fuerat* Poeta Saxo **1**.655; *non tibi sunt similes per se Venus atque Diana | sed si iungantur, sunt tibi consimiles* Ripoll **5**.21. Most examples are lexically and syntactically more complex, employing a very wide range of vocabulary and construction to express the idea of comparison. For the greatly increased category of comparisons expressing superiority to the exemplar see: *Append. Tibull.* **1**; 'Laus Pis.' **1**; Stat. **1a**.130 ff.; Claud. **3a**, **3b**; Sid. **2a**; Sid. **4a**, **4b**; Sid. **5** (implied); Prisc. **1**; Venant. **4**; Einh. (?) **1**; Ermold. **2**; Sed. **3**.10; Benzo **1**; Baudri **2a**.19 ff.,67 ff.; Baudri **3**; Hil. **1a**; Hil. **1b** and **1c** (implied); Archipoeta **1**; Ripoll. **1**; Ripoll. **2**; Ripoll **5**; CB **2**; CB **4**; CB **6b**; CB **6e**; CB **6 f.**; CB **7b**; CB **7c**; CB **7d**; CB **8**; G. Vins. **1**; G. Vins. **2**. There are also a number of identifications with an exemplar, or combinations of comparison and identification within the same context. Particularly frequent is the comparison (or less often identification) of the person praised in respect of particular characteristics possessed by the exemplar.

Lexical and syntactical features

1. Adjectives and adverbs, often in comparative form, or in conjunction with a negative: *non . . . tantos, Append. Tibull.* **1**. *quid ultra . . . quantum . . . quantumque*; *minus*; *nec talem* Stat. **1b**; *non talis* (2×) Stat. **1c**; *sic* Stat. **1c**; *nec minor* Stat. **2**. *qualis* Claud. **1**. *sic . . . sic*; *tali* Claud. **2**. *minorem* Claud. **3a**. *non . . . melius* Sid. **1**. *haud ita*; *segnius*; *nec sic* (2×); *non sic* Sid. **2a**, **2b**. *sic* Sid. **3b**, **3c**, **3d**. *nec minor* Sid. **5**. *non tantum* Prisc. **1**. *similis* Paul. Diac. **1**. *non . . . maior* Poeta Saxo **1**. *qualis* Ermold. **1**. *ut*; *ceu*; *similis*; *sic*; *veluti* Sed. **2**. *doctior* Sed. **3**. *ut* (repeated) MLat. Anon. **1**. *pluris* (2×); *nec tanti . . . neque tanti* Baudri **2a**. *pluris*; *nulli secundus* Baudri **3**. *velut* (2×); *ut* Primas **1**. *facundior . . . forcior . . . mansuetior . . . largior* Archipoeta **1**. *similem* Serlo

1. *minor* MLat. Anon. **2.** *affinis* Ripoll **3.** *similes*; *consimiles*; *simile* Ripoll **5.** *Veneri secundam* CB **1.** *sic* (2×) CB **2.** *par* CB **6a.** *praestantior*; *plus* CB **6e.** *fortior* CB **7b.** *doctior . . . fortior . . . dicior* CB **7c.** *similem* CB **7g.** *non aliter* Girald. **1.**

2. Prepositional constructions: *cum Constantino et Theodosio* Poeta Saxo **1.** *cum Scipione*; *cum Salomone* Benzo **1.**

3. Nominal constructions: *mihi dulcis imago prosiluit* Stat. **1a**; *nec turbine tanto* Sid. **2a**; *haud alio . . . vultu* Sid. **3e**; *Davides exemplo, Carm. Cant.* **1**; *super ora belli Absalonis* CB **2**; *nunquam tanti cordis* CB **7a**. In *pares esse Paridis* CB **7e**, the following genitive indicates that *pares* is here to be construed as a noun.

4.Verbal constructions, with many verbs of action and movement. Verbs of outdoing, equalling, yielding, falling short, or similar are common: *vincis*; *cedit* 'Laus Pis.' **1.** *emineat . . . premit*; *exsto* Stat. **1a.** *aequas* Stat. **2.** *mallet . . . praefert . . . victum fatetur . . . credit minorem . . . spernit . . . damnat*; *vincis* Claud. **3a.** *cessit . . . frustra sibi . . . tribuit palmam*; *vetuisses . . . insultaturus*; *vincit*; *dormitat* Sid. **2a.** *aequiperet*; *vincat* Sid. **3a.** *post erant* Sid. **4a**; *latebant* Sid. **4b.** *vincunt . . . promeruitque*; *cesserit* Prisc. **1.** *victa* Venant. **4.** *superat . . . vincit . . . edit . . . superat* Einh. (?) **1.** *prefertur* Poeta Saxo **1.** *cedet*; *exstas* Ermold. **2.** *cuius in aspectu nihil est . . .* Sed. **3.** *victor habes palmam. transcendens . . . transilis* Benzo **1.** *multos . . . valet . . . Aristoteles* Baudri **2b.** *exuperet* Ripoll **1.** *vincere* Ripoll **2.** *superas*; *superat* Ripoll **5.** *suppero* CB **7d.** Of related semantic type are the imperatives: *conde . . . titulos* Sid. **1.** *Veneris desine formam* Ripoll **4.** *tace . . . quiesce . . . desine . . . subsiste* G. Vins. **1.** Other verbs express similarity: *Traiani ingenium . . . refers* Venant. **1** *dicor similis . . . similor . . . conferor* Paul. Diac. **1.** *nomine reddis avum* Theod. **1.** *reddit . . . similem* Serlo **1.** *forma refert Paridem* MLat. Anon. **2.** *deam Cithaream representat* Ripoll **3.** *confert* G. Vins. **1.** Conditional constructions are extremely frequent: *si vidisses . . . erraret . . . si . . . foret . . . conspecta . . . liquisset . . . nisi me . . . placasset . . . sumeret . . . cecidisset* Stat. **1a.** *isset . . . si passus* Stat. **2.** *si petisses . . . poneret . . . solveret . . . conficeret* Claud. **3a.** *si . . . dedissent . . . vetuisses* Sid. **2a.** *si affuit . . . latebant* Sid. **4b.** *esset . . . impenderet . . . isset, si spectasset . . . non domuisset . . . occiderat*; *si iudicio . . . quarta fuisset . . . me damnasset . . . ambisset . . . esset* Sid. **5.** *posses deducere . . . si . . . foret . . . si prestiterint* Baudri **2a.** *si redirent . . . non foret* Hil. **1a.** *si regnaret . . . foret* Hil. **1b.** *si esset . . . ferret* Hil. **1c.** *si non esset . . . esset* Primas **1.** *cuperet | si videret, | et doleret* Ripoll **1.** *pro qua non curasset . . . Helene consortium* CB **6b.** *si vidisset . . . nec luderet . . . nec sumeret . . . vel falleret . . . coleret . . . videret* G. Vins. **2.**

There appears to be only one instance in which comparison is conveyed by juxtaposition, without explicit syntactical links: CB **5** *Delium flagrantem | . . . Daphne respuit, rennuit, | puduit amplexari. | michi refragari | nittitur, que petitur*, i.e. (just as) Daphne repulsed Apollo, (so) she whom I entreat, resists me.

There are a number of identifications with an exemplar: *Martino . . . novo* Venant. **2.** *alter Achilles*; *altera nata Venus* Venant. **3.** *Greca cerneris Homerus, Latina Vergilius,* | *in Hebrea quoque Philo, Tertullus in artibus,* | *Flaccus crederis in metris, Tibullus in eloquio* Petr. Gramm. **1.** *ego, pater, ille tuus prodigus sum filius*; *suus . . . secundus Lazarus* Gottsch. **1.** *novus Karolus* Sed. **1.** *filius Isaac sic Ludewicus erat* Sed. **2.** *inveni magnum . . . Homerum* Sed. **3.** *tu . . . Iulius ipse* Benzo **1.** *ego sum tibi filius ille,* | *qui pavi porcos . . .* Baudri **1.** *ut possis credi sisque Sibilla mihi*; *vive Diana* Baudri **2a.** *iste Cato rigidus, Tullius iste foret.* | *hunc facerent verba Ciceronem, facta Catonem* | *. . . iste videtur et est et dicitur alter Homerus* Baudri **2b.** *Iulius alter erat* Baudri **3.** *insano,* | *homocide, Daciano* Primas **1.** *Ionas tuus* Archipoeta **2.** *plangite . . .* | *miles, Alexandrum, plex, Marcum, clere, Maronem* Serlo **2.** *nec sit Daphnes Phebo* CB **1.** *o verecunda Tindaris!* CB **2.** *ave . . . Blanziflōr et Helena, Venus generosa*; *estne illa Helena, vel est dea Venus?* CB **3.** *tuo . . . Paridi* CB **6a.** *si tu esses Helena, vellem esse Paris* CB **6c.** *que vix potest corrigi,* | *ut Tyndaris sit illa* CB **6d.** *cuius Paris . . . sum* CB **7f.** *Tullius eloquio, conflictu Cesar, Adrastus* | *consilio, Nestor mente, rigore Cato* M. Vend. **1.** *forma Tersites, ad fraudes Argus, ad equum* | *Tyresias, Verres crimine, fraude Synon* M. Vend. **2.** Identification is clearly linked to possession of individual attributes of the exemplar only in M. Vend. **1** and **2**, but there is some similarity to these examples in *in artibus . . . in metris . . . in eloquio* in Petr. Gramm. **1**, and in *hunc facerent verba Ciceronem, facta Catonem* in Baudri **2b**.

In the above examples identification may be expressed in different ways: by a supporting adjective or possessive, as in *Martino . . . novo* Venant. **2**; *alter Achilles*; *altera nata Venus* Venant. **3**; *suus . . . secundus Lazarus* Gottsch. **1**; *novus Karolus* Sed. **1**; *alter Homerus* Baudri **2b**; *Iulius alter* Baudri **3**; *Ionas tuus* Archipoeta **2**; *tuo . . . Paridi* CB **6a**; *cuius . . . Paris . . . sum* CB **7f**; by a pronoun: *Iulius ipse* Benzo **1**.8. Additionally, or separately, identification may be expressed by forms of the verb 'to be', often in conjunction with other verbs: *ego . . . ille tuus prodigus sum filius* Gottsch. **1**; *filius Isaac . . . erat* Sed. **2**; *ego sum tibi filius ille* Baudri **1**; *ut possis credi sisque Sibilla michi* Baudri **2a**; *iste Cato rigidus, Tullius iste foret,* | *. . . iste videtur et est et dicitur alter Homerus* Baudri **2b**; *Iulius alter erat* Baudri **3**; *nec sit Daphnes Phebo* CB **1**; *estne illa Helena, vel est dea Venus?* CB **3**; *ut Tyndaris sit illa* CB **6d**; *cuius Paris . . . sum* CB **7f**. A verb is understood in M. Vend. **1** and **2**. For other verbs see: *cerneris, crederis* Petr. Gramm. **1**; *inveni . . . magnum Homerum* Sed. **3**; *vive Diana* Baudri **2a**. Identification is expressed in Primas **1** by means of the apposition of the name *Daciano* with *insano, homocide,* by the apostrophe in *o verecunda Tindaris!* CB **2**, and *Blanziflōr et Helena, Venus generosa!* CB **3**. As in the exemplary comparisons, conditional verbal forms are also found: see Baudri **2b**.28 and CB **6c**.

There may be combinations of comparison and identification with an exemplar within the same context. The most striking examples are those in which parallel passages or verses correspond to each other. Thus Petrus Grammaticus couches his praise of Paulus Diaconus in a series of hyperbolic identifications of the poet with Homer, Virgil, Philo, Tertullus, Horace and Tibullus, each in his own particular sphere, whereas in his response Paulus Diaconus converts the identifications into comparisons: *dicor similis Homero, Flacco et Vergilio, | similor Tertullo sive Philoni Memphitico, | tibi quoque, Veronensis o Tibulle, conferor.* This at once minimizes the praise and prepares the way for his rejection of it. In the parallel verses of the eulogy in Sed. **3**, the Muse identifies Gunther in the first verse with Homer, but in the following verse declares him to surpass Apollo in musical skill, so that the god is naught beside him. Likewise in Serlo **2**, the poet's lament for the death of Robert of Gloucester is expressed in ll. 11–14 in identifications with Alexander, Marcus Aurelius and Virgil, but in ll. 25–8 his attributes are compared with the positive qualities of Solomon, Nero, Paris and Nestor. There are other less uniformly structured instances: thus in Sedulius **2** the parallels between the members of the Carolingian dynasty and the biblical exemplars of Solomon, Abraham, Isaac and Jacob are largely conveyed by means of comparative phrases: *pacifer ut Salemon ... Abrahae similis ... proles Isaac ceu benedicta micas ... veluti Iacob benedictus et heres,* whereas the emperor Louis the Pious himself is directly identified with Isaac: *filius Isaac sic Ludewicus erat.* Conversely in Baudri **2b** the identifications with Cato and Cicero in ll. 27–9 and with Homer in l. 31 are interrupted by a comparative phrase describing the poet as alone equal in worth to many Aristotles: *multos iste valet solus Aristoteles.* Baudri **2a** describes Constantia as more dear to him than Helen to Paris, Venus to Mars, Juno to Jove, Euridice to Orpheus, and Daphne and Io as of lesser worth. The lack of a direct comparison with these figures is in accord with the rejection of unworthy pagan models elsewhere in the poem, and it is no doubt significant that the poet's true praise of Constantia resides in the identification of her with the positive models of the Sibyl as embodiment of knowledge – *ut possis credi sisque Sibilla michi* – and of Diana as symbol of chastity – *si mea vivere vis, vives mea, vive Diana.* These examples suggest that combinations of identification and comparison were a deliberate stylistic procedure and that in such combinations, identification may have a particularly emphatic function.

In many exemplary comparisons, a parallel is drawn, not directly with the exemplary figure itself, but indirectly with one of its distinguishing qualities or aspects. Reference to one aspect of a single figure is less frequent than that to a unique combination of exemplary attributes belonging to different figures, which the subject praised possesses. Of the first type, referring to a single figure, are the following: *Veneris sortita figuram* Claud. **4**; *vincit et eloquii magnum dulcedine Marcum* Einh. (?) **1**; *illic Daviticae pollet virtutis* *honore* Poeta Saxo **1**; *capillos,* | *quos Febi crinis vincere non poterit* Ripoll **2**; *huius crinis* | *. . . nobis deam* | *Cithaream* | *representat omnibus* Ripoll **3**; *Veneris vel desine formam* Ripoll **4**. A particular variation on this motif is that in Ripoll **1**: Venus herself would desire such hair, since it is more beautiful than her own: *fore suum* | *crinem tuum* | *Venus ipsa cuperet,* | *si videret,* | *et doleret,* | *suum quod exuperet.*

In the praise of a woman, the attributes of two exemplary figures may be combined: *Aurorae vincis digitos umerosque Dianae* Claud. **3b**.270; *cuius in ingenio seu formae corpore pulchro* | *arte Minerva fuit, victa decore Venus* Venant. **4**; *non tibi sunt similes per se Venus atque Diana* | *sed si iungantur, sunt tibi consimiles* | *. . . arte tua superas Venerem, candore Dianam* Ripoll **5**; *facie Tyndaride* | *ac Veneri secundam* CB **1**.

In panegyric of male subjects, on the other hand, multiple combinations of attributes are very common: *vim Laertiadae, brevitatem vincis Atridae* | *. . . inclita Nestorei cedit tibi gratia mellis* 'Laus Pis.' **1**; *possidet hic veterum quidquid laudatur in ullo:* | *Antoninum huius pietas, sapientia Marcum,* | *et mitem Nervam lenissima pectora vincunt,* | *promeruitque Titus non tantum mente benigna;* | *gloria magnanimi Traiani cesserit isti* Prisc. **1**; *est tibi Daviticae mansuetudo vitae.* | *. . . iudicium sapiens de Salomone trahis,* | *. . . Traiani ingenium de pietate refers.* | *quid repetam maturum animum, qui tempore nostro* | *antiqui Fabii de gravitate places?* Venant. **1**; *vir tuus iste fuit* | *qui virtute Petrum praebet tibi, dogmate Paulum,* | *hinc Iacobi tribuens, inde Iohannis opem* Venant. **2**; *nomine reddis avum, Salomonem stemmate sensus,* | *viribus et David, sive Ioseph specie* Theod. **1**; *ex filis illis virtutem format Achillis,* | *format Priamidem Pirithoique fidem* Serlo **1**; *forma refert Paridem, manus Hectora, sensus Ulixem:* | *in tribus iste tribus non tulit esse minor* MLat. Anon. **2**; *egregius sanguis te confert Bartholomaeo,* | *mite cor Andreae, pretiosa juventa Johanni,* | *firma fides Petro, perfecta scientia Paulo,* | *ista simul nulli* G. Vins. **1**. In an unusual example, Serlo **2** ascribes to Robert of Gloucester the positive aspects of Solomon, Nero, Paris and Nestor, distinguishing them from the associated negative characteristics: *mens Salomonis ei, non crimen: posse Neronis,* | *non mens, non Paridis dedecus, imo decor* | *os Paridem non mens, non etas Nestora sed mens* | *fecit eum, iuvenem forma, sophia senem.*

Explicit comparisons with exemplars may be textually linked with implied comparisons with such figures in specific incidents of mythological narrative, or more generally with related narrative episodes.[18] Thus in the panegyric of Messalla in *Append. Tibull.* **1**, the comparison with Ulysses prompts an account of the latter's adventures, with a return to comparison at the end of the passage in the line *sit labor illius, tua dum facundia maior.* In Stat. **1a** there is both an explicit comparison of the bride with Venus and Diana in ll. 112–

---

[18] See also Prop. **4, 5, 8, 11a** and **11b** and Ov. **6, 7** and **11**.

16 and also implied comparisons with the female figures who feature in the stories alluded to: in ll. 130–6 that of Phoebus and Daphne, of Bacchus and Ariadne, and the seduction of Leda, Europa and Danae by Jove; in ll. 213–17 the union of Paris and Helen and of Peleus and Thetis; in ll. 242–6 the story of Ilia and Mars, of Lavinia and Turnus, and the vindication of Claudia's chastity. Likewise in Claud. **3a** there is in ll. 6–9 and 16 f. a series of explicit comparisons of the emperor Honorius with Castor, Achilles, Apollo, Bacchus, Adonis and Hippolytus, and also in ll. 31–9 a comparison with Hercules in the allusion to the conquest of the Amazon Hippolyte: she would have submitted more readily to you, Honorius, than to Hercules. In Sid. **2a** the list of heroes whom Maiorianus surpasses is interspersed with details of episodes attaching to them: after *Eryx Siculus* in l. 161 there follows an account of the defeat of Amycus by Pollux in boxing; after *Arcas* (Parthonopaeus) in l. 166 the defeat of his mother Atalanta in the race against Hippomenes; after *Telamone creatum* in l. 185 the exploits of Ajax in the Trojan war; in ll. 195–197 the ravages of Pallas' thunderbolt. In the passage from l. 189 to 195, narrative details are interwoven with the comparisons with the blows delivered by Metabus, Achilles, Theseus and Pallas. In ll. 230 ff. Maiorianus' slaughter of a barbarian wedding-party permits an allusion to the battle of the Lapiths and Centaurs at the wedding of Pirithous and Hippodamia. In Sid. **5** the heroines of old who would have submitted to Ruricius and the heroes who would have contended for the love of Hiberia are each cited in conjunction with a brief reference, which gives the most salient feature of the story attaching to them. Of this same type is G. Vins. **2**, in which the list of those seduced by Jove is accompanied by mention of the disguise adopted by the god in each case. Examples of this kind make for greater variety and a wider frame of reference; they also introduce a more dynamic element, with many verbs of action and movement.

Many different combinations of voice are illustrated in the exemplary comparisons and identifications. Examples of first-person singular voice are rare, except in combination with apostrophe and third person. Apostrophe is common, including instances in which exemplary comparison or identification is applied to the person addressed: *Append. Tibull.* **1**; 'Laus Pis.' **1**; Stat. **2**; Venant. **1**; Petr. Gramm. **1**; Theod. **1**; Ermold. **2**; Sed. **2**; Benzo **1**; Hil. **1a**, **1b**; Archipoeta **1**; Ripoll **1**, **5**; CB **6a**, **6c**; G. Vins. **1** has double apostrophe, that of Innocent III, the object of the panegyric, and that of the ecclesiastical authorities whom the pope surpasses.

There are examples which are entirely in the third person: the epitaphs Claud. **4**, MLat. Anon. **2**, and Baudri **3**; instances of panegyric, of Theodosius in Claud. **1**, of Consentius in Sid. **4**, of Charlemagne in Einh.(?) **1** and Poeta Saxo **1**, of Charles, son of Louis the Pious in Ermold. **1**, of Conrad II in *Carm. Cant.* **1**, of king Louis VII in Serlo **1**; also in the third person are CB **6b**, **6d**, **6e**, and the praise of ideal beauty in Girald. **1**. Largely in the third person are:

the epitaph Venant. **4**, which however also apostrophizes the funereal stone and the spectator, the panegyric of Anastasius in Prisc. **1**, with the exception of the phrase *et, loquar ut breviter quod sentio corde sub imo*, and G. Vins. **2**, apart from apostrophe of three of the exemplary figures.

Most frequent, however, are complex and varying combinations of voice. Poets may refer to themselves in the first or third person: thus Gottsch. **1** combines first person with apostrophe in *ego, pater, ille tuus prodigus sum filius* (cf. *ego sum tibi filius ille* in Baudri **1**), but also refers both to God and himself in the third person: *benedictus sit excelsus genitor et genitus,* | . . . *per quem suus est secundus suscitatus Lazarus*. In association with his name, Primas **1** uses the third person – *Primas esset velut Pelox* – but in association with other first-person verb forms also the first person in *perissem . . . proclamabam . . . eram enim ut Zacheus*. Yet a different combination, linking third person with apostrophe, is found in Archipoeta **2**: *ecce Ionas tuus plorat,* | *culpam suam non ignorat*.

In Claud. **3a** the comparison of Honorius with Castor and Achilles occurs in the poet's address to the emperor himself: 6 *te Leda mallet quam dare Castorem;* | *praefert Achilli te proprio Thetis*; this is followed by third-person comparisons with Apollo, Bacchus, Adonis and Hippolytus, with a return to second-person address in the comparison with Hercules beginning at l. 31 *tu si nivalis per iuga Caucasi* | *saevas petisses pulcher Amazonas...*; the comparison with Aurora and Diana in l. 270, *Aurorae vincis digitos umerosque Dianae*, is contained in an address by Venus to the bride. In Serlo **2** the identification of Robert with Alexander, Marcus Aurelius and Virgil is expressed in a second-person exhortation to Gloucester to lament, whereas comparison with the qualities of Solomon, Nero, Paris and Nestor is in third-person form.

Passages may be signalled as direct speech, giving greater prominence to comparisons and identifications included in them. They too may illustrate varying combinations of voice. Thus in Stat. **1a** the speech of Venus in address to Cupid includes direct comparisons of the bride with Venus herself, Diana, Daphne and Ariadne, and by implication also with Leda, Europa and Danae. In comparing the bride with herself, Venus speaks in the first person; the comparison with Daphne is linked with apostrophe of Phoebus, those with Ariadne and the implied comparisons are in the third person. The panegyric of Maiorianus in Sid. **2a**, with its list of heroes whom Maiorianus surpasses, gains particular force by being placed in the mouth of the wife of Aëtius, who is bitterly opposed to his claim to the ruler's favour; in this instance the comparisons are expressed in the third person, except that those with Castor, Pollux, Alcon and Bellerophon are framed in apostrophe of Maiorianus, inset within the speech itself. In Sid. **3a**, the words of Rome highlight the potential comparison of Avitus with Trajan, and the authority of Jupiter himself lends weight to the comparisons with Hercules, Hippolytus and Fabricius;

the comparison with Trajan is combined with apostrophe of Gaul, and that with Fabricius is introduced by apostrophe of Pyrrhus. In Sid. 5, the speech of Cupid lists the heroines of old who would have submitted in love to Ruricius, to which Venus responds, by addressing Hiberia herself, with a list of heroes who would have contended for her favour. In Venant. 3, the two examples of identification, *alter Achilles* and *altera nata Venus*, are placed in the mouth of Cupid and Venus respectively. In the fictive dialogue between the poet and the Muse in Sed. 3, praise of Gunther is reinforced by being uttered, not by the poet, but by the Muse herself. Ripoll 4 is the first verse of a dialogue between *amicus* and *amica*. In CB 3.8.4 the identification with *Blanziflŏr*, *Helena* and *Venus* is couched in apostrophe, whereas that in 14.4 occurs in direct speech, signalled as such by *unde dixi sepius*.

The placing of examples does not seem to be significant in longer poems such as the earlier examples of panegyric and epithalamium, except perhaps in Sid. 5. The passage from l. 65 to l. 90, containing the list of heroines who would have submitted to Ruricius, and the list of heroes who would have contended for Hiberia, concludes the exchange between Cupid and Venus. The end of the comparisons in l. 90 is followed by two and a half further lines spoken by Venus, after which the narrative resumes, until a short final blessing by Venus in ll. 131–3 concludes the whole poem. More certain examples of what is probably deliberate placing are found in shorter poems. Thus Ripoll 4 is the opening stanza in an alternating dialogue between *amicus* and *amica* – this seems to be the only instance of initial placing among the examples. There are several instances of central or near-central placing. Thus the dialogue between the poet and the Muse in Sed. 3 consists of four four-line verses. The first and last of these are assigned to the poet, whereas the two central verses, spoken by the Muse, contain the identification with Homer and the comparisons with Apollo respectively. In MLat. Anon. 1 the bulk of the poem (6 out of 10 verses) is taken up with the exemplary comparisons, which are framed by two prefatory and two concluding verses. A somewhat similar pattern is seen in Archipoeta 1: the comparisons at the centre of the poem are preceded by four verses and followed by five verses, including the last, in which the poet commends his poem and himself as deserving of reward. The versicle in *Carm. Cant.* 1 containing the comparisons with David and the Messiah occurs towards the centre of the work. Hil. 1b begins at the midpoint of the poem, being preceded by seven verses and followed by six verses.

There are several examples of final or near-final placing: in Claud. 3a, a poem of 41 lines, the comparison with Hercules in ll. 31–9 occurs at the end of the poem, followed only by two lines of comment: she who is about to be united with you is fortunate indeed. The passage in the panegyric Ripoll 5 is likewise followed by only two further lines of comment. In Hil. 1c the implied comparison with Ganymede takes up the two final verses of the poem. In Hil.

1a the comparison with Ganymede forms the penultimate verse of the poem, being followed in the final verse by the pun on *Anglicum* | *Angelicum*, which was no doubt felt to be a suitable conclusion. CB **4** forms the final stanza of the poem in both the Arundel and the CB MS (although the total number of stanzas differs in each case). In G. Vins. **2** the lines quoted form the climax of the sample description of beauty. Benzo **1** is a special case: it is placed at the end of book VI of his *prosimetrum*. The five verses containing the exemplary figures make up the bulk of the poem; they are followed in verse 6 by a prayer for the emperor, and in verses 7–8 by a plea for recognition of faithful service, including that by the poet himself.

The diversity in types of example, the wide range of exemplary figures drawn from mythology, history, historical legend, the Bible, the Church and the authorial canon, and individual groupings of figures from more than one sphere, the direct and indirect references to mythological figures, the great variety of lexical and syntactical features associated with both exemplary comparisons and identifications, the differing combinations of comparison and identification and of expressions of voice within the same context, all lend very considerable stylistic variety to the examples examined, which in the main are more diverse and less strictly structured than those in the Classical poets.

5

The Troubadour Poets

Most of the poets' dates are uncertain, and therefore only an approximate chronological arrangement can be attempted, with the following rough groupings of poets who make use of exemplary comparisons:[1] poets of the twelfth century; those writing at the turn of the twelfth and thirteenth centuries; those whose poetic activity extends into the first decades of the thirteenth century; those falling entirely within the thirteenth century. Those poets writing in the twelfth century begin (in approximate chronological order) with Marcabru and include Rigaut de Berbezilh, Raimbaut d'Orange, Bernart de Ventadorn, Raimon Jordan, Arnaut de Mareuil, Arnaut Daniel, Bertran de Born, Folquet de Marseille, Guiraut de Bornelh, Garin d'Apchier, Guiraut de Salinhac and Guiraudo lo Ros. Those twelfth-century poets whose poetic activity extends into the early years of the thirteenth century include Gaucelm Faidit, Peire Vidal, Guillem Magret, Raimbaut de Vaqueiras, perhaps also La Comtessa de Dia, and Uc de la Bacalaria (but the dating of these two poets is very uncertain). Poets active in the first two decades of the thirteenth century are: Peirol, Peire Ramon de Tolosa, Guilhem Adémar, Raimon de Miraval, Aimeric de Peguilhan, Elias de Barjols, Pons de Capduelh, and Guiraut de Calanso. Poets writing in the later thirteenth century are: Falquet de Romans, Aimeric de Belenoi, Azalais d'Altier, Paulet de Marselha and Peire Cardenal. This group also includes the two Italian troubadours Bonifacio Calvo and Bartolomeo Zorzi, and the two Catalan troubadours Cerverí de Girona and Guilhem Raimon de Gironela, all of whom adopted the *langue d'oc*, the language of the troubadours, as their linguistic medium. Of uncertain date, and therefore placed at the end, are the examples ascribed to Daude or Bernart de Pradas, Uc de Pena, Jordan Bonel, and those transmitted anonymously.

It is necessary also to bear in mind that many troubadour poets, including some to whom a substantial œuvre is attributed, have no examples of exemplary comparisons in their extant œuvre. These include the earliest attested troubadour, Guilhem de Peitieus, more usually known as Guillaume IX, Duke of Aquitaine (1071–1126), and among the twelfth-century poets: Jaufre Rudel, Peire d'Alvernhe, Berenguer de Palazol and Guilhem de Saint-Didier. Thirteenth-century poets with no exemplary comparisons include le

---

[1] In the examples cited, abbreviated references are given to the incipit of the poem, to its classification, to the numbering in Pillet/Carstens (=PC) and Distilo (=D) where appropriate, and to the edition used. Most examples are derived from isostrophic lyric forms, a few from heterostrophic *descort*, some from longer isometric forms treating related themes.

Monge de Montaudon, Elias Cairel, Cadenet, Jausbert de Puycibot, Bertran d'Alamanon, Peire Bremon Ricas Novas, Uc de Saint-Circ, and the Italian poets writing in the *langue d'oc*, Rambertino Buvalelli, Lanfranc Cigala, Percivalle Doria and Sordello (see n. 3).

Exemplary comparisons are attested in a range of different types of poem: *canso, sirventes, sirventes-canso, planh, tenso, partimen, alba, descort, estampida, dansa, pastorela, salut* and related instances, and single stanzas (*coblas*).[2] The examples have been selected in order to illustrate their chronological spread, the range of lyric and other genres in which they occur, their place and function in the structure of the poem, and the relative popularity of particular categories of exemplary figures. It was not possible to cite all the extant references to the most frequently occurring figures such as Andrieu of France, Floris and Blancheflor, and Tristan: in any case many of these serve only as illustrative examples and are not in the form of explicit comparisons.[3]

Twelfth-Century Poets

In a *tenso* with Catola, Marcabru rejects his opponent's defence of the positive worth of love:

Marcabru 1

> *Amics Marchabrun* . . . (*tenso*). PC 293.6 and 451.1, D Ugo Catola 24640,
> Gaunt/Harvey/Paterson 6

> Catola, non entenz razon: IV   13
> non saps d'Amors cum trais Samson?
> Vos cuidaz e·ill autre bricon
> qe tot sia ver qant vos diz.
>
> [Catola, you do not understand reason: do you not know concerning love how it betrayed Samson? You and those other fools think that everything is true which it tells you.]

Stanza IV in a poem of fourteen 4-l. stanzas.   14 Samson: an allusion to the motif of love's famous victims – see also Peire Vid. **1**.52 ff. *Salamo, Davi, Samso*; Falq. Rom. **1**.43 *Salamos*; Couci **2**.9 f. n. *Salemons*; Veldeke **2**.1 n. *Salomône*; Chiaro **2b**.21 *Vergilio*. Samson as an exemplar of strength see Arn. Mar. **4**.45; Oc. Anon. **1**.4. Solomon as an exemplar of wisdom, cf. Peire Card. **2**.8; Zorzi **1**.60; Oc. Anon. **1**.1.

---

[2] See the designations of poems in the headings and the Glossary of Technical Terms.
[3] See for instance the *partimen, Uns amics et un'amia* (Guil. Tor 13) between Guil. Tor and Sordello, in which the former cites Andrieu as an example of the folly of dying for love.

Rigaut de Berbezilh **1**

Atressi con l'orifanz . . . (canso). PC 421.2, D 22410, Varvaro 2

Ben sai c'Amors es tan granz   III 23
que leu mi pot perdonar
s'ieu failli per sobramar
ni reingnei com Dedalus,
que dis qu'el era Iezus
e volc volar al cel outracuidanz,   28
mas Dieus baisset l'orgoill e lo sobranz.

[I well know that Love is so great that it can readily pardon me if I have erred through loving to excess or have acted like Daedalus who said he was Jesus and in his overweening presumption wished to fly to heaven, but God humbled his pride and his arrogance.]

23–9: the first 7 ll. of an 11-l. stanza in a poem of five stanzas + *tornada*. 26 *Dedalus*: this is the reading of most MSS; one MS has *Micarus*, one *Ycarus*, and one late MS *Magus*, an emendation which incorrectly associates the passage with Simon Magus. The link *Dedalus . . . Iezus* presupposes rather a source in a medieval Christian reworking of the Daedalus/Icarus myth (known from Ovid, *Met.* VIII.183 ff.), intended as a warning example.

Rigaut de Berbezilh **2**

Atressi con Persavaus . . . (canso). PC 421.3, D 22420, Varvaro 3

Atressi con Persavaus   I 1
    el temps que vivia,
que s'esbait d'esgardar
tant qu'anc non saup demandar
        de que servia   5
    la lansa ni·l grazaus,
    et eu sui atretaus,
Miels de dompna,   quan vei vostre cors gen,
        qu'eissamen
    m'oblit quan vos remir   10
e·us cug preiar, e non fatz, mais consir.

[Like Perceval when he lived, who stood amazed in contemplation, so that he was quite unable to ask what purpose the lance and the grail served, and I am the same, Best among Ladies, when I see your beautiful person, for in the same way I forget myself when I gaze at you and wish to entreat you and do not do so, but am lost in thought.]

The first stanza in a poem of five 11-l. stanzas + *tornada.*   1 ff. At the Grail castle, Perceval observed the bleeding lance but failed to ask its significance, or to ask whom the Grail served, questions which would have released the Fisher King from his suffering. See Chrétien, *Conte du Graal*, 3213 ff.   8 *Miels de dompna*: this *senhal* occurs in the same position in every stanza and at the beginning of the *tornada*.

Raimbaut d'Orange 1

> *Non chant per auzel . . .* (*canso*).
> PC 389.32, D 20720, Pattison 27

De midonz fatz dompn' e seignor   IV   25
  cals que sia·il destinada.
car ieu begui de la amor
  ja·us dei amar a celada.
Tristan, qan la·il det Yseus gen
  e bela, no·n saup als faire,   30
et ieu am per aital coven
  Midonz, don no·m posc estraire.

[I make my lady sovereign mistress and lord, whatever the fate ordained
may be. For I drank of love and must indeed love you in secret. Tristan,
when fair and lovely Iseut gave it (*sc.* the drink of love) to him, could not
do otherwise; and I love my lady by virtue of a like pledge, to which I am
inextricably bound.]

The fourth stanza in a poem of six 8-l. stanzas + *tornada*.   29 f. *Tristan,
qan la· il det Yseus gen . . .*: the Tristan story is the most widely diffused of
all medieval legends. It is preserved in OF in the fragmentary versions of
Thomas and Béroul, in the *Lai du Chèvrefeuille* of Marie de France, and the
13th-century Prose *Tristan*, in German in Eilhart von Oberge and Gottfried
von Strassburg, and in later Italian, Old Norse and Middle English versions. Its
diffusion explains the number of allusions in the vernacular lyric (see Index
of Proper Names *s.vv.* Tristan; Iseut/Isolde/Isalde/Ysalde/Isaotta). In versions
containing the episode of the love potion, e.g. that preserved in Eilhart and
Gottfried von Strassburg, it is Brangæne who mistakenly hands the potion
prepared by Iseut's mother to compel love between Iseut and king Mark, to
Tristan. Raimbaut has no doubt made the change (seen also in the less specific
allusion *car ieu begui de l'amor*) deliberately, in order to indicate that it is the
lady herself, like Iseut, who compels involuntary love, and not chance and an
external agency. Other refs. to the love potion: Aim. Peg. **1**.30 f.; Zorzi **2**, n. on
ll. 50 ff.; Daude Prad. (?) **1**.21; Oc. Anon. **2**.3. See also Guil. A. Novella **5**.26 *ara
sai eu q'eu ai begut del broc | don bec Tristan c'anc pois garir non poc* (now I
know that I have drunk from the vessel from which Tristan drank, so that he
could never thereafter be cured).   33 *don no·m posc estraire*: lit. 'from
which I cannot detach/extricate myself'. It is uncertain whether *don*, either
'from which' or 'from whom', refers to *coven* or to *midonz*; in the latter case
the line would mean: 'my lady, from whom I cannot detach myself/to whom
I am inextricably bound'.

Bernart de Ventadorn 1

> *Can vei . . .* (*canso*). PC 70.43, D 3070, Appel, *Bern.Vent.* 43

Anc non agui de me poder   III   17
ni no fui meus de l'or' en sai
que·m laisset en sos olhs vezer

en un miralh que mout me plai.   20
miralhs, pus me mirei en te,
m'an mort li sospir de preon
c'aissi·m perdei com perdet se
lo bels Narcisus en la fon.

[I never had power over myself, nor was I mine from that hour onwards when she let me gaze into her eyes, into a mirror which is greatly pleasing to me. Mirror, since I gazed at my reflection in you, sighs from the depths have caused my death, for I was lost, just as beautiful Narcissus was lost in the spring.]

The third stanza in a poem of seven 8-l. stanzas + *tornada*.   23 f. The story of Narcissus, derived from Ovid, *Met.* III. 407 ff., was probably known from the OF *lai de Narcisse*, dating from c. 1165–1175. See also Peirol **1.**20 and Index of Proper Names *s.v.* Narcissus, for exs. in other branches of the Romance lyric (for OF also *s.v.* Echo) and one ex. in the German lyric.]

Bernart de Ventadorn **2**

Tant ai mo cor . . . (canso).
PC 70.44, D 3080, Appel, *Bern. Vent.* 44

        plus trac pena d'amor   IV   45
        de Tristan l'amador,
que·n sofri manhta dolor
    per Izeut la blonda.

[I suffer more pains of love than Tristan the lover, who endured much sorrow on that account for the sake of Iseut the golden-haired.]

45–8: the last 4 ll. of a 12-l. stanza in a poem of six stanzas + *tornada*.   46 *Tristan*, 48 *Izeut*: see Raimb. Or. **1.**29 f. n.

Bernart de Ventadorn **3**

Ab joi mou lo vers . . . (canso).
PC 70.1, D 2660, Appel, *Bern.Vent.* 1

        Anc sa bela bocha rizens   VI   41
        non cuidei baizan me trais,
        car ab un doutz baizar m'aucis,
        si ab autre no m'es guirens;
            c'atretal m'es per semblansa   45
            com de Pelaus la lansa,
    que del seu colp no podi' om garir,
    si autre vetz no s'en fezes ferir.

[I never thought her beautiful smiling mouth would in kissing betray me, for with a sweet kiss she has killed me, unless she cures me with another; for the same befalls me, it seems, as from the lance of Peleus (see n.), in that a man could not recover from its blow, unless he let himself be wounded by it a second time.]

The sixth stanza in a poem of seven 8-l. stanzas + 4-l. *tornada* (with a second

tornada in one MS).   45 ff. the story of the lance of Peleus is derived
from Ovid: *Rem. Am.* 47 f. *vulnus in Herculeo quae quondam fecerat hoste,*
vulneris auxilium Pelias hasta tulit (the Pelian spear which once inflicted a
wound on its Herculean foe, bore relief to the wound); *Met.* XIII. 171 f. (in a
speech of Achilles) "*ego Telephon hasta | pugnantem domui, victum orantemque*
refeci" ("I conquered the warring Telephus with my spear, and healed him,
vanquished and pleading"); see also *Tristia* V.ii.156 f. *Pelias hasta* is thus the
Pelian spear of Achilles, the adj. *Pelias* being derived from the topographical
name *Pelion*, birthplace of *Peleus*, father of Achilles, and of Achilles (also
known by the patronymic *Pelides*). In the Romance lyric texts, the adj. has
been interpreted as a proper name, no doubt by association with the name
Peleus and the connection with Achilles is obscured. See the OF ex., Wilart
de Corbie **1**, and the Italian exs. Jacopo Mostacci **1** n.; Chiaro Davanzati **3a**
and **3b**.43–6; Giovanni d'Arezzo **1**; Tomaso da Faenza **1**; *Il Mare Amoroso*
1a.104 ff. Only in Bernart, Wilart, and *Mar. Am.* is the wound from the lance
explicitly associated with a kiss; reference to the kiss is lacking in Chiaro **3b** and
Giovanni d'Arezzo **1**, but appears to be implied, though not expressly stated,
in J. Mostacci **1**, Chiaro **3a**, and T. Faenza **1**.   45 f.: the syntax of these
ll. is (perhaps deliberately) ambiguous, and has been differently interpreted.
If a specific antecedent subject is implied, it should logically be *sa bela bocha*
rizens, since it is the mouth, like the lance, which is the source of the wound,
the kiss being the equivalent of the blow; it seems to have been understood in
this way by *Mar. Am.* **1a**.104 (*q.v.*): *ma quella* (*sc. bocca*) *mi fu lancia di Pelùs*.
The OF version of this stanza (Appel, *Ventadorn*, p. 7), on the other hand,
takes the construction to be impersonal: *se ua de moi par sanblance | con de*
peleus la lance (lit.: it happens to me, it seems, as with the lance of Peleus),
which seems to confirm that an impersonal interpretation is probably correct.

Raimon Jordan **1**

Quan la neus chai . . . (*canso*). PC 404.8, D 21540, Asperti 8

Qu'ieu·lh servirai hueimais, cossi que·m an,   VI   26
e serai li leials e ses enjan
mielhs qu'Elena no fo al frair' Ector
e, s'a lieis platz, mon servir no·m soan,
qu'anc non amet Hero tant Leander.   30

[For I shall serve her henceforth, whatever befalls me, and will be true to
her without inconstancy, more so than was Helen to the brother of Hector
(Paris), and if it pleases her, may she not spurn my service, for Leander
never loved Hero so greatly.]

The final stanza in a poem of six 5-l. stanzas + *tornada*.   28 *Elena . . . al fraire*
Ector: for the names of Helen and Paris in the troubadour and other vernacular
lyric, see Index of Proper Names, *s.v.*; the story was probably known chiefly
from the OF *roman d'antiquité* – see Arn. Mar. **3b**, general n. on names.   28,
30 *Ector* and *Leander* are instances of isolated rhyme (*rim estramp*), rhyming
from stanza to stanza. The need to place these names in rhyming position

no doubt explains the circumlocution for the name Paris, the poet's unusual comparison of his loyalty with that of the female figure of *Elena* in l. 28 and the word-order in l. 30: it is very common for the subject to be placed at the end of the phrase, preceded by the object, particularly in verse – see Arn. Mar. **3b**.155,156 f.,163; Guir. Born. **1**.30; Guir. Sal. **2**.16; Raimb. Vaq. **1**.12; Falq. Rom. **3c**.43; Zorzi **2**.121, Jensen, *Syntaxe*, §§840 f., 848, and OF Anon. **9**.15. 30 *Hero . . . Leander*: known from Ovid, *Her.* XVIII and XIX; see also Arn. Mar. **3b**.150.

Raimon Jordan **2**

Vert son li ram . . . (canso). PC 404.13, D 21590, Asperti 13

E pus li platz que·m retenh' a sa part,   IV 19
a lieis mi do, liges, ses tot reguart,
que ja d'aquo non aia mais duptansa
qu'ieu ja mon cor de lieis biais ni mut;
enans l'am mais – s'ela·m guart ni m'aiut-
no fes Andrius la reina de Fransa.   24

[And since it pleases her that she should retain me at her side, I surrender myself to her, as liege, without any reservation, for may she never fear that I might ever turn my heart away from her or change its inclination; rather do I love her more – may she protect and aid me – than Andrieu loved the queen of France.]

The fourth stanza in a poem of six 6-l. stanzas + *tornada.*   24 *Andrius*: see Index of Proper Names, *s.v.* Andrieu (of France/Paris); for references to this lost tale, see Asperti, p. 490 n. 24. See also Guil. Berg., ed. Riquer 28.41 ff. (not syntactically in the form of an explicit comparison): in the presence of the lady, who offers only hope long deferred, the poet can barely support himself, so sorrowful is he, when he remembers Andrieu. There are two further references lacking the name, but probably inspired by the motif of the hopeless love of Andrieu for the queen of France: Aim. Peg. 29.18 ff. *pus descobrir non l'aus ma fin'amansa,* | *qu'atressi puesc la reyna de Fransa* | *amar* (since I do not dare to reveal to her my true love, I might just as well love the queen of France); Guil. Tor 1.23 *entendre lai on volrai* | *puosc assaz; mas qe m'enanza* | *pois q'il s'amor m'estrai?* | *ensi puosc amar, si·m plai,* | *la reïna de França* (I can indeed set my thoughts wherever I will, but what does it profit me, since she withholds her love from me? I may just as well, if it pleases me, love the queen of France). See also Guil. Magr. **1**.2; CB **6e** and n.

Raimon Jordan **3**

D'amor no·m puesc . . . (canso). PC 404.3, D 21490, Asperti 3

Aital astr' ai cum Nicola de Bar,   II 9
– que si visques lonc temps savis hom fora –
qu'estet lonc temps mest los peichos e mar
e sabia que·i morria qualqu'ora.

[I have the same star as Nicola of Bari – who, had he lived long, would have been a wise man – who dwelt for a long time among the fishes in the sea and knew that he would die there some day.]

9–12: the first 4 ll. of an 8-l. stanza in a poem of five stanzas + *tornada*.

This unusual example refers to Nicola, the hero of a Sicilian folk tale, who lived both on sea and on land and finally perished in the sea (see Asperti, pp. 228 ff., nn. 9–16). He is here confused with St. Nicholas of Bari, patron saint of sailors.

Arnaut de Mareuil 1

Aissi cum selh . . . (canso). PC 30.5, D 1710, Johnston 2

Juli Cezar conquis la senhoria   V
per son esfors de tot lo mon a randa,   30
non ges qu'el fos senher ni reis d'Irlanda,
ni coms d'Angieus, ni ducx de Normandia,
ans fo bas hom, seguon qu'ieu aug retraire,
mas quar fon pros e francs e de bon aire,
pujet son pretz tan quant pugar podia.   35

Per que·m conort, enquer (s'ieu tant vivia)   VI
aia de vos tot quan mos cors demanda;
pus us sols hom ses tor e ses miranda
conquis lo mon ni·l tenc en sa baylia,
aissi ben dei, segon lo mieu vejaire,   40
de vostr' amor de dreg estr' emperaire,
com el del mon ses dreg que no·i avia.

[Julius Caesar won absolute sovereignty over the whole world through his efforts, not that he was lord or king of Ireland, or count of Anjou or duke of Normandy, but was a man of low degree, as I hear tell, but because he was valiant and true, and of noble disposition, he increased his renown as greatly as it lay within his power to increase it. Therefore I console myself with the thought – if I live long enough – that I may yet receive from you all that my heart seeks: since a single man without stronghold or watch-tower conquered the world and held it in his power, so should I, as it seems to me, by right be emperor of your love, as he was of the world, without possessing any right thereto.]

The two final stanzas in a poem of six stanzas + *tornada*.   29 *Juli Cezar*: see Guir. Cal. **1**.49; Andr. Contr. **1**.40 n.

Arnaut de Mareuil 2

Belh m'es . . . (canso). PC 30.10, D 1760, Johnston 17

Pus blanca es que Elena,   III   17
belhazors que flors que nais . . .

[She is more fair than Helen, more beautiful than a budding flower . . .]

17 f.: the first 2 ll. of an 8-l. stanza in a poem of four stanzas.   17 *Elena*: see Raim. Jord. **1**.28 n.

Two examples of the *salut*, a missive of greeting and praise addressed to the lady, in longer forms made up of rhymed couplets, contain lists of fabled lovers whom the poet outdoes in his joy or love. Since the two passages coincide in part in theme, and in the citation of exemplary figures, most names are discussed under **3b**.

Arnaut de Mareuil **3a**

Dona, genser . . . (*salut*).
PC p. 36, no. III, Bec, Arn. Mar, *Saluts* 1

> e †Rodocesta† ni Biblis,
> Blancaflor ni Semiramis,
> Tibes ni Leida ni Elena   155
> ni Antigona ni Esmena
> ni·l bel Yzeus ab lo pel bloy
> non agro la mitat de joy
> ni d'alegrier ab lurs amis,
> com yeu ab vos, so m'es avis.   160

[And neither Rodocesta (?) nor Biblis, Blancaflor nor Semiramis, Thisbe nor Leda or Helen, nor Antigone or Esmena, nor the beautiful Iseut with the golden hair had half the joy and delight with their lovers that I have with you, it seems to me.]

153 *Rodocesta*: this form, instated by Bec against the testimony of his base MS R, occurs in 2 MSS: *re de seta ni bel ris* R; *canc chirox ni semi ramis* G; *ne dido tristan ne biblis* L; *e rodo cesta nibiblis* N; *ni rodocesta ni biblis* c. The name *Rodocesta* appears to have some similarity to names of Greek origin, but is not identifiable, and in view of the disparity between the variants, it is impossible to conjecture what name stood in this position originally.

Arnaut de Mareuil **3b**

Tant m'abellis . . . (*salut*).
PC p. 36, no. IV, Bec, Arn. Mar., *Saluts* 3

> q'anc, domna, ço sapchaz,   146
> non fo neguns amans
> qe tant be, ses engans,
> ames com eu am vos:
> neih Leandier Eros   150
> ni Paris Elenan,
> ni Pirramus Titban,
> ni Floris Blancaflor,
> qe·n traich manta dolor,
> ni Lavina Eneas,   155
> no neich Cleopatras
> cel qe fo reis de Tyr.
> non ac tan ferm desir,
> ni crei qe tant ames

lo reis *Etiocles*   160
Salamandra tant be,
ni tan per bona fe,
ni anc Yseut Tristan,
qe·n sofri maint afan,
ni Berenguiers Quendis,   165
ni Valensa Seguis,
ni, pel meu essien,
Absalon Florissen,
ni anc Iris, ço cre,
no amet Biblis re,   170
avers so q'eu am vos.

[For know this, lady, never was there any lover who loved so well, without disloyalty, as I love you: not even Leander Hero, nor Paris Helen, nor Pyramus Thisbe, nor Floris Blancaflor, on account of which he suffered much sorrow, nor Aeneas Lavinia, nor even he who was king of Tyre Cleopatra. I do not think king Etiocles had so firm a desire or loved Salamandra so well, or with such true faith, nor ever Tristan Iseut, who suffered much anguish from it, nor Berenguiers Quendis, nor Valensa Seguis, nor, as I believe, Absalom Florissen, nor ever did Iris, I think, at all love Biblis, by comparison with my love of you.]

For the variable word-order in the placing of names see Raim. Jord. **1**.30 n. 150 *Leandier Eros*: see Raim. Jord. **1**.30 n.   151 *Paris Elenan*: see Raim. Jord. **1**.28 n.   152 *ni Pirramus Titban* (see *Tibes* **3a**.155): cf. Guir. Sal. **1**.27; Raimb. Vaq. **1**.12 and Index of Proper Names, *s.v.* Pyramus, Thisbe. The story was derived from Ov., *Met.* IV.55 ff., but was probably known mainly from the OF *Piramus et Tisbé*.   153 *Floris Blancaflor* (see *Blancaflor* **3a**.154): the lovers in the OF *Floire et Blancheflor* (*Flores* is the usual nom. form of the m. name in the text). For the same motif see also Falq. Rom. **2b**.17; **3a**.137 f. 156 f.: *cel qe fo reis de Tyr* probably refers to Apollonius of Tyre, hero of a popular Latin narrative (see the obscure ref. to *Apoloine de Tir* as exemplar in the Oc. Anon. *descort* PC 461.5, Mahn, *Gedichte*, no. 282); the name *Cleopatras*, not associated with Apollonius, and no doubt dictated by the requirements of rhyme, was known either from historical legend, or perhaps from the *Roman d'Alexandre*, where it occurs as the name of the second wife of Philip of Macedon, father of Alexander the Great.   160 *Etiocles*: MS *ociocles*. 163 *Yseut Tristan*: see Raimb. Or. **1**.29 f. n.   169 f. *Iris . . . Biblis* (see **3a**.153 n.): for the first name, the sole MS has *iris*, emended by Bec to *Itis*, but see *Hyris– Biblis*, Aim. Bel. **1**.46 f. In Ov., *Met.* IX. 453 ff., it is her brother Caunus whom Byblis loves, and *Iris*, the messenger of the gods, has no part in the story. Poli, *Aim. Bel.*, pp. 159–61, explains the substitution of the name *Iris/Hyris* for that of Caunus, as probably deriving ultimately from the enumeration in the *ensenhamen* of G. de Cabrera, ll. 163–5 (Pirot, *Recherches*, p. 552): *Ni sabs d'Ytis | ni de Biblis, | ni de Caumus nuilla faisson* (you know nothing at all of Itys, nor of Biblis or Caunus), in which *Biblis* and *Caumus* occur together, as is correct, but in which *Ytis*, from an entirely different story (see Catull. 1.14 n.), could have been misunderstood as connected with *Biblis*. Poli assumes that Arn. Mar. knew the passage in G. de Cabrera, took over the pair *Ytis – Biblis*, but substituted *Iris* for *Ytis*. However, as there is the testimony of only one MS, it is impossible to be certain what the original form of the name in the passage was, but it at least seems likely that Aim. Bel. took the pair *Hyris – Biblis* from a version of Arn. Mar. containing the form *Iris*.   The main sources of the other clearly identifiable names in **3a** and **3b** are probably: the OF *roman d'antiquité*; *Floire et Blancheflor*; *Piramus et Tisbé*; the Tristan story. The following names occur in these works: *Roman d'Eneas*: Eneas, Lavinia, Helene/Eleine, Paris; *Roman de Troie*: Eneas, Heleine, Leandes/Léandre; *Roman de Thèbes*: Antigone, Eneas, Éthiocles, Salamandre/Salamaundre, Semiramis, Ysmeine; *Floire et Blancheflor*: Absalon, Antigone, Biblis, Blanceflor, Eneas, Floire, Heleine/Elaine, Lavine, Leda, Paris, Ysmeine; *Piramus et Tisbé*: Piramus, Tisbé; *Tristan story*: Izeut, Tristan. *Eros* (Hero) was no doubt derived from Ovid; *Valensa – Seguis* (see Comt. Dia 2.10) and *Florissen* are probably from lost romances (see Chambers, *Proper Names*, pp. 264 and 128; *Valensa* is interpreted as a m. name derived from Oc. *valensa* f., 'valour', 'prowess'). *Berenger(s)* occurs in the *Chanson de Roland* as the name of one of the twelve peers, but the name *Quendis* seems not to be attested.

One further example of the *salut* contains the poet's boast of prowess in the service of love:

Arnaut de Mareuil **4**

Bona dompna . . . (salut).
Bec, Arn. Mar., *Saluts* 7 (not in PC or D)

> Car, cant vos disses qu'ieu diçia   41
> asatz, e molt petit fazia,
> mi dest dels fagz tal volontat,
> que s'ieu agues Rolant trobat,
> o Sanson, cel que fo tan forz,   45
> cascus d'elz fora pres o morz.

[For when you said that I spoke much and did little, you gave me such a desire for deeds, that if I had encountered Roland, or Samson, he who was so strong, each of them would have been taken captive or put to death.]

44 *Rolant*: hero of the *Chanson de Roland*, companion of *Olivier*; for these names, see Guir. Born. 2.40 n.   45 *Sanson*: see Marc. 1.14 n.

Arnaut Daniel **1**

Quan chai . . . (canso). PC 29.6, D 1640, Toja 3

> tals m'abelis   VI   45
> don ieu plus ai de ioia
> non ac Paris
> d'Elena, sel de Troia.

[Such a one pleases me, from whom I have more joy than Paris – the hero
of Troy – had from Helen.]

45–8: the last 4 ll. of an 8-l. stanza in a poem of seven stanzas + *tornada*.
47 *Paris*, 48 *Elena*: see Raim. Jord. **1**.28 n.

The stanza which includes these lines is lacking in one of the 4 MSS of the
poem and is treated differently by eds.: Toja includes it as part of the poem,
Perugi (II, p. 131) rejects it, whereas Eusebi (p. 18) retains it as a possible
alternative version of stanza V; none of these decisions materially affects the
readings or sense of the passage.

Arnaut Daniel **2**

En breu . . . (canso). PC 29.9, D 1570, Toja 11

q'il m'es plus fin' et ieu lieis certz   IV   31
que Talant' e Meleagre.

[For she is more true to me and I (more) faithful to her than Atalanta and
Meleager.]

31 f.: the last 2 ll. of an 8-l. stanza in a poem of six stanzas + *tornada*.   32 *Meleagre*: a *rim estramp*, rhyming only with the final line of the other stanzas
and the *tornada*. For the story of Atalanta and Meleager, see Ovid, *Met.*, VIII.
298 ff.

Arnaut Daniel **3**

Er vei . . . (canso). PC 29.4, D 1510, Toja 13

q'eu no vuoill ies qan pens sas grans valors,   III   20
valer ses lieis on plus valc Alixandres.

[For I do not at all wish, when I think of her great excellence, to achieve
renown without her where Alexander achieved his greatest renown.]

20 f.: the last 2 ll. of a 7-l. stanza in a poem of six stanzas + *tornada*.   21 *Alixandres*: cf. MLat. Anon. **1**.8.1n. The story of Alexander was known from the
Roman d'Alexandre, surviving in a 12th-century Franco-Provençal fragment
and later OF versions. For a similar motif, with ref. to Hector, see Gaut. Darg.
1.21 f.   The establishment of the text of this poem is fraught with difficulty
(see Eusebi, p. 90), and editorial decisions vary. The readings adopted in l. 21
by Perugi (II, p. 453) and Eusebi (p. 93) appear out of keeping with the basic
meaning of the topos, which is 'I would not wish to enjoy Alexander's renown
without her'. Therefore Toja's version is textually preferable.   21 Like
Meleagre in **2**, *Alixandres* is an isolated rhyme, rhyming with the last line of
each stanza and of the *tornada*.

Bertran de Born, rejected by his chosen lady and unable to find her equal,
seeks instead to create an imaginary lady (*dompna soiseubuda*), made up of
the individual qualities of different beauties; the hair alone is compared with
that of an exemplary figure:

Bertran de Born **1**

Dompna, puois de mi . . . (*canso*). PC 80.12, D 3760, Gouiran 7

<blockquote>
pois tenc ma carrieira,   IV   34
no·m biais,
ves Rocacoart m'eslais
als pels N'Agnes, qe·m dara·n;
q'Iseuz, la dompna Tristan,   38
que fon per totz mentauguda,
no·ls ac tant bels a saubuda.
</blockquote>

[Then I pursue my course, I do not turn aside, I hasten to Rochechouart for the hair of lady Agnes, who will give me some of it, for Iseut, Tristan's lady, who was celebrated by all, had not such beautiful hair, as is well known.]

34–40: the last 7 ll. of a 10-l. stanza in a poem of seven stanzas + *tornada*. 38 *Iseuz . . . Tristan*: see Raimb. Or. **1**.29 f. n.

In two poems, the poet refers to Mathilda, daughter of Henry I, with a *senhal*, identifying her with Helen:

Bertran de Born **2a**

Casutz sui . . . (*canso*). PC 80.9, D 3730, Gouiran 3

<blockquote>
car m'atrais   I   7
ab un esgart en biais
una gaia, fresca Elena.
</blockquote>

[For with a sideways glance a gay new Helen has attracted me.]

Lines 7–9 of a 12-l. stanza in a poem of five stanzas + *tornada*.   9 *Elena*: see Raim. Jord. **1**.28 n.

Bertran de Born **2b**

Ges de disnar . . . (*canso*). PC 80.19, D 3830, Gouiran 2

<blockquote>
c'aitan volgra volgues mon pro na Lana   I   7
cum lo seigner de Peitau.
</blockquote>

[For I could wish that lady Lana might be as favourably disposed towards me as the lord of Poitou.]

The last 2 ll. of an 8-l. stanza in a poem of five stanzas + *tornada*.   7 *volgues mon pro*: lit. 'might desire my advantage'.   *Lana*: an abbreviation of *Elena*; see **2a**.9.

A lament for the death in 1186 of count Geoffrey of Brittany (referred to with the *senhal* of *Rassa* in the poem). The poet expresses the wish that Alexander and renowned epic heroes such as Raoul de Cambrai, Roland and Oliver and Guillaume d'Orange may keep the count company in heaven and compares him with king Arthur and Gauvain:

Bertran de Born **3**

A totz dic . . . (*planh*). PC 80.6a, D 3690, Gouiran 22

S'Artus, lo segner de Cardoil,   V   33
cui Breton atendon e mai,
agues poder qe tornes sai,
Breton i aurian perdut   36
e Nostre Segner gazagnat.
si lor i tornava Galvain,
non lur auria esmendat
qe mais no lur agues tolut.   40

[If Arthur, the lord of Carlisle, whom the Bretons await now and henceforth (see n.), had the power to return to earth, the Bretons would have
lost thereby and our Lord would have gained. If Gauvain were to return
to them there, He would not have recompensed them for the greater good
He had taken away from them.]

The fifth stanza in a poem of seven stanzas + *tornada*.   33 *Artus*: see
also Gauc. Faid. **3**.16; Peire Vid. **5a**.12, **5b**.39; Guir. Cal. **2**.7.   34 *e mai*:
Gouiran takes *mai* as a substantive, and interprets the phrase as 'in May',
but this makes little sense; the adverb *mai(s)* is well attested in the sense
'henceforth' (see e.g. Peire Vid. **5b**.40), and it is therefore better with Paden *et
al.*, p. 351 to assume an elliptical construction with a second verb understood,
i.e. 'whom the Bretons await and (will await) henceforth'.   36 f. i.e. to
the Bretons Arthur would be a poor exchange for Geoffrey, and God would
have gained by retaining Geoffrey in heaven.   38 *Galvain*: an isolated
rhyme (*rim estramp*). Gauvain, nephew of king Arthur, is a celebrated knight
of the Round Table, e.g. in the romances of Chrétien de Troyes; see also Peire
Vid. **4**.17, 49; Aim. Peg. **2**.14; Peire Card. **2**.7; Oc. Anon. **1**.6.   *tornava* might
equally well be transitive, i.e. 'if He were to return Gauvain to them there'.

Folquet de Marseille **1**

Sitot me soi . . . (*canso*). PC 155.21, D 7520, ed. Stroński 11

Per so, Amors, mi soi ieu recrezutz   V   33
de vos servir, que mais no·n aurai cura;
q'aissi cum prez' om plus laida peintura   35
de loing, no fai qand l'es de prez venguz,
prezav' ieu vos mais qand no·us conoissia,
e s'anc vos volc, mais n'ai qu'er no volria:
c'aissi m'es pres cum al fol qeridor
que dis c'aurs fos tot qant el tocaria.   40

[Therefore, Love, I have renounced my service of you, so that I will no
longer make it my care; for just as one prizes more highly an ugly picture
from a distance, but does not do so when one has come close, so I prized
you more when I did not know you, and if ever I desired you, I have in
consequence more than I could now wish, for I have suffered the same fate

as the foolish petitioner, who asked that everything he touched be turned to gold.]

The final stanza in a poem of five stanzas + 2 *tornadas*; *qeridor* 39 is an isolated rhyme.   The final line contains an indirect allusion to the story of Midas, related in Ovid, *Met.* XI.92 ff.: granted the fulfilment of any wish by Bacchus, Midas asked that all he touched might be turned to gold, but when his food and drink turned to gold, prayed that he might be set free from his wish. 39 f.: cf. other similar comparisons in Folquet, in which an unnamed representative type serves as exemplar: 11.2 f. *aissi cum cel qu'a tot perdut e jura | que mais non joc* (like the man who has lost everything and swears he will not play again); 11.7 f. (referring to Love) *a lei de mal deutor | c'ades promet mas re no pagaria* (like the bad debtor, who promises at the moment, but would never pay anything); 1.29 f. *aissi com sel qu'estiers no pot gandir | que vai totz sols entre cinc cens ferir* (like the man who cannot otherwise save himself, but goes forth alone in the midst of five hundred to attack); 7.18 ff. *aissi quom sel qu'e mieg de l'albre estui, | qu'es tan poiatz que no sap tornar jos, | ni sus non vai, tan li par temeros* (like the man who is halfway up the tree, and has climbed so far that he cannot turn back, nor does he climb higher, so perilous does it seem to him).

For a poem attributed both to Folquet de Marseille and Falquet de Romans, see under the latter, no. **3c**.

Guiraut de Bornelh refuses to name his lady, in order not to injure her reputation by idle talk:

Guiraut de Bornelh **1**

Quar non ai . . . (canso). PC 242.28, D 11930, Sharman 35

c'ab faillimen	II 26
s'estrai sse	
cilh cui quer be,	
cui eu sui plus fis	
qu'Elena Paris.	30

[For she from I seek favour, to whom I am more true than Paris to Helen, distances herself from wrongdoing.]

26–30: the last 5 ll. of a 15-l. stanza in a poem of six stanzas + *tornada*. 26 *faillimen*: in the context this probably alludes also to the wrong the poet would commit, were he to name the lady, which would cause her to reject him. 30 For the word-order, with the subject at the end of the clause and line, see Raim. Jord. **1**. 30 n.   *Elena Paris*: see Raim. Jord. **1**.28 n.

The subject of a lament, not named and referred to only with a *senhal* as *Hygnaure*,[4] is usually thought to be the poet Raimbaut d'Orange:

---

[4] For this *senhal*, probably derived from the OF *Lai d'Ignaure*, see Sharman, pp. 8 ff.

Guiraut de Bornelh **2**

       S'anc iorn . . . (*planh*). PC 242.65, D 12290, Sharman 61

> c'anc non vi ni ia non veirai,   V 36
> tant non irai,
> d'un sol home tant bel assai,
> ni non deu dire cavalliers
> que tant en valgues Oliviers.   40

[For I never saw, and shall surely never see – however far I go – such fair endeavour on the part of a single man, nor ought any knight to say that Oliver was of such worth.]

36–40: the last 5 ll. of an 8-l. stanza in a poem of eight stanzas + two *tornadas*. 40 *Oliviers*: companion of Roland in the *Chanson de Roland*; see also Arn. Mar. 4.44 n.; Gar. Apch. 1.17 f.; Peire Vid. 2.13; Cerverí 1.47.

Garin d'Apchier **1**

       L'autrier trobei . . . (*sirventes*). PC 162.3, D 7750, Latella 8

> Eu no m'apel ges Olivier   III 17
> ni Rothlan, qe q'el se·n dises;
> mas valer lor cre maintas ves
> quant cossir de leis q'eu enquier;   20
> e non sai el mon cavalier
> q'eu adoncs no·l crezes valer;
> e volria tal fieu aver
> a partir regisme o enpier.

[I am not called Oliver or Roland, whatever may be said in that respect, but I many times consider myself to be equal to them in worth, when I think of her whose love I seek. And I do not know any knight in the world whom I do not then consider myself to equal; and I would wish to have a fief such that it surpasses realm or empire.]

17 *Olivier*: see Guir. Born. 2.40 n.   24 *partir*: usually 'divide', 'separate', 'set apart'; the line seems to mean that the possession of the fief, i.e. the lady's love, would set aside that of realm or empire, consigning it to a position of no importance.

This unusual example making up the final stanza of the poem, the only reference to the theme of love in the poet's work, which is otherwise entirely didactic and satirical in nature, is linked to two stanzas to which it seems to bear little relation. The ed. (p. 229) suggests that it may display 'un'intenzione parodica', which seems very likely, particularly since the figures of Roland and Oliver are prototypes of valour rather than of love. If that is so, it is testimony to the fact that such exemplary comparisons were so popular that they could be exaggerated and parodied.

Guiraut de Salinhac **1**

En atretal esperansa . . . (canso).
PC 249.5, D 14430, Strempel, Anhang I, pp. 71 f.

Mas denan totas s'enansa   IV   22
vas pretz, vas valor, vas sen,
e miels parla e plus gen,
so dizo·l pros e·l savay;   25
et ieu am la miels e may
no fes Piramus Tibe.
tan l'am que d'als no·m sove.

[But she surpasses all others in renown, merit, and sense and speaks better
and more pleasingly, as both the worthy and the unworthy affirm, and I
love her better and more than Pyramus loved Thisbe. I love her so much
that I am not mindful of anything else.]

The fourth stanza in a poem of six stanzas.   22 f. *s'enansa*: lit.'advances'; in
association with the prepositions *denan* 'in front of', and *vas* 'towards', the lit.
meaning is: 'she advances in front of all others towards renown'.   27 *Piramus Tibe*: see Arn. Mar. **3b**.152 n.

This poem is ascribed in two MSS to Guir. Sal., in one to El. Barj., in one to
El. Cair., and is anonymous in another. It is not included by Stroński under
El. Barj. (see ed., p. XXXII), or by Jaeschke under El. Cair. (see ed., pp. 48 f.,
206–9). Strempel treats it as an uncertain attribution.

Guiraut de Salinhac **2**

Aissi cum selh . . . (canso).
PC 249.1, D 14400, Strempel, Anhang II, p. 76

quar tal dona m'a s'amor autreyada   II   12
que genser es a mos ops per un cen
e val trop mais a lau de tota gen,
fin e leials e senes cor truan,   15
per qu'ieu l'am mais no fetz Auda Rotlan.

[For such a lady has granted me her love, who is a hundred times more
kind to me, and is accounted of much greater worth in the praise of all
the world, true and loyal, and without a false heart, so that I love her more
than Roland loved Aude.]

12–16: the last 5 ll. of an 8-l. stanza in a poem of four stanzas.   13 *genser,*
14 *trop mais*: the comparatives are explained by the fact that stanza I is a
complaint of a false lady.   16 For the word-order, with the subject at the
end of the clause and line, see Raim. Jord. **1**.30 n.   *Auda*: the betrothed of
Roland in the *Chanson de Roland*; see also Zorzi **2**.121 n.

This poem is ascribed in three MSS to Guir. Sal., in two to Aim. Peg. in one to
Arn. Dan., and in one to P. Brem. (see Arn. Dan., ed. Toja, p. 22, and Aim. Peg.,
ed. Shepard/Chambers, p. 29). Strempel treats it as an uncertain attribution.

Guiraudo lo Ros 1

A ley de bon servidor (*canso*). PC 240.2, D 11590, Finoli 4

Ai, belh cors francx ab honor,   III   19
la genser qu'el mon remanh,
ieu muer si cum fetz el banh
Serena, lo vielh auctor,
que per servir sofri greu penedensa;
tot enaissi abelhis et agensa
fin Amor, que·m vol a tort aucir,   25
que nueg e iorn mi nafron siey cossir,
mas hieu·m conort qu'ab merce truep guirensa.

[Ah, beautiful, noble, honoured lady, the most pleasing in the world, I am
dying, as there died in the bath *Serena*, the author of old, who on account
of service suffered a grievous penance; in just the same way it pleases and
seems good to perfect love to desire unjustly to kill me, for night and
day its cares afflict me, but I console myself that with mercy I may find
deliverance.]

The third stanza in a poem of five 9-l. stanzas.   20 *qu'el mon remanh*:
lit. 'who remains in the world'.   21 f. *Serena*: a substitution, probably
scribal, for the name of Seneca, whose death in the bath was known from the
De consolatio philosophiae of Boethius. There may be confusion with Annaeus
Serenus, to whom *De tranquillitate animi* and other works by Seneca are
addressed.   23 Seneca was banished in AD 41 on a false charge of adultery
with Julia Livilla.

In a 13th-century *tenso* between Guiraut Riquier, Jordan, Raimon Isarn and
Paulet de Marselha (see Paul. Mars., ed. I. de Riquer, pp. 178 ff.), Giraudo
lo Ros is cited as an exemplary lover: 19 *Guiraut Riquier, anc Giraudet lo
Ros | no fon destretz per sidons en tal guia | coma yeu soy per la genser c'anc fos*
(Guiraut Riquier, even Giraudet lo Ros did not suffer such distress for the sake
of his lady as I suffer for the sake of the most lovely one who ever lived) – for
trouvère exs. of poets as exemplars see Eustache le Peintre 1.34 *li Chastelains
ne Blondiaus*, and OF Anon. 4.1 *li chastelains de Couci*.

Poets Writing at the Turn of the
Twelfth and Thirteenth Centuries

Gaucelm Faidit affirms his own constancy and his hopes of the lady:

Gaucelm Faidit 1

Ges no·m tuoill . . . (*canso*). PC 167.29, D 8120, Mouzat 26

e si per estz fals brais   V   61
qe fan lausenjador
no·is camja ni s'irais,

pro m'estai mieils d'amor
q'a Floris el palais.   65

[And if despite that perfidious outcry which the slanderers raise, she does
not change and is not provoked, I am more fortunate in love than Floris
at the palace.]

61–5: the last 5 ll. of the final 13-l. stanza in a poem of five stanzas + *tornada*.
65 *Floris*: see Arn. Mar. **3b**.153 n.

Gaucelm Faidit **2**

Coras qe·m des . . . (*canso*). PC 167.17, D 7990, Mouzat 39

Car cel Andrieus, c'om romanssa,   V   41
non trais anc tant greu martire
per la reïna de Franssa
cum ieu per vos cui desire.

[For that Andrieu who is celebrated in romance, never experienced such
grievous torment for the queen of France as I experience for you whom I
desire.]

41–4: the first 4 ll. of a 10-l. stanza in a poem of seven stanzas + *tornada*.
41 *Andrieus*: see Raim. Jord. **2**.24 n.

A lament for the death of Richard Cœur de Lion in 1199:

Gaucelm Faidit **3**

Fortz chauza es . . . (*planh*). PC 167.22, D 8050, Mouzat 50

Mortz es lo reis, e son passat mil an   II   10
c'anc tant pros hom non fo, ni no·l vi res,
ni mais non er nulls hom del sieu semblan,
tant larcs, tant rics, tant arditz, tals donaire,
q'Alixandres, lo reis qui venquet Daire,
non cre que tant dones ni tant meses,   15
ni anc Karles ni Artus plus valgues,
c'a tot lo mon si fetz, qui·n vol ver dir,
als us doptar et als autres grazir.

[The king is dead, and a thousand years have passed since there ever was,
or anyone has seen, such an excellent man, nor will there ever again be
his like, so liberal, so powerful, so valiant, so prodigal, that I do not think
that Alexander, the king who vanquished Darius, gave or spent so much,
or that Charlemagne or Arthur were of greater worth, for if the truth is
told, out of the whole world he made himself feared by some and loved
by the rest.]

The second stanza in a poem of six 9-l. stanzas + *tornada*.   14 *Alixandres*:
see Arn. Dan. **3**.21 n. Here Alexander exemplifies munificence, as in Raimb.
Vaq. **4**.100.   *Daire*: see Perr. Ang. **1**.40 n.   16 *Karles*: the central figure,
based on Charlemagne, in the *Chanson de Roland*; see Raimb. Vaq. **5**.74.
Artus: see Bertr. Born **3**.33 n.

Peire Vidal 1

Ajostar e lassar . . . (*canso*). PC 364.2, D 18690, Avalle 3

hai baro!   IV   51
co·m te en sa preizo
Amors, que Salamo,
e Davi   atressi
venquet e·l fort Samso,   55
e·ls tenc en son grillo,
qu'anc non ac rezemso
tro a la mort; e pus mi te,
ad estar m'er a sa merce.

[Alas! how Love holds me in his prison, he who vanquished Solomon and
David likewise and Samson the strong and held them as his captives, so
that there was no redemption until death; and since he holds me, I must
remain at his mercy.]

51–9: the final ll. of a 15-l. stanza in a poem of six stanzas + 3 *tornadas*.
53 *Salamo*, 54 *Davi*, 55 *Samso*: for the motif of love's victims see Marc. **1**.14 n.
56 *en son grillo*: lit. 'in his prison'.

Peire Vidal 2

Drogoman senher . . . (*sirventes*). PC 364.18, D 18850, Avalle 29

D'ardimen vaill Rotlan et Olivier   III   13
e de domnei Berart de Mondesdier.

[In boldness I equal Roland and Oliver and in the service of ladies Berart
de Mondesdier.]

The first 2 ll. of a 6-l. stanza in a poem of seven stanzas + *tornada*.   13 *Rotlan*:
see Arn. Mar. **4**.44 n.; *Olivier*: see Guir. Born. **2**.40 n.   14 *Berart de Mondesdier*: a gallant lover in the *Chanson des Saisnes* by Jean Bodel (see Avalle,
p. 225); see also Raimb. Vaq. **4**.102.

Peire Vidal 3

Si·m laissava . . . (*sirventes-canso*). PC 364.43, D 19100, Avalle 32

E s'ieu podi' acabar   II   11
so que m'a fait comensar
mos sobresforcius talens,
Alexandres fon niens
contra qu'ieu seria: 15
e s'a Dieu plazia,
que m'en denhes aiudar,
ja·l sieus verais monumens
lonjamen non estaria
sotz mal serva senhoria.   20

[And if I could accomplish that which my strenuous desire has caused me
to undertake, Alexander was nothing by contrast with what I should be:

and if it were pleasing to God, so that He deigned to help me, his true Sepulchre would indeed not long remain under an evil servile rule.]

The second stanza in a poem of seven stanzas + *tornada*.   14 *Alexandres*: see Arn. Dan. **3**.21 n.   16 ff. These lines make it clear that the poet's desire is to free the Holy Sepulchre, in pagan hands after the fall of Jerusalem in 1187, which explains the comparison of himself with Alexander.

Peire Vidal **4**

Neus ni gels . . . (*sirventes-canso*). PC 364.30, D 18960, Avalle 34

A l'uzatge·m tenh de Galvanh   III   17
que quan non son aventuratz,
ieu m'esfortz tan deves totz latz
qu'ieu prenc e conquier e gazanh.
[. . .]

Las aventuras de Galvanh   VII   49
ai totas e d'autras assatz.

[I follow the usage of Gauvain, so that when I am not favoured by fortune, I make such efforts on every hand that I seize and conquer and gain. [. . .] I have attempted all the exploits of Gauvain and others (in addition).]

17 ff., 49 f.: the opening ll. of stanzas III and VII in a poem of nine 8-l. stanzas + *tornada*.   17, 49 *Galvanh*: see Bertr. Born **3**.38 n.

Peire Vidal **5a**

Pus tornatz sui . . . (*canso*). PC 364. 37, D 19050, Avalle 40

E sel que long'atendensa   II   10
blasma, fai gran falhizo;
qu'er an Artus li Breto
on avion lur plevensa.

[And he who criticizes long expectation, makes a great mistake, for now the Bretons have their Arthur, in whom they placed their trust.]

10 ff.: the first 4 ll. of a 9-l. stanza in a poem of seven stanzas.   A reference to the Bretons' expectation of the return of king Arthur, which is realized in the birth of Arthur, son of Geoffrey of Brittany, in 1187; see also **5b**.39 and Bertr. Born **3**.33 n.

Peire Vidal **5b**

Ges pel temps . . . (*sirventes-canso*). PC 364.24, D 18910, Avalle 31

despos Artus an cobrat en Bretanha,   IV   39
non es razos que mais jois mi sofranha.

[Since they have regained Arthur in Brittany, there is no reason why I should lack joy henceforth.]

39 f.: the last 2 ll. of a 10-l. stanza in a poem of seven stanzas + 3 *tornadas*; see **5a**.10 ff. n.

In a poem in a form which repeats the same rhyme vowels in each stanza (*coblas unissonans*), the poet chooses -*el* : -*el* as the rhyming syllable in the last 2 ll. of the stanza, which no doubt explains some of the names in this position:

Peire Vidal **6**

Be·m pac . . . (*canso*). PC 364.11, D 1870, Avalle 36

siei dig an sabor de mel,   II   19
don sembla Sant Gabriel.

[. . .]
don m'a leyal e fizel   III   29
e just pus que Dieus Abel.

[. . .]
am la mais per San Raphel,   V   49
que Jacobs no fetz Rachel.

[Her words have the sweetness of honey so that she resembles Saint Gabriel. [. . .] Therefore I am loyal and faithful to her, and indeed more so than Abel to God. [. . .] I love her more by Saint Raphael than Jacob loved Rachel.]

In II, III and V the two final ll. of a 10-l. stanza in a poem of seven stanzas + 2 *tornadas.*   29 lit. 'so that she has me loyal and faithful and indeed more so than God (had) Abel'.   30 *Abel*: for Abel's faith in God see Heb. 11:4; cf. Zorzi **2**.35.

Guillem Magret **1**

Atrestan be·m tenc . . . (*canso*). PC 232.2, D 10620, Naudieth 1

Atrestan be·m tenc per mortal   I   1
cum selh qu'avia nom Andrieu,
dompna, pus chauzimens no·m val
ab vos de cui tenc so qu'es mieu.

[I consider myself just as fated to die as the one with the name of Andrieu, lady, since mercy is of no avail with you, from whom I hold whatever is mine.]

The first 4 ll. of a 10-l. stanza in a poem of five stanzas.   2 *Andrieu*: see Raim. Jord. **2**.24 n.   3 f.: i.e. because of the lady's resistance, mercy is powerless to help the poet.

Guillem Magret **2**

Trop mielhs m'es pres . . . (*canso*). PC 223.7, D 10680, Naudieth 4

Trop mielhs m'es pres qu'a'n Golfier de las Tors: I   1
[. . .]
et am dona aital cum la volria
tener elh bratz, quar mi seri' honors;
et ai senhor aital cum ops m'avia,   5
et ai trobat pus avinen leo
quez elh no fetz e de maior preyzo.

[It has fared much better with me than with sir Golfier de las Tors [. . .]

and I love a lady such that I could wish to hold her in my arms, for it would be an honour for me, and I have a lord of the kind I needed, and I have found a more pleasing lion than he, of greater bounty.]

The first 7 ll. of a 9-l. stanza (l. 2 is missing in the MS) in a poem of five stanzas.   7 *preyzo*, lit. 'prey', 'booty'.

This unusual example refers to a hero of the First Crusade, said to have rescued a lion from a snake, whereupon the lion followed at his side, bringing him his prey as food; for this narrative motif in a medieval work see Chrétien de Troyes, *Le Chevalier au lion* (*Yvain*). The choice of this exemplary figure results in an awkward comparison of the lady with the lion, and explains the word *preyzo*, appropriate to the lion, but hardly to the lady (for a similar ex., implying the identification of the lady with the lion, with ref. to *Yvain*, see Perr. Ang. 2.35). Gauc. Faid. 53.47 ff. more fittingly compares his devotion to the lady with that of the lion to Golfier de las Tors, whereas Uc Pena, in a reference to another episode attaching to the same hero, compares his state when the lady bids him rejoice with that of Golfier de las Tors when he transmitted a message to the Crusaders at Antioch (*Cora qe·m desplagues* . . ., ll. 33–40, Kolsen, 1925, p. 66).

There are a particularly high number of exemplary figures in Raimbaut de Vaqueiras, so that not all the occurrences can be quoted *in extenso*, but they are cited, if only briefly, in order to show the wide range of literary reference in his work.

Raimbaut de Vaqueiras **1**

Era·m requier . . . (*canso*). PC 392.2, D 20850, Linskill 10

Anc non amet tan aut cum eu negus   9
ni tant pro dompn', e car no·i trob pareill
m'enten en lieis e l'am al sieu conseill
mais que Tisbe non amet Pyramus.   12
[. . .]

Anc Persivals qand en la cort d'Artus   III   17
tolc las armas al cavallier vermeill
non ac tal gauch cum eu del sieu conseill,
e·m fai morir si cum mor Tantalus.   20
[. . .]

Bella dompna, aitant arditz e plus   IV   25
fui qan vos quis la joia del cabeill
e qe·m dassetz de vostr' amor conseill
no·n fo del saut a Tir Emenadus.

[No one ever loved in such a high place as I, nor such an excellent lady, and since I cannot find her equal, I set my thoughts on her and love her in accordance with her counsel, more than Pyramus loved Thisbe. [. . .]

> Never did Perceval, when at Arthur's court he stripped the armour from the Red Knight, experience such joy as I have from her counsel, and she makes me die as Tantalus died. [. . .] Beautiful lady, when I sought the gift of a lock of hair and that you might give me counsel on my love for you, I was as bold and even more so than was Emenadus at the assault upon Tyre.]

9 ff., 17 ff., 25 ff.: in each case the first 4 ll. of an 8-l. stanza in a poem of five stanzas + 2 *tornadas*.   11, 19, 27 *conseill*: the rhyme scheme demands two rhyme words in -*eill* in each stanza, so that the word occurs in each of five stanzas. Its meaning is explained by the first stanza, in which the poet seeks counsel from the lady, who advises him to love the best of all ladies, who will bring him honour; the poet follows her advice by choosing her.   12 For the word-order, with the subject at the end of the clause and line, see Raim. Jord. **1**.30 n.   *Tisbe* . . . *Pyramus*: see Arn. Mar. **3b**.152 n.   17 *Persivals*: see also Rig. Berb. **2**.1.   18 For this episode see Chrétien, *Conte du Graal*, 866 ff.   20 *Tantalus*: cf. Ovid, *Ars Am.* II.605 f., *Met.* IV.458 f.; X.41 f.; see Liechtenstein **1a**.113 ff.; MHG Anon. **1**.1 ff.; Calvo **1**.55, and the *partimen*, Bertoni, *Trovatori d'Italia*, p. 476: 26 *Q'entrels amanz es aitals l'us e·l cors,* | *c'on plus s'aman, maier es lur langors,* | *si no·s vezon, q'il moron eissamenz* | *com Tantalus qe zo que plus l'agenza* | *ve e non a aiuda ni valenza* (for such is the custom and way among lovers, the more they love one another, the more they languish if they do not see each other, so that they die just like Tantalus, who sees that which is most pleasing to him and has no help or succour). 28 *Emenadus*: a lieutenant of Alexander in the *Roman d'Alexandre*.

Other comparisons with famous lovers:

Raimbaut de Vaqueiras **2a**

No puesc saber . . . (*canso*). PC 392.25, D 21130, Linskill 6

lieys qu'ieu am mais que non amet vasletz   II   12
Guis de Nantuelh la piussel' Ayglentina.

[. . .]

amada·us ai mays qu'Andrieus la reyna.   IV   29

> [She whom I love more than the young hero Gui de Nanteuil loved the maiden Aiglentine. [. . .] I have loved you more than Andrieu loved the queen.]

12 f.: ll. 4–5 of II; 29: l. 5 of IV. The poem consists of five 8-l. stanzas + *tornada*. 13 *Guis de Nanteuil*: the hero of the OF poem *Gui de Nanteuil*; cf. Aim. Peg., ed. Shepard/Chambers 33.45 ff., for a comparison of Guilhem de Malespina with Gui de Nanteuil.   29 *Andrieus*: see Raim. Jord. **2**.24 n.

Raimbaut de Vaqueiras **2b**

Engles, un novel descort . . . (*descort*).
PC 392.16, D 21030, Linskill 17

Ses doptansa,   II   23
Andreus de Fransa
no·s saup tan gen rendre,
qu'alegransa
·m fo fermansa.

[. . .]

e si prendre·m denha,   V   53
a tapi li venrai,

Si cum Tristans, que·s fes guaita,   VI   55
tro qu'Yzeus fo vas si traita.

[Without a doubt, Andrieu of France did not surrender so graciously, for
the assurance was gladness to me. [. . .] And if she deigns to accept me, I
will come to her secretly, like Tristan, who acted as watchman until Iseut
came to him.]

23 ff.: ll. 7–11 in a 12-l. section of the *descort*.   53 ff.: the end of section VI
and the beginning of section VI.   24 *Andreus de Fransa*: see Raim. Jord.
2.24 n.   54 *a tapi*: a reference to Tristan's secret assignations with Iseut
after his banishment from Mark's court.   55 f. *Tristans . . . Yzeus*: see
Raimb. Or. **1**.29 f. n.   56 *fo vas si traita* lit. 'was drawn towards him',
the construction necessitated by the incidence of 6 rhymes in *-aita* in this
monorhyme section.

Raimbaut de Vaqueiras **2c**

Leu pot hom . . . (*canso*). PC 392.23, D 21110, Linskill 7

et anc Floris de Blanchaflor   VI   58
non pres comjat tant doloiros
cum eu, dompna, si·m part de vos.

[And never did Floris take such a sorrowful parting from Blancheflor as I,
lady, if I part from you.]

58–60: the last 3 ll. of the final stanza in a poem of six 10-l. stanzas + 2 *tornadas*.
58 *Floris*: see Arn. Mar. **3b**.153 n.   59 *comjat tant doloiros*: this may refer
to the grief of Floire when he is sent away by his father on a false pretence, in
order to separate him from Blancheflor (*Floire et Blancheflor* 340 ff.), or to his
lament when he is made to believe she is dead (*ib.* 691 ff.) – but see Ziltener,
p. 779 n. 1.

Raimbaut de Vaqueiras **2d**

Kalenda maia . . . (*estampida*).
PC 392.9, D 20940, Linskill 15

qar per gençor   vos ai chauzida   VI   77
e per meilhor,   de prez complida,

	blandida,	
	servida	80
genses	q'Erecs Enida.	
	Bastida,	
	finida,	
n'Engles	ai l'estampida.	

[For I have chosen you as the most excellent and the best, of perfect merit, and I have wooed and served you better than Erec Enida. I have composed and finished, Sir *Engles*, the *estampida*.]

77–84: the last 8 ll. of the final stanza in a poem of six 14-l. stanzas.   81 *Erecs, Enida*: known from the *Erec* of Chrétien de Troyes, c. 1170. See Guil. R. Giron. **1**.48 ff., Oc. Anon. **3**.113; cf. Appel, *Prov. Inedita*, p. 322 *Donna, pos vos ay chausida* (*dansa*): 9 *que Erex non amet Henida | tan ni Yseutz Tristan | con yeu, vos* . . . (for Erec did not love Enida as much, nor Tristan Iseut, as I love you . . .).

Comparisons with other male figures:

Raimbaut de Vaqueiras 3a

D'amor no·m lau . . . (*canso*).
PC 392.10, D 20960, Linskill 5

    mas trahitz sui si cum fo Ferragutz,   II 11
    qu'a Rotlan dis tot so major espaut.

[But I am betrayed as was Ferragu, who revealed his most vulnerable spot to Roland.]

11 f.: ll. 3–4 of an 8-l. stanza in a poem of five stanzas.   11 f.: this episode is narrated in the 12th-century *Chronique du Pseudo-Turpin*.

Raimbaut de Vaqueiras 3b

Gerras ni plaich . . . (*canso*).
PC 392.18, D 21060, Linskill 13

    anc Tibauz ab Lodoyc   I 10
    no fetz plait ab tans plazers
    cum eu, qan sos tortz m'esders.

[Never did Thibaut make a treaty with Louis with such pleasure, as I (with Love) when it redressed the wrongs committed against me.]

10–12: the last 3 ll. of I in a poem of six 12-l. stanzas + 2 *tornadas*.   10 *Tibauz*: in the OF poem *Folque de Candie*, the Saracen Thibaut rejoiced when Louis, the son of Charlemagne, promised to restore him to his inheritance upon conclusion of the treaty; see the ref. to the lovers in this poem in Duchesse de Lorraine **1**.15.

Raimbaut de Vaqueiras 3c

Ja no cujei . . . (*canso*). PC 392.20, D 21080, Linskill 14

    e si·m des sos cors gens   III 40
    so c'ab son conseill qier,

vencut agr' a sobrier
d'aventura Galvaing.

[And if her gracious person were to grant me what I seek from her counsel,
I would have far exceeded Gauvain in good fortune.]

40 ff.: ll. 8–11 of a 16-l. stanza in a poem of seven stanzas+2 *tornadas*.
43 *Galvaing*: see Bertr. Born **3**.38 n.

In praise of the Marquis of Montferrat, the poet's patron:

Raimbaut de Vaqueiras **4**

Valen marques . . . Epic letter, Linskill, p. 308

E qui vol dir per vertat ni comtar,   99
Aleyxandres vos laisset son donar
et ardimen Rotlan e·lh dotze par
e·l pros Berart domney e gent parlar.

[And if one wishes to tell and recount truly, Alexander bequeathed you
his generosity, and Roland and the twelve peers a bold spirit, and noble
Berart service of ladies and fair speech.]

100 *Aleyxandres*: see Arn. Dan. **3**.21 n., and for the motif of largesse, Gauc.
Faid. **3**.14 and n.   101 *Rotlan*: see Arn. Mar. **4**.44 n.; *e·lh dotze par*: see the
Chanson de Roland, 547 and *passim*.   102 *Berart*: see Peire Vid. **2**.14 n.

In praise of the exploits of the Marquis and other Crusaders on the Fourth
Crusade in 1205:

Raimbaut de Vaqueiras **5**

No m'agrad' . . . (*sirventes-canso*).
PC 392.24, D 21120, Linskill 22

Anc Alixandres non fetz cors   VII   73
ni Carles ni·l reis Lodoics
tan honrat, ni·l pros n'Aimerics   75
ni Rotlans ab sos poignadors
non saubron tan gen conquerer
tan ric emperi per poder
cum nos, don poja nostra leis.

[Neither Alexander nor Charlemagne nor king Louis ever carried out such
a glorious expedition, nor would valiant sir Aimeric or Roland with his
warriors be able so nobly to conquer with their might such a powerful
empire as we have won, as a result of which our faith is in the ascendant.]

73–9: the first 7 ll. of a 12-l. stanza in a poem of seven stanzas+3 *tornadas*.
73 *Alixandres*: see Arn. Dan. **3**.21 n.   74 *Carles*: see Gauc. Faid. **3**.16.
Lodoics: see above **3b**.10 n. 75 *n'Aimerics*: father of Guillaume d'Orange, hero
of the OF poem *Aymeri de Narbonne*.   76 *Rotlans*: see **4**.101 n.

Poems ascribed to a woman, and written in the female voice, may use the
same exemplary comparisons as those in male poets:

La Comtessa de Dia **1**

Estat ai . . . (*canso*).
Beatriz de Dia PC 46.4, D 2070, Rieger, *Trobairitz* 36

Ben volria mon cavallier   II   9
tener un ser en mos bratz nut,
q'el s'en tengra per ereubut
sol q'a lui fezes cossellier;
car plus m'en sui abellida
no fetz Floris de Blanchaflor.   14

[I would dearly like one evening to hold my knight in my arms, naked, for
he would thus consider himself full of joy, were I only to serve as his pillow,
for I have taken greater delight in him than Floris took in Blancheflor.]

9–14: the first 6 ll. of an 8-l. stanza in a poem of three stanzas.   14 *Floris* . . .
Blanchaflor: see Arn. Mar. **3b**.153 n.; here the poet identifies herself with the
male lover.

La Comtessa de Dia **2**

A chantar m'er . . . (*canso*).
Beatriz de Dia PC 46.2, D 2050, Rieger, *Trobairitz* 35

D'aisso·m conort car anc non fi faillenssa,   II   8
amics, vas vos per nuilla captenenssa,
anz vos am mais non fetz Seguis Valenssa.

[I console myself with this, for I was never at fault in my conduct towards
you, my friend, but love you more thanValensa loved Seguis.]

8–10: the first 3 ll. of a 7-l. stanza in a poem of five stanzas + *tornada*.
10 *Seguis* . . . *Valenssa*: see **1**.14 n. (for the word-order see Raim. Jord. **1**.28 n.);
for the names, see under Arn. Mar. **3b** n. As in **1**.14, it seems that the poet
identifies herself with the male lover.

Uc de la Bacalaria **1**

Per grazir . . . (*alba*). PC 449.3, D 24550, Riquer, *Trovadores* II, 211

Qu'ieu·us jur pels sans evangelis   II   12
que anc Andrieus de Paris,
Floris, Tristans ni Amelis
no fo vas amor tant fis.

[For I swear to you on the holy Gospels that never was Andrieu of Paris,
Floris, Tristan or Amelis so true to love.]

The first 4 ll. of an 8-l. stanza in a poem of four stanzas + 3-l. refrain.
13 *Andrieus de Paris*: see Raim. Jord. **2**.24 n.   14 *Floris*: see Arn. Mar.
3b.153 n. *Tristans*: see Raimb. Or. **1**.30 n.   *Amelis*: one of the eponymous
heroes of the OF *Ami et Amile*, who are examples of friendship rather than of
love.

Poets Whose Activity Extends into the First Decades of the Thirteenth Century

Peirol 1

Mout m'entremis . . . (canso). PC 366.21, D 19390, Aston 15

Ja no partrai de lieys mos cossiriers;   III 15
per mal que·m do non li puesc mal voler,
quar tant la fai sens e beltatz valer
segon l'afan folley saviamen.
Mal o ai dig, ans folley follamen,
quar anc Narcis, qu'amet l'ombra de se,   20
si be·s mori, no fo plus fols de me.

[I will never turn my thoughts away from her; whatever suffering she may cause me, I cannot wish her ill, for good sense and beauty lend her such worth, that according to the measure of the torment I was wisely foolish. I have expressed it ill, rather was I foolishly foolish, for never was Narcissus, who loved his own reflection, even though he died, more foolish than I.]

The third stanza in a poem of six stanzas + *tornada.*   20 *Narcis*: see Bern.Vent. **1**.23 f. n.

Peire Raimon de Tolosa 1

Ar ai ben . . . (canso). PC 355.3, D 18350, Cavaliere 2

merce vos clam, que merces   IV 28
mi val' e ma bona fes;
qu'ieu serai de bon celar
e plus fis, si Dieus m'ampar,
que no fo Landrics a N'Aya.   32

[I beg mercy of you, that mercy and my loyalty may be of advantage to me, for I will practise concealment and be more true, if God protects me, than was Landric to lady Aya.]

28–32: the last 5 ll. of an 8-l. stanza in a poem of five stanzas + *tornada.*
32 *Landrics . . . N'Aya*: a pair of lovers from a lost tale; see also Pons Capd. **2**.42 and Paul. Mars. **1**.4. *N'Aya* is an isolated rhyme (*rim estramp*).

Guilhem Adémar 1

Pois vei . . . (canso).
Rambertino Buvalelli, PC 281.7, D 15000, Almqvist 11

Dompna, s'ieu sui enojos   VII 61
de clamar merce vas vos,
sapchatz: cocha m'o fai far.
per que no·us deu enojar;
q'ie·us am plus senes mesura   65
que no fetz Paris Elena.

[Lady, if I am importunate in begging you for mercy, know that it is pressing desire which causes me to do it; therefore it should not be irksome to you, for I love you more without measure than Paris loved Helen.]

VII is the first of 2 *tornadas* in a poem of six 10-l. stanzas.   The poem is also ascribed to *Rambertins de Bonarel* (probably for Rambertino Buvalelli) and is included under doubtful attributions in Melli's edition of the latter poet.   66 *Paris Elena*: see Raim. Jord. 1.28 n.

Raimon de Miraval 1

Be m'agrada . . . (*canso*). PC 406.13, D 21740, Topsfield 11

Per servir en ric seingnoriu   VI   41
es bons servire benanans;
per qu'eu·s voill servir totz mos ans,
et anc servidor menz antiu
non ac la bell'a cui servi Tristans,   45
anz vos farai de bels servisis tans,
tro mos servirs me fass'en grat venir
o vos digatz: "mon servidor azir".

[Through serving a powerful lord, a good servant is made happy. Therefore I wish to serve you all the years of my life, and never did the beautiful one whom Tristan served have a less faint-hearted servant – rather will I render you such a degree of praiseworthy service until my service causes me to be admitted to favour, or you say: "I hate my servant".]

The final stanza in a poem of six stanzas+3 *tornadas*.   44 *antiu*: lit. 'full of shame', 'shamefaced', 'bashful'; cf. Fr. *honteux* in: *jamais honteux n'eut belle amie* 'faint heart never won fair lady'.   45 *Tristans*: see Raimb. Or. 1.29 f. n.

Raimon de Miraval 2

Trop an chauzit . . . (*canso*). PC 406.45, D 22060, Topsfield 46

car ab sol un bais de secor   IV   32
seri'eu gais e d'amor benanan
plus que no fo per s'amia Tristan.

[For with one kiss alone to sustain me, I would be more joyful and happy in love than was Tristan for the sake of his loved one.]

32–5: ll. 5–7 of a 9-l. stanza in a poem of five stanzas.   34 *Tristan*: see 1.45 n.

This poem, in one MS ascribed to Raim. Mir., in the other preserved anonymously and lacking stanzas IV and V, is included by Topsfield under uncertain attributions. The rhyme *benanan : Tristan* might perhaps suggest imitation of *benanans : Tristans* in **1**.

Aimeric de Peguilhan **1**

Ades vol . . . (canso). PC 10.2, D 360, Shepard/Chambers 2

Et ieu dobli la balansa,   IV   25
que·l doble tenc lieis plus car
totz jorns qu'aissi sai doblar
doblamen ma malanansa;
mas assatz doblet plus gen
Tristans quan bec lo pimen,   30
quar el guazanhet s'amia,
per so per qu'ieu pert la mia.

[And I have doubled the scales, for I hold her doubly dear, every day that
I am thus able to double my ill fortune doubly; but Tristan doubled his in
a much more favourable way when he drank the potion, for he gained his
lady by that through which I lose mine.]

The fourth stanza in a poem of five stanzas + *tornada.*   30 f. *Tristans . . .*
s'amia: see Raimb. Or. **1.29** f. n.

A lament for the death in 1220 of *Guillems Malespina marques:*

Aimeric de Peguilhan **2**

Era par ben . . . (planh).
PC 10.10, D 440, Shepard/Chambers 10

De bos mestiers el mon par non li say,   II   10
qu'anc no fon tan larcs, segon mon parer,
Alexandres de manjar ni d'aver,
qu'elh non dis non qui·l quis ni trobet plai;
ni ges Galvains d'armas plus non valia
ni non saup tan Ivans de cortezia,   15
ni·s mes Tristans d'amor en tan d'assay.

[For good actions I do not know his like in this world, for in my view,
Alexander was not so munificent in dispensing hospitality and riches, for
he never said no to anyone who entreated him or disputed it. Nor was
Gauvain at all more proficient in arms, nor was Yvain so well versed in
courtliness, nor did Tristan submit to so many tests for the sake of love.]

10–16: the first 7 ll. of a 9-l. stanza in a poem of five stanzas + *tornada.*
12 *Alexandres:* see Arn. Dan. **3.21** n.; Gauc. Faid. **3.14** n. See also Aim. Peg.,
Shepard/Chambers 26.31 f., in praise of Frederick II: *hueymais cre ben, quom*
que·y anes duptan, | *lo fag qu'om di d'Alixandr' en comtan* (now I indeed believe,
although I used to doubt them, the deeds which men recount of Alexander).
14 *Galvains:* see Bertr. Born **3.38** n. In another poem (Shepard/Chambers
44.36 ff.), Aim. Peg. boasts that neither *Ectors ni Tideüs* could equal him in
jousts of love, but in one MS these names have been replaced by *Galvain ni*
Artus.   15 *Ivans:* Yvain, hero of *Le Chevalier au lion* (*Yvain*) by Chrétien
de Troyes; see Index of Proper Names, *s.v.* (rare exs. in other branches of the
lyric).   16 *Tristans:* see **1.30** f. n.

Aimeric de Peguilhan **3a**

Qui sofrir . . . (*canso*).
PC 10.46, D 800, Shepard/Chambers 46

e si·m fai tant amar   II 26
c'anc en plus greu balanssa
non fo Andrieus de Franssa.

[And it (*sc.* a new love) makes me love so much that Andrieu of France was never in a state of more grievous suspense.]

26–8: the last 3 ll. of a 14-l. stanza in a poem of five stanzas + *tornada*. 29 *Andrieus de Franssa*: see Raim. Jord. **2**.24 n.

Aimeric de Peguilhan **3b**

S'ieu tan ben . . . (*canso*).
PC 10.49, D 830, Shepard/Chambers 49

Quar m'es del cor tan pres,   III 25
sai be que desmezur;
mas son cors fresc e pur
fora dregz qu'en blasmes,
qu'es blancs aissi cum nieus,
qu'ieu, ges plus que N'Andrieus,   30
non ai poder di mi.

[For she is so close to my heart, I well know that I lack moderation, but it would be right that I should impute the blame to her fair and pure body, which is as white as snow, so that no more than sir Andrieu have I power over myself.]

25–31: the first 7 ll. of a 12-l. stanza in a poem of five stanzas + *tornada*. 30 *N'Andrieus*: see **3a**. 29 n.

Elias de Barjols **1**

Bon' aventura . . . (*canso*). PC 132.6, D 6670, ed. Stroński 9

Si tan gen muri Andrieus,   IV 28
non amet miels en son cor
qu'ieu fas lieys qu'ai encobida.

[If Andrieu died so well, he did not love more in his heart than I love her whom I have desired.]

28–30: the first 3 ll. of a 9-l. stanza in a poem of five stanzas + *tornada*. *Andrieus* is an isolated rhyme (*rim estramp*), rhyming only from stanza to stanza. 28 *Andrieus*: see Raim. Jord. **2**.24 n.   *gen*: because he died for love.

Pons de Capduelh **1a**

Qui per nesi cuidar . . . (*canso*). PC 375.18, D 20020, Napolski 6

Domna, genser qu'ieu sai,   VI 41
mais vos am ses bausia,
non fetz Tristanz s'amia,
e nuill pro non i ai.

[Lady, more excellent than any I know, I love you more without falsehood than Tristan loved his lady, and I have no advantage from it.]

41–4: the *tornada* of a poem of five stanzas.   43 *Tristanz s'amia*: see Raimb. Or. **1**.29 f. n.

Pons de Capduelh 1b

Astrucs es cel . . . (canso). PC 375.3, D 19870, Napolski 23

e pois en leis non faill neguna res   II   12
de tot quant taing a ric pretz cabalos,
be·m deu valer s'amors, car fis amans
li sui trop meillz non fo d'Iseut Tristans.

[And since in her nothing is lacking of all that which pertains to excellent supreme worth, love of her should indeed bring me advantage, for I am a faithful lover to her, far more than was Tristan to Iseut.]

12–15: ll. 3–6 of a 9-l. stanza in a poem of five stanzas + *tornada*.   15 *Iseut Tristans*: see **1a**.43 n.

Pons de Capduelh 2

Humils e francs . . . (canso). PC 375.10, D 19940, Napolski 15

Vostr'om son, domna gaja,   VI   41
et am vos mais que Landrics no fes Aja,
e sobre totz port las claus d'amar be,
per qu'ieu aillors non posc virar mon fre.

[I am your vassal, joyous lady, and I love you more than Landric loved Aja; above all others I hold the keys of loving well, so that I cannot turn my attention elsewhere.]

41–4: the *tornada* in a poem of five 8-l. stanzas.   44 *fre*: lit. 'reins'. 42 *Landrics . . . Aja*: see P. R. Tolosa **1**.32 n.

Guiraut de Calanso 1

Los grieus dezirs . . . (canso). PC 243.8a, D 12530, Ernst 1

Tezaur e gaug e dompna e senhor   VI   46
fas tot de vos e lais los mals d'alhor,
qu'anc non ac pus de son bel conquerir
jois ni plazers Sesars ni Alissandres.   49

[I make (my) treasure and joy and lady and lord wholly of you, and I abandon the sorrows of elsewhere, for never did Caesar or Alexander experience more joy or pleasure from their splendid conquests.]

46–9: the *tornada* in a poem of five 9-l. stanzas; *Alissandres* 49 is an isolated rhyme (*rim estramp*).   47 *los malhs d'alhor*: the sorrows attaching to another love.   49 *Sesars*: see Arn. Mar. **1**.29 n.   *Alissandres*: see Arn. Dan. **3**.21 n.; for Alexander in association with the motif of conquest see OF Anon. **11**.18 n.

A lament for the death in 1211, at the age of 21, of Ferdinand, son of Alfonso VIII:

Guiraut de Calanso **2**

Belh senher Dieus . . . (*planh*). PC 243.6, D 12500, Ernst 11

> Belh senher Dieus, quo pot esser sufritz   I   1
> tan estranhs dols cum es del jov'enfan,
> del filh del rei de Castella prezan,
> don anc nulhs oms jorn no·s parti marritz
> ni ses cosselh ni dezacosselhatz;   5
> qu'en lui era tot lo pretz restauratz
> del rei Artus, qu'om sol dir e retraire,
> on trobavan cosselh tug bezonhos.
> ar es mortz selh que degr'esser guizaire,
> lo mielhs del mon de totz los joves bos.

[Dear Lord God, how can such severe grief be borne as that for the young Infante, the esteemed son of the king of Castile, from whom no one ever departed sorrowful, without help or deprived of support, for in him was restored all the excellence of king Arthur, of whom men tell and narrate, in whom all the needy found help. Now he is dead, he who should be a guide, the best in the world of all good young men.]

The first stanza in a poem of five stanzas + *tornada*.　　　7 *Artus*: see Bertr. Born **3**.33 n.

Poets Writing in the Later Thirteenth Century

Falquet de Romans **1**

Ma bella dompna . . . (*canso*).
PC 156.8, D 7630, Arveiller/Gouiran 2

> qe meill no·n pres a Raol de Cambrais   I   6
> ne a Flori, qan poget el palais,
> com fez a mi, car soi fins et verais,
> 　　　ma bella dompna.
> [. . .]
> et morrai tot aissi com fes N'Andreus   II   16
> et valgra mais q'agues mort vint romeus,
> 　　　ma bella dompna.
> [. . .]
> qe per amor fu vencuz Salamos,   V   43
> aissi soi eu, cortesa res, per vos,
> 　　　ma bella dompna.

[For it did not fare better with Raoul de Cambrai or with Floris, when he ascended to the castle, than with me, for I am faithful and true, my beautiful lady. [. . .] And I shall die just as did Sir Andrieu, and it would be better that I should have killed twenty pilgrims, my beautiful lady. [. . .] For Solomon was vanquished by love, and so am I, courtly one, for you, my beautiful lady.]

6 ff., 16 f., 43 f.: the final ll. of an 8-l. stanza (in 43 f. of the final stanza), followed by the refrain phrase *ma bella dompna*, in a poem of five stanzas (the eds. number the refrain as l. 9 of each stanza). Each stanza has eightfold repetition of the same rhyme (I *-ais*; II *-eus*; V *-os*), which no doubt explains *romeus* in l. 17.   6 *Raol de Cambrais*: the hero of a *chanson de geste*, not usually cited as a lover; the name is no doubt explained by rhyming constraints (see above).   7 *Flori*: see Arn. Mar. **3b.**153 n.   16 *N'Andreus*: see Raim. Jord. **2.**24 n.   43 *Salamos*: for the theme of love's victims see Marc. **1.**14 n.

Falquet de Romans 2a

Una chanso sirventes . . . (*sirventes-canso*).
PC 156.14, D 76803, Arveiller/Gouiran 3

anc no fo de joi tan ricx   II   17
Floris, quan jac ab s'amia.

[Never was Floris so full of joy, when he lay with his loved one.]

17 f.: the last 2 ll. of a 9-l. stanza in a poem of five stanzas + *tornada*.   18 *Floris*: see **1.**7 n.

Falquet de Romans 2b

Cantar vuoill . . . (*canso*).
PC 156.3, D 7590, Arveiller/Gouiran 4

E sapciatç c'anc plus coralmen   III   17
non amet Floris Blanciflor
c'ieu am lieis ce·m val e·m socor.

[And know that Floris never loved Blancheflor so truly as I love her who benefits and sustains me.]

16–18: the first 3 ll. of an 8-l. stanza in a poem of four stanzas + *tornada*.
17 *Floris Blanciflor*: see **1.**7 n.

Falquet de Romans 3a

Domna, eu pren comjat . . . (*salut*).
PC p. 135, Arveiller/ Gouiran 14

qe tan vos soi ferms e leials   135
qe Tristan fo vers Ysout fals
contra mi, e vers Blanchaflor
Floris ac cor galiador.
[. . .]
e se·m teneç en tal balança,   181
compainz serai Andreu de França
qe mori per amor s'amia.

[For I am so firm in faith and loyal to you that Tristan was false to Iseut compared with me, and to Blancheflor Floris showed a treacherous heart. [. . .] And if you keep me in such suspense, I shall be the companion of Andrieu of France who died for love of his loved one.]

This poem is sometimes given the designation *comjat* 'poem of leave-taking', on the strength of its first line ('lady, I take leave of you'), but in subject-matter and structure it has all the characteristics of the *salut*, and is so designated in one MS (see Arveiller/Gouiran p. 155).   136 *Tristan . . . Ysout*: see Raimb. Or. **1.29** f. n.   137 f. *Blanchaflor . . . Floris*: see **1.7** n.   182 *Andreu de França*: see Raim. Jord. **2.24** n.

Falquet de Romans 3b

Aucel no truob . . . (*sirventes-canso*).
PC 156.2, D 7580, Arveiller/Gouiran 5

Tan l'am de bon talan   III   23
qe·l cor me ressautella;
    qez ainch no amet tan
Tristanz Ysolt la bella.

[So greatly do I love her with true intent that my heart trembles, for never did Tristan love Iseut the beautiful so greatly.]

23–6: the first 4 ll. of an 11-l. stanza in a poem of five stanzas + 2 *tornadas*. 26 *Tristanz Ysolt*: see **3a**.136 n.

Falquet de Romans 3c

Meravil me . . . (*canso*). Folq. Mars.
PC 155.13, D 7450, Arveiller/Gouiran 16

Q'ie·us sui garens   41
    plus vos am ses engan
no fetz Yseutz son bon amic Tristan.

[For I bear witness to you: I love you more without breach of faith than her dear friend Tristan loved Iseut.]

41–3: the *tornada* in a poem of five 8-l. stanzas.   43 *Yseutz . . . Tristan*: see **3a**.136 n.; for the word-order see Raim. Jord. **1.30** n.

The poem is attributed both to Folq. Mars. and Falq. Rom. (and also to Pons Capd.). Both Stroński in his ed. of Folq. Mars., and Arveiller/Gouiran in their ed. of Falq. Rom. include it under doubtful attributions (see in particular p. 195 of the latter ed. for a survey of the MS tradition). Since Folq. Mars. has no other instances of comparisons with named exemplars (see Folq. Mars. **1.39** f. n. on the incidence of representative types in comparisons in his work), whereas Falq. Rom. has several, including two referring to Tristan, the example has been included here, although the attribution remains uncertain.

Aimeric de Belenoi **1**

S'a midons plazia . . . (*descort*). PC 9.20, D 340, Poli 4

Que anc Hyris   III   46
Iorn de Biblis
No fo tan enveyos;

Ni Blancaflor   IV
Tan greu dolor   50
Per Flori non senti,
Quan de la tor
L'emperador
Per s'amistat eyssi,
Qu'ieu per amor   55
De la gensor
Vas cuy ieu vau cor cli,
Tan gran tristor
Senes secor
E per tal no·m defuy.   60

[For never was Hyris so desirous of Biblis, nor did Blancaflor feel such grievous sorrow – on account of Floris, when he came out of the emperor's tower for love of her – as the great sadness without remedy which I feel for the love of the most fair whom I approach with submissive heart – and yet I did not flee.]

Sections III and IV of the *descort* each contain 18 ll.; ll. 46–8 form the end of III, ll. 49–60 the first 12 ll. of IV.   46 f. *Hyris . . . Biblis*: see Poli, pp. 159 ff., and Arn. Mar. **3b**.169 f. n.   49 *Blancaflor*, 51 *Flori*: see Arn. Mar. **3b**.153 n. 52–4: the tower is that in which Blancheflor was imprisoned, but there is no episode in the extant versions of the story corresponding to these lines.

In this *salut* the poet, a woman, exhorts a lady to reinstate her lover in her favour, and in l. 6 gives her own name as *N'Azalais d'Altier*. Uc de St. Circ mentions *N'Azalais d'Autier* as the recipient of one of his songs (Jeanroy/ Salverda de Grave 14.46 f.), which permits an approximate dating of mid-13th century.

Azalais d'Altier **1**

Tanz saluts e tantas amors . . . (*salut*). PC 42a, Rieger, *Trobairitz* 43

ez aquil qe non o sabran,   55
cuidaran si qe per talan
q'autrui amar vos l'azires
e de vos amar lo lunges,
ez intrares in folla bruda,
si esz per canzairitz tenguda;   60
q'esqern fai de si mal retraire
Brizeida, qar ilh fo cangiaire
sos cors, qar laiset Troilus

per amar lo fil Tideus.
autressi·us er en mal retrach   65
si·us partes de lui sens forfach.

[And those who do not know will think that out of a desire to love another you hate him and debar him from loving you, and you will become the object of foolish rumour if you are held to be changeable; for scorn makes Briseida ill spoken of, because she was fickle, since she left Troilus to love the son of Tydeus (Diomedes). In the same way you will be ill spoken of, if you part from him without any transgression on his side.]

55 *non . . . sabran*: lit. 'will not know'.   58 lit.: 'distance him from loving you'.   62 ff. This unusual warning example is derived from an invented episode, without classical antecedent, in the *Roman de Troie*, which later served as source for *Il Filostrato* of Boccaccio and Chaucer's *Troilus and Criseyde*. The form *Brizeida* is a generalization of the accusative of the Greek name *Briseis*, but the figure here designated as *Brizeida* has no connection with the classical *Briseis*, referred to, for instance, in *Iliad* 12 and Propertius 7 and 8.   64 *lo fil Tideus*: in the *Roman de Troie* the appellation *li fiz Tideüs* occurs beside *Diomedés*.

Paulet de Marselha 1
                        Belha dompna . . . (dansa). PC 319.4, D 16630, I. de Riquer 9

Belha dompna plazens: Ay!   I 1
dic soven quar no·us ai,
quar vos am, que qu'ieu n'aya,
mais qu'Enricx no fes N'Aya.

[Beautiful, charming lady: Alas! I often say, since I do not possess you, for I love you, whatever may befall me in consequence, more than Enricx loved lady Aya.]

These lines form the head refrain in a poem of three 12-l. stanzas.
3 f. *n'aya*: *N'Aya*: a punning rhyme.   4 *Enricx*: substituted in the MS for *Landrics*; see P. R. Tolosa 1.32 n., and Pons Capd. 2.42.

Peire Cardenal 1
                        De tant tenc . . . (cobla). PC 461.79, D 25870 (Anon.), Lavaud 6

De tant tenc per nesci Andreu   I 1
car mori de zo don vieurai;
qu'el mon non a donna soz Dèu
qu'en traisses mal s'ela non trai.

[In this much I consider Andrieu foolish, because he died of that of which I shall live, for there is no lady in the world for whom I would suffer pains, if she does not suffer them.]

The first 4 ll. of a single 7-l. stanza.   1 *Andreu*: see Raim. Jord. 2.24 n.

Peire Cardenal 2

Alexandris fon . . . (coblas). PC 461.14, D 25330 (Anon.), Lavaud 83

Alexandris fon le plus conquerens   I   1
e le plus larcs de nostres ansesors,
e Tristantz fon de totz los amadors
lo plus leals e fes mais d'ardimens,
etz Ectors fon le meillers, ses falhensa,   5
de cavalliers en faz e en parvensa,
e plus cortes Gualvanz totes sazos,
e plus savis fon le reis Salamos.

Si eu agues aquetz bons fazemens,   II
miels m'estera c'als dos emperadors   10
ni als dos reis, sitot an grans onors
ni gran poder de terras ni d'argens,
que fora rix de bella captenensa,
larcx e leials et arditz ses temensa,
savis e pros, umilz e amoros,   15
e for'en Dieu servir m'entensios.

[Alexander was the greatest conqueror and the most liberal of our prede-
cessors, and Tristan was of all lovers the most true, and carried out most
bold deeds, and Hector was the best of knights, without a doubt, in deeds
and bearing, and Gauvain the most courtly at all times, and the most wise
was king Solomon. If I had these good accomplishments, I would be more
fortunate than the two emperors or the two kings, although they have
great honour, and are powerful in lands and wealth, for I would be rich
in good conduct, liberal and true and bold without fear, wise and valiant,
humble and dedicated to love, and to serve God would be my intent.]

These two stanzas make up the whole poem.   1 *Alexandris*: see Arn.
Dan. 3.21 n.; Gauc. Faid. 3.14 n.   3 *Tristantz*: see Raimb. Or. 1.29 f. n.
5 *Ectors*: rarely cited in the vernacular lyric (see Index of Proper Names, *s.v.*).
7 *Gualvanz*: see Bertr. Born 3.38 n.   8 *Salamos*: for Solomon as exemplar
of wisdom see Zorzi 1.60; Oc. Anon. 1.1.   10 f.: i.e. the German and
Byzantine emperors and the kings of France and England.

Bonifacio Calvo 1

Scotz, qals mais . . . (partimen). PC 101.11a, D 5590, Branciforti 19

mais vostres mals encomenza   IV   51
totz iornz e non pot fenir,
per qe vos er ses bistenza,
– zo·m par, e no·us pot fallir –
qom Tantalus a murir: 55
e d'aizo aiatz plivensa.

[But your trouble begins every day and has no end, so that you will be

bound without delay – so it seems to me, and it cannot fail to befall you –
to die like Tantalus, and of that be assured.]

51–6: the last 6 ll. of a 14-l. stanza in a poem of six stanzas.   55 *Tantalus*:
see Raimb. Vaq. **1**.20 n.

In a dispute between Scot and Bonifacio (described in the MS as a *tenzo*, but
in reality a *partimen*, with a set subject of debate), stanza IV contains the
reply of Scot to the assertion of Bonifacio that he would prefer to see and
talk to the lady, but not be allowed anything further, rather than enjoy her
love without seeing her or talking to her and never being loved in return, the
position adopted by his opponent.

Bartolomeo Zorzi **1**

S'ieu trobes . . . (*sirventes*). PC 74.15, D 3290, Levy 2

Domn', Amors m'a faig enprendre   VII   55
tan gran ponh' en vos amar
[. . .]
quar la beutatz d'Ansalon   59
e·l sabers de Salomon
si pod en vos conparar,
per qu'om no·s pot trop lauzar
ni·l vostr' onranz' escoissendre.

[Lady, Love has caused me to undertake a great endeavour in loving you
[. . .] for the beauty of Absalom and the wisdom of Solomon can be
equalled in you, so that one cannot praise you too much, or destroy your
honour.]

55–63: the first 2 ll. and last 5 ll. of the final stanza in a poem of seven
9-l. stanzas + 2 *tornadas*.   59 *Ansalon*: for the beauty of Absalon see 2
Sam. 14:25, and for the name, without ref. to the motif, Arn. Mar. **3b**.168.
60 *Salomon*: see Marc. **1**.14 n.   62 *no·s = no·us*.   63 *escoissendre*: lit.
'tear'; i.e. even inadequate praise cannot detract from the lady's honour. The
unusual choice of verb is dictated by the necessity to find three rhymes in
-*endre* in each of 7 stanzas, and one in each of the 2 *tornadas*.

Bartolomeo Zorzi **2**

Atressi cum lo camel . . . (*canso*). PC 74.2, D 3160, Levy 3

Don per calor e per gel   III   33
senes voluntat truanda
m'auretz mielhs que dieus Abel
non ac a son mandamen.

[. . .]

car si neis ma mortz vos platz,   VIII   118
ieu la volh sofrir en patz,
          car ie·us am
mais que no fetz Sarra Abram.   121

[Therefore through fire and ice, without base desire, you will hold me more firmly than God held Abel in his power. [...] For if even my death is pleasing to you, I am ready to suffer it in patience, for I love you more than Abraham loved Sarah.]

33–6: the first 4 ll. of a 16-l. stanza in a poem of seven stanzas + 2 *tornadas*; 118–21: the last 4 ll. of the first *tornada*, which is made up of 9 ll.   35 *Abel* (see Peire Vid. **6.**30 n.), 121 *Sarra Abram*: the comparisons, with the names in rhyme, are no doubt prompted by rhyming constraints. Each of the seven stanzas has the rhyme *-el* : *-el* in ll.1 and 3, and each of the seven stanzas and both *tornadas* conclude with the rhyme *-am* : *-am*, with the name *Abram* occurring in rhyme also in II.31.   121 For the word-order, with the subject at the end of the clause and line, see Raim. Jord. **1.**30 n.

In addition to the biblical comparisons, stanza IV of the poem refers to the Tristan story and that of Roland; ll. 50–4: *l'amoroseta bevanda* | *non feric* ... | *Tristan n'Iseut plus fortmen,* | ... *cum ilh me ab doutz purven* (the love potion did not wound Tristan and Iseut as grievously ... as she has wounded me with her beautiful appearance); ll. 55–60 my only desire has been to do what pleases her, and if I was given leave to do so, I experienced greater joy than Roland formerly received from Aude: 60 *qu'anz non pres d'Alda Rotlan* (an isolated rhyme); see also Guir. Sal. **2.**16.

Cerverí de Girona **1**

> *Cosselhier, bail' e jutge* ... (*sirventes*).
> PC 434.3, D 22740, ed. Coromines 106

La don' als Cartz e Sobrepretz an sen;   VII 45
e nostre Reys, cor, ab mais d'ardimen
qu'Alixandres, Oliviers ne Rotlans:
qu'ab pauc dels sieus, es fortz otra·ls pus grans.

[The lady of the Thistles and Sobrepretz have good sense, and our king a heart with more bravery than Alexander, Oliver or Roland, for with few of his followers he is powerful beyond the greatest men.]

45–8: the second of two *tornadas* in a poem of five 8-l. stanzas.   45 *la don' als Cartz*: the wife of the Viscount of Cardona, referred to by the family's heraldic emblem of the thistle.   46 *nostre Reys*: the king of Aragon, either James I, d. 1276, or Peter III, 1276–85.   47 *Alixandres*: see Arn. Dan. **3.**21 n.; *Oliviers*: see Guir. Born. **2.**40 n.; *Rotlans*: see Arn. Mar. **4.**44 n.

Cerverí de Girona **2**

> *Ar' agues eu* ... (*sirventes*). PC 434a.3, D 23030, ed. Coromines 75

Almenz pendray aytan d'enfortimen,   V 29
pus le moutos lo pres contra·l fort ors,
que li diray: "vos am e vos azor
e vos mercey"; e si d'ayço·m repren
car li suy fis, leyals e vertaders,

> eu li diray que totz aytals volers
> s'es mes en mi d'amor, con en Tristan.   35

[At least I will take so much courage, since the sheep took courage when confronting the strong bear, to say to her: "I love and adore you and plead for mercy"; and if she reproaches me on that account, since I am faithful, loyal and true towards her, I will say to her that just such a desire born of love has established itself in me as in Tristan.]

The final stanza in a poem of five stanzas + 2 *tornadas*. *Tristan* is an isolated rhyme.   35 *Tristan*: see Raimb. Or. **1**.29 f. n.

Cerverí de Girona 3

En may . . . (*pastorela*). PC 434.6b, D 22800, ed. Riquer 13

> Car Floris ab Blanxaflor   II   13
> ne Paris ne Elena
> no·m pogren dar gaug major . . .

[For Floris together with Blancaflor, nor Paris nor Helen could give me greater joy . . .]

13 *Floris* . . . *Blanxaflor*: see Arn. Mar. **3b**.153 n.   14 *Paris* . . . *Elena*: see Raim. Jord. **1**.28 n.

The MS text of this stanza is unsatisfactory. Coromines (no. 89) emends ll. 13–15 so that they read 'for Blancheflor to Floris, nor Helen to Paris could give greater joy . . .', which is more rational, but requires too much editorial intervention. Since what is important is the names of the famous lovers, and their placing at the head of the stanza, two of them in rhyme, the more conservative text of Riquer has been preferred, and the example restricted to the first three lines of the 12-l. stanza.

Guilhem Raimon de Gironela 1

Gen m'apareill . . . (*canso*).
PC 230.1, D 11060, Appel, *Prov. Inedita*, p. 148

> car es de bos aips complida,   V   45
>   deu esser enantida
>   sa valors, s'ap si m'acueill;
> enquer er meils que d'Enida,
> can Erecs l'ac enrequida,
>   quar mais la tem e l'am meils.   50

[Since she has the sum of praiseworthy qualities, her worth will be enhanced if she admits me to her favour; it will be even greater than that of Enida, when Erec had exalted her in rank, for I revere her more and love her more truly.]

25–50: the final 6 ll. of the last of five 10-l. stanzas, followed by a *tornada*. 45 *complida*: lit. 'full', but also with the sense of 'complete', 'perfect'(see Raimb. Vaq. **2d**.78).   48 f. *Enida* . . . *Erecs* – see Raimb. Vaq. **2d**.81 n. 49 *enrequida* lit. 'made more powerful/rich', i.e. when he made her his queen.

Of Uncertain Date

Daude de Pradas (?) **1**

Sitot m'ai pres . . . (canso). Bernart
de Pradas PC 65.3, D 2560 (one MS only),
Schutz, Appendice 1, p. 87

quar viu d'Amor et ab luy renh,   I 5
que daus totz latz me li' e·m senh,
per qu'ieu totz temps la servirai,
que d'als no·m pens ni puesc ni·m plai,
qu'em poder m'a quon ac Andrieu:
Dieu prec, no·n prenda dan tan grieu.   10
[. . .]
Beure·m fai ab l'enap Tristan   III 21
Amors, e eisses los pimens,
e si·n des a lieys, qu'ieu am tan,
obrera·n plus cortezamens,
quar sols suy sieus, sol mi destrenh.   25

[For I live on love and dwell with it, for on every hand it binds and sets its mark on me; therefore I will always serve it, for I can think, do, or take pleasure in nothing other, since it has me in its power as it had Andrieu: I pray God that I may not suffer such grievous injury from it. [. . .] Love causes me to drink from Tristan's goblet and (to partake of) the same spiced potion, and if it were to administer it to her, whom I love so much, it would act in a more fitting manner, for I alone am its captive, and I alone the one whom it constrains.]

5–10: the last 6 ll. of stanza I; 21–5: the first 5 ll. of stanza III. The poem consists of five 10-l. stanzas + *tornada*.   9 *Andrieu*: see Raim. Jord. 2.24 n. 21 *Tristan*: see Raimb. Or. 1.29 n.   22 *los pimens*: the pl. of *pimen* 'spice', 'spiced drink'.

Uc de Pena **1**

Si anc me fe amors . . . (canso).
PC 456.2, D 24720, Appel, Prov. Inedita, p. 313

Anc Lanselotz, quan sa dona·l promes   III 25
que faria per elh tot son coman,
si·l mostrava un fin' leial aman,
no poc aver de si eix sovinensa,
bona domna, ta fort s'er' oblidatz,
tro que merces lo y ac adregz esguartz   30
lay on razos non li valia re,
per qu'ieu aten de vos aital merce.

[Lancelot too, when his lady promised him that she would grant all his wishes, if he showed himself towards her a true, faithful lover, lost all awareness of himself, excellent lady, so greatly had he become distracted, until mercy had rightly looked on him with favour, there where reason was of no avail to him – therefore I expect like mercy from you.]

The third stanza in a poem of five stanzas + *tornada*.   26: lit. 'that she would do for him all he asked'.

The poet draws a parallel between himself and Lancelot, the hero of the *Chevalier de la Charette* of Chrétien and of vastly expanded 13th-c. versions of the exploits of Lancelot, e.g. in the OF Prose Lancelot. As the poet is robbed of all power by the lady's beauty and can only be rescued from his suffering by mercy, so Lancelot was plunged into distraction by his overwhelming love for queen Guinivere, but after many trials was restored by mercy. There is an indirect reference to the sufferings of Lancelot (unnamed) in an Anon. *salut* (M. Pelaez, *Studi Romanzi* 16 (1921), p. 69: *souenz mi fai morir e viure,* | *si com fist la reina Geniure* | *uns dels chavaliers de sa cortz* (often it causes me to die and live, as queen Guinivere caused one of the knights of her court to die and live). See OF Gille Vin. **1**.33 f. n.; Sicil. Anon. **4**.57 n.; *Mar. Am.* **3**.31 ff. n.

Jordan Bonel **1**

Anc mais aissi . . . (canso).
PC 273.1a, D 14870, Kolsen, *Archiv* 142 (1921), pp. 130–5

Ai, si m'auci, per tal coven morrei,   VI   31
qu'aissi s'en vai l'arma tot en rizen.
anc gensor fi no fetz hom qu'ieu farei,
mas ad Andrieu en pres tot eissamen,
　　car elh mori d'aital esfrei: 35
　　ma don'auci atressi me.

[Ah, if she kills me, I will die in such a manner that the soul will thus depart smiling. No man ever made a better end than I shall make, but just the same fate befell Andrieu, for he died of such distress: my lady kills me likewise.]

The final stanza in a poem of six stanzas + *tornada*.   31 *per tal coven*: lit. 'through such an agreement/resolve', i.e. the poet is resolved to die a beautiful death for the sake of love.   34 *Andrieu*: see Raim. Jord. **2**.24 n.

Oc. Anon. **1**

Lo sen volgra . . . (cobla). PC 461.154, D 26550, Kolsen 1917, p. 294

Lo sen volgra de Salamo   1
e de Rotlan lo ben-ferir
e l'astre de sel qe pres Tir
e la gran forssa de Samso
e que sembles Tristan d'amia   5
e Galvanh de cavalaria

e·l bon saber de Merlin volgra mai
qu'eu feira dret del tort que vei c'om fai.

[I could wish for the intellect of Solomon and the power to strike of
Roland, and the favourable star of him who captured Tyre (Alexander),
and the great strength of Samson, and that I might resemble Tristan in
the matter of love and Gauvain in chivalry, and further I could wish for
the knowledge of Merlin, so that I could put right the wrong I see men
doing.]

A single stanza.   1 *Salamo*: see Marc. 1.14 n.   2 *Rotlan*: see Arn. Mar.
4.44 n.   3 *sel qe pres Tir*: see *Alixandres*, Arn. Dan. **3.21 n.**   4 *Samso*: see
Marc. **1.14 n.**   5 *Tristan*: see Raimb. Or. 1.29 f. n.; *d'amia*: lit. 'in respect
of a loved one'.   6 *Galvanh*: see Bertr. Born 3.38 n.   7 *Merlin*: the
diviner and magician of the Arthurian cycle.

Oc. Anon. 2

Bona dona . . . (*cobla*). PC 461.58,
D 25680, see Bartsch, *ZRP* 4 (1890), p. 510,
Kolsen, 1939, p. 190

Bona dona, vostre preç fo triaç,   I   1
plus fo traiç lo jorn e enganaç
non fo Tristan, qe d'amor fo temptatz,
eç eu qe bic del vin qe fo tempraç,
e fo tan fortz qe mos cors fo turbaç,   5
si qe anc pois non fo treis jorns en paç,
ni anc convenç no fo per mi trencaç.

[Esteemed lady, your worth was supreme; I was betrayed and deceived by
love that day more than was Tristan, who was led astray by love, and I
drank of the wine which was tempered, and it was so powerful that my
heart was thrown into confusion, so that ever after I was not at peace for
the space of three days, nor was the bond ever broken by me.]

A single stanza, the vocabulary and syntax of which are no doubt largely determined by the choice of a decasyllabic line with monorhyme in -*aç*; Bartsch (B)
prints a diplomatic text, Kolsen (K) emends too drastically.   1 *bona dona*
B: *si be, dona* K (the introduction of the concessive conjunction 'although'
is inappropriate in the largely paratactic structure of the stanza).   *triaç*: lit.
'chosen', 'singled out'.   3 *Tristan* B: *Tristans* K; see Raimb. Or. 1.29 f. n.
4 *Eç eu qe bic del uin qe fo tempraç* B: *E bic del vin, qe ges no fo tempraç* K (the
introduction of the negative *no* destroys the sense); the relative pronoun *qe*
(disregarded in the translation) seems syntactically redundant (but without
it the line lacks the necessary number of 10 syllables, strictly observed in the
other lines).   *tempraç*: i.e. the wine was modified by an element making it
into a love potion.

Oc. Anon. 3

Si trobes tan leial messatge (designated in the text, l. 11, as *complainta*).
Kolsen, *SM* 10 (1937), 193–203

e trauch per vos trop major pena   111
que no fesz Paris per Helena;
ni Floris, Herecs ni Tristantz,
ni Andrieus ne nuillz fins amantz
no trais tan grant mal per amor   115
q'ieu no·l traga cen tantz pejor.

[And I suffer for your sake far greater pains than Paris suffered for the sake of Helen; neither Floris, Erec, nor Tristan, nor Andrieu or any other perfect lover suffered such great sorrow for the sake of love, but I suffer it a hundred time worse.]

A poem of 194 lines in couplets.   112 *Paris . . . Helena*: see Raim. Jord.
1.28 n.   113 *Floris*: see Arn. Mar. 3b.153 n.   *Herecs*: see Raimb. Vaq.
2d. 81 n.   *Tristantz*: see Raimb. Or. 1. 29 f. n.   114 *Andrieus*: see Raim.
Jord. 2.24 n.

Conclusion

Most of the exemplary comparisons cited occur in instances of the *canso* on the theme of love. In addition, the following types of poem are represented among the examples: *sirventes*: Gar. Apch. 1; Peire Vid. 2; Zorzi 1; Cerverí 1; Cerverí 2; *sirventes-canso*: Peire Vid. 3; Peire Vid. 4; Peire Vid. 5b; Raimb. Vaq. 5; Falq. Rom. 2a; Falq. Rom. 3b; *coblas* (single or paired stanzas): Peire Card. 1; Peire Card. 2; Oc. Anon. 1; Oc. Anon. 2; *planh*: Bertr. Born 3; Guir. Born. 2; Gauc. Faid. 3; Aim. Peg. 2; Guir. Cal. 2; *tenso*: Marc. 1; *partimen*: Calvo 1; *salut*: Arn. Mar. 3a; Arn. Mar. 3b; Arn. Mar. 4; Falq. Rom. 3a (see n.); Azalais 1; Oc. Anon. 3, designated in the text as *complainta*, is similar to a *salut*; the epic letter Raimb. Vaq. 4 also has some formal similarity to a *salut*, but with panegyric of a male subject; *descort*: Raimb. Vaq. 2b; Aim. Bel. 1; *estampida*: Raimb. Vaq. 2d; *dansa* + refrain: Paul. Mars. 1; *alba*: Uc Bac. 1; *pastorela*: Cerverí 3. That exemplary comparisons were considered a stylistic adornment is indicated by the fact that a number of poets employ them in more than one poem.[5] This is in marked contrast to the trouvère lyric, in which a single poem containing an exemplary comparison is the norm.

Most examples express comparison (or contrast) with an exemplar, but as in the classical poets, a comparison may be made, not directly with the figure itself, but with one or more of its attributes. This occurs frequently in the

---

[5] See Rig. Berb.; Bern. Vent.; Raim. Jord.; Arn. Mar.; Arn. Dan.; Bertr. Born; Guir. Born.; Guir. Sal.; Gauc. Faid.; Peire Vid.; Guil. Magr.; Raimb. Vaq.; Comt. Dia; Raim. Mir.; Aim. Peg.; Pons Capd.; Guir. Cal.; Falq. Rom.; Peire Card.; Zorzi; Cerverí.

context of panegyric. There are several instances in a *planh*: Richard Cœur de Lion surpassed the generosity of Alexander and the excellence of Charlemagne and Arthur (Gauc. Faid. **3**); the Marquis of Malespina exceeded Alexander in generosity, Gauvain in chivalry, Yvain in courtliness and Tristan in love (Aim. Peg. **2**); the Infante Ferdinand possessed all the renown of Arthur (Guir. Cal. **2**). The Marquis of Montferrat has the generosity of Alexander, the bold spirit of Roland, and the courtly manners of Berart (Raimb. Vaq. **4**); the king of Aragon is braver than Alexander, Oliver, and Roland (Cerverí **1**); the poet's lady possesses the beauty of Absalom and the wisdom of Solomon (Zorzi **1**). Other instances are associated with the poet himself: he equals Roland and Oliver in boldness, and Berart de Mondesdier in the service of ladies (Peire Vid. **2**); his deeds in the Holy Land would outstrip those of Alexander (**3**). Two examples are expressed in hypothetical form: if the poet possessed the qualities of Alexander, Tristan, Hector, Gauvain and Solomon, he would be more fortunate than reigning kings and emperors (Peire Card. **2**); the poet wishes for the intellect of Solomon, the fighting power of Roland, the good fortune of Alexander, the strength of Samson, the love of Tristan, the chivalry of Gauvain, and the knowledge of Merlin, in order to right the wrongs of the world (Oc. Anon. **1**). There is one unusual example: in creating his imaginary lady, Bertr. Born (**1**) seeks out the hair of lady Agnes which exceeds that of Iseut in beauty.[6] Bern. Vent. **3** is an unique example, in that the lady's kiss is compared with the wound inflicted by the lance of Peleus.

By contrast with the classical poets, there are very few instances of identification with an exemplar. The clearest example is *una gaia fresca Elena* in Bertr. Born **2a**, which identifies the lady praised with Helen – see also *pro na Lana* in **2b**, with a s*enhal*[7] based on an abbreviated form of the name. In Peire Vid. **5a** and **5b**, the name *Artus*, that of the son of Geoffrey of Brittany, prompts identification with the legendary Arthur, whose return the Bretons await. Possession of the name confers on Arthur of Brittany the qualities of its original bearer: now that the Bretons have a new Arthur, they need no longer await the old.

Exemplary comparisons are associated with a range of themes, which are of two main types: firstly, the poet's love, grief, or joy is equal to, or exceeds that of famous lovers; secondly, the subjects of panegyric or lament, or on occasion the poet himself, equal or surpass named exemplars, either in their entirety or in their individual characteristics. There are also specific motifs attaching to the theme of love, and exemplified in particular figures. The nature of love is excessive: *Dedalus* Rig. Berb. **1**. It is ineluctable, like the attraction induced by

---

[6] This has some similarity to the classical motif of hair which a god would desire – see Ovid **4** and **15**, Ripoll **1**, **2**, **3** and n.

[7] The names of exemplary figures may be used elsewhere as a *senhal*, e.g *Tristan*, Bertr. Born, 25.52, 57; *Floris*, Comt. Dia 34.33; see also n. on *Hygnaure*, Guir. Born. **2**.

the love potion: *Tristan* Raimb. Or. **1**. It robs the poet of his senses or strength: *Persavaus* Rig. Berb. **2**; *Narcisus* Bern.Vent. **1**; *Narcis* Peirol **1**; *N'Andrieus* Aim. Peg. **3b**; *Lanselotz* Uc Pena **1**. It will cause the poet's death: *Nicola de Bar* Raim. Jord. **3**; *Andrieu* Guil. Magr. **1**; Jord. Bon. **1**; *N'Andreus* Falq. Rom. **1**; *Andreu de França* Falq. Rom. **3a** – see also Daude Prad. (?) **1**; *Tantalus* Raimb. Vaq. **1**; Calvo **1**. Love is preferable to power: *Alixandres* Arn. Dan. **3**. It is associated with secrecy: *Tristan* Raimb. Or. **1**; Raimb. Vaq. **2b**. It subjected famous victims: *Samson* Marc. **1**; *Salamo, Davi, Samso* Peire Vid. **1**; *Salamos* Falq. Rom. **1**. It is surprising that exemplary comparisons hardly occur in connection with the theme of beauty, or in general praise of the lady, perhaps because of the predominance of male exemplars, but see *Elena* Arn. Mar. **2**; Bertr. Born **2a**, and *Lana* **2b**; *Iseuz* Bertr. Born **1**; *Ansalon* Zorzi **1**; *Enida* Guil. R. Giron. **1**.

Exemplary figures may have more than one function. In Rig. Berb. **2**, Perceval exemplifies mental distraction, in Raimb. Vaq. **1**, joy. In Bern.Vent. **1**, Narcissus illustrates the fatal power of love, in Peirol **1** its folly. Samson is cited as a victim of love in Marc. **1** and Peire Vid. **1**, but in Arn. Mar. **4** and Oc. Anon. **1** as an example of great strength. Solomon is likewise a victim of love in Peire Vid. **1**, but an exemplar of wisdom in Peire Card. **2**, Zorzi **1**, and Oc. Anon. **1**. Alexander exemplifies power in Arn. Dan. **3**, feats of arms in Peire Vid. **3** and Raimb. Vaq. **5**, joy in his conquests in Guir. Cal. **1**, and liberality in Gauc. Faid. **3**, Raimb. Vaq. **4**, and Aim. Peg. **2**.

Comparison with exemplary figures may include brief reference to narrative motifs or episodes: Perceval at the Grail castle, Rig. Berb. **2**; his encounter with the Red Knight, Raimb. Vaq. **1**; Emenadus and the assault on Tyre, Raimb. Vaq. **1**; Tristan and the love potion, Raimb. Or. **1**; Aim. Peg. **1**; Daude Prad. (?) **1**; Oc. Anon. **2**; his secret assignations with Iseut, Raimb. Vaq. **2b**; the fate of Narcissus, Bern. Vent. **1**; Peirol **1**; the amphibious existence of Nicola de Bar, Raim. Jord. **3**; Golfier de las Tors and the lion, Guil. Magr. **2**; Floris at the palace, Gauc. Faid. **1**; Falq. Rom. **1**; issuing from the tower, Aim. Bel. **1** (see n.); Ferragu's vulnerable spot, Raimb. Vaq. **3a**; Thibaut's treaty with Louis, Raimb. Vaq. **3b**; Brizeida's abandonment of Troilus, Azalais **1**; Lancelot's mental distraction, Uc Pena **1**; see also Folq. Mars. **1**.39 f. n.

The exemplary figures cited by the troubadours are derived from the following main sources: classical literature and legend, usually, however, transmitted through medieval adaptations, e.g. the *roman d'antiquité*, the OF *Pyramus et Tisbé*, and *Narcisus*; the Bible; historical legend (but the historical names were probably known chiefly from poetic works); the *Roman d'Alexandre*; the *chanson de geste* and related works; the Arthurian romances; the Tristan story; other medieval narratives, including some now lost. There are a few unusual examples: *Nicola de Bar*, the hero of a Sicilian folk tale in Raim. Jord. **3**; *Brizeida*, the heroine of an invented episode without classical precedent in the *Roman de Troie*, in Azalais 1; a hero of the first Crusade, *Golfier de las Tors*, in Guil. Magr. 2.[8]

Classical literature and legend: *Pelaus* Bern. Vent. 3; *Antigona* Arn. Mar. 3a; *Biblis* Arn. Mar. 3a; 3b (+*Iris*); Aim. Bel. 1 (+*Hyris*); *Dedalus* Rig. Berb. 1; *Elena* Arn. Mar. 2; 3a; Bertr. Born 2a (see also *Lana* 2b); *Paris – Elena* Arn. Mar. 3b; Arn. Dan. 1; Guir. Born. 1; Guil. Ad. 1; Cerverí 3; Oc. Anon. 3; *Elena – al fraire Ector* Raim. Jord. 1; *Ectors* Peire Card. 2; *Esmena* Arn. Mar. 3a; *Hero – Leander* Raim. Jord. 1; Arn. Mar. 3b; *Lavina – Eneas* Arn. Mar. 3b; *Leida* Arn. Mar. 3a; *Narcisus* Bern. Vent. 1; Peirol 1; *Ociocles* (=*Etiocles*) Arn. Mar. 3b; *Talant' e Meleagre* Arn. Dan. 2; *Serena* (=Seneca) Guir. Ros 1; *Tantalus* Raimb. Vaq. 1; Calvo 1; *Tibes* Arn. Mar. 3a; *Pirramus – Titban* Arn. Mar. 3b; Guir. Sal. 1; Raimb. Vaq. 1. *Brizeida* Azalais 1 is derived fom the classical name *Briseis* (see n.). For the figure of Midas (unnamed) see Folq. Mars. 1.39 f. n.

The Bible: *Abel* Peire Vid. 6; Zorzi 1; *Absalon* Arn. Mar. 3b; Zorzi 1; *Davi* Peire Vid. 1; *Jacobs – Rachel* Peire Vid. 6; *Salomo* Peire Vid. 1, Peire Card. 2; Zorzi 1; Oc. Anon. 1; *Samson* Marc. 1; Arn. Mar. 4; Peire Vid. 1; Oc. Anon. 1; *Sarra – Abram* Zorzi 2.

Historical legend: *Cleopatras* Arn. Mar. 3b (or perhaps from the *Roman d'Alexandre*, see 3b.156 f. n.); *Juli Cezar* Arn. Mar. 1; *Sesars* Guir. Cal. 1; *Semiramis* Arn. Mar. 3a.

The *Roman d'Alexandre*: *Alixandres* Arn. Dan. 3; Gauc. Faid. 3; Peire Vid. 3; Raimb. Vaq. 4; 5; Aim. Peg. 2; Guir. Cal. 1; Peire Card. 2; Cerverí 1; *sel qe pres Tir* Oc. Anon. 1; *Emenadus* Raimb. Vaq. 1.

The *chanson de geste* and related works: *Aimerics* Raimb. Vaq. 5; *Amelis* Uc Bac. 1; *Berart de Mondesdier* Peire Vid. 2; *Berart* Raimb. Vaq. 4; *Karles* Gauc. Faid. 3; Raimb. Vaq. 5; *Ferragutz* Raimb. Vaq. 3a; *Guis de Nantuelh – Ayglentina* Raimb. Vaq. 2a; *Lodoyc(s)* Raimb. Vaq. 3b; 5; *Raol de Cambrais* Falq. Rom. 1; *Tibauz* Raimb. Vaq. 3b; *Oliviers* Guir. Born. 2; *Rolant* Arn. Mar. 4; Raimb. Vaq. 4; 5; Oc. Anon. 1; *Olivier – Rothlan* Gar. Apch. 1; Peire Vid. 2; Cerverí 1; *Auda – Rotlan* Guir. Sal. 2; Zorzi 2.121 n.

Arthurian romances: *Artus* Bertr. Born 3; Gauc. Faid. 3; Peire Vid. 5a; 5b; Guir. Cal. 2; *Erecs – Enida* Raimb. Vaq. 2d; Guil. R. Giron. 1; *Herecs* Oc. Anon. 3; *Persavaus* Rig. Berb. 2; Raimb. Vaq. 1; *Galvain* Bertr. Born 3; Peire Vid. 4; Raimb. Vaq. 3c; Aim. Peg. 2; Peire Card. 2; Oc. Anon. 1; *Ivans* Aim. Peg. 2; *Lanselotz* Uc Pena 1; *Merlin* Oc. Anon. 1.

The Tristan story: *Tristan(s)* Uc Bac. 1; Aim. Peg. 2; Peire Card. 1; Daude Prad. (?) 1; Oc. Anon. 1 (see 5 n.); Oc. Anon. 2; Oc. Anon. 3; *Tristan – Izeut* Bern. Vent. 2; Arn. Mar. 3b; Raimb. Vaq. 2b; Pons Capd. 1b; Falq. Rom. 3a;

---

[8] In the following lists most orthographical variants and the varying order of paired names are disregarded after the first example under each name or pair of names. Figures customarily paired are listed separately if they also occur singly.

3b; **3c**; *la bell' a cui servi Tristans* Raim. Mir. **1**; *s'amia* – *Tristan* Raim. Mir. **2**; Aim. Peg. **1**; Pons Capd. **1a**.

Floire et Blancheflor: *Blancaflor* Arn. Mar. **3a**; *Floris* (for the form with final -*s*, see Arn. Mar. **3b**.153 n.) Gauc. Faid. **1**; Uc Bac. **1**; Falq. Rom. **1**; Oc. Anon. **3**; *Floris* – *Blancaflor* Arn. Mar. **3b**; Raimb. Vaq. **2c**; Comt. Dia. **1** (the female speaker identifies herself with *Floris*, not with *Blanchaflor*); Falq. Rom. **2b**; **3a**; Aim. Bel. **1**; Cerverí **3**; *Floris* – *s'amia* Falq. Rom. **2a**.

The story of Apollonius of Tyre: *cel qe fo reis de Tir* Arn. Mar. **3b**.

Lost narratives: *Andrieu(s)* Guil. Magr. **1**; Aim. Peg. **3b**; El. Barj. **1**; Falq. Rom. **1**; Peire Card. **1**; Daude Prad. (?) **1**; Jord. Bon. **1**; Oc. Anon. **3**; *Andrieus de Paris* Uc Bac. **1**; *Andrius de Fransa* Raimb. Vaq. **2b**; Aim. Peg. **3a**; *Andrius* – *la reina de Fransa* Raim. Jord. **2**; Gauc. Faid. **2**; *Andreus* – *la reyna* Raimb. Vaq. **2a**; *Andreu de França* – *s'amia* Falq. Rom. **3a**; *Berenguiers* – *Quendis* Arn. Mar. **3b**; *Valensa* – *Seguis* Arn. Mar. **3b**; Comt. Dia **2** (see n. on names); *Landrics* – *Aya* P. R. Tolosa **1**; Pons Capd. **2**; Paul. Mars **1** (see **4** n.).

Medieval legend: *Nicola de Bar* Raim. Jord. **3**; *Golfier de las Tors* Guil. Magr. **2**.

As in the classical poets, where it is extremely common, a circumlocution or generic designation may replace the name: *al fraire Ector* Raim. Jord. **1**; *cel qe fo reis de Tir* Arn. Mar. **3b**; *la bell' a cui servi Tristans* Raim. Mir. **1**; *s'amia* Raim. Mir. **2**; Aim. Peg. **1**; Pons Capd. **1a**; Falq. Rom. **2a**, in the first three instances designating Yseut, in the last Blancheflor; *sel qe pres Tir* Oc. Anon. **1**. All these examples are occasioned by metrical constraints, permitting *Tristan(s)* to appear in rhyme in Raim. Mir. **1** and **2**, and placing the paraphrases themselves in rhyme in the other cases. Folq. Mars. **1**.29 f. *c'aissi m'es pres cum al fol qeridor | que dis c'aurs fos tot qant el tocaria* is a special case, in which the circumlocution is used to obscure the identity of the specific exemplar usually associated with the narrative details, replacing it with a generalized type.

Famous lovers are usually cited in pairs, but there are also instances where the female name (or a circumlocution representing it) is omitted: Gauc. Faid. **1**; Guil. Magr. **1**; Raimb. Vaq. **2b**.24 ff.; Uc Bac. **1**; Aim Peg. **3a**; **3b**; El. Barj. **1**; Falq. Rom. **1**.7,16; Peire Card. **1**; **2**.3; Daude Prad. (?) **1**.9,21; Jord. Bon. **1**; Oc. Anon. **2**; Oc. Anon. **3**.113 f. Figures may be grouped together. There are double pairs of lovers in *Elena* – *al fraire Ector . . . Hero* – *Leander* Raim. Jord. **1**, and *Floris* – *Blanxaflor . . . Paris* – *Elena* Cerverí **3**; three pairs in *Tristan* – *Ysout, Blanchaflor* – *Floris, Andreu de França* – *s'amia* in Falq. Rom. **3a**; four male figures in *Andrieus de Paris, Floris, Tristans ni Amelis* Uc Bac. **1**, and lists of female figures in Arn. Mar. **3a**, and of paired lovers in **3b**, made up of classical and medieval names, with the addition in **3b** of *Absalon*, and of legendary/historical names; Oc. Anon. **3** combines the classical names *Paris* – *Helena* with the medieval names *Floris, Herecs, Tristantz, Andrieus*. Other figures appearing together in particular contexts, are: *Rolant o Sanson* Arn.

Mar. 4; *Artus . . . Galvain* Bertr. Born 3; *Sesars ni Alissandres* Guir. Cal. 1; *Ansalon . . . Salomon* Zorzi 1. There are also larger groupings: *Alixandres . . . Karles ni Artus* Gauc. Faid. 3; *Salamo et Davi . . . e·l fort Samso* Peire Vid. 1; *Rotlan et Olivier e . . . Berart de Mondesdier* Peire Vid. 2; *Aleyxandres . . . Rotlan e·lh dotze par e·lh pros Berart* Raimb. Vaq. 4; *Alixandres . . . ni Carles ni·l reis Lodoics . . . ni·l pros n'Aimerics ni Rotlans* Raimb. Vaq. 5; *Alexandres . . . Galvains . . . Tristans . . . Ivans* Aim. Peg. 2; *Alexandris . . . Tristantz . . . Ectors . . . Gualvanz . . . le reis Salamos* Peire Card. 2; *Alixandres, Oliviers ne Rotlans* Cerverí 1; *Salamo . . . Rotlan . . . sel qe pres Tir . . . Samso . . . Tristan . . . Galvanh . . . Merlin* Oc. Anon. 1.

In most poems the exemplary comparison or comparisons are contained within one stanza or part of a stanza, but there are also instances in which other stanzas of the poem contain further examples: Peire Vid. 6. II *Sant Gabriel*; III *Abel*; V *Jacobs – Rachel*; Raimb. Vaq. 1.II *Tisbe – Pyramus*; III *Persivals, Tantalus*; IV *Emenadus*; Raimb. Vaq. 2a.II *Guis de Nantuelh – Ayglentina*; IV *Andrieus – la reyna*; Raimb. Vaq. 2b (*descort*), II *Andreus de Fransa*; VI *Tristans . . . Yzeus*; Falq. Rom. 1.I *a Raol de Cambrais ne a Flori*; II *N'Andreus*; V *Salamos*; Zorzi 2.III *Abel*; IV (see 121 n.) *Tristan*; *Alda – Rotlan*; VIII *Sarra – Abram*; Daude Prad. (?) 1. I *Andrieu*; III *Tristan*.

As the above examples show, poets may combine exemplary figures from more than one sphere, mostly within one stanza, but also in different stanzas of the same poem. Such combinations tend to occur particularly in genres other than the *canso*: in *coblas*, Peire Card. 2; Oc. Anon. 1; in a *sirventes*, Peire Vid. 2 and Cerverí 1; in a *sirventes-canso*, Raimb. Vaq. 5; in a *planh*, Gauc. Faid. 3 and Aim. Peg. 2; in a *descort*, Aim. Bel. 1; in a *salut*, Arn. Mar. 3a, 3b, and 4; in a poem akin to the *salut*, Oc. Anon. 3; in an epic letter, Raimb. Vaq. 4.

Exemplary comparisons may occupy, or form the main focus of, a whole stanza: Rig. Berb. 1; 2; Raimb. Or. 1; Bern. Vent. 1; Raim. Jord. 1; Bertr. Born 3; Guir. Ros 1; Aim. Peg. 1; 2; Uc Pena 1; Oc. Anon. 2; of one section of a *descort*: Aim. Bel. 1.IV; of two stanzas: Arn. Mar. 1; Peire Card. 2; of a *tornada*: Pons Capd. 1a; Falq. Rom. 3c. They may be placed at the beginning of the stanza: Marc. 1; Rig. Berb. 1; Raim. Jord. 3; Arn. Mar. 2; Gar. Apch. 1; Gauc. Faid. 2; Peire Vid. 2; 3; 4. III,VII; 5a; Guil. Magr. 1; Raimb. Vaq. 5; Comt. Dia 2; Uc Bac. 1; El. Barj. 1; Falq. Rom. 2b; 3b; Peire Card. 1; Zorzi 2.III; Cerverí 3; Daude Prad. (?) 1.III; in the first half of the stanza in three consecutive stanzas: Raimb. Vaq. 1; at the beginning of a *tornada*: Pons Capd. 2; in a head refrain: Paul. Mars. 1. They may be placed at the centre of the stanza: Raimb. Vaq. 2a; Raim. Mir. 1; at the centre of a *tornada* Cerverí 1. They may be placed at the end of the stanza: Bern. Vent. 2; 3; Raim. Jord. 2; Arn. Dan. 1; 2; 3; Bertr. Born 1; 2b; Guir. Born. 1; 2; Guir. Sal. 2; Gauc. Faid. 1; Peire Vid. 1; 5b; 6.II, III,V; Raimb. Vaq. 2c; 2d; 3b; Peirol 1; P. R. Tolosa 1; Aim. Peg. 1; 3a; Falq. Rom. 1.I, II, V; 2a; Calvo 1; Zorzi 1; Cerverí 2; Guil. R. Giron. 1; Daude

Prad. (?) 1.I; Jord. Bon. 1; towards the end of the stanza: Guir. Sal. 1; Gauc. Faid. 3; Guir. Cal. 2; at the end of a section in a *descort*: Aim. Bel. 1.III; at the end of a *tornada*: Guil. Ad. 1; Guir. Cal. 1; Zorzi 2.VIII; at the end of a refrain: Paul. Mars. 1. In addition, the stanzas containing the exemplary comparisons may themselves be placed in prominent position. The comparisons occur in the first stanza: Rig. Berb. 2; Bertr. Born 2a; Guil. Magr. 1; 2; Raimb. Vaq. 3b; Guir. Cal. 2; Peire Card. 2; Daude Prad. (?) 1.I; in a single stanza: Peire Card. 1; Oc. Anon. 1; in Bertr. Born 2b the identification is placed in the first stanza. They may occur in the central stanza, i.e. in the second of three stanzas Comt. Dia 1; in the third of five stanzas Rig. Berb. 1; Guir. Ros 1; Aim. Peg. 3b; Falq. Rom. 3b; Daude Prad. (?) 1.III; Uc Pena 1. They are placed in a final stanza: Raim. Jord. 1; Gar. Apch. 1; Gauc. Faid. 1; Raimb. Vaq. 2c; 2d; 5; Raim. Mir. 1; Falq. Rom. 1.V; Zorzi 1; Cerverí 2; Guil. R. Giron. 1; Jord. Bon. 1; in the two final stanzas: Arn. Mar. 1; in a *tornada*: Guil. Ad. 1; Pons Capd. 1a; 2; Guir. Cal. 1; Falq. Rom. 3c; Zorzi 2.VIII; Cerverí 1.[9] These examples show that overall, there is a stronger tendency towards final placing of comparisons in both stanza and poem.

Most names are placed in emphatic position as rhyme words, and may also rhyme with another name (indicated by: between names): Marc. 1 *Samson.* Rig. Berb. 1 *Dedalus*; Rig. Berb. 2 *Persavaus.* Raim. Jord. 3 *Nicola de Bar.* Arn. Mar. 2 *Elena*; Arn. Mar. 3a *Biblis: Semiramis*; *Elena: Esmena*; Arn. Mar. 3b *Eros*; *Blancaflor*; *Tristan*; *Elenan: Titban*; *Eneas: Cleopatras*; *Quendis: Seguis.* Arn. Dan. 1 *Paris.* Bertr. Born 1 *Tristan*; Bertr. Born 2a *Elena*; Bertr. Born 2b *Lana.* Guir. Born. 1 *Paris*; Guir. Born. 2 *Oliviers.* Gar. Apch. 1 *Olivier.* Guir. Sal. 1 *Tibe*; Guir. Sal. 2 *Rotlan.* Peire Vid. 1 *Salamo: Samso*; *Davi*; Peire Vid. 2 *Olivier: Berart de Mondesdier*; Peire Vid. 4 *Galvanh* (2×); in Peire Vid. 6 *Sant Gabriel*, *Abel*, *Rachel* rhyme within stanzas I, III, and V respectively, and also with each other. Guil. Magr. 1 *Andrieu*; Guil. Magr. 2 *Golfier de las Tors.* In Raimb. Vaq. 1 *Pyramus*, *Emenadus* rhyme within stanzas I and IV respectively, and also with the pair *Artus: Tantalus* in III; Raimb. Vaq. 2a *Ayglentina*; Raimb. Vaq. 2b *Andreus de Fransa*; Raimb. Vaq. 2c *Blanchaflor*; Raimb. Vaq. 2d *Enida*; Raimb. Vaq. 3a *Ferragutz*; Raimb. Vaq. 3c *Galvaing*; Raimb. Vaq. 5 *Lodoics: Aimerics.* Comt. Dia 1 *Blanchaflor*; Comt. Dia 2 *Valenssa.* Uc Bac. 1 *Andrius de Paris: Amelis.* Guil. Ad. 1 *Elena.* Raim. Mir. 1 *Tristans*; Raim. Mir. 2 *Tristan.* Aim. Peg. 3a *Andrieus de Franssa*; Aim. Peg. 3b *N'Andrius.* Pons Capd. 1b *Tristans*; Pons Capd. 2 *Aja.* Falq. Rom. 1 *Raol de Cambrais*; *N'Andreus*; *Salamos*; Falq. Rom. 2b *Blanciflor*; Falq. Rom. 3a *Blanchaflor*; *Andreu de França*; Falq. Rom. 3c *Tristan.* Aim. Bel. 1 *Hyris: Biblis.* Paul. Mars. 1 *N'Aya* (in punning rhyme with *n'aya*). Peire Card. 1 *Andreu*; Peire Card. 2

---

[9] See also Folq. Mars. 1, in which the (obscured) comparison with Midas is placed in the last two lines of the final stanza.

Salamos. Daude Prad. (?) 1.I *Andrieu*; III *Tristan*. Zorzi 1 *Ansalon*: *Salomon*; Zorzi 2 *Abel*; *Abram*. Cerverí 3 *Blanxaflor*; *Elena*. Guil. R. Giron. 1 *Enida*. Oc. Anon. 1 *Salamo*: *Samso*; Oc. Anon. 3 *Helena*; *Tristantz*. Names in isolated rhyme (*rim estramp*): Raim. Jord. 1 *Ector*; *Leander*. Arn. Dan. 2 *Meleagre*; Arn. Dan. 3 *Alixandres*. Bertr. Born 3 *Galvain*. P. R. Tolosa 1 *N'Aya*. El. Barj. 1 *Andrius*. Guir. Cal. 1 *Alissandres*. Cerverí 2 *Tristan*; see also *qeridor* Folq. Mars. 1.

Names at the head of the line: Raimb. Or. 1 *Tristan*; Bern. Vent. 1 *lo bels Narcisus*; Arn. Mar. 1 *Juli Cezar*; Arn. Mar. 3a *Blancaflor, Tibes*; Guir. Ros 1 *Serena*; Peire Vid. 3 *Alexandres*; Raimb. Vaq. 2b *Andreus de Fransa*; Raimb. Vaq. 4 *Aleyxandres*; Aim. Peg. 1 *Tristans*; Aim. Peg. 2 *Alexandres*; Falq. Rom. 2a, 3a *Floris*; Falq. Rom. 3b *Tristanz*; Azalais 1 *Brizeida*; Peire Card. 2 *Alexandris*. Both at the head and end of line: Raimb. Vaq. 2a *Guis de Nantuelh . . . Ayglentina*; with a name also at the centre of the line: Uc Bac. 1 *Floris, Tristans ni Amelis*.

Comparison with the exemplar is usually conveyed explicitly by a variety of lexical and syntactical means. There are two main types of syntactical construction, that expressing likeness to, and that expressing superiority to, the exemplar. In the first type, likeness to the exemplar is expressed predominantly by means of adjectives, pronouns, adverbs, conjunctions, and, less often, verbs such as *valer, semblar* and *comparar*, which have a comparative sense: *s'ieu failli . . . com Dedalus* Rig. Berb. 1; *atressi con Persavaus . . . et eu sui atretaus . . . qu'eissamen m'oblit* Rig. Berb. 2; *Tristan . . . no·n saup als faire, et ieu am per aital coven midonz* Raimb. Or. 1; *c'aissi·m perdei com perdet se lo bels Narcisus en la fon* Bern. Vent. 1; *c'atretal m'es . . . com de Pelaus la lanza* Bern. Vent. 3; *aital astr' ai cum Nicola de Bar* Raim. Jord. 3; *Juli Cezar conquis la senhoria . . . de tot lo mon . . . aissi ben dei . . . de vostr' amor . . . estr' emperaire, com el del mon* Arn. Mar. 1; *eu no m'apel ges Olivier ni Rothlan, . . . mas valer lor cre maintas ves . . .* Gar. Apch. 1; *ieu muer si cum fetz el banh Serena . . . tot enaissi abelhis et agensa a fin'amor, que·m vol a tort aucir* Guir. Ros 1; *co·m te en sa preizo Amors, que Salamo, e Davi atressi venquet . . .* Peire Vid. 1; *d'ardimen vaill Rotlan et Olivier . . .* Peire Vid. 2; *don sembla Sant Gabriel* Peire Vid. 6; *atrestan . . . cum selh qu'avia nom Andrieu* Guil. Magr. 1; *e·m fai morir si cum mor Tantalus* Raimb. Vaq. 1; *a tapi li venrai, si cum Tristans* Raimb. Vaq. 2b; *mas trahitz sui si cum fo Ferragutz* Raimb. Vaq. 3a; *et morrai tot aissi com fes N'Andreus; qe per amor fu vencuz Salamos, aissi soi eu . . . per vos* Falq. Rom. 1; *q'esqern fai de si mal retraire Brizeida . . . autressi·us er en mal retrach* Azalais 1; *per qe vos er . . . qom Tantalus a murir* Calvo 1; *quar la beutatz d'Ansalon e·l sabers de Salomon si pod en vos conparar* Zorzi 1; *que totz aytals volers s'es mes en mi d'amor, con en Tristan* Cerverí 2; *qu'em poder m'a quon ac Andrieu* Daude Prad. (?) 1.9; *beure·m fai ab l'enap Tristan amors, e eisses los pimens* Daude Prad. (?) 1. 21 f. (in this ex., drinking the same potion stands metaphorically for sharing the fate of Tristan); *per tal coven morrei . . . mas ad Andrieu en pres tot eissamen, car elh mori d'aital esfrei* Jord. Bon. **1**.

There may also be other more varied constructions expressing likeness to the exemplar: *a l'uzatge·m tenh de Galvanh* Peire Vid. **4**; *Aleyxandres vos laisset son donar* Raimb. Vaq. **4**; *qu'en lui era tot lo pretz restauratz del rei Artus* Guir. Cal. **2**; *compainz serai Andreu de França* Falq. Rom. **3a**. In Uc Pena **1**, the link between the poet and the exemplar is established firstly by the opening phrase *anc Lanselotz*, and secondly by the conclusion drawn in the result clause: *per qu' ieu aten de vos aital merce*. In Oc. Anon. **1**, potential likeness is expressed in the form of a wish, followed by a purpose clause: *qu'eu feira dret del tort que vei c'om fai*. In Peire Card. **2**, likeness to a range of exemplars is hypothetical, expressed by the conditional construction beginning *si eu agues aquetz bons fazemens . . .*, followed by the list of qualities the poet would thus possess, making him comparable to the preceding list of exemplary figures. In Marc. **1** the comparison between the poet's opponent in the dialogue and Samson as victim of love is conveyed implicitly by the question *non saps d'amor cum trais Samson?* – this is the sole instance of an implicit comparison among the examples cited.

There is a second larger group of examples expressing superiority to the exemplar, predominantly by means of comparative adverbs, or, less often, comparative adjectives, in either positive or negative constructions: *plus trac pena d'amor de Tristan* Bern. Vent. **2**; *serai li leials . . . mielhs qu'Elena no fo al fraire Ector . . . qu'anc non amet Hero tant Leander* Raim. Jord. **1**; *l'am mais . . . no fes Andrius la reina de Fransa* Raim. Jord. **2**; *pus blanca es que Elena* Arn. Mar. **2**; *don ieu plus ai de ioia non ac Paris . . .* Arn. Dan. **1**; *q'il m'es plus fin' et ieu lieis certz que Talant' e Meleagre* Arn. Dan. **2**; *q'Iseuz . . . no·ls ac tant bels* Bertr. Born **1**; *cui eu sui plus fis qu' Elena Paris* Guir. Born. **1**; *ni non deu dire cavalliers que tant en valgues Oliviers* Guir. Born. **2**; *et ieu am la miels e may no fes Piramus Tibe* Guir. Sal. **1**; *per qu'ieu l'am mais no fetz Auda Rotlan* Guir. Sal. **2**; *pro m'estai mieils d'amor q'a Floris . . .* Gauc. Faid. **1**; *cel Andrieus . . . non trais anc tant greu martire per la reïna de Franssa cum ieu per vos* Gauc. Faid. **2**; *q'Alixandres . . . no cre que tant dones ni tant meses, ni anc Karles ni Artus plus valgues* Gauc. Faid. **3**; *don m'a leyal e fizel e just pus que Dieus Abel*; *am la mais . . . que Jacobs no fetz Rachel* Peire Vid. **6**; *trop mielhs m'es pres qu'a'n Golfier de las Tors . . . et ai trobat pus avinen leo quez elh no fetz* Guil. Magr. **2**; *anc Persivals . . . non ac tal gauch cum ieu . . .* Raimb. Vaq. **1**; *lieys qu'ieu am mais que non amet vasletz Guis de Nantuelh la piussel' Ayglentina*; *amada·us ai mays qu'Andrieus la reyna* Raimb. Vaq. **2a**; *Andreus . . . no·s saup tan gen rendre* Raimb. Vaq. **2b**; *et anc Floris de Blanchaflor non pres comjat tant doloiros cum eu . . .* Raimb. Vaq. **2c**; *qar per gençor vos ai chausida . . . servida genses q'Erecs Enida* Raimb. Vaq. **2d**; *anc Tibauz ab Lodoyc no fetz plait ab tans plazers cum eu* Raimb. Vaq. **3b**; *anc Alixandres non fetz cors . . . tan*

honrat . . . ni Rotlans ab sos poignadors non saubron tan gen conquerer tan ric
emperi . . . cum nos Raimb. Vaq. **5**; *anc Andrieus . . . no fo vas amor tant fis* Uc
Bac. **1**; *car plus m'en sui abellida no fetz Floris de Blanchaflor* Comt. Dia **1**; *vos*
am mais non fetz Seguis Valenssa Comt. Dia **2**; *quar anc Narcis . . . no fo plus*
fols de me Peirol **1**; *qu'ieu serai . . . plus fis . . . que no fo Landrics a N'Aya* P. R.
Tolosa **1**; *q'ie·us am plus . . . que no fetz Paris Elena* Guil. Ad. **1**; *et anc servidor*
menz antiu non ac la bell' a cui servi Tristans Raim. Mir. **1**; *seri'eu gais . . . plus*
que no fo . . . Tristan Raim. Mir. **2**; *qu'anc no fon tan larcs . . . Alexandres . . .*
ni ges Galvains d'armas plus non valia ni non saup tan Ivans de cortezia, ni·s
mes Tristans . . . en tan d'assay Aim. Peg. **2**; *c'anc en plus greu balanssa non fo*
Andrieus de Franssa Aim. Peg. **3a**; *qu'ieu ges plus que N'Andrieus, non ai poder*
de mi Aim. Peg. **3b**; *si tan gen muri Andrieus, non amet miels . . . qu'ieu fas*
lieys El. Barj. **1**; *mais vos am . . . non fetz Tristanz s'amia* Pons Capd. **1a**; *car fis*
amans li sui trop meillz non fo d'Iseut Tristans Pons Capd. **1b**; *et am vos mais*
que Landrics no fes Aja Pons Capd. **2**; *qu'anc non ac pus de son bel conquerir*
jois ni plazers Sesars ni Alissandres Guir. Cal. **1**; *qe meill no·n pres a Raol de*
Cambrais . . . com fez a mi Falq. Rom. **1**; *anc no fo de joi tan ricx Floris* Falq.
Rom. **2a**; *qez ainch no amet tan Tristanz Ysolt* Falq. Rom. **3b**; *plus vos am . . .*
no fetz Yseutz son bon amic Tristan Falq. Rom. **3c**; *anc Hyris . . . de Biblis no fo*
tan enveyos; ni Blancaflor tan greu dolor per Flori non senti Aim. Bel. **1**; *quar*
vos am . . . mais qu'Enricx no fes N'Aya Paul. Mars. **1**; *m'auretz mielhs que*
dieus Abel non ac a son mandamen; car ie·us am mais que no fetz Sarra Abram
Zorzi **2**; *e nostre Rey, cor, ab mais d'ardimen qu'Alixandres . . .* Cerverí **1**; *car*
Floris ab Blanxaflor ne Paris ne Elena no·m pogren dar gaug major Cerverí **3**;
enquer er meils que d'Enida, . . . quar mais la tem e l'am meils Guil. R. Giron.
1; *plus fo traiç lo jorn e enganaç non fo Tristan* Oc. Anon. **2**; *e trauch per vos*
trop major pena que no fesz Paris per Helena; ni Floris, Herecs ni Tristantz, ni
Andrieus . . . no trais tan grant mal per amor q'ieu no·l traga cen tantz pejor
Oc. Anon. **3**. There may also be a combination of different syntactical types
expressing likeness and superiority within the same example: *aitant arditz e*
plus fui . . . no·n fo . . . Emenadus Raimb. Vaq. **1**.

As in the first group, there are also more varied constructions: in Arn. Mar.
4, the poet's humorous boast of superiority is conveyed in a conditional structure: if he were to encounter Roland or Samson, both would be vanquished.
In Bertr. Born **3**, paired conditional constructions stress the supreme worth
of Geoffrey: neither Arthur nor Gauvain could compensate for his loss, i.e.
he surpassed them both. In the conditional construction in Raimb. Vaq. **3c**,
the motif of outdoing the exemplar is expressed verbally in the phrase *vencut*
agr' . . . d'aventura Galvaing. It may also be expressed by words explicitly
indicating contrast: *ni anc Iris . . . no amet Biblis re, avers so q'eu am vos* Arn.
Mar. **3b**; *Alexandres fon niens contra qu'ieu seria* Peire Vid. **3**; *qe Tristan fo vers*
Ysout fals contra mi Falq. Rom. **3a**. Unusually, Aim. Peg. **1** contrasts himself

unfavourably with Tristan: *quar el guazanhet s'amia, per so per qu'ieu pert la mia,* and Peire Card. 1 presents an exemplar in a negative light: *de tant tenc per nesci Andreu | car mori de zo don vieurai.*

The vast majority of exemplary comparisons are presented from a first-person authorial standpoint, and are couched in, or contain, first-person singular verbal and pronominal forms. Exceptions in the *canso* are extremely rare, found only in the third-person description of beauty in Arn. Mar. **2**, and the praise of Arthur of Brittany in Peire Vid. **5a**. There are also first-person formulations in a *salut* in Arn. Mar. **3a**, **3b**, and **4**, and Falq. Rom. **3a**; in a *descort* Raimb. Vaq. **2b**, and Aim. Bel. **1**; in an *estampida* Arn. Mar. **2d**; in a *sirventes-canso* in Peire Vid. **3**, **4**, and **5b**, and Falq. Rom. **2a** and **3b**; in a *sirventes* Gar. Apch. **1** and Cerverí **2**. In the *sirventes-canso* Raimb. Vaq. **5**, the subject of the comparison with epic heroes are the Crusaders, designated by the first-person plural *nos*, among whom the poet includes himself.

The introduction of a first-person singular pronoun, not obligatory in conjunction with the verb, serves to emphasize the comparison or contrast between the poet and the exemplar: *cui eu sui plus fis qu'Elena Paris* Guir. Born. **1**; *lieys qu'ieu am mais que non amet vasletz | Guis de Nantuelh la piussel' Ayglentina* Raimb. Vaq. **2a** (compare the example without first-person pronoun in l. 29: *amada·us ai mays qu'Andrieus la reyna*); *et ieu am la miels e may no fes Piramus Tibe* Guir. Sal. **1**; *per qu'ieu l'am mais no fetz Auda Rotlan* **2**; *qu'ieu ges plus que N'Andrieus, | non ai poder di mi* Aim. Peg. **3b**.[10] The first-person singular pronoun without a verb has a similarly emphatic function, as in *anc Persivals . . . non ac tal gauch cum ieu del sieu conseill* Raimb. Vaq. **1**.17.[11]

In the main, exemplary comparisons in the more objective genres tend to be couched in third-person forms, as in Bertr. Born **3** and Guir. Cal. **2**, both examples of the *planh*, and the epic letter Raimb. Vaq. **4**. The *salut* Azalais **1** combines third person with apostrophe. Elsewhere, although the comparison itself is in the third person, there may be formulaic first-person phrases associated with it for purposes of emphasis, e.g. in examples of the *planh*: *c'anc non vi ni ia non veirai* Guir. Born. **2**; *q'Alixandres . . . non cre que tant dones ni tant meses* Gauc. Faid. **3**; *de bos mestiers el mon par non li say . . . segon mon parer* Aim. Peg. **2**. The *sirventes* Cerverí **1** alludes to the object of praise as *nostre Rey*. Generalizing third-person formulations in association with comparisons are extremely rare: *e sel que long'atendensa blasma, fai gran falhizo* Peire Vid. **5a** (in an instance of identification, rather than of comparison); *e qui vol dir per vertat ni comtar* Raimb. Vaq. **4**; *qui·n vol ver dir* Gauc. Faid. **3**.17.

[10] See also Rig. Berb. **1**.25; **2**.7; Arn. Mar. **3b**.171; Arn. Dan. **1**.46; Guir. Ros **1**.21; Peire Vid. **3**.15; Guil. Ad. **1**.65; Raim. Mir. **2**.33; Aim. Peg. **1**.32; El. Barj. **1**.30; Falq. Rom. **1**.44; **2b**.19; Zorzi **2**.120 f.; Daude Prad. (?)**1**.7,23; Uc Pena **1**.32; Oc. Anon. **2**.4; Oc. Anon. **3**.116.

[11] See also Arn. Mar. **3a**.160; Gauc. Faid. **2**.44; Raimb. Vaq. **2c**.60; **3b**.12; Aim. Bel. **1**.55 f.

There is no direct speech, except in the fictive dialogues of the *tenso* in Marc. 1, the *partimen* in Calvo 1, the few words attributed to the lady in Raim. Mir. 1.48, and the short phrase in Cerverí 2. Apostrophe is extremely common, mostly in protestations of the following type addressed to the lady: *domna, genser qu'ieu sai,* | *mais vos am ses bausia,* | *no fetz Tristanz s'amia* Pons Capd. 1a; *qe per amor fu vencuz Salamos,* | *aissi soi eu, cortesa res, per vos,* | *ma bella dompna* Falq. Rom. 1.43 ff. – the poem in which this comparison occurs is entirely in apostrophe, in that each of the five stanzas begins with the appellation *ma bella dompna*, which is then repeated as a refrain phrase at the end of the stanza; the whole of the refrain in Paul. Mars. 1 is an address to the lady.[12] Comt. Dia 2 addresses instead the male lover: *car anc non fi faillenssa,* | *amics, vas vos, . . .* | *anz vos am mais non fetz Seguis Valenssa.* There are a few other objects of apostrophe: *n'Engles* in Raimb. Vaq. 2d.84, and the poet's patron in 4; the recipient of the *salut* in Azalais 1; the mirror of the lady's eyes in Bern. Vent. 1.21. In spite of the high incidence of apostrophe, exemplary comparison referring to the person apostrophized is very rare – only Raimb. Vaq. 4, Azalais 1, Calvo 1 and Zorzi 1 fall into this category.

If the exemplary comparisons of the troubadour lyric are compared with those in the epics of Homer and Virgil, and with those in the classical, post-classical, and medieval Latin poets, there are certain striking differences, chief of which are the use of a literary language based on the vernacular, and a decisive shift towards presentation from a first-person authorial standpoint. A first-person stance prevails almost entirely in the examples in the love poems, which make up the bulk of the corpus, with only rare exceptions, such as the praise of beauty in Arn. Mar. 2, or of Iseut's hair in Bertr. Born 1. The comparisons are used mainly to stress the extent of the poet's love, constancy, or suffering, and it is predominantly in the genres of panegyric and lament that third-person presentation is found. A first-person standpoint, not, however, one exclusively associated with the theme of love, is already foreshadowed to some extent in Catullus, Propertius, Horace, and Ovid, and to a lesser degree in the later and medieval Latin lyric, but in the troubadour lyric it has become dominant.

By comparison particularly with classical epic and lyric poets, there is a very considerable increase in the repertoire of exemplary figures, and the areas from which they are drawn. This extends still further a development already present in the later and, more particularly, the medieval Latin poets. There are no longer comparisons with divinities or their attributes, although this feature may still persist under classical influence in contemporaneous Latin

---

[12] See also Rig. Berb. 2.7–11; Arn. Mar. 1.37, 41; **3a**.160; **3b**.171; **4**.41–3; Guir. Ros 1.19 ff.; Gauc. Faid. 2.44; Guil. Magr. 1.3 f.; Raimb. Vaq. 1.25 ff.; **2a**.29; **2c**.60; **2d**.77 ff.; P. R. Tolosa 1.28 f.; Guil. Ad. 1.61 ff.; Raim. Mir. 1.43 ff.; Pons Capd. 2.41 f.; Guir. Cal. 1. 46 f.; Falq. Rom. **3a**.135 ff., 181 ff.; **3c**.41 ff.; Zorzi 1.59 ff.; **2**.33 ff., 118 ff.; Uc Pena 1.29 ff.; Oc. Anon. 3.111 f.

poetry – see for instance Baudri 2a, Giraldus Cambrensis 1, and the examples in the Ripoll and Carmina Burana collections.

Exemplary comparisons are, with only very rare exceptions, now always placed in emphatic position: they either take up, or form the main focus of, a whole stanza, section of a *descort*, or *tornada*, or they are placed in initial, final, or occasionally central position in these elements of the poem. The stanzas containing exemplary comparisons are themselves prominently placed, in initial, central, or – predominantly – final position. The other decisive difference is the dominance of rhyme, a development already established to a limited extent in some of the examples in medieval Latin poets. This permits the names of exemplars to be strongly emphasized by being placed in rhyming position, rhyming also with other names, or as isolated rhymes, rhyming only from stanza to stanza, which singles them out still further. The developments which mark the troubadour lyric as distinct from the different stages of the Latin lyric are taken over in part and continued in other branches of the medieval vernacular lyric.

6

The Trouvère Poets

In Northern France, the troubadour lyric became known and imitated from about 1160, and among the features taken over was the use of exemplary comparisons.[1] Many of the examples from troubadour poets cited in the previous chapter belong to the second half of the twelfth century, whereas among the trouvère poets who employ exemplary comparisons, only Chrétien (fl. c. 1160–1185), and Guillaume de Ferrières (d. 1204) can be assigned to this period. There are a few poets from the turn of the twelfth and thirteenth centuries (Le Chastelain de Couci, Guiot de Provins, Blondel de Nesle and Eustache le Peintre), but a poet with a substantial œuvre such as Gace Brulé (fl. c. 1179–1212) has no instances of exemplary comparisons in his work (for a probably spurious example ascribed to him in one manuscript see p. 219). Similarly, the considerable poet Gontier de Soignies, probably also writing at the turn of the twelfth and thirteenth centuries, has no exemplary comparisons proper in his work.[2] The vast majority of poets who employ exemplary comparisons belong to the thirteenth century. Those writing in the first half of the century include Thibaut de Blaison, Moniot d'Arras, Gautier de Dargies, Andrieu Contredit d'Arras, Gille le Vinier, Jean de Neuville, Thibaut de Champagne, Perrin d'Angicourt, Wilart de Corbie, and the anonymous author of the *lais* in the Prose *Tristan*. To the second half of the thirteenth century belong Richard de Fournival, Raoul de Soissons, Le Comte de Bretagne, Adam de la Halle, and the examples of the *jeu parti*. At the end of the chapter are grouped together all examples of uncertain authorship and date, including those attributed to the Duchesse de Lorraine and Gace Brulé, and those transmitted anonymously, of which there are a far greater number than in the troubadour lyric. Some of the anonymous items in particular make it clear that exemplary comparisons seem to have become a well-worn device, which may be used in brief formulations solely in order to provide a rhyme.

It was chiefly the troubadour *canso* on themes of love which was imitated in the Old French lyric and it is therefore mainly in the *chançon* that instances

---

[1] Many of the dates of the poets are uncertain and only a rough chronological ordering can be attempted. In the examples cited, abbreviated references are given to the incipit of each poem, to its classification, to the numbering in the bibliography of Raynaud (=R), updated by Spanke and Linker (see pp. 364 f.), and to the standard edition.

[2] He refers only to his hope as like that of the Bretons for the return of Arthur (6.41 f.), and to *ceus de Troie* as witness, in their exploits for the sake of *Elaine* (15.38 ff.), to the power of *fine amors*.

of exemplary comparisons occur. The general areas from which the exemplars are derived remain largely the same in both branches of the lyric, but there is in the trouvère lyric a more restricted repertoire of names, with a concentration on those which were better known, and much less syntactical and stylistic variety in the formulation of comparisons. There is thus not only a difference of timespan between the two branches of the lyric, but also considerable divergence in the range and choice of exemplary comparisons and the manner of their expression.

The Second Half of the Twelfth Century

Chrétien de Troyes **1**

D'Amors ke m'ait tolut a moy (*chançon*).
R 1664 (for the edition of the text, see below)

Onkes del bovraige ne bui	IV 28
dont Tristans fut enpoisonneis,	
maix plux me fait ameir ke lui	30
Amors et bone volonteis.	
se m'en doit savoir *bon* greit,	
quant de riens esforciés n'en sui	
fors de tant ke mes ieuls en crui	
per cui seux en la voie entreis	35
dont ains n'issi ne ne recrui.	

[I never drank of the potion by whose magic Tristan was intoxicated, but Love and firm desire cause me to love more than he did. Thus it should be accounted to my credit, since I am in no way compelled in this, except in so far that I trusted my eyes – through them I have entered on the path, from which I never departed or drew back.]

The fourth of six stanzas.   The MS transmission of this poem is very complex. The edition by Zai in *Les Chansons courtoises de Chrétien de Troyes* (pp. 75–100) presents all the substantive and graphic variants, but establishes an eclectic text. Therefore the version of MS C, as in Frank, *Trouvères et Minnesänger* 5b, has been preferred, but with one exception. In l. 32, MS C has a negative construction: *se ne m'en doit savoir mal greit* (thus it should not be held against me), but this makes no sense in the context. A positive construction, i.e. lacking the negative particle, is attested in other MSS e.g. *men deuroit sauoir* U, *men deuez sauoir* KNPV; also, C is alone in having *mal*, as against *bon* (or a graphic variant) in other MSS. The emendation conveys the sense required by the context, i.e. the poet's love, freely entered upon, is of greater worth than that of Tristan, compelled by the potion. It is confirmed by the wording of Veldeke **1**, which is modelled on a version of this stanza (see Veldeke **1**.5 ff. and n.).   28 f. *bovraige . . . enpoisonneis*: the noun *bovraige* is a neutral designation, but the association here with *enpoisonneis*, which has stronger negative connotations, lends it a specialized sense. The verb is derived from *poison*, denoting either 'drink', 'potion' in general, or 'philtre', 'magic potion'. See *beverage* Couci **1**.19; *poisûn* Veldeke **1**.3; *poison, empoisonnez, Jeux-partis* **1a**.41 f.   *Tristans*: refs. to Tristan, and to Iseut (though as in the case of other f. names, these are less frequent), are particularly common in the OF lyric (see Index of Proper Names, *s.v.*), no doubt because of the strong OF traditions of the story. For the diffusion of the legend in general, and the significance of the love potion, see Raimb. Or. **1**.29 f. n.

Guillaume de Ferrières (Le Vidame de Chartres) **1**

> *D'Amours vient joie et honours . . . (chançon).*
> R 663, Petersen Dyggve 1945, p. 21

par biau servir est dame a droit conquise.   II   16

Mieuz ameroie itel conquerement   III   17
qu'Espaigne au jor que li bons rois l'ot prise,
Charlemainnes, qui en fist son talant.

[A lady is rightly conquered by faithful service. I would prefer such a conquest to (that of) Spain when the good king had captured it, Charlemagne, who ruled it at will.]

The last l. of II and the first 3 ll. of III in a poem of five 8-l. stanzas + 3-l. *envoi.*   19 *Charlemainnes*: see Gauc. Faid. **3**.16 n. For the motif of conquest in a religious context, see OF Anon. **11**.17 ff. (*Alixandre*), and for the related motif of love as preferable to status or power Gaut. Darg. **1**.21 f. (*Hector*); Andr. Contr. **1**.39 f. (*Julius Cesaire*).   *qui en fist son talant*: lit. 'did with it in accordance with his wishes'; see the similar construction, OF Anon. **11**.19.

Poets Writing at the Turn of the Twelfth and Thirteenth Centuries

Le Chastelain de Couci **1**

> *La douce voiz du louseignol . . . (chançon).* R 40, Lerond 3

Tant ai en lui ferm assis mon corage   III   17
qu'ailleurs ne pens, et Diex m'en lait joïr!
c'onques Tristanz, qui but le beverage,
pluz loiaument n'ama sanz repentir.

[I have fixed my heart so firmly on her that I do not turn my thoughts elsewhere – and God grant that I may experience joy thereby – for never did Tristan, who drank the potion, love more faithfully and unreservedly.]

17–20: the first 4 ll. of an 8-l. stanza in a poem of five stanzas.   18 *ailleurs*: frequently used, as here, as an indirect designation of another object of love. 19 *Tristanz, qui but le beverage*: see Chrétien **1**.28 f. n.   20 *sanz repentir*: lit. 'without repentance/regret'.

Le Chastelain de Couci **2**

> *Quant li estez . . . (chançon).* R 1913, Lerond 11

> Se j'avoie le sens qu'ot Salemons,   II   9
> si me feroit Amours pour fol tenir;
> quar tant est fors et crueuz sa prisons,
> qu'ele me fait assaier et sentir.

> [If I had the sense which Solomon possessed, yet would Love cause me to
> be considered foolish, for so strong and cruel is its imprisonment, which
> it makes me undergo and suffer.]

9–12: the first 4 ll. of an 8-l. stanza in a poem of five stanzas.   9 f. For
Solomon as the victim of love, see Thib. Ch. **2**.34; for the theme of love's
victims in general see Marc. **1**.14 n.; see also *Jeux-partis* **1a**.45 *Aristotes*; *Jeux-partis* **1b**.49 *Cesar*.

Guiot de Provins **1**

> *Contre lo novel tens (chançon).* R 287, Orr 2

> Chancenette, va t'ant,   VII   43
> lez m'amie t'envoi.
> di li que je li mant: 45
> cuer et cors li outroi;
> s'ele me porte foi
> la leiauté Tristant   48
> porra trover en moi.

> [Little song, be on your way, I send you to my loved one. Relate the message
> I send her: I surrender heart and body to her. If she is true to me, she will
> find Tristan's loyalty in me.]

This *envoi* addressed to the song is the last of seven 7-l. stanzas, i.e. it is not
formally distinct from the rest of the poem.   48 *Tristant*: see Chrétien
1.28 f. n.

The MS transmission of the five-stanza poem ascribed to Blondel de Nesle in
which the following examples occur is very complicated (see Lepage, p. 207),
and there are two alternative final stanzas attested, both containing exemplary
comparisons. The first, Lepage V (=**1a**), occurs in three MSS, the second,
Lepage V^{bis} (=**1b**), in five MSS.

Blondel de Nesle **1a**

> *L'amour dont sui espris (chançon).* R 1545, Lepage 11

> de granz mauz m'a fait oir,   V   53
> dont Tristans soffri tant:
> d'ameir sens decevoir.

> [She has made me heir to great ills, from which Tristan suffered so much:
> loving without inconstancy.]

53–5: the last 3 ll. of an 11-l. stanza.   54 *Tristans*: see Chrétien **1**.28 f. n.

Blondel de Nesle **1b**

> por li maintendrai l'us V^{bis} 60
> d'Eneas et Paris,
> Tristan et Pyramus,
> qui amerent jadis;
> or serai ses amis.
> or pri deu de lasus 65
> qu'a lor fin soie pris.

[For her I will follow the example of Aeneas and Paris, of Tristan and Pyramus who loved in former times; now I will be her lover. I now pray God above that I may attain the same end (?).]

60–6: the last 7 ll. of an 11-l. stanza. The stanza was obviously composed by an author who felt that the reference to Tristan in stanza V (**1a**) was insufficient and therefore added three further exemplars.   60 *por li maintendrai l'us*: cf. Peire Vid. **4**.17 *a l'uzatge·m tenh de Galvanh.*   61 *Eneas, Paris,* 62 *Pyramus*: classical names were probably known in the main from the OF *roman d'antiquité* or from other OF versions of classical stories. For *Eneas* see in particular the OF *Eneas*, for *Pyramus* the OF *Pyramus et Tisbé*; see also general n. on names, including classical names, Arn. Mar. **3b**.   62 *Tristan*: see **1a**.54 n.   66 i.e. 'that I may love as did Aeneas, Paris, Tristan and Pyramus' (?).

Eustache le Peintre **1**

Cil qui chantent de flor ... (*chançon*). R 2116, Gambini 2

> Onques Tristans n'ama de tel maniere, V 33
> li Chastelains ne Blondiaus autresi,
> con j'ai fet vos, tres douce dame chiere
> et oncor aim, c'onques nus n'ama si.

[Never did Tristan love in such a way, nor the Chastelain or Blondel likewise, as I have loved you, very sweet dear lady and whom I still love, so that none ever loved thus.]

The first 4 ll. of the final stanza in a poem of five 8-l. stanzas.   33 *Tristans*: see Chrétien **1**.28 f. n.   34 *li Chastelains ne Blondiaus*: the literary personae of the poets have themselves become exemplars, to be ranked together with Tristan (for *li Chastelains* as exemplar see also OF Anon. **4**.1). This is taken further in the later 13th century, when both poets are made the subject-matter of legend, Couci in the *Roman du Castelain de Couci et de la dame de Fayel* (a version of the story of the eaten heart), and Blondel in the *Récits* of le Ménestrel de Reims (c. 1260), in which he appears as the minstrel of Richard Cœur de Lion. For a troubadour ex. of poets as exemplary lovers see under Giraudo lo Ros **1**.23 n.

Poets Writing in the First Half of the Thirteenth Century

Thibaut de Blaison **1**

Quant je voi esté venir (chançon). R 1477, Newcombe 6

Tout cest mal et cest torment   IV   34
    me sui je quis
quant je vi premierement
    l'amoreus ris;
adonques fui si espris
    d'amer loiaument,
c'onques tant n'ama Paris   40
    Elaine au cors gent.

[I brought all this pain and torment upon myself when I first saw her lovely smile; I was then so inflamed with the desire to love faithfully that never did Paris love Helen of the fair form so greatly.]

34–41: the first 8 ll. of an 11-l. stanza in a poem of five stanzas.   35 *quis*: lit. 'sought out'.   40 f. *Paris, Elaine*: see Blondel de Nesle **1b**.61 n.

Moniot d'Arras **1**

Amors me fait renvoisier . . . (chançon).
R 810=796, Rosenberg/Tischler 126

Trestuit li bien c'on porroit deviser   VI   46
sont en celui a cui del tout m'otroie;
bien set son cuer envers autrui celer
et envers moi volentiers le desploie.
non pluz c'on puet Tristan n'Yseut la bloie   50
de lor amour partir ne dessevrer,
n'iert ja l'amours de nous deux dessevree.

[All the good qualities which one could recount are found in him, to whom I surrender myself entirely; he well knows how to conceal his heart from others, and freely reveals it to me. No more than one can part or sever Tristan or Iseut the fair from their love, will the love between us two be severed.]

The last stanza of a woman's song with complaints of a jealous husband, in a poem of 6 stanzas + 2-l. refrain (omitted here).   46 f. These ll. form a contrast to the previous stanza, in which the husband is described as possessing no qualities worthy of love.   50 *Tristan, Yseut la bloie*: see Chrétien **1**.28 f. n.; see also Moniot, ed. Petersen Dyggve 13.II: the features of his lady are so beautiful that the poet surpasses Tristan in loving (20 *qu'en bien amer Tristan pas*).

Gautier de Dargies **1**

La douce pensee (*descort*), R 539, Raugei 19

Qui voit sa crigne bloie III 15
qui samble que soit d'or
et son col qui blanchoie
desouz son biau chief sor,
c'est ma dame, ma joie
et mon riche tresor; 20
certes je ne voudroie
sanz li valoir Hector.

[Whoever sees her fair hair, which seems as if made of gold, and the whiteness of her throat below her lovely blond head, it is my lady, my joy and my rich treasure; indeed I would not wish without her to be the equal of Hector.]

15–22: the third section of a *descort*. 21 f.: for a similar motif cf. Arn. Dan. 3.20 f.; for related motifs see Guil. Ferr. 1.19 n. 22 *Hector*: see Peire Card. 2.5 n.; the name is prompted by the demands of the rhyme.

Andrieu Contredit d'Arras **1**

Bonne, belle et avenant (*chançon*).
R 262, Nelson/van der Werf 16

je n'ai doleur ne contraire V 36
puis que j'ai si bel repaire,
ou mes fins cuers est manans.
je sui plus riches cent tans
que ne fu Julius Cesaire. 40

[I have neither sorrow nor distress, since I have such a fair refuge, in which my true heart is a dweller. I am more powerful a hundred times than was Julius Caesar.]

The last 5 ll. of the final stanza in a poem of five 8-l. stanzas + 4-l. *envoi*. 36 *contraire*: lit. 'vexation', 'annoyance'. 40 *Julius Cesaire*: for a similar motif, see Guir. Cal. 1.49; there is a very similar formulation in Martin le Beguin R 1329 (ed. Dyggve, *Neuphil. Mitteilungen* 31(1930), 20 f.): 42 *mais se ja li puis plaire,* | *dont ere jou plus riche que Cesaire* (but if I can please her, then I shall be more powerful than Caesar); for related motifs see Guil. Ferr. 1.19 n.

Gille de Vinier (participant in a Crusade in 1250, d. 1252), remembering his lady's promise to reward him on his return, announces his departure to her. He leaves his heart with her, and asks that her heart may accompany him to fortify his courage:

Gille le Vinier **1**

Aler m'estuet . . . (chançon). R 410, Metcke 1

Del gentil cuer Genievre la roïne   V   33
fu Lanselos plus preus et plus vaillans;
pour li emprist mainte dure aatine   35
si en souffri paines et travaus grans;
mais au double li fu guerredonans
aprés ses maus Amors loiaus et fine.
en tel espoir serf et ferai toustans
celi a qui mes cuers est atendans.   40

[Through the gentle heart of Guinivere the queen, Lancelot was braver and more valiant. For her sake he undertook many a difficult challenge and endured hardship and great labours, but true and perfect love rewarded him doubly after his sufferings. With such a hope I serve – and always will – her to whom my heart aspires.]

The final stanza in a poem of five 8-l. stanzas + 4-l. *envoi.*   33 *Genievre,*
34 *Lanselos*: see n., Uc Pena **1**.

Jean de Neuville **1**

L'an que la froidure faut (chançon). R 393, Richter 1

Se je l'aim a son plaisir,   III   17
a grant tort m'en avient maus;
car je l'aim pluz et desir
c'onques ne fist Menelaus   20
Helaine, qui tant d'assaus
fist ceus de Troies sentir.

[If I love her in accordance with her wishes, it is a great injustice that suffering should befall me as a result, for I love and desire her more than ever Menelaus did Helen, who caused the people of Troy to suffer so many assaults.]

The first 6 ll. of the final stanza in a poem made up of three 8-l. stanzas. 20 f. *Menelaus – Helaine*: this appears to be a rare, if not unique ex., perhaps necessitated by the rhyme, of the name of Menelaus in association with the theme of love. Helen usually occurs together with Paris (see e.g. Thib. Bl. 1.40 f.). For classical names in general see Blondel de Nesle **1b**.61 n.]

Thibaut, count of Champagne (b. 1201, d. 1253), was the great-grandson of Eleanor of Aquitaine (granddaughter of the first attested troubadour, Guilhem IX) and grandson of Marie de Champagne, like Eleanor a renowned patron of poets. He acceded through the maternal line to the throne of Navarre in 1234.

Thibaut de Champagne **1**

Por conforter ma pesance (chançon). R 237, Wallensköld 1

Por conforter ma pesance   I   1
    faz un son.
bons ert, se il m'en avance,
    car Jason,
cil qui conquist la toison,   5
n'ot pas si grief penitance.
    é! é! é!

[To alleviate my sorrow, I am fashioning a song; it will be good if it helps me in this, for Jason, he who won the fleece, did not experience such grievous suffering. Oh! oh! oh!]

1–7: the first stanza in a poem of five 6-l. stanzas + refrain line, followed by 2-l. *envoi* + refrain.   4 *Jason*: the story of Jason and the Golden Fleece was known from Ovid, *Met.* VII.1 ff.

Thibaut de Champagne **2**

Li rosignous chante tant (chançon). R 360, Wallensköld 5

Onques fierté n'ot si grant   III   15
vers Pompee Julius
que ma dame n'en ait plus
vers moi, qui muir desirrant.
    [. . .]

Je ne cuit pas que serpent   V   29
n'autre beste poigne plus
que fet Amors au desus;
trop par sont si coup pesant.
plus tret souvent que Turs ne Arrabiz,
n'onques oncor Salemons ne Daviz
ne s'i tindrent ne q'uns fous d'Alemaigne.   35

[Never did Julius show such great arrogance towards Pompey, but my lady shows more towards me, who am dying of desire. [. . .] I do not think that a serpent or other creature stings more sharply than victorious Love; his blows are exceedingly powerful; he shoots arrows more thick and fast than Turk or Arab and neither Solomon nor David could withstand them, any more than a fool from Germany.]

A poem of five 7-l. stanzas + three 3-l. *envois*.; 15–18 are the first four ll. of III; 29–35 make up stanza V. The final rhyme in -*aigne* links all the stanzas and the first two *envois*.   16 *Julius*: see Index of Proper Names, *s.v.* Julius/Julius Caesar.   31 *au desus*: lit. 'on top', i.e. Love prevails/has the upper hand in the contest.   34 *Salemons ni Daviz*: for the theme of Love's victims, see Couci **2**.9 f. n.

Thibaut de Champagne **3**

Tout autresi con l'ente . . . (chançon). R 1479, Wallensköld 21

Pleüst a Dieu, pour ma dolor garir,   II   11
qu'el fust Tisbé, car je sui Piramus;
mès je voi bien ce ne puet avenir:
ensi morrai que ja n'en avrai plus.

[Might it please God – to cure my sorrow – that she were Thisbe, for I am
Pyramus; but I see indeed that cannot happen: thus I shall die and gain
nothing further from it.]

The first 4 ll. of a 10-l. stanza in a poem of 5 stanzas + 4-l. *envoi.*   14 The
line seems to mean that the poet will derive no reward other than death for
his love and sorrow.   12 *Tisbé . . . Piramus*: see Blondel de Nesle **1b**.61 n.

Thibaut de Champagne **4**

A enviz sent mal . . . (chançon). R 1521, Wallensköld 22

Se ma dame ne prent oncor conroi   V   33
de moi, qui l'aim par si grant couvoitise,
mult la desir et, s'ele me desprise,
Narcisus sui, qui noia tout par soi.

[If my lady still gives no heed to me, who love her with such great longing,
I (yet) desire her greatly and if she scorns me, I am Narcissus, who alone
was the cause of his drowning.]

The first 4 ll. of the final stanza in a poem of five 8-l. stanzas + 4-l. *envoi.*
36 *Narcisus*: see Rich. Fourn. **1**.10,15; Raoul Soiss. **1**.59; *Jeux-partis* **2**.42; OF
Anon. **9**.16. The story, derived from Ov., *Met.* III.407 ff. was probably known
from the 12th-century OF *lai de Narcisse.* See also Bern. Vent. **1**.23 f. n.

Thibaut de Champagne **5**

Chançon ferai . . . (chançon). R 1596, Wallensköld 23

Douce dame, s'il vos plesoit un soir,   IV   32
m'avrïez vos plus de joie doné
c'onques Tristans, qui en fist son pouoir
n'en pout avoir nul jor de son aé.

[Sweet lady, if it were to be your pleasure one evening, you would have
given me more joy than ever Tristan, who felt the greatest joy of which he
was capable, was able to experience any day of his life.]

The first 4 ll. of IV in a poem of five 8-l. stanzas + 3-l. *envoi*, with a variable
refrain throughout, included by ed. in the numbering.   34 *Tristans*: see
Chrétien **1**.28 f. n.   *qui en fist son pouoir*: lit. 'who did all in his power in this
respect'.

Thibaut de Champagne **6**

L'autrier par la matinee (pastourelle). R 529, Wallensköld 52

"Sire, par sainte Marie,   IV   31
vous en parlez por noient.

mainte dame avront trichie
cil chevalier soudoiant.
trop sont faus et mal pensant,   35
pis valent de Guenelon.
je m'en revois en meson,
que Perrinez, qui m'atent,
m'aime de cuer loiaument.
abessiez vostre reson!"   40

["Sir, by saint Mary, you speak of this in vain; those treacherous knights
have certainly betrayed many a lady, they are very false and ill-intentioned,
they are worse than Guenelon. I am going home, because Perrinez, who
is waiting for me, loves me truly from his heart. Put an end to your
arguments!"]

The fourth stanza in a poem of five 10-l. stanzas + 3-l. *envoi*.   In an
encounter typical of the *pastourelle*, the poet tries to persuade the shepherdess to abandon her shepherd, alleging the superiority of knights as lovers.
33 *avront*: lit. 'will have', i.e. expressing a supposition.   36 *Guenelon*: the
traitor in the *Chanson de Roland*; see also OF Anon. **8.15**. Ad. Halle (**26.26**)
describes the action of a faithless lady, who has abandoned him for another,
as *oevre de Guenelon*; see also Philippe de Remi, ed. Suchier, *salut* 241 ff. (II,
p. 204), of the personified figures *Envie* and *Felonie*: *pis valent ne fist Guenelons*.

Perrin d'Angicourt 1
                           J'ai un joli souvenir (*chançon*). R 1270, Steffens 3

s'en souspir,   IV 35
e d'amoureus cuer m'aïr,
quant el n'esclaire
moi qui ne li puis guenchir,
ains me fait plus maus souffrir,
qu'Alixandres ne fist Daire.   40

[Thus I sigh and with loving heart am distressed, since she affords no
relief to me, who cannot turn from her, but makes me suffer more ills
than Alexander made Darius suffer.]

The last 6 ll. of a 10-l. stanza in a poem of 5 stanzas + 6-l. *envoi*.   36 Oc. *ira*,
OF *ire* have the primary sense of 'anger', but particularly in the love lyric have
also acquired the sense of 'grief'/'sorrow'; thus the OF verb *s'aïrier*, primarily
'be angered', may on occasion have the sense of 'be sorrowful'. For the latter
sense in this verb, see Kleiber, *Le mot «ire» en ancien français*, p. 441 n. 46.
40 *Alixandres*: see Arn. Dan. **3.21** n.   *Daire*: see Gauc. Faid. **3.14**; for the
paired names in association with love, see Guillaume de Machaut (14th c.),
ed. Chichmaref, p. 180: *Aucuns parlent de · X· plaies d'Egipte | et des meschiés
qu'Alixandres fist Daire, | mais vraiment, c'est chose tres petite | contre ce que
ma dame me fait traire* (some speak of the ten plagues of Egypt and the
harm which Alexander inflicted upon Darius, but truly it is a small matter

by comparison with that which my lady makes me suffer). Both names were known from the *Roman d'Alexandre*.

Perrin d'Angicourt 2

Bien m'est du tens . . . (chançon). R 1767, Steffens 23

> sa cruautés me confont et desvoie   V   31
> ne ne me let cuidier ma guerison;
> et neporquant fu jadis, ce dist on,
> Yvains li preus qui tant fist toute voie
> que par servir ot l'amor du lion.   35

[Her cruelty confounds and bewilders me [lit. leads me astray] and does not allow me to hope for my salvation; and yet formerly, as they say, there was (the example of) Yvain the valiant, who did so much in every way that through rendering service he gained the love of the lion.]

The final 5 ll. in the last of five 7-l. stanzas.   Stanza IV of this poem contains a hypothetical comparison with Solomon: 26 *se j'avoie tout le sens Salemon, | en li servir trestout l'enplieroie* (if I had the wisdom of Solomon, I would apply it all in serving her).   34 *Yvains*: see Aim. Peg. **2**.15 n. 35 There is an implied comparison here between the lady and the lion; for the motif of a lion's devotion, in which the identification of the lady with the lion is explicit, see Guil. Magr. **2**.6 f. n.

Perrin d'Angicourt 3

Tres haute Amors . . . (chançon). R 1098, Steffens 30

> las! je morrai s'ele ne m'assoage!   III   21
> s'ele m'ocit, trop fera grant outrage,
> plus sent por li de mal qui me guerroie,
> k'ainc n'ot Paris por Elene de Troie.

[Alas! I shall die if she does not relieve my suffering. If she causes my death, she will commit a very great wrong. I suffer for her sake the onslaught of more pain than ever Paris experienced for the sake of Helen of Troy.]

The last 4 ll. of III in a poem of five 8-l. stanzas.   24 *Paris . . . Elene de Troie*: see Blondel de Nesle **1b**.61 n.]

The poem is ascribed to both Perrin and to Thibaut de Champagne. In 6 MSS, ll. 23 f. read: *tant sent por li de mal qui me guerroie | s'espoir n'estoit, souffrir ne le porroie* (I suffer the onslaught of so much pain on her account, that if there were not hope, I could not endure it). This is the reading adopted by Steffens, whereas 3 MSS have the comparison, as above. For other instances of versions with and without a comparison, see OF Anon. **1** and **10f**.

Wilart de Corbie 1

Cil qui me prient de chanter (chançon). R 791, Boogaard 1971, 2

> S'acointance mar acointai: III   27
> helas, une foiz la besai,

maugré sien, qu'onc nel vout graer;
[...]

Las, pour quoi me mis a l'essai   IV   34
de besier ma dame au vis cler?
La lance Pelee trouvai
el besier que je li donai,
qui durement me puet grever;
car se ne me repuis vanter
la endroit ou je me navrai,   40
bien sai qu'a la mort avendrai.
Dex m'i lest oncore assener.

[I fared ill in seeking closer acquaintance with her: alas, I once kissed her, against her will, for she would never willingly grant it. [. . .] Alas, why did I venture on the attempt to kiss my lady of the fair face? I discovered the lance of Peleus in the kiss which I gave her, which may wound me grievously, for if I cannot again boast (of another kiss) in the very place in which I was wounded, I well know that I will face death. May God permit me yet to attain it.]

Lines 5–7 of III, and stanza IV in a poem of five 8-l. stanzas + 2-l. refrain (included by ed. in l. numbering, but here omitted).   36 *la lance Pelee*: for the lance of Peleus, which has the power both to wound and cure, see Bernart de Ventadorn **3.45** ff. n.; in the OF example, the power of a second kiss to cure is less clearly expressed.   41 *avendrai*: lit. 'will come to/ arrive at'.

In the prose version of the Tristan story (c. 1250) there are lyric *lais* sung by Tristan and Iseut respectively:

Prose *Tristan* **1a**

> *Je fis canchonnetes et lais (lai lyrique).* Fotitch, *Lais* 1

Chil autre vont d'amours chantant,   VII   25
et j'em plour et me vois vantant
c'onques jour n'ama nus hon tant
con fist Tristans, s'il muert pour tant.
[...]

Asses ai fui et couru,   X   37
mais nus ne m'i a secouru.
mors et Amours m'ont acoru,
ainc tel mal n'ot d'Ynde Poru.   40

[Those others sing of love; and I weep because of it and boast, that no man ever loved as much as did Tristan, and yet he is dying. [...] I have fled and run far, but no one has come to my aid. Death and love have hastened towards me; Porus of India never experienced such suffering.]

This example of the *lai lyrique*, attested in 19 MSS of the narrative, has in the

Vienna MS, which forms the basis of the text in Fotitch, 31 monorhyme verses (with differing numbers of verses in other MSS). It is designated in the text as *lai mortel* and purports to be that sung by Tristan himself as he was dying, which gives added point to the comparison in ll. 27 ff.   25 *vont... chantant*, 26 *me vois vantant*: forms of *aler* 'to go' + pres. part. express a durative sense, i.e. 'they continue to sing', 'I continue to boast'.   28 *Tristans*: see Chrétien 1.28 f. n.   40 *Poru*: this is a clear case of the use of a name to provide a rhyme. Gk. *Poros*, Lat. *Porus* is a Westernized adaptation of the name of an Indian king, opponent of Alexander the Great in 327 BC. It was known from the *Roman d'Alexandre*.

Prose *Tristan* **1b**

Li solaus luist et clers et biaus (*lai lyrique*). Fotitch, *Lais* 2

Ne fist pas tel perte jadis   XXI   81
Adans, quant perdi paradis
com a fait Yseut, et, tans dis
com muert, fenist cans plus de dis.   84

[Adam did not suffer such a loss in former times when he lost paradise, as Iseut has suffered, and meanwhile (lit. on so many days) as she is dying she finishes more than ten songs.]

This example of the *lai lyrique*, attested in 18 MSS, has 31 monorhyme verses in the Vienna MS (with differing numbers of verses in other MSS); it is sung by Iseut before her death, lamenting the loss of Tristan. Like Tristan in **1a**, Iseut refers to herself in the third person.   82 *Adans*: Biblical comparisons are relatively rare in the love lyric, but for a similar comparison with Adam see Duchesse 1.13 f.   83 f. The construction in l. 84 is occasioned by the requirements of the monorhyme form, in this instance with a punning rhyme between *dis*, the pl. of *di* 'day', in *tans dis*, and *dis*, the numeral 'ten'. In other MSS, *dis* in l. 84 is understood as the pl. of *dit*, indicating the words of the text, as opposed to the melody (*chant*), as in MS G: *com meurt fenissent chans et dis* (as she dies, melodies and words end).

The Later Thirteenth Century

Richard de Fournival **1**

Puis k'il m'estuet . . . (*chançon*). R 805, Lepage 9

Si com Eqo ki sert de recorder   II   8
che k'autres dist, qant par sa sourquidanche
ne la deigna Narchisus resgarder,   10
      k'el secha toute d'ardure
      fors la vois ki encor dure,
ausi perdrai tout fors merchi crïer
et secherai de duel et de pesanche.

Mais Amours ki Narchisus fist mirer,   III   15
qant pour Equo en vaut prendre venganche,
s'ausi pour moi le fesist enamer
     tel ki n'eüst de li cure,
     mis aroit a sa droiture
le grant orgueil ki le fait reveler,   20
et en venroit plus tost a repentanche.

[Like Echo, who is able to repeat what others say, when Narcissus through his arrogance did not deign to regard her, so that she was entirely consumed by her burning passion, except for the voice which still remains, in the same way I shall lose everything except pleading for mercy, and will be consumed by grief and sorrow. But if Love, which caused Narcissus to admire his reflection, when it wished to take vengeance for Echo, in the same way for my sake caused her to love one who paid no heed to her, it would have reduced to its right measure the great pride which makes her resist, and she would in consequence the sooner be moved to repentance.]

The second and third stanzas in a poem of 7 stanzas + 2-l. *envoi*. The next stanza begins with a *revocatio* (*las, k'ai je dit?* alas, what have I said?), since it is quite impossible that anyone could not love such a lady who is the height of beauty and perfection.   8 ff. *Eqo ... Narchisus*: for Narcissus see Thib. Ch. 4.36 n.

This is an unusual example, in that the poet identifies himself, not with Narcissus, as is customary, but with Echo, and the lady with Narcissus.

Richard de Fournival 2

         Talent avoie d'amer (*chançon*). R 760, Lepage 15

C'est la maison Dedalu   IV   25
     u a sa devise
     set cascun entrer,
et tout issont detenu,
     car en nule guise
     ne pueent trouver   30
         ne assener
par u l'entree fu.

Je ne me kier pas mesler   V   33
     de plus haute emprise
     que la Theseü,   35
q'amors sans corde noer
     n'iert ja par moi prise,
     car mains a eü
         plus de vertu
que ains ne pot finer.   40

[It is the house of Daedalus where at will everyone is able to enter, and in which all are detained, for they can in no way find or reach the place where the entrance was. I do not seek to embark on a greater enterprise than that of Theseus, for I will never engage in love without securing a (guiding) thread, for many a one who had greater courage was never able to attain his goal.]

The two final stanzas of the poem.   25 *la maison Dedalu*: for the construction of the labyrinth, see Ovid, *Met.* VIII.155 ff. Guil. Magr. 3 *Ma dompna·m ten pres* likewise compares the bondage of love to imprisonment in the labyrinth: 9 *q'en la maiso de Dedalus | m'a mes amors aman reclus* (for my love has enclosed me as lover in the house of Daedalus).   36. Lit.: 'for love without tying a cord will never be undertaken by me'.   *corde*: a reference to the thread given by Ariadne to Theseus to guide him out of the labyrinth (see Ov., *Met.* VIII.169 ff.).

Raoul de Soissons 1

Rois de Navare . . . (chançon). R 2063, Winkler 10

Rois, a qui j'ai amour et esperance,   VII   55
de bien chanter avez assez raison;
maiz mi plourer sunt ades en saison,
quant je ne puis veoir ce que j'aim plus
c'onques n'ama son ombre Narcisus.

[King, in whom I place love and hope, you have good reason to sing fittingly, but my laments are now in season, when I cannot see the one whom I love more than ever Narcissus loved his reflection.]

The *envoi* in a poem of six 9-l. stanzas.   The poem is in response to one by Thibaut de Champagne (see Winkler pp. 89–91). The fact that the recipient is addressed as *Rois de Navare* dates the poem to post 1234, the year in which Thibaut acceded to the throne of Navarre.   56 *bien*: the adv. is explained by the fact that Thibaut's poem is in praise of love.   58 *ce que*: lit. 'that which', a common form of indirect reference to the lady.   59 *Narcisus*: the final word and rhyme of the poem. See Thibaut de Ch. 4.36 n.

Raoul de Soissons 2

Sens et reson . . . (chançon). R 2106, Winkler 11

Chançon, a la melz amee   VI   56
et a la meilleur du païs
di que plus avroie conquis
amor haute desiree
c'onques n'ot Tristan ne Paris,   60
se s'amor m'avoit donee.

[Song, say to the best loved and the best lady in the land, that I would have won a greater prize of supreme love desired than ever Tristan or Paris enjoyed, if she had given me her love.]

The first 6 ll. of the final 11-l. stanza, which takes the form of an *envoi*. 60 *Tristan*: see Chrétien **1**.28 f. n.   *Paris*: for classical names see Blondel de Nesle **1b**.61 n.   61: the ppf. tense is in accord with stanza III, a complaint of the lady's continuing hard-heartedness, but the final ll. of the *envoi* none the less express the hope of mercy.

Raoul de Soissons (?) **3**

Se j'ai esté lonc tens . . . (*chançon*). R 1204, Winkler, Anhang 15

car quant je pens a son tres douz visage,	II 16
de mon penser aim meuz la conpaignie	
c'onques Tristan ne fist d'Iseut s'amie.	
[. . .]	

Si puisse je sentir sa douce alaine	IV 28
et reveoir sa bele contenance;	
com je desir s'amor et s'acointance	
plus que Paris ne fist onques Elaine!	

[For when I think of her very sweet face, I love the company of my thoughts more than Tristan loved that of Iseut his loved one. [. . .] May I feel her sweet breath and see again her beautiful countenance, how I desire her love and her society more than Paris ever desired Helen!]

16–18: the last 3 ll. of II; 28–31: the first 4 ll. of IV; the stanzas have 9 ll. This poem occurs in the MSS B, N and V, with I–III only in V. MSS B and N have I–V, with three further lines in B, which may be either an *envoi*, or part of a sixth stanza (see Rosenberg/Tischler, *Chansons des Trouvères*, pp. 1039 f.). The question of attribution is problematic: in N the poem is ascribed to Thierri de Soissons, which in this manuscript (and also in MS K) appears to be an error for the name Raoul de Soissons. In B and V, the poem is anonymous, but in the added lines in B, Raoul de Soissons is one of the persons addressed, which, while suggesting some link with the poet, indicates that this version of the poem was not held to be composed by him (the extra lines could of course be an inauthentic addition). It is perhaps unlikely that the poet would have repeated the comparisons with Tristan and Paris occurring in one of his undoubtedly authentic poems (see **2** above), particularly since they are here couched in repetitive formulations. The poem is therefore perhaps unlikely to be by Raoul de Soissons, and may be by an imitator. It is included by Winkler under dubious examples in the appendix, but treated as authentic by Rosenberg/Tischler.   18 *Tristan . . . Iseut*; 31 *Paris . . . Elaine* see **2**.60 n.

Le Comte de Bretagne **1**

Chanter me fet ma dame . . . (*chançon*).
R 357, Bédier p. 487 (no. 2)

Dex! s'el savoit con je l'aim finement,	IV 28
je sai de voir que de melz m'en seroit,	
car onc Tristen n'ama si loiaument	30
la bele Iseut que touz jors desiroit,	
et je autresi sui sorpris et destroit	
de la meilleur qui soit el mont vivant,	
ne ja ne croi que ja si bele soit.	

[Oh God, if she knew how truly I love her, I am certain that it would fare better with me, for never did Tristan love the beautiful Iseut, whom he always desired, so faithfully, and I likewise am overpowered and constrained by the best lady living in the world, and I do not believe that there is such a beautiful one anywhere.]

The first 7 ll. of IV in a poem of five 9-l. stanzas.   30 *Tristen . . . Iseut*: see Chrétien **1**.28 f. n.

Adam de la Halle uses exemplary figures in two poems as a warning against incorrect behaviour in love; although set in a lyric context, these instances are more akin to moral *exempla* than to exemplary comparisons proper:

Adam de la Halle **1**

Hé! las, il n'est mais nus . . . (chançon), R 149, Marshall 5

Cele ki par fierté destraint   IV   25
trop son ami, fait a blasmer,
et cil, s'il l'ounor de li fraint:
moienement couvient aler.
Dedalus, k'ensi vaut ouvrer,
          le senefie,   30
et ses fix ki par sa folie
fu tous ars par trop haut voler.

[She who out of pride constrains her lover too greatly is to be blamed, as is he, if he injures her honour: it is necessary to proceed with moderation. Daedalus, who was intent on acting thus [i.e. without moderation] is an illustration of this, and his son, who through his folly was consumed in flames by flying too high.]

The fourth stanza in a poem of 5 stanzas + 4-l. *envoi*.   25 *destraint*: i.e. causes suffering by keeping him at a distance.   29 *Dedalus*: for Daedalus in association with the motif of excess in love see Rig. Berb. **1**.   31 *ses fix*: Icarus.

Adam de la Halle **2**

De canter ai volenté . . . (chançon). R 1018, Marshall 17

Pour chou fait mal quant ele ne m'asaie: V   33
adont saroit a qui douner merchi.
mais jou ne sai comment a chou l'atraie;   35
bele dame est, ne s'abaisseroit si.
pour coi je douc Lucifer ne pourtraie,
ki pour sa grant biauté s'enorguelli,
          et qu'ele ne face ausi
          vers moi, ki l'aim d'amour vraie.   40

[Therefore she acts ill when she does not put me to the test; then she would know to whom to grant mercy; but I do not know how to induce her to do this – she is a beautiful lady, she would not humble herself so much.

Therefore I fear she may resemble Lucifer, who grew arrogant because of his great beauty, and may act likewise towards me, I who love her with true love.]

33–40: the last of five stanzas, followed by a 4-l. *envoi.*   37 *Lucifer*: in Is. 14:12 an epithet of the king of Babylon, the epitome of arrogance vanquished. In medieval theology, in conjunction with Luke 10:18, the name became a synonym for the devil, cast out from heaven because of his overweening pride. For beauty as the cause of Lucifer's downfall see *Jeux-partis* 27.32 *grant biautés enorgeilli | Lucifer, ki trop vilment | dedens enfer en kaï* (great beauty made Lucifer proud, who most shamefully fell down into hell in consequence).

Jeux partis

The *jeu parti* (Oc. *joc partit*), most instances of which belong to the 13th century, consists of an exchange between two poets, debating on a set subject in alternate stanzas. Exemplars may be cited as illustration of the argument. Of the following examples, **1a** and **2** can be assigned to the later thirteenth century, **1b** may belong to the early fourteenth century (see Långfors, *Jeux-partis*, p. LVII on the possible identification of Thibaut de Bar).

Jeux-partis **1a**

Jehan de Bretel à Jehan de Grieviler, *Grieviler, par quel raison.* (*jeu parti*). R 1890, Långfors, *Jeux-partis* 39

D'Amour et de sa poison,   VI   41
Sire, estes empoisonnez.
je voi bien que vous parlez
a guise de son prison.
Aristotes tout son sens i perdi,   45
ja sages hom n'avra d'amer bon cri;
vuide est Amours, li sage y sont perdant
de leur pourfit qui le vont poursivant.

[Sir, by Love and its philtre you are intoxicated; I see clearly that you speak in the manner of its prisoner. Aristotle lost all his sense through this; no wise man will gain a good reputation from love. Love is vain, the wise who pursue it forfeit their advantage thereby.]

41–8: the final stanza.   41 f. *poison… empoisonnez*: see Chrétien **1**.28 f. n. 45 *Aristotes*: see also the reference in *Jeux-partis* 116.1 ff. to the story of Aristotle ridden like a horse by Phyllis, probably known from the *Lai d'Aristote* by Henri d'Andeli. For the theme of Love's victims see Couci **2**.9 f. n.

Jeux-partis **1b**

Rolant à Thibaut de Bar, *Thiebaus de Bair, li rois
des Allemans.* (*jeu parti*). R 259, Långfors, *Jeux-partis* 171

li grans Cesar, qui tant ot de pooir,   V   49
Amors lou fist venir a son servaige
por la belle plaixant, au cler visaige,
Cleopatras, ke tant fist a loeir.
por ceu di je c'amors n'ait point de peir.
je ferai ce que ma dame me prie:
Amours lou vuelt et volanteit l'otrie.   55

[Love made the great Caesar, who had so much power, submit to its
bondage for the sake of the beautiful charming one, fair of face, Cleopatra,
who was so much praised. Therefore I say that love has no peer. I shall do
what my lady asks of me: Love wills it and desire assents.]

49–55: the last 7 ll. of the final 11-l. stanza.   49 *li grans Cesar*: Antony. In
contrast to **1a**, the victim of Love and its servitude is here presented positively.
52 *Cleopatras*: see Arn. Mar. **3b**.156 n.

Jeux-partis **2**

Jehan de Marli à Jehan de Grieviler, *Or coisisiés, Jehan
de Grieviler.* (*jeu parti*). R 861 and 770, Långfors, *Jeux-partis* 100

Maistre Jehan, vous volés resambler   VI   41
chel Narcisu dont on va tant parlant,
qui la mort eut par son ombre mirer;
autant vaut çou que vous m'alés contant:
songiers ne vaut a amours tant ne qant,   45
mais qant d'ami est amie sentie,
autres deduis tant cuer ne glorefie,
         bien l'os prover.

[Master Jehan, you wish to resemble that Narcissus of whom so much is
told, who met his death through admiring his reflection. Of like worth is
that which you are recounting to me: dreams are of no use at all to love,
but when the lover experiences the lady's presence, no other joy so exalts
the heart, as I venture to prove.]

41–8: the final stanza, followed only by a 4-l. *envoi*.   42 *Narcisu*: see Thib.
Ch. **4**.36 n.

Examples of Uncertain Date, Including
Those Transmitted Anonymously

The following example occurs in a poem surviving in one MS ascribed to Gace
Brulé (fl. c. 1179–1212); it is placed by the editor under doubtful attributions.

Gace Brulé (?) **1**

Ire d'amors . . . (chançon). R 230, Petersen Dyggve, Gace *14

Pertenopés nous moustre sens doutance IV 22
perde d'amors est griés a andureir.
li maltalent d'amors et la pesence,
ki n'ait sentit les duels ne seit ameir. 25
Amors se veult servir et honoreir.
k'an veult joïr, gairt soi de mesprenance:
mefais d'amours ne fait a perdoneir.

Haute Amor ait desdaig et grant viltance, V
quant a[s] siens voit ses comans refuseir: 30
per Gingamur en avons la provence.

[Pertenopés shows us without any doubt, loss of love is hard to endure.
The distress and pain of love, whoever has not experienced these sorrows, knows nothing of love. Love demands to be served and honoured.
Whoever wishes to enjoy its benefits, let him refrain from error: wrong
behaviour in love cannot be pardoned. Noble Love experiences scorn and
great contempt, when it sees its servants refusing to obey its commands:
in Gingamur we have the proof of this.]

The text breaks off after the first 3 ll. of V.   22 *Pertenopés*: the hero of
Partonopeus de Blois, a popular 12th-century narrative. The name is reminis-
cent of that of Parthenopaeus, one of the Seven against Thebes, but there is no
connection with the classical figure. The fairy Melior makes Partonopeus vow
never to look at her during their nocturnal encounters, but given a lantern by
his mother, he does so and is banished from her presence. After many adventures he defeats her other suitors and finally wins her.   24 f. The syntax
of these ll. is defective; l. 25 should perhaps read *qui n'en ait . . .* (whoever has
not experienced the sorrows of these . . .).   25 *ne seit ameir*: lit. 'does
not know how to love'.   31 *Gingamur*: the hero of *Giugemar*, a narrative
lai by Marie de France (12th century). Guigemar resists love and is punished
by being wounded while killing a white doe, who prophesies that his wound
will never heal until it is cured by a lady, destined like him to undergo great
suffering before they are finally reunited.

Duchesse de Lorraine **1**

Par maintes fois . . . (chançon). R 1640, Rosenberg/Tischler 193

Par maintes fois avrai esteit requise I 1
c'ains ne chantai ansi con je soloi,
car je suix si aloingnie de joie
que j'en devroie estre plus antreprise,
et a mien voil moroie an iteil guise 5
con celle fist cui je sanbler voroie:
Didol, qui fut por Eneas ocise.

Ahi, amins! tout a vostre devise   II 8
que ne fis jeu tant con je vos veoie?
jant vilainne cui je tant redotoie   10
m'ont si greveit et si ariere mise
c'ains ne vos pou merir vostre servise.
s'estre poioit, plus m'an repantiroie
c'Adans ne fist de la pome c'ot prise.

Ains por Forcon ne fist tant Afelisse   III 15
con je por vos, amins, s'or vos ravoie;
mais ce n'iert jai, se premiers ne moroie.
mais je [ne] puis morir en iteil guise,
c'ancor me rait Amors joie promise.
si vuel doloir an leu de mener joie: 20
poinne et travail, ceu est ma rante assise.

[Many times I may have been asked (to sing), since I have never sung as I used to, for I am so distanced from joy that I should be even more prevented from singing; and if my wish were granted, I would die in the same way as the one I would wish to resemble, Dido, who was slain for the sake of Aeneas. Ah! my friend, why did I not act entirely according to your wishes while I still saw you? The evil ones whom I so much dreaded have so greatly injured and held me back that I was never able to reward you for your service. If it were possible, I would feel greater remorse than did Adam on account of the apple which he had taken. Never did Afelisse do so much for Forcon, as I would do for you, my friend, if you were now restored to me, but this can never be, if I were not first to die – but I cannot die in such a manner, for Love might again promise me joy. Thus I will grieve instead of being joyful: pain and torment is my allotted due.]

Stanzas I–III of a 4-stanza poem. The poem is in the female voice, and whereas some critics have doubted whether it was actually written by a woman, others posit various possible female identifications. Of these perhaps the most likely is that with Marguerite de Champagne, daughter of Thibaut de Champagne (*q.v.*), who married Ferri III, Duke of Lorraine in 1255 (see Doss-Quinby, *Women Trouvères*, pp. 28–30 and 126). Stanza IV also contains an identification: 25 *or seu Fenis, lasse soule et eschise* (now I am a Phoenix, weary, alone and estranged).   1 *avrai*: the future auxiliary expresses the idea of probability, i.e. 'I will have been asked'; cf. also 19 *rait*, the 3rd. pres. subj. of *ravoir*, expressing a more doubtful possibility.   1 f. The transl. in Rosenberg/Tischler 'maintes fois on m'aura demandé pourquoi je ne chante plus . . .' is inaccurate, because *requerre* does not have the sense of 'ask/question', but that of 'ask/request', and the conjunction *que* does not have the sense of 'why'.   5 *a mien voil*: 'in accordance with my wishes'.   7 *Didol . . . Eneas*: for classical names see Blondel **1b**.61 n.   *ocise*: when abandoned by Aeneas, Dido fell on his sword.   10 *jant vilainne*: a circumlocution for the *losengeor*, the treacherous slanderers who spy on and come between the lovers.   14 *Adans*: see Pr. *Trist.* **1b**.82 n.   15 Folque (Fouque) and Anfelise are the lovers in the OF epic poem *Folque de Candie. Tibauz* in Raimb. Vaq. **3b**.10 is derived from the same poem.   16 *s'or vos ravoie*: lit. 'if I now had you again'.

OF Anon. **1**

Grant piece ait . . . (chançon). R 194,
Jeanroy/Långfors, *Chansons satiriques et bachiques* 19

Grant piece ait ke ne chantai maix	I	1
ne ke de chanteir n'oi talent,		
maix or soustien d'Amors lou faix,		
por coi tous merris chant;		
car onkes Tristans n'amait tant		5
ne nel tint Amors de si près		
com or fait moi tout a elaix.		

[It is long since that I ever sang or had the desire to sing, but now I bear the burden of Love, and therefore I sing very sorrowfully, for never did Tristan love so much, nor did Love hold him so closely as it now holds me with all its force.]

The first 7 ll. of a 10-l. stanza in a 3-stanza poem, according to MS C. MS O has only stanzas I and II, with considerable textual variations, so that the name of Tristan has been suppressed, and 5 f. reads: *car sanz guierredon n'ama tant* | *nuns hons* (for no man ever loved so much without reward). For other instances of versions with and without an exemplary comparison, see Perr. Ang. **3**; OF Anon. **10f**.   5 *Tristans*: see Chrétien **1**.28 f. n.

OF Anon. **2**

L'on dit q'amors . . . (chançon). R 1937, Rosenberg/Tischler 39

Estre cuidai de lui amee	III	21
quant entre ses braz me tenoit;		
cum plus iere d'amors grevee,		
a son parler me refaisoit;		
a sa voiz iere si sanee		25
cum Piramus quant il moroit:		
navrez en son flanc de s'espee,		
au nom Tisbé les iauz ovroit.		

[I thought I was loved by him when he held me in his arms; when I was most oppressed by love, I was restored by his words; at the sound of his voice I was cured, like Pyramus when he was dying: wounded in his side by his sword, at the name of Thisbe he opened his eyes.]

The final stanza of the poem, which is a woman's lament at abandonment by her faithless lover. The 2-l. refrain is omitted here.   26 ff. *Piramus . . . Tisbé*: see Blondel **1b**.61 n. It is noteworthy that the female speaker identifies herself with Pyramus, and not with Thisbe. See Ov., *Met.* IV.145 f.: *ad nomen Thisbes oculos a morte gravatos* | *Pyramus erexit visaque recondidit illa* (at the name of Thisbe, Pyramus raised his eyes, heavy with death, and when he had looked at her, closed them again).

OF Anon. **3**

La froidor ne la jalee (*chançon*). R 517, Rosenberg/Tischler 40

Ma chanson isi define,   V   41
ke joie ait vers moi fineir;
car j'ai el cors la rasine
ke ne puis desrasineir,
ke m'est a cuer enterine,   45
    sens fauceir.
Amors m'ont pris en haïne
    por ameir.
j'ai beüt del boivre ameir
k'Isoth but, la roïne.   50

[My song here ends, since joy is finished for me, for I have within my being the root which I cannot uproot, for it is implanted in my heart in very truth. Love has conceived hatred towards me, because I love. I have drunk of the bitter potion which Iseut the queen drank.]

The final stanza of a woman's song, a complaint of the torments of love, with considerable morphological word play: *define–fineir*; *rasine–desrasineir*; *amors–ameir*; there is also a semantic contrast between the homophones *ameir* 'to love' and *ameir* 'bitter', and between the opposing pairs *cors–cuer* and *amors–haïne*. 49 f. In contrast to OF Anon. **2** (*q.v.*), the speaker compares herself to a female exemplar.   50 *Isoth*: the love potion is usually cited, not in association with Iseut, as here, but with Tristan – see Chrétien 1.28 f. n.

OF Anon. **4**

Li chastelains de Couci ama tant (*chançon*, designated
in l. 3 as *conplainte*). R 358, Spanke, *Liedersammlung* 10

Li chastelains de Couci ama tant   I   1
qu'ainz por amor nus n'en ot dolor graindre;
por ce ferai ma conplainte en son chant,
que ne cuit pas que la moie soit maindre.

[The Chastelain de Couci loved so much that no one ever suffered greater sorrow from love; therefore I will compose my complaint in (the form of) his song, for I do not think that my sorrow is less.]

The first 4 ll. of an 8-l. stanza in a poem of 5 stanzas.   This poem has the form and melody of Couci R 679 (Lerond 1), *A vous, amant, plus k'a nulle autre gent,* | *est bien raisons que ma doleur conplaigne*, a lament at parting from the lady on departure as a Crusader. The anonymous poem laments the death of the lady, brought about by the cruel separation of the lovers by her family. 1 *Li chastelains de Couci*: for the poet as exemplary lover see Eustache 1.34 n.

OF Anon. **5**

Quant voi blanchoier la flor (*chançon*). R 1980, Spanke, *Liedersammlung* 22

Elaine por qui Paris II 10
   ot tant de torment,
n'ot onques, ce m'est avis,
   de biauté autant
con cele ou mes cuers s'atent.

[Helen, for whom Paris suffered so much torment, never, I believe, possessed such great beauty as the one to whom my heart aspires.]

The first 5 ll. of a 9-l. stanza in a poem of 5 stanzas. 10 *Elaine . . . Paris*: see Blondel **1b**.61 n.; the beauty of Helen, see OF Anon. **6**.49.

OF Anon. **6**

Souvent souspire (*chançon*). R 1506, Spanke, *Liedersammlung* 29

plus ai dolor que cil de Troie; II 25
   ne croie
   que voie
le jor que sire en soie.
[. . .]

   si me demaine IV 46
   com sien demaine,
plus est fiere que chastelaine.
onques ni fu si bele Elaine, 49
ne n'ot onques si douce alaine.

[I have more sorrow than him of Troy; I do not think I shall see the day that I shall master it. [. . .] She exercises power over me as her liege, she is more proud than the mistress of a castle. Helen was never so beautiful, nor ever had such sweet breath.]

II.25 ff.: the last 4 ll. of the stanza; IV.46 ff.: ll. 4–8 of the stanza. The poem consists of 5 stanzas of 14 ll., each with only one rhyme: I -*ire*; II -*oie*; III -*ie*; IV -*aine*; V -*ere* (but with two unrhymed ll.). The need for so many identical rhyming syllables has clearly prompted the insertion of *Troie* and *Elaine* as rhyme words, and explains the designation *cil de Troie* for Paris; for classical names, see Blondel **1b**.61 n. 49 *Elaine*: see OF Anon. **5**.10 ff.

OF Anon. **7**

Ichi comans | . . . | *le gentil lai des amans* (*lai*).
R 635, Jeanroy/Brandin/Aubry, *Lais et descorts* 20

Jou aim plus dis tans VI 67
ke ne fist Tristrans.
[. . .]
Dame belle, blance et blonde, IX 149
plus belle ke Soramonde . . .

[I love ten times more than did Tristan. [. . .] Beautiful Lady, of fair complexion and blond hair, more beautiful than Soramonde . . .]

The *lai*, of *lai-descort* type, consists of 10 heterometric sections; VI has 3 rhymes in *-ans*, IX is a monorhyme section, with 12 rhymes in *-onde*, which no doubt explains the choice of an unusual exemplar of female beauty. 68 *Tristrans*: see Chrétien **1**.28 f. n.   150 *Soramonde*: a f. name in the *chanson de geste*, e.g. in the 13th-century *Aimeri de Narbonne*, ed. Demaison 4597 *et Soramonde, la bele o le cler vis*, and as a variant form of a f. name in the 12th-century *Fierabras* and the 14th-century *Hugues Capet*.

OF Anon. **8**

Uns hons qui a en soi . . . (*chançon*). R 1886, *Archiv* XLIII (1868), p. 392

por bien servir ne doit on pais mal rendre,   II 14
mais sil ki sont pire ke Guenillon,
k'en autre rien n'ont lor entendement
fors k'en tous tans nuit et jor abaissant
loial amor par fauce traïxon.   18

[One should not repay good service with evil, but (there are) those who are worse than Guenelon, who have their purpose fixed on nothing else but at all times, night and day, bringing low faithful love by false treachery.]

The final 5 ll. of II, in a poem of three 9-l. stanzas (+ the beginning of a fourth). 15 *sil ki sont pire ke Guenillon*: for the general significance of the name, see Thib. Ch. **6**.36 n. Here it is used to refer to the *losengeor*, who attempt to disrupt the love relationship. See also *la gent Guenelon* designating the same figures: Jehan de Maisons 8.17, Petersen Dyggve, *Trouvères et Protecteurs de Trouvères*, p. 88; Adam de Givenci, Jeanroy/Brandin/Aubry, *Lais et descorts* 11.28.

OF Anon. **9**

Costume et us (*chançon*).
R 2123, Jeanroy/Långfors, 'Chansons inédites', p. 310 (no. 14)

Amis et druz   II 10
puet lire a son talant,
    mais il n'est nus
qui l'aint si lëaument,
    car je l'aim plus
qu'Aude n'ama Rolant;   15
    ainz Narcisus,
Tristans ne Piramus
n'amerent tant.

[She can choose friend and lover as she wishes, but there is none who loves her so faithfully, for I love her more than Roland loved Aude; never did Narcissus, Tristan or Pyramus love so much.]

The second of three 9-l. stanzas. I and II have fivefold repetition of the rhyming syllable *-us*, including in I the name *Artus* in rhyme (8 f. *et dout ne soit Artus | ce que j'atent* (and I fear that it may be Arthur that I await), i.e. his hope, like that of the Bretons for Arthur, is vain.   15 *Aude*: the betrothed of Roland in the *Chanson de Roland*; see Guir. Sal. **2**.16 n. Particularly in verse (see the Oc. exs. Raim. Jord. **1**.30 n.) the word-order object–verb–subject is common. 16 *Narcisus*: see Thib. Ch. **4**.36 n.; 17 *Tristans*: see Chrétien **1**.28 f. n.; *Piramus*: see Blondel **1b**.62 n.

Brief Anonymous Examples[3]

Under this heading, brief examples of a similar nature are grouped together.

OF Anon. **10a**

> *De cuer dolant et ploin d'ire (chançon).*
> R 1500, Jeanroy/Långfors, 'Chansons inédites' p. 315 (no. 20)

. . . ma tres doucete amie   III   25

[. . .] qui si m'a en son demainne,

plus l'ain que Paris Helainne.   27

[My very sweet love . . . who has me in her power, I love her more than Paris loved Helen.]

These lines occur in the second half of III in a poem of of five 10-l. stanzas, each of which has the rhyme in -*ainne*: I *certainne* : *poinne*; II *estrainne* : *prochainne*; III *demainne* : *Helainne*; IV *fonteinne* : *vilainne*; V *semainne* : *remeinne*.

OF Anon. **10b**

> *Quant voi le dous tans comencier (chançon).*
> R 1271, *Archiv* XLII (1868), p. 256

car ie l'am plux c'onke Paris Helainne,   II   16

cors ait bien fait et avenant,

euls vairs riants, bouchete tainte en grainne.

[For I love her more than Paris ever loved Helen; she has an elegant and charming figure, bright smiling eyes, a mouth of rosy hue.]

The final 3 ll. of II, in a poem of five 9-l. stanzas, with the rhyme scheme *aaab bcdcd*, the *d* rhyme the same in all stanzas: I *poene* : *fontainne*; II *Helainne* : *grainne*; III *serainne* : *semaine*; IV *poene* : *estrainne*; V *certaine* : *plainne*.

OF Anon. **10c**

> *Or seux liés* . . . *(chançon).* R 1386, Rosenberg/Tischler 43

mis me seux en sa saixine: III   25

bien puet aligier ma poene,

car je l'ain plux d'amor fine

ke Paris ne fist Helenne.

[I have submitted myself to her power; she is well able to relieve my sufferings, for I love her with true love more than Paris loved Helen.]

---

[3] For Paris and Helen in OF Anon. **10a**, **10f**, see Blondel **1b**.61 n.; for Tristan and/or Iseut (including the circumlocution in **10h**) in OF Anon. **10f**–**10j**, see Chrétien **1**.28 f. n.

The last 4 ll. of III in a poem of three 8-l. stanzas + 2-l. refrain, (omitted here). The rhyme scheme is *abababab*, the *a* rhyme in *-ine*, the *b* rhyme in *-aine* (with varying graphic representation) in all three stanzas: I *premerainne : fontainne : lointaine : plainne*; II *moinne : voinne : plainne : semainne*; III *moinne : regne : poene : Helenne.*   25 Lit.: 'I have placed myself under her feudal sove-reignty'.

OF Anon. 10d

De lors que j'acointai Amors (chançon). R 144.
Jeanroy/Långfors, *Chansons satiriques et bachiques* 18 (see **10e**)

Et moi c'an chaut, tan seus jolis,   II 9
j'ains la millour de son païs,
c'onke tant nen amait Paris
            Helainne.

[And what does it matter to me, I am so joyful, I love the best one of her country, for never did Paris love Helen so much.]

Four quatrains + identical 2-l. head- and end-refrain. The first line of the head-refrain is *Hé! trikedondene!*, which is given as the first line in Raynaud and Spanke under R 144, but the true first line of the poem, correctly given in Linker as *De lors que j'acointai Amors*, allies it closely to OF Anon. **10e**. The poem has the rhyme scheme *aaabRbb*, with the *b* rhyme the same throughout: I *et poinne*; II *Helainne*; III *ne voine*; IV *ma poinne*; Refr. *trikedondene* (2×).

OF Anon. 10e

Quant primes me quintey d'amors (chançon).
R 2017b, *Romania* XIX (1890), p. 102

je em la plus bele du pays;   II 5
kaunt je m'ene pens si sui jolis.
je l'em plus ke ne fist Paris
            Heleyne.

[I love the most beautiful one in the country; when I think of her, I am joyful. I love her more than Paris loved Helen.]

The poem consists of eight quatrains, rhyming *aaab* + 1-l. refrain (incomplete) The *b* rhyme is the same in all stanzas: I *e peyne*; II *Heleyne*; III *ne veyne*; IV *en greyne*; V *sa alayne*; VI *a payne*; VII *k'en reclayme*; VIII *si n'eyme*. As in the previous ex. (see n.) the refrain probably had *trikedondene* as the final word in rhyme.   6 *ene* is ambiguous, either 'of her' or 'of that'.

OF Anon. 10f

Aucunes gens m'ont enquis (chançon). R 1528.
See Gillebert de Berneville, ed. Fresco, pp. 142 f.

c'onkes n'amait tant Paris   IIIbis 25
ne Tristans, j'en sui tout fis,
com je fais . . .

[For never did Paris or Tristan, of that I am certain, love as much as I do.]

The Gillebert de Berneville poem (Fresco 8) consists in MSS M and T of six 9-l. stanzas + 5-l. *envoi* and one-l. refrain, with five stanzas in MS a. MS C has three stanzas only, with I and II in accord with the other MSS, but III, the only one with an exemplary comparison, is a *unicum*, which however follows the same rhyme scheme as I and II. For other instances of versions with and without a comparison see Perr. Ang. 3; OF Anon. 1.

OF Anon. 10g

Jolif, plain de bone amor (chançon). R 1942, Spanke, *Liedersammlung* 13

ja dex ne mi doint a li   IV   29
n'a sa joie recovrer,
s'onques riens poi tant amer:
du lignage Tristan sui.   32

[May God not grant that I gain her favour or joy from her, if ever I was able to love anything as much: I am of the lineage of Tristan.]

The last 4 ll. of IV in a poem of five 8-l. stanzas.   29 f. lit.: 'may God not grant that I attain to her or to her joy'.

OF Anon. 10h

Chanter ne me seut agreer (chançon). R 756, *Archiv* XLII (1868), p. 257

Onkes celle n'ot tant biauteit   V   33
cui Tristans provait a l'essai,
ne tant valour ne tant bonteit . . .

[She whose worth Tristan put to the test never had such beauty, or such excellence or such goodness . . .]

The first 3 ll. of V in a poem of five 8-l. stanzas + 4-l. *envoi*.

OF Anon. 10i

Pour ce que (tant se) mes cuers . . . (chançon).
R 1975, *Archiv* XLIII (1868), p. 299

k'onques Tristans n'amait autant Isot   I   6
com je fais vos, amie.
mes amors et les vos
ne departiront mie.

[For never did Tristan love Isot as much as I love you, dear one. My love and yours will never part.]

The last 4 ll. of the first 9-l. stanza in a poem of five stanzas.

OF Anon. 10j

Hareu! ne fin de proier (chançon). R 1294, *Archiv* XLII (1868), p. 326

Amors, plux me greveis   III   17
k'Isot ke morte en fut.

[Love, you oppress me more than Isot, who died in consequence.]

The first two ll. of III in a poem of five 8-l. stanzas.   18 *Isot*: unusually, the male poet compares himself with a female exemplar.

Secular Exemplars in a Religious Context

OF Anon. **11**

L'estoile qui tant est clere (chançon). R 902, Järnström, *Chansons pieuses* 26

Cele estoile est fille et mere   II   13
a Jhesu le Creatour;
qui l'aimme et li porte honour,   15
bien emploie cel usaige.
ne conquist en son aage
Alixandre l'emperere
qui dou mont fist son plaisir,
tant com fait en li servir.   20

[This star is the daughter and mother of Jesus the Creator; whoever loves her and does her honour, employs this service to a good end. Alexander the emperor who ruled the world as he pleased, did not conquer as much as is attained by serving her.]

The first 8 ll. of a 12-l. stanza in a poem of three stanzas celebrating the Virgin Mary.   17 ff. For *Alixandre* see Perr. Ang **1**.40 n.; for the motif of conquest cf. Guil. Ferr. **1**.19 n.   19 See the related construction with *talant*, Guil. Ferr. **1**.19.

Secular exemplary figures, together with motifs of the love lyric, occur in a hagiographic context in the *Miracles* of Gautier de Coinci (1177/8–1236): Koenig II, mir. 9 (the Empress of Rome, with etymological word play on the name of Tristan): 298 *vostre amors me fait endurer | tant tristre moys et tant tristre an | que plus sui tristres que Tristran. | plus vous aim, dame, et plus i bé | que Pyramus n'ama Tysbé | ne que Tristrans Ysot la blonde* (love of you causes me to endure so many sad months and so many sad years that I am more sad than Tristan. I love you more, lady, and aspire to this love more than Pyramus loved Thisbe, or Tristan Ysot the fair); Koenig I, mir. 44 (saint Léocade): 298 *ains n'enbraça Paris Helainne | si doucement con je fis li* (never did Paris embrace Helen so tenderly as I embraced her).

Conclusion

Exemplary comparisons occur mainly in the genre of the *chançon*, but there are also instances in the following types of poem: *descort* (Gaut. Darg. 1); *pastourelle* (Thib. Ch. 6); *lai lyrique* (Pr. *Tristan* **1a, 1b**); *jeu parti* (*Jeux-partis* **1a, 1b, 2**); *lai* (OF Anon. **7**); the author of OF Anon. **4**, a *chançon* in the form of Couci R 679, designates his poem as *conplainte*. As in the troubadours, the exemplary figures are derived from the following areas: classical literature and legend; the Bible; historical legend; the *chanson de geste* and related works; the Tristan story; Arthurian romances; other medieval narratives. There are no comparisons with divinities or their attributes. As in the troubadours, classical and historical figures are probably derived from medieval adaptations of classical themes and historical legend.[4]

Most instances take the form of explicit comparison, and in the above examples identification with an exemplar occurs only in Thib. Ch. **3**.11 f. *pleüst a Dieu, . . . qu'el fust Tisbé, car je sui Piramus*, and *id.* **4**.35 f. *mult la desir et, s'ele me desprise, Narcisus sui, qui noia tout par soi* (but see n. on Duchesse 1.IV.25). Comparison with an attribute of an exemplar occurs in Guiot **1**.48 f. *la leiauté Tristant porra trover en moi*, and Thib. Ch. **2**.15 ff. *onques fierté n'ot si grant | vers Pompee Julius | que ma dame n'en ait plus | vers moi*; OF Anon. **5**.10 ff. *Elaine . . . | n'ot onques . . . | de biauté autant | con cele ou mes cuers s'atent*; OF Anon. **10h**.33 ff. *onkes celle n'ot tant biauteit | . . . ne tant valour ne tant bonteit*. The most commonly occurring motif is that of the poet's love or suffering, or more rarely his joy, real or imagined, as equalling or surpassing those of the exemplar. The motif of like or greater love occurs in Chrétien **1**; Couci **1**; Guiot **1**; Blondel **1b**; Eustache **1**; Thib. Bl. **1**; J. Neuv. **1**; R. Soiss. **1**; R. Soiss. (?) **3**; Comte Bret. **1**; OF Anon. **1**; OF Anon. **7**; OF Anon. **9**; OF Anon. **10a**; OF Anon. **10b**; OF Anon. **10c**; OF Anon. **10d**; OF Anon. **10e**; OF Anon. **10f**; OF Anon. **10i**. In Pr. *Trist.* **1a**.27 f. Tristan, referring to himself in the third person, rejects the notion that anyone ever equalled his love: *c'onques jor n'ama nus hon tant con fist Tristans*. The poet's grief equals or surpasses that of the exemplar: Blondel **1a**; Thib. Ch. **1**; Perr. Ang. **1**; **3**; Pr. *Trist.* **1a**.39 f.; Pr. *Trist.* **1b**.81 ff.; Duchesse **1**.13 f.; OF Anon. **3**; OF Anon. **4**; OF Anon. **6**; OF Anon. **10j**. He is doomed to suffer the fate of Narcissus, Thib. Ch. **4**, or that of Echo, Rich. Fourn. **1**.8 ff. If the lady were to be kind, his joy would be greater than that of Tristan, Thib. Ch. **5**. R. Soiss. **2** is similar: the poet would have won a greater prize of love than Tristan or Paris, if the lady were to grant her love. Some comparisons are associated with the theme of power: Guil. Ferr. **1** would prefer the conquest of the lady to Charlemagne's conquest of Spain; in OF Anon. **11** the motif of Alexander's conquest is transferred to the religious sphere; without the lady, Gaut. Darg. **1** would not wish to equal Hector; in his love, Andr. Contr. **1** is more powerful than Caesar. The same exemplar may have a positive or negative function according to context: thus in Andr. Contr. **1**, Caesar represents supreme power, but in Thib. Ch. **2** arrogance; in R. Soiss. **1** and OF Anon. **9** Narcissus is a positive example of love, but in Thib. Ch. **4** and *Jeux-partis* **2** he is presented negatively as the cause of his own death.

Most exemplars are associated with the male poet, and in references to exemplary pairs of lovers, the female name may be omitted altogether, as in Chrétien **1**; Couci **1**; Guiot **1**; Blondel **1a**; Blondel **1b**; Eustache **1**; Thib. Ch. **5**; Pr. *Trist.* **1a**; R. Soiss. **2**; OF Anon. **1**; OF Anon. **6**.25 ff.; OF Anon. **7**; OF

---

[4] See pp. 150 f., 188 f.

Anon. **9**.16 f.; OF Anon. **10f**; OF Anon. **10g**; in OF Anon. **10h** the female name is replaced by a circumlocution. Where the object of the exemplar's love is named in a paired formula, the female name is grammatically subordinate, being part of the predicate – see, for instance, Thib. Bl. **1**.40 f.; J. Neuv. **1**.20 f; Perr. Ang. **3**.24; R. Soiss. (?) **3**.18; Comte Bret. **1**.30 f.; OF Anon. **2**.28; OF Anon. **9**.15 (but with emphatic placing of the female name before the verb); OF Anon. **10a**.28; OF Anon. **10b**.16; OF Anon. **10c**.27 f.; OF Anon. **10d**.11 f.; OF Anon. **10e**.7 f.; OF Anon.**10i**.6. Only occasionally is the lady the sole, or dominant, part of the comparison: she is more beautiful than Helen, OF Anon. **5**.10 ff.; OF Anon. **6**.49 f.; more beautiful than Soramonde, OF Anon. **7**.149 f. Because of the dominant tradition of male exemplars, the lady may be likened to a male figure: she shows the arrogance of Caesar towards Pompey, Thib. Ch. **2**.15 ff.; she causes the poet to suffer greater ills than Alexander inflicted on Darius, Perr. Ang. **1**.39 f.; she is potentially compared with Lucifer in Ad. Halle **2**.37. Likewise in poems in the female voice, the speaker may compare herself with a male figure: with Adam in Pr. *Trist.* **1b** and Duchesse **1**.13 f., with Pyramus in OF Anon. **2**.25 f., but with Dido and Afelisse in Duchesse **1**.7, 15, and with Iseut in OF Anon. **3**.50 and, by implication, in Moniot **1**.50. Exceptionally, in OF Anon. **10j**.17 f. the male poet compares his grief with that of Iseut.

Most exemplars represent positive models, but there are also those which have a negative function: in Gace (?) **1**, Pertenopés teaches the folly of wrong conduct in love, Gingamur that of disobeying love's commands; in Ad. Halle **1**, Daedalus and Icarus represent immoderate desires, whereas in Rich. Fourn. **2** the maze built by Daedalus symbolizes love itself, from which there is no escape; in Ad. Halle **2**, Lucifer embodies arrogance; Guenelon represents the archetypal traitor in Thib. Ch. **6** and OF Anon. **8**.

There are a few, mainly brief, allusions to narrative motifs associated with the exemplar: the love potion, Chrétien **1**; Couci **1**; OF Anon. **3**; Lancelot's service of Guinevere, Gille Vin. **1**; Jason and the fleece, Thib. Ch. **1**; the death of Narcissus, Thib. Ch. **4**; *Jeux-partis* **2**; the fate of Echo, Rich. Fourn. **1**; the thread of Ariadne, *id.* **2**; Yvain and the lion, Perr. Ang. **2**; the flight of Icarus, Ad. Halle **1**; the death of Pyramus OF Anon. **2**.26 ff.

The names[5] are derived from the following main sources:

Classical legend and literature: *Didol* – *Eneas* Duchesse **1**.7; *Eneas* Blondel **1b**.61. *Aristotes, Jeux-partis* **1a**.45. *Dedalu(s)* Rich. Fourn. **2**.25; Ad. Halle **1**.29. *Hector* Gaut. Darg. **1**.22. *Jason* Thib. Ch. **1**.4. *la lance Pelee* Wil. Corb. **1**. *Eqo* – *Narchisus* Rich. Fourn. **1**.8 ff., 15 f; *Narcisus* Thib. Ch. **4**.36; R. Soiss. **1**.59; *Jeux-partis* **2**.42; OF Anon. **9**.16. *Paris* – *Elaine* Thib. Bl. **1**.40 f.; *Paris* – *Elene*

---

[5] In the lists of names, graphic variants and differences in the order of paired names are disregarded. Figures customarily paired are also listed separately if they occur singly.

de Troie Perr. Ang. **3**.24 (but the names are omitted in 6 MSS – see n.); R. Soiss. (?) **3**.31; OF Anon. **5**.10; OF Anon. **10a**.28; OF Anon. **10b**.16; OF Anon. **10c**.28; OF Anon. **10d**.11 f.; OF Anon. **10e**.7 f. *Menelaus – Helaine* J. Neuv. **1**.20 f.; *Paris* Blondel **1b**.61; R. Soiss. **2**.60; OF Anon. **10f**.25; *cil de Troie* OF Anon. **6**.25; *Elaine* OF Anon. **6**.49. *Tisbé – Piramus* Thib. Ch. **3**.12; OF Anon. **2**.26 ff.; *Pyramus* Blondel **1b**.62; OF Anon. **9**.17 (*la*) *Theseü* Rich. Fourn. **2**.35.

The Bible: *Salemons ne Daviz* Thib. Ch. **2**.34; *Salemons* Couci **2**.9; *Adans* Pr. *Trist.* **1b**.82; Duchesse **1**.14. *Lucifer* Ad. Halle **2**.37.

Historical legend: *Alixandres – Daire* Perr. Ang. **1**.40; *Alixandre* OF Anon. **11**.18. *Julius Cesaire* Andr. Contr. **1**.40; *Pompee – Julius* Thib. Ch. **2**.16; *Cesar – Cleopatras, Jeux-partis* **1b**.49 ff. *Poru* Pr. *Trist.* **1a**.40.

The *chanson de geste*: *Forcon – Afelisse* Duchesse **1**.15. *Aude – Rolant* OF Anon. **9**.15. *Charlemainnes* Guil. Ferr. **1**.19. *Guenelon* Thib. Ch. **6**.36; OF Anon. **8**.15. *Soramonde* OF Anon. **7**.150.

Arthurian romances: *Genievre – Lanselos* Gille Vin. **1**.33 f.; *Yvains* Perr. Ang. **2**.34.

The Tristan story: *Tristan n'Yseut la bloie* Moniot **1**.50; *Tristan – d'Iseut s'amie* Raoul. Soiss. (?) **3**.18; *Tristen – la bele Iseut* Comte Bret. **1**.30 f.; *Tristan – Isot* OF Anon. **10i**.6; *Tristans* Chrétien **1**.29; Couci **1**.19; Guiot **1**.48; Blondel **1a**.54; Blondel **1b**.62; Eustache **1**.33; Thib. Ch. **5**.34; Pr. *Trist.* **1a**.28; R. Soiss. **2**.60; OF Anon. **1**.5 (but the name of Tristan is omitted in one MS – see n. *ad loc.*); OF Anon. **7**.68; OF Anon. **9**.17; OF Anon. **10f**.26; OF Anon. **10g**.32; OF Anon. **10h**.34; *Yseut* Pr. *Trist.* **1b**.83; *Isot*(*h*) OF Anon. **3**.50; OF Anon. **10j**.18.

Other medieval narratives: *Pertenopés* Gace (?) **1**.22; *Gingamur* Gace (?) **1**.31.

Medieval authors: *li Chastelains ne Blondiaus* Eustache **1**.34; *li chastelains de Couci* OF Anon. **4**.1.

There are a few groupings of figures from different spheres: *d'Eneas et Paris,* | *Tristan et Pyramus* Blondel **1b**.61 f.; *Tristan ne Paris* Raoul. Soiss. **2**.60; *Aude – Rolant*; *Narcisus, Tristans ne Piramus* OF Anon. **9**.16 ff. Circumlocutions replace a name in *ses fix* (Icarus) Ad. Halle **1**.31; *cil de Troie* OF Anon. **6**.25; *celle . . . cui Tristans provait a l'essai* OF Anon. **10h**.33 f.

Most poems contain in one stanza or part of a stanza a single exemplary comparison, but there are a few exceptions: Thib. Ch. **2**.III *Pompee – Julius*, V *Salemons ne Daviz*; Pr. *Trist.* **1a**.VII *Tristans*, X *Poru*; Rich. Fourn. **1**.II, III *Eqo – Narchisus*; Rich. Fourn. **2**.IV *la maison Dedalu*, V *la Theseü*; R. Soiss. (?) **3**.II *Tristan – Iseut*, IV *Paris – Elaine*; Gace (?) **1**.IV *Pertenopés*, V *Gingamur*; Duchesse **1**.I *Didol – Eneas*, II *Adans*, III *Forcon – Afelisse*; OF Anon. **6**.II *cil de Troie*, IV *Elaine*; OF Anon. **7**.VI *Tristrans*, IX *Soramonde*. By comparison with the troubadours, few poets employ exemplary comparisons in more than one poem.[6]

Exemplary comparisons are usually placed in prominent position, both within the stanza and in the structure of the poem as a whole. Comparisons which occupy, or form, the main focus of, a complete stanza occur only in Gille Vin. 1; Wil. Corb. 1.IV; Rich. Fourn. 1.II. Comparisons may be placed at the beginning, or in the first half, of a stanza: Chrétien 1; Guil. Ferr. 1; Couci 1; Couci 2; Eustache 1; Thib. Ch. 2.III; Thib. Ch. 3; Thib. Ch. 4; Thib. Ch. 5; Pr. *Trist.* 1b; Rich. Fourn. 2.IV, V; *Jeux-partis* 2; Gace (?) 1.IV, V; Duchesse 1.III; OF Anon. 4; OF Anon. 5; OF Anon. 10h; OF Anon. 10j; they may be placed at the end of the stanza: Blondel 1a; Moniot 1; Andr. Contr. 1; Thib. Ch. 1; Thib. Ch. 2.V; Perr. Ang. 1; Perr. Ang. 2; Perr. Ang. 3; Pr. *Trist.* 1a.VII, X; Raoul. Soiss. (?) 3.II; Ad. Halle 1; Ad. Halle 2; Duchesse 1.I, II; OF Anon. 2; OF Anon. 3; OF Anon. 9; OF Anon. 10c; OF Anon. 10d; OF Anon. 10e; OF Anon. 10g; at the end of an *envoi*: Guiot 1; R. Soiss. 1. Comparisons are placed in the first stanza of the poem: Thib. Ch. 1; OF Anon. 1; OF Anon. 4; OF Anon. 10i; in the second stanza: Couci 2; Thib. Ch. 3; OF Anon. 5; OF Anon. 6.25; OF Anon. 8; OF Anon. 9; OF Anon. 10b; OF Anon. 10e; OF Anon. 11; in the third, i.e. central, stanza of a five-stanza poem: Guil. Ferr. 1; Couci 1; Thib. Ch. 2.15 ff.; Perr. Ang. 3; OF Anon. 10a; OF Anon. 10j; in Rich. Fourn. 1, comparisons are placed in the second and third stanzas of a seven-stanza poem, in Duchesse 1 in stanzas I, II, and III of a four-stanza poem (with an identification in the final stanza). More often, comparisons are placed at or near the end of the poem: in a penultimate stanza: Thib. Bl. 1; Thib. Ch. 5; Thib. Ch. 6; Perr. Ang. 1; Ad. Halle 1; OF Anon. 6.49; OF Anon. 10g; in a final stanza (* = placing of the comparison at or near end of stanza or *envoi*): Blondel 1a*; Blondel 1b; Eustache 1; Moniot 1*; Andr. Contr. 1*; Gille Vin. 1; J. Neuv. 1; Thib. Ch. 2.29 ff.*; Thib. Ch. 4; Perr. Ang. 2*; R. Soiss. 2; Ad. Halle 2*; *Jeux-partis* 1a; *Jeux-partis* 1b; *Jeux-partis* 2; OF Anon. 2*, OF Anon. 3*, OF Anon. 10c*; OF Anon. 10f; in an *envoi*: Guiot 1*; R. Soiss. 1*; in the two final stanzas: Rich. Fourn. 2.

The names themselves are frequently placed in emphatic position in rhyme: *Salemons* Couci 2.9. *Trist(r)ant* Guiot 1.48; OF Anon. 7.68. *Paris* Blondel 1b.61; Thib. Bl. 1.40; R. Soiss. 2.60; OF Anon. 5.10; OF Anon. 10f.25. *Pyramus* Blondel 1b. 62; Thib. Ch. 3.12; OF Anon. 9.17. *Hector* Gaut. Darg. 1.22. *Julius Cesaire* Andr. Contr. 1.40; *Julius* Thib. Ch. 2.16. *Menelaus* J. Neuv. 1.20. *Jason* Thib. Ch. 1.4. *Daviz* Thib. Ch. 2.34. *Guenelon* Thib. Ch. 6.36; OF Anon. 8.15. *Daire* Perr. Ang. 1.40. *Poru* Pr. *Trist.* 1a.40. *Dedalu* Rich. Fourn. 2.25. *la Theseü* Rich. Fourn. 2.35. *Narcisus* R. Soiss. 1.59; Anon 9.16. *Elaine/Helaine* R.

---

[6] See Couci; Thib. Ch.; Perr. Ang.; Rich. Fourn.; R. Soiss.; Ad. Halle; for the troubadour poets, see chapter 5, n. 5.

Soiss. (?) **3**.31; OF Anon. **6**.49; OF Anon. **10a**.28; OF Anon. **10b**.16; OF Anon. **10c**.28; OF Anon. **10d**.12; OF Anon. **10e**.8. *Afelisse* Duchesse 1.15. *Soramonde* OF Anon. 7.150. *Rolant* OF Anon. 9.15. *Isot* OF Anon. **10i**. See also *Yseut la bloie* Moniot 1.50; *d'Iseut s'amie* R. Soiss. (?) 3.18; *Elene de Troie* Perr. Ang. 3.24; *cil de Troie* OF Anon. 6.25. Among these examples there are several in which it seems that only the need for a particular rhyming syllable has resulted in the choice of name: *Hector* Gaut. Darg. 1; *Menelaus* J. Neuv. 1; *Poru* Pr. *Trist.* **1a**; *cil de Troie* OF Anon. 6; *Soramonde* OF Anon. 7; *Elaine* OF Anon. 6; OF Anon. **10a**; OF Anon. **10b**; OF Anon. **10c**; OF Anon. **10d**; OF Anon. **10e**; *Paris* OF Anon. **10d**; OF Anon. **10e**. All the names cited rhyme within the stanza in which they occur; there are no instances, as in the troubadours, of rhymes between names, or of isolated rhyme, in which the name rhymes only from stanza to stanza.

Names may be placed at the head of the line: *Charlemainnes* Guil. Ferr. 1.19; *Tristan(s)* Blondel **1b**.62; OF Anon. 9.17; *li Chastelains* Eustache 1.34; *Elaine/Helaine* Thib. Bl. 1.41; J. Neuv. 1.21; OF Anon. 5.10; *Narcisus* Thib. Ch. 4.36; *Yvains* Perr. Ang. 2.34; *Adans* Pr. *Trist.* **1b**.82; *Dedalus* Ad. Halle 1.29; *Aristotes, Jeux-partis* **1a**.45; *Cleopatras, Jeux-partis* **1b**.52; *Pertenopés* Gace (?) 1.22; *Didol* Duchesse 1.7; *li chastelains de Couci* OF Anon. 4.1. See also *d'Eneas* Blondel **1b**.61; *la bele Iseut* Comte Bret. 1.31; *li grans Cesar, Jeux-partis* **1b**.49; *c'Adans* Duchesse 1.14; *k'Isoth* OF Anon. 3.50; *qu'Aude* OF Anon. 9.15; *ne Tristans* OF Anon. **10f**.26.

By comparison with the troubadour poets, there is considerably less syntactical variety in the structure of the exemplary comparisons in the trouvère lyric, and there is overall a far higher proportion of examples expressing superiority, rather than equivalence, to the exemplar. Straightforward comparison expressing similarity by means of comparative adverbs is rare: *si com Eqo . . . | ausi perdrai tout fors merci crïer | et secherai de duel et pesanche* Rich. Fourn. 1.8 ff.; *a sa voiz iere si sanee | cum Piramus quant il moroit | . . . au nom Tisbé les iauz ovroit* OF Anon. 2.25 ff. In some instances similarity is conveyed by nominal and verbal phrases in association with the name: *la leiauté Tristant | porra trover en moi* Guiot 1.48 f.; *de granz mauz m'a fait oir, | dont Tristans soffri tant* Blondel **1a**.53 f.; *por li maintendrai l'us | d'Eneas et Paris, Tristan et Pyramus* Blondel **1b**.60 ff.; *la lance Pelee trouvai | el besier que je li donai* Wil. Corb. 1; *du lignage Tristan sui* OF Anon. **10g**.32; *j'ai beüt del boivre ameir | k'Isoth but, la roïne* OF Anon. 3.49 f. A verb may convey equivalence or resemblance: *certes je ne voudroie | sanz li valoir Hector* Gaut. Darg. 1.20 f.; *vous volés resambler | chel Narcisu . . . Jeux-partis* 2.41 f.; *celle . . . cui je sanbler vorroie: | Didol qui fut por Eneas ocise* Duchesse 1.6 f.; *pour coi je douc Lucifer ne pourtraie, | ki pour sa grant biauté s'enorguelli, | et qu'ele ne face ausi vers moi* Ad. Halle 2.37. Some verbs convey the more explicitly didactic idea of signification or proof: *Dedalus . . . le senefie* Ad. Halle **1**.29 f.; *Pertenopés nous moustre* Gace (?) **1**.22; *per Gingamur en avons la provence* Gace (?) **1**.31.

In the majority of examples, superiority to the exemplar is expressed predominantly by means of constructions containing the comparative adverb *plus*; there are also instances of the comparative adverb *mieuz*; of the adverbs *tant, autant, si, ausi, autresi, com*; of the comparative adjectives *graindre, maindre, pire*, and the comparative adverb *pis*; of the verb *valoir*: *plux me fait ameir ke lui* | *Amors Chrétien* **1**.30 f.; *mieuz ameroie itel conquerement* | *qu'Espaigne . . .* Guil. Ferr. **1**.17 f.; *c'onques Tristanz . . .* | *plus loiaument n'ama sanz repentir* Couci **1**.19 f.; *onques Tristans n'ama de tel maniere, . . .* | *con j'ai fet vos* Eustache **1**.33 ff.; *c'onques tant n'ama Paris* | *Elaine* Thib. Bl. **1**.40 f.; *non pluz c'on puet Tristan n'Yseut la bloie* | *de lor amour partir ne dessevrer,* | *n'iert ja l'amours de nous deux dessevree* Moniot **1**.50 ff.; *je sui plus riches cent tans* | *que ne fu Julius Cesaire* Andr. Contr. **1**.39 f.; *car je l'aim pluz et desir* | *c'onques ne fist Menelaus Helaine* J. Neuv. **1**.19 ff.; *car Jason,* | *. . . n'ot pas si grief penitance* Thib. Ch. **1**.4 ff.; *onques fierté n'ot si grant* | *vers Pompee Julius* | *que ma dame n'en ait plus vers moi* Thib. Ch. **2**.15 ff.; *m'avrïez vos plus de joie doné* | *c'onques Tristans . . .* | *n'en pout avoir nul jor de son aé* Thib. Ch. **5**.33 ff.; *pis valent de Guenelon,* Thib. Ch. **6**.36; *ains me fait plus maus souffrir* | *qu'Alixandres ne fist Daire* Perr. Ang. **1**.39 f.; *plus sent por li de mal qui me guerroie,* | *k'ainc n'ot Paris por Elene de Troie* Perr. Ang. **3**.23 f.; *c'onques jor n'ama nus hon tant* | *con fist Tristans* Pr. Trist. **1a**.27 f.; *onc tel mal n'ot d'Ynde Poru* Pr. Trist. **1a**.40; *ne fist pas tel perte jadis* | *Adans . . . com a fait Yseut* Pr. Trist. **1b**.81 ff.; *je ne me kier pas mesler* | *de plus haute emprise* | *que la Theseü* Rich. Fourn. **2**.33 ff.; *ce que j'aim plus* | *c'onques n'ama son ombre Narcisus* R. Soiss. **1**.58 f.; *plus avroie conquis* | *amor haute desiree* | *c'onques n'ot Tristan ne Paris* R. Soiss. **2**.58 ff.; *de mon penser aim meuz la conpaignie* | *c'onques Tristan ne fist d'Iseut s'amie* R. Soiss. (?) **3**.17 f.; *com je desir s'amor et s'acointance* | *plus que Paris ne fist onques Elaine* R. Soiss. (?) **3**. 30 f.; *car onc Tristen n'ama si loiaument* | *la bele Iseut . . . et je autresi sui sorpris et destroit . . .* Comte Bret. **1**.30 ff.; *plus m'an repantiroie* | *c'Adans ne fist,* Duchesse **1**.13 f.; *ains por Forcon ne fist tant Afelisse* | *con je por vous, amins, s'or vos ravoie* Duchesse **1**.15 f.; *car onkes Tristans n'amait* | *tant ne nel tint Amors de si près* | *com or fait moi* OF Anon. **1**.5 ff.; *qu'ainz por amor nus n'en ot dolor graindre* | *. . . que ne cuit pas que la moie soit maindre* OF Anon. **4**.2 ff.; *Elaine . . .* | *n'ot onques . . .* | *de biauté autant* | *con cele ou mes cuers s'atent* OF Anon. **5**.10 ff.; *plus ai dolor que cil de Troie* Anon. **6**.25; *onques ni fu si bele Elaine* OF Anon. **6**.49; *jou aim plus dis tans* | *ke ne fist Tristrans* OF Anon. **7**.67 f.; *plus belle ke Soramonde* OF Anon. **7**.150; *sil ki sont pire ke Guenillon* OF Anon. **8**.15; *car je l'aim plus* | *qu'Aude n'ama Rolant;* | *ainz Narcisus,* | *Tristans ne Piramus* | *n'amerent tant* OF Anon. **9**.14 ff.; *plus l'ain que Paris Helainne* OF Anon. **10a**.28; *car ie l'am plux c'onke Paris Helainne* OF Anon. **10b**.16; *car je l'ain plux d'amor fine* | *ke Paris ne fist Helenne* OF Anon. **10c**.27 f.; *c'onke* *tant nen amait Paris* | *Helainne* OF Anon. **10d**.11 f.; *je l'em plus ke ne fist Paris* | *Heleyne* OF Anon. **10e**.7 f.; *c'onkes n'amait tant Paris* | *ne Tristans* | *com je fais* OF Anon. **10f**.25 ff.; *onkes celle n'ot tant biauteit* OF Anon. **10h**.33; *k'onques Tristans n'amait tant* | *com je fais vos* OF Anon. **10i**.6 f.; *Amors, plux me greveis* | *k'Isot* OF Anon. **10j**.17 f.; *ne conquist en son aage* | *Alixandre l'emperere* | . . . *tant com fait en li servir* OF Anon. **11**.17 ff.

There are a few syntactically less straightforward examples: in Couci **2**.9 f. a potential comparison with the exemplar is couched in the hypothetical construction *se j'avoie le sens qu'ot Salemons,* | *si me feroit amours pour fol tenir*, which conveys the didactic motif of the universality of love's folly, alluding both to the theme of Solomon's wisdom and that of love's victims. There is a similar allusion to the theme of love's assaults on its victims in Thib. Ch. **2**.34 ff.: *n'onques oncor Salemons ne Daviz* | *ne s'i tindrent ne q'uns fous d'Alemaigne*, i.e. if neither Solomon nor David could withstand love's darts, it is thereby implied that the poet would be equally defenceless. In Gille Vin. **1**.39 f. the link between Lancelot's service of Guinevere and the poet's hope of like reward is expressed solely by the adjective *tel* in *en tel espoir serf et ferai toustans* | *celi a qui mes cuers est atendans*. In Perr. Ang. **2**.33 ff. the syntactic link with the poet, conveyed by the adverb *neporquant*, is more tenuous still: *et neporquant fu jadis, ce dist on,* | *Yvains li preus qui tant fist toute voie* | *que par servir ot l'amor du lion*, which implies that faithful service will result in winning the lady's love. *Jeux-partis* **1b**.53 f. is similar: after the description of Antony's subjection to Cleopatra, a causal link with the poet's situation is established in the phrase *por ceu di je c'amors n'ait point de peir.* | *je ferai ce que ma dame me prie*. In *Jeux-partis* **1a**. 49 ff. there is no syntactic link between the allusion to the folly of love and the statement *Aristotes tout sens i perdi*, but textual juxtaposition makes the connection clear.

The majority of exemplary comparisons are couched in, or contain, first-person singular verbal and pronominal forms and are presented from a first-person authorial standpoint, with an admixture of third-person forms necessitated by the reference to the exemplary figures. In Pr. *Trist.* **1a** Tristan refers to himself both in the third and the first person: 27 *c'onques jor n'ama nus hon tant* | *con fist Tristans*; 39 f. *mors et amours m'ont acoru,* | *ainc tel mal n'ot Poru*; in Pr. *Trist.* **1b** Yseut likewise refers to herself in the third person: 81 ff. *ne fist pas tel perte jadis* | . . . *com a fait Yseut*. There appear to be very few examples of a first-person plural pronoun: Moniot **1**.52 *n'iert ja l'amours de nous deux dessevree*; Gace (?) **1**.22 *Pertenopés nous moustre sens doutance*; Gace (?) **1**.31 *per Gingamur en avons la provence*. There are second-person forms in apostrophe in instances of the *envoi*, with address to *Rois* (= *Rois de Navarre*, as in the first line of the poem) in R. Soiss. **1**, and to the song in Guiot **1** and R. Soiss. **2**. There is apostrophe of the lady in Eustache **1**.35; Thib. Ch. **5**.32 f.; OF Anon. **7**.149 f.; OF Anon. **10i**.7 ff.; apostrophe of Love in OF Anon. **10j**.17; of the male lover in Duchesse 1.II, III. There is direct address in dialogue in the *pastourelle* Thib. Ch. **6**, and in *Jeux-partis* **1a**, **1b** and **2**. Only in *Jeux-partis* **2** and OF Anon. **7**.149 f. is the person apostrophized also the subject of an exemplary comparison. There is a higher proportion of third-person forms in association with motifs of a more generalizing and didactic nature: love's victims, Thib. Ch. **2**.V (Solomon and David); *Jeux-partis* **1a** (Aristotle); the bondage of love (the maze of Daedalus), Rich. Fourn. **2**.IV; lack of moderation (Daedalus, Icarus), Ad. Halle **1**; the treachery of the *losengeors* (Guenelon), OF Anon. **8**.

Since the troubadour lyric was imitated by the trouvères, there are, as might be expected, considerable parallels between the troubadour and the trouvère lyric in the use of exemplary comparisons. The two branches of the lyric coincide in the following respects: there are very few instances of identification with an exemplar, comparisons being greatly preferred; the exemplars are derived from the same main areas of classical and historical legend and medieval narrative, with a few examples from the Bible; figures from different spheres may be combined; they may be linked with brief references to narrative situations; the comparisons are predominantly associated with the theme of love, usually presented from the male lover's perspective, with an overwhelming preponderance of male exemplars; there are relatively few comparisons which have the lady as their main focus, or beauty as their theme; the comparisons may express either likeness to, or superiority to, the exemplar, with, however, a preponderance of syntactical constructions expressing superiority (but see below); the exemplars may have more than one function; the comparisons are mostly placed within the confines of one stanza, with emphatic placing of the comparison itself within the stanza, and of the stanza in the structure of the poem as a whole, with a tendency towards final placing in both stanza and poem (but final, as opposed to initial placing within the stanza is more common in the troubadour lyric); names may be placed prominently in rhyme or at the head of the line; most comparisons are presented from an authorial first-person standpoint.

However, there are also considerable differences between the troubadour and the trouvère lyric in the use of exemplary comparisons. There is in the latter an overall reduction and simplification: there is a narrower range of lyric poems attested in which exemplary comparisons occur (poems of panegyric and lament are almost wholly lacking among the examples), so that all the instances cited occur in association with the theme of love (even OF Anon. **11** transfers a motif of secular love to the religious sphere); in contrast to the troubadours, there are few poets who employ exemplary comparisons in more than one poem. There are fewer comparisons with the attributes of the exemplar; there is a less wide range of names represented, with a concentration on the better known names in each sphere, those of Paris, Helen, and Tristan being particularly frequent; there is overall much less stylistic and syntactical variety in the structure of examples; there are only rare instances in which an exemplary comparison takes up, or forms the main focus of, a whole stanza; the preponderance of the motif of outdoing, rather than equalling the exemplar, is much more strongly marked, with a predominance of stereo-typed constructions with *plus*; apostrophe is much less common; there are no rhymes between names, or instances of a name as an isolated rhyme; in many examples it seems that exemplary comparisons are viewed merely as a convenient device for providing a rhyme.

7

The German Poets

This chapter spans the period from the second half of the twelfth century to the beginning of the fourteenth century. The earliest recorded instances of exemplary comparisons in the German lyric, in Herger, Friedrich von Hausen, Heinrich von Veldeke and Bernger, belong to the second half of the twelfth century. Heinrich von Morungen (probably attested 1217 and 1218), and Walther von der Vogelweide, who is directly attested only in 1203, but who refers to events at the end of the twelfth century and the beginning of the thirteenth, were writing at the turn of the twelfth and thirteenth centuries. Wolfram von Eschenbach also belongs to the same period, but the one example ascribed to him is not likely to be authentic and must therefore be considered as of uncertain authorship and date. To the first half of the thirteenth century belong Reinmar von Zweter, Bruder Wernher, Otto von Botenlouben and Der Marner. The main body of exemplary comparisons, however, is attested in the work of poets of the second half of the thirteenth century: Ulrich von Liechtenstein, Konrad von Würzburg, Der von Gliers, Tannhäuser, Der wilde Alexander, Boppe, Der junge Meissner, Der Dürinc, Der Henneberger and Sigeher. Rudolf von Rotenburg, for whom there is no certain attestation, and the *Leich* ascribed by MS C to Ulrich von Gutenburg (see below) certainly also belong to the thirteenth century. The example from the *Wartburgkrieg* and MHG Anon. 1 are of uncertain date, but probably no earlier than the thirteenth century. Der Goldener and Frauenlob span the end of the thirteenth and the beginning of the fourteenth century. The poets are cited in rough chronological order, in so far as this can be ascertained; Rudolf von Rotenburg and the *Leich*[1] ascribed to Ulrich von Gutenburg are placed together with the other main late thirteenth-century examples of the *Leich*, with Tannhäuser, who satirizes the use of exemplary comparisons and the citation of names in the genre, at the end of the group.

The poems preserved from the second half of the twelfth century are largely polystrophic poems (examples of the *Lied*) on themes of love, following the tradition set by the Romance lyric. During this period, the German lyric was decisively influenced both thematically and formally by the poetry of the troubadours and the trouvères: there is evidence that a few poets were directly acquainted with the troubadour lyric, but most derived their knowledge indirectly via the medium of the trouvère lyric. At first German poets imi-

---

[1] For the designations of the genres, see Glossary of technical terms.

tated specific Romance poems directly: it is therefore significant that among the earliest recorded examples of exemplary comparisons in the medieval German lyric there are two instances (Veldeke 1, Bernger 1) which are based on a stanza in a poem by Chrétien de Troyes. In the thirteenth century the French influence becomes more widely diffused, but is clearly seen in the development of the secular *Leich.*

From the second half of the twelfth century, there is also evidence for the separate category of didactic lyrics customarily designated as *Spruchdichtung*, or more accurately as *Sangspruchdichtung*.[2] Although MHG *spruch* is a general term and not the designation of a specific genre or category, NHG *Spruch* has customarily been used to designate a particular type of stanza or group of stanzas, which in the main treat didactic, political and religious themes from a non-personal objective standpoint, predominantly in stanza structures which are longer and more weighty than those characteristic of the *Minnelied*, but largely, as in the latter, of tripartite type. The basic unit is a single stanza (*Spruchstrophe/Sangspruchstrophe*), which usually forms part of a series of stanzas on different topics in the same metrical form, but within the series, stanzas may also be linked thematically in loose groupings of various kinds. The *Spruch/Sangspruch* thus differs from the *Minnelied*, which is essentially polystrophic, consisting of a limited number of stanzas making up a relatively unified whole. It has thematic similarities to the troubadour *sirventes*, but it is formally a separate phenomenon, and remains relatively unaffected by Romance influence. Herger 1 and Walther 1 are early examples of the use of exemplary comparisons in this type of lyric, but the bulk of the examples belong to the thirteenth century.

The secular *Leich* on themes of love, in heterostrophic forms, in contradistinction to the isostrophic *Lied*, is essentially a development of the thirteenth century, as a counterpart to the cultivation of the *descort* by the troubadours from the beginning of the thirteenth century, and of *descort* and *lai* by the trouvères in the thirteenth century. Of the authors to whom examples of the secular *Leich* containing exemplary comparisons are ascribed, the earliest, Otto von Botenlouben, is attested between 1197 and 1244. Konrad von Würzburg (d. 1287) and Tannhäuser, who refers to events between 1225 and 1266, belong to the later thirteenth century. Der von Gliers is probably the Wilhelm von Gliers attested 1267 to 1308 or 1314. The *Leich* of Frauenlob is a late example. Rotenburg, who is of uncertain date, is placed with the other thirteenth-century examples. The *Leich* ascribed to Ulrich von Gutenburg is a special case, since there is a very marked discrepancy between the six-stanza poem ascribed to him in MSS B and C, which is modelled on a poem by Blon-

---

[2] On the terminology, see Tervooren, *Sangspruchdichtung*, pp. 81 ff.

del de Nesle[3] and is therefore in accord with late twelfth-century attestations of the poet's name, and the lengthy and mannered *Leich* preserved solely in MS C, which is certainly a late example of the genre.[4] It must therefore be assumed that this *Leich* has been incorrectly ascribed to Gutenburg.

Poets of the Twelfth and Early Thirteenth Centuries

Herger **1**

Ich sage iu, lieben süne mîn (*Spruchstrophen*).
MF 25,13. Spervogel 12–16 AC

Dô der guote Wernhart   AC 15   IV   1
an dise welt geborn wart,
dô begonde er teilen al sîn guot.
dô gewan er Rüedegêrs muot,
Der saz ze Bechelære   5
und pflac der marke menegen tac.
der wart von sîner vrumecheit sô mære.

[When the worthy Wernhart was born into this world, he began to distribute all his goods. He acquired the spirit of Rüedegêr – his seat was at Bechelære and he governed the march for many a day. He became so renowned on account of his probity.]

The fourth of five related 7-l. strophes preserved in the Spervogel ascription in MSS A and C, but thought to be by an earlier poet, customarily as in MF, but probably mistakenly, designated as Herger on the dubious evidence of the occurrence of this name in Spervogel 18. The strophes lament the death of generous patrons, among them *von Hûsen Walther*, father of the poet Friedrich von Hausen, last attested 1173.   4 *Rüedegêrs muot*: Rüedegêr is a character in the Dietrich epics and the *Nibelungenlied*, but it is particularly in the latter that he is praised for his generosity and nobility of character (e.g. 1692–1696, 2153 f., 2194–2199).   5 *Bechelære*: Bechelâren in the *Nibelungenlied*, now Pöchlarn, at the confluence of the Erlaf and the Danube in Lower Austria.

Friedrich von Hausen **1**

Ich muoz von schulden . . . (*Lied*). MF 42,1

Ich muoz von schulden sîn unvrô,   I   1
sît si jach, dô ich bî ir was,
ich mohte heizen Enêas
und solte aber des wol sicher sîn,
si wurde niemer mîn Tidô.   5
wie sprach si dô?
aleine vrömidet mich ir lîp,

---

[3] See Sayce, *Romanisch beeinflußte Lieder* 7 (MF 77,36).
[4] See Ehrismann, *ZfdP* 33 (1901), pp. 395–7; Schweikle, *Mittelhochdeutsche Minnelyrik*, p. 525; Sayce, *Medieval German Lyric*, pp. 372 ff.

si hât iedoch des herzen mich
beroubet gar vür alliu wîp.

[I am rightly bound to be sad, since she said, when I was with her, I might
be called Aeneas, but I should be very sure she would never be my Dido.
Why did she then speak (thus)? Although she is cold towards me, yet she
has robbed me of my heart, surpassing all other women.]

The first of a total of six stanzas in the same form; B has I–III, V, VI; C has I–IV,
and in a later position V, VI.   3 *Enêas*, 5 *Tidô*: Hausen was acquainted
with the OF lyric – see 'Mîn herze und mîn lîp die wellent scheiden'(MF 47,
9), which is based on 'Ahi, Amors, com dure departie' by Conon de Béthune
(see *Romanisch beeinflußte Lieder* 2), but as comparisons with Aeneas and/or
Dido in association with love are rare in the Romance lyric (see Index of
Proper Names), it is more likely that this unusual example of identification
was inspired by knowledge of Veldeke's adaptation of the OF *Eneas*, in which
both names frequently occur in similar rhyming combinations, e.g. 35.37 f.
Enêas: was; 58.5 f. *Didô: unfrô.*

Heinrich von Veldeke 1

Tristan muose . . . (Lied). MF 58,35.
Sayce, *Romanisch beeinflußte Lieder* 5

Tristan muose sunder sînen danc   I 1
stæte sîn der küniginne,
wan in der poisûn dar zuo twanc
mêre dan diu kraft der minne.
des sol mir diu guote danc   5
wizzen, daz ich solken tranc
nie genam und ich si doch minne
baz danne er, und mac daz sîn.
wolgetâne,
valsches âne   10
lâ mich wesen dîn
und bis du mîn.

[Tristan was compelled to be faithful to the queen against his will, for the
love potion forced him into it, more than the power of love. Therefore the
fair one should give me credit for this, in that I never drank such a potion,
and yet I love her more than Tristan, if that were possible. Beautiful one,
without falsehood, let me be yours and be mine.]

The first of two stanzas in the same form (1–2 A, 10–11 BC), here given
according to MS C. Ll. 1–8 are closely modelled textually on Chrétien 1,
which is imitated also in Bernger 1 (*qq.v.*); ll. 9–12 also show knowledge of the
troubadour lyric (see 9 f. n.). The metrical form coincides only in part with the
Chrétien stanza.   1 *Tristan*, 2 *küniginne*: for the diffusion of the Tristan
story cf. Raimb. Or. 1.29 f. n. and Index of Proper Names *s.v.* Tristan, Iseut/
Isolde/Isalde/Isaotta.   3 *poisûn*: cf. Chrétien 1.29 *enpoisonneis*. Whereas
the motif of the poet's love surpassing that of Tristan is very common, ref.

to the love potion in association with it is rare: apart from Chrétien, this ex., and that in Bernger **1**, see the troubadour exs. Raimb. Or. **1**.29 f. n. 5 ff.: these ll. show that Veldeke knew a version of the stanza in which the poet claims credit for his voluntary love, as opposed to that compelled by the love potion, and confirm the reading adopted in Chrétien **1**.32 (*q.v.*).   9 f. *wolgetâne, valsches âne*: the direct address, with appellations modelled on examples of the *senhal*, imitates a type of *tornada* customary in the troubadour, but not the trouvère, lyric; for an exact parallel in apostrophe in a *tornada*, see Gauc. Faid. 9.46 *Bel Ses Enjans* (Beautiful one without falsehood).

Heinrich von Veldeke **2**

Diu minne . . . (single stanza). MF 66,16

Diu minne betwanc Salomône,	1
der was der alrewîseste man,	
der ie getruoc küniges krône,	
wie mohte ich mich erwern dan,	
Si twunge ouch mich gewalteclîche,	5
sît si sölhen man verwan	
der sô wîse was und ouch sô rîche?	
den solt sol ich von ir ze lône hân.	

[Love vanquished Solomon, who was the very wisest man who ever wore a king's crown. How could I then guard against her assailing me also mightily, since she conquered such a man who was so wise and also so powerful? This is the reward I am destined to receive from her in recompense.]

In the earliest attested examples of the German lyric, a single stanza, as here, and elsewhere in the work of Veldeke, is the norm.   1 *Salomône*: an allusion to the theme of Love's illustrious victims; see Zweter **2**.1 ff. (Adam, Samson, Solomon); *Gutenburg (?) **1a**.41 (Alexander); Dürinc **1**.9 ff. (Parzival, Adam, Samson, David, Solomon); *Frauenlob (?) **7**.1 ff.(Adam, Samson, David, Solomon, Absalon, Alexander, Virgil, Aristotle, Parzival + other un-characteristic exs. – *qq.v.*); see also *Rotenburg **1**.45 (Parzival); Frauenlob **5** (Gahmuret, Paris). Romance examples: Marc. **1**.14 n.; with explicit reference to the poet, as in Veldeke, and in the asterisked exs. above: Peire Vid. **1**.53 ff.; Falq. Rom. **1**.43 f.; Couci **2**.9 ff.; Thib. Ch. **2**.34 f.; Chiaro **2b**.21 n.

Bernger von Horheim **1**

Nu enbeiz ich doch . . . (Lied).
MF 112,1. Sayce, Romanisch beeinflußte Lieder 6

Nu enbeiz ich doch des trankes nie,	I B, 5 C I	1
dâ von Tristran in kumber kam.		
noch herzeclîcher minne ich sie		
danne er Ysalden, daz ist mîn wân.		
Daz habent diu ougen mîn getân,		5
daz leite mich, daz ich dar gie,		
dâ mich die Minne alrêst vie,		

der ich deheine mâze hân.
sô kumberlîche gelebte ich noch nie.

[Now I never partook of the potion, as a result of which Tristan was plunged into grief. I love her more intensely than he loved Isolde, that is my belief. My eyes were the cause. That led me to venture there where love, in which I know no moderation, first captured me. I have never lived in such a sorrowful state.]

The first of three stanzas; like Veldeke 1, it is modelled textually on Chrétien 1, but unlike the former, it also imitates the metrical form of the OF poem exactly. Text according to MS B.   1 *trankes*: see Veldeke 1.3 n.   2 *Tristran*, 4 *Ysalden*: see Veldeke 1.1 n. The f. name is missing in the Chrétien stanza; the form *Ysalt* occurs (among other forms) in OF texts, e.g. the *Cligés* of Chrétien; *Isalde* is attested in the *Tristan* of Eilhart.

Heinrich von Morungen 1
Mir ist geschehen als einem kindelîne (*Lied*). MF 145,1

Grôz angest hân ich des gewunnen,   III   1
daz verblîchen süle ir munt sô rôt.
des hân ich nu niuwer klage begunnen,
sît mîn herze sich ze sülher swære bôt,
Daz ich durch mîn ouge schouwe sülhe nôt   5
sam ein kint, daz wîsheit unversunnen
sînen schaten ersach in einem brunnen
und den minnen muoz unz an sînen tôt.

[I consequently feel great anguish that her mouth, which is so red, may grow pale; I have therefore begun a new lament, since my heart laid itself open to such grief, in that I see such sorrow through my eyes, like a youth, unmindful of wisdom, who saw his reflection in a spring and must love it until his death.]

The third of four stanzas ascribed in MS e to Reinmar. MSS C and Ca contain the first stanza only under Morungen. Each of the first three stanzas uses the theme of vision and illusion to express grief: I the poet resembles the child who, snatching at his reflection in a mirror, breaks it and destroys his happiness; II Love brings the poet a dream vision of the lady, perfect in beauty, except in her red mouth.   2 *verblîchen*: the red mouth symbolizes beauty and joy, its growing pale the loss of perfection, and grief.   6 ff.: an indirect, but clear reference to the story of Narcissus, in which the designation *ein kint* may perhaps replace the name in order to link the image with that of the reflection in the mirror associated with *kindelîne* in the opening lines of the poem, or may merely indicate uncertain recollection of the myth. In *Met.* III.351, Narcissus is said to have attained his sixteenth year, and is several times referred to as *puer*.   For Narcissus, see Bern. Vent. 1.23 f. n.; in Bern. Vent. 1 Narcissus' reflection is linked to the mirror of the lady's eyes, in Petrarch 11 to the lady's own reflection in the mirror.

Heinrich von Morungen **2**

Ich wæne, niemen lebe . . . (*Lied*). MF 138,17

Ich wæne, si ist ein Vênus hêre, die ich dâ minne,   III   1
wan si kan sô vil.
si benimt mir beide vröide und al die sinne.

[I believe that she, whom I love, is a sovereign Venus, for she has the power
to do so much. She robs me both of joy and of all my senses.]

The first lines of III in a poem, which in MS C consists of five 8-l. stanzas, with
the second stanza attested singly also in MS A.   1 *Vênus*: cf. Wolfram (?)
1.10; comparison or identification with Venus is uncommon in the vernacular
lyric (see *Mar. Am.* **1a**.134 n.). For similar identifications in the MLat. lyric, see
Venant. **3**.103 *altera nata Venus*; CB **3**.8.4 *Blanziflôr et Helena, Venus generosa*
(in apostr.); CB **14**.4 *estne illa Helena, vel est dea Venus?*

Heinrich von Morungen (?) **3**

Diu vil guote (*Lied*). MF 136,25

Ascholoie   V   1
diu vil guote heizet wol.
erst von Troie
Paris, der si minnen sol.
Obe er kiesen solde under den schœnesten, die nu leben   5
sô wurde ir der apfel, wær er unvergeben.

[The most fair one is called Ascholoie. He is of Troy, Paris, who should
love her. If he had to choose among the most beautiful now alive, the apple
would be hers, if it had not been awarded.]

The poem has a maximum of five 6-l. stanzas, with a differing number and
order of stanzas in MSS A, C and p. Stanza V is a *unicum* in A, and forms the
conclusion to the poem.   1 *Ascholoie*: perhaps an imperfectly remembered
classical name, chosen to provide a rhyme for *Troie*; cf. *Acheloia* 'daughter of
Acheloüs', referring to Callirhoe, *Met.* IX.413.   3 f. implies identification
of *diu vil guote* with Helen; for MLat. identifications with Helen, see Morungen
2.1 n. The identification then prompts the ref. to the judgement of Paris in
5 f.: Paris decided the contest between Juno, Pallas and Venus in favour of the
latter, because she had promised him Helen as reward. Line 6 further implies
that the lady surpasses not only Helen, but all three goddesses; for an explicit
comparison with Helen, see Rotenburg **2**.204 ff.

Walther von der Vogelweide **1**

Philippes künic, die nâhe spehenden
zîhent dich (*Spruchstrophe*). L. 19,17

Denke an den milten Salatîn: III   7
der jach, daz küniges hende dürkel solten sîn,
sô wurden si erforht und ouch geminnet.
gedenke an den künic von Engellant,   10

wie tiure man den lôste dur sîne milten hant.
ein schade ist guot, der zwêne frumen gewinnet.

[Remember generous Saladin: he said that a king's hands should be open, then they would be feared and also loved. Remember the king of England, at what a high price he was ransomed by his generous hand. One loss is good, which gains two benefits.]

The *Abgesang* of a 12-l. stanza in a group of five in the same form, the first three relating to king Philip.   7 *Salatîn*: cf. Wernher **1**.11; Goldener **1**.2; frequently cited as exemplar of generosity, e.g. Würzburg (ed. Schröder III, 23.31 ff.), contrasting the generosity of Saladin with the miserliness of present-day lords; Sunnenburg (ed. Masser 53), in praise of an unnamed king of Bohemia.   8 *dürkel*: lit. 'perforated', 'porous'.   10 Richard Cœur de Lion.   12 *zwêne frumen*: in ll. 5 f. Philip is said not to understand how to win *prîs und êre* (renown and honour) through giving.

Walther von der Vogelweide (?) **2**

Ich bin nû sô rehte vrô (*Lied*). L. 118,24

Dar zuo enkunde nieman mir   IV 1
gerâten, daz ich schiede von dem wâne.
kêrt ich mînen muot von ir,
wâ fünde ich danne *eine sô wol getâne*,
Diu sô wære valsches âne?   5
si ist schœner unde baz gelobt denne Helêne und Dijâne.

[No one could persuade me to abandon the hope. If I were to turn my thoughts from her, where should I then find one so lovely and who was so free of falsehood? She is more beautiful and more praised than Helen and Diana.]

The fourth stanza of five in MSS C and E; MS F has I, II, III.4–6, and IV. 1 f.: a reference to the hope expressed at the end of the preceding stanza that the lady may favourably acknowledge the poet's song and avert his sorrow. 4 *eine sô wol getâne*: MSS *ein(e) so schœn(e) wip*, but a rhyme in -*âne* is required, as in ll. 2 and 6.   6 *Helêne*: see Morungen (?) **3**.3 f. n.   *Dijâne*: the name is no doubt prompted by rhyming constraints. Diana as exemplar is very rare in the vernacular lyric (but see Petrarch **7**.1 in a ref. to Diana and Actaeon). Ziltener, *Repertorium* 8679 f. cites 2 exs. in OF reworkings of classical narrative.

Wolfram von Eschenbach (?) **1**

Guot wîp, ich bitte dich minne (*Lied*). MF 9,4

Ir schœne vröide machet.   V 1
durliuhtec rôt
ist ir munt als ein rubîn.
[. . .]
Vênus diu götinne,   10

lebt si noch,
si müeste bî ir verblichen sîn.

[Her beauty inspires joy. Her mouth is of a luminous red, like a ruby. [...]
If Venus the goddess were still alive, she would pale beside her.]

The first three and last three lines of V in a six-stanza poem ascribed to
Wolfram solely in MS C and unlikely to be by him.   10 ff. cf. Morungen
2.1 n.   12 *verblichen*: a similar idea is expressed by the verb *perde*, in
reference to Helen, in Petrarch **8.44**.

Thirteenth-Century Poets

Reinmar von Zweter **1**

Tristram der leit . . . (*Spruchstrophe*). Roethe 25

Tristram der leit vil grôze nôt,   1
von eines wîbes minne   lac er vil jæmerlîchen tôt:
daz quam von sînen triuwen: der selben minne ûz eime glase er tranc.
Daz selbe ouch ich getrunken hân
ûz mîner vrouwen ougen,   des ich in grôzem kumber stân: 5
des mac mir niht gehelfen   des meien schîn noch cleiner vogellîn sanc.

[Tristram suffered very great anguish, because of the love of a woman he
lay most pitiably dead. That arose from his constancy; he drank that same
love from a goblet. I have drunk the same draught from my lady's eyes, so
that I am beset by great sorrow; therefore neither the splendour of May
nor the song of little birds can avail me.]

The first 6 ll. (the *Aufgesang*) of a 12-l. stanza in a sequence of single stanzas,
mostly on didactic subjects, in the so-called *Frauen-Ehren-Ton*.   1 *Tristram*: see Veldeke **1.1** n.   3 ff. For refs. to the love potion, cf. Veldeke
1.3 n.

Reinmar von Zweter **2**

Der edel wîse vrî Adam (*Spruchstrophe*). Roethe 103

Der edel wîse vrî Adam   1
von eines wîbes minne   schaden an sîner wirde nam:
sîn wîsheit wart verlistet,   sîn vrîheit seic in eigenschefte joch.
Samson ouch sîne kraft verlôs
von eines wîbes minne,   die er im ze trût erkôs.   5
diu Salomônis wîsheit,   swie ganz diu wære, ein wîp verschriet si doch.

[Noble, wise and free Adam suffered injury to his worth from the love
of a woman: his wisdom was deceived by trickery, his freedom sank low,
reduced to the yoke of servitude. Samson also lost his strength as the result
of love of a woman, whom he chose as the object of his love. Solomon's
wisdom, however perfect it was, a woman yet destroyed it.]

The *Aufgesang* of a 12-l. single stanza in the same series as **1**. The rest of the

stanza praises love only if it is the source of virtue.   1 ff. For the theme
of love's illustrious victims see Veldeke **2**.1 n.; for Adam's nobility, see Boppe
1.11 n.   3 *seic in eigenschefte joch*: lit. 'sank into the yoke of servitude'.

Bruder Wernher 1

"Nu râtent alle . . ." (Spruchstrophe).
Holz/Saran/Bernouilli, Bruoder Wirner 31

"Nu râtent alle, die nu leben unde ouch bî guoten witzen sint,   1
in welhem lande vrouwe Êre habe ein reine, gebende kint,
daz niht wan milter werke phlege, baz dan ie milter man gephlac?"
als ich daz wort hie vor gesprach, dô wart ein vil gemeine ruof,
dô riefen iene unde dise: "Got milter herren nie geschuof   5
den graven Wilhalm von Hunesburc, der ist der gerenden ôstertac!
dar ne hœret niuwan bieten zuo
die hende, swer sîn guot entfâhen welle."
nu saget, wer sô grôze milte in al der werlde tuo?
swaz man der gebenden ieman vür gezelle,   10
des milten Salatînes hant gesæte umb êre nie sô wîten schaz
noch nie man, der ie wart geborn, des sî in al der werlde traz.

["Now let all now living and of right mind consider in which land lady
Honour has a virtuous, munificent child, who carries out nothing but
works of generosity, more than any generous man ever did?" When I
formerly spoke thus, there was a common cry, this one and that one cried:
"God never created a more generous lord than Wilhalm von Hunesburg, he
is the Easter day of suppliants! One needs only to stretch out one's hands,
if one wishes to receive his bounty." Now say, who practises such great
generosity in the whole world? Whoever among the munificent anyone
may enumerate, the hand of generous Saladin never spread abroad for
honour's sake so large a treasure, nor anyone who ever lived – let this hold
true, in all the world's despite.]

A single stanza in a series in the same form. The text is based on the diplomatic edition of MS J by Holz in Holz/Saran/Bernouilli, but the idiosyncratic
orthography of the MS is modified in accordance with that customary in the
edition of MHG texts.   11 *des milten Salatînes hant*: cf. Walther **1**.7 n.

Otto von Botenlouben 1

Mir hât ein wîp herze unde lîp (Leich). KLD I, p. 310

Peir der mære   dulde swære   J 21   59
dur Afrîen   sîn amîen   von Navâr.
Mei von Lône   lie die krône
und die sinne   durch die minne   drîzec jâr.
er was sorgen rîch,   daz was kumberlîch,   doch ungelîch   K 22   63
der swære mîn,   die mir tuot schîn   von der ich dulde disen pîn.

[Peir the famed suffered sorrow on account of his lady Afrie of Navarre.
Mei of Lone forsook the crown and his senses on account of love for thirty

years. He had abundant suffering, that was grievous, yet not comparable
to the grief which she inflicts on me, she for whom I suffer this torment.]

Two contiguous units in a *Leich* made up of a succession of short units and
particularly characterized by a proliferation of internal rhyme. The poem is
transmitted in MSS A and C, but it is perhaps significant that ll. 59–64 are
omitted in A, which suggests that the names were not familiar to the compiler
or had perhaps become garbled. Apart from the possible exception of *Mei*
(see below) they appear in fact not to be attested – they might be from a lost
tale, or did the poet perhaps invent them, giving them the look of Romance
names, for the sake of the rhyme?   61 *Mei*: the reading is uncertain,
because the initial letter or letters of the word are faint in the MS, and it is
not certain whether a correction has been attempted. KLD prints *Mei*, but see
Kornrumpf's added n. ⟨Mei *aus* Plei *gebessert oder* Plei?⟩, i.e. either *Mei* or
Plei could be intended. If *Mei* is correct, a ref. to the tale of *Mai und Beaflor*
might have been expected, but the details are dissimilar: Mai does penance
for eight years, not thirty, when he discovers his mother's calumnies and plots
against the life of Beaflor, which cause her to flee, but he does not renounce
the crown or lose his senses.

Der Marner 1

Guot wahter wîs (*Tagelied*). Strauch/Brackert III

"Troie wart zerstœret ê,   II   20
Tristranden wart von minne dur Isalden dicke wê.
noch hât Minne werden
man, der wirbet frouwen gruoz,
dem sol er werden,
ob ich alsus warten muoz: 25
ez ist vor tage niht einen vuoz."

["Troy was formerly destroyed, Tristan often suffered grief for the sake
of love of Isalde. Love still has a man of worth who aspires to a lady's
greeting; it shall be granted him, if I am able thus to keep watch: it is not
a foot distant from day."]

The last 7 ll. of II in a dawn song consisting of three 13-l. stanzas. In II.17
the song sung by the watchman to warn the lovers of the approach of dawn
is described as *ein tageliet*, a designation appropriate to the poem itself. The
lovers whom he guards are implicitly compared to those of Troy and Tristan
and Isolde.   20 The allusion to the destruction of Troy refers obliquely to
Paris and Helen, who were its cause.   21 *Tristranden... Isalden*: cf. Veldeke
1.1 n.; there is a similar allusion in a 14th-century dawn song by Peter von
Arberg (*Tagelieder*, ed. Hausner, 48) in the words of the departing knight: *"des
muoz ich in Tristrams minne varn | unt scheiden von Isalden"* ("therefore I must
depart in Tristram's love and part from Isalde"). As in Marner, this is linked to
the theme of Troy, but with an inaccurate pairing of Hector and Dido: *"Hector
von Troijen geschach alsam, | do er die schœnen Dido muoste varen lan."* ("the
same befell Hector of Troy when he had to abandon beautiful Dido").

Der Marner **2**

Ein wunderlîchez kunder (*Spruchstrophe*). Strauch/Brackert XIV,13

Ein wunderlîchez kunder   1
Gorgôn ez geheizen was.
wîlent, swer daz houbet sach, der wart ein stein.
bî der zît ein ritter lebte, der hiez Antêus,
Den nam des michel wunder,   5
daz nieman vor im genas.
er wart dô in sînem muote des enein,
daz er machte ein kristallînen schilt und truoc den sus
Vor sînen ougen, er ersach ez dur den schilt und streit
mit im, er sluoc ez sô manlîchen,   10
daz man ez noch von im seit.
ir werden fürsten, merkent disen list:
dem ritter sult ir iuch gelîchen,
swâ ein valschez houbet ist,
sehet ez dur êren klâren schilt,   15
und slaht ez, wan ez keiner arger dinge niht bevilt.

[There was a wondrous monster called Gorgon. Formerly, whoever looked upon the head was turned to stone. At that time there lived a knight called Antaeus; he wondered greatly that no one could survive in its sight. He resolved that he would make a crystal shield, and he bore it in front of his eyes in such a way that he looked at it through the shield and fought with it. He slew it so manfully that the tale is still told of him. You noble princes, take heed of this stratagem: you should be like that knight. Where there is a treacherous head, look at it through the clear shield of honour and slay it, for it never shrinks from any evil deed.]

A single stanza in a series.   2 *Gorgôn*: one of three snake-haired sisters, especially Medusa.   4 *Antêus*: the slayer of Medusa was Perseus, here confused with Antaeus, a giant who defeated all comers, until Hercules slew him.

Der Marner **3**

Mariâ blüendez mandelrîs (*Spruchstrophe*). Strauch/Brackert XV,1

du vil wîsen Salomônes wol gezierter küneges trôn,   5
Du Jûdith, diu des siges prîs
gewan, als uns wart schîn,
du Hester, küniginne wîs,
nu sich dîn volc in nœten sîn,
daz sol gegen Asvêrus versüenen dînes mundes dôn.   10
Du reiniu Jahel hâst geslagen tôt den Sisoran.
du bist ouch diu dem slangen sîne maht benan.
du schœner leitestern,
du bist diu wîse Abigahel   die sünder müezen dîn begern,
wan dich minte Dâvît,   der Gôljam ze tôde ersluoc   15

wîslîch genuoc
und im sîn houpt entruoc.

[You ornate royal throne of most wise Solomon, you Judith, who won
the prize of victory, as was made manifest to us, you Esther, wise queen,
now look upon your people in distress, the sound of your voice shall seek
reconciliation with Ahasuerus. You pure Jael slew Sisora. You are also the
one who robbed the serpent of his power. You beautiful guiding star, you
are wise Abigail, sinners must desire you, for David loved you, he who slew
Goliath with clever skill, and robbed him of his head.]

Lines 5–17 of a 20-l. single stanza, placed at the head of a series in the same
form. It illustrates a particular type of identification known as typology, i.e. the
interpretation of events and persons of the Old Testament as prefigurations
of those of the New.   5 *du vil wîsen Salomônes wol gezierter küneges trôn*:
Mary is here identified with the throne of Solomon because she is chosen by
God's divine wisdom, paralleled on earth by the wisdom of Solomon, to bear
Christ; cf. Walther L. 4.32 *Salomônes hôhen thrônes | bistû, frowe, ein selde hêre
und ouch gebieterinne* (you are the sovereign dwelling place of Solomon's high
throne, lady, and its queen).   6 *Jûdith*: Judith released the Israelites from
the assaults of the Assyrians by killing their commander Holofernes (Judith
13).   8 *Hester*: Esther, Jewish consort of Ahasuerus, king of the Medes
and Persians, prevailed on him to rescind the decree authorizing Haman to
exterminate the Israelites (Esther 6–8); cf. Frauenlob **2.**III,3.2 (*Hester* as the
image of womanly perfection).   11 *Jahel*: Jael delivered the Israelites from
the Canaanites by slaying their commander Sisora (Judg. 4:17 ff.).   *Sisoran*,
15 *Gôljam* are exemplars of the evil annihilated by Mary, like the serpent
(Satan) in 12.   14 *Abigahel*: persuaded David not to destroy her husband
Nabal, and after the latter's death was taken as wife by David (I. Sam. 25:14 ff.;
39 ff.).   15 *Dâvît*: ancestor of Christ through the lineage of Jesse and
type of Christ; cf. Heinzelin von Konstanz (Cramer I, p. 376), in apostrophe
of Christ: *du David, der Golyas trauw | mit siner kraft verzwicket* (you David,
who transfixed the bold assurance of Goliath with his strength); Mönch von
Salzburg (*Geistliche Lieder*, ed. Spechtler 10.46), in apostrophe of Mary: *durch
dich kam David von Jesse* (through you David came from Jesse); see also *ib.*
53 ff. (comparison or identification of Mary with Esther, Judith, Tamar, Ruth,
Susannah and Abigail).

Ulrich von Liechtenstein

The *Frauendienst*, a narrative in 8-l. stanzas with couplet rhyme, which purports to relate the poet's exploits in the service of love, contains in total 57
isostrophic poems and one *Leich*, prose and verse letters (designated as *brief*),
and three so-called *buochel*. The lyric MS C preserves the poems and the *Leich*
separately from the narrative, but with some omissions and the addition of
two poems not contained in the narrative MS M. **1a** and **1b** below form part

of the third *buochel*, a lengthy missive addressed by the poet in part to his heart and mind, in part to the lady. It has thematic and formal similarities to the Romance *salut*, which may also contain exemplary comparisons – see Arn. Mar. **3a, 3b, 4**; Falq. Rom. **3a**; Azalais **1**. The *buochel* is sent by the poet to the lady, together with the poem which immediately follows it in the narrative, and with which it is thematically connected (see Liechtenstein **2**):

Ulrich von Liechtenstein **1a**

Wol her, friunt, an mînen rat
Frauendienst, ed. Spechtler pp. 253–60

sus so het ich beide	110
herzenliebe und herzenleide,	
hellewizze und himelriche,	
dem marterer vil geliche,	
den man da nennet Tantalus,	
des not ist ouch gestalt alsus.	115
er swebet uf einem (breiten) se	
und ist im doch vor durste we,	
ouch hat er vil groze quale	
von hunger ze allem male,	
swie nahen sinem munde si	120
der wunsch von edelem obze bi.	
waz dane? ez fliuhet ie von dan,	
sa swanne er wil reichen dran.	
[...]	
gelich dem armen manne	127
het ich freude and da bi not,	
hie daz leben, da den tot.	

[Thus I had both heartfelt joy and heartfelt grief, torments of hell and (joy of) heaven, just like the sufferer named Tantalus, whose anguish is of the same kind. He is afloat upon a wide lake, and yet he suffers pangs of thirst. He also suffers great torment from hunger at all times, however near to his mouth is the choicest of magnificent fruit. What of it? it ever flees away, as soon as he wishes to grasp it. [...] Like this poor man, I had joy and at the same time distress, life on one side, death on the other.]

114 *Tantalus*: in Homer, *Od.* XI.582 ff. Tantalus stands up to his chin in water, but when he tries to drink, the water is swallowed up; overhanging trees bear pears, pomegranates, apples, figs and olives, which elude him as he tries to grasp them; Ov. *Met.* IV.458 *tibi, Tantale, nullae | deprenduntur aquae, quaeque inminet, effugit arbor* (by you, Tantalus, no water can be caught, any tree which overhangs flees from you); *Met.* X.41 *nec Tantalus undam | captavit refugam* (Tantalus did not catch the fleeing water). Ov. *Am.* II ii.43 *quaerit aquas in aquis et poma fugacia captat | Tantalus* (Tantalus seeks water in the midst of water, and catches at fleeing fruit); cf. OF *Roman d'Eneas* 2747 ff.; Veldeke, *Eneasroman* 104.16 ff.; see also MHG Anon. **1.1–4**.

Ulrich von Liechtenstein **1b**

Frauendienst, ed. Spechtler p. 256

vil saelic vrowe here,   139
ir habt mir also sere
gehoehet minen senenden sin
und alle mine sinne hin
von mir gefuoret so
beidiu verre und so ho,
als ich in dem himel si   145
oder aber vil nahen da bi.
Alexander maere
der edel wunderaere
dem geschach nie vreuden halp so vil
do er über der sterne zil   150
von griffen chla gefüeret wart.
wol mich miner saeliclichen vart,
da ich gewan so hohen gewin,
des ich so hohe getiuret bin.

[Most blessed illustrious lady, you have raised my yearning thoughts to
such a degree and so transported all my senses far from me and lifted
them so high, as if I were in heaven or very near. Famed Alexander, the
illustrious man of marvels, never experienced half so much joy when he
was transported by the claws of gryphons beyond the bounds of the stars.
Praised be my blessed journey, through which I gained such a great prize,
by which my worth is so much enhanced.]

147 ff. The Middle Ages inherited from a Greek source of c. AD 300, via later
Latin adaptations, an amalgam of fact and fantasy relating to Alexander the
Great, including legends that he journeyed in a capsule to the bottom of
the sea, and to the heavens, drawn by gryphons; this episode occurs in the
Basle version of Lamprechts *Alexander*, probably dating from the end of the
13th century, but preserved in a 15th-century MS (see Werner, *Die Basler
Bearbeitung von Lambrechts Alexander* 4281 ff.); it is frequently depicted in
medieval art, e.g. in the floor mosaic of the cathedral of Otranto; see also
Gutenburg **1a**.41 n. For exs. based on the historical Alexander, see Sigeher
1.1 n.; MLat. Anon. **1**.1,8; Arn. Dan. **3**.21 n.

Ulrich von Liechtenstein **2**

Wol mich der sinne . . . (*Lied*, designated in
the text as *tanzwise*). *Frauendienst*, ed. Spechtler p. 261

Min hende ich valde   mit triuwen algernde uf ir füeze,   III   1
daz si als Ysalde   Tristramen getroesten mich müeze
und also grüeze,
daz ir gebaere   min swaere   mir büeze,
daz si mich scheide   von leide,   si liebe, si süeze.   5

[I join my hands together, bowing in faithful supplication at her feet, that she may bring me consolation as did Ysalde to Tristan, and may receive me in such a way that her conduct may remedy my grief, that she may free me from suffering, the sweet, the dear one.]

The third stanza in a five-stanza poem – for its placing in the narrative, see introduction to Liechtenstein above. The poem was clearly well known, since it is preserved not only in the MS of the *Frauendienst*, and in the lyric MS C under Liechtenstein, but also, with the exception of the last stanza, under Veldeke in C, and in MS A under the poet Niune. It is noteworthy that this is the only exemplary comparison in any of the lyric poems in the work, which is no doubt explained by its close link with the preceding *buochel*, which contains the comparisons with Tantalus (**1a**) and Alexander (**1b**).   **2** *Ysalde Tristramen*: see Veldeke **1.1** n.   **3** *grüeze*: lit. 'may greet me'; the lady's greeting represents acceptance of the poet's service and therefore the promise of reward.

Konrad von Würzburg 1

Vênus diu feine diust entslâfen (Leich). Schröder III,2

Her Mars der rîhset in dem lande,   15
der hât den werden got Amûr
verhert mit roube und ouch mit brande:
des sint die minne worden sûr,
die man hie vor vil suoze erkande,
dô Riwalîn und Blantschiflûr   20
vil kumbers liten von ir bande.

[Sir Mars reigns in the land, he has ravaged the noble god Amor with pillage and fire: as a result those loves have become bitter, which were formerly seen to be so sweet, when Riwalîn and Blantschiflûr suffered much grief from their bonds.]

The first seven ll. of an 8-l. section in the *Leich*, which is unusual in treating the general subject of the conflict between Venus and Mars, without reference to personal themes.   **20** *Riwalîn und Blantschiflûr*: the parents of Tristan in the *Tristan* of Gottfried von Strassburg; in ll. 55 ff. of the *Leich*, Paris is cited as example of those led astray by the god of war.

Der von Gliers 1

Ich klage mich vil leide (Leich). SM², p. 59

Möht ich die welt betwingen gar,   XIII   1
alse Rôme Julius betwanc,
ich wære doch iemer fröide bar,
si eine spræche "habe danc!"
ich wolde niht ein keiser sîn,   5
daz ich die lieben frowen mîn
gesæhe niemer zallen tagen:
sone wolde ich niht der krône tragen.

[Could I conquer the whole world as Julius conquered Rome, I would

always be without joy, unless she alone spoke her thanks. I would not wish
to be an emperor, if I could never at any time see my dear lady: then I
would not wish to wear the crown.]

The first 8 ll. of a 12-l. unit making up the first half of XIII, which is the
penultimate section of the first *Leich*.   2 *Julius*: see Index of Proper
Names, *s.v.* Julius/Julius Caesar.   4 "*habe danc*": lit. 'accept thanks'.

Der von Gliers 2

Si prîsent alle sunder strît (*Leich*). SM², p. 65

Der Minne dienen ist ein nôt,	III 9
die man wunderkûme tragen mag.	10
durh si lîdet meniger tôt,	
der ir doch mit herzetriuwe pflag,	
sam Tristan, der mich riuwen muoz,	
swie mir der riuwe niemer buoz	
werde. sam tet Pyramus	15
und ouch der kiusche Ypolitus.	

[To serve love is pain which one can scarcely bear. Because of it, many a
one, who devoted himself to it with heartfelt constancy, suffers death, like
Tristan, for whom I feel sorrow, although my grief can never be cured.
Pyramus acted likewise and also chaste Hippolytus.]

The central unit of three, making up the third section of the second *Leich*.
13 *Tristan*: see Veldeke **1.2** n.   15 *Pyramus*: on the source of the story in
Ovid, see Arn. Mar. **3b**.152 n. There is a German poem treating the story of
Pyramus and Thisbe in a 14th-century MS (see *ZfdA* 6 (1848), 504–17), but
German authors probably derived their knowledge of the story mainly from
school excerpts from Ovid and MLat. and OF sources (see Kugler, VL², 259 ff.);
see der j. Meissner **1.13**; **2.18**.   16 *Ypolitus*: for the death of Hippolytus,
the result of a false accusation of unchastity, see Sid. **5.76** f. n. This exemplar
is out of keeping with the rest of the passage, which suggests that the need for
a rhyme has prompted the inappropriate inclusion of the name.

Der von Gliers 3

Kunde ich mit fuoge mînen muot (*Leich*). SM², p. 70

Owê, senelichiu nôt,	IX 17
wie dû mih fröiden hâst behert!	
Grâlant, den man gar versôt,	
wart nie grœzzer nôt beschert	20
danne mir, ich wænne, ane mînen tôt.	

[Alas, pangs of longing, how you have robbed me of joy! Gralant, who was
boiled, did not suffer greater distress than I am destined to suffer, I think,
until my death.]

The first five lines of the third unit of eight lines in IX, which forms the
penultimate section of the third *Leich*.   19 *Grâlant*: the name is that of
the hero of the OF *Lai de Graelent*, but the story differs; the name occurs also,

without ref. to the story, in Gottfrieds *Tristan*, 3583 ff., in which Tristan plays *einen leich* ... | *von der vil stolzen friundîn* | *Grâlandes des schœnen* (a lay ... of the most proud lady of Gralant the fair). There is a close parallel to l.19 in 'Der Weinschwelg' (Der Stricker, *Verserzählungen* II, p. 56) 334 f. *Grâlanden sluoc man unde sôt,* | *und gab in den frouwen ze ezzen* (Gralant was killed and boiled, and given to the ladies to eat). In the *Lai d'Ignaure*, the faithless lover's heart is given to twelve ladies to eat, to all of whom he had professed devotion. Such stories are variants on the widely diffused motif of the lover's heart given to the lady to eat, e.g. in the *Herzmære* of Konrad von Würzburg.

Ruodolf von Rotenburg 1

Ein hôher muot mich singen tuot (*Leich* III). KLD I, p. 366

Parcifal der leit dur minne	D 10	45
grôzen kumber unde nôt;		
Melioth pflac der selben sinne,		
wande ez ime Amûr gebôt;		
Glîes und ein kuniginne		
minten sich unz an den tôt.		50
Noch minne ich herzeclîcher	B 11	
dich lieben sælikeit		
mit ganzer stætekeit.		53
[...]		
Daz diu maget Lavîne iht wære	D 12	57
schœner danne mîn frouwe sî,		
oder Pallas diu wîten mære,		
des gelouben bin ich frî.		60

[Parzival suffered great grief and distress on account of love; Melioth was of the same disposition, for Love commanded him in this. Cliges and a queen loved each other until death. I love you, dear blessed one, even more, with absolute constancy. [...] That the maiden Lavinia was in any respect more beautiful than my lady, or Pallas the widely famed, that I do not at all believe.]

Ll. 45–50 make up a complete section; ll. 51–3 are the first half of the following section, and ll. 57–60 form the first four lines of the next section. 45 *Parcifal*: the name occurs in the *Conte del Graal* of Chrétien in the form *Percevaus/Perceval*, and in the German version of the story by Wolfram as *Parzival*. For Parzival as a victim of love, see Veldeke 2.1 and Dürinc 1.11. 47 *Melioth*: Meliot is the name of a vassal of Gauvain in the OF *Perlesvaus*; the name *Melôt* in Gottfrieds *Tristan* is phonologically a less exact parallel. 49 *Glîes* (cf. Rotenburg 2.239): hero of the *Cligés* of Chrétien; he loves Fénice, who is forced to marry another, but after many setbacks, the pair are finally united. There are fragments of a German version attributable to Ulrich von Türheim (see VL^2 10, 29 ff.). Rudolf von Ems, *Alexander*, 3239 ff. (including the form *Clîesen*, with medial vocalization of *g* as in Rotenburg) refers also

to a version by Konrad Fleck, of which there is no trace.   57 *Lavîne*: cf.
Gutenburg **1d**.25 n. 59 *Pallas*: cf. Frauenlob **1**.V.5 n.

Ruodolf von Rotenburg **2**

Ich tæte gerne schîn den grôzen pîn . . . (*Leich* V).
KLD I, p. 372

Ich wil der schœnen künden	F 14	181
daz mir ist rehte als ê was Gûrâze		
der in des sêwes ünden		
ertranc dâ von daz er âne mâze		
minnet eine frouwen.		185
[. . .]		
Sô sêre nie bevangen	F 16	191
enwart noch ritter Gâwân von minnen,		
ich sî in ir getwangen		
noch vaster. wolde si sich des versinnen,		
sô möhte ichs noch von ir vil süezen lôn gewinnen.		195
[. . .]		
Ob ich von ir eine	G 18	201
verdirbe, daz ist kleine;		
wie lützel mich des wundert!		
jâ lâgen tûsent hundert		
ze Troje von Elênen tôt.		205
noch gerner mac man lîden durch mîne frouwen nôt,		
wan got ein bezzer wîp nie werden gebôt.		
[. . .]		
Glîes leit vil manigen tac von liebe grôze swære;	D 50	239
Alienor desselben pflac. wie ungerne ich verbære		
ich endiende ir baz ald alse wol! der lîp ist mir unmære		
ob ich si dicke mîden sol, bî der ich gerne wære.		

[I will make known to the beautiful one that I am in the very same state as was formerly Guraz, who drowned in the waves of the sea, because he loved a lady without moderation. [. . .] Gawan the knight was never so much the captive of love, but I am held even more firmly in her bonds; if only she were willing to take account of it, I might yet receive a sweet reward from her in recompense. [. . .] If I alone perish for her sake, that is of no account and how little cause of wonder to me! – thousands of hundreds lay dead at Troy because of Helen. One may be more ready to suffer pain for the sake of my lady, for God never commanded a better woman to be created. [. . .] Cliges suffered great grief for many a day because of love; Alienor did likewise – how reluctantly would I forsake serving her better or as well! Life is indifferent to me if I must be often separated from her, with whom I would wish to be.]

This *Leich* is very much longer than other examples, and it is likely that an original shorter version has been expanded by a less competent poet. The comparisons take up complete units (except that l. 185 has a final phrase, here omitted, linking it syntactically to the following unit). Whereas ll. 181–5 are probably original, ll. 201–7 and ll. 239–42 are likely to be later additions; the introduction of Helen in l. 205 may have been inspired by the exemplars of beauty in *Leich* III (see Rotenburg 1.57 ff.), particularly since the theme is expanded in the three following units in the same form and which together with it make up a complete section of the *Leich*: her beauty is supreme (ll. 208–14); it surpasses that of goddesses (ll. 215–21); she wins universal acclaim (ll. 222–8). Lines 239 ff. appear to be based on *Leich* III (see Rotenburg 1.49 f.), with the repetition of *Glîes*, and the addition of a second name in *Alienor desselben pflac*, as a parallel to *Melioth pflac der selben sinne.* 182 *Gûrâze*: cf. Boppe 1.12; with a ref. to the story also in *Der Weinschwelg* 344 *mir ist baz denne Curâze,* | *der von minne in dem sê ertranc* (I am more fortunate than Curaz, who drowned in the sea because of love). The name occurs without ref. to the story in Tannhäuser (see n. on names, Tannhäuser 1), and in the *Flore und Blanscheflur* of Konrad Fleck as the name of a count. 192 *Gâwân*: *Gâwân/ Gâwein* are the predominant MHG forms of the name, beside *Gauvains* in the romances of Chrétien. 205 *Elênen*: see Raim. Jord. 1.28 n.; Morungen (?) 3.3 f. n. 239 *Glîes*: see Rotenburg 1.49 n. 240 *Alienor*: *Alienor/ Elienor* is frequently attested as a f. name in OF narrative (see Flutre, and West 1970 *s.v.*); a m. name *Elienor/Helienor*, that of a figure in *Guiron li Courtois*, is recorded in West 1978. The name is unlikely to be derived from *Helenor* (from Virgil) in the *Eneasroman* of Veldeke, as stated by Kreibich, *Minneleich*, p. 140 n. 265, since the second syllable is dissimilar.

The *Leich* ascribed in MS C to Ulrich von Gutenburg (for the ascription see pp. 239 f. and n. 4) is divided into two halves, each consisting of six sections. Each of the first five sections in the second half has structural correspondences with its counterpart in the first half (this explains the MF numbering in Ib, IIb, IVb and Vb below), but is not identical with it. The final section in each half is structurally unique.

Ulrich von Gutenburg(?) **1a–1d**

Ze dienest ir, von der ich hân (*Leich*). MF 69,1

1a	Nieman darf des wunder nemen,	MF V 33
	daz si mich hât gebunden.	
	ich enmac ir kreften niht gestemen:	35
	sô ist si obe, sô bin ich unden.	
	swaz ich nu tuon,	
	si hât bejaget an mir den ruon,	
	ich muoz ir jehen.	
	nu wol eht [ ], ez ist noch ie beschehen.	40
	Alexander der betwanc	
	diu lant von grôzer krefte;	
	doch muoste er sunder sînen danc	
	der minne meisterschefte	

sîn undertân   45
umb eine vrouwen wolgetân,
die er erkôs:
er enwart ouch nie mê sigelôs.
    In einem wilden walde er sach
sînes herzen küniginne.   50
des muoste er lîden ungemach,
er hete sîne sinne
vil nâch verlorn.
daz ich die schœnen hân erkorn
ze mîme leben,   55
des wirt mir lîhte ein lôn gegeben.

[No one should marvel that she has bound me. I cannot withstand her
strength: thus she is above and I below. Whatever I may now do, she has
achieved victory over me – I must yield to her. Now so be it, it has happened
at all times. Alexander subjugated lands by means of great strength, yet he
had to be subject, against his will, to the sovereignty of love, for the sake
of a lovely woman whom he saw (see n.): he was never again vanquished.
In a wild forest he saw the queen of his heart; in consequence he had to
suffer pain, he almost lost his senses. Since I have chosen the beautiful one
as my lady, I may perhaps be granted a reward.]

MF V.33–56 consists of the three concluding 8-l. units in a sequence of seven
such equal units, which make up the fifth section.   38 Lit.: 'she has
achieved glory in me'.   41 *Alexander*: for the theme of Love's victims, see
Veldeke **2.**1 n.; *Cesar* (*Jeux-partis* **1b.**49 ff.) is a comparable historical instance.
41 ff. As Vogt indicated (MF III/2, p. 416), this appears to be a conflation of
two episodes in the Strassburg version of Lamprechts *Alexander* (see Kinzel
ed.): forest episode, 5162–5358, and Candacis episode 5511–6461. The ref.
is mainly to the latter, and the exchange between Candacis and Alexander
6172 ff., in which Candacis lists Alexander's military conquests, contrasting
them with his present subjection: "*nû hât dich bedwungen | âne fehten ein wib.*"
[. . .] *ih sprah, mir wêre vil zorn, | daz ich hette verlorn | beide witze unde sin.*
("now a woman has subjugated you without a fight." [. . .] I said that I was very
angry that I had lost both my wits and senses.). The setting is derived from
the encounter with the flower maidens in the forest episode.   47 *erkôs*:
the verb *erkiesen* can mean both 'see'/'perceive' and 'choose'. If the former
meaning is intended, it is semantically related to *sach* in l. 49; if the latter
meaning is intended, it would be a parallel to *erkorn* in l. 54.   55 Lit. 'for
my life', 'as mine'.

1b   Mîn leben wirt müelich unde sûr,   MF Ib   21
          sol ich si lange mîden.
          daz Floris muose durch Planschiflûr
          sô grôzen kumber lîden,
              Daz enwas ein michel *wunder* niet,   MF IIb   1

wan si grôz ungeverte schiet,
als ez der alte heiden riet.
   Si wart vil verre über mer gesant,
des muost er in mangiu vrömdiu lant.   5
dâ er si in eime turne vant
   Von guoten listen wol behuot,
dâ wâget er leben unde guot;
des gewan er sît vil hôhen muot.
   Daz trœstet mich und tuot mir wol   10
von mînem kumber, den ich dol.
ez geschiht gar, swaz geschehen sol.
   Si sol wol wizzen âne wân,
swiez mir dar umbe sol ergân,
wær si versendet zEndîân,   15
Dar wære mîn varn vil bereit.

[My life will be arduous and bitter if I must long remain distant from her. That Floris had to suffer such great distress on account of Blancheflor, that was not a great marvel, for they were separated by an impassable distance, as the heathen of old decreed. She was sent far across the sea, therefore he had to venture into many strange lands. There where he found her in a tower, well guarded with great cunning, he risked life and worldly goods, and as a result later attained much joy. That consoles me and brings me relief for the distress I suffer. That which is fated to happen, will happen. She should truly know, whatever may befall me in consequence, if she were banished to India, I would gladly travel thither.]

This passage comprises the end of MF section Ib, which is made up of six 4-l. units, and the first five units + one line of the sixth unit of MF IIb, which is made up of seven 3-l. units.   MF Ib.23 *Floris . . . Planschiflûr*: the passage shows detailed knowledge of the story preserved in the OF *Floire et Blancheflor*, and in German in a fragmentary LG version, and in the *Flore und Blanscheflur* of Konrad Fleck. The pagan father of Floire (*der alte heiden* IIb.3) causes the Christian Blancheflor to be sold to merchants from Babylon (Cairo), in order to separate the lovers and prevent a marriage between them. Blancheflor is shut up in a tower by the emir of Babylon, from which she is finally rescued by Floire. For Romance refs. and the form *Floris*, see Arn. Mar. **3b**.153 n.   IIb.1 *wunder*: MS *kumber*.

1c   Ir vert mit   der vrouwen sit   de la Roschi bîse: MF IVb 17
die gesach nie man,   er schiede dan   vrô, rîche unde wîse.
ich wæne wol, ir sî alsam.
wer möhte ir danne wesen gram?

[Her nature resembles that of the lady de la Roschi bise: no man could see her without departing thence glad, rich and wise. I truly think she is similar. Who could then be ill-disposed to her?]

The final unit in a sequence of five which make up MF IVb.   IVb.17 *de la*

Roschi bîse: this place name occurs in the *chanson de geste* (see Langlois, *Table des noms propres*, p. 566), but without association with a similar episode.

1d	Sît ich der sælde niene habe,	MF Vb 17
	daz si mir sanfte lône,	
	ich enwil doch niht wesen abe,	
	ich werde enbunden schône,	20
	als ichs ger.	
	ich muoz iemer wesen der,	
	der umbe ir heil	
	ir treit ein schœnez leben veil.	
	Turnus der wart sanfte erlôst	25
	von kumberlîchem pîne:	
	daz was sînes herzen sunder trôst,	
	daz er lac dur Lavîne	
	sô schône tôt.	
	der endet schiere sîne nôt	30
	in eime tage,	
	die ich nu mange jâr trage.	

[Since I have not the good fortune that she graciously rewards me, yet I will not depart from the endeavour to be released from suffering, as I desire. I must always be the one, who for the sake of her perfection offers her worthy service (see n.). Turnus was gently released from painful grief; that was his sole consolation that he suffered such a beautiful death for Lavinia's sake. He swiftly put an end to his distress in the space of a day, distress which I have now borne for many a year.]

The final two 8-l. units in a section consisting of four such units (as opposed to seven units in the corresponding section in the first half – see MF V under **1a** above).   19 f. lit. 'I will not depart (i.e. by giving up the service of the lady) from being released . . .'   23 f.: *heil* has the primary sense of wholeness and hence of good fortune; *ein schœnez leben* seems to refer to the praiseworthy nature of love service, which enhances both the lady and the poet.   25 *Turnus*: MS *Turius* . . . 28 *Lavîne*; cf. Rotenburg **1**.57. The names may be derived directly from the *Roman d'Eneas*, or from Veldeke's adaptation of the work; the form *Lavine* occurs in both versions, with 5 exs. in rhyming position in *Eneas*, and many exs. in Veldeke, e.g. 10891 *mîne*: *Lavîne*.

Tannhäuser 1
                              Ich lobe ein wîp . . . (*Leich* IV). For the text, see below.

	Ich lobe ein wîp, diu ist noch bezzer danne guot,	I 1
	sist schœne und ist schœner vil und hôchgemuot,	
	si hât vor allen valschen dingen sich behuot;	
	ich gehôrte nie wîp sô wol geloben, als man si tuot.	
	Ysalde wart sô schœne nie	II 5
	noch *Djone*, diu ein gütin was.	

Medea swaz diu noch ie begie
des half ir mit wîsheit frou Pallas.

[I praise a woman who is even better than good; she is beautiful and much
more beautiful and joyful; she has guarded against all falsehood; I have
never heard a woman praised as highly as she is praised. Isalde was not
so beautiful nor Dione (see n.), who was a goddess. Whatever Medea did,
lady Pallas assisted her with wisdom.]

The first two strophes of the fourth *Leich* ascribed in MS C to Tannhäuser, and
here given according to C. The edition of Siebert in *Der Dichter Tannhäuser* introduces too many emendations and is therefore disregarded.   5 *Ysalde*: cf.
Veldeke **1**.1 n.; Bernger **1**.2 n.   6 *Djone* (MS *trone*): the name of the mother
of Venus, but often applied to Venus herself; cf. Ov. **4**.33 n.   Lines II.5 f.
introduce conventional comparisons in accord with the hyperbolic praise of
ll. 1–4; the tone for the central part of the *Leich* is set by II.7 f., with the introduction of the contrasting figure of Medea and the ironical reference to
the wisdom of Pallas. In sections III – XV there follows a jumble of (a) classical, (b) medieval and (c) otherwise unknown or invented names,[5] including
a number elsewhere associated with the theme of love, and real or invented
allusions to narrative details, often incongruously combined. The overall accumulation is no doubt intended to satirize the exaggerated use of literary
allusion in general, probably also that of exemplary comparisons in the *Leich*
in particular. This is made clear in the final part, with the injunction to forget
those of old and turn instead to praise of the lady, as she takes part in the
dance with her companions, whose peasant names – *Matze, Jutze, Elle* – form
a deliberate realistic contrast to those in the earlier part of the poem.

Der wilde Alexander **1**

Her Gâwein . . . (Spruchstrophe). KLD I, p. 9

Her Gâwein stîc noch strâze vant,	24	1
dô er ze Gâlois in daz lant		
hin wider rîten wolde.		
sô mac Burgou Gâlois wol sîn:		
dâ kund ich nie gekomen în,		5
doch versuochte ichz alse ich solde.		
mir wart dâ gruoz und rede verzigen;		
si sâhen hin ûz unde swigen		
und heten ir herren sô verspart		
und teten alle dem gelîch		10

---

[5] Figures represented (disregarding aberrant MS spellings): (a) Achilles, Dido, Hector, Helen, Juno, Menelaus, Paris, Pyramus, Sibille, Thisbe, Venus; (b) Artus, Blanschiflur, Curaze
(see Rotenburg **2**), Gahmuret, Galogriant, Gawan, Ginofer, Lanzlet, Lunet, Parcifal, Tristran, Wigol/Wigoleis, Ysalde, Ywein, Willebrant, perhaps also Opris (see Siebert, *Der Dichter
Tannhäuser*, p. 141); (c) Amabilia (cf. Lat. adj *amabilis*), Amarodia, Amye (OF subst.), Avenant
(OF adj.), Invidia (Lat. subst.), Latricia, Palatrica, Porhtram, Sarmena.

als ez wære kuninc Ermenrîch
und ich der zornic Eckehart.

[Sir Gawein could find neither path nor road when he wished to ride back
into the land of Galois. In this respect Burgou may indeed be Galois: I
could never find a way in there, yet I tried as I was bound to do. Greeting
and converse were denied me there: they looked out and were silent, and
had so barricaded their lord in, and all acted in such a way, as if he were
king Ermenrich and I angry Eckehart.]

A single stanza in a series of twenty-four didactic stanzas in the same form. It
combines an exemplar drawn from courtly narrative with two figures from the
heroic epics of the Dietrich cycle, in order to censure the poet's treatment at a
lord's court. 1–3 In the *Wigalois* of Wirnt von Gravenberg, ed. Kapteyn 1167 ff.,
Gawein wishes to return to his wife and son in his father-in-law's kingdom of
Galois, but is unable to do so, because he had left the magic girdle, necessary
for access, with his wife. The comparison between the poet and Gawein is
here implicit, whereas that in 11 f. is explicit.   1 *Gâwein*: see Rotenburg
2.192 n.   2 *Gâlois*: a medieval designation of Wales.   4 *Burgou*, 9
ir herren: may refer either to Markgraf Heinrich of Burgau, Bavaria, attested
from 1241, d. 1293, or to an earlier bearer of the title, d. 1282.   11 f. In the
Dietrich epics, *Eckehart* is a follower of Dietrich and defender of the Harlunge
against their uncle, the treacherous *Ermenrîch*; in one version he avenges their
death upon the latter.

Boppe 1

Hæt ich . . . (*Spruchstrophe*). Alex I,18

Hæt ich des küniges Salomônes wîsheit ganz,   1
und Absolônes schœne dâ bî sunder schranz
und gewalt des rîchen küniges Davîdes;
wære ich dâ bî noch sterker, danne sich was Samsôn
kunde vürbringen als Hôrant süezen dôn   5
und wære gewaltig alles goltgesmîdes;
wære ich als Aristôtiles
und künde kunst als Virgilîus zouberîe,
vil wol möht ich mich trœsten des;
wære ich der beste in Artûs massenîe,   10
wære ich als Adam edel gar
und Gûrâz was, trût den vrouwen allen
[. . .]
und Gawin, wem möhte daz missevallen?
hæt ich tugent als Sêneca, daz wære ze der welte ein wunne,   15
und daz ich wære zen füezen snel
als Azahel,
hie vür næme ich, daz sich min lieb gegen mir lieblich versunne.

[Had I Solomon's wisdom undiminished and in addition the beauty of
Absalon unimpaired and the power of mighty king David, if in addition I

were even stronger than was Samson, could bring forth like Horant sweet melody, and if I commanded all the goldsmith's art, if I were like Aristotle and as proficient in skill as Virgil in magic, I would indeed be able to renounce all this (see n.); if I were the best in Arthur's retinue, were I noble like Adam, and like Guraz dear to all women [. . .] and Gawain, to whom could that be displeasing? Had I virtue like Seneca, that would be a joy in worldly life, and were I fleet of foot like Asael, I would accept in exchange that my loved one might be lovingly disposed towards me.]

A single stanza in a series in the same form. The catalogue of exemplars, in a series of hypothetical conditions, combines figures drawn from the Bible, the ancient world and Arthurian romance with one from another medieval narrative (*Gûrâz*), and one from Germanic heroic epic (*Hôrant*),[6] in order to illustrate the theme of the supremacy of love over all else. 1 *Salomônes*: cf. Boppe **2**.17. 2 *Absolônes schœne*: cf. II. Sam. 14.25 and Index of Proper Names, *s.v.*; Frauenlob (?) **7**.6. 3 *Davîdes*: cf. Boppe **2**.10 n.; Goldener **1**.3. 4 *Samsôn*: cf. Boppe **2**.16. 5 *Hôrant*: a famed minstrel in the heroic poems *Dukus Horant* and *Kudrun*. 7 *Aristôtiles*: cf. Frauenlob (?) **7**.11. 8 *Virgilîus*: the medieval legend of Virgil as magician is attested in 12th-century Latin authors such as Gervais of Tilbury and Alexander Neckham (cf. similar legends attaching to Alexander the Great, as in Liechtenstein **1b**). 9 lit. 'I would be well able to console myself for (the loss of) this'. 10 *der beste in Artûs massenîe*: for Arthur himself as exemplar cf. Frauenlob **6b**.13. Sigeher MS C 19 praises two knights as worthy to be admitted to the Round Table. 11 *Adam*: cf. Zweter **2**.1. Adam is noble, because made in the image and likeness of God (Gen. 1.26 f.). 12 *Gûrâz*: cf. Rotenburg **2**.182 n. 13 The MS text of this line is corrupt and has therefore been omitted. 14 *Gawin*: the comparison is rendered unintelligible by the preceding corrupt line, but for Gauvain/Gawan as exemplar cf. Rotenburg **2**.192 n. 15 *Sêneca*: not customary as exemplar in the lyric, but see the possible allusion Guir. Ros. **1**.21 f. n. 17 *Azahel*: for the swiftness of Asael, see II. Sam. 2.18.

Boppe 2

Zâhî, waz hôher . . . (*Spruchstrophe*). Alex II.1

Zâhî, waz hôher tugende hât	1
got dem künic gegeben	
von Rôme, der durch nieman lât,	
er minne got und rechtez leben,	
vrouwen und wîbes tugent, zucht, stæten muot, bescheidenheit.	5
sîne vuore unde sînen rât	

---

[6] Cf. Anon. (14th century), Kiepe, *Gedichte 1300–1500*, p. 75, in the third of three related stanzas in the *Langer Ton* of Frauenlob, each based on a series of hypothetical conditions: Were I as beautiful as Absalom, could sing like Horant, were as noble as Adam, as learned as Aristotle, as proficient in magic as Virgil, strong as Samson, wise as Solomon, yet I would grieve when I reflected that I must become food for worms.

gelîche ich schône und eben
künic Karlen sunder missetât,
der nâch dem rechten kunde streben:
gotliep als Dâvît und Jôsîas, den schande meit,   10
vrom als Jûdas Makkabêus, küen als Jonatas,
kiusche als Sâmûêl, der gotes prophête was,
gedultic als Iôb,
diemüetic als Moîses, milte und guot als was Jâcôb,
gerecht gegen got als Simeôn, strîtbær als Jerôboâm,   15
stark als Samsôn,
wîse als Salomôn,
ein helt als Jôsuê, dem got den sunnen hiez stên und den *môn*.
dise tugend alle got hât an den künic Karlen geleit.

[Ah, what exalted virtues God has given to the king of Rome, who for no
one's sake deviates from loving God and a righteous way of life, excellence in ladies and women, propriety, constancy, understanding. I liken
his conduct and his counsel, without risk of error, truly and exactly to
king Charlemagne, who was well able to strive for what is right; pleasing
to God like David and Josiah, untainted by dishonour, valiant like Judas
Maccabaeus, bold like Jonathan, pure like Samuel, who was the prophet of
God, patient like Job, meek like Moses, gentle and good as was Jacob, just
towards God like Simeon, ready for battle like Jeroboam, strong like Samson, wise like Solomon, a hero like Joshua, for whom God bade sun and
moon stand still. God has invested all these virtues in king Charlemagne.]

A single stanza which is not part of a series, but this may be an accident of
transmission. It is an instance of double panegyric, of the unnamed 'king of
Rome', usually taken to be Rudolf von Habsburg, and of Charlemagne, with
whom he is compared.   8, 19 *Karlen*: see Sed. **1**.5 n.   10 *Dâvît*: cf.
Boppe **1**.3; for David as exemplar of virtue, see Venant. **1**.78 n.   *Jôsîas*: cf. II.
Kgs. 22.1 f.   11 *Jûdas Makkabêus*: cf. 1 Macc. 3.1 ff.   *Jonatas*: cf. I. Sam.
13.3; 14.1 ff.   12 *Sâmûêl*: cf. I. Sam. 12.1 ff.   13 *Iôb*: cf. Job 1.20 f.; 2.10.
14 *Moîses*: cf. Num. 12.3 *erat enim Moyses vir mitissimus*.   *Jâcôb*: cf. Gen.
33.10 f.   15 *Simeôn*: there is no appropriate OT ref., but cf. Luke 2.25 *Et
ecce homo... cui nomen Simeon, et homo iste iustus, et timoratus*.   *Jerôboâm*:
Jeroboam is cited only as an evil king, e.g. I. Kgs. 14.7 ff.   16 *Samsôn*:
cf. Boppe **1**.4.   17 *Salomôn*: cf. Boppe **1**.1.   18 *môn*: MS *tron*. The
emendation is confirmed by the reference to the biblical passage Josh. 10.12 f.

Der junge Meissner **1**
                    Swa wiplich wip ... (*Spruchstrophe*). Peperkorn I.5, p. 44

Swa wiplich wip lieplichen tougen lieben man   1
geblicket an
und er sie wider blicket,
liebe wirt verstricket.
in minnen strick gar sunder wer   werden sie verzwicket,   5

so daz ir lip, ir mut, ir leben   hilt minne sam minne diebe.
[. . .]
Piramus leit durch Thisbe not,   13
ein swert er zu dem herzen bot.
von blute rot   15
verwt er sich tot;
diz wag unminne nicht ein lot.
sam tet vrou Thisbe: daz geschach   von rechter minne, liebe.

[Whenever a womanly woman lovingly and secretly looks at a dear man, and he in turn looks at her, love becomes entwined. They are caught in love's snare without all defence, so that their person, their spirit, their life hides love like thieves of love. [. . .] Pyramus suffered grief for the sake of Thisbe, he pointed a sword at his heart. With red blood he stained himself in death; this was in no degree equivalent to lack of love. Thisbe also acted thus: that sprang from true affection, love.]

The first *Stollen* and the *Abgesang* of the stanza, part of a series.   13 *Piramus . . . Thisbe*: see Gliers 2.15 n.   17 lit. 'this did not weigh by the smallest weight in the scale of lack of love'.

Der junge Meissner 2

"Die minne ist . . ." (*Spruchstrophe*). Peperkorn I.6, p. 45

"Die minne ist aller tugende gar ein voller hort!"   1
du warez wort!
geblümet bist du, minne.
wer gar sine sinne
gerichten kan uf den bejag,   wie er din gewinne: 5
gar uf sin houbet ze eime cranze   heil er haben müze!
[. . .]
er sol mit minnen werben eben,   13
durch minne nieman sol sin leben
dem tode geben.   15
ein widerstreben
daz sol er halten unverweben:
sam Piramus und Thisbe, daz   in cummer iht begrüze.

["Love is a full treasure-house of all excellence": a true saying! You are adorned with blessings, Love. Whoever can set his thoughts on that prize, how he may win you, may he be granted good fortune as a garland on his head! [. . .] He should pursue love with moderation, no one should surrender his life to death for the sake of love. He should hold fast to undiminished resistance, so that grief may not, as with Pyramus and Thisbe, draw near him.]

The first *Stollen* and the *Abgesang* of the stanza. In contrast to **1**, this example interprets the actions of Pyramus and Thisbe negatively, as is also common. 1 cf. Walther L. 14.8 *minne ist aller tugende ein hort*.   17 *unverweben*: lit. 'not interwoven'.   18 *begrüze*: lit. 'greet'.

Der Dürinc **1**

Spil minnen wunder volbringen man git (single stanza). See
KLD I, p. 54 and KLD II, pp. 55–9. For the following text see below.

War quam gwin der vil wisen ze male	9
die Venus verschriet?	
riet si e sus Parcifalen,	
entrisenden sin si nam gar	
Adam Sampsone in ir ziten,	
boug wirde in ir schœne.	14
[. . .]	
künde girde troug Dauiden	
Salmone da sam.	18

[Where has straightway vanished the profit of the most wise, whom Venus
cut down? She formerly counselled Parzival thus, she completely robbed
fleeting sense from Adam, Samson in their time, she laid low worth in its
prime. [. . .] Eager desire betrayed David and Solomon likewise.]

Ll. 9–14 and 17 f. form part of the *Abgesang* of a single syntactically and
metrically complex stanza, imperfectly rendered in MS C, and considerably
emended in KLD I.[7] The first part of the stanza appears to contain the poet's
complaint of the pains inflicted by love, and praise of the lady. If this interpretation is correct, this forms a transition to the general theme of love's victims,
as a parallel to the poet's own sufferings. Because of the unsatisfactory nature
of the text, only those lines relevant to the theme of love's victims and their
names are given here; see Veldeke 2.1 n., and for *Parcifalen* Rotenburg 1.45 n.

Der Henneberger (*MS J Der Hynnenberger*)

The stanzas from which the following excerpts are taken are preserved in MS
J in an East Central German dialect, with idiosyncratic scribal features. Only
the lines relevant to the two exemplary figures are included, rendered on the
basis of the diplomatic edition by Holz in vol. I of *Die Jenaer Handschrift*,
ed. Holz/Saran/Bernouilli. The division into metrical units and lines is not
certain.

Der Henneberger **1**

Rv̊mere hetten eynen kvninc . . . (*Spruchstrophe*).
Holz/Saran/Bernouilli, Der Hynnenberger 10

Rv̊mere hetten eynen kvninc, troianus was er genant,	1
Truwe vnd ere, milte was ym wol bekant.	
[. . .]	
Der rv̊mer kvninc vragete syne man	7
An synem ende tugentlicher mere,	
Ob er icht lasters hette began.	

---

[7] In 'Exemplary comparisons in the medieval lyric', p. 16, I mistakenly referred to two stanzas.

Sie sprachen alle, her were scanden lere. 10
Ir vursten, herren set iuch vůr
an iuweme hoesten vreudentage:
Nu vragent waz ir habent getan,
vnde scaffet daz man uch nach todhe klage.

[The Romans had a king called Trajan, uprightness and honour, generosity were (qualities) very well known to him. [. . .] The king of the Romans asked his subjects at the end of his life for a true account, whether he had committed any evil: they all declared that he was free of dishonour. You princes, lords, look to the future, in the day of your greatest felicity: now ask what things you have done, and act in such a way that you will be mourned after death.]

A single stanza in a series. Lines 3–6 lament the lack of the virtues listed in l. 2 in Trajan's heirs and the noblemen of the present. 1 *troianus*: for Trajan (*Trajanus*) as exemplar of virtue cf. Sid. **3**.116n.

Der Henneberger 2

Untruwe, kvndicheit . . . (Spruchstrophe).
Holz/Saran/Bernouilli, Der Hynnenberger 11

Untruwe, kvndicheit, dartzů vbermůt, 1
Die dre die ne synt tzůr sele noch tzů den eren gůt.
[. . .]
Her lucifer vůrstozen wart durch vbermůt 7
vaste in die tiefen helle. daz ist dir ouch vil vnvůrspart:
Du valscher man, du bist wol syn geselle . . .

[Falsehood, cunning and in addition pride, these three do not profit the soul or honour. A wise man should be unwilling to embrace them [. . .] Sir Lucifer was cast out on account of pride into the far depths of hell. You also will in no way be spared that, you faithless man, you are indeed his associate . . .]

Ll. 1 f. and 7 ff. of a single stanza in the same series as **1** (the end of the stanza is omitted). 7 *Lucifer*: see Ad. Halle **2**.37 n.; cf. Rumelant, MS J 87, which castigates Singauf for boasting of his poetic skill, alluding to Lucifer (unnamed) as warning: *sich hielt ein engel al tzů ho | Den got vůrstiez, der wart unvro. | Swer alsus tůt, dem geschiht also* (an angel aspired much too high; God cast him out and he was made unhappy; whoever acts thus will suffer the same fate). In Wolfram, MS J 30 (part of a poetic contest – see *Wartburgkrieg* **1** n.), Lucifer, likewise unnamed, speaks in the first person, citing as warning example his expulsion from the angelic company as punishment for pride.

Sigeher 1

Ein Alexander fuort ein her (Spruchstrophe). Brodt 18

Ein Alexander fuort ein her, 1
dâ sîn ein *Persân* getorste wol erbîten,
in hôher wirde mit kostlîcher zer,

mit der wer,
als man künige sol anrîten.   5
nu fuort eins Alexanders muot
eins Alexanders her gesamnet wîten,
eins Alexanders lîp unt ouch sîn guot,
wol behuot
ze ganzen êren zallen zîten: 10
ein Beheim wert,
Otacker, der des rîches erbe noch sol wîten.
ob ers gert,
sîn wirt eben berge unt tal unt alle lîten.
sus sol ein Stoufer hiure hôher stîgen danne vert   15
unt sîn swert
sol umb êre als ê Alexander strîten.

[An Alexander led an army where a Persian dared to await him, in great splendour, with costly array, and armed with the defence appropriate to the march against kings. Now the spirit of an Alexander commands the army of an Alexander, assembled from afar, the person and wealth of an Alexander, safeguarded at all times in perfect honour: a noble Bohemian, Ottokar, who shall yet widen the heritage of the realm. If he so desires it, for him shall be made low mountains and valley and all hills. In the same way a Hohenstaufen shall ascend higher today than yesterday, and his sword shall fight for honour, as did Alexander formerly.]

A single strophe in a group of four in the same form, at the end of the Sigeher entry in MS C. To praise of the historical Alexander in ll. 1–5 (the first *Stollen*) corresponds in ll. 6–10 (the second *Stollen*) that of an unnamed hero comparable to Alexander in spirit, army, person, wealth and honour. This leads to the disclosure of the name of Ottokar in l. 12.   1 *Alexander*: for Alexander as exemplar of military prowess see e.g. Gutenburg **1a**.41 f., Frauenlob **6b**.17. 2 *ein Persân getorste*: *ein pſone getorſte* C, with the indeterminate noun 'person', where a specific designation is required as a parallel to *ein Alexander*. Brodt omits *ein* and emends to the pl.: *Persâne getorsten*. It is, however, likely that 1 f. refers to the Persian campaign of Alexander the Great against Darius (*ein Persân*).   12 *Otacker*: Ottokar II of Bohemia (1253–1278).   14 Cf. Isa. 40.4 *omnis vallis exaltabitur, et omnis mons et collis humiliabitur*. Brodt emends *berge* C to the sg. in line with the Biblical passage.   15 *ein Stoufer*: probably a ref. to Konradin's expedition to Italy in 1267.

Der Goldener **1**

Der hoen tugent ein voller schrin (*Spruchstrophe*). Cramer I, p. 255

Der hoen tugent ein voller schrin,   1
der rechten milte ein Salatin,
der zucht ein maget, ein koning David der truwen,
der eren luter spiegelglas,
[. . .]

wol veret der eren gerende man, 13
der sich in tugenden werden kan,
von Brandenburch markgreve Otto de lange.

[A full treasury of elevated virtue, in true generosity a Saladin, in proper conduct a maiden, a king David in righteousness, the clear mirror of honour [...]. He fares well, the man who aspires to honour, who acquires worth through virtue, margrave Otto der Lange of Brandenburg.]

The first four and the last three ll. of a 15-l. stanza in a series.   2 *Salatin*: see Walther 1.7 n.   3 *David*: see Boppe 1.3; 2.10 n.

Frauenlob 1

Ouwe herzelicher leide (*Lied*). Stackmann/Bertau Lied 2, p. 563

Minne, wiltu solchen jamer   IV 1
uf mich erben mine zit?
Diner lüste selden amer
mir da kleine stiure git.
Nie dem herren Iwein wirs kein maget tetc,   5
wan die schöne vrou Lunete
half: des leben da trost an hete.

Ach, solt ich den apfel teilen,   V 1
den Paris der Minne gab,
Zwar, du müstest jamer seilen,
solte ich dadurch in min grab.
Pallas oder Juno müsten halden ir: 5
so reche ich min leide an dir,
die du hast geerbet mir.

[Love, do you wish to bequeath me such grief for my lifetime? The amber of the joys of your desires affords me little help in this. Never did any maiden inflict worse on sir Iwein, but fair lady Lunete provided help: his life found solace in that. Ah, if I had to award the apple, which Paris gave to Love (see n.), indeed you would have to bind grief to yourself, even were I consigned to my grave because of it. Pallas or Juno would have to receive it: thus I will avenge upon you the sufferings which you have bequeathed to me.]

The two final stanzas of a five-stanza poem.   IV.1 *Minne*: here the customary personification of love, but see V.2 n.   IV.5 f. *Iwein . . . Lunete*: in the *Iwein* of Hartmann von Aue, based on *Le Chevalier au lion* (*Yvain*) of Chrétien, Iwein kills the lord of a castle, guardian of an enchanted fountain, and is given a ring by Lunete, the servant of Laudine, the lord's widow, making him invisible to the lord's followers who seek revenge. Iwein is seized by love for Laudine, and Lunete persuades her to accept him as her husband and defender of her land.   V.2 *Minne*: here the noun designates both the personified figure of love, as in IV.1, and also Venus, as goddess of love. Paris decided the dispute between Pallas, Juno and Venus by awarding the apple to

Venus, because he had been promised Helen as reward. Were he to decide the contest, the poet would avenge himself on *Minne*/Venus by depriving her of the prize.   V.3 *seilen*: lit. 'bind with a rope'.   V.5 *Pallas*: see Rotenburg **1**.59; *müsten halden ir*: the eds. explain the construction as follows: *müste* (*i*)*n*, with *in*, acc. sg., referring back to *apfel* in l. 1, and *ir* as reflexive dat., i.e. 'to herself'.

Frauenlob 2

O wip, du hoher eren haft (*Leich*). Stackmann/Bertau III, p. 330

"Her Sin, nu bildet mir ein wip,   III,2   1
sit ich ouch trage eines mannes lip."
"ob ich erkenne ir bernden lobes künne,
Ich tunz mit willeclicher hege."
"nu secht, welch bilde ich an si lege."   5
"der hochsten ger ein erensedel, wünne,

Hast du gelesen, wie si gewesen   III,3   1
Hester hie vor?" "la mich genesen
und bilde selber deste baz!"

["Sir Mind, now fashion for me a woman, since I moreover bear the form of a man." "If I can discern the kinship of her blossoming merit, I will do it with willing diligence." "Now consider what image I should ascribe to her." "Of supreme desire the throne of honour, joy – have you read of what nature was Hester in former times? " "Let me desist, and fashion the image yourself so much the better."]

The second section, and the first half of the following section in the *Minneleich*, containing a dialogue in which the poet addresses his mind, seeking help in delineating the image of womanly perfection.   III,3.2 *Hester*: the question implies that Esther is an exemplar of womanly perfection; in Marner **3**.8 (see n.) she is a type of the Virgin.

Frauenlob 3

Swaz ie gesang . . . (*Spruchstrophe*). Stackmann/Bertau V,115, p. 457

Swaz ie gesang Reimar und der von Eschenbach,   1
swaz ie gesprach
der von der Vogelweide,
mit vergoltem kleide
ich, Vrouwenlob, vergulde ir sang,   als ich iuch bescheide.   5
sie han gesungen von dem feim,   den grunt han si verlazen.
Uz kezzels grunde gat min kunst, so gicht min munt.
ich tun iu kunt
mit worten und mit dönen
ane sunderhönen: 10
noch solte man mins sanges schrin   gar rilichen krönen.
sie han gevarn den smalen stig   bi künstenrichen strazen.
Swer ie gesang und singet noch

– bi grünem holze ein fulez bloch – ,
so bin ichz doch   15
ir meister noch.

[Whatever Reimar and von Eschenbach have sung, whatever von der Vogelweide has ever spoken, with gilded vesture, I, Frauenlob, gild their song,
as I set forth to you. They have sung of the froth, they have departed from
the base. My art proceeds from the bottom of the pot, thus speaks my
mouth. I make known to you in words and melodies without undue presumption: the treasure-chest of my song should yet be richly crowned.
They have trodden the narrow path beside ways abounding in poetic
skills. Whoever has ever sung and still sings – a rotten stump beside green
wood – , I am yet still their master.]

The *Aufgesang* and the first 4 ll. of the *Abgesang* of a stanza of 19 ll. in the series
of the *Langer Ton*. In this piece of poetic bravado, the poet boasts, in typically
ornate style, of outdoing famous poets of the recent past. Reimar is probably
Reinmar von Zweter (*q.v.*); *der von Eschenbach* refers, not to Wolfram's narrative works, but to his supposed role as participant in a poetic contest (see n.
on *Der Wartburgkrieg* 1); Walther von der Vogelweide is no doubt primarily
seen as the author of didactic and political poems (*gesprach* in l. 2 perhaps
refers to the genre of the *Spruch*). See also Frauenlob, ed. Stackmann/Bertau
V,117 G, which appears to be a reply by another poet to this stanza: it praises
her Walther unde zwen Reimar, ein Wolferam in contrast to the unfounded
boasts of another poet, probably Frauenlob himself.   6 f.: for this image
of the cooking-pot, cf. l.18 of the stanza, in which the poet describes himself
as *der künste ein koch* (a cook of arts/skills).

In the panegyric of princes, there are two instances of identification with
figures drawn from the *Willehalm* of Wolfram von Eschenbach (based on the
OF cycle of *Guillaume d'Orange*):

Frauenlob **4a**
          Komm, minnen schüler . . . (*Spruchstrophe*). Stackmann/Bertau V,9, p. 393

du Rennewart   15
in strites vart,
dich, helt, von der Hoye Gerhart,
meine ich. hete ich me kunst gelart,
daz vromte dir zu dime lobe.   din verch in tugenden gralet.

[You Rennewart in conduct of battle, of you, a champion, Gerhart von der
Hoye, I speak. Had I learned more skill, that would be of benefit to praise
of you. Your life attains the grail of virtue.]

The final lines of a 19-l. stanza in the *Langer Ton*.   15 *Rennewart* : in book
IV of the *Willehalm* of Wolfram von Eschenbach, Rennewart, a noble young
heathen of superhuman strength and bravery, a servant at the court of king
Louis, is given at his request to Willehalm, and is instrumental in securing the
latter's victory in the second battle.

Frauenlob **4b**

> *Ja tuon ich als ein wercman, der sin winkelmaz* (*Spruchstrophe*).
> Stackmann/Bertau V,13, p. 396

froun Eren diener Vivianz   18
ist Waldemar, der fürste stolz,   sin lob noch wunder wirket.

[The servant of lady Honour, Vivianz, such is Waldemar, the proud prince,
praise of him still achieves marvels.]

The final ll. of a 19–l. stanza in the *Langer Ton*.   18 *Vivianz*: nephew
of Willehalm and prototype of the virtuous young Christian knight, whose
death is lamented in book II of *Willehalm*.   19 This is explained by the
main image of the stanza: the poet attempts, like the carpenter with set square
(*winkelmaz*, l. 1) to measure praise of Waldemar, but this exceeds all normal
dimensions.

Frauenlob **5**

> *Ich han der Minne und ouch der Werlte kraft gewegen*
> (includes exchange between *Welt* and *Minne* in a series of
> alternating *Spruchstrophen*). Stackmann/Bertau IV,12, p. 384

daz han ich oft an dir ervarn,   Welt   IV,12   2
daz maniger schone und eben warp
mit stolzer fuge richliche, als du hast verjehen,
Der doch versmehet wart vor diner helfe tür,   5
[. . .]
als Gachmoret, der sich ie liez in fuge sehen: 8
Den totest du
davon, was daz maze und bescheidenheit? sprich nu!   10
[. . .]
Din lieb hat leit.   Welt   IV,14   9
ja triuge ich nicht sam du mit diner gunterfeit:
des Paris vil wol wart gewar
und maniger von derselben schar.

[I have often observed in you that many a one served love handsomely
and with measure, unstintingly in assured and fitting manner, as you have
decreed, who was scorned at the door of your help [. . .] like Gahmuret,
who always observed what was fitting: him you killed because of that (?),
was that moderation and wisdom? speak now! [. . .] Your joy contains
sorrow. I do not deceive like you with your counterfeit, as Paris became
very well aware and many a one of the same company.]

The stanzas consist of twelve lines. In IV,12, the essential parts of the comparison take up five of the eight ll. of the *Aufgesang* and the first two ll.
of the *Abgesang*; in IV,14 the example of Paris is contained in the *Abgesang*. 12.8 *Gachmoret*: Gahmuret, father of the hero in Wolfram's *Parzival*;
see Veldeke **2**.1 n.; Frauenlob **6a**.13 n., and on the possible origin of the name,
n. 9.   12.10 *davon*: MS *dauon*, emended by eds. to *davor*.   14.11 *Paris*:
see Veldeke **2**.1 n.

Frauenlob **6a**

Ich wil durch niemans vorchte schanden bi gestan (*Spruchstrophe*). Stackmann/Bertau V,47, p. 416

Ich wil durch niemans vorchte schanden bi gestan,   1
schande ist ein gran,
dar inne wirt geverbet:
daz kleit manigem erbet
und da bi manigen edelen man   eren gar verderbet,   5
daz er wiget ringer dan er wag,   e er getrug der kleider.
Swer rates ger, der volge dem, der ere hat,
fru unde spat,
so mag im wol gelingen.
wil er nach prise ringen,   10
so laze sich kein swachen rat   in die winkel dringen,
ge ab der vinster an daz liecht   und volge mir der beider
Alsam der tiure Parzifal,
dem da empfolhen wart der gral:
des lob erhal   15
berg unde tal,
bi hohen vürsten in dem sal,
vor schönen vrouwen über al,
si retten wol des heldes lop,   swaz laster was, daz meit er.

[I will not, for fear of any man, ally myself with shame; shame is a scarlet stain which acts as a dye: such a garment falls as portion to many a man and thereby completely destroys the honour of many a noble man, so that he is of lesser worth than before he wore these garments. Whosoever seeks advice, let him follow the one who possesses honour, early and late, then he may prosper. If he wishes to strive for renown, then let him not be thrust into corners by base advice, let him go from the darkness into the light and follow me in both, like esteemed Parzival, to whom the grail was entrusted; his praises resounded in hill and dale, among high princes in the chamber, in the company of beautiful women everywhere – they indeed declared the hero's praises. Whatever was evil, that he shunned.]

A single stanza in a series in the *Langer Ton*; the comparison takes up the *Abgesang*.   13 *Parzifal*: see Rotenburg 1.45 n.; see also Frauenlob VII, 27.1 ff. (with corrupt MS text): *Man saget von Parzifale,* | *von Titurel und Gachmurete,* | *von Ector* (MS *Eckart*) *und Achille,* | *von Gawein, der daz beste ie tete,* | *von Walwan* (variant of *Gawein*) *und von Lanzelot,* | *von Iweins krieg und von Wilhalmes tat* (they tell of Parzival, of Titurel and Gachmuret, of Hector and Achilles, of Gawein, whose actions were ever most excellent, of Walwan and of Lancelot, of Iwein's warfare and of Willehalm's deeds) – these were renowned for virtue and generosity, and were Arthur still alive, all the grail heroes such as Parzival might still be found.

Frauenlob **6b**

Sibilla sprach . . . (Spruchstrophe). Stackmann/Bertau IX,4, p. 511

Künig Artus mit ritterschaft	13
vil hohen pris erwarb;	
swie daz er doch erstorben si,	15
sin reinez lob doch nie verdarb	
künig Alexander, der ouch hie	
in hohen wirden starb.	
die fürsten nemen snöden schaz	
für ritterliche tat,	20
der ritterschaft mit swachem saz	
so gar verdrungen hat.	

[King Arthur won most high renown through chivalry; although he is dead, the unsullied reputation of king Alexander, who likewise died possessed of great honour on earth, never perished. The princes prefer base wealth to chivalric deeds; this with its unworthy rule has entirely supplanted chivalry.]

The *Abgesang* of a single stanza in a series; it begins with a Sibylline injunction to arrest the decay of honour, and exhorts princes and lords to pursue renown through chivalry.   13 *Artus*: see Boppe **1**.10 n.   17 *Alexander*: see Sigeher **1**.1 n.

Frauenlob (?) **7**

Adam den êrsten menschen . . . (Spruchstrophe). Ettmüller p. 102

Adam den êrsten menschen den betrouc ein wip.	1
Samsônes lip	
wart durch ein wip geblendet,	
Davit wart geschendet,	
her Salomôn ouch gotes richs durch ein wip gepfendet;	5
Absalôns schœne in niht vervienc, in het ein wip betœret.	
Swie gwaltec Alexander was, dem geschach alsus,	
Virgilius	
wart betrogen mit valschen sitten,	
Ôlofern versnitten;	10
dâ wart ouch Aristoteles von eime wibe geritten;	
Troya diu stat und al ir lant wart durch ein wip zerstœret.	
Achilli dem geschach alsam;	
der wilde Asahel wart zam;	
Artûses scham	15
von wibe kam;	
Parcival grôze sorge nam:	
sit daz ie vuogt der minnen stam,	
waz schadet, ob ein reinez wip mich brennet unde vrœret?	

[Adam the first man was deceived by a woman, Samson was deluded by a woman, David was disgraced, sir Solomon was also robbed of God's kingdom by a woman; Absalon's beauty was of no avail to him, a woman reduced him to folly. However powerful Alexander was, the same befell him. Virgil was deceived by trickery, Holofernes was cut down; Aristotle too was ridden by a woman; the city of Troy and all its land was destroyed by a woman. The same befell Achilles; unbridled Asael was tamed; Arthur's disgrace came from woman; Parzival suffered great grief. Since the kinship of love has at all times been the cause, what matter, if a lovely woman causes me to burn and freeze?]

This stanza in the *Langer Ton* of Frauenlob, preserved only in later MSS, is not included in the ed. of Stackmann/Bertau, since it is very unlikely to be by the poet himself, but it has been included as an extreme example of the listing of love's illustrious victims. In accumulating the names of as many victims as possible, the author has included some (Absalon, Achilles, Holofernes, Asael, Arthur) not usually associated with the theme (for the latter, and the names of victims, see Veldeke 2.1 n.). 6 *Absalônes schœne*: cf. Boppe 1.2 n. 7 *Alexander*: see Gutenburg 1a.41 n. 8 *Virgilius*: a ref. to the legend of Virgil left hanging in the basket by a courtesan (see Chiaro 2b.21 n.). 10 *Ôlofern*: see Marner 3.6 n. 11 *Aristoteles*: for this legend see *Jeux-partis* 1a.45 n. 12 *ein wip*: an indirect ref. to Helen (see Rotenburg 2.205 n.). 14 *Asahel*: cf. Boppe 1.17 n.; in the biblical account he is described as rash. 17 *Parcival*: see Rotenburg 1.45.

Der Wartburgkrieg 1

> *Was Pilat missewende vrî* (*Spruchstrophe*). Holz/Saran/Bernouilli,
> Her Wolveram 41 (see Simrock, *Wartburgkrieg*, p. 159)

Was Pilât missewende vrî? 1
er twuoc sîne hende darabe, er wolde unschuldic sî
eins tôdes den er schuof der megede kinde.
Ir hôhen, die die pfarren geben,
warumme ne vrâget ir niht umme der pfaffen leben? 5
Pilâtus glîchen muoz man an iuch vinden.
Lâzet ir mit Aurônes pfenninc iuwer pfaffen schallen,
unde stêt der missewende bî,
sô wolt ir wænen, daz got ein lugenære sî:
nein, er lieze ê daz himelrîche vallen. 10

[Was Pilate free of blame? He washed his hands of it, he claimed to be innocent of the death of the Virgin's child, which he brought about. You nobles who dispense benefices, why do you not inquire into the life of the priests? One must recognize the counterparts of Pilate in you. If you allow your priests to boast of Auron's pence and look on at the abuse, you must think that God is a liar: no, He would sooner let the heavens fall.]

One of a number of stanzas ascribed to Wolfram in MS J, complaining of the venality of priests (in J 31 they are described as worse than Judas – for a similar ex. cf. *Carmina Burana*, ed. Vollmann, 9. 1. 1 ff.). They form part of the original corpus of the so-called *Wartburgkrieg*, a complex of stanzas dating from the 13th to 15th centuries, making up a fictive poetic dialogue, with later accretions, with stanzas ascribed to well-known earlier poets such as Wolfram von Eschenbach, with whom they have no connection.   7 *Aurônes pfenninc*: the money derived from charging for the sacraments; Auron is the name of a devil.

MHG Anon. 1

> *Möhte zerspringen mîn herze mir gar (Lied)*.
> See KLD p. 276, Höver/Kiepe I, p. 245

Tantalus geselle bin ich nu gesîn,   II   1
dem turst sêre und tuon hunger wê,
doch sô *fliuhet* [ ] vor dem munde sîn,
grânât menger leie und ein tiefer sê.
Alsô sên ich dicke   lieplîch ougen blicke,   5
dâ von ich erschricke.   ach, daz tuot mir wê,
ach, daz tuot mir wê,   ach, daz tuot mir wê.
ach, daz tuot mir wê,   ach, daz tuot mir wê.
rât, edele Minne, daz sorge zergê.

[I have now been the companion of Tantalus, to whom thirst and hunger cause sharp pangs, yet pomegranates of many kinds, and a deep lake flee before his mouth. In the same way I often see lovely glances which make me tremble. Alas, that causes me pain, alas, that causes me pain, alas, that causes me pain, alas, that causes me pain, alas, that causes me pain. Help, noble Love, that sorrow may cease.]

The second of two 9-l. stanzas added at the end of a 13th-century Latin MS of Lucan. The text is given in a heavily emended version in KLD I, and in a virtual diplomatic version in Höver/Kiepe, neither of which is satisfactory for the present purpose; it is here rendered conservatively, but with the adoption of the customary standardized spelling.   1 *Tantalus*: MS *Tattalus*; cf. Liechtenstein **1a**.114 and n.   2 *dem*: MS *den.vn*.   3 *fliuhet*: *flussent tôfte* MS (the second unintelligible word is omitted). In support of *fliuhet*, see Liechtenstein **1a**.122 and *ibid*. 114 n.: Ov., *Met*. IV.459 *effugit*; *Met*. X.41 f. *undam . . . refugam*; *Am*. II ii.43 *poma fugacia*.   4 *grânât*: this fruit is mentioned in the Homeric version of the story (see Liechtenstein **1a**.114 n.).

Conclusion

The main types of poem containing exemplary comparisons, identifications and exemplary parallels are the following: (a) the isostrophic poem (*Lied*); (b) the heterostrophic *Leich*; (c) didactic stanzas (*Spruchstrophen*), usually single stanzas in a series in the same form, but occasionally part of loose thematic groupings. Examples of (a): Hausen **1**; Veldeke **1**; Bernger **1**; Morungen **1**, **2**; Morungen (?) **3**; Walther (?) **2**; Wolfram (?) **1**; Marner **1** (see n. on *tageliet*); Liechtenstein **2** (designated in the narrative as *tanzwîse*); Frauenlob

1; MHG Anon. 1. Related to this first category are Liechtenstein **1a** and **1b**, in couplets, part of a missive (*buochel*) addressed to the lady, with similarities to the Romance *salut*, which itself has affinities with the *canso*. There are two single stanzas, Veldeke **2** and Dürinc **1** (*qq.v*). Examples of (b): Botenlouben **1**; Würzburg **1**; Gliers **1, 2, 3**; Rotenburg **1, 2**; Gutenburg **1a–1d**; Tannhäuser **1**; Frauenlob **2**. Examples of (c): Herger **1**; Walther **1**; Zweter **1, 2**; Wernher **1**; Marner **2, 3**; Alexander **1**; Boppe **1, 2**; Der j. Meissner **1, 2**; Henneberger **1, 2**; Sigeher **1**; Goldener **1**; Frauenlob **3, 4a, 4b, 5, 6a, 6b**; Frauenlob (?) **7**; *Wartburgkrieg* **1**. If the polystrophic poems (*Lied + Leich*) on the one hand, and the predominantly monostrophic didactic stanzas on the other are considered as forming two separate groups, there are a roughly equal number of examples (taking comparisons and identifications together) in each, with a high incidence of exemplary figures in association with general didactic themes in the second group.

The most common stylistic type is explicit comparison, expressing either similarity or superiority to, or less often, contrast with, an exemplar; comparison is couched in hypothetical form in Gliers **1**. Comparison may be based on the possession of qualities or attributes of the exemplar: the spirit of Rüedeger in Herger **1**; the qualities of biblical exemplars in Boppe **2**; the qualities and attributes of Alexander in Sigeher **1**; there is a hypothetical comparison with the qualities of a series of exemplars in Boppe **1**; see also Goldener **1** below under identification.

Less frequently, comparison may be conveyed implicitly by textual juxtaposition, without a specific grammatical link, as in Marner **1**, in which the watchman's song implicitly associates the lovers he is guarding with those of Troy, and Tristan and Isolde; Rotenburg **2**. 204 ff. implies a comparison with Helen; Alexander **1** combines implicit comparison with Gawein, with explicit comparison with Ermenrich and Eckehart; comparison with the ideal of womanhood is implied in the question in Frauenlob **2**: *hast du gelesen, wie si gewesen | Hester hie vor?*; Frauenlob **6b** implies a contrast between the positive exemplars of Arthur and Alexander and princes of the present. In as far as it is possible to interpret the tortuous syntax satisfactorily, Dürinc **1** seems to be of this type, in that the poet's complaint of his sufferings is followed by the list of love's victims who gained no reward and were brought low by love. Related to such examples are those in which the citation of an exemplar is linked to an exhortation: thus in Walther **1**, Philip is urged to remember the generosity of Saladin and Richard Cœur de Lion, i.e. to follow their example; in Henneberger **1**, the noble example of Trajan is followed by the injunction to princes to act rightly, i.e. like Trajan, so that they may be mourned after their death (but see the similar instance of Marner **2**, in which a specific grammatical link, with a verb expressing similarity, reinforces the lesson: *ir werden fürsten, merkent disen list: | dem ritter sult ir iuch gelîchen*). Gutenburg **1a** is perhaps a marginal case: the link between the poet and Alexander is mainly implied by the close juxtaposition of the description of the poet's sufferings in ll. 33–9 with those of Alexander in ll. 41–53, but the phrase *ez ist noch ie beschehen* in l. 40 provides a tenuous link between the two passages.

There are also instances of identification with an exemplar: with Eneas and Dido in Hausen **1**; with Venus in Morungen **2**; with Rennewart in Frauenlob **4a**; with Vivianz in Frauenlob **4b**; in Goldener **1**, Otto is identified with Saladin and David in respect of their characteristic qualities; identity with Helen is implied in Morungen (?) **3**.3 f. Marner **3** is distinct from these examples in that the identification of Mary with a series of biblical exemplars is an instance of typological interpretation.

There are other instances which are more closely akin to general *exempla*, without explicit or implicit reference to a particular person or group of persons. Of this type is Zweter **2**, which after listing love's victims, describes love as good only if it is a source of virtue; in Würzburg **1**, Riwalin and Blantschiflur are positive examples of love in an earlier uncorrupted age; in Der j. Meissner **1**, Pyramus and Thisbe are presented positively as representing the highest ideal of love, but in **2** they illustrate the excesses to which love may lead; in Frauenlob **5**, in the debate between the world and love, the world accuses love of injustice and treachery towards lovers, citing Gahmuret and Paris as examples.

Many of the examples are associated with the theme of love, expressing either the extent of the poet's love or of his sufferings. Of this type are: Hausen **1**; Veldeke **1**; Bernger **1**; Morungen **1**; Zweter **1**; Botenlouben **1**; Liechtenstein **1a, 2**; Gliers **1, 2, 3**; Rotenburg **1**.45–53, Rotenburg **2**; Gutenburg **1b, 1d**; Boppe **1**; Frauenlob **1**; MHG Anon. **1**. Marner **1** is a special case in that the lovers are referred to obliquely in the third person by the watchman. The topos of the illustrious victims of love is associated with the theme in Veldeke **2**; Gutenburg **1a**; Frauenlob (?) **7**; there is probably a similar link also in Dürinc **1** (see n.); the topos occurs without reference to the poet himself in Zweter **2** and Frauenlob **5**. Exceptionally in Liechtenstein **1b** the exemplar of Alexander illustrates the poet's joy in love. Praise of the lady occurs in Morungen **2**, *id.* (?) **3**; Walther (?) **2**; Wolfram (?) **1**; Rotenburg **1**.57 ff.; Rotenburg **2**.201 ff.; Gutenburg **1c**; Tannhäuser **1**; praise of womankind in general is the theme of Frauenlob **2**; Marner **3** praises the Virgin.

In didactic stanzas, exemplars are cited in panegyric in Herger **1**; Wernher **1**; Boppe **2**; Sigeher **1**; Goldener **1**; Frauenlob **4a, 4b**; in an exhortation in Walther **1**; Marner **2**; Henneberger **1**; Frauenlob **6a**; in a boast of poetic supremacy in Frauenlob **3**. In association with the theme of censure, Frauenlob **6b** has the positive exemplars of Arthur and Alexander; Alexander **1** combines the positive exemplars of Gawein and Eckehart with the negative exemplar of Ermenrich; Henneberger 2 cites the negative exemplar of Lucifer, *Der Wartburgkrieg* 1 that of Pilate.

Exemplars may have differing functions: this is particularly the case with the main figures associated with the topos of the illustrious victims of love: Adam, Alexander, David, Samson, Solomon. Thus Adam is a victim in Zweter 2, Dürinc 1 and Frauenlob (?) 7, but an example of nobility in Boppe 1; Alexander is a victim in Gutenburg 1a and Frauenlob (?) 7, but a positive model in Sigeher 1 and Frauenlob 6b; David is a type of Christ in Marner 3, an example of power in Boppe 1, and of virtue in Boppe 2, but a victim in Dürinc 1 and Frauenlob (?) 7; Samson and Solomon are positive models in Boppe 1 and 2, and victims in Dürinc 1 and Frauenlob (?) 7, as is Solomon also in Veldeke 2. This may be the case also with the less frequently cited exemplars: thus Parzival is a victim in Rotenburg 1 and Dürinc 1, but an example to be followed in Frauenlob 6a. See also the differing presentation of Pyramus and Thisbe in Der j. Meissner 1 and 2.

The names of the figures in the exemplary comparisons are derived from the following sources: classical literature and legend; the names of classical authors; medieval courtly literature, together with a few names from Germanic epic; names of German authors; the Bible; history and historical legend.[8]

Classical literature and legend: *Enêas – Tidô* Hausen 1. *Lavîne* Rotenburg 1; *Turnus – Lavîne* Gutenburg 1d. *Vênus* Morungen 2; Wolfram (?) 1; Dürinc 1; *Minne* = Venus Frauenlob 1 (see 1.V.2 n.). *Mars*; *Amûr* Würzburg 1; *Amûr* Rotenburg 1. *Paris* Morungen (?) 3; Frauenlob 1, 5. *Ascholoie* Morungen (?) 3 seems to be intended as a classical name. *Helêne* Walther (?) 2; *Elênen* Rotenburg 2. *Dijâne* Walther (?) 2 (see n.). *Pallas* Rotenburg 1; Tannhäuser 1; Frauenlob 1. *Juno* Frauenlob 1. *Gorgôn*; *Antêus* Marner 2. *Tantalus* Liechtenstein 1a; MHG Anon. 1. *Pyramus* Gliers 2; *Piramus – Thisbe* Der j. Meissner 1, 2. *Ypolitus* Gliers 2. *Djone* (see n.); *Medea* Tannhäuser 1. *Achilli* Frauenlob (?) 7. See also *ein kint* for Narcissus, Morungen 1. Classical authors: *Aristôtiles* Boppe 1; Frauenlob (?) 7. *Virgilîus* Boppe 1; Frauenlob (?) 7. *Sêneca* Boppe 1.

The Bible: *Salomôn(e)* Veldeke 2; Zweter 2; Marner 3; Boppe 1, 2; Dürinc 1; Frauenlob (?) 7. *Adam* Zweter 2; Boppe 1; Dürinc 1; Frauenlob (?) 7. *Absalônes schœne* Boppe 1; Frauenlob (?) 7. *Samsôn* Zweter 2; Boppe 1, 2; Dürinc 1; Frauenlob (?) 7. *Dâvît* Marner 3; Boppe 1, 2; Dürinc 1; Goldener 1; Frauenlob (?) 7. *Lucifer* Henneberger 2. *Ôlofern* Frauenlob (?) 7. *Pilât*, *Wartburgkrieg* 1. *Hester* Marner 3; Frauenlob 2. *Jûdith*; *Asvêrus*; *Jahel*; *Sisoran*; *Abigahel*; *Gôljam* Marner 3. *Azahel* Boppe 1; Frauenlob (?) 7. *Jôsîas*; *Jûdas*

---

[8] After the first example of a name or names, insignificant orthographical variants are usually disregarded.

Makkabêus; *Jonatas*; *Sâmûêl*; *Iôb*; *Moîses*; *Jâcôb*; *Simeôn*; *Jerôboâm*; *Jôsuê* Boppe **2**.

Medieval literature: *Tristran – Ysalden* Bernger **1**; *Tristranden – Isalden* Marner **1**; *Ysalde – Tristramen* Liechtenstein **2**; *Tristan – der küniginne* Veldeke **1**; *Tristram . . . von eines wîbes minne* Zweter **1**; *Tristan* Gliers **2**; *Ysalde* Tannhäuser **1**. *Riwalîn – Blantschiflûr* Würzburg **1**. *Grâlant* Gliers **3**. *Glîes* Rotenburg **1**, **2**. *Parcifal* Rotenburg **1**; Dürinc **1**; Frauenlob **6a**; Frauenlob (?) **7**. *Melioth* Rotenburg **1** (see n.). *Gûrâz* Rotenburg **2**; Boppe **1**. *Gâwân* Rotenburg **2**; *Gâwein* Alexander **1**; *Gawin* Boppe **1**. *Floris – Planschiflûr* Gutenburg **1b**. *Artus* Boppe **1**; Frauenlob **6b**; Frauenlob (?) **7**. *Iwein – Lunete* Frauenlob **1**. *Rennewart* Frauenlob **4a**. *Vivianz* Frauenlob **4b**. *Gachmoret* Frauenlob **5**, see n. **9**. *Peir der mære – Afrîen . . . von Navâr*; *Mei von Lône* (see n.) Botenlouben **1**, *Alienor* Rotenburg **2** appear also to be Romance names, but are of uncertain origin, as is the designation *der vrouwen . . . de la Roschi bîse* Gutenburg **1c**. Germanic epic: *Rüedegêr* Herger **1**. *Ermenrîch*; *Eckehart* Alexander **1**. *Hôrant* Boppe **1**. German poets: *Reimar*; *der von Eschenbach*; *der von der Vogelweide*; *ich, Vrouwenlob* Frauenlob **3**.

History and historical legend: *Salatîn* Walther **1**; *Wernher* **1**; *Goldener* **1**. *den künic von Engellant* Walther **1**. *Alexander* Liechtenstein **1b**; Gutenburg **1a**; Sigeher **1**; Frauenlob **6b**; Frauenlob (?) **7**. *Julius* Gliers **1**. *dem künic . . . von Rôme*; *künic Karlen* Boppe **2**. *Troianus* Henneberger **1**.

The names of figures are thus, with a few exceptions, derived from the same general areas as in the other branches of the medieval lyric, and are in the main restricted to those which are better known. Most of the classical names, with the exception of *Pyramus, Thisbe, Ypolitus, Gorgôn, Antêus* occur in Veldeke's adaptation of the OF *Roman d'Eneas*; some names may have been known from other medieval adaptations of classical stories, e.g. that of Pyramus and Thisbe, or from the Romance lyric. The majority of the medieval names are derived either directly, or probably in the main indirectly, from OF sources. It is significant also that the few unexplained names – *Peir der mære – Afrîen von Navâr, Mei von Lône, Alienor, der vrouwen . . . de la Roschi bîse* are of OF type. Veldeke 1 and Bernger 1 took the name *Trist(r)an* directly from the Chrétien poem which was their source; Bernger also includes the name *Ysalden*, not present in the Chrétien stanza, but known from German adaptations of the story. Some of the Romance names occur in Germanized form: *Parzifal* (OF *Perceval/Percevaus*); *Gâwân/Gâwein* (OF predominantly *Gauvains*); *Iwein* (OF *Yvains*); *Rennewart* (OF *Rainouart*); *Vivianz* (OF *Vivien*); this suggests that they were derived indirectly from German adaptations of French works in which these forms are current. The form *Glîes*, with medial vocalization, is a Germanized variant of the name *Cligés*, ultimately derived from the eponymous work by Chrétien. The Romance names *Grâlant, Gûrâz* are mentioned incidentally in German poems. The paired names *Riwalîn –*

Blantschiflûr in Würzburg, although the f. name is of Romance origin, are derived from the *Tristan* of Gottfried. The names *Floris – Planschiflûr* in Gutenburg 1b occur in the context of detailed knowledge of the story, which may be
derived directly from the OF version, or indirectly from a German adaptation.
The name *Gachmoret* in Frauenlob is no doubt derived from Wolfram's *Parzival*, since there is no equivalent personal name[9] in Chrétien, Wolfram's main
source. By contrast, the names derived from specifically Germanic sources –
Rüedegêr, Ermenrîch, Eckehart, Hôrant are very few.

The exemplary figures may be paired or grouped together. Well-known
lovers usually appear as a pair, as in the examples of Tristan and Isolde above,
but see the general designations replacing the f. name in Veldeke 1, Zweter
1, Rotenburg 1, and the omission of the f. name in Gliers 2. Other pairs:
Enêas – Tidô Hausen 1; *Riwalîn und Blantschiflûr* Würzburg 1; *Floris – Planschiflûr* Gutenburg 1b; *Turnus – Lavîne* Gutenburg 1d; *Piramus – Thisbe* Der
j. Meissner 1 and 2. Other pairings or groupings may unite figures from the
same or a different sphere. Of the first type are: *den milten Salatîn . . . den
künic von Engellant* Walther 1; *Helêne und Dijâne* Walther (?) 2; *Lavîne . . .
oder Pallas* Rotenburg 1; *Pallas oder Juno* Frauenlob 1; of the second type:
sam tet Tristan . . . sam tet Pyramus | und ouch der kiusche Ypolitus Gliers
2; Goldener 1 compares Otto with Saladin and David, and in Frauenlob 6b
Arthur and Alexander are cited as examples to be emulated. Rotenburg 2 combines comparisons of the poet himself with medieval heroes with an implied
comparison of the lady with Helen; Alexander 1 combines within the same
context an implicit comparison with *Gâwein* with explicit comparisons with
two figures of Germanic epic.

In the listing of the victims of love, the basic grouping appears to consist
of biblical figures, as in Zweter 2 (Adam, Samson, Solomon). This may be
reduced to a single figure, as in Veldeke 2 (Solomon).[10] To Adam, Samson,
David and Solomon, Dürinc 1 adds Parzival; Frauenlob (?) 7 extends the list
still further, adding the three further biblical characters Absalon, Holofernes
and Asael, and Alexander, Virgil, Aristotle, Achilles, Arthur and Parzival. Similar to such examples in its listing of famous figures is Boppe 1, in which a
series of hypothetical conditions contains figures from the Bible (including
Solomon, Absalon, David, Samson and Adam), Antiquity, medieval Romance
and German narrative (see n.). Boppe 2 praises the subject of the panegyric
as resembling Charlemagne in possessing the qualities of OT figures (but see
n. on *Simeôn*). There is a list of solely biblical characters in Marner 3, as is
appropriate to the subject matter.

There are a number of instances which include a reference to details of

---

[9] But see the similar place name, from which the personal name may be derived: Chrétien,
 Conte del graal 467 *au roi Ban de Gomoret*; Hartmann, *Erec* 1977 *Beals von Gomoret*.
[10] Cf. Marcabru 1.14 (Samson); Falquet de Romans 1.43 (Solomon).

the narrative associated with the exemplar: the story of Narcissus (Morungen 1); that of Tantalus (Liechtenstein 1a and MHG Anon. 1); the killing of the Medusa (Marner 2); the death of Pyramus and Thisbe (Der j. Meissner 1); the judgement of Paris is linked to the implicit comparison with Helen in Morungen (?) 3; in Frauenlob 1 it is cited to express the poet's desire to avenge himself on *Minne*/Venus by depriving her of the prize. In the biblical identifications in Marner 3, details of the actions of Judith, Hester, Jael and David explain the choice of typological figure; *Wartburgkrieg* 1 presents and interprets the biblical narrative in order to justify the comparison drawn between Pilate and those nobles who stand idly by as the incumbents of their benefices sell the sacraments. There are two striking instances among the medieval examples: Gutenburg 1b shows detailed knowledge of the story of Floris and Blancheflor, and Der wilde Alexander 1 is based on a particular episode in the *Wigalois* of Wirnt von Gravenberg. The allusion to the motif of the love potion in Veldeke 1, Bernger 1 and Zweter 1 serves to stress the extent of the poet's love, and the description of the manner of death of *Grâlant* in Gliers 3, and of *Gûrâz* in Rotenburg 2 reinforces the comparison with the intensity of the poet's suffering. In the examples drawn from history or historical legend, there is a reference to Alexander's aerial flight in Liechtenstein 1b, and to a supposed actual episode in the life of Trajan in Henneberger 1. The obscure references to the story of *Mei von Lône* in Botenlouben 1, to that of Alexander's forest encounter in Gutenburg 1a, and that of *der vrouwen . . . de la Roschi bîse* in Gutenburg 1c add to the total of narrative allusions.

The comparisons and identifications may (a) form the sole or main focus of a stanza; be placed (b) in the first part of the stanza (coinciding wholly or in part with the *Aufgesang*); (c) in the second part of the stanza (coinciding wholly or in part with the *Abgesang*); (d) at the beginning and the end of the stanza. Examples of (a): Herger 1; Veldeke 1, 2; Morungen (?) 3; Marner 2; Boppe 1; Sigeher 1; Frauenlob 1.V; 3; Frauenlob (?) 7; *Wartburgkrieg* 1; MHG Anon. 1; in Marner 3 the typological identifications occupy the central part of the stanza, i.e. excluding the first 4 and the last 3 lines. Examples of (b): Hausen 1; Bernger 1; Morungen 2; Zweter 1; 2. Examples of (c): Morungen 1; Walther 1; Walther (?) 2; Wolfram (?) 1; Wernher 1; Marner 1; Der j. Meissner 1; 2; Dürinc 1; Frauenlob 1.IV; 4a; 4b; 5.IV,12 (end of *Aufgesang* + beginning of *Abgesang*), 5.IV,14; 6a; 6b; in Boppe 2 the comparisons are largely in the second part of the stanza. Examples of (d) Alexander 1; Goldener 1. Only Frauenlob 1 and 5 have comparisons in two stanzas. In the *leich*, comparisons may take up whole metrical units, as in Rotenburg 2 (but see n. on l. 185). The comparison is placed towards the beginning of the *leich* in Tannhäuser 1; at the beginning of a section or part of a section in Gliers 1; 3. Comparisons are placed in the central unit of a tripartite section in Gliers 2; at the end of a section or part of a section in Würzburg 1; Gutenburg 1c; 1d. They span more than one unit or part of a unit in Botenlouben 1; Rotenburg 1.45–53; Gutenburg 1a; Gutenburg 1b.Ib–IIb; in Frauenlob 2 the implied comparison spans the last l. of II and the beginning of III.

Names are given prominence by being placed at the head of the line or in rhyme. Beginning of the line: *Tristan* Veldeke 1; *Ascholoie*; *Paris* Morungen (?) 3; *Vênus* Wolfram (?) 1; *Tristram* Zweter 1; *Samson* Zweter 2; *Peir der mære*; *Mei von Lône* Botenlouben 1; *Tristranden* Marner 1; *Gorgôn* Marner 2; *Alexander* Liechtenstein 1b; *Grâlant* Gliers 3; *Parcifal*; *Melioth*; *Glîes* Rotenburg 1; *Glîes*; *Alienor* Rotenburg 2; *Alexander* Gutenburg 1a; *Turnus* Gutenburg 1d; *Ysalde*; *Medea* Tannhäuser 1; *her Gâwein* Alexander 1; *Piramus* Der j. Meissner 1; *Adam*; *Salmône* Dürinc 1; *her Lucifer* Henneberger 2; *Pallas* Frauenlob 1; *Hester* Frauenlob 2; *ich, Vrouwenlob* Frauenlob 3; *künig Artus*; *künig Alexander* Frauenlob 6b; *Adam*; *Samsônes*; *Davit*; *her Salomôn*; *Absalôns*; *Virgilius*; *Ólofern*; *Achilli*; *Artûses*; *Parcival* Frauenlob (?) 7; *Pilâtus, Wartburgkrieg* 1; *Tantalus* MHG Anon. 1.

Names in rhyme (: indicates names rhyming together): *Enêas*; *Tidô* Hausen 1; *Salomône* Veldeke 2; *Salatîn*; *den künic von Engellant* Walther 1; *Dijâne* Walther (?) 2; *Adam* Zweter 2; *Antêus* Marner 2; *Sisoran* Marner 3; *Tantalus* Liechtenstein 1a; *Ysalde* Liechtenstein 2; *Blantschiflûr* Würzburg 1; *Pyramus* : *Ypolitus* Gliers 2; *Gûrâze* Rotenburg 2; *Planschiflûr* Gutenburg 1b; *der vrouwen . . . de la Roschi bîse* Gutenburg 1c; *Lavîne* Gutenburg 1d; *Pallas* Tannhäuser 1; *Ermenrîch*; *Eckehart* Alexander 1; *Davîdes*; *Samsôn*; *Aristôtiles*; *Azahel* Boppe 1; *Jonatas*; *Iôb*; *Jâcôb*; *Jerôbôam*; *Samsôn* : *Salomôn* Boppe 2; *Parcifalen*; *Dauîden* Dürinc 1; *Salatîn* Goldener 1; *Lunête* Frauenlob 1; *der von Eschenbach*; *der von der Vogelweide* Frauenlob 3; *Rennewart* Frauenlob 4a; *Vivianz* (in a series of 6 rhymes in *-anz*) Frauenlob 4b; *Parzifal* Frauenlob 6a.

Within the individual examples cited in the chapter, the different stylistic types, i.e. expressing general similarity to the exemplar, similarity in respect of specific attributes, superiority to, or identification with the exemplar usually occur separately, and combinations are rare.[11] In the first type of comparison, likeness to the exemplar is expressed by means of adverbial constructions with (*al*) *sam* or *als*(*e*), by adjectives, nouns, and verbs and lexical repetition: *daz ich durch mîn ouge schouwe sülhe nôt* | *sam ein kint, daz . . .* | *sînen schaten ersach in einem brunnen* | *und den minnen muoz unz an sînen tôt* Morungen 1; *der selben minne ûz eime glase er tranc.* | *daz selbe ouch ich getrunken hân* | *ûz mîner vrouwen ougen* Zweter 1; *ir werden fürsten . . .* | *dem ritter sult ir iuch gelîchen* Marner 2; *dem marterer vil geliche,* | *den man da nennet Tantalus* Liechtenstein

---

[11] See *ich endiend ir baz ald also wol* (superiority + equivalence) Rotenburg 2.241; Boppe 1 combines potential likeness in general, likeness in respect of attributes, and superiority to the exemplar.

1a; *daz si als Ysalde Tristramen getroesten mich müeze* Liechtenstein **2**; *möht ich die welt betwingen gar* | *alse Rôme Julius betwanc* Gliers **1**; *durh si lîdet meniger tôt,* | . . . *sam Tristan* . . . | . . . *sam tet Pyramus* | *und ouch der kiusche Ypolitus* Gliers **2**; *daz mir ist rehte als ê was Gûrâze* Rotenburg **2**; *und teten alle dem gelîch* | *als ez wære kuninc Ermenrîch* | *und ich der zornic Eckehart* Alexander **1**; *künde vürbringen als Hôrant süezen dôn* | . . . *wære ich als Aristôtiles* | *und künde kunst als Virgilîus zouberîe* | . . . *wære ich als Adam edel gar* . . . *hæt ich tugent als Sêneca* . . . | *und daz ich wære zen füezen snel* | *als Azahel* Boppe **1**; *sîne fuore unde sînen rât* | *gelîche ich* . . . *künic Karlen* | . . . *gotliep als Davît und Jôsias* . . . (with repetition of *als*+a further 11 names) Boppe **2**; *her Lucifer vůrstozen wart* | . . . *daz ist dir ouch vil unvůrspart* : | *du valscher man, du bist wol sîn geselle* Henneberger **2**; *ge ab der vinster an daz liecht und volge mir der beider* | *alsam der tiure Parzifal* Frauenlob **6a**; *ir hôhen, die die pfarren geben,* | . . . *Pilâtus glîchen muoz man an iuch vinden* Wartburgkrieg **1**; *Tantalus geselle bin ich nu gesîn* MHG Anon. **1**. Likeness may also be indicated by the possession of the attributes of the exemplar: *dô gewan er Rüedegêrs muot* Herger **1**; *ir vert mit der vrouwen sit de la Roschi bîse* Gutenburg **1c**; *hæt ich des küniges Salomônes wîsheit ganz,* | *und Absalônes schœne dâ bî sunder schranz* | *und gewalt des rîchen küniges Davîdes* | . . . *hæt ich tugent als Sêneca* . . . Boppe **1**; *nu fuort eins Alexanders muot* | *eins Alexanders her gesamnet wîten,* | *eins Alexanders lîp und ouch sîn guot* Sigeher **1**. There are two examples in which the poet characterizes his fate as unlike that of the exemplar: *Mei von Lône lie die krône* | . . . *er was sorgen rîch, daz was kumberlîch, doch ungelîch* | *der swære mîn* Botenlouben **1**; *Turnus der wart sanfte erlôst* | *von kumberlîchem pîne* | . . . *der endet schiere sîne nôt* | *in eime tage,* | *die ich nu mange jâr trage* Gutenburg **1d**. These examples are closer to the notion of surpassing the exemplar.

In the second type of comparison, superiority to the exemplar is expressed predominantly by means of comparative adjectives and adverbs, in either positive or negative constructions: *des sol mir diu guote danc* | *wizzen, daz ich solken tranc* | *nie genam und ich si doch minne* | *baz danne er* Veldeke **1**; *nu enbeiz ich doch des trankes nie* | *dâ von Tristran in kumber kam.* | *noch herzeclîcher minne ich sie* | *danne er Ysalden* Bernger **1**; *si ist schœner unde baz gelobt denne Helêne und Dijâne* Walther (?) **2**; *Vênus diu götinne,* | *lebt si noch,* | *si müeste bî ir verblichen sîn* Wolfram (?) **1**; *des milten Salatînes hant gesæte umb êre nie sô wîten schaz* Wernher **1**; *Alexander maere* . . . | *dem geschach nie vreuden halp so vil* Liechtenstein **1b**; *Grâlant* . . . | *wart nie græzer nôt beschert* | *danne mir* Gliers **3**; *Glîes und ein küniginne* | *minten sich unz an den tôt.* | *noch minne ich herzeclîcher dich lieben sælikeit* | . . . *daz diu maget Lavîne iht wære* | *schœner dan mîn frouwe sî,* | *oder Pallas diu wîten mære,* | *des gelouben bin ich frî* Rotenburg **1**; *sô sêre nie bevangen* | *enwart noch ritter Gâwan von minnen,* | *ich sî in ir getwangen* | *noch vaster* . . . | *jâ lâgen tûsent hundert* | *ze Troje von Elênen tôt.* | *noch gerner mac man lîden durch mîne frouwen nôt* | . . . *Glîes leit* *vil manigen tac von liebe grôze swære* | ... *wie ungerne ich verbære* | *ich endiende ir <u>baz ald alse wol</u>* Rotenburg **2**; *Ysalde wart <u>sô schœne nie</u>* | *<u>noch</u> Djone, diu ein gütin was* Tannhäuser **1**; *wære ich dâ bî <u>noch sterker, danne</u> sich was Samsôn* Boppe **1**; *nie dem herren Iwein <u>wirs</u> kein maget tete* Frauenlob **1**; *swaz ie gesang Reimar und der von Eschenbach,* | *swaz ie gesprach* | *der von der Vogelweide,* | *<u>mit vergoltem kleide</u>* | *ich, Vrouwenlob, <u>vergulde</u> ir sang* ... | ... *so bin ichz doch* | *ir meister noch* Frauenlob **3**.

The simplest form of identification with an exemplar is conveyed by forms of the verb 'to be': *ich wæne, si <u>ist</u> ein Vênus hêre, die ich dâ minne* Morungen **2**; *du <u>bist</u> diu wîse Abigahel* Marner **3** (see n. on typological identification); *froun Eren diener Vivianz* | *<u>ist</u> Waldemar* Frauenlob **4b**. The verb may be understood, as in *der rechten milte ein Salatîn* | ... *ein koning David der truwen* Goldener **1**; in *ich mohte <u>heizen</u> Enêas* | ... *si <u>wurde</u> niemer mîn Tidô* Hausen **1**, the verbs function as equivalents of the verb 'to be'. In *du Rennewart* Frauenlob **4a**, the vocative pronoun *du* conveys identification; in Marner **3** *du Jûdith* ... *du Hester* ... *du reiniu Jahel*, the pronoun conveys typological identification (see n.). In Morungen (?) **3**, identification of the lady with Helen is implied by the affirmation that Paris would be worthy to love her.

There are some unusual examples: in Veldeke **2** the comparison with the fate of Solomon is expressed by a factual statement, followed by a logical deduction in the form of a question: *Diu minne <u>betwanc</u> Salomône* | ... *wie mohte ich mich erwern dan,* | *<u>si twunge ouch mich</u> gewalteclîche?* Frauenlob (?) **7** is similar, in that after a long list of victims of love, which concludes with Parzival, the connection with the poet is established in a question: *Parzival grôze sorge nam:* | *sit daz ie vuogt der minnen stam,* | *waz schadet, ob ein reinez wîp mich brennet unde vrœret?* In Frauenlob **2**, comparison is implied by the question '*hast du gelesen, wie sî gewesen* | *Hester hie vor?*'.

Many of the comparisons, particularly those associated with the theme of love, are presented predominantly from a first-person authorial standpoint, with third-person reference to the exemplar and to the lady. This is the case in Hausen **1** (in this instance the identification with *Enêas* links the name grammatically to the first person); Bernger **1**; Morungen **1**; **2**; Walther (?) **2**; Zweter **1**; Botenlouben **1**; Liechtenstein **2**; Rotenburg 1.57–60; Rotenburg **2**; Gutenburg **1a**; **1b**; **1d**; Tannhäuser **1**; Boppe **1**; MHG Anon. **1**; Frauenlob (?) **7** has 17 lines referring to love's victims in the third person, but concludes with a reference of the poet to himself in the first person, and to the lady in the third person in the final line. Gliers **1** is of the same basic type, except that the short phrase *habe danc* can be construed as being (as in SM^2) in direct, or (as in SM^1) in indirect speech. In Veldeke **2** and Gliers **2**, reference to a f. name is lacking. In the didactic examples, Frauenlob **3** combines first-person voice with third-person reference to the exemplars; Alexander **1** is similar, except that the potential identification with Eckehart is couched in the first person.

There may also be other combinations of person in examples presented from a first-person standpoint: Veldeke **1** combines third-person reference to the lady in ll. 5–8 with apostrophe in the plea addressed to her in ll. 9–12; Liechtenstein **1b** introduces the comparison with Alexander by addressing the lady directly; in Gliers **3**, the poet apostrophizes his suffering in the exclamation *owê, senelichiu nôt, | wie du mich fröiden hâst behert!*; Rotenburg **1**.45–53 combines first, second and third person. Frauenlob **1** combines first and second person in the poet's address to *Minne*; Frauenlob **2** is a dialogue between the poet and his mind, in which the implied comparison with *Hester* in ll. 6–8 is contained in a question addressed to the poet. Frauenlob **5** is made up of two speeches of *Welt* addressed to *Minne*, which combine first- and second-person forms. In Marner **2**, Henneberger **2**, and Wartburgkrieg **1**, exemplary comparison is expressed in the form of apostrophe. In Frauenlob **4a**, apostrophe occurs together with identification with an exemplary figure, and in Marner **3** a series of typological identifications is presented throughout in apostrophe.

Comparisons may be couched in solely third-person forms, as in Herger **1**; Wolfram (?) **1**; the implied comparison in Marner **1** (but see also below); Sigeher **1**; Goldener **1**. Predominantly third-person presentation may be associated with formulaic phrases in the first person: *ich wæne wol, ir sî alsam* Gutenburg **1c**; *sîne vuore... gelîche ich* Boppe **2**; *ich wil durch niemans vorchte schanden bi gestan* Frauenlob **6a**. There are combinations of third person with apostrophe in Walther **1**; Marner **2**; Der j. Meissner **2**; Henneberger **1**; **2**; *Wartburgkrieg* **1**. Direct speech is rare (for its possible occurrence in Gliers **1**, see above): it occurs in Frauenlob **2** and **5**, and in the poet's address to the audience and their reply in Wernher **1**. Marner **1** is ostensibly part of the song sung by the watchman to warn the lovers.

The German lyric was considerably influenced by that of the troubadours and trouvères, and therefore shares many features in common with these two branches of the Romance lyric in the use of exemplary comparisons (see in particular Veldeke **1** and Bernger **1**, based on a French model). It also has affinities with the medieval Latin lyric. There are, however, certain differences. There are a roughly equal number of explicit comparisons of likeness and of superiority in the German examples; if implicit comparisons of likeness are included, the total of the former type is higher, whereas in the other branches of the Romance lyric, including Italian, comparisons of superiority predominate. There are a number of comparisons of similarity in respect of attributes, particularly frequent in MLat., and common in the troubadour examples, but rare in OF. There are a number of identifications, something common in MLat., much less common in the troubadour lyric, and rare in OF. There is a considerable amount of detailed reference to narratives associated with the exemplars, a parallel in this respect to MLat.; in the troubadour and trouvère examples such references are usually brief. As in the troubadour lyric, several poets employ comparisons in more than one poem, and there are a number of instances in which the comparison forms the main focus of the stanza, whereas both features are rare in OF. Some instances are more akin to general *exempla*, a parallel in this respect to MLat. There is greater syntactical variety than in the OF examples. There are several instances in which comparison is suggested merely by textual juxtaposition, without explicit syntactical links. Above all, by comparison with the Romance lyric, there is a much greater element of third-person voice in the German examples, a reflection of the increasing generalizing and didactic element in the German lyric of this period. Tannhäuser is unique in satirizing the use of exemplary comparisons and allusions to the names of exemplary figures.

8

The Sicilian and Italian Poets

The beginnings of the Italian vernacular lyric can be traced to the so-called Sicilian school of poets gathered at the court of the emperor Frederick II at Palermo, approximately during the period 1230–1250. There is thus a considerable time-lag between the initial development of the Italian lyric in the vernacular and the troubadour lyric, on which it is based. This is in part a parallel to the chronological gap between the troubadour and trouvère lyric, but it is here much greater in extent. From about the end of the twelfth century, the troubadour lyric had become very widely known and imitated, and its overriding prestige and authority ensured the spread of its influence to Northern France, to German linguistic areas (where knowledge of it was, however, mainly transmitted indirectly via the trouvère lyric), and to Spain, but more particularly to Northern Italy, where from the end of the twelfth century the troubadour lyric was cultivated at the courts of powerful patrons. At first, Italian poets wrote poems not merely imitating troubadour poetry, but using the language of the troubadours as their medium.[1] As Jensen[2] points out, these developments were facilitated by the fact that the dialects of Southern France and Northern Italy were closely related and therefore mutually comprehensible. This assiduous cultivation of the troubadour lyric also resulted in the compilation of a large number of collective manuscripts of troubadour poetry in Northern Italy, many still in Italian libraries today.

Among the troubadour poets who are known to have been in Italy are Aimeric de Peguilhan, Elias Cairel, Gaucelm Faidit, Guilhem de la Tor, Peire Vidal, and Raimbaut de Vaqueiras.[3] The testimony of Dante and Petrarch shows that other troubadour poets were well known in Italy: Aimeric de Belenoi, Arnaut Daniel, Arnaut de Mareuil, Bernart de Ventadorn, Bertran de Born, Folquet de Marseille, Guiraut de Bornelh, Jaufre Rudel, Peire d'Alvernhe, and Raimbaut d'Orange.[4] Petrarch's knowledge of the troubadour poets is no

---

[1] Bonifacio Calvo and Bartolomeo Zorzi are examples, and are therefore treated as belonging to the troubadour tradition and included in chapter 5. Other Italian poets who wrote in the *langue d'oc*, Rambertino Buvalelli, Lanfranc Cigala, Percivalle Doria and Sordello appear to have no exemplary comparisons in their work.

[2] The Introduction in Jensen, *Sicilian School*, provides both an excellent general survey and an informed assessment of the linguistic factors determining the choice of poetic medium in Sicily and Northern Italy respectively.

[3] See Bertoni, *I Trovatori d'Italia*, pp. 3–34; Monteverdi, *La Poesia Provenzale in Italia*, pp. 51–117; Folena, 'Tradizione e cultura trobadorica'.

[4] Dante: *Inf.* xxviii.134 *Bertram dal Bornio*; *Purg.* xxvi.120 *quel di Lemosì* (Guiraut de Bor-

doubt in part explained by the fact that, as a result of his father's exile from Florence, the family moved in 1312 to Carpentras, near Avignon. Here he began his studies of grammar, and from 1316 to 1320 studied law in Montpellier.

It was probably Frederick II himself, a man of wide linguistic and literary culture, who encouraged the composition of poetry on the model of that of the troubadours at his Sicilian court. The court moved on occasion to other parts of Italy, and among the poets were also those who were not natives of Sicily or the South. The troubadour lyric was no doubt known from its cultivation in Northern Italy, perhaps also from manuscript collections or from contacts with individual troubadour poets. In Sicily, the problem of the linguistic medium to be adopted was more acute, in that Southern Italian dialects were much further removed from the language of the troubadours, making the latter much less readily comprehensible (see n. 2). This led to the decisive step, whose influence can hardly be overestimated, of composition, not in the idiom of the troubadours, but in an elevated variant of the local vernacular. Thus the foundations of the Italian lyric were laid.[5] The troubadour lyric was closely imitated in themes, images, key terminology, and metrical forms, but these were now transposed into a new linguistic medium. That the poetry of the Sicilian school was well known in Northern Italy is shown by the fact that when the poems came to be gathered in collections towards the end of the thirteenth and the beginning of the fourteenth century, they were transmitted in Tuscanized form in Northern Italian manuscripts, chief among them Vatican MS 3973 (A), in which Giacomo da Lentini is given pride of place. Therefore all that usually remains of the specifically Sicilian linguistic forms is to be found in the rhyme words, where Tuscanization would have disrupted the rhyme.[6] After the death of Frederick II in 1250, the conditions which had given birth to the Sicilian school came to an end, and it was also from about this date, or possibly somewhat earlier (but the evidence for this is sparse and controversial) that Northern Italian poets began to follow the Sicilian example and to write in

nelh); in *Purg.* xxvi.140–7 Arnaut Daniel speaks in Provençal, giving his name as *Arnaut*; *Par.* ix.94 *Folco*; in *De vulg. eloqu.* I.x Dante mentions Peire d'Alvernhe, and in II.vi cites incipits of poems by Guiraut de Bornelh, Arnaut Daniel, Bertran de Born, Folquet de Marseille, Aimeric de Belenoi, and Aimeric de Peguilhan. Petrarch: *Trionfo d'Amore* iv.40 ff.: *Arnaldo Daniello*; *l'un Piero e l'altro* (Peire Vidal and Peire Rogier); *e 'l men famoso Arnaldo* (Arnaut de Mareuil); *l'uno e l'altro Raimbaldo* (Raimbaut d'Orange and Raimbaut de Vaqueiras); *e 'l vecchio Pier d'Alvernha con Giraldo* (Guiraut de Bornelh); *Folco*; *Giaufré Rudel*; *Amerigo* (Aimeric de Peguilhan); *Bernardo* (Bernart de Ventadorn); *Ugo* (Uc de Saint-Circ); *Gauselmo* (Gaucelm Faidit). See also Bonagiunta **1a**.

[5] This explains Dante's comment, *De vulg. eloqu.* 1.xii.2 *quicquid poetantur Ytali sicilianum vocatur* (whatever the Italians compose in poetry is called Sicilian).

[6] There is only one complete poem, *Pir meu cori alligrari* by Stefano Protonotaro, and two other fragments of poems by Re Enzo preserved in Sicilian form in a 16th-century transcription from a lost MS (see Jensen, *Sicilian School*, pp. xxiii and 84–7).

their native idiom, rather than in the language of the troubadours. The cultivation of lyric poetry in the vernacular thus moved from the South to the North.

The selection in the following chapter encompasses poets of the Sicilian school, writing in the first half of the thirteenth century, and Tuscan and other Northern poets writing in the second half of the thirteenth century and the beginning of the fourteenth. Also included are extracts from the anonymous poem, *Il Mare Amoroso*, three otherwise unattested authors, Alberto di Massa di Maremma, La Compiuta Donzella and Maestro Torrigiano, and two anonymous items from the *Memoriali Bolognesi*. They are followed by later poets who use exemplary comparisons in their work: Lapo Gianni, probably late thirteenth or early fourteenth century, and Cino da Pistoia, c. 1270–1336/7; after them are placed two unidentified poets, Binduccio da Firenze, attested in an exchange of sonnets with Cino, and the so-called Amico di Dante. Other prominent later poets, Guido Guinizelli and Guido Cavalcanti, writing in the second half of the thirteenth century, and Dino Frescobaldi, who died before April 1316, appear not to employ exemplary comparisons, preferring instead other types of imagery. Dante, who was born in 1265 and died in 1321, illustrates the decline of exemplary comparisons in the lyric, though in the *Commedia* he makes very frequent use of them, including some commonly found elsewhere in the lyric. Finally, Petrarch (1304–1374), who belongs entirely to the fourteenth century, shows both direct knowledge of the troubadours and of the renewed influence of their poetry. His work marks a return to exemplary comparisons in the lyric, together with striking innovations, which far exceed mere stylistic procedures, in the use of identification in association with the myth of Daphne and Apollo. In all the poets cited, there is an almost complete restriction to the theme of love in instances of exemplary comparison and identification.

Poets of the Sicilian School

The identity and dates of many of the poets of the Sicilian school are unknown, many ascriptions are uncertain, and a very large number of items are transmitted anonymously. It can, however, be established that several of the poets included in the following section, such as Giacomo da Lentini, Pier della Vigna, and Guido delle Colonne, were distinguished court officials. In the main, the poems treat solely the love themes of troubadour poetry, disregarding other types of subject matter. The one significant formal development is the invention of the sonnet form, usually ascribed to Giacomo da Lentini, although it was only later that the term *sonetto*, originally a general designation, acquired its specific connotation.

Giacomo da Lentini **1**

Dal core mi vene (discordo). Antonelli 17

Or potess'eo,   II   27
o amore meo,
come romeo
venire ascoso,   30
e disïoso
con voi mi vedesse,
non mi partisse
dal vostro dolzore.

Dal vostro lato   35
[...] allungato,
be·ll' ò provato
mal che non salda:
Tristano Isalda
non amau sì forte;   40
ben mi par morte
non vedervi fiore.

[If I might now, O my love, come in secret, in the guise of a pilgrim, and,
pining, find myself together with you, I would not depart from your sweet
person. Separated from your presence, truly I have experienced grief which
does not heal: Tristan did not love Isalda so intensely; it seems indeed to
me death not to see you at all.]

The second and third parts of an isometric tripartite strophe.   27 ff. The
term *romeo* in 29 and the close proximity to the comparison with Tristan in
ll. 39 f., probably allude to the secret return of Tristan, disguised as a pilgrim,
to the court of Mark.   30 *ascoso*: lit. 'hidden'.   39 *Tristano Isalda*:
for the diffusion of the story and the variant names, see Raimb. Or. 1.29 f. n. It
is likely that comparisons with Tristan and/or Iseut in the Sicilian and Italian
poets are in the main modelled on those in the troubadour lyric, i.e. they do
not necessarily imply direct knowledge of the story. However, there are also
instances suggesting knowledge of narrative details, as in ll. 27–30 above, Re
Giov. 1.52 ff. (the marriage of Iseut and Mark, and the lovers' deception of
the latter); Binduccio 1.12 (Tristan's skill as harpist). The most common type
of comparison is, as in this example, that in which the poet's love is said to
exceed that of Tristan (with or without explicit mention of Iseut); cf. also Giac.
Pugl. 1.27 f.; Fil. Mess. 1.11 f.; Re Giov. 1.51–3; Sicil. Anon. 1.55 ff.; Bonagiunta
2a.30 ff.; **2b**.32 f. The theme of beauty surpassing that of famous exemplars
is much more common generally in the Sicilian and Italian lyric than in that
of the troubadours; for beauty surpassing that of Iseut, see Giac. Lent. 2.45 f.;
Sicil. Anon. **5b**.7 f.; Chiaro **1d**.5 ff.; D. Maiano 1.13 f.; Maestro Torr. 1.1 ff. is
unusual, in that Iseut is credited with poetic skill.

Giacomo da Lentini 2

Madonna mia, a voi mando (*canzone*). Antonelli 12

> più bella mi parete VI 45
> ca Isolda la bronda,
> amorosa, gioconda,
> che sovr' ogn' altra sete.

[You seem to me more beautiful than Isolda the fair, lovely, joyful, for you are supreme above all others.]

The last 4 ll. (the *sirma*) of an 8-l. stanza in a poem of 7 stanzas. 45 f.: see Giac. Lent. **1**.39 n.

Rinaldo d'Aquino 1

Poi li piace c'avanzi suo valore (*canzone*). Panvini, p. 99

> Altresì finamente III 31
> come Narciso in sua spera vedire
> per sè si 'nnamorao
> quando in l'aigua isguardao,
> così posso io ben dire 35
> che eo son preso de la più avenente.

[Just as truly as Narcissus, in gazing at his image, fell in love with himself, when he looked into the water, so I may indeed say that I am bound fast by the most lovely one.]

The final 6 ll. (the *sirma*) of III in a *canzone* of three 12-l. stanzas. 32 *Narciso*: for the story of Narcissus, derived from Ovid, *Met.* III.407–570, see Bern. Vent. **1**.23 f. n.; see Index of Proper Names, *s.v.*

Rinaldo d'Aquino 2

In gioi mi tegno tutta la mia pena (*canzone*). Panvini, p. 109

> In gioi mi tegno tutta la mia pena 1
> e contolami in gran bonaventura;
> come Parisi quando amav' Alena,
> così faccio, membrando per ogn'ura.
> Non cura – lo meo cor s'à pene, 5
> membrando gioi che vene,
> quanto più dole ed ell'ave più dura.

[I consider all my torment as joy and account it as great good fortune; like Paris when he loved Helen, so do I react, mindful at all times. My heart is not troubled if it suffers torments, mindful of joy to come, the more it suffers and the greater constancy it has.]

The first stanza in a *canzone* of five 7-l. stanzas. 3 *Parisi . . . Alena*: see Index of Proper Names and Raim. Jord. **1**.28 n. 4 *membrando*: the sense of the verb is made clear by ll. 6 f.: the poet constantly recalls the thought that future joy is dependent on the degree of suffering. 7 *dura*: Panvini takes this to be a f. noun, with the meaning 'persistence', 'constancy'.

Pier della Vigna **1**

Amore, in cui disio ed ho speranza (*canzone*). Contini I, p. 121

Or potess'eo venire a voi, amorosa,   II 9
com' lo larone ascoso, e non paresse:
  be'l mi ter[r]ia in gioia aventurusa,
se l'Amor tanto bene mi facesse.
  Sì bel parlante, donna, con voi fora,
e direi como v'amai lungiamente,
più ca Piramo Tisbia dolzemente,   15
ed amerag[g]io infinch'eo vivo ancora.

[If I might now come to you, lovely one, like the thief in secret, and it might not be seen – I would indeed consider it a happy gift of fortune, if Love were to grant me such a great boon. I would speak to you so eloquently, lady, and would say how I have long loved you, more tenderly than Pyramus loved Thisbe, and will love you as long as I still live.]

The second stanza in a *canzone* of five 8-l. stanzas.   9 f. See the closely similar formulation Giac. Lent. **1**.27 ff. and n., but in the present instance the textual allusion to one of Tristan's actual disguises is lacking, making a reference to the Tristan story less likely; 11 *aventurusa*: lit. 'caused by good fortune', cf. Chiaro **1c**.1 f.   15 *Piramo* (MSS *triamo*) *Tisbia*: see Arn. Mar. **3b**.152 n.

Guido delle Colonne **1**

La mia gran pena e lo gravoso afanno (*canzone*).
Contini I, p. 97

Se madonna m'ha fatto sof[e]rire   IV
†per gioi d'amore avere compimento,†
pen' e travaglia ben m'ha meritato.   30
  Poi ch'a lei piace, a me ben de' piacere
che 'nd' ag[g]io avuto tanto valimento;
sovr'ogne amante m'ave più 'norato,
  c'aggio aquistato – amar la più sovrana,
ché se Morgana – fosse infra la gente,   35
inver' madonna non paria neiente.

[If my lady has made me suffer, . . . (for the defective line 29, omitted in translation, see n.), she has well rewarded my sufferings and torment. Since it pleases her, it must indeed please me, for I have therefrom experienced such great benefit; she has honoured me more than any other lover, for I have obtained (the prize of) loving the most sovereign lady, for if Morgana were in the world, by comparison with my lady, she would seem nothing.]

The fourth of five 9-l. stanzas.   29 The MS reading is probably corrupt. Contini comments 'Salvo correzione, infinitiva con soggetto *gioi*', i.e. 'in order that the joy of love may attain fulfilment', but this is out of line with the construction in the preceding stanza, in which *avere compimento* is used absolutely, as is customary, without grammatical link to *gioi d'amore*, and in which its subject is the poet speaking in the first person: 22 *quella che lo meo core distringia,* | *ed ora in gioi d'amore m'inavanza.* | *soferendo ag*[*g*]*io avuto compimento* (she who constrained my heart, and now advances me in the joy of love; through suffering I have attained fulfilment).   35 *Morgana*: sister of Arthur (*Morgant la fee*) in the OF romances, occurring solely in the Sicilian and Ital. lyric as exemplar of beauty, or of magical power (see Index of Proper Names).

Giacomino Pugliese 1

La dolce cera piagente (*canzone*).
Jensen, *Sicilian School* 3, p. 100

Io non fuivi sì lontano,	IV 25
che 'l meo amor v'ubriasse,	
e non credo che Tristano	
Isaotta tanto amasse.	
Quando veggio l'avenente	
infra le donne aparire,	30
lo cor mi trae di martire	
e ralegrami la mente.	

[I have not been so far from you that my love could there forget you, and I do not think that Tristan loved Isaotta so much. When I see the lovely one appear among the ladies, she plucks my heart from sorrow and gladdens my mind.]

The last of four 8-l. stanzas. The poem is attributed to Giacomino Pugliese in MS A, and to Pier della Vigna in MSS C and D; Panvini therefore includes it as no. 13 under 'Poesie di dubbia attribuzione'.   25 f.: the previous stanza describes the lady's tears and her unwillingness to let the poet depart. 27 f. *Tristan . . . Isaotta*: cf. Giac. Lent. **1**.39 n.

Filippo da Messina 1

Oi Siri Deo, con forte fu lo punto (*sonetto*). Panvini, p. 235

Poi non son meo ma vostro, amor meo fino,	9
preso m'avete como Alena Pari,	
e non amò Tristano tanto Isolda	11
quant'amo voi, per cui penar non fino;	
oi rosa fresca che di magio apari,	
merzè vi chiamo: lo meo mal solda.	14

[Since I am not my own but yours, my perfect love, you have bound me fast as Helen bound Paris, and Tristan did not love Isolda as much as I love you, on whose account I do not cease to feel torment; ah, fresh rose blooming in May, I beg you for mercy: heal my suffering.]

9–14 form the sestet of the sonnet; punning rhymes: *fino*: *fino*; *Pari*: *apari*; *Isolda* : *solda*.   10 *Alena Pari*: for the names cf. Raim. Jord. **1**.28 n. For the punning rhyme *Pari*: *apari* see Chiaro **1b**. 21 n.; Bonagiunta **1a**.5 ff.; Guittone **2b**.8 n.; Alb. Mass. **1**.7 f. n.   11 *Tristano . . . Isolda*: cf. Giac. Lent. **1**.39 n.

Re Giovanni 1

Donna audite como (*discordo*). Panvini, p. 85

Fino amor m'à comandato	IV 47
ch'io m'allegri tuttavia,	
faccia sì ch'io serva a grato	
a la dolze donna mia,	50
quella c'amo più 'n celato	
che Tristano non facia	
Isotta, como cantato,	
ancor che *li* fosse zia.	
Lo re Marco era 'nganato	55
perchè *'n* lui si confidia:	
ello n'era smisurato	
e Tristan se ne godia	
de lo bel viso rosato	
ch'Isaotta blond' avia.	60

[True Love has commanded me always to be joyful and to act in such a way as to serve my sweet lady as I desire, she whom I love more secretly than Tristan loved Isotta, as is narrated, although she was his aunt. King Mark was deceived because he trusted him: he was excessive in this (i.e. in his trust), and Tristan was able to rejoice in the lovely rosy face of Isaotta the fair.]

The first 14 ll. of a 22-l. strophe in the *discordo*; ll. 61–4: although it was a sin, he could do no other, because of what was given to him on the ship, i.e. the love potion.   52 f. *Tristano . . . Isotta*: cf. Giac. Lent. 1.39 n.

Jacopo Mostacci 1

A pena pare – ch'io saccia cantare (*canzone*). Contini I, p. 142

La rimembranza – mi fa disïare	IV 43
e lo disïo mi face languire;	
ch[e s']eo non sono da voi confortato,	45
†tosto poria di banda pria venire:†	
†ca per voi l'aio e per voi penso avere,†	
como Pelëo non poria guarire	
quell' on che di sua lancia l'ha piagato	
se non [lo] fina poi di riferire.	50
Così, madon[n]a mia, similemente	
mi conven brevemente	
acostarme di vostra vicinanza,	
†che l'aggio là 'nde colse la mia lanza:†	
con quella credo tosto e brevemente	55
vincere pena e stutar disïanza.	

[Remembrance causes me to feel desire and desire causes me to languish, for if I am not relieved by you, I could soon already be lost (?): for I receive it from you and trust to receive it from you (?). As Peleus could not cure that man whom he wounded with his lance, if he did not go on to strike him again, so likewise, my lady, I must without delay approach your presence, that I may have it there where I took my lance/wound (?); with that I trust soon and without delay to vanquish pain and extinguish longing.]

Stanzas I–V of this poem in 14-l. stanzas occur anonymously in MS Palatino 418, I, II, and V only in MS Vat. Lat. 3973, attributed to Jacopo Mostacci. 48 *Pelëo*: *dipegio* MS. For the lance of Peleus, see Bernart de Ventadorn 3.45 ff. n.   The text of IV is very unsatisfactory, but it has been included, since it is the first extant example, and the only one among the Sicilian poets, of the comparison of the wound inflicted by the lady with that from the lance of Peleus, which has the power both to wound and heal. In spite of textual difficulties, the general sense is clear, and is in accord with that found in other instances of the comparison: the poet has received one blow, as from the lance, and hopes for another if he is to be cured. This appears to contain a veiled reference to the kiss, which inflicts a wound which can only be healed by another. For other exs. in Italian poets see Chiaro **3a** and **3b**; Giov. Arezzo. **1**; T. Faenza **1**; *Mar. Am.* **1a**.103 ff., with implicit allusion to the kiss, as here, in Chiaro **3a** and T. Faenza **1**.

Anonymous Items

Sicil. Anon. **1**

Del meo voler dir l'ombra (*canzone*). Panvini, Inghilfredi 3, p. 379

La mia fede è più casta   V 55
e più diritta c'asta,
che 'n segnoria s'è regata a serva
e più lealtà serva
che 'l suo dir non conserva
lo bon Tristano al cui pregio s'adasta.   60

[My faithfulness is more inviolate and more direct than a lance, since it has subjected itself as servant to a seigneurial power and maintains a loyalty greater than that with which praiseworthy Tristan, after whose merit it strives, keeps his word.]

The last 6 ll. (the *sirma*) of the final stanza in a *canzone* of five 12-l. stanzas + 6-l. *congedo*.   This poem is preserved anonymously, together with many others, in MS A, Vatican 3973, and the attribution to Inghilfredi in MS C, accepted by Panvini, is uncertain; it therefore seems preferable to treat it together with the other Sicilian anonymous items.   The vocabulary, syntax, and style of the poem, described in l. 2 as *scura rima*, is deliberately obscure, with a profusion of rare grammatical and punning rhymes, in imitation of the hermetic style known as *trobar clus* cultivated by Arnaut Daniel and other troubadour poets. As Panvini indicates, the very rare rhyme words in the first stanza of the poem, *'nungla* 3 ('claws into') and *ungla* 6 ('nail', 'claw') undoubtedly imitate the rhyming syllable *ongla* 'nail', which occurs in

all six stanzas of Arnaut Daniel's poem *Lo ferm voler q'el cor m'intra* (Toja 18);
in particular, *'nungla* is paralleled by *s'enongla*, with similar meaning, in Toja
18.31, and *carne et ungla* ('flesh and nail') in l. 6 by *carns et ongla* in Toja 18.17.
60 *Tristano*: cf. Giac. Lent. **1**.39 n.

Sicil. Anon. **2**

Fin amor di fin cor ven di valenza . . . (*sonetto*). Panvini, p. 582

Che fino amor non tiene sospecione,   9
e non porria cangiar la sua 'ntendenza
chi sente forza d'amorosa sprone;   11
e di ciò portan la testimonianza
Tristano e Isaotta cǫ ragione,
che non partir già mai di loro amanza.   14

[For true love does not harbour suspicion, and whoever feels the force of
love's spur could not change the focus of his love; and to this Tristan and
Isaotta rightly bear witness, for they never deviated from their love.]

9–14: the sestet of the sonnet.   10 *la sua 'ntendenza*: the noun, lit. 'intention', implies the focussing of desire on a particular object of love; in the translation, ll. 10 f. are transposed.   13 *Tristano . . . Isaotta*: cf. Giac. Lent. **1**.39 n.

Sicil. Anon. **3**

Guardando la fontana . . . (*sonetto*). Panvini, p. 613

Guardando la fontana, il buon Narciso   1
de lo suo viso forte 'namorao,
e 'n tanto che lo vide fue conquiso
e dismarito sì, che s'oblidao   4
pensando che 'nfra l'aqua foss' assiso
ed incarnato ciò c'allor mirao;
vogliendolo tenere, fue diviso
da tutte gioie, e sua vita finao.   8
Così cred'eo fenir similemente,
poi son venuto a la dolze fontana,
dov'è la spera di tutte belleze;   11
volendol' abrazzar, trovo neiente,
e sospiro la fresca ciera umana,
per cui follezo e pero in gran mateze.   14

[Gazing at the fountain, good Narcissus fell profoundly in love with his
own image, and in seeing it he was vanquished and so distraught that he
lost all awareness, thinking that what he then contemplated was present in
the water and a creature of flesh and blood; wishing to grasp it, he was severed from all joy and his life ended. Likewise I think I will come to a similar
end, since I have come to the sweet fountain in which is the image of all
beauty; wishing to embrace it, I find nothing, and I sigh for the living human face, for whose sake I am possessed by folly and perish in great frenzy.]

1 *il buon Narciso*: cf. Rin. Aq. **1**.32 n.   13 *sospiro*: MS *piago e sospiro.*   *la fresca ciera umana* stands in contrast to *neiente* in 12.

Sicil. Anon. **4**

Per gioiosa baldanza (*canzone*). Panvini, p. 557

e breve il mostreragio,   V   55
chè sì faragio
com fece Lanc[i]allotto ver Morgana,
quando il tenea in servagio
del bel visagio,
che torno, rotta la catena vana.   60

[And I will shortly show her that I will act as did Lancelot towards Morgana, when she held him in subjection to her beautiful face, so that I return, the ineffectual chain broken.]

The last 6 ll. (the *sirma*) of V in a *canzone* of six 12-l. stanzas + 6-l. *congedo*. The poem celebrates the return to joy and love of the lady, and the consequent breaking free from grief and despair, hence the reference to *catena* in 60. 57 *Lanc[i]allotto*: cf. *Mar. Am.* **3**.33; Uc Pena **1**.25 n.   *Morgana*: cf. Guid. Col. **1**.35 n.

There are brief references in the anonymous items, here grouped together, to paragons of beauty and perfection:

Sicil. Anon. **5a.**

Quando la primavera (*canzone*). Contini I, p. 167

tu ch'avanzi Morgana,   II   17
merzé, ché m'hai conquiso.

[You who surpass Morgana, mercy, for you have vanquished me.]

The last 2 ll. of the *sirma* in II, with the rhyme *sovrana : adorna : soggiorna : Morgana*, in a *canzone* of seven 9-l. stanzas.   17 *Morgana*: cf. Guid. Col. **1**.35 f. n.

Sicil. Anon. **5b**

Lo gran valor di voi, donna sovrana (*sonetto*, part of a *tenzone?*).
Panvini, p. 605

nè Blanziflor, nè Isaotta [o] Morgana   7
non ebero quanto voi di piacimento.

[Neither Blanziflor, nor Isaotta or Morgana had so much pleasing grace as you.]

The end of the octave of a sonnet which has the rhymes *sovrana : piana : Dïana : Morgana*. Santangelo emends l. 8 to restore an expected internal rhyme, also in -*a*.   7 *Blanziflor*: the heroine of the OF *Floire et Blancheflor*; cf. Arn. Mar. **3b**.153 n.; D. Maiano **1**.14; Casini, *Propugnatore* XV, II, p. 333 includes a 14th-century sonnet which cites *Florio* (together with *Pirramo*) as exemplary lover: *che non portò mai tante pene Florio* (for Florio never experienced such suffering); the story forms the main source of the *Filocolo* of Boccacio; cf. also 'Cantare di Fiorio e Biancifiore', Sapegno, *Poeti minori del Trecento*, 811. *Isaotta*: cf. Giac. Lent. **1**.39 n.; *Morgana*: cf. **5a**.17 n.

Sicil. Anon. **5c**

De la primavera *(discordo)*. Panvini, p. 466

Preziosa più c'Alena   XIV   101
o [più] che Pol*i*ssena.

[More precious than Helen or Polyxena.]

The first 2 ll. of a 4-l. section couched in apostrophe of the lady.   101 *Alena*:
cf. Rin. Aq. **2**.3 n.   102 *Polissena*: MS *ochepolla osena*, but the emendation is certainly correct, the unusual choice of name being dictated by the rhyme; cf. *Polixena* Petrarch **9**.11; cf. Ziltener, *Repertorium* 8784 (one ref.).

Tuscan and Northern Poets of the Second Half of the Thirteenth Century

A *tenzone* consisting of two sonnets: in the first, an anonymous poet praises Bonagiunta (addressed in l. 2 as *tu, Bonagiunta*), in the second Bonagiunta replies; the comparison with named poets occurs in each case in the second half of the octave. Each sonnet has grammatical and punning rhymes in *-pari* and *-mondo* in the octave, with the added complication in **1b** of internal rhyme in *-pari* in ll. 6 and 8, which imposes severe restraints on the choice of vocabulary and syntax, so that any translation can only be approximate and conjectural:

Bonagiunta **1a**

Poi di tutte bontà ben se' dispàri *(sonetto)*.
Bonagiunta IX, 1 Anonimo, Contini I, p. 275

Di ciausir motti Folchetti tu' pari   5
non fu, né Pier Vidal né 'l buon di 'Smondo:
però m'inchino a te sì com' fe' Pari
a Venùs, la duchessa di lor mondo.   8

[In choosing words Folquet was not equal to you, nor Peire Vidal, nor the excellent di 'Smondo: therefore I bow before you, as did Paris before Venus, the queen of their world.]

5 f. *Folchetti ... Pier Vidal*: both poets, particularly Folquet, were well known in Italy (see Introducton to the chapter and n. 4). The identity of *di 'Smondo* is uncertain.   7 *Pari*: cf. Rin. Aq. **2**.3 n., and for similar rhymes Fil. Mess. **1**.10 n.
8 *Venùs*: cf. *Mar. Am.* **1a**.134 *dea d'amare*; Alb. Mass. **1**.9 *d'amore la dea*.

Bonagiunta **1b**

Lo gran pregio di voi sì vola pari (*sonetto*).
Bonagiunta IX, 2, Contini I, p. 276

Però, chi vol valer, da voi impari   5
gli apari – che del mal fa[n] l'om rimondo,
che 'n voi commendan li due che son pari,
ma più che pari, – Folchetto né 'Smondo.   8

[Therefore, whoever wishes to prevail, let him learn from you the (poetic) procedures which render a man free from fault, which the two who are equal, or rather, more than equal, commend in you – Folquet and 'Smondo (?).]

6 *gli apari* lit. 'preparations', glossed in Contini's n. as 'gli apprestamenti, la technica'.

Bonagiunta **2a**

Oi, amadori, intendete l'affanno (*discordo*). Zaccagnini/Parducci, p. 69

E messire – Ivano   30
e 'l dolze Tristano
ciascun fue sotano
ver' me di languire.

[And sir Yvain and sweet Tristan, each was inferior, compared with me, in languishing for love.]

These lines make up the fourth section of the *discordo*.   30 *Ivano*: cf. Aim. Peg. 2.15 n.   31 *Tristano*: cf. Giac. Lent. 1.39 n.; *Tristano* in rhyme, cf. Giac. Pugl. 1 *lontano*: *Tristano*; Carnino Ghiberti di Firenze, Panvini, p. 265. 21 *quant'eo non amara | nessuno altro cristiano; | credo lo buon Tristano | tant' amor non portara* (no other Christian could love as I do; I think the fair Tristan could not experience such love).

Bonagiunta **2b**

Donna, vostre belleze (*ballata*). Zaccagnini/Parducci, p. 73

Ed eo similemente   III   31
'nnamorato son di vue
assai più che non fue – Tristan d'Isolda:
meo cor non solda – se non vostr' altura.

[And I likewise am much more in love with you than was Tristan with Isolda: nothing can cure my heart – save your supremacy.]

The last 4 ll. of III in a poem of three 10-l. stanzas + 4-l. head-refrain.   33 f. *Tristan d'Isolda*: cf. Giac. Lent. 1.39 n.; for the rhyme *Isolda*: *solda* cf. Giac. Lent. 1.38 f. *salda*: *Isalda*; Fil. Mess. 1.11 ff. *Isolda*: *solda*.

Chiaro Davanzati **1a**

Madonna, lungiamente . . . (*canzone*). Menichetti, p. 141

Madonna, lungiamente aggio portato   I   1
amore in core, e no·ll'ho discoverto

per tema non vi fosse a dispiacere;
   e ciascun giorno m'è più doplicato,
riguardando lo vostro viso aperto   5
che passa ogne altro viso di piacere
   e ave più valere – e 'nsegnamento
che non ebbe Morgana né Tisbia.

[Lady, I have long born love in my heart and have not revealed it, out of fear that it might be displeasing to you; and every day it has increased in me twofold, when gazing on your fair (lit. open) face, which surpasses every other face in grace, and has greater excellence and refinement than had Morgana or Thisbe.]

The first 8 ll. of stanza I in a *canzone* of five 11-l. stanzas. The comparison in 7 f. takes up the first 2 ll. of the *sirma*, which has the rhyme *Tisbia*: *sia*. 8 *Morgana*: cf. Guid. Col. **1**.35 n.   *Tisbia*: cf. Pier Vign. **1**.15 n.

Chiaro Davanzati **1b**

Di lontana riviera (*canzone*). Menichetti, p. 193

che non credo Tisbia,   II   20
Alèna né Morgana
avesson di bieltà tanto valore.

[For I do not think that Thisbe, Helen or Morgana had such excellence of beauty.]

The first three ll. of the *sirma* in II, in a *canzone* of five 13-l. stanzas. II has the rhyme sequence *sia*: *cortesia*: *Tisbia*: *mia*. The second line of the *sirma* in each stanza (here l. 21, ending in *Morgana*) is unrhymed. Reference to the lady is in the third person throughout. 20 *Tisbia*: cf. **1a**.8 n.   21 *Alèna*: cf. Rin. Aq. **2**.3 n.; see also the sonnet Chiaro 118.4 *amor mi prende com' Alèna Paro* (love takes possession of me as did Helen of Paris), in which *Paro* occurs in an elaborate sequence of grammatical and punning rhymes (see Fil. Mess. **1**.10 n.).   *Morgana*: cf. **1a**.8 n.

Chiaro Davanzati **1c**

Ringrazzo amore . . . (*sonetto*). Menichetti, p. 218

Ringrazzo Amore de l'aventurosa   1
gioia e del'allegrezza che m'ha data,
ché mi donò a servir la più amorosa
che non fue Tisbia o Morgana la fata,   4
che la sua bocca aulisce più che rosa
viso amoroso e gol'ha morganata.

[I thank Love for fortune's gift of joy and the gladness it has bestowed on me, in that it granted me the boon of serving her who is more lovely than was Thisbe or Morgana the fairy, for her mouth is more fragrant than a rose, she has a lovely face and a neck like that of Morgana.]

The comparison is placed at the end of the first half of the octave, and is reinforced by *morganata* in l. 6.   1 f. *aventurosa gioia*: lit. 'joy occasioned by good fortune'; cf. Pier Vign. **1**.11.   4 *Tisbia . . . Morgana*: cf. **1a**.8 n. 6 *morganata*: the adj. is derived from the name; the phrase is imitated in D. Maiano, ed. Bettarini 7.1 *Viso mirabil, gola morganata.*

Chiaro Davanzati **1d**

Lo disïoso core . . . (sonetto). Menichetti, p. 230

Lo disïoso core e la speranza	1
c'ho di voi, fina donna ed amorosa,	
mi fa di canto e di gran benenanza	
rinovellar la mia vita gioiosa,	4
poi che di voi non veggio simiglianza	
né pari di bieltà sì grazïosa:	
ch'Isotta né Tisbïa per sembianza,	
nesuna in gioia fue sì poderosa.	8

[The longing heart and the hope which I have from you, perfect and lovely lady, causes me with song and great gladness to renew my joyful life, since I see no likeness to you, nor any equal in such gracious beauty, for neither Isotta nor Thisbe had, as it seems, such power to confer joy.]

The comparison is placed at the end of the octave.   7 *Isotta*: cf. Giac. Lent. **1**.39 n.; *Tisbïa*: see **1a**.8 n.

Chiaro Davanzati (?) **1e**

Dacché parlar non possovi celato (sonetto). Menichetti, p. 395

ché di Morgana avete la scïenza	12
e d'Elena bellezza al mio parvente.	

[For you have the knowledge of Morgana and the beauty of Helen, so it seems to me.]

This sonnet is placed by the ed. under doubtful attributions.   12 *Morgana*: cf. **1a**.8 n.   13 *Elena*: cf. **1b**.21 n.; for the beauty of Helen cf. Guittone **2a**.7; Alb. Mass. **1**.8; Petrarch **8**.43 ff.; **9**.7 f.

Complaints of a faithless lady, who, while professing love for the poet, has turned to another lover:

Chiaro Davanzati **2a**

Da che mi conven fare (canzone). Menichetti, p. 104

Come Cain primero	VII 73
di far crudele e fero	
micidio fu, posso dire che sia	75
ella la prima ch'apare	
di sì gran fallo fare	
in tale guisa, sanza dir bugia.	

[As Cain was the first to commit a cruel and brutal homicide, I can say –

without uttering a lie – that she is the first to commit such great treachery in such a way.]

These ll. represent the two *piedi* making up the *fronte* of VII, in a *canzone* of nine 12-l. stanzas. The phrase *sanza dir bugia* in 78, displaced for the sake of the rhyme, belongs syntactically after *dire* in 75, and has therefore been transposed in the translation. The concluding lines of the stanza express the wish that the lady's guilt, like that of Cain, should be universally known. 73 *Cain*: cf. Lapo XIV.65 (Marti, 1969, p. 322) *farò com' fece Caino ad Abello* (: *quadrello*), i.e. the poet declares that in avenging himself upon Love, he will act as did Cain towards Abel.

Chiaro Davanzati 2b

Or tornate in usanza, buona gente (*canzone*). Menichetti, p. 108

> A Giuda ben la posso asumigliare   III   17
> che baciando ingannò Nostro Segnore;
>   mai nessuno omo non si può guardare
> da quei che vuole ingannar con amore.   20
>   Vergilio, ch'era tanto sapïente
> per falso amore si trovò ingannato.

[I can liken her to Judas who betrayed our Saviour with a kiss; but no man can guard against one with the will to deceive by means of love. Virgil, who was so wise, came to be deceived by false love.]

17–22 form the *fronte* and the first half of the *sirma* of III in a *canzone* of five 8-l. stanzas.   17 *Giuda*: cf. *Mar. Am.* **1b**.321.   21 *Vergilio*: a ref. to the legend (related e.g. in the 14th-century *Myreur des histors* of Jean d'Outremeuse) that Virgil, while being hoisted up in a basket by a courtesan, was left suspended in mid-air to the derision of onlookers; stanzas IV and V contain two explicit comparisons with love's victims: IV.31 *chi m'ha fatto torto | più grevemente che non fue Adamo*: *richiamo* (for a similar comparison with Adam, see Incontrino de' Fabrucci, Contini I, p. 382, and for the same pair of rhymes, but in a different context *Mem. Bol.* **2**); V.38 *ingannòmi l'amor come Sansone*: *stagione*); for the theme of love's victims, see Marc. **1.14** n. Unlike 17 f., IV.31 f., and V.38, the allusion to Virgil is not in the form of an explicit comparison, but of an exemplary parallel; cf. IV.26 *io non son lo primero cui avegna:* | *Salomone ingannato fue, non ch'altro*; Menichetti 118.10 *ch'Adamo – fu 'ngannato per amare.*[7]

---

[7] Cf. also biblical figures cited as general exemplifications, without reference to the poet: Menichetti XII.31 ff. Adam (patient suffering); XXXI. 46 ff. Adam (carnal love); LXI.59 f. Adam and Eve (sorrow turning to joy); XXXIII.53 ff. Lucifer (earthly desires, the source of evil). In XXXI.48 and LXI. 59 the formulations occur in association with the phrase *asempro e miri* 'example and mirror'. All these instances are more akin to *exempla*, than to comparison or exemplary parallel.

Chiaro Davanzati **3a**

Così m'aven com Paläùs sua lanza (*sonetto*). Menichetti, p. 277

Così m'aven com' Paläùs sua lanza,   1
ca del suo colpo om non potea guerire
mentre ch'un altro a simile sembianza
un'altra fiata non si fea ferire.   4
Così dich'io di voi, donna, i·leanza
che ciò ch'io presi mi torna i·languire:
se sumigliante nonn-aggio l'usanza,
di presente vedretemi morire.   8

[So it happens to me as from the lance of Peleus, for from its blow a man could not be healed unless with a second blow he let himself be struck in the same way a second time. Thus I say the same of you, lady, in sincerity, for that which I took (from you) turns to suffering: if I do not experience the same again, you will very soon see me die.]

The comparison takes up the octave of the sonnet.   6 f. These ll. appear to contain a veiled reference (lacking in **3b**.43–6) to the kiss, which causes suffering unless it is healed by another (*mentre*, lit. 'while', 'as long as'); for the lance of Peleus, see Bernart de Ventadorn **3**.45 ff. n.; J. Mostacci. **1**.48 n.

Chiaro Davanzati **3b**

Allegrosi cantari (*canzone*). Menichetti, p. 86

Ben è, la mia, gran doglia: IV   43
ch'io non posso guerire,
se quei che m'ha feruto
non mi sana com' Pelëùs sua lanza;
[. . .]
Non credetti svenire   V   57
com'io sono svenuto
tanto crudelemente,
tant'era alto per la vertù d'amore;   60
ben era, a lo ver dire,
fiorin d'oro venuto
d'amor, cui son servente;
prendea di lui tutora il frutto e 'l flore:
ca simile m'avene ch'a·lLuzefer legato,   65
che tutto il suo gran stato
perdé 'n un movimento.

[My sorrow is, indeed, very great: for I cannot be cured, unless she who has wounded me heals me like the lance of Peleus. [. . .] I did not think to fall from grace as I have fallen so cruelly, so exalted was I through the power of Love; indeed, in truth golden riches had come from Love, whose servant I am; I continually took from it the fruit and the flower, so that the same has happened to me as to Lucifer when bound, who lost all his high status in a moment.]

The first four ll. of the penultimate stanza and the first 11 ll. of the final stanza in a *canzone* of five 14-l. stanzas. The comparison with the lance of Peleus thus takes up the first *piede* of IV, and that with Lucifer is placed at the beginning of the *sirma* in V. The poem is closely packed with images of different kinds, but these are the only ones associated with a named figure.   62 *fiorin d'oro*: lit. 'gold florin' (of Florence); the designation *fiorino*, a diminutive of *fiore* 'flower', derives from the image of a lily on the coin; this no doubt explains the juxtaposition with *il frutto e 'l flore* in 64.   65 *ch'a·lLuzefer legato*: i.e. bound in hell after his fall; for traditions attaching to Lucifer, see Ad. Halle **2**.37 n.

Chiaro Davanzati **4**

Come Narcissi . . . (sonetto). Menichetti, p. 243

Come Narcissi, in sua spera mirando,	1
s'inamorao per ombra a la fontana;	
veggendo se medesimo pensando,	
ferìssi il core e la sua mente vana;	4
gittòvisi entro per l'ombrìa pigliando,	
di quello amor lo prese morte strana:	
ed io, vostra bieltate rimembrando	
l'ora ch'io vidi voi, donna sovrana,	8
inamorato son sì feramente	
che, poi ch'io voglia, non poria partire,	
sì m'ha l'amor compreso strettamente;	11
tormentami lo giorno e fa languire:	
com'a Narcissi paràmi piagente,	
veggendo voi, la morte soferire.	14

[As Narcissus, gazing at his mirror-image, fell in love with his reflection at the fountain; seeing himself, while lost in contemplation, he inflicted a wound on his own heart and his foolish mind; he threw himself into the water, in order to grasp the reflection; as a result of that love a strange death befell him, and I, remembering your beauty at the moment when I saw you, sovereign lady, am so intensely possessed by love that even though I wished it, I could not part from it, so closely has love constrained me; it torments me by day and causes me to languish; just as to Narcissus, it will seem to me pleasing, seeing you, to suffer death.]

   1 *Narcissi*: cf. Rin. Aq. **1**.32 n.

Dante da Maiano **1**

Rosa e giglio e flore aloroso (sonetto). Contini I, p. 479

E sprendïente siete come 'l sole,	9
angelica figura e dilicata,	
ch'a tutte l'altre togliete valore.	11
Se risplendete, l'alto Edeo lo vole;	
nulla bellezza in voi è mancata;	
Isotta ne passate e Blanziflore.	14

[And you are radiant like the sun, angelic and graceful figure, so that you detract worth from all others. If you are resplendent, supreme God wills it; no beauty is lacking in you; you surpass Isotta and Blancheflor in this.]

The sestet of the sonnet.   14 *Isotta*: cf. Giac. Lent. **1**.39 n.   *Blanziflore*: cf. Sicil. Anon. **5b**.7 n.

Dante da Maiano **2**

Convemmi dimostrar lo meo savere (*sonetto*). Bettarini 1

Amore prese e dè in vostro podere   5
lo core meo per voi, mia donna, amare,
ond'eo di core più v'amo che Pare
non fece Alèna co lo gran plagere.   8

[Love captured my heart and placed it in your power, so that I might love you, lady, therefore I love you from the heart more than Paris loved Helen who possessed most pleasing grace.]

The second half of the octave, which has the rhymes *cantare*: *parlare*: *amare*: *Pare*.   7 f. *Pare . . . Alèna*: see Rin. Aq. **2**.3 n.   8 *plagere*: a variant of the substantivized infinitive of *piacere* 'to please'.

Guittone d'Arezzo **1**

Ahi lasso, che li boni e li malvagi (*canzone*). Contini I, p. 210

Iulio Cesar non penò tempo tanto,   IV   37
né tanto mise tutto 'l suo valore
a conquistar del mondo esser signore,
talor non faccia in donna om altretanto;   40
e tal è che non mai venta dovene.

[Julius Caesar did not strive so long, nor so greatly devote all his prowess to conquering sovereignty over the world, as much as does a man in contending against a woman, and she is such that she is never vanquished thereby.]

37–41: the four-line *fronte*, with the rhyme *abab*, and the first l. of the *sirma* in IV, in a *canzone* of seven 12-l. stanzas + two *congedi* of 8 ll. and one of 3 ll. The poem aims to restore the good repute of women, unjustly held in low esteem and subordinated by men, who are less virtuous. The second *congedo* addresses a perfect lady, who surpasses all others.

Guittone d'Arezzo **2a**

Viso non m'è ch'eo mai potesse «Gioia» (*sonetto*). Leonardi 51

ché la grande beltà d'Alena en Troia
non fu pregiata più, sì como pare,   8
che la beltate e l'onor e 'l piacere
de voi aggio de fin pregio pregiato.
Ma, poi vi sete data en dispiacere   11
con dir noioso e con villan pensato,
eo vi dispregio e metto a non-calere,
e spiace me ciò che piacer m'è stato.   14

[For the great beauty of Helen of Troy was not more praised, as it seems, than I have praised with high praise your beauty and your honour and your pleasing qualities. But since you have yielded to displeasure with disagreeable words and with base thought, I dispraise you and consign you to indifference, and that which was pleasing to me displeases me.]

The comparison spans the end of the octave and the beginning of the sestet. 7 *Alena en Troia* (: *Gioia* : *Noia* : *croia*): cf. Rin. Aq. **2**.3 n.

Guittone d'Arezzo **2b**

Ai! como ben del mio stato mi pare (*sonetto*). Leonardi 65

Ed èmmi grave ciò; ma pur canpare 5
voi' dai noiosi e da lor noi' mi paro,
a onor de lei, che 'n beltate pare
no li fo Elena che amao Paro. 8

[And this is grievous to me, but yet I wish to escape the trouble-makers and I guard against the trouble they cause, in honour of her, who in beauty is such that Helen whom Paris loved was not equal to her.]

The second half of the octave. 6 *dai noiosi*: similar adjectival formulations are found in the troubadour lyric, e.g. Cercamon, ed. Tortoreto V.9 *li malvas enojos*; they refer to the figures designated by the Oc. substantive *lauzengier*, the slandering ill-wishers who attempt to disrupt the love relationship. 8 *Elena . . . Paro*: see **2a**.7 n. Every line of this sonnet has a rhyme based on the root *par-*, which explains the choice of the name *Paro*. For similar grammatical and punning rhymes, cf. Leonardi's n. to 7 f.; Fil. Mess. **1**.10 n.

Rustico Filippi **1**

Oi amoroso e mio fedele amante (*sonetto*). Mengaldo, LIV

Amore meo, cui piú coralmente amo, 9
ch'amasse già mai donna suo servente,
e che non fece Tisbïa Prïamo.

[My love, whom I love more truly than ever lady loved her servant, and (more) than Thisbe loved Pyramus.]

This sonnet, assigned to the lady, forms part of a *tenzone* of four sonnets between lady (*madonna*) and gentleman (*messere*). The comparison is placed in the first half of the sestet. 11 *Tisbïa Prïamo*: see Pier Vign. **1**.15 n.

Giovanni d'Arezzo **1**

Pelao con sua lancia . . . (*sonetto*). Santangelo, *Tenzoni*, p. 257

Pelao con sua lancia atoscicata 1
ferendo l'omo, no potea guarire
se non lo 'nde ferisse altra fiata;
sí mi vegio di voi, bella, venire: 4
che la feruta che m'avete data,
farámi d'esto secolo partire;

convene per voi essere sanata
che la pena facitemi sentire.   8

[Peleus, striking the man with his poisoned lance, could not cure him,
unless he struck him with it a second time; I see the same befalling me
through you, beautiful one, for the wound you have given me will cause
me to depart from this world; it must be cured by you, for you cause me
to feel this pain.]

The sestet of the sonnet is taken up with an appeal to the lady to act like
the pelican: as the pelican strikes and mortally wounds his offspring, so he
feels pity and saves him from death with his own blood (for another ex. of
this bestiary image applied to love, see *Mar. Am.* 255–262, Contini 1, p. 497).
1 *Pelao*: the initial *P*, left for the rubricator to insert, is missing in the MS;
for the lance of Peleus, see Bernart de Ventadorn 3.45 ff. n.; J. Mostacci 1.48 n.
5 *che la*: MS *dela*.

Tomaso da Faenza 1

Spesso di gioia nascie ed incomenza (*canzone*).
D'Ancona/Comparetti II, p. 43

Sperando morte, ond'eo poria gioire   III
la mia crudel feruta,   30
sì ch'io nom fosse in tutto a morte dato:
chè ricieputo l'ò per folle ardire,
laudando mia veduta,
e credendom aver gioioso stato.
Penzo ch'ancora porìa en zo' tornare,   35
sol per una semblanza,
che d'amoroso core,
perseverando da lei mi venisse,
C'a Pelleus la posso asimilgliare:
feruto di sua lanza   40
non gueria mai, s'altr'ore
con ella forte no' lo riferisse.

[Wishing for death, through which I might rejoice in my cruel wound,
yet so that I had not completely succumbed to death (?): for I received it
(the wound) through foolish aspiration, delighting in the sight I beheld,
and thinking to attain a state of joy. I believe it might yet return to that, if
I remain steadfast, through one sign which might come to me from her,
from a loving heart; for I can liken her to Peleus: the man wounded by
his lance would never be healed, unless once more he struck him forcibly
with it again.]

The third stanza in a *canzone* of five stanzas of fourteen lines.   This stanza
is tortuously and ambiguously expressed, perhaps in part through faults of
transmission, and any translation of ll. 29–38 is bound to be tentative, but as
with J. Mostacci 1 (*q.v.*) the general sense is clear: the poet's presumptuous
desire has caused him to be wounded by the lady, as by the lance of Peleus,

no doubt when, in expectation of joy, he dared to kiss her; he hopes for a sign of favour from her, i.e. another kiss, which like the second blow from the lance, would cure his malady.   39 *Pelleus*: for the lance of Peleus see Giov. Arezzo 1.1 n.

The unique work known as *Il Mare Amoroso* (*Amor mi' bello, or che sarà di me?*) (Contini I, p. 487), is made up of 334 mainly hendecasyllabic unrhymed lines. It is an address to the lady, containing a dense network of interlinked images. It has affinities with the love lyric and with the longer forms of the *salut*.[8]

Il Mare Amoroso **1a**

che se vi spiace ch'io vi deggia amare,	77
gittate via la vostra gran beltade,	
che mi fa forsenar, quando vi miro . . .	
[. . .]	
E se no'l fate, non m'en rimarraggio,	85
avegnamene ciò che può avenire:	
ch'io penso, se Narcisso fosse vivo,	
sì 'ntenderebbe in voi, a mia credenza,	
e non in sé medesmo come fece.	
[. . .]	
la bocca, piccioletta e colorita,	98
vermiglia come rosa di giardino,	
piagente ed amorosa per basciare.	100
E be·llo saccio, ch'i' l'aggio provato	
una fïata, vostra gran merzede;	
ma quella mi fu lancia di Pelùs,	
ch'avëa tal vertù nel suo ferire,	
ch'al primo colpo dava pene e morte,	105
e al secondo vita ed allegrezza:	
così mi die' quel bascio mal di morte,	
ma se n'avesse un altro, ben guerira.	
[. . .]	
e ben parete dea d'amare, e meglio	134
che la chiarita stella de la dia.	

[For if it displeases you that I am compelled to love you, cast aside your great beauty which drives me to frenzy when I look upon you [. . .] and if you do not do so, I will not desist, let what will befall me in consequence, for I think, if Narcissus were alive, he would fall in love with you, in my opinion, and not with himself as he did. [. . .] The mouth, very small and rosy, red like the garden rose, pleasing and lovely to kiss; and I know this well, for I experienced it once, thanks to your great favour, but it was to me the lance of Peleus, which had such power in its stroke that at the first

[8] For examples of the *salut* (in rhyming couplets) see Arn. Mar. **3a**; **3b**; **4**; Falq. Rom. **3a**; Azalais **1**.

blow it gave pain and death, and at the second life and gladness: in the same way that kiss gave me a mortal sickness, but if I were to have another, I would indeed be cured. [. . .] And you seem indeed to be the goddess of Love, and more beautiful than the resplendent day-star.]

Lines 80–4 contain the similes of the moth in the flame (going back to Folquet, ed. Stroński 11.9 ff. *co·l parpaillos. . .*) and of the salamander, frequent among bestiary images, e.g. Giac. Lent. 1.27 ff. (Contini I, p. 52). Line 89 is followed by an enumeration of the features of the lady's beauty, of which ll. 98–100 form part; the mention of the red mouth prompts the image of the lance of Peleus. The description of beauty continues from l. 109, and is concluded in ll. 134 f. by the comparison with Venus.   87 *Narcisso*: cf. Rin. Aq. 1.32 n. 103 *lancia di Pelùs*: see Bern. Vent. 3.45 ff. n.; J. Mostacci 1.48 n.   134 *dea d'amare*: cf. Alb. Mass. **1**.9; comparisons or identifications with Venus are not usual in the troubadour and trouvère lyric, but common in the Classical and MLat. poets, e.g. Claud. 4.3; Venant. 4.8; Ripoll 4.3; see also in the German lyric, Morungen **2**.1.   135 *la . . . stella de la dia*: a designation of the planet Venus.

Il Mare Amoroso **1b**

Ma non fuora dunqua gran malaventura   316
e smisurato male e gran peccato
se mi uccidete, poi che tanto v'amo?
Il vostro nome, ch'è chiamato dea,
saria mai sempre chiamato Giudea,   320
a simiglianza di Giuda giudeo
che tradì Gesù Cristo per un bascio.
Or non mi lasci Idio poter vedere
sì doloroso giorno com' quel fôra.

[But would it not therefore be a great misfortune and immeasurable ill and a great sin if you kill me, since I love you so much? Your name, which is that of goddess, would henceforth always be that of Giudea, like Judas the Jew who betrayed Jesus Christ with a kiss. May God then not let me be granted to see such a grievous day as that would be.]

319 ff. *dea . . . Giudea . . . Giuda giudeo*: the play on words, impossible to translate, is emphasized by the placing of the names at the end of the line. 321 *Giuda giudeo*: cf. Chiaro **2b**.17.

Other examples of comparison are expressed in the form of a wish or hypothesis:

Il Mare Amoroso **2**

Ed io vorrei bene, s'esser potesse,   209
che voi pareste a tutta l'altra gente
sì com parïa la Pulzella Laida.

[And I could wish, if it might be, that you might appear to everyone else as the Ugly Maiden appeared.]

211 *la Pulzella Laida*: the figure of the Ugly Maiden is described in Chrétien, *Conte du Graal* (*Perceval*), ll. 4610–4641, but it was probably known in Italy from Italian adaptations of Arthurian stories.

Il Mare Amoroso 3

E se non fosse ancora conquistata   31
la Val d'i Falsamanti di Morgana,
io la conquisterei per Lancialotto.

[And if the Valley of Faithless Lovers of Morgana was not yet conquered, I would conquer it in place of Lancelot.]

32 A reference to the *Val des Faux Amants* episode in the 13th-c. French material (see Uc Pena **1**.25 ff. n.). *Morgana*: cf. Guid. Col. **1**.35 n.

Il Mare Amoroso 4

Ma poi ch'i' non mi sento tal natura,   234
sapesse almeno volar sì com' seppe
lo saggio Didalùs anticamente . . .

[But since I do not possess such a nature, if I were at least able to fly as was wise Daedalus of old . . .]

This example occurs in a list of wishes for magic powers to gain the lady's love.   236 *Didalùs*: cf. Rig. Berb. **1**.26 n.; Ad. Halle **1**.29 n.

The work concludes with the epitaph composed by the poet and destined for his tomb:

Il Mare Amoroso 5

'Chi vuole amare, li convien tremare,   329
sì come 'l marinaio in mare amaro;
e chi no·m crede, mi deggia mirare,
che per amor son morto in amarore,
sì com' è morto Nadriano e Caedino;   333
però si guardi chi s'ha a guardare.'

['Whoever wishes to love must tremble, like the sailor in the bitter sea, and whoever does not believe me, may he look on me, for I have died for love in bitterness, as sir Andrieu and Kahedin died; therefore let him be on his guard, who needs to be on his guard.']

329 ff. In this passage, the disruptive MS interpolations, *bramare, chiamare* after *tremare*, and *per maraviglia* after *mirare* are omitted.   *amare– mare amaro– amor– amarore*: similar word-play on derivations from the roots *am-* and *mar-* are common in Oc. and OF.   333 *Nadriano*: a conflation of the title *Ne* 'sir' with an inaccurate rendering of the name *Andrieus*; cf. Raim. Jord. **2**.24 n., and for forms with the title, Aim. Peg. **3b**.30 *N'Andrieus*; Falq. Rom. **1**.16 *N'Andreus*.   *Caedino*: Kahedin, nephew of Mark in the Prose *Tristan*, hopelessly in love with Iseut.

Alberto di Massa di Maremma **1**

Donna, meo core . . . (*canzone*).
Contini I, p. 359

Donna, meo core in parte   I 1
vostr'amore ha diviso:
non d'amar è restato
   voi, cui no vé in parte
di valor e di viso   5
†. . . e in estato†
   alcuna donna pari
non Elena di Pari,
né d'amore la dea.

[Lady, love of you has divided my heart into parts: it has not ceased to love
you, to whom I have seen no lady in part equal in worth and appearance
and . . . in status (?), neither Helen of Paris, nor the goddess of love.]

The *fronte* and the first half of the *sirma* of I, in a *canzone* of six 12-l. stanzas.
The ll. contain punning rhymes of differing grammatical types: 1 *in parte*
(prep.+pl. subst.) : 4 *in parte* (prep.+sg. subst., used adverbially); 2 *diviso*
(pp.) : 5 *di viso* (prep.+subst.); 7 *pari* (undecl. adj.) : 8 *Pari* (proper name) –
for this type see Fil. Mess. **1**.10 n. It is clear that *restato* in 3 was intended to
be in punning rhyme with l. 6, with a paired formula, as in l. 5, but the first
element of the pair is missing; *estato* might be modelled on Oc. m. *estat* 'state',
'status'.   8 *Elena di Pari*: see Rin. Aq. **2**.3 n.; for the beauty of Helen cf.
Chiaro (?) **1**e.13 n.   9 *d'amore la dea* cf. Mar. Am. **1**a.134 n.

An exchange of sonnets (*tenzone*) between an anonymous poet and a poetess,
given the title La Compiuta Donzella di Firenze, 'the accomplished Maid of
Florence', in the MS. She is the first Italian woman poet known, and the only
one in the 13th century, and is now generally thought to have actually existed.
The *tenzone* must be seen in relation to Maestro Torrigiano **1**, which clearly
refers to the same learned poetess:

La Compiuta Donzella **1**

Gentil donzella . . . (*sonetto*). La Compiuta
Donzella III.1, Anonimo, Contini I, p. 436

Gentil donzella somma ed insegnata,   1
poi c'aggio inteso di voi tant' orranza,
che non credo che Morgana la fata
né la Donna del Lago né Gostanza   4
né fosse alcuna come voi presciata;
e di trovare avete nominanza
(ond'eo mi faccio un po[ca] di mirata
c'avete di saver tant'abondanza):   8
però, se no sdegnaste lo meo dire,
vorria venire a voi, poi non sia saggio

a ciò che 'n tutto mi poria chiarire 11
di ciò ch'eo dotto ne lo mio coraggio;
e so che molto mi poria 'nantire
aver contìa del vostro segnoraggio. 14

[Noble maiden, supreme and learned, since I have heard such renown ascribed to you, that I do not think that Morgana the fairy, nor the Lady of the Lake, nor Constanza were any of them as esteemed as you; and you are famed as a poet (on that account I marvel somewhat that you have such abundance of knowledge). Therefore, if you do not spurn my poetry, I would like to come to you, although I am not learned, so that you may in everything elucidate that of which I am uncertain in my mind; and I know that acquaintance with your supremacy could enhance my skill greatly.]

1 *insegnata*: modelled on Oc. *ensenhat* 'educated', 'of courtly education'. 3 *Morgana la fata*: cf. Guid. Col. 1.35 n.   4 *la Donna del Lago*: the fairy who took Lancelot from his cradle and brought him up, hence his name *Lanceloz del Lac*.   *Gostanza*: Contini takes this name to refer to Constance, wife of Henry VI, and mother of the emperor Frederick II, but since the other names are literary, it is more likely to be a reference (required by the rhyme) to a figure in later Franco-Italian or French adaptations of *chanson de geste* material, e.g. *Co(n)stance*, daughter of king Floire and queen Blanchefleur in *Berte aus grans piés* by Adenet le Roi (for another name probably derived from the latter work, see *Mem. Bol.* 1.26 n.). In her reply (Contini I, p. 436 *Ornato di gran pregio e di valenza*), La Compiuta Donzella praises the anonymous poet, disclaiming excessive praise of herself, but declaring her willingness always to serve those who love, and Love itself.

Maestro Torrigiano di Firenze **1**

Esser donzella . . . (sonetto).
Contini I, p. 439 (see also La Compiuta Donzella 1)

Esser donzella di trovare dotta 1
sì grande meraviglia par a 'ntendre,
ca, se Ginevra fosse od Isaotta,
ver lor di lei se ne poria contendre. 4
[. . .]
Ma, se difender voglio la natura,
dirò che siate divina Sibilla,
venuta per aver del mondo cura. 11
Ed eo ne tegno di meglior la villa
e credo ch'èci meglior'aventura,
che ci è aparita sì gran meravilla. 14

[To be a maiden learned in the composition of verse appears to signify a great marvel, for if Ginevra or Isaotta were alive, one could contend that she was superior to them. [. . .] But if I wish to defend Nature, I will say that you are the divine Sibyl, come to have care of the world; and I estimate the city more highly on that account, and think there is greater good fortune there, in that such a great marvel has there appeared.]

The comparison and the identification are placed in the first half of the octave and the first half of the sestet respectively.   3 *Ginevra . . . Isaotta*: an atypical example, since the figures are usually exemplars of beauty; for *Ginevra* cf. Uc Pena **1**.25 n.; for *Isaotta* cf. Giac. Lent. **1**.39 n.   10 *Sibilla*: rarely cited as exemplar in the vernacular lyric; see Baudri **2a**.54 n.   12 *la villa*: Florence.

Memoriali Bolognesi 1

> *"Mamma, lo temp' è venuto"* (*ballata*). Contini I, p. 770

"Matre, de flevel natura   III   21
te ven che me vai sconfortando
de quello ch'eo sun plu segura
non fo per arme Rolando
né 'l cavalier sens paura   25
né lo bon duxo Morando.
Matre, 'l to dir sia en bando,
ch'eo pur me voi' maritare."

["Mother, it is as a result of your timid nature that you are discouraging me from this, for I am more steadfast than was Roland because of his arms, or the knight without fear, or the good duke Morando. Mother, abandon your talk, for I nevertheless wish to marry."]

An anonymous dialogue between mother and daughter in five 8-l. stanzas alternating between the speakers + head-refrain of 4 ll. The item is entered in a vol. for 1282 in the series of legal registers known as the *Memoriali Bolognesi*. For the practice of using blank space for this purpose, see Contini I, pp. 765 f. 24 *Rolando*: the hero of the *Chanson de Roland*.   25 *'l cavalier sens paura*: Brunor, a knight of the Round Table in *Guiron le Courtois*, always referred to as *le bon Chevalier sens Paour*. This designation (like *Rolando* in 24 and *Morando* in 26) was probably known indirectly from Franco-Italian adaptations (see Contini I, p. 771 nn., and *Prosa del Duecento*, ed. Segre/Marti, *Il Novellino* LXIII, 'Del buon re Emeladus e del Cavaliere senza paura').   26 *lo bon duxo Morando*: probably derived from *Morando di Riviera* in book VI of *I Reali di Francia* by Andrea da Barberino, based in part on *Berte aus grans piés*, in which the name *Morans/Morant* occurs.   27 lit. 'let your words be abandoned'.

Memoriali Bolognesi 2

> *Io faccio prego all'alto Dio potente* (*sirventese*).
> Orlando, pp. 95 f.

E sète, bella, lọ fiorẹ della contrata   53
che ne lo core mi sète plantata:
non fue sí bella Morgana la fata
al meo parere.
[. . .]
Di voi servire ho disio e bramo,   69

piú che non ebe de lo pomo Adamo;
però a voi medesma mi richiamo
del mio tormento.

[And you, beautiful one, are the flower of the land, so that you are planted in my heart: Morgana the fairy was not so beautiful, it seems to me. [. . .] I have a greater desire and longing to serve you than Adam had for the apple; therefore I address the complaint of my torment to you (lit. to you yourself).]

The poem of 76 ll. is entered on the cover of a group of legal documents of 1299–1300 (see Orlando, p. 96). The designation *sirventese* is explained by the form, which is that of the so-called *sirventese caudato*, consisting of three long lines followed by a short line, with the rhyme scheme AAAb BBBc etc., usually used for didactic subject-matter.　　55 *Morgana la fata*: cf. Guid. Col. 1.35 n. 70 *Adamo*: Adam is rarely cited in association with the individual poet's love, but see, in a different context, Pr. *Trist.* 1b.82 f.; Duchesse 1.13 f.

Lapo Gianni, probably late 13th or early 14th century

Lapo Gianni 1

Sì come i Magi . . . (single stanza). Contini II, p. 602

Sì come i Magi a guida de la stella　　　　　　　　　　　　　1
girono inver' le parti d'Orïente
per adorar lo Segnor ch'era nato,
così mi guidò Amore a veder quella
che'l giorno amanto prese novamente　　　　　　　　　　　　5
ond' ogni gentil cor fu salutato.

[As the Magi, guided by the star, turned towards the realms of the East to adore the Saviour who was born, so Love guided me to look upon her, who on that day first assumed supremacy, through which every noble heart was graciously acknowledged.]

The *fronte* of a single 14-l. stanza.　　　　1 *i Magi*: cf. Guittone, ed. Leonardi 72.9 *così como guidò i Magi la stella,* | *guida me sua fazzon, gendome avante* (as the star guided the Magi, so her form guides me, proceeding before me). 5 *amanto*: lit. robe of authority.　　　　6 *salutato*: Oc. *saludar* 'to salute, 'greet' has in the love lyric the special sense of the gracious acknowledgement hoped for from the lady as a sign of favour.

Lapo Gianni 2

Amor, eo chero mia donna in domìno
(*sonetto doppio caudato*). Contini II, p. 603

bel mi trovasse come fu Absalone,　　　　　　　　　　　　16
Sansone pareggiasse e Salamone
[. . .]
giovane, sana, alegra e secura　　　　　　　　　　　　　　21
fosse mia vita fin che 'l mondo dura.

[I would be as beautiful as was Absalon and would equal Samson and Solomon [...] my life would be young, healthy, happy and secure as long as the world lasts.]

The poem is an expanded sonnet of 22 lines. The hypothetical comparisons with exemplars in ll.16 f. are part of a list of impossible wishes which constitute the poem.   16 *Absalone*: cf. CB **2**.5a.2 n.; 17 *Sansone ... Salamone*: these are the sole instances of these two names among all the detailed examples of exemplary figures cited in this chapter (but see ref. to *Sansone* in Chiaro **2b** n.). Here they probably represent the qualities of strength and wisdom respectively, their inclusion perhaps having been prompted by the need for a rhyme in -*one*.

Cino da Pistoia, c. 1270–1336/7

Cino da Pistoia 1
Se conceduto ... (sonetto). Marti, 1969, p. 570

Se conceduto mi fosse da Giove,	1
io non potrei vestir quella figura	
che questa bella donna fredda e dura	
mutar facesse de l'usate prove.	4
[...]	
Ma s'i' potesse far come quel dio,	9
'sta donna muterei in bella faggia,	
e vi farei un'ellera d'intorno;	
ed un ch'i' taccio, per simil desio,	12
muterei in uccel ched onni giorno	
canterebbe sull' ellera selvaggia.	14

[Even if it were granted me by Jove, I could not assume that form which would cause this beautiful, cold and hard-hearted lady to change from her customary attitude [...] But if I could act like that god, I would change that lady into a beautiful beech tree, and would there entwine an ivy around it; and one on whom I remain silent, with like desire I would change into a bird, who every day would sing on the wild ivy.]

The first half of the octave, and the sestet.   2 *vestir quella figura*: cf. *mutar* 4, *muterei* 10, 14: since the poet cannot be other than he is, nor the lady be made to change, he wishes that they both might be transformed. Marti considers that ll. 9 ff. allude to the story of Philemon and Baucis in Ovid, *Met.* VIII. 626–720. Granted a wish by Jove, as reward for their hospitality, in spite of humble circumstances, to Jove and Mercury in disguise, they choose never to be separated, and are transformed on death into an oak and a lime-tree, growing side by side from one double trunk. The supposed similarity is unconvincing, however, in that in the Cino example the poet and the lady are not united in love, and the wish for transformation comes solely from the poet and is expressed in hypothetical form. It is probably rather a creative adaptation of the idea of metamorphosis, influenced by other literary examples of

transformations: into a tree, e.g. Daphne and the laurel (Ov., *Met.* I. 452–567);
Petrarch **2**, **3**, **5**, **6**.167; into a bird, e.g. Homer, *Od.* **6**, Catullus **1**, and with ref.
to the poet, Horace **2**.   9 *quel dio*: Giove, as in l. 1.

Cino da Pistoia 2

Tutte le pene ch'io sento d'amore (*sonetto*). Marti, 1969, p. 451

Quella, che porta pregio di valore,   5
più che non fece d'arme Ettor di Troia,
è di tutt'avenantezza e bellore:
fra tutte l'altre donne al mondo è gioia.   8

[She who is renowned as of surpassing worth, more than was Hector of
Troy in (force of) arms, is perfect in grace and beauty: above all other
ladies in the world she is joy.]

The comparison is placed in the second half of the octave.   5 lit. 'she who
bears the renown of excellence'; *pregio* refers to public recognition of worth,
valore to innate excellence.   6 *Ettor di Troia*: Hector is usually cited in
praise of male figures, but the name is dictated here by rhyming constraints
(*moia* : *noia* : *Troia* : *gioia*).

Cino da Pistoia 3

Se tu sapessi ben . . . (*sonetto*). Marti, 1969, p. 608

Se tu sapessi ben com'io aspetto   1
stando gravato de lo tuo silenzo,
non potresti già più, questo sentenzo,
la regola tener di Benedetto.   4
Non sai tu, frate, quant'io son distretto
di quel Signore cui servir m'agenzo,
e pròvonde la pena di Lorenzo,
per mia sventura e per lo tuo difetto?   8

[If you truly knew how I wait, weighed down by your silence, you would
no longer be able, this I affirm, to keep to the rule of Benedict. Do you not
know, brother, how much I am oppressed by that lord whom it pleases me
to serve, and how as a result I suffer the torment of Laurence, on account
of my misfortune and your failure (to respond)?]

The octave of the sonnet; it has been suggested that this sonnet may be addressed to Dante (see Marti's n.).   4 *la regola . . . di Benedetto*: a ref.
to the imposition of silence, more strictly observed in some branches of the
Benedictine order.   6 *quel Signore*: Love.   7 *Lorenzo*: according to
one tradition, St. Laurence was roasted on a gridiron.

Cino da Pistoia 4

Amor, che viene armato . . . (*sonetto*). Marti, 1969, p. 798

Amor, che viene armato a doppio dardo   1
del più levato monte che si' al mondo,
e de l'auro ferìo il nostro, Gherardo,

> e 'l bel soggetto del piombo ritondo.   4
> Fu, quel che fece così duro e tardo
> lo core a quella di Peneo, il secondo . . .   6
> [. . .]
> E se d'Amor non semo amanti, †fôra
> come Dafne del Sol†: esser benegno
> così vuol questo; onde perciò l'onora.   14

[Love which comes, armed with double arrow, from the highest mountain in the world, and with the gold wounded our friend, Gherardo, and the fair subject with the blunt lead. This was the second (arrow), that which made the heart of the daughter of Peneus so hard and reluctant [. . .] And if we are not lovers of Love, it would be comparable to Daphne in relation to Apollo (?); to be well disposed, such is his (Love's) will, therefore honour him.]

The first six lines of the octave and the second half of the sestet. Ll. 7–11 are textually obscure and are therefore omitted. This sonnet is a reply to *Con sua saetta d'or percosse Amore* by Gherardo da Reggio (Marti, Cino CXLVIa, p. 796), in which the poet complains that he has been struck by Love's golden arrow, but the lady remains hard-hearted, and asks whether he should continue to love and honour her.   1 Cino completes the reference to Love's two arrows, associated with the story of Daphne and Apollo in Ovid, *Met.* I. 452–567. The sharp gold arrow, which compels love, strikes Apollo; the blunt lead arrow, which puts love to flight, strikes Daphne.   2 *del più levato monte*: Parnassus.   4 *ritondo* lit. 'rounded': cf. *Met.* I.471 *obtusum*. 6 *quella di Peneo*: Daphne, daughter of the river-god Peneus, referred to in Ovid by the patronymic *Peneia*. Pursued by Apollo, Daphne implores her father to transform her beautiful appearance, the cause of unsought-for love, and is turned into a laurel. See the refs. to the transformation of Daphne in Petrarch, e.g. **1**.34 ff.; **2**.13 f.; **3**.1 ff.; **5**.1; **6**.167.   12 f. This appears to imply: if struck, like Gherardo, by the golden arrow, it is necessary to submit to the sovereign power of Love; to resist would make us comparable to Daphne. 13 *del Sol*: a reference to Apollo's manifestation as sun/the sun-god Phoebus; see Petrarch **1**.34 n.   14 *l'onora*: this may be read as referring both to Love and the lady, i.e. in the honouring of Love, the lady is also honoured.

In an exchange of sonnets with Cino da Pistoia, an otherwise unidentified poet praises Cino:

Binduccio da Firenze **1**
Solo per acquistar vostra contia (sonetto). Marti, 1969, p. 812

> Però che siete d'Amor sì secreto,   9
> fra gli amanti cavalcate la rota
> più che non fe' tra' pittor Pollicreto;   11
> né 'l bon Tristan non seppe d'arpa nota,

né sì non seppe David l'alfabeto,
com' voi sapete me' cui l'Amor dota.   14

[Therefore, since you are so much the familiar of Love, among lovers you bestride (Fortune's) wheel, more than did Polycletus among artists; nor did good Tristan know a note of the harp, nor did David know the alphabet, by comparison with you who know to a greater degree those on whom Love bestows his gifts.]

In the octave of the sonnet, Binduccio asks Cino for advice, declaring himself forgotten by Love, whom he has served faithfully. This gives rise to the praise of Cino in the comparisons of the sestet. In his reply, *Solo per ritenir vostra amistia* (Marti, p. 814), Cino disclaims exaggerated praise, but the sonnet is mainly taken up with advice to Binduccio to persist undeterred in love.   11 *Pollicreto*: the Greek sculptor Polycletus, cited as an example of artistic excellence in general also in Petrarch, sonnet 77.1, but in association specifically with sculpture *Purg.* X.32.   12 *Tristan*: cf. Giac. Lent. 1.39 n.   13 *l'alfabeto*: in opposition to *nota*, denotes the rudiments of the poetic text, appropriate to David as psalmist. This is an unusual example in that in the vernacular lyric David is usually portrayed as a victim of love (cf. Marc. 1.14 n.), and in the MLat. lyric as exemplary ruler (cf. Venant. 1.78 n.).

Amico di Dante 1

              La pena che sentì . . . (sonetto). Contini II, p. 768

La pena che sentì Cato di Roma   1
in quelle secche de la Barberia,
lor ch'al re Giuba pur andar volia,
veggendo la sua gente istanca e doma,   4
non sembl' a·mme che fosse sì gran soma
d'assai, madonna, com' or è la mia:
che·sse serpente e sete malfacia
lui ed a' suoi, come Lucan li noma,   8
i' son punto e navrato da colui
che tutte cose mena a·ssu' piacere
e face a qual si vuole adoperare.   11

[The anguish which Cato of Rome felt in those deserts of Barbary, when he greatly desired to go to king Juba, seeing his followers weary and vanquished, does not seem to me to have been so very great in extent, lady, as is mine now, for if serpent and thirst harmed him and his men, as Lucan relates of them, I am pierced and wounded by the one (i.e. *Amore*), who directs all things at his pleasure and commands the actions of anyone at all at will.]

The comparison takes up the octave and the first half of the sestet of the sonnet. The episode is related in Lucan, *De bello civili*, book IX, and is referred to by Dante, *Inf.* xxv.94–6.   8 *li noma*: lit. 'names them'.

Dante (1265–1321)

The decline in the incidence of exemplary comparisons in the Italian lyric of the later thirteenth and early fourteenth centuries is illustrated in the lyric poems of Dante. There is only one such comparison, which moreover seems to have been mainly prompted by rhyming constraints:

Dante **1**

> *Così nel mio parlar voglio esser aspro (canzone).* Foster and Boyde, 80

> E m'ha percosso in terra, e stammi sopra   III   35
> con quella spada ond'elli ancise Dido,
> Amore, a cui io grido
> merzé chiamando, e umilmente il priego;
> ed el d'ogni merzé par messo al niego.

> [And he has struck me to the ground and stands over me with that sword with which he slew Dido, Love, to whom I cry, calling for mercy, and I entreat him humbly, but he stands opposed, it seems, to all mercy.]

These ll. form the *sirma* of stanza III in a *canzone* of six 13-l. stanzas + 5-l. *congedo.*   36 *Dido*: for love as the cause of Dido's death, cf. *Duchesse* **1**.6 f.

In the *Commedia*, by contrast, there are a considerable number of comparisons with exemplary figures drawn from the Bible, classical literature (above all Virgil, Statius and Ovid), history, and legend, which are outside the scope of the present study. Two in particular, however, utilize examples of the type attested in the vernacular love lyric: thus in *Inferno* xxxi.1–6, Virgil's rebuke and consolation are compared to the lance of Peleus, which both wounds and cures (see J. Mostacci **1**.48 n.; Bern. Vent. **3**.45–8 and n.; in *Purgatorio* xxvii.34–42, when the guiding angel bids Dante, transfixed with fear, enter the flames separating him from Beatrice, the poet's courage is restored at the sound of her name, as Pyramus, hearing the name of Thisbe, opens his eyes when at the point of death (see OF Anon. **2**.26 ff. n.).

Petrarch (1304–1374)

The standard numbering of individual poems, as in the edition of Santagata, is based on the roughly chronological ordering in Petrarch's own manuscript of the *Canzoniere (Rerum vulgarium fragmenta)*. The following excerpts do not follow this sequence, because it is more appropriate for the study of exemplary comparison and identification to group them according to the nature and provenance of the exemplary figures, i.e. **1–5** Apollo and Daphne; **6** Daphne; **7** Diana and Actaeon; **8** Helen; **9** Lucretia, Polyxena, Hypsipile, Argia; **10** Orpheus and Euridice; **11** Narcissus; **12** Tithonus and Aurora; **13** Pygmalion; **14** Automedon, Tiphys; **15** Scipio Africanus, and by implication, Aeneas, Achilles, Ulysses, Augustus, Agamemnon; **16** Julius Caesar, David. Of the examples referring to Laura, **1–6**, **8**, **9**, **11**, **13**, **15**, **16** were written while she was alive, **10** and **12** after her death.

Petrarch **1**

A qualunque animale alberga in terra (sestina). Santagata 22

Con lei foss'io da che si parte il sole,	VI 31
e non ci vedess'altri che le stelle,	
sol una nocte, et mai non fosse l'alba;	
et non se transformasse in verde selva	
per uscirmi di braccia, come il giorno	35
ch'Apollo la seguia qua giù per terra.	

[If only I might be with her from the moment the sun departs, and nothing other than the stars might see us, for one single night, and it might never be dawn; and she might not be transformed into a verdant bush, to escape from my arms, as on the day when Apollo pursued her here below on earth.]

The last stanza of the *sestina*, which is followed by a 3-l. *congedo*.   31–3: a reference to the situation of the dawn song. Oc. *alba* denotes both dawn and the poetic genre describing the parting of lovers at dawn; as in 33, the word *alba* may occur in final position, e.g. Raimb. Vaq. ed. Linskill, 25, which has *l'alba* at the end of the third and sixth lines, and the refrain *l'alba, oi l'alba* as the seventh line in each of four stanzas. In the *sestina*, the final word of each line is repeated in differing position in each stanza, which serves further to single out the word *alba*.   34 For Apollo and Daphne, and the transformation of Daphne into a laurel, see Ovid, *Met.* I. 452–567, and Petrarch **2**; **3**; **5**; **6**.167. Apollo is identified with the sun-god, Phoebus: see in particular **2**.6 *'l tuo viso*, 11 *di queste impression' l'aere disgombra*; **3**.2 *Phebo*, 7 *e 'l sol ci sta lontano*; **4**.2 ff., 4 *il Sole*. The first brief ref. to the myth in Petrarch appears to be sonnet 5.12 f. See also Cino **4** nn. 1, 6 and 13.

Petrarch **2**

Apollo, s'anchor vive . . . (sonetto). Santagata 34

Apollo, s'anchor vive il bel desio	1
che t'infiammava a le thesaliche onde,	
et se non ài l'amate chiome bionde,	
volgendo gli anni, già poste in oblio:	4
dal pigro gielo et dal tempo aspro et rio,	
che dura quanto 'l tuo viso s'asconde,	
difendi or l'onorata et sacra fronde,	
ove tu prima, et poi fu' invescato io.	8
et per vertù de l'amorosa speme,	
che ti sostenne ne la vita acerba,	
di queste impressïon' l'aere disgombra;	11
sì vedrem poi per meraviglia inseme	

seder la donna nostra sopra l'erba,
et far de le sue braccia a se stessa ombra.   14

[Apollo, if the fair desire still lives which inflamed you by the Thessalian
waters, and if you have not, with the passage of the years, by now forgotten
the beloved golden tresses, from sluggish ice and harsh inclement weather,
which persists when your face is hidden, protect now the honoured and
sacred foliage, in which first you and then I were caught; and by virtue
of the pleasing hope which sustained you in a bitter life, purge the air of
these vapours: so shall we then together see, by a marvel, our lady seated
on the grass, and with her arms casting shade upon herself.]

2 *a le thesaliche onde*: i.e. by the waters of Peneus, a name designating both
a river in Thessaly and its god, father of Daphne (see Cino 4.6 n.). 5 ff.: see
1.34 n.   8 *invescato*: lit. 'caught (like a bird) in lime'.   10 *la vita
acerba*: this may refer either to Apollo's banishment from Olympus and his
service as herdsman to Admetus, or to the suffering caused by love (see Tibull.
2.11 n.); in contrast to *la vita acerba*, *l'amorosa speme* in l. 9 therefore has either
a general sense or may refer specifically to hopes of love.   14 *braccia*:
metaphorically also the branches of the laurel.

Petrarch 3

Quando del proprio sito . . . (*sonetto*). Santagata 41

Quando dal proprio sito si rimove   1
l'arbor ch'amò già Phebo in corpo humano,
sospira et suda a l'opera Vulcano,
per rinfrescar l'aspre saette a Giove: 4
il qual or tona, or nevicha et or piove,
senza honorar più Cesare che Giano;
la terra piange, e 'l sol ci sta lontano,
che la sua cara amica ved'altrove.   8

[When from its proper place there departs that tree which Phoebus formerly loved in human form, Vulcan pants and sweats at his work, to make
ready Jove's sharp arrows; he now thunders, now snows, and now rains,
without honouring Caesar more than Janus; the earth weeps and the sun
stands far off, seeing his dear love elsewhere.]

The octave of the sonnet.   1 ff. When Laura is absent, the sun departs
and Jove sends winter instead of summer weather; see also sonnet 43 (the sun/
Apollo mourns Laura's absence).   2 *Phebo*, 7 *'l sol*: see **1.34 n.**   4 *l'aspre
saette*: i.e. lightning flashes.   6 *Cesare*: i.e. July, sacred to Julius Caesar
(*Julius mensis*); *Giano*: i.e. January, sacred to Janus (*Jani mensis*).

Petrarch 4

In mezzo di duo amanti . . . (*sonetto*). Santagata 115

In mezzo di duo amanti honesta altera   1
vidi una donna, et quel signor co lei
che fra gli uomini regna et fra li dèi;

et da l'un lato il Sole, io da l'altro era.   4
Poi che s'accorse chiusa de la spera
de l'amico più bello, agli occhi miei
tutta lieta si volse, et ben vorrei
che mai non fosse inver' di me più fera.   8
Sùbito in allegrezza si converse
la gelosia che 'n su la prima vista
per sì alto adversario al cor mi nacque.   11
A lui la faccia lagrimosa et trista
un nuviletto intorno ricoverse:
cotanto l'esser vinto li dispiacque.   14

[Between two lovers I saw a lady, virtuous and proud, and that lord with
her who reigns among men and among gods, and on one side the Sun, I
was on the other. Since she found herself enclosed by the rays of the more
handsome lover, she, most happy, turned to face me, and I could truly wish
she might never again behave with lofty pride towards me. Suddenly there
turned to gladness the jealousy which at first glance had arisen in my heart
on account of so high an adversary. His face, tearful and sad, was covered
over by a little cloud, so greatly did it displease him to be vanquished.]

1 *altera*: in association with *honesta*, *altera* has a positive sense, 'having a
proper sense of pride', whereas *fera* 'proud' in l. 8 expresses the effect of the
lady's pride on the lover.   4 *il Sole*: see 1.34 n.   5 *s'accorse*: 'became
aware'.

Petrarch 5

L'aura celeste . . . (*sonetto*). Santagata 197

L'aura celeste che 'n quel verde lauro   1
spira, ov' Amor ferì nel fianco Apollo,
et a me pose un dolce giogo al collo,
tal che mia libertà tardi restauro,   4
pò quello in me, che nel gran vecchio mauro
Medusa quando in selce transformollo;
né posso dal bel nodo omai dar crollo,
là 've il sol perde, non pur l'ambra o l'auro;   8
dico le chiome bionde, e 'l crespo laccio,
che sì soavemente lega et stringe
l'alma, che d'umiltate e non d'altr'armo.   11
L'ombra sua sola fa 'l mio cor un ghiaccio,
et di bianca paura il viso tinge;
ma li occhi ànno vertù di farne un marmo.   14

[The celestial breeze which breathes in that green laurel, where Love struck
Apollo in the heart and placed a sweet yoke about my neck, such that I
struggle in vain to recover my freedom (lit. that I am slow to recover . . .),
has that same power over me as had Medusa over the giant old Moor when
she changed him into stone; nor can I now free myself from that lovely

net, beside which the sun pales in splendour, and not merely amber or gold: I mean the blond tresses and the curly strands which so sweetly bind and draw tight my soul, which is armed solely with humility; her shadow alone turns my heart to ice and casts upon my face the pallid hue of fear, but the eyes have the power to turn them to marble.]

1 f.: cf. **1**.34 n. *L'aura* is a homophone of the name *Laura*.   2 *fianco*, lit. 'side'.   5 f. *nel gran vecchio mauro . . . Medusa*; cf. *Met.* IV.628 ff.: Atlas, king of Mauretania, a man of colossal size, was changed by Perseus, with the help of the head of Medusa, into Mount Atlas, because he refused him hospitality. Petrarch uses the image of Medusa elsewhere: 366.111 f. (in a prayer to the Virgin) *Medusa et l'error mio m'àn fatto un sasso| d'umor vano stillante* (Medusa and my error have turned me to stone, shedding vain tears) – here the Medusa stands for Laura, *l'error mio* for his worldly love; 179.9 f. if my humility did not move her, to look upon her would be like confronting the face of the Medusa (*andrei non altramente| a veder lei, che 'l volto di Medusa*).   6 *selce*: lit. 'flint'. 7 *nodo*, 9 *laccio*: both words designate a net or snare for trapping birds or animals; *crespo laccio*: lit. 'curly snare'.   11 lit. 'which I arm with humility and with nothing else'.   14 *farne*: the enclitic *ne* refers to *cor* and *viso*.

Petrarch 6

Nel dolce tempo de la prima etade (canzone). Santagata 23

Canzon, i' non fu' mai quel nuvol d'oro	161
che poi discese in pretïosa pioggia,	
sì che 'l foco di Giove in parte spense;	
ma fui ben fiamma ch'un bel guardo accense,	
et fui l'uccel che più per l'aere poggia,	165
alzando lei che ne' miei detti honoro:	
né per nova figura il primo alloro	
seppi lassar, ché pur la sua dolce ombra	
ogni men bel piacer del cor mi sgombra.	

[My song, I was never that golden cloud which then descended in precious rain, so that it in part extinguished Jove's fire, but I was indeed the flame which a lovely glance ignited, and I was the bird which soars higher through the air, raising up the one whom I honour in my poems: nor was I able, despite any new guise, to forsake the laurel first encountered, for its sweet shade banishes from my heart all pleasures of lesser worth.]

The *congedo* at the end of a poem of eight 20-l. stanzas.   161–5 refer to Jove's disguises: 161 f. as golden rain, to win Danae (*Met.* IV.610 f.; VI.113); 164 as flame to win Aegina (*Met.* VI.113; VII. 615–18); 165 (with less precise application of the parallel), as eagle to carry off Ganymede (*Met.* X.155–61). Danae: see Stat. **1**.135 f. n.; Aegina: see G. Vins. **2**.619 n.; Ganymede: see Hil. **1a**.22 f. n. 167 *alloro*: Laura; for the myth of Daphne and the laurel, see **1**.34 n.

Petrarch 7

Non al suo amante . . . (madrigale). Santagata 52

Non al suo amante più Dïana piacque,   1
quando per tal ventura tutta ignuda
la vide in mezzo de le gelide acque,
ch'a me la pastorella alpestra et cruda
posta a bagnar un leggiadretto velo,   5
ch'a l'aura il vago et biondo capel chiuda,
tal che mi fece, or quand'egli arde il cielo,
tutto tremar d'un amoroso gielo.

[Not more pleasing was Diana to her lover, when by just such a chance he saw her quite naked in the ice-cold waters, than was to me the Alpine rustic shepherdess, intent on washing a delicate veil which ties up her lovely blond hair against the breeze, so that at the moment when the sky burns hot, it caused me to tremble in every limb with an icy frisson of love.]

A single stanza, with the form ABA BCB CC, which has thematic affinities with the OF genre of the *pastourelle*, in which the poet relates his encounter with a rustic shepherdess – see Thib. Ch. **6**.   1–3 cf. *Met.* III.173 ff. Returning from the hunt, Actaeon chanced to see Diana bathing naked in a woodland pool; as punishment she turned him into a stag, so that he was torn to pieces by his own hounds.   2 *per tal ventura*: i.e. by just such a chance as befell the poet.

Petrarch **8**

Di pensier in pensier, di monte in monte (canzone). Santagata 129

I' l'ò più volte (or chi fia che mi 'l creda?)   IV   40
ne l'acqua chiara et sopra l'erba verde
veduto viva, et nel tronchon d'un faggio
e 'n bianca nube, sì fatta che Leda
avria ben detto che sua figlia perde,
come stella che 'l sol copre col raggio.   45

[I have many times (who will there be to believe me?) seen her living image in the clear water and on the verdant grass, and in the trunk of a beech tree and in a white cloud, in such a form that Leda would indeed have said that her daughter pales beside it, like a star which the sun eclipses with its radiance.]

The first six lines of IV, forming the *fronte*, in a *canzone* of five 13-l. stanzas + 7-l. *congedo*.   44 *sua figlia*: Helen; cf. **9**.7 f.; for the beauty of Helen cf. Chiaro (?) **1e**.13 n.   There is an oblique reference in ll. 69 f. of the *congedo*, to Laura/Daphne/laurel: *ove l'aura si sente | d'un fresco et odorifero laureto* (where the air is redolent of a fresh and fragrant laurel grove).

Petrarch **9**

In tale stella duo belli occhi vidi (sonetto). Santagata 260

Non si pareggi a lei qual più s'aprezza,   5
in qual' ch'etade, in quai che strani lidi:

non chi recò con sua vaga bellezza
in Grecia affanni, in Troia ultimi stridi;   8
no la bella romana che col ferro
apre il suo casto et disdegnoso petto;
non Polixena, Ysiphile et Argia.   11

[Let not that one be compared to her who is most praised, in whatever age, on whatever strange shores, nor her who with her surpassing beauty caused arduous toils to Greece and final lamentation to Troy: not the fair Roman who with the sword opened her chaste and scornful breast, not Polyxena, Hypsypile and Argia.]

The second half of the octave and the first half of the sestet.   5 *lei*: to Laura.   7 f. Helen; cf. **8**.44 n.   9 *la bella romana*: Lucretia, who, upon being raped by Tarquin, killed herself. In another instance, the poet submits his accusations against Love to the judgement of Reason; Love defends himself by contrasting the servile love to which he subjected Agamemnon, Achilles, Hannibal and Scipio, with the love for a worthy object which he has inspired in the poet: 360.97 *et a costui di mille | donne elette, excellenti, n'elessi una | qual non si vedrà mai sotto la luna, | benché Lucretia ritornasse a Roma* (and for this one, from among a thousand supreme and excellent women, I chose one, whose like will never be seen beneath the moon, even were Lucretia to return to Rome); cf. also sonnet 262, in words ascribed to Laura herself: 9 *né di Lucretia mi meravigliai, | se non come a morir le bisognasse | ferro, et non le bastasse il dolor solo* (nor did I marvel at Lucretia, save that she needed the sword to die, and that her grief alone did not suffice).   11 *Polixena*: Polyxena, daughter of Priam, who at the command of Achilles, to appease his shade, was sacrificed on his tomb (*Met.* XIII. 447 ff.); see Sicil. Anon. **5c**.102 n. *Ysiphile*: Hypsypile, daughter of king Thoas, whom she saved when all other men on Lemnos were killed. She ruled in his stead and welcomed the Argonauts to Lemnos, bearing Jason two sons (see *Her.* VI, her complaint of his desertion).   *Argia* (: *via*): daughter of Adrastus and wife of Polynices.

Petrarch **10**

Mia benigna fortuna e 'l viver lieto (*sestina*). Santagata 332

Or avess'io un sì pietoso stile   IX   49
che Laura mia potesse tôrre a Morte,
come Euridice Orpheo sua senza rime,
ch'i' viverei anchor più che mai lieto!
S'esser non pò, qualchuna d'este notti
chiuda omai queste due fonti di pianto.   54

[Had I but a style able to arouse such pity, that I might snatch my Laura from Death, as did Orpheus his Euridice without rhymed verse, so that I might again live more than ever happy! If it cannot be, may one of these nights now close these two founts of tears.]

The ninth stanza in a double *sestina* of 12 stanzas + 3-l. *congedo*.   50 f. See Ov., *Met.* X.3 ff.; see also the vision of Laura as Euridice in the final stanza of

Standomi un giorno... (Santagata 323); the name of Euridice is not mentioned, but the reference to the snake bite which caused her death (*Met.* X.8–10) makes the identification clear: 69 *punta poi nel tallon d'un picciol angue,* | *come fior colto langue,* | *lieta si dipartio, nonché secura.* | *Ahi, nulla, altro che pianto, al mondo dura!* (bitten then in the heel by a small snake, as a plucked flower droops, happy she departed and secure. Alas, nothing other than lament remains in the world).   51 *senza rime*: for suggested interpretations see Santagata 332.51 n. Since *rime* had been placed at the end of a line in stanza I, the form of the double *sestina* + *congedo* required its repetition in the same position (with differing order of lines) in each of the following stanzas and the *congedo*, i.e. a total of 13 occurrences of the word. The demands of this technical *tour de force* may suffice to explain the obscurity of the phrase.

Petrarch **11**

Il mio adversario . . . (sonetto). Santagata 45

Il mio adversario in cui veder solete	1
gli occhi vostri ch'Amore e 'l ciel honora,	
colle non sue bellezze v'innamora	
più che 'n guisa mortal soavi et liete.	4
Per consiglio di lui, donna, m'avete	
scacciato del mio dolce albergo fora:	
misero exilio, avegna ch'i' non fôra	
d'abitar degno ove voi sola siete.	8
Ma s'io v'era con saldi chiovi fisso,	
non devea specchio farvi per mio danno,	
a voi stessa piacendo, aspra et superba.	11
Certo, se vi rimembra di Narcisso,	
questo et quel corso ad un termino vanno,	
benché di sì bel fior sia indegna l'erba.	14

[My enemy, in whom you are wont to see your eyes, which Love and heaven honour, makes you in love with beauties not his own, beauties gentle and joyous, surpassing mortal form. At his prompting, lady, you have banished me from my sweet refuge, a wretched exile, although I would not be worthy to live where you alone dwell. But had I been fixed there with firm bonds, a mirror would not make you, causing hurt to me, pleasing to yourself, harsh and proud. Indeed, if you remember Narcissus, your conduct and his lead to the same end, although the grass would be unworthy of so beautiful a flower.]

1 *il mio adversario*: explained by *specchio* in l. 10.   6 *mio dolce albergo*: Laura's heart.   9 *chiovi*: lit. 'nails'.   12 *Narcisso*: cf. Rin. Aq. 1.32 n.; Bern. Vent. 1.23 f. n. (in association with the mirror of the lady's eyes).   14 *di sì bel fior*: on death Narcissus was changed into a flower with yellow centre surrounded by white petals (*Met.* III. 509 *croceum per corpore florem* | *inveniunt foliis medium cingentibus albis*); were Laura likewise to be changed into a flower, its (earthly) setting would be unworthy of it.

Petrarch **12**

Quand'io veggio . . . (*sonetto*). Santagata 291

Quand'io veggio dal ciel scender l'Aurora   1
co la fronte di rose et co' crin d'oro,
Amor m'assale, ond'io mi discoloro,
et dico sospirando: Ivi è Laura ora.   4
O felice Titon, tu sai ben l'ora
da ricovrare il tuo caro tesoro:
ma io che debbo far del dolce alloro?
che se 'l vo' riveder, conven ch'io mora.   8

[When I see Aurora descending from heaven with rosy brow and golden
hair, Love assails me, so that I grow pale, and say with sighs: there now is
Laura. Oh happy Tithonus, you well know the hour when you will regain
your dear treasure: but I, what can I do to recover the sweet laurel? – for
if I wish to see it again, I must die.]

The octave of the sonnet.   1 *l'Aurora*: the goddess of dawn, married to
Tithonus, whom she carried off from earth to her palace in the furthermost
East. There is elaborate play on the rhymes in -*ora*, -*oro*, the identification
of Laura with Aurora being suggested by the rhyme *l'Aurora*: *Laur(a) ora*.
2 *la fronte di rose* . . . *crin d'oro*: attributes applicable to both Aurora and Laura.
5 *l'ora*: the hour of night, when Aurora returns to heaven and to Tithonus.
7 *del dolce alloro*: for the identification Laura/Daphne/laurel see **1.34** n.

Petrarch **13**

Quando giunse a Simon l'alto concetto (*sonetto*). Santagata 78

Pigmalïon, quanto lodar ti dêi   12
de l'imagine tua, se mille volte
n'avesti quel ch'i' sol una vorrei.   14

[Pygmalion, how you must have rejoiced in your creation, if a thousand
times you obtained from it that which I could wish for only once.]

The second half of the sestet.   This sonnet, like 77, describes a drawing
of Laura by Simone Martini. The poet wishes that the artist had been able
to give Laura's image, which is of gentler and more merciful aspect than in
life, a voice and understanding, that she might respond.   12 *Pigmalïon*:
see *Met.* X.243 ff. Pygmalion fell in love with the statue of a beautiful woman
he had created, and in answer to his prayers, Venus brought the figure to life.
14 *quel ch'i' sol una vorrei*: i.e. a response to my pleas.

Petrarch **14**

Dodici donne honestamente lasse (*sonetto*). Santagata 225

Non cose humane, o visïon mortale: 12
felice Autumedon, felice Tiphi,
che conduceste sì leggiadra gente!   14

[Not human forms or mortal vision, happy Automedon, happy Tiphys,
who conveyed so graceful a company!]

The second half of the sestet, which has the rhyme s*chifi* : *Tiphi.*   The poet describes a vision of twelve ladies, like twelve stars, with Laura, their sun, at the centre, first in a boat, surpassing even the vessel which carried Jason in pursuit of the golden fleece or that which brought Paris to Troy, and secondly in a carriage. This explains the identifications in l. 13.   13 *Autumedon*: Automedon, the charioteer of Achilles; Tiphys, the helmsman of the *Argo*, vessel of the Argonauts; cf. Ovid **6**.5 ff., in which the two names are also paired.

Petrarch 15

Se Vergilio et Homero . . . (*sonetto*). Santagata 186

Se Vergilio et Homero avessin visto	1
quel sole il qual vegg'io con gli occhi miei,	
tutte lor forze in dar fama a costei	
avrian posto, et l'un stil coll'altro misto:	4
di che sarebbe Enea turbato et tristo,	
Achille, Ulixe et gli altri semidei,	
et quel che resse anni cinquantasei	
sì bene il mondo, et quel ch'ancise Egisto.	8
Quel fiore anticho di vertuti et d'arme	
come sembiante stella ebbe con questo	
novo fior d'onestate et di bellezze!	11
Ennio di quel cantò ruvido carme,	
di quest' altro io: et oh pur non molesto	
gli sia il mio ingegno, e 'l mio lodar non sprezze!	14

[If Virgil and Homer had seen that sun which I see with my eyes, they would have devoted all their powers to bestowing fame on her, mingling the one style with the other; I declare that Aeneas would be troubled and sad, Achilles, Ulysses and the other demi-gods, and he who ruled the world so well for fifty-six years, and he whom Aegisthus slew. That antique flower of virtue and of arms, what a similar fate he shared with that new flower of honour and beauty! Ennius sang of him an unpolished song, of that other I sing: and oh, may my poetic talent yet not be injurious to her, and may my praise be not detraction!]

4 *et l'un stil* . . .: i.e. mingling the elegiac and the tragic style (Santagata, p. 810 n.).   7 *et quel che resse* . . .: Augustus.   8 *et quel ch'ancise* . . .: Agamemnon.   9 *quel fiore anticho* . . .: Scipio Africanus.   12–14: the implication is that Scipio and Laura, although both of surpassing excellence, are celebrated by poets of lesser stature, whereas only Homer and Virgil would be worthy to sing of Laura; see also sonnet 187, contrasting Achilles, fortunate in being celebrated by Homer, with Laura, dependent on the poet's deficient style (*mio stil frale*), although worthy of Homer, Orpheus and Virgil.

Petrarch **16**

Que' che 'n Tesaglia . . . (sonetto). Santagata 44

Que' che 'n Tesaglia ebbe le man' sì pronte   1
a farla del civil sangue vermiglia,
pianse morto il marito di sua figlia,
raffigurato a le fatezze conte;   4
e 'l pastor ch'a Golia ruppe la fronte,
pianse la ribellante sua famiglia,
et sopra 'l buon Saùl cangiò le ciglia,
ond' assai può dolersi il fiero monte.   8
Ma voi che mai pietà non discolora,
et ch'avete gli schermi sempre accorti
contra l'arco d'Amor che 'ndarno tira,   11
mi vedete straziare a mille morti:
né lagrima però discese anchora
da' be' vostr'occhi, ma disdegno et ira.   14

[He whose hands were so ready in Thessaly to stain it red with the blood
of his fellow-citizens, lamented, when he was dead, over the husband of
his daughter, recognized by his well-known features; and the shepherd
who smote the brow of Goliath, lamented over his rebellious family, and
wept over Saul, as a result of which the proud mountain has great cause
to grieve. But you whom pity never moves, and who have your defences
always ready against Love's bow which he draws in vain, see me tormented
by a thousand deaths: though no tear yet fell from your lovely eyes, but
only disdain and displeasure.]

1–4 Julius Caesar at Pharsalus defeated his son-in-law Pompey; the latter fled
to Egypt, but was killed by ministers of Ptolemy and his head sent back to
Caesar. In sonnet 155, Caesar and Jove are cited as examples of those moved
to pity, just as the poet is moved by Laura's tears. In sonnet 102, by contrast, Caesar exemplifies feigned sorrow in his apparent grief at the death
of Pompey, and Hannibal feigned indifference to reverses of fortune – in the
same way the poet disguises his anguished lament with a semblance of joy.
5 f. *'l pastor*: David. Absalom's conspiracy against David: II. Sam. 15. David's
lament for Absalom: II. Sam. 18.33.   7 David's lament for Saul: II. Sam.
1.17.   8 David's curse on the mountains of Gilboa, the place of Saul's
death: II. Sam. 1.21.   9 lit. 'you to whom pity never gives the pallor of
sorrow'.   14 *disdegno et ira*: both words are semantically modelled on
their Oc. equivalents: *desdenh* denotes the lady's proud spurning of the lover;
ira has a very wide range of meanings including 'anger', 'vexation', 'sorrow',
and here denotes her displeasure at his presumption.

Conclusion

The primary sources from which the names in the exemplary comparisons in the Sicilian and Italian lyric up to the end of the thirteenth century (including Dante in his lyric poems, but excluding the *Commedia*) are derived, coincide in the main – with some exceptions – with those utilized in the troubadour and trouvère lyric. The troubadour lyric formed the model for the vernacular poetry of the Sicilian school, which then paved the way for the composition of poetry in the vernacular also in Tuscany and the North. It is therefore likely that the use of exemplary comparisons, together with the names of the exemplary figures occurring in them, was initially derived indirectly from knowledge of the troubadour lyric, or from imitations of that lyric, rather than directly from the primary sources of the names listed below. In contradistinction to earlier poets, Petrarch displays direct knowledge of both the troubadour lyric and of classical myth and history.

The exemplary comparisons and identifications are contained mainly in examples of the *sonetto* (which is an adaptation of the *canzone* strophe), and the *canzone* itself, with more instances in the former than the latter, particularly in the later poets. In addition, the following types of poem are also represented: *discordo* (4 exs.); *sestina* (2 exs.); *ballata* (2 exs.); *madrigale* (1 ex.); *sirventese* (1 ex., see n. *Mem. Bol.* 2); there is one single stanza (Lapo 1). *Il Mare Amoroso* is in a series of unrhymed, mainly hendecasyllabic, lines, but has thematic and formal affinities with the Oc. *salut*, and is presented from the first-person authorial standpoint customary in the lyric. Among the sonnets, there is the extended form of Lapo 2, and paired sonnets, sometimes referred to as together forming a *tenzone* – see Bonagiunta 1a and 1b; Donzella 1, Cino 4, and Binduccio 1 also form one half of a pair (see nn.).

Few poets make use of identification with an exemplar (for Petrarch's distinctive usage, see below). Most examples express similarity to, or contrast with, an exemplar, on occasion with emphasis on particular attributes: thus in Bonagiunta 1a, it is the poet's skill in choice of words which likens him to Folquet and Peire Vidal, and in Binduccio 1, Cino's supreme knowledge of love exceeds the proficiency of Tristan in music and that of David in words; in Chiaro (?) 1e, the lady praised has the knowledge of Morgana and the beauty of Helen; in Guittone 2a the beauty of Helen was less praised than the beauty, honour and pleasing qualities of the lady celebrated by the poet (see also Alb. Mass. 1, Petrarch 8 and 9).

The examples of comparison or contrast are very largely associated with the theme of love: most frequently the poet's love exceeds that of named figures; his fate mirrors that of doomed lovers (Narcissus, Rin. Aq. 1; Sicil. Anon. 3; Chiaro 4; Andrieus and Kahedin, *Mar. Am.* 5; Dido, Dante 1); more unusual is the comparison with the fall of Lucifer (Chiaro **3b**), or, in a different context, with the pains suffered by St. Laurence, Cino **3**; the poet's reactions are comparable to those of an exemplary figure (Paris, Rin. Aq. **2**; Lancelot, Sicil. Anon. **4**, *Mar. Am.* **3**). In the case of lovers customarily paired, it is unusual for the female name to be omitted, as it may be in the troubadour and trouvère lyric – only Sicil. Anon. **1** and Bonagiunta **2a**, in which solely the name of Tristan occurs, seem to be of this type. A few examples are associated with the theme of poetic skill: Bonagiunta **1a** and **1b**; Maestro Torr. **1**; this is also the case in Donzella **1**, but in her reply, the poetess describes her art as serving love and those who love; in Binduccio **1**, Cino is praised primarily for his supreme knowledge of love, but the exemplars chosen, Tristan as harpist and David as psalmist, indicate the close link between the theme of love and its expression in art; in Petrarch **15**, the poet disparagingly compares himself with Ennius, in order to indicate that his skill is insufficient to celebrate Laura, worthy only of Homer and Virgil.

Whereas in the troubadour and trouvère lyric the theme of the lady's beauty and perfection is relatively rare, no doubt because of the dominance of male exemplars, it has become much more prominent in the Sicilian and Italian lyric. The lady is thus the focus of the comparison in Giac. Lent. **2**; Guid. Col. **1**; Sicil. Anon. **5a**; **5b**; **5c**; Chiaro **1a**; **1b**; **1c**; **1d**; D. Maiano **1**; Guittone **2a**; **2b**; Alb. Mass. **1**; Cino **2**; Petrarch **7**; **8**; **9**; see also *Mar. Am.* **1a**.134 f. In Donzella **1** and Maestro Torr. **1**, the lady is praised for her learning and poetic skill, but among the ideal figures with whom she is compared, *Morgana* in the former, and *Isaotta* in the latter, are elsewhere praised as exemplars of beauty (for *Morgana* see Chiaro **1a**; **1b**; **1c**; Chiaro (?) **1e**; *Mem. Bol.* **2**; for *Isaotta* Chiaro **1d**; D. Maiano **1**). In *Mar. Am.* **1a**.134, the *comparatum* is *dea d'amare*, in Alb. Mass. **1**.9 *d'amare la dea*, in Petrarch **7**.1 *Dïana*, which are the only instances of divine exemplars.

There are a few unusual examples: the lady is negatively compared with Cain in Chiaro **2a**, and with Judas in Chiaro **2b** and *Mar. Am.* **1b**; *Mar. Am.* **2** expresses the wish that the lady might appear to others like the ugly figure of *la Pulzella Laida*. In Cino **2**, the lady is inappropriately compared with *Ettor di Troia* (but this was probably simply occasioned by the need for a rhyme in -*oia*), and in *Mem. Bol.* **1**, the female speaker likens herself to male heroes. In Petrarch **11**, Laura's fate, if she persists in self-love, is compared with that of Narcissus, usually an exemplar of the male lover. A few examples are more general in nature and more closely akin to *exempla* than to exemplary comparisons: thus in Sicil. Anon. **2**, *Tristano* and *Isaotta* bear witness to the indissolubility of love; in Guittone **1**, the comparison with Julius Caesar is applied to men in general, in their attempt to subordinate women; Chiaro **2b** combines the specific comparison with Judas with a general reference to Virgil as victim of love (see also **2b**. 21 n.); in the first part of Petrarch **16**,

Caesar and David serve as general examples of those moved to pity, but in the sestet a specific contrast is drawn with Laura, who is never so moved. Cino 1 is an unique example, in that it combines types of metamorphosis paralleled in classical literature, in this instance that into a tree (the lady) and that into a bird (the poet) – see n.

The exemplary figures may have more than one function, but this seems to be less common than in the troubadour lyric, no doubt because of the almost exclusive concentration on themes of love: thus in Guittone 1, Julius Caesar is cited for his arduous efforts to conquer the world, but in Petrarch 16 as one capable of pity; Tristan is almost invariably the perfect lover, but in Binduccio 1 he is praised for his musical skill; Virgil is presented as a victim of love in Chiaro 2b, but as a supreme poet in Petrarch 15.

There likewise seem to be comparatively few references to narrative situations associated with the exemplars: Giac. Lent. 1, Re Giov. 1, and Binduccio 1 refer to details of the Tristan story; Rin. Aq. 1, Sicil. Anon. 3, Chiaro 4 , and *Mar. Am.* 1a include details of the story of Narcissus, Petrarch 7 of the encounter between Diana and Actaeon; Sicil. Anon. 4 refers to Lancelot's escape from captivity, *Mar. Am.* 3 to his conquest of the *Val d'i Falsamanti*; Amico 1 refers to Cato's sufferings in N. Africa (and, very unusually, cites an actual source in Lucan); Petrarch 16 alludes to Caesar's defeat of Pompey.

The main sources from which the names in the exemplary comparisons are derived are the following: classical literature and legend; the Bible; history and historical legend; the Tristan story; Arthurian romances; other Romance narratives.[9]

Classical literature and legend: *Parisi– Alena* Rin. Aq. 2; Fil. Mess. 1; D. Maiano 2; Guittone 2b; Alb. Mass. 1;[10] *Pari* Bonagiunta 1a; *Alena* Sicil. Anon. 5c; Chiaro 1b; (?)1c; *Alena en Troia* Guittone 2a; see also *Leda . . . sua figlia* Petrarch 8; *chi recò con sua vaga bellezza| in Grecia affanni, in Troia ultimi stridi* Petrarch 9. *Piramo– Tisbia* Pier Vign. 1; R. Filippi 1; *Tisbia* Chiaro 1a; 1b; 1c; 1d. *Narciso* Rin. Aq. 1; Sicil. Anon. 3; Chiaro 4; *Mar. Am.* 1a; Petrarch 11. *Polissena* (emended) Sicil. Anon. 5c (see also under Petrarch 9 below). *Venùs* Bonagiunta 1a; cf. *dea d'amare, Mar. Am.* 1a.134; *d'amore la dea* Alb. Mass. 1. *Vergilio* Chiaro 2b; Petrarch 15. *Pelëo* J. Mostacci 1; see variant spellings of the name: Chiaro 3a; 3b; Giov. Arezzo 1; T. Faenza 1; *Mar. Am.* 1a. *Didalùs, Mar. Am.* 4. *Sibilla* Maestro Torr. 1. *Ettor di Troia* Cino 2. *Dafne* Cino 4; see *ibid.*, *quella di Peneo* (on the pattern of the patronymic *Peneia*), and the indirect

---

[9] Except for the variants *Isalda/Isolda/Is(a)otta*, the names are normally given in the orthographical form, and in the case of paired names, in the order, of their first occurrence. Names usually paired are cited separately if they occur singly.

[10] Unusually in *Cantilene e ballate*, ed. Carducci CXIV, Paris is paired both with *Oenone*, whom he abandoned, and with *Elena*, to exemplify the poet's desertion of one object of love for another.

refs. Petrarch **1–6**. *Pollicreto* Binduccio **1**. *Dido* Dante **1**. *Apollo* Petrarch **1**; **2**; **5**; cf. *Phebo* Petrarch **3**, and *il Sol(e)* replacing the name Cino **4** and Petrarch **3**; **4**. *Medusa* Petrarch **5**. *Dïana* Petrarch **7**. *Polixena, Ysiphile, Argia* Petrarch **9**; see also *ibid.*, the circumlocution under *Alena* above, and *la bella romana* for Lucretia. *Euridice – Orpheo* Petrarch **10**. *l'Aurora – Titon* Petrarch **12**. *Pigmalïon* Petrarch **13**. *Autumedon, Tiphi* Petrarch **14**. *Vergilio, Homero, Enea, Achille, Ulixe, Ennio* Petrarch **15**; see also *nel gran vecchio mauro* (Atlas) Petrarch **5**; *quel ch'ancise Egisto* (Agamemnon) Petrarch **15**.

The Bible: *Cain* Chiaro **2a**. *Giuda* Chiaro **2b**; *Giuda giudeo, Mar. Am.* **1b**. *Adamo, Mem. Bol.* **2**; cf. also Chiaro **2b**.21 n. *Luzefer* Chiaro **3b**. *I Magi* Lapo **1**. *Absalone, Sansone, Salamone* Lapo **2** (see n.); cf. also *Sansone* Chiaro **2b**.21 n. *David* Binduccio **1**; cf. *e'l pastor ch'a Golia ruppe la fronte* Petrarch **16**. *Saùl* Petrarch **16**.

History and historical legend: *Iulio Cesar* Guittone **1**; cf. *que' che 'n Tessaglia ebbe le man' sì pronte | a farla del civil sangue vermiglia* Petrarch **16**. *Lorenzo* Cino **3** (cf. also *ibid. Benedetto*). *Cato di Roma* Amico **1**. See also *quel che resse anni cinquantasei | sì bene il mondo* (Augustus); *quel fiore anticho di vertuti et d'arme* (Scipio) Petrarch **15**; *il marito di sua figlia* (Pompey) Petrarch **16**.

The Tristan story: *Tristano – Isalda* Giac. Lent. **1**; *Tristan(o) – Isolda* Fil. Mess. **1**; Bonagiunta **2b**; *Tristano – Isaotta* Giac. Pugl. **1**; Re Giov. **1**; Sicil. Anon. **2**; *Tristano* Sicil. Anon. **1**; Bonagiunta **2a**; Binduccio **1**. *Isolda* Giac. Lent. **2**; *Isaotta* Sicil. Anon. **5b**; Chiaro **1d**; D. Maiano **1**; Maestro Torr. **1**. *Caedino, Mar. Am.* **5**.

Arthurian romances and later continuations: *Morgana* Guido Col. **1**; Sicil. Anon. **4**; **5a**; **5b**; Chiaro **1a**; **1b**; (?) **1e**; *Morgana la fata* (cf. also *morganata*) Chiaro **1c**; Donzella **1**; *Mem. Bol.* **2**. *Lancialotto* Sicil. Anon. **4**; *Mar. Am.* **3**. *La Donna del Lago* Donzella **1**. *Ginevra* Maestro Torr. **1**. *Ivano* Bonagiunta **2a**. *la Pulzella Laida, Mar. Am.* **2**.

Other medieval narratives: *Blanziflor* Sicil. Anon. **5b** (see n. on *Florio*); D. Maiano **1**. *Nadriano, Mar Am.* **5**. *Gostanza* Donzella **1**; *Rolando, Morando, Mem. Bol.* **1**; see also *ibid.* 25 *'l cavalier sens paura*.

Troubadour poets: *Folchetti, Pier Vidal* Bonagiunta **1a**; *Folchetto* Bonagiunta **1b**.[11]

Figures, mainly from different sources, are often grouped together for purposes of emphasis: *Alena – Pari . . . Tristano – Isolda* Fil. Mess. **1**; *nè Blanziflor, nè Isaotta* [*o*] *Morgana* Sicil. Anon. **5b**; *Tisbia Alèna né Morgana* Chiaro **1b**; *Tisbia o Morgana la fata* Chiaro **1c**; *Morgana . . . Elena* Chiaro (?) **1e**; *Isotta . . . e Blanziflore* D. Maiano **1**; *Nadriano e Caedino, Mar. Am.* **5**; *Morgana la fata né la Donna del Lago né Gostanza* Donzella **1**; *Ginevra . . . od Isaotta . . . divina Sibilla*

---

[11] Cf. Eustache **1** and OF Anon. **4** for the trouvère poets le Chastelain de Couci and Blondel de Nesle as exemplary lovers, but not explicitly as poets.

Maestro Torr. 1; *Rolando né 'l cavalier sens paura né lo bon duxo Morando, Mem. Bol.* 1; *Absalone, Sansone . . . e Salamone* Lapo 2; *Pollicreto*; *né 'l bon Tristan . . . né . . . David* Binduccio 1; *non Polixena, Ysiphile et Argia* Petrarch 9.

The proper names are frequently placed in rhyme (* indicates grammatical or punning rhyme): *salda* : *Isalda** Giac. Lent. 1; *pena* : *Alena* Rin. Aq. 2; *lontano* : *Tristano* Giac. Pugl. 1; *Pari* : *apari**; *Isolda* : *solda** Fil. Mess. 1; *Narciso* : *conquiso* : *assiso* : *diviso* Sicil. Anon. 3; *Morgana* : *vana* Sicil. Anon. 4; *sovrana* : *adorna* : *soggiorna* : *Morgana* Sicil. Anon. 5a; *sovrana* : *piana* : *Dïana* : *Morgana* Sicil. Anon. 5b. *Alena* : *Polissena* Sicil. Anon. 5c; *pari* : *Pari** Bonagiunta 1a; *Ivano* : *Tristano* : *sotano* Bonagiunta 2a; *Isolda* : *solda** Bonagiunta 2b; *Tisbia* : *sia* Chiaro 1a; *sia* : *cortesia* : *Tisbia* : *mia* (*Morgana* is unrhymed, see n.) Chiaro 1b; *data* : *Morgana la fata* : *morganata* Chiaro 1c; *Adamo* : *richiamo*; *Sansone* : *stagione* Chiaro 2b. 21 n.; *valore* : *Blanziflore* D. Maiano 1; *cantare* : *parlare* : *amare* : *Pare* D. Maiano 2; *Gioia* : *Noia* : *croia* : *Alena en Troia* Guittone 2a; *canpare* : *pare*; *paro* : *Paro** Guittone 2b; *amo* : *Priamo* R. Filippi 1; *pari* : *Pari** Alb. Mass. 1; *insegnata* : *Morgana la fata* : *presciata* : *mirata*; *orranza* : *Gostanza* : *nominanza* : *abondanza* Donzella 1; *dotta* : *Isaotta*; *Sibilla* : *villa* : *meravilla* Maestro Torr. 1; *sconfortando* : *Rolando* : *Morando* : *en bando*, Mem. Bol. 1; *contrata* : *plantata* : *Morgana la fata*; *bramo* : *Adamo* : *richiamo*, Mem. Bol. 2; *Absalone* : *Salamone* Lapo 2; *Ettor di Troia* : *gioia* Cino 2; *silenzo* : *sentenzo* : *m'agenzo* : *Lorenzo* Cino 3; *secreto* : *Pollicreto* : *alfabeto* Binduccio 1; *Cato di Roma* : *doma* : *soma* : *noma* Amico 1; *Dido* : *grido* Dante 1; *Apollo*; *collo* : *transformollo* : *crollo* Petrarch 5; *creda* : *Leda* Petrarch 8; *Argia* : *via* Petrarch 9; *fisso* : *Narcisso* Petrarch 11; *l'Aurora* : *Laura ora** : *l'ora* : *mora* Petrarch 12; *schifi* : *Tiphi* Petrarch 14; see also 15 *visto* : *misto* : *tristo* : *Egisto*. In *Mar. Am*, although there is no rhyme, several of the names are placed at the end of lines : *Pelùs* 1a; *Giudea, Giuda giudeo* 1b; *la Pulzella Laida* 2; *Morgana, Lancialotto* 3; *Caedino* 5. There are also instances of names at the head of lines: *Isaotta* Giac. Pugl. 1; *Isotta* Re Giov. 1; *Tristano* Sicil. Anon. 2; *Alèna* Chiaro 1b; *Vergilio* Chiaro 2b; *Iulio Cesar* Guittone 1; *Pelao* Giov. Arezzo 1; *Sansone* Lapo 2; *Achille, Ennio* Petrarch 15; in apostrophe: *Apollo* Petrarch 2; *Pigmalïon* Petrarch 13. As in the troubadour lyric, but not in that of the trouvères, a name may rhyme with another name. In several of the above examples, the proper name follows one or more words in the same rhyme series, which suggests that the choice of name is frequently determined by the need for a particular rhyme.[12]

---

[12] Poets may even introduce exemplary comparisons in inappropriate contexts for the sake of a rhyme: e.g. Guittone, ed. Egidi, 238 (political) *vostro son più non fu d'Enida Erecche* (*Mecche* 'Mecca': *pecche* : *Erecche*); Monte Andrea, ed. Minetti, 99 (political) *ed è più certo ch'è d'Alèna Paro* (in a series of grammatical and punning rhymes in *-paro* – see Fil. Mess. 1.10 n.); Cecco Angiolieri, ed. Lanza, 92 (a complaint of poverty) *e son più vil che non fu pro Tristano* (*mano* : *Tristano* : *foretano* : *villano*).

The stylistic device of identification usually takes the form of conferring the name of an exemplar on a new subject, which is thereby stated to be endowed with the attributes of the exemplar: of this straightforward type are *dirò che siate divina Sibilla* Maestro Torr. **1**; *felice Autumedon, felice Tiphi* Petrarch **14**. In *ma quella mi fu lancia di Pelùs, Mar. Am.* **1a**, the demonstrative *quella* appears to refer to *bocca*, thus identifying the lady's mouth with the lance, in its ability to inflict a wound with its kiss. In those poems of Petrarch, on the other hand, which allude to the myth of Daphne and Apollo, identifying Laura with Daphne and the laurel, the name of Daphne never occurs, but the identification is posited, as it were, as established fact. Laura is thus presented both as herself, and at the same time as Daphne and the laurel. She may be primarily identified with Daphne, as in **4**, with both Daphne and laurel in **1**, **2**, and **3**, or with the laurel in **6** and **12** – but in these examples too there is undoubtedly an implicit allusion to other aspects of the myth. Such complex affiliations are in part achieved by specific linguistic means, which serve to link the past of myth with present reality: the exclusive use of third-person formulations[13] in association with the figure of Laura/Daphne/laurel, which permits the combination of grammatical subjects and objects with differing semantic reference; the use of indicative verb forms in factual statements; combinations within the same context of past and present tense, in conjunction with precise temporal and local reference. In these poems, Petrarch's use of identification is quite different from that found elsewhere. The resulting examples are expressions of the highest poetic art, which cannot be reduced to, or analysed merely as, stylistic devices.

Most examples illustrate explicit comparison. There are two main types, that which expresses likeness to, or less often contrast with, an exemplary figure, and that, much more frequent, in which the subject is said to surpass the exemplary figure. Comparison is expressed primarily by means of adverbs: *altresì*; *così*; *come*; *sì come*; *similemente*; by verbs or verbal constructions: *asimigliare*; *simile m'avene*; *parere*; *pareggiare*; by nominal constructions: *a simiglianza di*; *come sembiante stella . . . con*; or by demonstratives *quello*; *quella*; *questo*.

Explicit comparison: *altresì finamente | come Narciso . . . | per sè si 'nnamorao | . . . così posso io ben dire | che eo son preso de la più avenente* Rin. Aq. **1**; *in gioi mi tegno tutta la mia pena | . . . come Parisi quando amav' Alena* Rin. Aq. **2**; *preso m'avete como Alena Pari* Fil. Mess. **1**; *como Pelëo non poria guarire | quell'on che di sua lancia l'ha piagato | . . . così, madon[n]a mia, similemente | mi conven brevemente | acostarme di vostra vicinanza* J. Mostacci **1**; *guardando la fontana, il buon Narciso | de lo suo viso forte 'namorao | . . . vogliendolo tenere,*

---

[13] It is noteworthy that only in poems without reference to the myth, as in **11** and **16**, is Laura (unnamed) addressed in the second person, and that the name Laura itself, as in **10** and **12**, or the punning reference *L'aura* in **5**, occurs in the context of third-person reference.

fue diviso | *da tutte gioie, e sua vita finao* | . . . *così cred'eo fenir similemente* Sicil. Anon. **3**; *chè sì faragio* | *come fece Lanc*[*i*]*allotto ver Morgana* Sicil. Anon. **4**; *m'inchino a te sì com' fe' Pari* | *a Venùs* Bonagiunta **1a**; *come Cain primero* | *di far crudele e fero* | *micidio fu, posso dire che sia* | *ella la prima ch'apare* | *di sì gran fallo fare* Chiaro **2a**; *a Giuda ben la posso asumigliare* | *che baciando ingannò Nostro Segnore* Chiaro **2b**; *così m'aven com' Pelàùs sua lanza* | . . . *così dich'io di voi* . . . Chiaro **3a**; *se quei che m'ha feruto* | *non mi sana com' Pelëùs sua lanza*; *ca simile m'avene ch' a·lLuzefer legato* Chiaro **3b**; *come Narcissi* . . . | *s'inamorao per ombra a la fontana* | . . . *com' a Narcissi paràmi piagente,* | *veggendo voi, la morte soferire* Chiaro **4**; *Pelao con sua lanza atoscicata* | *ferendo l'omo, no potea guarire* | *se no lo 'nde ferisse altra fiata;* | *sí mi vegio di voi , bella venire* Giov. Arezzo **1**; *c'a Pelleus la posso asimilgliare* T. Faenza **1**; *e ben parete dea d'amare,* Mar. Am. **1a**; *il vostro nome ch'è chiamato dea* | *saria mai sempre chiamato Giudea,* | *a simiglianza di Giuda giudeo,* Mar. Am. **1b**; *che per amor son morto in amarore,* | *sì com' è morto Nadriano e Caedino,* Mar. Am. **5**; *sì come i Magi a guida de la stella* | *giron inver' le parti d'Orïente* | . . . *così mi guidò Amore a veder quella* . . . Lapo **1**; *e m'ha percosso in terra, e stammi sopra* | *con quella spada ond'elli ancise Dido* Dante **1**; *l'aura celeste che 'n quel verde lauro* | *spira* . . . *pò quello in me, che nel gran vecchio mauro* | *Medusa quando in selce transformollo* Petrarch **5**; *certo, se vi rimembra di Narcisso,* | *questo et quel corso ad un termino vanno* Petrarch **11**; *quel fiore anticho di vertuti et d'arme* | *come sembiante stella ebbe con questo* | *novo fior d'onestate et di bellezze* Petrarch **15**; this is preceded in ll. 5–8 by a passage implicitly placing Laura above the heroes celebrated by Virgil and Homer, and is followed by an implicit comparison between the poet and Ennius: *Ennio di quel cantò ruvido carme,* | *di quest' altro io.* In a few examples, similarity is expressed by possession of an attribute of the exemplar, e.g. *ché di Morgana avete la scïenza* | *e d'Elena bellezza* Chiaro (?) **1e**; *non sai tu, frate, quant'io son distretto* | . . . *e pròvonde la pena di Lorenzo?* Cino **3**. An implicit comparison is expressed in Sicil. Anon. **2**: *e non porria cangiar la sua 'ntendanza* | *chi sente forza d'amorosa sprone;* | *e di ciò portan la testimonianza* | *Tristano e Isaotta co ragione,* but this is a special case: the generalizing third-person formulations, and the use of the word *testimonianza* show its close similarity to an *exemplum*, rather than to an exemplary comparison proper.

Some examples of comparison are expressed in terms of a wish or hypo-thesis: *ed io vorrei bene, s'esser potesse,* | *che voi pareste a tutta l'altra gente* | *sì com parïa la Pulzella Laida,* Mar. Am. **2**; *e se non fosse ancora conquistata* | *la Val d'i Falsamanti di Morgana,* | *io la conquisterei per Lancialotto,* Mar. Am. **3**; *sapesse almeno volar sì com' seppe* | *lo saggio Didalùs anticamente,* Mar. Am. **4**; *bel mi trovasse come fu Absalone,* | *Sansone pareggiasse e Salamone* Lapo **2**; *e se d'Amor non semo amanti,* †*fòra* | *come Dafne del Sol*† Cino **4**; *or avess' io un sì pietoso stile* | *che Laura mia potesse tôrre a Morte,* | *come Euridice Orpheo sua* . . . Petrarch **10**.

In other instances, there is a contrast with the exemplar, expressed by an adversative statement introduced by *ma*, or clauses containing contrasting elements: *o felice Titon, tu sai ben l'ora* | *da ricovrare il tuo caro tesoro:* | *ma io che debbo far del dolce alloro?* Petrarch 12; *Pigmalïon, quanto lodar ti dêi* | *de l'imagine tua, se mille volte* | *n'avesti quel ch'i' sol una vorrei* Petrarch 13; (Caesar and David were moved to pity) *ma voi che mai pietà non discolora,* | ... *mi vedete straziare a mille morti:* | *né lagrima però discese anchora* | *da' be' vostr' occhi, ma disdegno et ira* Petrarch 16.

The motif of outdoing the exemplar is expressed by means of positive constructions containing the adverb + conjunction *più che*; forms of the verbs *avanzare*; *passare*; *se contendre*; *perdre*; the adjective *sotano*. Much more frequent, however, are constructions containing negative particles in conjunction with *sì*; *come*; *più*; *tanto*; *altretanto*; *quanto*; with the verbs *parere*; *se pareggiare*; with the undeclined adj. *pari*, or the indef. pronoun *alcuna*; cf. also the negative form *nesuna*; contrast with the exemplar may be expressed by *ver*, *inver*: *Tristano Isalda* | *non amau sì forte* Giac. Lent. 1; *e direi como v'amai lungiamente,* | *più ca Piramo Tisbia dolzemente* Pier Vign. 1; *e non credo che Tristano* | *Isaotta tanto amasse* Giac. Pugl. 1; *e non amò Tristano tanto Isolda* | *quant' amo voi* Fil. Mess. 1; *quella c'amo più 'n celato* | *che Tristano non facia* | *Isotta* Re Giov. 1; *la mia fede è più casta* | ... *e più lealtà serva* | *che 'l suo dir non conserva* | *lo bon Tristano* Sicil. Anon. 1; *di ciausir motti Folchetti tu' pari* | *non fu, né Pier Vidal* ... Bonagiunta 1a; *e messire– Ivano* | *e 'l dolze Tristano* | *ciascun fue sotano* | *ver me di languire* Bonagiunta 2a; *ed eo similimente* | *'nnamorato son di vue* | *assai più che non fue –* Tristan d'Isolda Bonagiunta 2b; *ond'eo di core più v'amo che Pare* | *non fece Alèna* co lo gran plagere D. Maiano 2; *Iulio Cesar non penò tempo tanto,* | ... *talor non faccia in donna om altretanto* Guittone 1; *cui più coralmente amo,* | ... *e che non fece Tisbïa Prïamo* R. Filippi 1; *ca, se Ginevra fosse od Isaotta* | *ver lor di lei se ne poria contendre* Maestro Torr. 1; *de quello ch'eo sun plu segura* | *non fo per arme Rolando* | *né 'l cavalier sens paura* | *né lo bon duxo Morando,* Mem. Bol. 1; *di voi servire ho disio e bramo* | *più che non ebe de lo pomo Adamo,* Mem. Bol. 2; *fra gli amanti cavalcate la rota* | *più che non fe' tra' pittor Pollicreto;* | *né 'l bon Tristan non seppe d'arpa nota,* | *né sì non seppe David l'alfabeto* | *com' voi sapete me' cui l'Amor dota* Binduccio 1.

The motif occurs frequently in association with praise of the lady: *più bella mi parete* | *ca Isolda la bronda* Giac. Lent. 2; *ché se Morgana – fosse infra la gente,* | *inver madonna non paria neiente* Guido Col. 1; *tu ch'avanzi Morgana* Sicil. Anon. 5a; *nè Blanziflor, nè Isaotta* [*o*] *Morgana* | *non ebber quanto voi di piacimento* Sicil. Anon. 5b; *preziosa più c'Alena* | *o* [*più*] *che Polissena* Sicil. Anon. 5c; *lo vostro viso aperto* | *che passa ogne altro viso di piacere* | *e ave più valere – e 'nsegnamento* | *che non ebbe Morgana né Tisbia* Chiaro 1a; *che non credo Tisbia* | *Alèna né Morgana* | *avesson di bieltà tanto valore* Chiaro 1b; *la più amorosa* | *che non fue Tisbia o Morgana la fata* Chiaro 1c; *ch'Isotta né Tisbïa per sembianza,* | <u>*nesuna*</u> *in gioia fue* <u>*sì*</u> *poderosa* Chiaro **1d**; *nulla bellezza in voi è mancata;* | *Isotta ne* <u>*passate*</u> *e Blanziflore* D. Maiano **1**; *ché la grande beltà d'Alena en Troia* | <u>*non fu pregiata più*</u> *. . .* | *che la beltate e l'onor e 'l piacere* | *de voi* <u>*aggio de fin pregio pregiato*</u> Guittone **2a**; *a onor de lei, che 'n beltat* <u>*pare*</u> | <u>*no li fo*</u> *Elena* Guittone **2b**; *voi, cui* <u>*no vé*</u> *in parte* | *. . .* <u>*alcuna dona pari,*</u> | <u>*non*</u> *Elena di Pari,* | <u>*né*</u> *d'amore la dea* Alb. Mass. **2**; *che* <u>*non credo*</u> *che Morgana la fata* | <u>*né*</u> *la Donna del Lago* <u>*né*</u> *Gostanza* | <u>*né fosse alcuna come voi*</u> *presciata* Donzella **1**; <u>*non fue sí bella*</u> *Morgana la fata,* Mem. Bol. **2**; *quella, che porta pregio di valore,* | <u>*più che non fece*</u> *d'arme Ettor di Troia* Cino **2**; <u>*non*</u> *al suo amante* <u>*più*</u> *Dïana piacque,* | *. . .* <u>*ch'a me*</u> *la pastorella alpestra et cruda* Petrarch **7**; *sì fatta che Leda* | *avria ben detto che sua figlia* <u>*perde*</u> Petrarch **8**; <u>*non si pareggi a lei qual più s'aprezza,*</u> | *. . .* <u>*non chi*</u> *recò con sua vaga bellezza* | *in Grecia affanni, in Troia ultimi stridi;* | <u>*no*</u> *la bella romana . . .* | <u>*non*</u> *Polixena, Ysiphile et Argia* Petrarch **9**.

    In the *canzone* and related stanzaic forms, comparisons may be placed at the beginning of the poem: Rin. Aq. **2**; Chiaro **3a**; Giov. Arezzo **1**; Lapo **1**; Petrarch **7**; at the beginning of other stanzas: Chiaro **2a**; **2b**; **3b**.IV; Guittone **1**; Petrarch **10**; at the end of the poem: Rin. Aq. **1**; Sicil. Anon. **1**; Bonagiunta **2b**; T. Faenza **1**; see also (in a non-stanzaic form) *Mar. Am.* **5**; in a final stanza: Giac. Pugl. **1**; at the beginning of the *sirma*: Chiaro **1a**; **1b**; **3b**.V; at the end of a stanza: Giac. Lent. **2**; Pier Vign. **1**; Guido Col. **1**; Sicil. Anon. **4**; **5a**; T. Faenza **1**; Dante **1**; at the end of the *fronte*: Petrarch **8**. In the sonnet, comparisons may be placed in the first half of the octave: Chiaro **1c**; Donzella **1** (+one l. of the second half); Maestro Torr. **1** (with the identification with *Sibilla* in the first half of the sestet); in the second half of the octave: Sicil. Anon. **5b**; Bonagiunta **1a** and **1b**; Chiaro **1d**; Guittone **2b**; Cino **2**; **3**; Petrarch **12**; they may take up the whole of the octave and the first half of the sestet: Petrarch **5**; the end of the octave and the beginning of the sestet: Guittone **2a**; they may spread over octave and sestet: Sicil. Anon. **3**; Chiaro **4**; Amico **1**; Petrarch **9** (the second half of the octave and the first half of the sestet); Petrarch **16**. Final placing is common: in the sestet: Fil. Mess. **1**; Binduccio **1**; in the second half of the sestet, i.e. the concluding lines of the sonnet: Sicil. Anon. **2**; Chiaro (?) **1e**; D. Maiano **1**; Cino **4**; Petrarch **11**; **13**; **14**; **15**. In the *discordo*, the comparison is placed in the third part of a tripartite section in Giac. Lent. **1**; in Bonagiunta **2a** it takes up a whole section.

    Most examples are presented from a first-person authorial standpoint,[14] and, as in the troubadour lyric, poets may make use of the first-person singular pronoun, not obligatory with the verb, to reinforce either comparison or contrast. Of the first type are Rin. Aq. **1**.35 f. *così posso io ben dire* | *che eo son preso de la più avenente*; Sicil. Anon. **3**.9 *così cred'eo fenir similemente*; of the

---

[14] A feminine first-person voice in association with an exemplary comparison is the exception: see *Mem. Bol.* **1** (but the speaker compares herself with male exemplars), and R. Filippi **1**.

second, Petrarch **12**.5 ff. (in this instance coupled with a parallel construction with the second-person pronoun *tu*) *O felice Titon, tu sai ben l'ora* | . . . *ma io che debbo far del dolce alloro?* Exceptions to the first-person standpoint are extremely rare: thus in Sicil. Anon. **2** and in Guittone **1**, the comparisons occur in the context of third-person generalizing statements without personal reference. Unusually, there is a first-person plural form in association with a comparison in *e se d'Amor non semo amanti, fôra* | *come Dafne del Sol* Cino **4**.[15]

Apostrophe is extremely common (* = with exemplary comparison, parallel, or identification referring to the person addressed). Apostrophe of the lady: Giac. Lent. **1**; **2***; Pier Vign. **1**; Fil. Mess. **1**.9 f.*; J. Mostacci **1**; Sicil. Anon. **5a***; **5b***, **5c***; Bonagiunta **2b**; Chiaro **1a***; **1d***; **3a**; **4**; Chiaro (?)**1e***; D. Maiano **1***; D. Maiano **2**; Guittone **2a***; Giov. d'Arezzo **1**; *Mar. Am.* **1a**.77 ff., 134*; **1b**; **2**; Alb. Mass. **1***; *Mem. Bol.* **2***; Amico **1**; Petrarch **11***; **16*** (see above, n. 13). Apostrophe of the male lover occurs in R. Filippi **1**. Other objects of apostrophe: Bonagiunta **1a*** (l. 2 *tu, Bonagiunta*); Bonagiunta **1b** (unnamed poet); Donzella **1*** (*gentil donzella*); Maestro Torr. **1**.10* (unnamed poetess, but see below under third-person reference); Cino **3** (*tu, frate*); Binduccio **1*** (*Cino*); Petrarch **2** (*Apollo*); **12** (*Titon*); **13** (*Pigmalïon*); **14*** (*Autumedon* . . . *Tiphi*). Direct speech occurs only in the fictive dialogue between mother and daughter in *Mem. Bol.* **1**.

There are also examples of indirect third-person reference to the lady: Rin. Aq. **1**; Guido Col. **1**; Giac. Pugl. **1**; Re Giov. **1**; Sicil. Anon. **3**; **4**; Chiaro **1b**; **1c**; **2a**; **2b**; Guittone **2b**; T. Faenza **1**; Maestro Torr. **1**.3 f. (see above); Lapo **1**; Cino **2**. There is a considerable degree of third-person reference in Petrarch: *la pastorella alpestra et cruda* **7** is a straightforward instance, which is in accord with the genre of the *pastourelle*, of which the poem shows knowledge (see *ad loc.*). Other third-person references are similarly of more usual kind: the poet's vision of Laura in nature in **8**, the description of her as surpassing all others in beauty and worth in **9**, or as *questo* | *novo fior d'onestate et di bellezze* in **15**. In other instances, the identity of Laura with Daphne and laurel, which lies behind the examples, makes the varying third-person reference to aspects of the figure grammatically and semantically much more complex. For instance in **1**.31 ff. *Con lei foss'io da che si parte il sole,* | *e non ci vedess' altri che le stelle,* | *sol una nocte, et mai non fosse l'alba;* | *et non se transformasse in verde selva* | *per uscirmi di braccia, come il giorno* | *ch'Apollo la seguia qua giù per terra,* the pronoun *lei* in the first line appears initially to refer from the perspective of the present to the poet's object of love, Laura, but with the phrase *et non se transformasse in verde selva,* there is a transition to Daphne as implied subject of the

---

[15] Cf. Petrarch **1** *e no ci vedess' altri che le stelle,* in which the first-person plural refers to the poet and Laura, in an allusion to the situation of the dawn song; Petrarch **2** *sì vedrem poi . . . seder la donna nostra sopra l'erba,* in which the plural refers to Apollo and the poet, in association with the identification of Laura with Daphne and the laurel.

verb *se transformasse*; this then gives rise to a shift from the present to a precise moment of the past in the temporal clause *come il giorno | ch'Apollo la seguia qua giù per terra*, in which *la* clearly refers to Daphne; retrospectively it now seems that *lei* in the first line designates a figure who is both Laura and Daphne.

There is in the incidence of exemplary comparison and identification in the Sicilian and Italian lyric up to the end of the thirteenth century (i.e. excluding Petrarch, whose usage is in every respect distinctive) a restriction both in type of poem and range of themes and exemplars. This is analogous to developments in the trouvère poets, by comparison with the troubadour lyric. Most instances treat the theme of love, and even those few examples which occur in association with the celebration of poetic skill are implicitly linked to this theme. Comparisons which refer the didactic motif of Love's victims explicitly to the poet himself are rare (see Chiaro **2b** n. 21).[16] The panegyric of male figures, attested in the troubadours, but not the trouvères, seems to be lacking in the Italian lyric of this period.[17] As in the troubadour and trouvère lyric, there are few examples of identification, except in Petrarch, whose usage of it is distinctive. The tendency, already seen in the troubadour poets, and greatly increased in the trouvère poets, to prefer the motif of superiority to the exemplar to that of comparablity is again evident. Because of the restriction of theme, it is rare for exemplars to have more than one function, and there are relatively few references to narrative situations. The Sicilian and Italian poets draw in the main on the same sources as the troubadour and trouvère lyric, but once more, as in the trouvères, there is a restriction to better known figures. Classical figures such as Biblis, Hero and Leander, names derived from the *chanson de geste*, the classical period of Arthurian romance, the *Roman d'Alexandre* are either missing altogether, or sparsely represented; some names such as *Rolando, Lancialotto, Caedino, Morgana, la Donna del Lago, la Pulzella Laida, Morando* are derived from later poems, or later continuations or adaptations of earlier material: of these, only *Rolando* and *Lancialotto* are paralleled in the troubadours and trouvères.[18] The story of Floire and Blancheflor, references to which are very common in the troubadours and trouvères, is represented only by two instances of *Blanziflor(e)*, and one of *Florio* (see Sicil. Anon. **5b** n.), and *Andrieus*, very common in the troubadour, but not the trouvère, lyric, occurs only once in the form *Nadriano* (*Mar. Am.* **5**). It is noteworthy that Petrarch in the fourteenth century draws mainly on classical examples, with a few biblical and historical instances, and disre-

---

[16] See in the troubadour lyric, Peire Vid. **1**; Falq. Rom. **1**.43 ff.; in the trouvère lyric, Couci **2**.

[17] It is attested in didactic non-lyric genres, e.g. the *Tesoretto* of Brunetto Latini, in which the dedicatee is praised as a second Solomon, resembling Alexander, Achilles, Hector, Lancelot and Tristan, possessing the eloquence of Cicero and the morals of Scipio and Cato. Troubadour exs.: Guir. Born. **2**; Gauc. Faid. **3**; Raimb. Vaq. **4**; **5**; Aim. Peg. **2**; Guir. Cal. **2**; Cerverí **1**.

[18] Ziltener 8704 and 9012 cites two instances of *Morge la fee* in narrative works.

gards medieval narrative altogether as a source. Most of the circumlocutions replacing names occur in Petrarch, no doubt under classical influence.

In the troubadour lyric, and to a lesser extent in that of the trouvères, it is common for poets to compose more than one poem containing exemplary comparisons, or poems containing more than one such comparison. Among the Sicilian and Italian poets there are several poets who utilize comparisons in more than one poem.[19] There appears to be among the examples only one instance of a poem containing comparisons in different stanzas: the comparison of the lady with Judas in Chiaro **2b** is linked by a reference to Virgil in the same stanza with the theme of love's victims, and this is followed by explicit comparisons with Adam and Samson as victims in two other stanzas. The most striking difference between the Sicilian and Italian lyric and the other branches of the Romance lyric is the emergence of the sonnet form. Of the examples cited, more than half occur in sonnets, and although the concision of the form mostly restricts the incidence of more than one comparison, there are a few exceptions: in Fil. Mess. **1**, a one-line comparison with Paris and Helen occurs in conjunction with that with Tristan; Bonagiunta **1a** links the comparison with *Folchetti* and *Pier Vidal* with that with the submission of Paris to Venus; in Maestro Torr. **1** the comparison with *Ginevra* and *Isotta* in the first half of the octave is combined with the identification with *Sibilla* in the first half of the sestet. In Petrarch **15**, the explicit comparison of the poetic fate of Laura with that of Scipio is framed by two implicit comparisons: that of Laura as surpassing the heroes celebrated by Virgil and Homer, and that of the poet himself with Ennius. Petrarch **5** combines the explicit comparison with Medusa with implicit identification of Laura with Daphne and the laurel at the beginning of the sonnet. There is considerable variety in the placing of comparisons in *canzone*, sonnet and other forms, and particularly skilful use is made of the structural elements of the sonnet in this respect. As in the troubadours and trouvères, there is a tendency towards final placing in both stanzas and formal divisions of the sonnet, and also in the poems as a whole.

---

[19] See Giac. Lent.; Rin. Aq.; Bonagiunta; Chiaro; Guittone; Lapo; Cino; Petrarch; see also, in a non-lyric form, *Mar. Am.*

Conclusion

The instances of exemplary comparison and, later, of identification with an exemplar discussed in the book cover a wide chronological spread from Homer to Petrarch, a range of languages and types of poem, yet there are many basic similarities which persist throughout, combined with developments characteristic of a particular stage in the tradition. The choice and portrayal of particular exemplars reflects the literary, historical, legendary, religious, and cultural traditions prevailing in a particular society at a particular time. These are usually mainly transmitted through the medium of writing, but they are no doubt also influenced by oral tradition. The epics of Homer have their origins in a pre-literate period, and are based on oral-formulaic traditions which predate written texts.

The general function of exemplary comparisons and identifications is that of emphasis and embellishment, lending weight and the authority of tradition to the expression of praise or blame. This may have different realizations, according to the type of work. In the epics of Homer and Virgil, the placing and function of examples is largely determined by the demands of the narrative. Indeed it is probable that exemplary comparison was originally a device of narrative. In non-narrative and lyric verse, the placing of examples is largely determined by the relative degree of prominence attaching to specific parts of the poetic structure, for instance the beginning and end of a stanza or poem. The wide range of types of poem and subject-matter in this very large group is matched by a correspondingly wide range of variations on the basic function of emphasis and embellishment. In both narrative and non-narrative verse, exemplary and other names may be placed at the beginning or end of lines, or sometimes in both positions.

In later and medieval Latin verse, exemplary comparisons and identifications are attested in poems in a variety of verse forms. In the different branches of the vernacular lyric, comparisons and identifications are firstly associated with isostrophic forms such as the *canso*, and the heterostrophic forms of *descort* and related types, and their equivalents in other languages, and secondly, with the monostrophic forms of the German *Sangspruch* and the Sicilian/Italian sonnet, which is a specialized adaptation of a single stanza of the formal type characteristic of the *canzone*; some examples occur in longer poems in couplet form. The introduction of rhyme in later Latin examples and its use in all the branches of the vernacular lyric had a decisive effect in enabling the names of exemplars to be singled out by being placed in rhyming position, on occasion rhyming with other names or made the subject of punning rhyme.

Homeric epic

Exemplary comparisons are first attested in Homeric epic as one type of simile. In Homer and Virgil they serve to enhance the status of characters, to focus attention on a particular character or one newly introduced, on key stages in the action, or a key theme, and their linkage with other similes or passages may emphasize their significance. Where they are placed in speech, they are more graphic and immediate, and may present a temporal or individual perspective differing from that of the epic narrator. In the *Iliad*, the exemplary comparisons are brief and descriptive, by contrast with the extensive dynamic similes which characterize the rest of the work, and all are explicitly formulated as similes by means of grammatical markers. Those of the *Odyssey* are in the main similar, except that a few have a more active element, and there is one implied simile, expressed solely by textual juxtaposition and lexical, semantic, and syntactic parallelism. Particularly in the *Iliad*, exemplary comparisons may form part of a sequence of related similes or passages. The majority of examples in the *Iliad* are set in the third-person epic narrative, but there are two examples in speech. Of these, *Iliad* 11 contains a hypothetical comparison. In the *Odyssey*, there are four examples in speech, and of these, two are presented explicitly from a first-person perspective: in the examples in speech, comparison is formulated in apostrophe in one instance each in the *Iliad* and the *Odyssey*, with a further instance of implied comparison in apostrophe in the latter. The authority of the speaker may lend further weight to the example, as in the praise of Penelope and censure of Clytemnestra in the *Iliad*, spoken by the shade of Agamemnon in the underworld. Two instances in speech in the *Odyssey* stand in ironic contrast to events already revealed in the narrative, in that the speakers are unaware that Odysseus has returned, disguised as a beggar. In the first instance, Penelope reveals to Odysseus in disguise her suffering and longing for death, just before they are due to be reunited. In the second, Antinous warns the disguised Odysseus that he will suffer the fate of the Centaur Eurytion, if he persists in the foolish attempt to string the bow, whereas the hearer or reader knows that Odysseus will be the victor in the contest, and that it is Antinous himself who will perish. The higher number of non-divine exemplary figures in the *Odyssey* permits increased allusion to related characters and stories; thus here the reference to Eurytion introduces an account of the battle of the Lapiths and Centaurs.

The *Iliad* and the *Odyssey* presuppose a world ruled by the gods, and the gods themselves therefore represent the highest ideal of exemplarity. In the *Iliad*, the warring heroes Aias, Hector, Meges, Pylaemenes, Aeneas, Idomeneus,

Meriones, and Automedon are compared directly with Ares; Briseis and Cassandra are compared directly with Aphrodite, and there is a hypothetical comparison of the unnamed daughter of Agamemnon with Aphrodite and Athena (*Il.* 11). There are also comparisons in respect of divine attributes: Agamemnon has eyes and head like those of Zeus, a waist like that of Ares, a breast like that of Poseidon; Hector has the eyes of Ares (and also of the non-divine figure of the Gorgon); the hair of Euphorbus resembles that of the Graces; Hector and Odysseus are equal to Zeus in counsel. In the *Odyssey*, there are direct comparisons of Helen and Nausicaa with Artemis, and of Penelope with Artemis and Aphrodite; Euryalos and Odysseus are compared with Ares; there are two comparisons in respect of divine attributes: Hermione has the form of Aphrodite; Odysseus likens Nausicaa to Artemis in beauty, stature and form. There are also comparisons with non-divine figures: Penelope compares herself with Aëdon, and is contrasted with Clytemnestra; there is an implied comparison of Odysseus with the Centaur Eurytion. This survey shows that in Homer the exemplars are predominantly divine figures, but that there are no direct comparisons with Zeus, the supreme deity; the only non-divine figures in the *Iliad* are the Gorgon, and in the *Odyssey*, Aëdon and the negative exemplars of Clytemnestra and Eurytion. The subject to which the comparison is applied (the *comparandum*) is predominantly male in the *Iliad*, but predominantly female in the *Odyssey*. In both the *Iliad* and the *Odyssey*, the different styles of naming, e.g. patronymic, indication of patrilineal descent, name plus descriptive epithet, and in the *Iliad* also name plus descriptive phrase, serve to reinforce the significance of the exemplary figures and the comparisons. Names are frequently placed in prominent position, at the beginning or end of lines, or sometimes in both positions.

Virgil, the Aeneid

By contrast with Homer, all the main instances of exemplary comparisons in Virgil's *Aeneid* have a dynamic, active element, in line with other similes in the work and the dominant (i.e. non-exemplary) type of simile in Homer. Verg. 1 is based on a Homeric model (see *Od.* 3). Six examples occur in the narrative, and there are also five brief passages in speech: of these, one contains a hypothetical comparison, and four have instances of identification. There is no instance of identification in Homer. All the passages in speech express the subjective viewpoint of the speaker. There are now only three comparisons with named deities: Dido is likened to Diana (in the passage based on the *Odyssey*), and Aeneas correspondingly to Apollo; Turnus is compared with Mavors (Mars). The other exemplars are non-divine figures: Dido in her frenzy is like Pentheus and Orestes; Aeneas is likened to Agaeon, and Turnus boasts that he will confront Aeneas boldly, even if he should surpass Achilles (this is the first instance of the motif of outdoing the exemplar, albeit in hypothetical form); there is an implied comparison of Camilla with Hippolyte and Penthesilea. For the first time there are instances of identification: of Turnus with Achilles, once in the words of the Sibyl, and once in the words of Turnus himself; Aeneas is identified with Paris, once dismissively by Iarbas, and once in Juno's prediction of the evils of the coming war. The majority of subjects to whom comparisons and identifications are applied are, as in the *Iliad*, male. As in Homer, exemplary names may be reinforced by the addition of descriptive epithets, phrases, or in the case of Agaeon, a relative clause, indicating the nature and significance of the figure. Of the examples in speech, three serve to enhance the characters, but in two instances the opinion of the speaker denigrates Aeneas. Again, as in Homer, names may be placed at the beginning or end of lines.

Latin poets from Catullus to Ovid

In the verse of non-epic type attested in the Latin poets from Catullus to Ovid, there is a wider range of subject-matter, a general increase in the repertoire of exemplary figures (including a few historical or legendary/historical figures), together with a decrease in divine exemplars, and greater syntactical variety in their presentation. Exemplary comparisons remain the dominant type, but there are also identifications in Propertius and Ovid, with one hypothetical identification in Catullus, and one negated identification in Horace. The theme of outdoing the exemplar is attested in Propertius, Horace and Ovid, but comparisons of likeness predominate. The formal evidence seems to suggest that exemplary comparisons may have originally been associated with epic narrative, since some early examples, e.g. two of those in Catullus, are in poems in elegiac couplets, akin to the weightier metre of the epic hexameter. This may also in part explain why there are relatively few examples in Horace (beside widespread mythological reference elsewhere in his work), since the short lines of many of his poems are ill-adapted to accommodate them.

Comparison and identification must now be seen against the general background of mythological reference, in that examples are frequently linked with parallels in characters and stories of myth, which serves to reinforce their significance: this is particularly striking in Propertius and Ovid. There are no longer any direct comparisons with divine figures, but many instances of indirect or implied comparison, or comparisons with divine attributes. Thus in Catullus, Junia is described as coming to her husband, as Venus came to submit to the judgement of Paris; when Catullus appears to imply a comparison of himself with Juno, in that like her, he is the victim of a lover's infidelity, he hastily retracts it, declaring it to be inappropriate for men to be compared with gods. In Tibullus, Apollo as herdsman serves as example to justify the poet's desire to till the fields to be near his mistress, but not as an object of comparison. Propertius declares Cynthia to be worthy of Jove, thus implying a comparison with Juno, and to have the bearing of the sister of Jove and Pallas. He cites Jove, Achilles and Hector as examples of vigour undiminished by love, but significantly identifies himself in this respect solely with the last two. Figures are often grouped together to emphasize the comparison: thus Propertius describes the tears and grief of his mistress as exceeding those of Briseis, Andromache, Procne, and Niobe.

Mainly as a consequence of the wider range of subject-matter, including in particular the theme of love, there is now greater variety of voice and person, resulting in new types of comparison and identification. There is a very considerable increase in the first-person authorial voice and presentation from a first-person perspective, together with a related increase in second-person address. Allied to this is an increase in instances of the poet himself as *comparandum*, and of female figures as both *comparandum* and exemplar. There are examples of comparison in apostrophe in Propertius, Horace and Ovid. As in Homer and Virgil, different types of naming – proper names, patronymics, designations of parental descent or of topographical origin, or combinations of these, and circumlocutions replacing the name which reveal details of the story associated with the exemplar – lend stylistic variety. Examples may be placed at or near the beginning of poems or books, or at or near the end, and names, exemplary and other tend, as in epic narrative, to be placed in prominent position, at the beginning or end of lines, or sometimes in both positions.

In general, the function of exemplary comparisons and identifications in this group of poets is that of emphasis, lending weight to praise or blame, but in particular, they may be a vehicle for the praise of the poet himself or his mistress, they may serve to raise the mundane to a higher level, to express humorous exaggeration or an ironic contrast, or to temper criticism. The more varied types of use show that exemplary comparisons and identifications had become firmly established as a stylistic device.

Latin poets from Antiquity to the Middle Ages

The Latin poets from Antiquity to the Middle Ages span an extensive chronological period and geographical area. By comparison with the earlier Latin poets, there is a wider range of poets, of types of poem, and of exemplary figures. Exemplary comparison and identification occur chiefly in the context of panegyric, praise of poetic skill, epithalamium, religious poetry, occasional verse, funeral lament and epitaph, and love and the praise of beauty. There are considerable developments in exemplary comparison and identification during the period: figures from classical myth are still common, and some authors use them exclusively, but exemplars from history or historical legend, the Bible, the Church, and the canon of classical authors are now added to the repertoire. Reference to related characters and episodes of narrative seem to occur mainly in association with mythological exemplars, as in Propertius and Ovid, and to a lesser extent with classical historical or legendary/historical figures. Groupings of figures from more than one sphere are common, particularly in reference to a male *comparandum*, which is the commonest type. A female *comparandum* occurs particularly in the epithalamium, and the love poetry of the Ripoll and *Carmina Burana* collections. There is a small number of direct comparisons or identifications with deities, for instance with Mars and Apollo in panegyric, with Venus in epithalamium, and with Venus and Diana in praise of a perfect woman, and comparison with divine attributes persists, beside frequent comparison with the attributes of non-divine figures. There is an increase in the instances of identification, and a few instances of combinations of comparison and identification. In the *Carmina Burana*, identifications with an exemplar occur in all types of poem, but exemplary comparisons are found only in the love poems. Almost half the examples of comparison now express the motif of surpassing the exemplar. There is greater stylistic, lexical, and syntactical variety than in the earlier Latin poets, including differing combinations of voice, and passages of speech, but a first-person perspective is relatively rare, except in some of the love poems. There is an increased incidence of comparison in apostrophe. In passages in speech, the choice of speaker, e.g. of Venus in the epithalamium, lends extra authority to what is expressed. Variety of naming, and indirect references replacing a proper name appear to occur almost solely in association with figures of classical mythology. As in the classical poets, names are placed at the beginning or end of lines, or in both positions, but now with instances of names in rhyme at the end of lines.

The placing of examples does not seem to be significant in longer poems, but in shorter poems there is one example of initial placing, and several examples of central or final placing. Instances of exemplary comparison and identification in panegyric, praise of poetic skill, epithalamium, funeral lament and epitaph, and love poetry illustrate the primary function of praise, which is particularly emphasized when the *comparandum* is compared or identified with several figures or their qualities. Exemplary figures are also cited in support of exhortation, and pleas or prayers for mercy. The motif of censure is infrequent, but the poetic theorists give examples to illustrate both praise and blame.

The vernacular lyric

There is a radical development in the next stage, represented at first by the troubadour lyric. There is a shift to the medium of the vernacular; to the dominance of rhyme, which allows most names to be placed in rhyming position; to a primary concentration on the theme of love and love service; and predominantly to presentation from a first-person viewpoint (for exceptions under these headings, see below under individual branches of the vernacular lyric). There is much less variety of naming than in the classical and post-classical poets: figures are referred to mainly by proper name, on occasion with the addition of a title of rank or descriptive adjective, with some circumlocutions and general designations replacing the name.

The troubadour lyric

The troubadour lyric is attested from the beginning of the 12th century, with instances of exemplary comparison from mid-century onwards, with a considerable number in poets writing in the second half of the century. Most instances of exemplary comparisons occur in the isostrophic *canso* and related formal types, with examples also in heterostrophic forms such as *descort*, and poems made up of couplets. The main theme with which they are associated is that of love, but themes of panegyric or lament are also attested. Comparison of attributes is common, particularly in the latter group, in which the subject of the comparison may be said to possess the distinguishing attributes of several exemplary figures. There are few examples of identification, and any references to related narrative works are mostly brief. Not all the well-attested poets use exemplary comparisons, but that they were considered a stylistic adornment is suggested by those poets who use them in more than one poem, or in more than one stanza of an individual poem. The *comparandum* is predominantly male.

There are now no comparisons with dcities or their attributes. Classical and historical exemplars persist, but are now probably mainly derived from vernacular adaptations of earlier material, rather than from the original sources. The few Biblical exemplars, including David, Solomon, and Samson as examples of Love's famous victims, are now cited almost exclusively in association with the theme of love. There are new vernacular sources from which exemplary figures are derived: the *chanson de geste* and related works, Arthurian romances, the Tristan legend, and other medieval narratives, some now lost. The name of an exemplary figure, e.g. Tristan, may be used as a *senhal*. Groupings of figures from different spheres are common. Because of the dominance of male exemplars, in allusions to pairs of lovers, the female name may be omitted, or replaced by a general designation, and in the few poems purporting to present a female viewpoint, the woman may compare herself to a male exemplar. According to context, exemplars may represent different qualities: thus Solomon is cited both as victim of love and exemplar of wisdom. There is a considerable range of lexical and syntactical features, and apostrophe of the lady is very common, but speech is rare. In spite of the high incidence of apostrophe, there are few examples of comparison in apostrophe. A first-person stance prevails almost entirely in the love poems. Names may be placed at the head of a line, but much more frequently at the end of lines in rhyming position, rhyming with other names, or rhyming only from stanza to stanza, which singles them out still further.

The placing of examples is significant: they may form the main focus of a stanza or other structural unit, or be placed in initial, central, or final position, with a strong tendency towards final placing in both stanza and poem. For the first time, more than half the comparisons express the motif of surpassing the exemplar. The examples mainly illustrate the primary function of praise: the poet's love or grief equals or exceeds that of famous lovers, more rarely they serve to stress the beauty or perfection of the lady; the subjects of panegyric or lament equal or exceed one or more exemplars or their attributes. The choice of the motif of superiority, rather than equality, to one or more exemplars may add further emphasis. Among the examples included, there is only one expressing censure: the woman poet Azalais exhorts a lady not to follow the negative example of Brizeida in rejecting her lover.

The trouvère lyric

The trouvère lyric was fundamentally influenced by that of the troubadours, on which it is mainly modelled, but by contrast with the latter, there are very few poets attested before 1160, with the majority belonging to the thirteenth century, and many anonymous items. Some poets to whom a substantial œuvre is ascribed have no examples of exemplary comparisons. Overall there is a restriction in the type of poem in which such comparisons are set, most examples occurring in the *chançon* and other isostrophic forms, with rare examples in heterostrophic *descort* and related types. There is an almost exclusive restriction to the theme of love, in which the poet praises his love as equalling or surpassing that of famous exemplars; there are a few instances of the praise of beauty. Examples of male panegyric, common in the troubadour lyric, are lacking. There is a reduction in the repertoire of exemplars to those better known; there is much less syntactical and stylistic variety. There are no longer comparisons with deities or their attributes, and few comparisons with attributes, and there are only rare examples of identification. The lady is seldom the *comparandum*, and as in the troubadour lyric, where pairs of lovers are cited, the female name may be omitted, or is grammatically subordinate, being placed in the predicate; the lady may be compared with male exemplars; in one instance the male poet, exceptionally, compares himself with Iseut. In one poem a woman author compares herself to Dido and Afelisse, but also to Adam. In four other instances ascribed to a woman, in one she praises her lover, likening their love to that between Tristan and Iseut, in one she compares herself to Adam, in one to Pyramus, and in one to Iseut.

In the later poems, particularly in the anonymous items, exemplary comparisons seem to have become a stereotyped device, often used merely to provide a rhyme. Reference to narrative motifs connected with the exemplar are usually brief. The sources from which a more limited range of exemplary figures are drawn are basically the same as in the troubadour lyric, with classical and legendary/historical figures probably derived indirectly from medieval adaptations. Now all the biblical figures cited are associated with the theme of love, and there is one innovation: two medieval poets, Le Chastelain de Couci and Blondel de Nesle are cited as exemplary lovers; there are a few groupings of figures from different spheres. Exemplary comparisons are usually placed in one stanza of a poem, with few poems having examples in more than one stanza; it is rare also for poets to use exemplary comparisons in more than one poem. Most examples are presented from a first-person standpoint, with instances of direct speech only in the dialogue of the *jeu parti* and one *pastourelle*. Comparison in apostrophe is rare. There is a higher incidence of third-person formulations in examples of a generalizing nature, more akin to *exempla*. Names are placed in rhyme, but there are no rhymes between names or in isolated rhyme, as in the troubadours. Now the majority of exemplary comparisons express the motif of surpassing the exemplar, often in syntactic structures of a repetitive and stereotyped kind. Their main function is that of praise, but they may express censure, occasionally of the lady (she shows the arrogance of Caesar or potentially that of Lucifer), but more often in general condemnations of false conduct in love.

The German lyric

In the German lyric, the instances of exemplary comparisons and identifications span the period from the second half of the 12th century to the beginning of the 14th, with relatively few poets belonging to the 12th century, the turn of the 12th and 13th centuries, and the first half of the 13th century, and most to the second half of the 13th century and beyond. The German lyric differs from the troubadour and trouvère lyric, in that there is a twofold strand of development, that of the *Minnesang* on the one hand, and that of *Spruchdichtung* on the other. To the first group belong mainly polystrophic poems on the theme of love, i.e. instances of the *Minnelied*, and in the 13th century, of the heterostrophic *Leich*, both decisively influenced thematically and formally by the Romance lyric; related to these are the so-called *buochel* in rhyming couplets in the *Frauendienst* of Ulrich von Liechtenstein, which are influenced by the Romance *salut*. Very few poets show direct knowledge of the troubadour lyric, most deriving their knowledge of it indirectly from the lyric of the trouvères. Thus it is significant that two of the earliest examples of exemplary comparisons are based on a poem by Chrétien de Troyes.The second group, that of *Spruchdichtung*, is largely monostrophic, consisting predominantly of single stanzas of a longer and weightier type, usually forming part of a series of stanzas in the same metrical form treating a range of themes, but within the series there may be loose thematic groupings of varying kinds. The themes of *Spruchdichtung* are mainly panegyric, exhortation, and occasionally censure; the theme of love is usually treated generally, without reference to the poet himself. Although some of the themes may coincide with those of the troubadour *sirventes*, the latter is of the same formal type as the *canso*, and there appears to be no evidence of Romance textual or formal influence on the German didactic stanzas, except that of an indirect kind, in that they take over the tripartite stanza structure characteristic of the *Minnesang* and ultimately derived from the Romance lyric.

The exemplars are in the main derived from the same general areas as in the troubadour and trouvère lyric, but there are no figures from the *chanson de geste* and related narratives. Exemplars from classical and historical/legendary sources, Arthurian romances and the Tristan story may be derived, not directly from Romance adaptations of earlier material, as in the troubadour and trouvère lyric, but indirectly from German adaptations of Romance or other versions of the stories, as narrative details and the Germanized form of some proper names may make clear. Biblical figures are not cited solely as instances of love's illustrious victims, but also as positive exemplars of virtue. There are a few exemplars derived from the Germanic heroic tradition, and a few names of classical and German authors. There are instances of comparison or identification of a female *comparandum* with female divinities or their attributes. Figures from the same or different spheres may be combined. In pairs of lovers, as in the troubadour and trouvère lyric, the female name may be omitted or replaced by a general designation. There may be detailed reference to associated narrative situations in the longer forms of the *Spruchstrophe*, the *buochel* of Liechtenstein, and the *leich* ascribed to Gutenburg.

There are different combinations of voice, with instances of apostrophe, and of direct speech in dialogue and exhortation, and, in association with the theme of love, a high proportion of presentation from a first-person standpoint (but none of a female first person), and of a third-person standpoint in the didactic stanzas. Comparison in apostrophe is very rare; exceptionally, Marner **3** consists of a series of typological identifications in apostrophe. The *comparandum* is usually male, except in instances praising the lady and her beauty. The comparisons may form the sole or main focus of a stanza, or be placed at the beginning or end of the stanza or poem. There are a few rhymes between names. Most examples in both *Minnesang* and *Spruchdichtung* illustrate the primary function of praise, with a few instances of censure in the latter, in keeping with the increased didactic element.

The German lyric is similar to the medieval Latin lyric, in the following respects: the comparison or identification of female figures with female divinities; particularly in the didactic stanzas, there are a higher number of identifications, many comparisons with attributes of the exemplar, detailed references to associated narrative situations, and instances more akin to general *exempla* (a feature found also in the OF lyric). Overall, there is also a roughly equal balance between comparisons of likeness, and those of superiority to the exemplar.

The Sicilian and Italian lyric

The Sicilian and Italian lyric was initially modelled on the troubadour lyric, but with a considerable chronological gap between its first recorded beginnings from about 1230, and the troubadour lyric, attested from the beginning of the 12th century. The troubadour lyric, in its original linguistic form, was well known and cultivated in N. Italy in the 12th century, and when from the end of the century it was imitated by Italian poets, they likewise wrote in the *langue d'oc*. It was only at the court of Frederick II at Palermo from c. 1230 that Sicilian and other poets began to write in an elevated form of the local vernacular, thus laying the foundations of the Italian lyric proper. The reason for this difference is that N. Italian dialects and the *langue d'oc* were linguistically similar and mutually comprehensible, whereas the dialects of Sicily were linguistically more remote from the *langue d'oc*, which therefore could no longer serve as a common poetic medium. After about 1250 or possibly somewhat earlier, N. Italian poets also began to write in Italian, and when Sicilian poets were collected in N. Italian manuscripts, the texts were Tuscanized, leaving only the rhymes in Sicilian form.

By comparison with the troubadour lyric, the Sicilian and Italian lyric shows a narrower range of themes and exemplars. The dominant theme is that of love, with a few poets linking this to the theme of poetic skill. There is a higher proportion of the theme of praise of the lady and her beauty than in the troubadour lyric, and consequently of female *comparanda* and exemplars. There are two comparisons with Venus, designated as *dea d'amare* and *d'amare la dea* respectively, and one, in Petrarch, with Diana. There is no panegyric of male figures, as in the troubadours. Most instances of exemplary comparison occur in the *canzone* and the *sonetto*, with a few in *discordo* and other types, and several in the *Mare amoroso*, a longer poem in unrhymed lines, akin to the troubadour *salut*. Most occur within one stanza, and several poets employ them in more than one poem; they are usually placed in a structurally significant section, with a strong tendency towards final placing in structural element, stanza and poem. Several prominent 13th-century poets have no exemplary comparisons, and Dante has only one in his lyric poetry, while using many, often of a type found elsewhere in the lyric, in the *Commedia*. There are few identifications, except in Petrarch, whose use of it is unique. There are a few examples which are more akin to general *exempla*.

The exemplars coincide in the main with those found in the troubadour lyric, but with a restriction to better known figures in classical literature and legend, classical authors, history and historical legend, the Bible, the Tristan story, a few other medieval narratives (with only one instance of the name *Rolando* from the *chanson de geste*), and a few troubadour poets; reference to Arthurian narratives is usually derived, not from earlier versions of the material, as in the troubadour and trouvère lyric, but from later continuations and adaptations. Figures from different sources may be grouped together for emphasis. Petrarch shows direct knowledge of both the troubadours and classical authors; he disregards medieval exemplars altogether and restricts himself largely to classical figures, with a few others from history and the Bible. There are a few references in other poets to narrative details of the Tristan story, to episodes of Roman history in Amico **1** and Petrarch **16**, and oblique allusions to the myth of Daphne and Apollo in Petrarch. Most examples are presented from a first-person male standpoint; a first-person female perspective is extremely rare, and in one instance the speaker compares herself with male exemplars; there is considerable use of apostrophe, but only one instance of speech in dialogue. There are a number of instances of comparison or identification in apostrophe. Petrarch's individual use of the third person in association with Laura/Daphne/laurel permits multiple semantic reference. There are rhymes between names, and names in grammatical and punning rhyme. As in the troubadour lyric, and more particularly in the lyric of the trouvères, the majority of comparisons express the motif of surpassing, rather than equalling, the exemplar. Most examples serve to express praise, but there are a few instances of actual or hypothetical comparison with negative figures such as Cain and Judas.

Certain features remain similar in all the classical, post-classical, and medieval examples included in the survey: the basic function of exemplary comparison, and later identification, to emphasize and lend authority to praise and censure; the overall predominance of male exemplars and of a male *comparandum*; the placing of comparisons and later, identifications, in emphatic position, in epic according to the demands of the narrative, in non-narrative, particularly lyric, poems, according to the relative prominence of structural elements, e.g. the beginning or end of stanza or poem; the placing of names at the beginning or end of lines, or in both positions. The main developments are the following: the introduction of identification with an exemplar, not found in Homer, and represented by only four short instances in speech in

Virgil; overall the greater range of types of poem and themes associated with comparison and identification, but with a restriction in the main to the theme of love in the vernacular lyric (with the exception of German *Spruchdichtung*); the increase in the incidence of the theme of beauty in the Sicilian and Italian lyric; the increase in the repertoire of exemplary figures, including not only figures of classical mythology (which remain the main type in Petrarch), but also those derived from the canon of classical authors, history, historical legend, the Bible, history of the Church, and medieval literature; the gradual decrease in divine exemplars, which are not attested in the the poetry of the troubadours and trouvères, but comparison or identification with male and female deities or their attributes survives in the medieval Latin lyric, with a few rare instances of comparison or identification of a female *comparandum* with a female divinity among the German and Italian poems; the existence of a greater generalizing element in the trouvère, German, and in part the Sicilian and Italian lyric, with instances similar to *exempla*; the introduction of rhyme, which permits even greater emphasis on the names; the greater stylistic and syntactical variety of expression, including the wider range of person and voice, and the increase in presentation from a first-person viewpoint; the gradual introduction of comparisons expressing the surpassing of the exemplar, which is attested in one hypothetical example in speech in Virgil and which then becomes the dominant type, exceeding comparisons of equality, except in the German lyric.

Similes of all kinds are an archetypal feature of world literature. The book examines one particular type of simile and its individual manifestations in different languages and literatures. In so doing it reaffirms the supreme importance of detailed textual and linguistic analysis in the study of literary and stylistic phenomena. The establishment of the precise details of the particular then forms the basis for general conclusions. This is shown to be true both within the confines of one language and literature, and by extension within groupings of interrelated languages and literatures. The results of such a study may thus transcend the boundaries of time, space, and established cultural and literary traditions.

Bibliography

The Bibliography is constituted as follows:

i) General reference works.

ii) Separate bibliographies for each chapter, including for chapters 4–8 general and reference works, collected editions, and editions of individual poets.

For chapters 1–3 see note on the texts, p. ix.

References to Loeb editions of classical poets, mainly in chapters 1–3, with a few in chapter 4, are given in summary form, without details of editors/translators or publisher (Harvard University Press).

GENERAL

Grant, Michael and Hazel, John, *Who's who in Classical Mythology*. London and New York, 2002.

Lausberg, Heinrich, *Handbuch der literarischen Rhetorik*. 2 vols. 2nd ed., Munich, 1960.

The Oxford Classical Dictionary. 3rd rev. ed., Oxford University Press, 2003.

The Oxford Dictionary of the Christian Church. 3rd rev. ed., Oxford University Press, 2005.

Preminger, Alex *et al.*, *The New Princeton Encyclopedia of Poetry and Poetics*. Princeton University Press, 1993.

CHAPTER 1. HOMER: THE *ILIAD* AND THE *ODYSSEY*

General

Macleod, Colin, 'A Use of Myth in Ancient Poetry', in *Collected Essays*. Oxford, Clarendon Press, 1983, pp. 159–70.

Moulton, Carroll, *Similes in the Homeric poems*. Göttingen, 1977. (Hypomnemata 49).

Editions

Homer, *Iliad*. 2 vols. I Books 1–12. II Books 13–24. 2nd ed., 1999. *Odyssey*. 2 vols. I Books 1–12. II Books 13–24. 2nd ed., 1995. (Loeb).

CHAPTER 2. VIRGIL: THE *AENEID*

Editions

Virgil, 2 vols. I *Eclogues. Georgics. Aeneid*, Books 1–6. Rev. ed., 1999. II *Aeneid*, Books 7–12, *Appendix Vergiliana*. Rev. ed., 2000. (Loeb).

CHAPTER 3. LATIN POETS FROM CATULLUS TO OVID

Editions of individual poets

Catullus. Tibullus. *Pervigilium Veneris.* Rev. ed., 1988. (Loeb).

Horace, *Odes and Epodes.* Rev. ed., 1968. *Satires. Epistles. The Art of Poetry.* 1926. (Loeb).

Ovid, 6 vols. I *Heroides. Amores.* Rev. ed., 1977. II *Art of love. Cosmetics. Remedies for love. Ibis. Walnut-tree. Sea fishing. Consolation.* Rev. ed., 1979. III *Metamorphoses,* Books 1–8. Rev. ed., 1977. IV *Metamorphoses,* Books 9–15. Rev. ed., 1984. V *Fasti.* Rev. ed., 1989. VI *Tristia. Ex Ponto.* Rev. ed., 1988. (Loeb).

Propertius, *Elegies.* Rev. ed., 1999. (Loeb).

Tibullus – see under Catullus.

CHAPTER 4. LATIN POETS FROM ANTIQUITY TO THE MIDDLE AGES

The bibliography is largely restricted to items relevant to texts included in the chapter.

General

Bittner, Franz, *Studien zum Herrscherlob in der mittellateinischen Dichtung.* Diss. Würzburg. Volkach, 1962.

Brinkmann, Hennig, *Geschichte der lateinischen Liebesdichtung im Mittelalter.* Halle a/S., 1925. Repr. Darmstadt, 1979.

Brunhölzl, Franz, *Geschichte der lateinischen Literatur des Mittelalters.* 2 vols. I Munich, 1975. II Munich, 1992.

Dronke, Peter, *Medieval Latin and the rise of European love-lyric.* 3rd ed., Oxford, Clarendon Press, 1965–6.

—— *Latin and Vernacular Poets of the Middle Ages.* Variorum, Gower House, Croft Road, Hampshire, 1991.

—— *The Medieval Lyric.* 3rd ed., Cambridge, D. S. Brewer, 1996.

Georgi, Annette, *Das lateinische und deutsche Preisgedicht des Mittelalters in der Nachfolge des genus demonstrativum.* Berlin, 1969. (Philologische Studien und Quellen 48).

Latzke, Therese, 'Der Fürstinnenpreis', *MJ* 14 (1979), 22–65.

Moos, Peter von, *Consolatio. Studien zur mittellateinischen Trostliteratur über den Tod und zum Problem der christlichen Trauer.* 4 vols. Munich, 1971–2.

Raby, F. J. E., *A History of Secular Latin Poetry in the Middle Ages.* 2 vols., 2nd ed., Oxford, Clarendon Press, 1957.

Sayce, Olive, *Plurilingualism in the Carmina Burana. A Study of the Linguistic and Literary Influences on the Codex.* Göppingen, 1992. (GAG 556).

Spitzmuller, Henry, *Poésie latine chrétienne du Moyen Âge, III–XV siècle.* [Paris and Bruges], 1971.

Steger, Hugo, *David, rex et propheta. König David als vorbildliche Verkörperung des Herrschers und Dichters im Mittelalter. Bilddarstellungen des achten bis zwölften Jahrhunderts.* Nürnberg, 1961.

Szövérffy, Josef, *Weltliche Dichtungen des lateinischen Mittelalters: ein Handbuch.* I *Von den Anfängen bis zum Ende der Karolingerzeit*. Berlin, 1970.

Collected editions

Analecta hymnica medii aevi, ed. Dreves, Guido Maria and Blume, Clemens. 55 vols. Leipzig, 1886–1922.
——— Blume, Clemens, *Ein Jahrtausend lateinischer Hymnendichtung. Eine Blütenlese aus den Analecta hymnica von G. M. Dreves*. Leipzig, 1909.
Appendix Tibulliana, ed. Tränkle, Hermann. Berlin, 1990. (Texte und Kommentare 16). (Tränkle).
The Arundel Lyrics: Meyer, Wilhelm (ed.), *Die Arundel-Sammlung mittellateinischer Lieder*. Abhandlungen der königlichen Gesellschaft der Wissenschaften zu Göttingen, phil.-hist. Klasse, NF XI. 2, 1908. See also under Hugo Primas, ed. McDonough.
Baehrens, P. H. Emil (ed.), *Poetae latini minores*. 6 vols. Leipzig, 1879–86. (*PLM*).
Carmina Burana (CB): Mit Benutzung der Vorarbeiten Wilhelm Meyers, hrsg. von Alfons Hilka und Otto Schumann. I *Text*. 1. *Die moralisch-satirischen Dichtungen*. Heidelberg, 1930. 2. *Die Liebeslieder*, hrsg. von Otto Schumann. Heidelberg, 1941. 3. *Die Trink- und Spielerlieder. Die geistlichen Dramen. Nachträge*, hrsg. von Otto Schumann und Bernhard Bischoff. Heidelberg, 1970. II *Kommentar*. 1. *Einleitung* (*Die Handschrift der Carmina Burana*). *Die moralisch-satirischen Dichtungen*. Heidelberg, 1930.
——— Vollmann, Benedikt Konrad, *Carmina Burana*. Texte und Übersetzungen. Mit den Miniaturen aus der Handschrift und einem Aufsatz von Peter und Dorothee Diemer. Frankfurt a.M., 1987. (Bibliothek deutscher Klassiker 13). (Vollmann).
The Cambridge Songs: *A Goliard's Song Book of the Eleventh Century*, ed. Karl Breul. Cambridge, 1915.
——— *Carmina Cantabrigiensia. Die Cambridger Lieder*, ed. Karl Strecker. Berlin, 1926. Repr. Berlin, Zurich, Dublin, 1966. (*MGH Scriptores*, XL). (*Carm. Cant.*, ed. Strecker).
——— *Carmina Cantabrigiensia*, ed. Walther Bulst. Heidelberg, 1950.
Faral, Edmond, *Les Arts poétiques du XIIᵉ et du XIIIᵉ siècle. Recherches et Documents sur la technique littéraire du Moyen Âge*. Paris, 1924. Repr. Geneva and Paris, 1982. (Faral).
Godman, Peter, *Poetry of the Carolingian Renaissance*. London, 1985.
Minor Latin Poets. 2 vols. Rev. ed., 1934–5. (Loeb). (*MLP*).
Oxford Book of Medieval Latin Verse, ed. F. J. E. Raby. Oxford, Clarendon Press, 1959. (*OBMLatV*).
The Ripoll Lyrics: D'Olwer, Lluis Nicolau, 'L'escola poètica de Ripoll en els segles X–XIII', Institut d'Estudis Catalans, Secció històrico-arqueològico. Anuari MCMXV–XX, vol. VI (1923), 3–84.
——— Latzke, Therese, 'Die carmina erotica der Ripollsammlung', *MJ* 10 (1975), 138–201. (Latzke).
——— See Dronke, P., 'The Interpretation of the Ripoll Love Songs', *Romance Philology* 33, 1 (August 1979), 14–42 for corrections to Latzke's text and further bibliography.

Spitzmuller, Henry (ed.), *Poésie latine chrétienne du Moyen Âge*. Bruges, 1971.

Werner, Jakob, *Beiträge zur Kunde der lateinischen Literatur des Mittelalters*. 2nd ed., Aarau, 1905. (Werner, *Beiträge*).

Editions of individual poets or works

Archipoeta: *Die Gedichte des Archipoeta*, kritisch bearbeitet von Heinrich Watenphul, hrsg. von Heinrich Krefeld. Heidelberg, 1958. (Watenpfuhl/Krefeld).

—— *Der Archipoeta: Lateinisch und deutsch*, ed. Heinrich Krefeld. Berlin, 1992. (Schriften und Quellen der alten Welt 41).

Baudri de Bourgueil: *Les Œuvres poétiques de Baudri de Bourgueil (1046–1130)*, ed. Phyllis Abrahams. Paris, 1926.

—— *Baldricus Burgulianus, Carmina*, ed. Karlheinz Hilbert. Heidelberg, 1979. (Hilbert).

—— *Baldricus Burgulianus, Carmina*, ed. Jean-Yves Tilliette. I Paris, 1998–.

Benzo of Alba: *Benzo von Alba, Ad Heinricum IV imperatorem libri VII*, ed. Hans Seyffert. Hannover, 1996. (*MGH Scriptores*, LXV). (Seyffert).

[Cicero], *Rhetorica ad Herennium*. 1954. (Loeb).

Claudian: *Claudii Claudiani Carmina*, ed. Theodor Birt. Berlin, 1892. Rev. ed., Berlin, 1961. (*MGH AA*, X).

Disticha Catonis see *Minor Latin Poets* II (Loeb).

Hilarius of Orléans: N. M. Häring, 'Die Gedichte und Mysterienspiele des Hilarius von Orléans', *SM*, ser. 3a, XVII (1976), 913–68.

—— *Hilarii Aurelianensis Versus et Ludi, Epistolae, Ludus Danielis Belouacensis*, ed. W. M. Bulst and M. L. Bulst-Thiele. Leiden, 1989. (Bulst/Bulst-Thiele).

Hildebert of Le Mans: *Hildeberti Cenomannensis Episcopi Carmina*, ed. A. Brian Scott. Leipzig, 1969. Rev. ed., 1996.

Hugh Primas: McDonough, C. J., *The Oxford Poems of Hugh Primas and the Arundel Lyrics*, ed. from Bodleian Library MS. Rawlinson G. 109 and British Library MS. Arundel 384. Toronto, 1984. (McDonough).

'Laus Pisonis' see *Minor Latin Poets* I. (Loeb).

Mathieu de Vendôme: *Mathei Vindocinensis Opera*, ed. Franco Munari. 3 vols. Rome. I 1977. II 1982. III 1988. (Munari).

Serlo of Wilton: *Serlon de Wilton, Poèmes latins*, ed. J. Öberg. Stockholm, 1965. (Öberg).

Sidonius Apollinaris: *Gai Sollii Apollinaris Sidonii Epistulae et carmina*, ed. Christian Luetjohann. Berlin, 1887. (*MGH AA*, VIII).

—— *Sidoine Apollinaire*, ed. A. Loyen. 3 vols. Paris, 1960–70.

Statius, 2 vols. I *Silvae*. Rev. ed., 2003. (Loeb).

Venantius Fortunatus: *Venantii Honori Clementiani Fortunati . . . opera poetica*, ed. Friedrich Leo. Berlin, 1881. (*MGH AA*, IV. 1).

—— George, Judith W., *Venantius Fortunatus. A Latin Poet in Merovingian Gaul*. Oxford, Clarendon Press, 1992.

—— *Venantius Fortunatus: Personal and Political Poems*, transl. with notes and introduction by Judith George. Liverpool University Press, 1995.

Walter of Châtillon: Strecker, Karl, *Die Lieder Walters von Châtillon in der Handschrift 351 von St. Omer*. Berlin, 1925.

—— *Moralisch-satirische Gedichte Walters von Châtillon aus deutschen, englischen, französischen und italienischen Handschriften*. Heidelberg, 1929.

CHAPTER 5. THE TROUBADOUR POETS

Bibliography and reference

Chambers, Frank M., *Proper Names in the Lyrics of the Troubadours*. The University of North Carolina Press. Chapel Hill, 1971. (Chambers, *Proper Names*).

Dictionnaire des Lettres Françaises: Le Moyen Âge. Rev. ed., [Paris], Fayard, 1992.

Distilo, Rocco, *Per le concordanze della lirica trobadorica. Incipit/Explicit*. Vol. I. Rome, 2000–. Part of a project to update and supplement the bibliography of Pillet/Carstens and the *Répertoire métrique* of Frank (*qq.v.*). (=D before numbering of troubadour poems).

Flutre, Louis-Fernand, *Table des noms propres avec toutes leurs variantes figurant dans les romans du Moyen Âge écrits en français ou en provençal et actuellement publiés et analysés*. Poitiers, 1962. (Flutre).

Frank, István, *Répertoire métrique de la poésie des troubadours*. 2 vols. Paris, 1966. (Frank, *Rép. métr.*).

Pillet, Alfred and Carstens, Henry, *Bibliographie der Troubadours*. Halle a/S., 1933. (=PC before numbering of troubadour poems).

Ziltener, Werner, *Repertorium der Gleichnisse und bildhaften Vergleiche der okzitanischen und französischen Versliteratur des Mittelalters*. Berne. I 1972. II 1983. III 1989. (Ziltener, *Repertorium*).

General

Akehurst, F. R. P. and Davis, Judith M. (eds.), *A Handbook of the Troubadours*. University of California Press, 1995.

Gaunt, Simon and Kay, Sarah (eds.), *The Troubadours. An Introduction*. Cambridge University Press, 1999.

Hackett, W. M., 'Ire, courroux et leurs dérivés en ancien français et en provençal', *Études de langue et de littérature du Moyen Âge offertes à Félix Lecoy*. Paris, 1973, pp. 169–80. See also Kleiber under chapter 6.

Jensen, Frede, *Syntaxe de l'ancien occitan*. Tübingen, 1994. (Beihefte zur *ZRP* 257). (Jensen, *Syntaxe*).

Pirot, François, *Recherches sur les connaissances littéraires des troubadours occitans et catalans des XII*[e]* et XIII*[e]* siècles*. Barcelona, 1972. (Pirot, *Recherches*).

Collected editions

Appel, Carl, *Provenzalische Inedita aus Pariser Handschriften*. Wiesbaden, 1892. (Appel, *Prov. Inedita*).

Bartsch, K., 'Die provenzalische Liederhandschrift Q', *ZRP* 4 (1880), 502–20.

Bertoni, Giulio, *I trovatori d'Italia*. (Biografie, testi, traduzioni, note). Modena, 1915.

Kolsen, Adolf, '25 bisher unedierte provenzalische Anonyma', *ZRP* 38 (1917), 286–310. (Kolsen, 1917).

—— *Dreissig Stücke altprovenzalischer Lyrik zum ersten Mal kritisch bearbeitet.* Halle a/S., 1925. (Kolsen, 1925).

—— 'Zwei provenzalische "partimen" und zwei "coblas"', *SM* 12 (1939), 183–91. (Kolsen, 1939).

Mahn, C. A. F., *Gedichte der Troubadours in provenzalischer Sprache.* 4 vols. Berlin 1856–73. (Mahn, *Gedichte*).

Nelli, René and Lavaud, René, *Les Troubadours.* Texte et traduction. 2 vols. I *L'Œuvre épique: Jaufre, Flamenca, Barlaam et Josaphat.* II *L'Œuvre poétique: le trésor poétique de l'Occitanie.* 2nd ed., Bruges, 2000.

Pelaez, M., 'Il Canzoniere Provenzale L (Cod. Vaticano 3206)', *Studi Romanzi* 16 (1921), 6–206.

Rieger, Angelica, *Trobairitz: der Beitrag der Frau in der altokzitanischen höfischen Lyrik.* Edition des Gesamtkorpus. Tübingen, 1991. (Beihefte zur *ZRP* 233). (Rieger, *Trobairitz*).

Riquer, Martín de, *Los Trovadores. Historia literaria e textos.* 3 vols. Barcelona, 1983. (Riquer, *Trovadores*).

Editions of individual poets

Aimeric de Belenoi: Dumitrescu, Maria, *Poésies du troubadour Aimeric de Belenoi.* Paris, 1935. (Dumitrescu).

—— Poli, Andrea, *Aimeric de Belenoi, le Poesie.* Edizione critica. Prefazione di Maurizio Perugi. Florence, 1997. (Poli).

Aimeric de Peguilhan: Shepard, William P. and Chambers, Frank M., *The Poems of Aimeric de Peguilhan.* Evanston, Ill., Northwestern University Press, 1950. (Shepard/Chambers).

Arnaut Daniel: Toja, Gianluigi, *Arnaut Daniel, Canzoni.* Edizione critica. Florence, 1960. (Toja).

—— Perugi, Maurizio, *Le Canzoni di Arnaut Daniel.* Edizione critica. 2 vols. Milan, 1978. (Perugi).

—— Eusebi, Mario, *Arnaut Daniel: Il Sirventese e le Canzoni.* Milan, 1984. (Eusebi).

Arnaut de Mareuil: Johnston, R. C., *Les Poésies lyriques du troubadour Arnaut de Mareuil,* publiées avec une introduction, une traduction, des notes et un glossaire. Paris, 1935. (Johnston, *Arn. Mar.*).

—— Bec, Pierre, *Les Saluts d'amour du troubadour Arnaud de Mareuil,* textes publiés avec une introduction, une traduction et des notes. Toulouse, 1961. (Bec, *Arn. Mar., Saluts*).

Arnaut Guilhem de Marsan: Sansone, Giuseppe E., *Testi didattico-cortesi di Provenza.* Bari, 1977, pp. 111–80.

Azalais d'Altier: Rieger, *Trobairitz* (see under Collected editions).

Bartolomeo Zorzi: Levy, Emil, *Der Troubadour Bertolome Zorzi.* Halle a/S., 1883. (Levy).

Bernart de Ventadorn: Appel, Carl, *Bernart von Ventadorn, seine Lieder,* mit Einleitung und Glossar. Halle a/S., 1915. (Appel, *Bern. Vent.*).

Bertran de Born: Gouiran, Gérard, *L'amour et la guerre: L'œuvre de Bertran de Born.* Édition critique, traduction et notes. 2 vols. Aix-en-Provence, 1985. (Gouiran).

—— Paden, William D. Jr., Sankovitch, Tilde and Stäblein, Patricia H., *The Poems of the Troubadour Bertran de Born.* University of California Press, 1986. (Paden *et al.*).

Bonifacio Calvo: Branciforti, F., *Le Rime di Bonifacio Calvo.* Università di Catania, 1955. (Branciforti).

Cerverí de Girona: Riquer, Martín de, *Obras Completas del Trovador Cerverí de Girona.* Texto, traducción y comentarios. Barcelona, 1947. (Riquer, *Cerverí*).

—— Coromines, Joan, *Cerverí de Girona, Lírica.* 2 vols. Barcelona, 1988. (Coromines, *Cerverí*).

Comtessa de Dia, La, see Rieger, *Trobairitz* under Collected editions.

Daude de Pradas: Schutz, A. H., *Poésies de Daude de Pradas*, publiées avec une introduction, une traduction et des notes. Toulouse and Paris, 1933. (Schutz).

Elias de Barjols: Stroński, Stanislas, *Le Troubadour Elias de Barjols.* Édition critique, publiée avec une introduction, des notes et un glossaire. Toulouse, 1906. (Stroński, *El. Barj.*).

Falquet de Romans: Arveiller, Raymond and Gouiran, Gérard, *L'Œuvre poétique de Falquet de Romans, troubadour.* Édition critique, traduction, notes. Université de Provence – Centre d'Aix, 1987. (Arveiller/Gouiran).

Folquet de Marseille: Stroński, Stanisław, *Le troubadour Folquet de Marseille.* Édition critique. Cracow, 1910. Repr. 1968. (Stroński, *Folq. Mars.*).

Garin d'Apchier: Latella, Fortunata, *I sirventesi di Garin d'Apchier e di Torcafol.* Edizione critica. Modena, 1994. (Latella).

Gaucelm Faidit: Mouzat, Jean, *Les poèmes de Gaucelm Faidit, troubadour du XIIe siècle.* Paris, 1965. (Mouzat).

Giraudo lo Ros: Finoli, Anna Maria, 'Le poesie di Giraudo lo Ros', *SM* 15 (1974), 1051–1106. (Finoli).

Giraut see Guiraut.

Guilhem Adémar: Almqvist, Kurt, *Poésies du Troubadour Guilhem Adémar*, publiées avec introduction, traduction, notes et glossaire. Uppsala, 1951. (Almqvist).

Guilhem Augier Novella: Calzolari, Monica, *Il trovatore Guillem Augier Novella.* Edizione critica. Modena, 1986. (Calzolari).

Guillem de Berguedà: Riquer, Martí de, *Las poesias del trobador Guillem de Berguedà.* Text, traducció, introducció i notes. Barcelona, 1996. (revised version of his 2-vol. ed. of 1971).

—— Forner, Climent, *Guillem de Berguedà, Huguet de Mataplana, Guillem Ramon de Gironella, Obra Poètica.* Edicions de l'Albí, 1986.

Guilhem Magret: Naudieth, Fritz, *Der Trobador Guillem Magret.* Halle a/S., 1914. (Beihefte zur *ZRP* 52, pp. 81–144). (Naudieth).

Guilhem de Montanhagol: Ricketts, Peter T., *Les Poésies de Guilhem de Montanhagol, troubadour provençal du XIIIe siècle.* Pontifical Institute of Mediaeval Studies, Toronto, 1964.

Guilhem Raimon de Gironela: Appel, *Prov. Inedita*, pp. 146–52 (see under Collected editions). See also under Forner above.

Guilhem de Saint-Didier: Sakari, Aimo, *Poésies du troubadour Guillem de Saint-*

Didier, publiées avec introduction, traduction, notes et glossaire. Helsinki, 1956. (Mémoires de la Société Néophilologique de Helsinki XIX). (Sakari).

Guilhem de la Tor: Blasi, Ferruccio, *Le Poesie di Guilhem de la Tor*. Geneva and Florence, 1934. (Blasi).

Guiraut de Bornelh: Kolsen, Adolf, *Sämtliche Lieder des Trobadors Giraut de Bornelh*. Mit Übersetzung, Kommentar und Glossar kritisch herausgegeben. 2 vols. Halle a/S. I 1910. II 1935. (Kolsen, Guiraut de Bornelh).

——Sharman, Ruth Verity, *The cansos and sirventes of the troubadour Giraut de Borneil*. A critical edition. Cambridge University Press, 1989. (Sharman).

Guiraut de Calanso: Ernst, Willy, 'Die Lieder des provenzalischen Trobadors Guiraut von Calanso', *RF* 44 (1930), 255–406. (Ernst).

Guiraut de Salinhac: Strempel, Alexander, *Giraut de Salignac, ein provenzalischer Trobador*. Diss. Rostock. Leipzig, 1916. (Strempel).

Huguet de Mataplana – see under Forner above.

Jordan Bonel: Kolsen, Adolf, 'Des Jordan Bonel Kanzone *Anc mais aissi finamen non amet* (B. Gr. 275,1)', *Archiv* 142 (1921), 130–5. (Kolsen 1921).

Lanfranc Cigala: Branciforti, Franco, *Il canzoniere di Lanfranco Cigala*. Florence, 1954. (Biblioteca dell'*Archivum Romanicum*. Serie I, vol. 37). (Branciforti).

Marcabru: Gaunt, Simon, Harvey, Ruth and Paterson, Linda, *Marcabru*. A critical edition. Cambridge: D. S. Brewer, 2000. (Gaunt/Harvey/Paterson).

Paulet de·Marselha: Riquer, Isabel de, 'Las Poésias del Trovador Paulet de Marselha', *Boletín de la Real Academia de Buenas Letras de Barcelona* 38 (1979–82), 133–205. (I. de Riquer).

Peire Cardenal: Lavaud, René, *Poésies complètes du troubadour Peire Cardenal (1180– 1278)*. Texte, traduction, commentaire, analyse des travaux antérieurs, lexique. Toulouse, 1957. (Lavaud).

——Vatteroni, S., 'Le poesie di Peire Cardenal' (in progress), *Studi Mediolatini e Volgari*: I vol. 36 (1990), 74–259. II vol. 39 (1993), 105–219. III vol. 40 (1994), 119–202.

Peire Raimon de Tolosa: Cavaliere, Alfredo, *Le poesie di Peire Raimon de Tolosa*. Introduzione, testi, traduzioni, note. Florence, 1935. (Cavaliere).

Peire Vidal: Avalle, D'Arco Silvio, *Peire Vidal, Poesie*. Edizione critica e commento. 2 vols. Naples, 1960. (Avalle).

Peirol: Aston, S. C., *Peirol, troubadour of Auvergne*. Cambridge University Press, 1953. (Aston).

Pistoleta: Niestroy, Erich, *Der Trobador Pistoleta*. Halle a/S., 1914. (Beihefte zur *ZRP* 52, pp. i–xvi, 1–77).

Pons de Capduelh: Napolski, Max von, *Leben und Werke des Trobadors Ponz de Cap- duoill*. Halle a/S., 1879. (Napolski).

Raimbaut d'Orange: Pattison, Walter T., *The Life and Works of the Troubadour Raim- baut d'Orange*. University of Minnesota Press, Minneapolis, 1952. (Pattison).

Raimbaut de Vaqueiras: Linskill, Joseph, *The Poems of The Troubadour Raimbaut de Vaqueiras*. The Hague, 1964. (Linskill).

Raimon Jordan: Asperti, Stefano, *Il trovatore Raimon Jordan*. Edizione critica. Modena, 1990. (Asperti).

Raimon de Miraval: Topsfield, L. T., *Les Poésies du troubadour Raimon de Miraval.* Paris, 1971. (Topsfield).

Rambertino Buvalelli: Melli, Elio, *Rambertino Buvalelli, Le Poesie.* Edizione critica con introduzione, traduzione, note e glossario. Bologna, 1978. Repr. 1993.

Rigaut de Berbezilh: Varvaro, Alberto, *Rigaut de Berbezilh, Liriche.* Bari, 1960. (Varvaro).

—— Braccini, Mauro, *Rigaut de Barbezieux, le Canzoni.* Testi e commento. Florence, 1960. (Braccini).

Sordello: Boni, Marco, *Sordello, Le Poesie.* Nuova edizione critica con studio introduttivo, traduzioni, note e glossario. Bologna, 1954. (Boni).

Uc de la Bacalaria: Riquer, *Trovadores* II, pp. 1059–62 (see under Collected editions).

Uc de Pena: Appel, *Prov. Inedita*, p. 314 (see under Collected editions).

Uc de Saint-Circ: Jeanroy, A. and Salverda de Grave J.-J., *Poésies de Uc de Saint-Circ*, publiées avec une introduction, une traduction et des notes. Toulouse, 1913.

Narrative works

Le Roland occitan: Gouiran, Gérard and Lafont, Robert, *Le Roland occitan. Roland à Saragosse. Ronsasvals.* Paris, 1991.

See also under chapter 6, list of OF narrative works, knowledge of whose subject-matter was widely diffused in other branches of the lyric.

CHAPTER 6. THE TROUVÈRE POETS

Bibliography and reference

Dictionnaire des Lettres Françaises: Le Moyen Âge – see under chapter 5.

Petersen Dyggve, Holger, *Onomastique des trouvères.* Helsinki, 1934. (*Annales Academiae Scientiarum Fennicae*, Ser. B. Tom. XXX,1).

Doss-Quinby, Eglal, *The lyrics of the trouvères: a research guide (1970–1990).* New York, 1994.

Flutre, *Table des noms propres* – see under chapter 5.

Langlois, Ernest, *Table des noms propres de toute nature compris dans les chansons de geste imprimées.* Paris, 1904. Repr. New York, 1971.

Linker, Robert White, *A Bibliography of Old French Lyrics.* University, Mississippi, Romance Monographs Inc., 1979. A reworking and updating of Raynaud and Spanke (*qq.v.*), with the addition of items previously excluded, e.g. motets, rondeaux. (Linker).

Moisan, A., *Répertoire des noms propres de personnes et de lieux cités dans les chansons de geste françaises et les œuvres étrangères dérivées.* Geneva, 1986.

Raynaud, Gaston, *Bibliographie des chansonniers français des XIIIe et XIVe siècles.* Comprenant la description de tous les manuscrits, la table des chansons classées par ordre alphabétique de rime et la liste des trouvères. 2 vols. Paris, 1884. (See Spanke).

Spanke, Hans, *Raynauds Bibliographie des altfranzösischen Liedes.* Neu bearbeitet und ergänzt. I Leiden, 1955. A corrected and expanded version of vol. II of Raynaud, *Bibliographie.* (Spanke did not live to complete the two further vols. planned, II dealing with the MSS., III with the history of the OF lyric.) (Spanke). Superseded by Linker (*q.v.*).

West, G. D., *An Index of Proper Names in French Arthurian Verse Romances*. University of Toronto Press, 1970. (West 1970).

—— *An Index of Proper Names in French Arthurian Prose Romances*. University of Toronto Press, 1978. (West 1978).

Ziltener, *Repertorium* – see under chapter 5.

General

Bec, Pierre, *La lyrique française au Moyen Âge (XIIe–XIIIe siècles). Contribution à une typologie des genres poétiques médiévaux. Études et Textes*. I *Études*, Paris, 1977. II *Textes*, Paris, 1978. (Bec, *Lyrique française*).

Dragonetti, Roger, *La technique poétique des trouvères dans la chanson courtoise*. Bruges, 1960.

Kleiber, Georges, *Le mot 'ire' en ancien français (XIIe–XIIIe siècles). Essai d'analyse sémantique*. Paris, 1978. See also Hackett under chapter 5.

Collected editions

Bec, Pierre, *La lyrique française au Moyen Âge*. II *Textes* (see above under General).

Brakelmann, J., 'Die altfranzösische Liederhandschrift Nro. 389 der Stadtbibliothek zu Bern. Fonds Mouchet 8 der Pariser kaiserlichen Bibliothek', *Archiv* 42 (1868), 73–82, 241–392; 43 (1868), 241–394.

Doss-Quinby, Eglal, Grimbert, Joan Tasker, Pfeffer, Wendy and Aubrey, Elizabeth, *Songs of the Women Trouvères*. Edited, translated and introduced. Yale University Press, 2001. (Doss-Quinby *et al.*, *Women Trouvères*).

Frank, István, *Trouvères et Minnesänger: recueil de textes pour servir à l'étude des rapports entre la poésie lyrique romane et le Minnesang au XIIe siècle*. Saarbrücken, 1952. (Frank, *Trouvères et Minnesänger*). See also under chapter 7.

Järnström, E., *Recueil de chansons pieuses du XIIIe siècle*. I Helsinki, 1910. (*Annales Academiae Scientiarum Fennicae*, Ser. B. Tom. III,1). (Järnström, *Chansons pieuses*).

—— Järnström, E. and Långfors, Arthur, *Recueil de chansons pieuses du XIIIe siècle*. II Helsinki, 1927. (*Annales Academiae Scientiarum Fennicae*, Ser. B. Tom. XX,4).

Jeanroy, Alfred, Brandin, Louis and Aubry, Pierre, *Lais et descorts français du XIIIe siècle. Texte et musique*. Paris, 1901. (Jeanroy/Brandin/Aubry, *Lais et descorts*).

Jeanroy, A. and Långfors, A., 'Chansons inédites tirées du manuscrit français 846 de la Bibliothèque nationale', *Archivum Romanicum* 2 (1918), 296–324 (nos. 1–28); 3 (1919), 1–27 (nos. 29–58), 355–67 (textual notes and versification). (Jeanroy/Långfors, 'Chansons inédites').

Jeanroy, A., and Långfors, A., *Chansons satiriques et bachiques du XIIIe siècle*. Paris. Repr. 1965. (CFMA). (Jeanroy/Långfors, *Chansons satiriques et bachiques*).

Långfors, Arthur, *Recueil général des Jeux-partis français*. 2 vols. Paris, 1926. (SATF). (Långfors, *Jeux-partis*).

Meyer, Paul, 'Rotruenge en quatrains', *Romania* 19 (1890), 102–6.

Petersen Dyggve, Holger, *Trouvères et Protecteurs de Trouvères dans les Cours Seigneuriales de France. Vieux-Maisons, Membrolles, Mauvoisin, Trie, L'Isle Adam, Nesle,*

Harnes. Helsinki, 1942. (=*Annales Academiae Scientiarum Fennicae*, Ser. B. Tom. L,2, pp. 39–247). (Petersen Dyggve, *Trouvères et Protecteurs de Trouvères*).

Rosenberg, Samuel N., Tischler, Hans, with the colloboration of Marie-Geneviève Grossel, *Chansons des Trouvères. Chanter m'estuet*. Édition critique de 217 textes lyriques d'après les manuscrits, mélodies, traduction, présentation et notes. Paris, 1995. (Rosenberg/Tischler).

Spanke, Hans, *Eine altfranzösische Liedersammlung. Der anonyme Teil der Lieder-handschriften K N P X*. Halle a/S., 1925. (Romanische Bibliothek XXII). (Spanke, Liedersammlung).

Tarbé, Prosper, *Les Chansonniers de Champagne au XIIe et XIIIe siècles*. Avec une biobibliographie des chansonniers. Reims, 1850. Repr. Geneva, 1980.

Editions of individual poets

Adam de la Halle: Marshall, J. H., *The Chansons of Adam de la Halle*. Edited with Introduction, Notes and Glossary. Manchester University Press, 1971. (Marshall).

Andrieu Contredit d'Arras: Nelson, Deborah and van der Werf, Hendrik, *The Songs Attributed to Andrieu Contredit d'Arras*. With a translation into English and the extant melodies. Amsterdam, 1992. (Nelson/van der Werf).

Blondel de Nesle: Lepage, Yvan G., *L'Œuvre lyrique de Blondel de Nesle. Textes*. Édition critique, avec introduction, notes et glossaire. Paris, 1994. (Lepage).

Le Chastelain de Couci: Lerond, Alain, *Chansons attribuées au Chastelain de Couci (fin du XIIe–début du XIIIe siècle)*. Édition critique. Paris, 1964. (Lerond).

Chrétien de Troyes: Zai, Marie-Claire, *Les Chansons courtoises de Chrétien de Troyes*. Édition critique avec introduction, notes et commentaire. Bern and Frankfurt a.M., 1974. (Zai).

Le Comte de Bretagne: Bédier, Joseph, 'Les chansons du Comte de Bretagne', *Mélanges de linguistique et de littérature offerts à M. Alfred Jeanroy par ses élèves et ses amis*. Paris, 1928, pp. 477–95. (Bédier).

Eustache le Peintre: Gambini, Maria Luisa, *Le Canzoni di Eustache le Peintre*. Edizione critica. Fasano (Brindisi), 1997. (Gambini).

Gace Brulé: Petersen Dyggve, Holger, *Gace Brulé, Trouvère Champenois*. Édition des chansons et étude historique. Helsinki, 1951. (Mémoires de la Société Néophilolo-gique de Helsinki XVI). (Petersen Dyggve, Gace).

Gautier de Coinci: Långfors, Arthur, *Miracles de Gautier de Coinci. Extraits du Manu-scrit de L'Ermitage*. Helsinki, 1937.

——— Koenig, V[ernon] Frédéric, *Gautier de Coinci, Les Miracles de Nostre Dame*. 4 vols. I Geneva and Lille, 1955. II Geneva and Paris, 1961. III Geneva and Paris, 1966. IV Geneva and Paris, 1970.

Gautier de Dargies: Raugei, Anna Maria, *Gautier de Dargies, Poesie*. Edizione critica. Florence 1981. (Raugei).

Gille le Vinier: Metcke, Albert, *Die Lieder des altfranzösischen Lyrikers Gille le Vinier*. Halle a/S., 1906. (Metcke).

Gillebert de Berneville: Fresco, Karen, *Gillebert de Berneville, les poésies*. Édition cri-tique. Geneva, 1998. (TLF). (Fresco).

Guillaume de Ferrières (Le Vidame de Chartres): Petersen Dyggve, Holger, 'Personnages historiques figurant dans la poésie lyrique française des xii͏ᵉ et xiii͏ᵉ siècles. Chansons du Vidame de Chartres', *Neuphilologische Mitteilungen* 46 (1945), 21–55. (Petersen Dyggve 1945).

Guiot de Provins: Orr, John, *Guiot de Provins, Œuvres*. Manchester and Paris, 1915. Repr. Geneva, 1974. (Orr).

Jean de Neuville: Richter, Max, *Die Lieder des altfranzösischen Lyrikers Jehan de Nuevile*. Halle a/S., 1904. (Richter).

Moniot d'Arras: Petersen Dyggve, Holger, 'Moniot d'Arras et Moniot de Paris, trouvères du xiii͏ᵉ siècle, édition des chansons et étude historique', *Mémoires de la Société Néo-philologique de Helsinski (Helsingfors)* 13 (1938), 7–252. (Moniot, ed. Petersen Dyggve).

—— see under Collected editions, Rosenberg/Tischler 126.

Perrin d'Angicourt: Steffens, Georg, *Die Lieder des Troveors Perrin von Angicourt*. Kritisch herausgegeben und eingeleitet. Halle a/S., 1905. (Steffens).

Philippe de Remi: Suchier, Hermann, *Œuvres poétiques de Philippe de Remi, sire de Beaumanoir*. 2 vols. Paris, I 1884, II 1885.

Raoul de Soissons: Winkler, Emil, *Die Lieder Raouls von Soissons*. Halle a/S., 1914. (Winkler).

Richard de Fournival: Lepage, Yvan G., *L'Œuvre lyrique de Richard de Fournival*. Édition critique. Ottawa, 1981. (Lepage).

Thibaut de Blaison: Newcombe, Terence H., *Les Poésies de Thibaut de Blaison*. Geneva, 1978. (TLF). (Newcombe).

Thibaut de Champagne: Wallensköld, A., *Les Chansons de Thibaut de Champagne, Roi de Navarre*. Édition critique. Paris, 1925. (SATF). (Wallensköld).

—— Brahney Kathleen J., *The Lyrics of Thibaut de Champagne*. Edited and translated. New York and London, 1989. (Brahney).

Vidame de Chartres see Guillaume de Ferrières.

Wilart de Corbie: Boogaard, N. H. J. van den, 'Les Chansons attribuées à Wilart de Corbie', *Neophilologus* 55 (1971), 123–41. (Boogaard 1971).

Narrative works

La Chanson de Roland: Segre, Cesare, *La Chanson de Roland*. Edizione critica. Milan and Naples, 1971. See also *Le Roland occitan*, under chapter 5.

Chrétien de Troyes: *Les Romans de Chrétien de Troyes*, édités d'après la Copie de Guiot: I *Erec et Enide*, ed. M. Roques. Paris, 1963. (CFMA 80). II *Cligés*, ed. A. Micha. Paris, 1978. (CFMA 84). III *Le Chevalier de la Charrete*, ed. M. Roques. Paris, 1981. (CFMA 86). IV *Le Chevalier au lion (Yvain)*, ed. M. Roques. Paris, 1960. (CFMA 89). V–VI *Le Conte du Graal (Perceval)* ed. F. Lecoy. 2 vols. Paris, I 1972. II 1975. (CFMA 100, 103).

Floire et Blancheflor: Leclanche, Jean-Luc, *Le conte de Floire et Blancheflor*. Paris, 1980. (CFMA).

Lai d'Ignaure: Lejeune, Rita, Renaut [de Beaujeu], *Le Lai d'Ignaure ou Lai du Prisonnier*. Brussels, 1938.

Narcisus: Pelan, M. M. and Spence, N. C. W., *Narcisus (poème du XII͏ᵉ siècle)*. Paris, 1964.

—— Thiry-Stassin, Martine and Tyssens, Madeleine, *Narcisse. Conte ovidien français du XIIᵉ siècle*. Édition critique. Paris, 1976.

—— Mancini, Mario, *Il Lai di Narciso*. 2nd ed., Parma, 1990.

Piramus et Tisbé: de Boer, C., *Piramus et Tisbé. Poème du XIIᵉ siècle*. Paris, 1921. (CFMA).

Prose *Tristan*: Curtis, Renée L., *Le Roman de Tristan en prose*, 3 vols. I Munich, 1963. II Leiden, 1976. III Cambridge, D. S. Brewer, 1985.

—— Fotitch, Tatiana, *Les lais du roman de Tristan en prose d'après le manuscrit de Vienne 2542*. Édition critique. Partie musicale par Ruth Steiner. Munich, 1974. (Fotitch, *Lais*).

Roman d'Alexandre: Armstrong, E. C. *et al.*, *The Medieval French Roman d'Alexandre*. 7 vols. Princeton and Paris, 1937–76.

Roman d'Eneas. Übersetzt und eingeleitet von Schöler-Beinhauer, Monica. Munich, 1972. (Klassische Texte des romanischen Mittelalters in zweisprachigen Ausgaben 9).

Roman de Thèbes: Constans, L., *Le Roman de Thèbes. Publié d'après tous les manuscrits*. 2 vols. Paris, 1890. (SATF).

—— Mora-Lebrun, Francine, *Le Roman de Thèbes. Édition du manuscrit S (Londres, Brit. Libr., Add. 34114)*. Traduction, présentation et notes. Paris, 1995.

Roman de Troie: Constans, L., *Le Roman de Troie*. 6 vols. Paris, 1904–12. (SATF).

CHAPTER 7. THE GERMAN POETS

Reference works

Chandler, Frank W., *A Catalogue of Names of Persons in the German Court Epics. An Examination of the Literary Sources and Dissemination, together with notes on the etymologies of the more important Names*. Ed. with an Introduction and an Appendix by Martin H. Jones. London, 1992. (King's College London; Medieval Studies VIII).

Gillespie, George T., *A Catalogue of Persons named in Germanic Heroic Literature (700–1600)*. Oxford, 1973.

Kern, Manfred and Ebenbauer, Alfred, *Lexikon der antiken Gestalten in den deutschen Texten des Mittelalters*. Berlin and New York, 2003.

Wittstruck, Wilfried, *Der dichterische Namengebrauch in der deutschen Lyrik des Spätmittelalters*. Munich, 1987. (Münstersche Mittelalter-Schriften 61).

General

Bartsch, Karl, *Albrecht von Halberstadt und Ovid im Mittelalter*. Quedlinburg and Leipzig, 1861. (Bibliothek der gesammten deutschen National-Literatur 38).

Holznagel, Franz-Josef, 'Mittelalter', in *Geschichte der deutschen Lyrik*, ed. Holznagel, F.-J. *et al.* Stuttgart (Reclam), 2004, pp. 11–93.

Kern, Manfred, *Edle Tropfen vom Helikon. Zur Anspielungsrezeption der antiken Mythologie in der deutschen höfischen Lyrik und Epik*. Amsterdam, 1998. (Amsterdamer Publikationen zur Sprache und Literatur).

Kreibich, Christina, *Der mittelhochdeutsche Minneleich. Ein Beitrag zu seiner Inhalts-analyse.* Würzburg, 2000. (Würzburger Beiträge zur deutschen Philologie 21).

Kugler, Hartmut, 'Ovidius', VL² VII, 247–73.

Lecouteux, Claude, *Kleine Texte zur Alexandersage.* Göppingen, 1984. (GAG 368).

Lienert, Elisabeth, *Deutsche Antikenromane des Mittelalters.* Berlin, 2001. (Grundlagen der Germanistik 39).

Maurer, Friedrich, 'Der Topos von den "Minnesklaven". Zur Geschichte einer thematischen Gemeinschaft zwischen bildender Kunst und Dichtung im Mittelalter', *DVjs* 27 (1953), 182–206.

Sayce, Olive, *The Medieval German Lyric 1150–1300.* Oxford, Clarendon Press, 1982.

—— 'Exemplary comparisons in the medieval German lyric', in *Blütezeit. Festschrift für L. Peter Johnson zum 70. Geburtstag*, hrsg. Mark Chinca *et al.* Tübingen, 2000, pp. 3–28.

Schweikle, Günther, *Minnesang.* 2. korrigierte Auflage, Stuttgart and Weimar, 1995. (Sammlung Metzler 244).

Tervooren, Helmut, *Sangspruchdichtung.* Stuttgart and Weimar, 1995. (Sammlung Metzler 293).

*Verfasserlexikon*²: *Die deutsche Literatur des Mittelalters, Verfasserlexikon.* Begründet von Wolfgang Stammler, fortgeführt von Karl Langosch. Zweite völlig neu bearbeitete Auflage . . . hrsg. von Kurt Ruh *et al.*, 1977–. (VL²).

Wachinger, Burghart, *Sängerkrieg. Untersuchungen zur Spruchdichtung des 13. Jahrhunderts.* Munich, 1973. (MTU 42).

Yao, Shao-Ji, *Der Exempelgebrauch in der Sangspruchdichtung vom späten 12. Jahrhundert bis zum Anfang des 14. Jahrhunderts.* Würzburg, 2006. (Würzburger Beiträge zur deutschen Philologie 32).

Collected editions

Backes, Martina: *Tagelieder des deutschen Mittelalters. Mittelhochdeutsch/Neuhochdeutsch.* Ausgewählt, übersetzt und kommentiert. Einleitung von Alois Wolf. Stuttgart, 1992. (Reclam).

Bartsch, Karl: *Die Schweizer Minnesänger.* Frauenfeld, 1886. (SM¹). See also under Schiendorfer.

Cramer, Thomas: *Die kleineren Liederdichter des 14. und 15. Jahrhunderts.* 4 vols. Munich, 1977–85. (Cramer).

Frank, István, *Trouvères et Minnesänger* (see under chapter 6).

Hausner, Renate, *Owe do tagte ez. Tagelieder und motivverwandte Texte des Mittelalters und der frühen Neuzeit.* I Göppingen, 1983. (GAG 204).

Höver, Werner and Kiepe, Eva, *Gedichte von den Anfängen bis 1300. Nach den Handschriften in zeitlicher Folge herausgegeben.* Munich, 1978. (Epochen der deutschen Lyrik 1). (Höver/Kiepe).

Holz, Georg, Saran, Franz, Bernouilli, Eduard, *Die Jenaer Handschrift.* 2 vols. Leipzig, 1901. I *Getreuer Abdruck des Textes.* II *Übertragung, Rhythmik und Melodik.* (Holz/Saran/Bernouilli).

Kiepe, Eva and Hansjürgen, *Gedichte 1300–1500.* Nach Handschriften und Frühdrucken herausgegeben. Munich, 1972. (Epochen der deutschen Lyrik 2). (Kiepe).

Kraus, Carl von, *Deutsche Liederdichter des 13. Jahrhunderts*. I *Text*. Zweite Auflage, durchgesehen von Gisela Kornrumpf. Tübingen, 1978. II *Kommentar*, besorgt von Hugo Kuhn. Zweite Auflage, durchgesehen von Gisela Kornrumpf. Tübingen, 1978. (KLD).

Moser, Hugo and Tervooren, Helmut, *Des Minnesangs Frühling* (MF). Unter Benutzung der Ausgaben von Karl Lachmann und Moriz Haupt, Friedrich Vogt und Carl von Kraus bearbeitet. I *Texte*. 38., neu revidierte Auflage. Stuttgart, 1988. II *Editionsprinzipien, Melodien, Handschriften, Erläuterungen*. 36., neugestaltete und erweiterte Auflage. Mit vier Notenbeispielen und 28 Faksimiles. Stuttgart, 1977. See also *Des Minnesangs Frühling, Kommentare*. III 1–2. Stuttgart, 1981.

Sayce, Olive, *Romanisch beeinflußte Lieder des Minnesangs*. Mit Übersetzungen, Kommentar und Glossar. Göppingen, 1999. (GAG 664).

Schiendorfer, Max, *Die Schweizer Minnesänger*. Nach der Ausgabe von Karl Bartsch neu bearbeitet und herausgegeben. I *Texte*. Tübingen, 1990. (SM²). See also under Bartsch.

Schweikle, Günther, *Mittelhochdeutsche Minnelyrik*. Texte und Übertragungen, Einführung und Kommentar. Stuttgart, 1993.

Simrock, Karl, *Der Wartburgkrieg*. Herausgegeben, geordnet, übersetzt und ediert. Stuttgart and Augsburg, 1858.

Wachinger, Burghart, *Deutsche Lyrik des späten Mittelalters*. Deutscher Klassiker Verlag, 2006. (Bibliothek deutscher Klassiker 191).

Editions of individual poets

Boppe: Alex, Heidrun, *Der Spruchdichter Boppe*. Edition – Übersetzung – Kommentar. Tübingen, 1998.

Der junge Meissner: *Der Junge Meißner. Sangsprüche, Minnelieder, Meisterlieder*, hrsg. von Günter Peperkorn. Munich, 1982. (MTU 79).

Friedrich von Sunnenburg: *Die Sprüche Friedrichs von Sunnenburg*, hrsg. von Achim Masser. Tübingen, 1979. (ATB).

Frauenlob: *Heinrichs von Meissen des Frauenlobes Leiche, Sprüche und Lieder*. Erläutert und hrsg. von Ludwig Ettmüller. Quedlinburg and Leipzig, 1843. Repr. Amsterdam, 1966.

—— *Frauenlob (Heinrich von Meissen), Leichs, Sangsprüche, Lieder*. Auf Grund der Vorarbeiten von Helmuth Thomas hrsg. von Karl Stackmann und Karl Bertau. 2 vols. I *Einleitungen, Texte*. II *Apparate, Erläuterungen*. Göttingen, 1981.

Konrad von Würzburg: *Konrad von Würzburg, kleinere Dichtungen*, hrsg. von Edward Schröder. III *Die Klage der Kunst, Leiche Lieder und Sprüche*. 4. Auflage, Dublin and Zürich, 1970.

Der Marner: *Der Marner*, hrsg. von Philipp Strauch. Strassburg, 1876. Mit einem Nachwort, einem Register und einem Literaturverzeichnis von Helmut Brackert. Repr. Berlin, 1965.

Der Mönch von Salzburg: *Die geistlichen Lieder des Mönchs von Salzburg*, hrsg. von Franz Viktor Spechtler. Berlin and New York, 1972.

Reinmar von Zweter: *Die Gedichte Reinmars von Zweter*, hrsg. von Gustav Roethe. Leipzig, 1887. Repr. Amsterdam, 1967.

Rudolf von Fenis: *Rudolf von Fenis, die Lieder*. Unter besonderer Berücksichtigung des romanischen Einflusses, mit Übersetzung, Kommentar und Glossar, hrsg. von Olive Sayce. Göppingen, 1996. (GAG 633).

Sigeher: Brodt, Heinrich Peter, *Meister Sigeher*. Breslau, 1913. (Germanistische Abhandlungen 42). (Brodt).

Tannhäuser: *Der Dichter Tannhäuser. Leben – Gedichte – Sage*, hrsg. von Johannes Siebert. Halle a/S., 1934.

Walther von der Vogelweide: *Walther von der Vogelweide. Leich, Lieder, Sangsprüche*. 14., völlig neubearbeitete Auflage der Ausgabe Lachmanns mit Beiträgen von Thomas Bein und Horst Brunner, hrsg. von Christoph Cormeau. Berlin and New York, 1996.

Narrative works

Eilhart, *Tristan*: *Eilhart von Oberge*, hrsg. von Franz Lichtenstein. Strassburg and London, 1877. Repr. Hildesheim and New York, 1973.

Gottfried, *Tristan*: *Gottfried von Straßburg, Tristan*. Nach der Ausgabe von Reinhold Bechstein hrsg. von Peter Ganz. 2 vols. Wiesbaden, 1978.

Heinrich von Veldeke, *Eneasroman. Mittelhochdeutsch/Neuhochdeutsch*. Nach dem Text von Ludwig Ettmüller ins Neuhochdeutsche übersetzt, mit einem Stellenkommentar und einem Nachwort von Dieter Kartschoke. Stuttgart, 1986. (Reclam, Universalbibliothek 8303).

Konrad Fleck: Sommer, Emil, *Flore und Blanscheflur. Eine Erzählung von Konrad Fleck*. Quedlinburg and Leipzig, 1846.

Lamprechts Alexander: Werner, Richard Maria, *Die Basler Bearbeitung von Lambrechts Alexander*. Tübingen, 1881.

——— Kinzel, Karl, *Lamprechts Alexander*. Nach den drei Texten mit dem Fragment des Alberic von Besançon und den lateinischen Quellen hrsg. und erklärt. Halle a/S., 1884.

Mai und Beaflor. Eine Erzählung aus dem dreizehnten Jahrhundert. Leipzig, 1848. Repr. Hildesheim, 1974. (Dichtungen des deutschen Mittelalters VII, lacking name of editor).

Das Nibelungenlied. Mittelhochdeutscher Text und Übertragung. Hrsg., übersetzt und mit einem Anhang versehen von Helmut Brackert. 2 vols. Frankfurt a.M., 1987. (Fischer Taschenbücher 6038–9).

Strassburger Alexander see *Lamprechts Alexander*.

Der Stricker: *Der Stricker, Verserzählungen*. 2 vols. I hrsg. von Hanns Fischer, 4. rev. Auflage besorgt von Johannes Janota. Tübingen, 1979. II Mit einem Anhang: *Der Weinschwelg*, hrsg. von Hanns Fischer, neu bearbeitet von Johannes Janota. Tübingen, 1997. (ATB).

Ulrich von Liechtenstein: *Ulrich von Liechtenstein, Frauendienst*, hrsg. von Franz Viktor Spechtler. Göppingen, 1987. (GAG 485).

Wigalois: *Wigalois der Ritter mit dem Rade von Wirnt von Gravenberg*, hrsg. von J. M. N. Kapteyn. I *Text*. Bonn, 1926.

CHAPTER 8. THE SICILIAN AND ITALIAN POETS

General

Berra, Claudia, *La similitudine nei 'Rerum Vulgarium Fragmenta'*. Lucca, 1992.

Catenazzi, Flavio, *L'influsso dei Provenzali sui temi e immagini della poesia siculo-toscana*. Brescia, 1977.

Colussi, Giorgio (ed.), *Glossario degli antichi volgari italiani*. Helsinki, 1983–.

Delcorno Branca, Daniela, *I romanzi italiani di Tristano e la Tavola ritonda*. Florence, 1968.

—— *Tristano e Lancillotto in Italia: studi di letteratura arturiana*. Ravenna, 1998.

Folena, Gianfranco, 'Cultura e poesia dei Siciliani', in Cecchi, E., Sapegno, N. (eds.), *Storia della letteratura italiana*. I, Milan, 1965, 273–347.

—— 'Tradizione e cultura trobadorica nelle corti e nelle città venete', in *Storia della cultura veneta dalle origini al Trecento*. Vicenza, 1976, 453–562.

Fratta, Aniello, *Le fonti provenzali dei poeti della scuola siciliana. I postillati del Torraca e altri contributi*. Florence, 1996.

Hainsworth, Peter and Robey, David, *The Oxford Companion to Italian Literature*. Oxford University Press, 2002.

Mölk, Ulrich, 'Die sizilianische Lyrik', in *Neues Handbuch der Literaturwissenschaft*. VII *Europäisches Hochmittelalter*, ed. H. Krauss. Wiesbaden, 1981, 49–57.

Monteverdi, Angelo, *La poesia provenzale in Italia*. Lezioni di filologia romanza raccolte dall'assistente Dr. Costanza Pasquali. Rome, 1955–6.

Ortiz, Ramiro, 'La materia epica di ciclo classico nella lirica italiana delle origini', *Giornale storico della letteratura italiana* 79 (1922), 1–31; 80 (1922), 241–94; 81 (1923), 241–71; 85 (1925), 1–93.

Pagani, Walter, *Repertorio tematico della Scuola Poetica Siciliana*. Bari, 1968.

Rosa, Alberto Asor et al., *Letteratura italiana: storia e geografica*. I *L'età medievale*. Turin, 1987.

Savona, Eugenio, *Repertorio tematico del dolce stil nuovo*. Bari, 1973.

Stussi, Alfredo, 'Versi d'amore in volgare tra la fine del secolo XII e l'inizio del XIII', *Cultura neolatina* 59 (1999), 1–69 (2 items in hybrid linguistic form in MS of the Archivo Storico Arcivescovile, Ravenna, as possible evidence for early vernacular love poetry in N. Italy).

Varvaro, Alberto, 'Il regno normanno-svevo', in Rosa et al., *Letteratura italiana* I (*q.v.*), 79–99.

Vitale, Maurizio, *La lingua del Canzoniere (Rerum Vulgarium Fragmenta) di Francesco Petrarca*. Padua, 1996.

Collected editions

Bartoli, Adolfo, Casini, Tommaso, *Il Canzoniere Palatino 418 della Biblioteca Nazionale di Firenze*. Bologna, 1881.

Bertoni, Giulio, 'I trovatori minori di Genova'. Introduzione, testo, note e glossario. *Gesellschaft für romanische Literatur*, 2. Jg. (1903), 1, 3. Repr. Rome, 1967.

—— *I trovatori d'Italia (Biografie, testi, traduzioni, note)*. Modena, 1915. Repr. Geneva, 1974.

Casini, Tommaso, 'Rime inedite dei secoli XIII e XIV', *Propugnatore* 15, 2 (1882), 331–49.

—— *Il Canzoniere Laurenziano Rediano 9.* Bologna, 1900.

Carducci, Giosuè, *Cantilene e ballate, strambotti e madrigali nei secoli XIII e XIV.* Pisa, 1871.

Contini, Gianfranco, *Poeti del Duecento.* 2 vols. Milan and Naples, 1960. (Contini).

—— *Poeti del dolce stil novo.* Milan, 1991.

D'Ancona, A., Comparetti, D., *Le antiche rime volgari secondo la lezione del Codice Vaticano 3793.* Vol. II. Bologna, 1881. (D'Ancona/Comparetti).

Egidi, Francesco, *et al., Il libro de varie romanze volgare, Cod. Vat. 3793.* Rome, 1908. (diplomatic ed.).

Frati, Lodovico, *Rimatori bolognesi del Trecento.* Bologna, 1915.

Jensen, Frede, *The Poetry of the Sicilian School.* Edited and translated. New York, 1986. (Jensen, *Sicilian School*).

Marti, Mario, *Poeti giocosi del tempo di Dante.* Milan, 1956.

—— *Poeti del dolce stil nuovo.* Florence, 1969. (Marti, 1969).

Orlando, Sandro, *Rime dei Memoriali Bolognesi 1279–1300.* Turin, 1981. (Orlando).

Panvini, Bruno, *Le rime della Scuola Siciliana.* I *Introduzione– Testo critico– Note.* Florence, 1962. II *Glossario.* Florence, 1964. (Panvini).

Santangelo, Salvatore, *Le tenzoni poetiche nella letteratura italiana delle origini.* Florence, 1928. (Biblioteca dell'*Archivum Romanicum* 9). (Santangelo, *Tenzoni*).

Sapegno, Natalino, *Poeti minori del Trecento.* Milan, 1952.

Segre, Cesare and Marti, Mario, *La prosa del Duecento.* Milan and Naples, 1959.

Vitale, Maurizio, *Rimatori comico-realistici del Due e Trecento.* 2 vols. Repr. Turin, 1965. (Vitale).

Zaccagnini, Guido, *I rimatori pistoiesi dei secoli XIII e XIV.* Pistoia, 1907.

Zaccagnini, Guido and Parducci, Amos, *Rimatori siculo-toscani del Dugento, serie I: Pistoiesi, Lucchesi, Pisani.* Bari, 1915. (Zaccagnini/Parducci).

Editions of individual poets or works

Cecco Angiolieri: Lanza, Antonio, *Cecco Angiolieri, Le Rime.* Rome, 1990.

Chiaro Davanzati: Menichetti, Aldo, *Chiaro Davanzati, Rime.* Edizione critica con commento e glossario. Bologna, 1965. (Menichetti).

Dante, Alighieri: Petrocchi, Giorgio, *La Commedia secondo l'antica vulgata.* Florence, 1994.

—— *De vulgari eloquentia. Opere minore* II, ed. Mengaldo, Pier Vincenzo. Milan and Naples, 1979.

—— Foster, Kenelm and Boyde, Patrick, *Dante's Lyric Poetry.* Edited and translated. Clarendon Press, 1967.

Dante da Maiano: Bettarini, Rosanna, *Dante da Maiano, Rime.* Florence, 1969. (Bettarini).

Dino Frescobaldi: Brugnolo, Furio, *Dino Frescobaldi, Canzoni e Sonetti.* Turin, 1984.

Giacomino Pugliese: Santangelo, Margherita, *Le poesie di Giacomino Pugliese.* Testo e studio critico. Palermo, 1937.

Giacomo da Lentini: Antonelli, Roberto, *Giacomo da Lentini, Poesie*. Edizione critica. Rome, 1979. (Antonelli).

Guido Cavalcanti: De Robertis, Domenico, *Guido Cavalcanti, Rime. Con le rime di Jacopo Cavalcanti*. Turin, 1986.

—— Cassata, Letterio, *Guido Cavalcanti, Rime*. Edizione critica, commento, concordanze. Anzio, 1993.

Guido Guinizelli: Edwards, Robert, *The Poetry of Guido Guinizelli*. Edited and translated. New York and London, 1987.

—— Pelosi, Pietro, *Guido Guinizelli, Rime*. Naples, 1998.

Guittone d'Arezzo: Egidi, Francesco, *Le Rime di Guittone d'Arezzo*. Bari, 1940.

—— Leonardi, Lino, *Guittone d'Arezzo, Canzoniere. I sonetti d'amore del codice Laurenziano*. Turin, 1994. (Leonardi).

Lai di Narciso, Il, ed. Mancini – see under chapter 6.

Lapo Gianni: Iovine, Francesco, *Lapo Gianni, Rime*. Rome, 1989.

Monte Andrea: Minetti, Francesco Filippo, *Monte Andrea da Fiorenza, Le Rime*. Edizione critica. Florence, 1979.

Onesto da Bologna: Orlando, Sandro, *Onesto da Bologna, Le Rime*. Edizione critica. Florence, 1974.

Panuccio del Bagno: Ageno, Franca Brambilla, *Le Rime di Panuccio del Bagno*. Florence, 1977.

Petrarch: Santagata, Marco, *Francesco Petrarca, Canzoniere*. Milan, 1996. (Santagata).

Rinaldo d'Aquino: Tallgren, O. J., 'Les poésies de Rinaldo d'Aquino, rimeur de l'école sicilienne du XIIIe siècle', *Mémoires de la Société néo-philologique de Helsingfors* 6 (1917), 175–303.

Rinuccino da Firenze: Carrai, Stefano, *I sonetti di Maestro Rinuccino da Firenze*. Florence, 1981.

Rustico Filippi: Mengaldo, Pier Vincenzo, *Rustico Filippi, Sonetti*. Turin, 1971.

Glossary of Technical Terms

Abgesang   The German designation of the third metrically and musically distinct part of a tripartite stanza. See *canso*.

alba   The Oc. term, lit. 'dawn', designates a poem describing the parting of lovers at dawn after a nocturnal meeting. It has equivalents in the OF *aube*, MHG *tageliet* (modern German *Tagelied*).

Aufgesang   The German designation of the first part of a tripartite stanza structure, made up of two metrically and musically identical elements (*Stollen*), the equivalent of the *pedes* in the *canso* (*q.v.*).

ballata (It.)   A lyric form, originally that of a dancing song, formally related to the *canzone*, but with a head refrain, which may be repeated also after each stanza.

canso (Oc.), *chançon* (OF), *canzone* (It.).   *Lied/Minnelied* are the modern German equivalents (the MHG term *liet* is ambiguous, denoting in the singular 'stanza', and in the pl. 'stanzas', 'verses', and only secondarily 'poem'). The terms denote a polystrophic poem, originally intended to be sung (as the Romance terms imply), made up of isostrophic stanzas of tripartite structure, consisting of two metrically identical sets of lines, set to the same melody, which together make up the first part of the stanza, followed by a metrically differing third part, set to a different melody. In *De vulg. eloqu.*, Dante describes this stanza structure as consisting of two *pedes* (sing. *pes*), making up the *frons*, followed by the *cauda*. The corresponding modern Italian terms are *piede*, pl. *piedi*, *fronte* and *sirma*. See *Aufgesang*, *Abgesang*.

cobla (Oc.)   A single stanza, either part of a poem, or an isolated single stanza, in which case it is more accurately described as *cobla esparsa*.

comparandum   The subject to which a comparison is applied.

comparatio   The stylistic figure of comparison.

comparatum   The figure with whom the subject is compared.

congedo see *tornada*.

dansa (Oc.)   A lyric form, originally that of a dancing song, normally consisting of three stanzas, with a head refrain, which may be repeated at the end of the stanzas.

descort (Oc./OF), *discordo* (It.)   A heterostrophic poem on the theme of love, with many short rhyming units, formally distinct from the isostrophic *canso*. See *lai*, *leich*.

dôn (MHG), modern German *Ton*   The term denotes an individual metrical and musical structure. In combination with descriptive attributes, it may refer to a specific structure occurring in the didactic lyric – see e.g. Frauenlob **6**, in the so-called *Langer Ton*.

envoi see *tornada*.

estampida (Oc.)   A formal type well attested as a textless dance tune. The extant Oc. textual exs. have links with *descort*, but unlike the latter are isostrophic, with many short rhyming units suggesting the rhythm of the dance.

exemplum   In its technical sense, as a term of rhetoric, denotes 'example', 'exemplary story', 'warning example'.

frons, fronte see under *canso*.

joc partit (Oc.), *jeu parti* (OF), *partimen* (Oc.)   A poem of debate on a set theme between two participants, in alternating stanzas.

lai (OF)   A term with widely differing connotations. There are two types of *lai* attested in the OF exs.: Anon. **7**, designated in the text as *lai*, is of heterostrophic type, with thematic and formal similarities to *descort* (*q.v.*); Pr. *Trist.* **1a, 1b** are exs. of the *lai lyrique/lai arthurien*, an isostrophic lyric poem in monorhyme stanzas inserted in a prose romance.

langue d'oc   Occitan, comprising the dialects of S. France, as distinct from the dialects of N. France, which together constitute the *langue d'oïl*; the distinction derives from the designation of the word 'yes' in each group, *oc* in the former, *oïl* in the latter. The former general term Old Provençal, used to describe the poetic medium of the troubadours and the poets themselves, is linguistically inaccurate, in that the Provençal dialect forms only part of the S. dialect group.

leich (MHG), modern German *Leich*   A type of heterostrophic poem influenced by Oc. *descort* and OF *lai*; like the *lai* it may treat both secular and religious themes.

Lied see *canso*.

madrigale (It.)   A 14th-century poetic form consisting of two or more tercets followed by a couplet (see Petrarch **7**).

Minnelied see *canso*.

Minnesang   A modern German collective term for medieval German lyrics on the theme of love. It is distinguished from *Spruchdichtung/Sangspruchdichtung* (*q.v.*).

Occitan see *langue d'oc*.

octave see *sonetto*.

pastourelle (OF)   A Romance lyric genre, much more common in OF than Oc., which recounts in first-person form an encounter between the poet and a shepherdess.

pedes, piedi see under *canso*.

planh (Oc.)   A poem of lament, usually funeral lament.

Provençal see *langue d'oc*.

rim estramp (Oc.)   An isolated rhyme which has no equivalent in the stanza in which it occurs, but only in other stanzas of the poem. The device is frequently used to single out proper names.

salut (Oc.)   A missive of greeting and praise in rhyming couplets addressed to the lady, with themes analogous to those of the *canso*.

Sangspruchdichtung see *Spruchdichtung/Sangspruchdichtung*

senhal (Oc.)   A pseudonym, which may be a poetic invention or the name of an exemplary character, e.g. Tristan, used to replace the name of the lady or another subject addressed or referred to, frequently in a *tornada* (*q.v.*).

sestet see *sonetto*.

sestina (It.)   A poem of six stanzas of six hendecasyllabic lines, with three-line *congedo* (*q.v.*). The lines do not rhyme within the stanza, but with lines in the other stanzas, according to a strict pattern of rotation. (See Petrarch **1**).

sirma see under *canso*.

sirventes (Oc.)   A poem treating predominantly moral, political, satirical, and also personal themes. The *sirventes* is not structurally differentiated from the *canso* and may imitate the form of a specific *canso*. The *sirventes-canso* combines themes of both *canso* and *sirventes*, and usually contains a more pronounced personal element than the *sirventes*.

sirventese (It.) see n., *Mem. Bol.* **2**.

sonetto (It.)   The term, lit. 'little song', was originally general in meaning and only later acquired the specific connotation 'sonnet'. It represents a specialized development of the *canzone* (see *canso*), consisting of fourteen hendecasyllabic lines, divided into the octave, made up of two sets of four lines, which correspond to the *pedes* constituting the *frons/fronte* in the *canso*, followed by the sestet, which corresponds to the *cauda/sirma*, divided into two sets of three lines.

Spruchdichtung/Sangspruchdichtung   The terms denote the medieval German didactic lyric, in contradistinction to the *Minnesang* (*q.v.*). The themes coincide in the main with those of the *sirventes* (*q.v.*), but the *Spruch/Sangspruch* differs formally from *canso*, *Minnelied*, and *sirventes*, which are made up of a limited number of stanzas forming a relative unity, in that the basic unit is an independent or relatively independent single stanza (*Spruchstrophe/Sangspruchstrophe*), which may, however, also be linked with other stanzas in loose groupings of various kinds, within a series of stanzas on different topics in the same metrical form. See *dôn*.

Stollen see *Aufgesang*.

tageliet see *alba*.

tenso (Oc.), *tenzone* (It.)   A poem of debate between two participants in alternating stanzas. In the Italian lyric, it may take the form of paired sonnets.

Ton see *dôn*.

tornada (Oc.), *congedo* (It.), *envoi* (Fr.)   A short stanza, consisting of a variable number of lines, with the repetition of rhymes occurring in the penultimate stanza, which forms the conclusion of a poem. It may sum up the central theme and be addressed to the lady, the song, or a patron. It is not customary in the *Minnesang*, but see Veldeke **2**, which imitates a type of *tornada* common in the troubadour lyric.

Index of Poets and Works

Adam de la Halle   216–17
Aimeric de Belenoi   177
Aimeric de Peguilhan   171–2
Alberto di Massa di Maremma   212
Alexander, Der wilde   261–2
'Amico di Dante'   319
Andrieu Contredit d'Arras   205
Anon.: MLat. 105–6, 116; Oc. 184–6; OF 221–
    8; MHG 276; Sicil. 296–9
Appendix Tibulliana   85
Archipoeta   113–15
Arnaut Daniel   151–2
Arnaut de Mareuil   148–51
Arundel Lyrics   120–1
Azalais d'Altier   177–8

Bartolomeo Zorzi   180–1
Baudri de Bourgueil   108–10
Benzo of Alba   107–8
Bernger von Horheim   242–3
Bernart de Ventadorn   144–6
Bertran de Born   152–4
Binduccio da Firenze   318–19
Blondel de Nesle   202–3
Bonagiunta   299–300
Bonifacio Calvo   179–80
Boppe   262–4

Carmina Burana   118–24
Carmina Cantabrigiensia   106
Catullus   38–45
Cerverí de Girona   181–2
Chastelain de Couci, Le   201–2
Chiaro Davanzati   300–5
Chrétien de Troyes   200–1
Cino da Pistoia   316–18
Claudian   88–91
Comte de Bretagne, Le   215–16
Comtessa de Dia, La   168

Dante   320
Dante da Maiano   305–6
Daude de Pradas   183
Donzella, La Compiuta   312–13
Duchesse de Lorraine, La   219–21

Dürinc, Der   266

Einhard (?)   101–2
Elias de Barjols   172
Ermoldus Nigellus   103–4
Eustache le Peintre   203

Falquet de Romans   174–6
Filippo da Messina   294
Folquet de Marseille   154–5
Frauenlob   269–75
Friedrich von Hausen   240–1

Gace Brulé (?)   218–19
Garin d'Apchier   156
Gaucelm Faidit   158–9
Gautier de Coinci   228
Gautier de Dargies   205
Geoffroi de Vinsauf   126–7
Giacomo da Lentini   291–2
Giacomino Pugliese   294
Gille le Vinier   205–6
Giovanni d'Arezzo   307–8
Giraldus Cambrensis   124–5
Gliers, Der von   253–5
Goldener, Der   268–9
Gottschalk   102–3
Guido delle Colonne   293–4
Guilhem Adémar   169–70
Guilhem Raimon de Gironela   182
Guillaume de Ferrières   201
Guillem Magret   162–3
Guiot de Provins   202
Guiraudo lo Ros   158
Guiraut de Bornelh   155–6
Guiraut de Calanso   173–4
Guiraut de Salinhac   157
Guittone d'Arezzo   306–7

Heinrich von Morungen   243–4
Heinrich von Veldeke   241–2
Henneberger, Der   266–7
Herger   240
Hilarius of Orléans   111–12
Homer   9–28

Horace 56–62
Hugh Primas 112–13

Jacopo Mostacci 295–6
Jean de Bretel 217
Jean de Grieviler 217–18
Jean de Marli 218
Jean de Neuville 206
Jeux partis 217–18
Jordan Bonel 184

Konrad von Würzburg 253

Lapo Gianni 315–16
'Laus Pisonis' 86

Maestro Torrigiano di Firenze 313–14
Marcabru 142
Mare Amoroso, Il 309–11
Marner, Der 248–50
Matthieu de Vendôme 125–6
Meissner, Der junge 264–5
Memoriali Bolognesi 314–15
Moniot d'Arras 204

Otto von Botenlouben 247–8
Ovid 62–76

Paulet de Marselha 178
Paulus Diaconus 100–1
Peire Cardenal 178–9
Peire Raimon de Tolosa 169
Peire Vidal 160–2
Peirol 169
Perrin d'Angicourt 209–10
Petrarch 320–30
Petrus Grammaticus 100
Pier della Vigna 293
'Poeta Saxo' 102
Pons de Capduelh 172-3
Priscian 97–8
Propertius 46–56
Prose *Tristan* 211–12

Raimbaut d'Orange 144
Raimbaut de Vaqueiras 163–7
Raimon Jordan 146–8
Raimon de Miraval 170
Raoul de Soissons 214–15
Re Giovanni 295
Reinmar von Zweter 246–7
Richard de Fournival 212–14
Rigaut de Berbezilh 143
Rinaldo d'Aquino 292
Ripoll lyrics 116–17
Ruodolf von Rotenburg 255–7
Rustico Filippi 307

Sedulius Scottus 104–5
Serlo of Wilton 115–16
Sidonius Apollinaris 91–7
Sigeher 267–8
Statius 86–8

Tannhäuser 260–1
Theodulf of Orléans 101
Thibaut de Bar 218
Thibaut de Blaison 204
Thibaut de Champagne 206–9
Tibullus 45–6
Tomaso da Faenza 308–9

Uc de la Bacalaria 168
Uc de Pena 183–4
Ulrich von Gutenburg 257–60
Ulrich von Liechtenstein 250–3

Venantius Fortunatus 98–100
Virgil 29–37

Walther von der Vogelweide 244–5
Wartburgkrieg, Der 275–6
Wernher, Bruder 247
Wilart de Corbie 210–11
Wolfram von Eschenbach (?) 245–6

Index of Proper Names

The index lists reference to all personal names and their nominal and adjectival derivatives, and all variant names and alternative designations replacing proper names in the textual examples of explicit comparison or identification with an exemplary figure and exemplary parallels, together with all instances of proper names or their variants in non-exemplary usage. Topographical, generic, and ethnic names are included only if they serve to identify the figure. In order to distinguish the incidence of particular exemplary figures at different periods, examples are classified according to chapters (see below). The headword is normally given according to the standard form customary in English: thus some Greek names, e.g. Patroclus, occur with Latin endings. Variant names, e.g. *Pelides* for *Achilles*, and alphabetically distant variant forms, e.g. *Ysalde* for *Isalde*, are listed, with a cross-reference to the headword, which records all occurrences of the name and its variants in full, with the exception of longer examples of periphrasis, indicated by 'see periphrasis' before the reference.

Key to Classification of Chapters
[1] = Homer: The *Iliad* and the *Odyssey* (pp. 9–28) [2] = Virgil: The *Aeneid* (pp. 29–37) [3] = Latin Poets from Catullus to Ovid (pp. 38–83) [4] = Latin Poets from Antiquity to the Middle Ages (pp. 84–140) [5] = The Troubadour Poets (pp. 141–98) [6] = The Trouvère Poets (pp. 199–237) [7] = The German Poets (pp. 238–87) [8] = The Sicilian and Italian Poets (pp. 288–342)

Order of references: (i) chapter number at left; (ii) author/work (for abbreviations, see pp. x–xiv); (iii) bold number referring to numbered examples in the book; (iv) line-reference within the example; (v) parenthetical number referring to the page of the book. *Symbols preceding the reference*: (C) = comparison with an exemplar or one or more of its attributes; (I) = identification with an exemplar; (EP) = exemplary parallel.

Abel
[4] (C) MLat. Anon. **1**.3.1 (p. 105)
[5] (C) Peire Vid. **6**.30 (p. 162); (C) Zorzi **2**.35 (p. 180)
Abigail
[7] (I) Marner **3**.14 (p. 249)
Abraham
[4] (C) Sed. **2**.55 (p. 105)
[5] (C) Zorzi **2**.121 (p. 180)
Absalon
[4] (C) CB **2**.5a.2 (p. 119)
[5] (C) Zorzi **1**.59 (p. 180); for (C) Arn. Mar. **3b**.168 see n. (p. 150)
[7] (C, hypothetical) Boppe **1**.2 (p. 262); (EP) Frauenlob (?) **7**.6 (p. 274)
[8] (C, hypothetical) Lapo **2**.16 (p. 315)
Achaeans
[1] *Il.* **4**.211 (p. 12); *Od.* **6**.528 (p. 20)
Achelous
[4] Sid. **5**.87 (p. 96)
Achilles
[1] *Il.* **9**.131 (p. 13)
[2] (C) Verg. **7**.438 (p. 34); (I) Verg. **8a**.89 (p. 34); (I) Verg. **8b**.742 (p. 34)
[3] (C) *filium Thetidis* Hor. **1**.14 (p. 56); (EP) Prop. **8**.29 (p. 51); Ov. **7**.741 (p. 66); *armatique*

Ov. **17**.256 (p. 71). (I) *Pelides* Prop. **8**.34 (p. 51). (C) *Aeacides* Ov. **7**.736 (p. 66); (EP) Ov. **6**.17 (p. 66)
[4]   (C) Claud. **3**.7 (p. 90); (I) Venant. **3**.50 (p. 99); (C) Serlo **1**.11 (p. 115); (C) *Achilleos* . . . *actus* Baudri **3**.1 (p. 110). (C) *Aeacida* Sid. **1**.150 (p. 91). (C) *Pelidae* Sid. **2a**.191 (p. 92)
[7]   (EP) Frauenlob (?) **7**.13 (p. 274)
[8]   Petrarch **15**.6 (p. 329)
Actaeon
[8]   *suo amante* Petrarch **7**.1 (p. 325)
Adam
[6]   (C) Pr. *Trist.* **1b**.82 (p. 212); (C) Duchesse **1**.14 (p. 220)
[7]   (C, hypothetical) Boppe **1**.11 (p. 262); (EP) Zweter **2**.1 (p. 246); (EP) Dürinc **1**.13 (p. 266); (EP) Frauenlob (?) **7**.1 (p. 274)
[8]   (C) *Mem. Bol.* **2**.70 (p. 315); see also Chiaro **2b**.21 n. (p. 303)
Admetus
[3]   Tibull. **2**.11 (p. 46)
Adonis
[4]   (C) Claud. **3**.16 (p. 90)
Adrastus
[4]   (I) M. Vend. **1**.52.61 (p. 46)
Aeacides see **Achilles**
Aëdon
[1]   see *Od.* **6**.518 n. (p. 19); see also **Pandareos**
Aegaeon see **Briareus**
[2]   (C) Verg. **4**.565 (p. 31)
Aegides see **Theseus**
Aegiale
[4]   (C) Stat. **2**.48 (p. 88)
Aegina
[4]   (C) *Asopo genitam* G. Vins. **2**.619 (p. 127)
[8]   see Petrarch **6**.164 n. (p. 324)
Aegisthus
[8]   Petrarch **15**.8 (p. 329)
Aelia Galla
[3]   Prop. **11b**.38 (p. 52)
Aeneas
[1]   *Il.* **6c**.XIII.500 (p. 13)
[2]   Verg. **1**.494 (p. 29); Verg. **2**.142, 150 (p. 30); Verg. **3**.466 (p. 31); Verg. **4**.569 (p. 32); Verg. **6**.324 (p. 33); see *Veneris partus suus et Paris alter* (periphrasis + identification) Verg. **9b**.321 (p. 35)
[4]   (C) Ermold **2**.34 (p. 104); (C) *Veneris soboles* Ermold. **2**.33 (p. 104); Sid. **5**.88 (p. 96)
[5]   (C) Arn. Mar. **3b**.155 (p. 149)
[6]   (C) Blondel **1b**.61 (p. 203); Duchesse **1**.7 (p. 219)
[7]   (I, hypothetical) *Enêas* Hausen **1**.3 (p. 240)
[8]   Petrarch **15**.5 (p. 329)
Afelisse (for **Anfelise**)
[6]   (C) Duchesse **1**.15 (p. 220)
Afrie von Navarre
[7]   Botenlouben **1**.60 (p. 247)
Agamemnon
[1]   *Il.* **1**.477 (p. 11); *Il.* **11**.388 (p. 14)
[2]   see under **Orestes**
[8]   *quel ch'ancise Egisto* Petrarch **15**.8 (p. 329)
Agenor
[4]   G. Vins. **2**.617 (p. 127)

Agnes
[5] (C) Bertr. Born 1.37 (p. 153)
Ahasverus
[7] Marner 3.10 (p. 249)
Aias/Ajax
[1] *Il.* 4.206, 211 (p. 12)
[3] (C) *Telamonius* Ov. 7.737 (p. 66)
[4] (C) *Telamone creatum* Sid. 2a.185 (p. 92)
Aiglentine
[5] Raimb. Vaq. 2a.13 (p. 164)
Aimerics
[5] (C) Raimb. Vaq. 5.75 n. (p. 167)
Alcestis
[4] Sid. 5.67 (p. 95)
Alcides see **Hercules**
Alcinous
[1] *Od.* 2.VI.17 (p. 18)
Alcmene
[3] Prop. 8.25 (p. 51)
[4] (C) G. Vins. 2.615 (p. 127); Claud. 2.536 (p. 89)
Alcon
[4] (C) Sid. 2.183 (p. 92)
Alexander
[4] (C) Sid. 2.202 (p. 92); (C) MLat. Anon. 1.8.1 (p. 106); (C) Archipoeta 1.6.1 (p. 113); (I) Serlo 2.13 (p. 115)
[5] (C) Gauc. Faid. 3.14 (p. 159); (C) Peire Vid. 3.14 (p. 160); (C) Raimb.Vaq. 4.100 (p. 167); (C) Raimb. Vaq. 5.73 (p. 167); (C) Aim. Peg. 2.12 (p. 171); (C) Guir. Cal. 1.49 (p. 173); (C) Cerverí 1.47 (p. 181); (EP) *cel qe pres Tir* Oc. Anon. 1.3 (p. 184); (EP) Arn. Dan. 3.21 (p. 152); Peire Card. 2.1 (p. 179)
[6] (C) OF Anon. 11.18 (p. 228); Perr. Ang. 1.40 (p. 209)
[7] (C) Liechtenstein 1b.147 (p. 252); (I) Sigeher 1.6, 7, 8 (p. 268); (C) Sigeher 1.16 f. (p. 268); (EP) Gutenburg 1a.41 (p. 257);(EP) Frauenlob 6b.17 (p. 274); (EP) Frauenlob (?) 7.7 (p. 274); Sigeher 1.1 (p. 267)
Alienor
[7] (C) Rotenburg 2.240 (p. 256)
Amazon
[2] (C) Verg. 5.659 f. (p. 32); (I) Verg. 5.648 (p. 32)
[4] Claud. 3a.32 (p. 90)
Amelis
[5] (C) Uc Bac. 1.14 (p. 168)
Amor/Amors/Amore/Amûr (personified) see also **Cupid**
[3] Ov. 6.7, 8, 17 (pp. 65, 66); Ov. 9.1 (p. 67)
[5] Marc. 1.14 (p. 142); Rig. Berb. 1.23 (p. 143); Folq. Mars. 1.33 (p. 154); Guir. Ros. 1.25 (p. 158); Peire Vid. 1.53 (p. 160); Zorzi 1.55 (p. 180); Daude Prad. (?) 1.5, 22 (p. 183)
[6] Chrétien 1.31 (p. 200); Couci 2.10 (p. 202); Gille Vin. 1.38 (p. 206); Thib. Ch. 2.31 (p. 207); Pr. *Trist.* 1a.39 (p. 211); Rich. Fourn. 1.15 (p. 213); *Jeux-partis* 1a.41, 47 (p. 217); *Jeux-partis* 1b.50, 55 (p. 218); Gace (?) 1.26, 29 (p. 219); Duchesse 1.19 (p. 220); OF Anon. 1.3, 6 (p. 221); OF Anon. 3.47 (p. 222); OF Anon. 10j.17 (p. 227)
[7] Würzburg 1.16 (p. 253); Rotenburg 1.48 (p. 255)
[8] Pier Vign. 1.12 (p. 293); Chiaro 1c.1 (p. 301); Lapo 1.4 (p. 315); Cino 4.1, 12 (p. 317); Binduccio 1.9, 14 (pp. 318 f.); Dante 1.37 (p. 320); Petrarch 5.2 (p. 323); Petrarch 11.2 (p. 327); Petrarch 12.3 (p. 328); Petrarch 16.11 (p. 330); *quel Signore cui servir m'agenzo* Cino 3.6 (p. 317); *colui che tutte cose mena a·ssu' piacere* Amico 1.9 ff. (p. 319)

Amphion

[4] *Amphioniae... arti* Sid. **4a.**120 (p. 95)

Amphitrion

[4] G. Vins. **2.**614 (p. 127)

Amymone

[3] (C) Ov. **3.**5 (p. 64)

Andrew, St.

[4] (C) G. Vins. **1.**11 (p. 126)

Andrieu (of France/Paris)

[5] (C) Raim. Jord. **2.**24 (p. 147); (C) Gauc. Faid. **2.**41 (p. 159); (C) Guil. Magr. **1.**2 (p. 162); (C) Raimb. Vaq. **2a.**29 (p. 164); (C) Raimb. Vaq. **2b.**24 (p. 165); (C) Uc Bac **1.**13 (p. 168); (C) Aim. Peg. **3a.**28 (p. 172); (C) Aim. Peg. **3b.**30 (p. 172); (C) El. Barj. **1.**28 (p. 172); (C) Falq. Rom. **1.**16 (p. 174); (C) Falq. Rom. **3a.**182 (p. 175); (C) Peire Card. **1.**1 (p. 178); (C) Daude Prad. (?) **1.**9 (p. 183); (C) Jord. Bon. **1.**34 (p. 184); (C) Oc. Anon. **3.**114 (p. 186)

[8] (C) *Nadriano*, see n. *Mar. Am.* **5.**333 (p. 311)

Andromache

[3] (C) Prop. **7.**2 (p. 50); Prop. **8.**31 (p. 51); (C) *Hectoris uxor* Ov. **18.**19 (p. 71); see periphrasis (C) Ov. **20.**44 and n. (p. 72). (C) *Thebana* Ov. **19.**29 (p. 71)

Andromeda

[3] (C) *Cepheia ... Andromede* Prop. **1.**3 f. (p. 47)

Antaeus

[7] see (C) *Antêus* Marner **2.**4 (for Perseus) (p. 249)

Antigone

[5] (C) Arn. Mar. **3a.**156 (p. 149)

Antiopa

[3] (C) *Antiopae Nycteidos* Prop. **3.**5 (p. 48)

[4] (C) G. Vins. **2.**617 (p. 127)

Antoninus

[4] (C) Prisc. **1.**46 (p. 97)

Aphrodite see **Venus**

[1] (C) *Il.* **11.**389 (p. 14); (C) *Il.* **12a.**282 (p. 14); (C) *Il.* **12b.**XXIV.699 (p. 14); (C) *Od.* **1.**14 (p. 17); (C) *Od.* **5.**37 (p. 19)

Apollo

[2] (C) Verg. **2.**144 (p. 30)

[3] (C) Ov. **4.**31 (p. 64); (I) Ov. **11.**23 (p. 68); (C) Ov. **15.**421 (p. 69); (EP) Tibull. **2.**11 (p. 46). (I) *Phoebus* Ov. **11.**188 (p. 68); (EP) Ov. **11.**25 (p. 68)

[4] (C) Claud. **2.**537 (p. 89); (C) Claud. **3a.**8 (p. 90); (C) Ermold. **1.**533 (p. 103); (C) Sed. **3.**11 (p. 105); CB **2.**7a.1 (p. 119). (C) *Paean* Sid. **1.**154 (p. 91). (C) *Phoebus* Sid. **4a.**122 (p. 95); (C) Sed. **3.**10 (p. 105); (C) Ripoll. **2.**10 (p. 116); (EP) CB **1.**5.6 (p. 118); Stat. **1a.**130 (p. 86). (EP) *Delium* CB **5.**2.1 (p. 121)

[8] Petrarch **1.**36; see also **1.**34 n. (p. 321); Petrarch **2.**1 (p. 321); Petrarch **5.**2 (p. 323). *Phebo* Petrarch **3.**2 (p. 322). *del Sol* Cino **4.**13 (p. 318); see also *e 'l sol* Petrarch **3.**7 (p. 322); *il Sole* Petrarch **4.**4 (p. 323) and Petrarch's distinctive usage (p. 336; pp. 340–1 and n. 15)

Apollonius (?)

[5] (C) *cel qe fo reis de Tyr* Arn. Mar. **3b.**157 (p. 149)

Aragon, king of

[5] Cerverí **1.**46 (p. 181)

Arcas see **Parthenopaeus**

Ares

[1] (C) *Il.* **1.**479 (p. 11); (C) *Il.* **2.**349 (p. 12); (C) *Il.* **4.**208 (p. 12); (C) *Il.* **5.**605 (p. 12); (C) *Il.* **6a.**627 (p. 12); (C) *Il.* **6b.**V.576 (p. 13); (C) *Il.***6c.**XIII.500 (p. 13); (C) *Il.* **8.**784 (p. 13); (C) *Od.* **8.**115 (p. 22); (C) *Od.* **9.**518 (p. 22); (C) *Enyalius Il.* **7.**651 (p. 13); (C) *Il.* **9.**132 (p. 13)

Index of Proper Names

Argia
[8] (C) Petrarch **9**.11 (p. 326)
Argus
[3] (C) Prop. **2**.20 (p. 47)
[4] (I) M. Vend. **2**.53.7 (p. 125)
Ariadne
[3] (C) *Gnosia* Prop. **1**.2 (p. 47). (C) *Cressa* Ov. **2**.16 (p. 63). (EP) *Gnosida* Ov. **11**.25 (p. 68)
[4] (C) *Gnosida* Stat. **1a**.133 (p. 86). *Cressa* Sid. **5**.66 (p. 95)
Aristotle
[4] (C) Baudri **2b**.30 (p. 110)
[6] (EP) *Jeux-partis* **1a**.45 (p. 217)
[7] (C, hypothetical) Boppe **1**.7 (p. 262); (EP) Frauenlob (?) **7**.11 (p. 274)
Artemis see **Diana**
[1] (C) *Od.* **2**.122 (p. 17); (C) *Od.* **3**.102 (p. 18); (C) *Od.* **4**.151 (p. 18); (C) *Od.* **5**.37 (p. 19); *Od.* **6**.XX.61, 80 (p. 20)
Arthur
[5] (C) Bertr. Born **3**.33 and 36 f. n. (p. 154); (C) Gauc. Faid. **3**.16 (p. 159); see n. (I) Peire Vid. **5a**.12 (p. 161); see n. (I) Peire Vid. **5b**.39 (p. 161); (C) Guir. Cal. **2**.7 (p. 174); Raimb. Vaq. **1**.17 (p. 163)
[7] (C, hypothetical) Boppe **1**.10 (p. 262); (EP) Frauenlob **6b**.13 (p. 274); (EP) Frauenlob (?) **7**.15 (p. 274)
Asael
[7] (C, hypothetical) Boppe **1**.17 (p. 262); (EP) Frauenlob (?) **7**.14 (p. 274)
Ascholoie
[7] Morungen (?) **3**.1 n. (p. 244)
Asopus
[4] G. Vins. **2**.619 (p. 127)
Atalanta
[3] (C) Ov. **5**.29 (p. 65). (C) *Schoeneida* Ov. **2**.13 (p. 63); (EP) Ov. **14**.123 (p. 69)
[4] Sid. **5**.68 (p. 95)
[5] (C) Arn. Dan. **2**.32 (p. 152)
Athena see **Pallas**
[1] (C) *Il.* **11**.390 (p. 14)
[4] (C) *violatae Phoebados ultrix* Sid. **2a**.194 (p. 92); *Tritonidos* Sid. **3c**.198 (p. 183)
Atlas
[4] *gigas* Sid. **3c**.583 (p. 94)
[8] *nel gran vecchio Mauro* Petrarch **5**.5 (p. 323)
Atreus
[1] see *Il.* **11**.388 (p. 14)
[4] see (C) *brevitatem . . . Atridae* 'Laus Pis.' **1**.61 (p. 86)
Aude
[5] Guir. Sal. **2**.16 (p. 157)
[6] OF Anon. **9**.15 (p. 224)
Augustine
[4] (C) G. Vins. **1**.15 (p. 126)
Augustus
[4] (C) CB **7c**.4b.5 (p. 123)
[8] *quel che resse anni cinquantasei sì bene il mondo* Petrarch **15**.7 f. (p. 329)
Auron
[7] *Wartburgkrieg* **1**.7 (p. 275)
Aurora
[3] (EP) Ov. **4**.43 (p. 65)
[4] (C) Claud. **3b**.270 (p. 91)
[8] Petrarch **12**.1 (p. 328); *o felice Titon . . . il tuo caro tesoro* Petrarch **12**.6 (p. 328)

Automedon
[3] (I) Ov. **6.**8 (p. 65); (C) Ov. **7.**738 (p. 66); (EP) Ov. **6.**5 (p. 65)
[8] (I) Petrarch **14.**13 (p. 328)
Aya
[5] P. R. Tolosa **1.**32 (p. 169); Pons Capd. **2.**42 (p. 173); Paul. Mars. **1.**4 (p. 178)

Bacchus
[3] (C) Ov. **4.**32 (p. 64); (I) Ov. **11.**24 (p. 68); (C) Ov. **15.**421 (p. 69); (EP) Ov. **11.**25 (p. 68); with the meaning 'wine' Prop. **1.**9 (p. 47)
[4] (C) *Liberum* Claud. **3a.**9 (p. 90); (C) *Semeleius Euhan* Sid. **2b.**231 (p. 93); Stat. **1a.**133 (p. 86)
Baldine
[4] (C) CB **8.**8 (p. 123)
Bartholomew, St.
[4] (C) G. Vins. **1.**10 (p. 126)
Bellerophon
[3] (C) *quique ab equo praeceps in Aleïa decidit arva* Ov. **17.**257 (p. 71)
[4] (C) Baudri **2a.**116 n. (p. 109); (C) *Bellerophonteis . . . opimis* Sid. **2a.**184 (p. 92); *Stheneboeius heros* Sid. **5.**74 (p. 96)
Bellona
[4] Claud. **1.**121 (p. 89)
Benedict, St.
[8] *Benedetto* Cino **3.**4 (p. 317)
Berart (de Mondesdier)
[5] (C) Peire Vid. **2.**14 (p. 160); (C) Raimb. Vaq. **4.**102 (p. 167)
Berenguiers
[5] (C) Arn. Mar. **3b.**165 (p. 150)
Biblis
[5] (C) Arn. Mar. **3a.**153 (p. 149); Arn. Mar. **3b.**170 (p. 150); Aim Bel. **1.**47 (p. 177)
Blancheflor
[4] (I) CB **3.**8.4 (p. 120)
[5] (C) Arn. Mar. **3a.**154 (p. 149); (C) Aim. Bel. **1.**49 (p. 177); Arn. Mar. **3b.**153 (p. 149); Raimb. Vaq. **2c.**58 (p. 165); Comt. Dia **1.**14 (p. 168); Falq. Rom. **2b.**18 (p. 175); Falq. Rom. **3a.**137 (p. 175); Cerverí **3.**13 (p. 182); *s'umia* Falq. Rom. **2a.**18 (p. 175)
[7] (EP) Gutenburg **1b.**1b.23 (p. 258)
[8] (C) Sicil. Anon. **5b.**7 (p. 298); (C) D. Maiano **1.**14 (p. 305)
Blancheflor 2
[7] (EP) Würzburg **1.**20 n. (p. 253)
Blondel
[6] (C) Eustache **1.**34 (p. 203)
Breton
[5] Bertr. Born **3.**34, 36 (p. 154); Peire Vid. **5a.**12 (p. 161)
Briareus see **Aegaeon**
[4] (C) Primas **1.**77 (p. 112)
Brimo
[3] (C) Prop. **6.**12 (p. 49)
Briseis
[1] *Il.* **12a.**282 (p. 14)
[3] (C) Prop. **7.**1 (p. 50); Prop. **8.**29 (p. 51)
Brizeida
[5] Azalais **1.**62 n. (p. 177)
Brunhild
[4] *Brunichildis* Venant. **3.**101 (p. 99)

Burchard
[4] Baudri **3.2** (p. 110)

Caedino see **Kahedin**
Caesar see also **Julius/Julius Caesar**
[3] (Octavian) Hor. **5.3** (p. 58)
[4] (Julius Caesar) (C) Poeta Saxo **1.656** (p. 102); (I) M. Vend. **1.52.61** (p. 125). (title of Louis the Pious) Sed. **2.53** (p. 105); (of Heinrich IV) Benzo **1.1, 19** (p. 107)
[5] (Julius Caesar) (C) *Sesars* Guir. Cal. **1.49** (p. 173)
[6] (Antony) (EP) *Jeux-partis* **1b.49** (p. 218)
[8] *Cesare* 'month of July' Petrarch **3.6** (p. 322)
Cain
[8] (EP) Chiaro **2a.73** (p. 302)
Calchas
[3] (C) Ov. **7.737** (p. 66)
Callisto
[4] (C) G. Vins. **2.616** (p. 127)
Calypso
[4] Sid. **5.67** (p. 95)
Camilla
[2] Verg. **5.649, 657** (p. 32)
[4] Sid. **2a.189** (p. 92)
Camillus
[4] (C) Poeta Saxo **1.655** (p. 102)
Cardona, Viscountess of
[5] *la don' als Cartz* Cerverí **1.45** n. (p. 181)
Carolus see **Charles (Charlemagne)**
Cassandra
[1] *Il.* **12b.699** (p. 14)
[3] (C) Ov. **2.17** (p. 63)
[4] see *violatae Phoebados* Sid. **2a.194** n. (p. 92)
Castile, son of king of
[5] Guir. Cal. **2.3** (p. 174)
Castor
[3] See (C) *Ledae partu gratior, una tribus* Prop. **4.30** and n. (p. 48)
[4] (C) Claud. **3a.6** (p. 90); (C) Sid. **2a.182** (p. 92)
Cato
[4] (C) Einh. (?) **1.72** n. (p. 101); (C) Poeta Saxo **1.656** (p. 102); (C) *Catones* Benzo **1.10** n. (p. 107); (I) Baudri **2b.28, 29** (p. 110); (C) Serlo **1.15** (p. 115); (I) M. Vend. **1.52.62** (p. 125)
[8] (C) Amico **1.1** (p. 319)
Catola
[5] Marc. **1.13** (p. 142)
Catullus
[3] Catull. **4.135** (p. 41)
Cavalier sens paura, il
[8] (C) *Mem. Bol.* **1.25** n. (p. 314)
Centaur
[1] *Od.* **10.295** (p. 22)
[3] Prop. **6.10** (p. 49)
Cepheus see **Andromeda**
Charites see **Graces**
Charles (Charlemagne)
[4] (I) Sed. **1.5** f. (p. 104); (C) *Karolos* Benzo **1.15** (p. 107); Sed. **2.51, 55** (pp. 104 f.); Poeta Saxo **1.660** (p. 102)

[5] (C) Gauc. Faid. **3**.16 (p. 159); (C) Raimb. Vaq. **5**.74 (p. 167)
[6] *Charlemainnes* Guil. Ferr. **1**.19 (p. 201)
[7] (C) *künic Karlen* Boppe **2**.8, 19 (p. 264)
Chastelain de Couci, Le
[6] (C) Eustache **1**.34 (p. 203); (EP) OF Anon. **4**.1 (p. 222)
Chiron
[3] (EP) Ov. **6**.17 (p. 66)
[4] Stat. **1b**.216 (p. 87); *magistri* Sid. **1**.150 (p. 91)
Chloe
[3] Hor. **3**.6 (p. 57)
Christ/Jesus/Jesus Christ
[4] Sed. **3**.12 (p. 105)
[5] *Iezus* Rig. Bcrb. **1**.27 (p. 143)
[6] OF Anon. **11**.14 (p. 228)
[8] *Mar. Am.* **1b**.322 (p. 310); *lo Segnor* Lapo **1**.3 (p. 315); *Nostro Segnore* Chiaro **2b**.18 (p. 303)
Cicero
[4] (I) Baudri **2b**.29 (p. 110); (I, hypothetical) Baudri **2b**.28 (p. 110); (C) Serlo **1**.13 (p. 115);
 (C) *Cicerones* Benzo **1**.9 n. (p. 107); (C) *Tulliane* Archipoeta **1**.5.1 (p. 113); (I) *Tullius* M.
 Vend. **1**.52.61 (p. 125)
Circe
[4] Sid. **5**.67 (p. 95)
Cisseis see **Hecuba**
Claudia
[4] (C) Stat. **1c**.245 (p. 87)
Cleopatra
[5] Arn. Mar. **3b**.156 (p. 149)
[6] *Jeux-partis* **1b**.52 (p. 218)
Cliges
[7] (C) Rotenburg **1**.49 (p. 255); (C) Rotenburg **2**.239 (p. 256)
Clytemnestra
[1] (C) Τυνδαρέου κούρη 'daughter of Tyndareus' *Od.* **7**.199 (p. 21)
[2] *matrem* Verg. **3**.472 (p. 31)
Consentius
[4] Sid. **4b**.169 (p. 95)
Constance
[8] (C) *Gostanza* Donzella **1**.4 n. (p. 312)
Constantine
[4] (C) Poeta Saxo **1**.662 (p. 102)
Corinna
[3] Ov. **1**.9 (p. 62)
[4] CB **6f**.8.7 (p. 122)
Creon
[4] Sid. **2**.192 (p. 92)
Cressa see **Ariadne**
Cupid see **Amor**
[3] Catull. **3**.133 (p. 40); Ov. **9**.3 (p. 67)
[4] Venant. **3**.47 (p. 99)
Cydippe
[3] (EP) Ov. **14**.123 (p. 69)
Cynthia
[3] Prop. **1**.8 (p. 47); Prop. **3**.8 (p. 48)
Cypris see **Venus**
Cytharea see **Venus**

Dacian
[4] (I) Primas 1.47 (p. 112)
Daedalus see also **Icarus**
[5] see Rig. Berb. 1.26 n. (p. 143)
[6] (EP) Rich. Fourn. 2.25 (p. 213); (EP) Ad. Halle 1.29 (p. 216)
[8] (C, hypothetical) *Mar. Am.* 4.236 (p. 311)
Danae
[4] (C) G. Vins. 2.620 (p. 127); (C) Baudri 2a.21 n. (p. 108); see also (C, implied) Stat. 1a.136 n.
      (p. 87); (C, implied) CB 4.5.4 (p. 120); Sid. 5.90 n. (p. 96)
[8] see Petrarch 6.161 ff. n. (p. 324)
Daniel
[4] (C) MLat. Anon. 1.3.3 (p. 105)
Daphne
[3] (EP) Ov. 11.25 (p. 68)
[4] (C) Stat. 1a.131 (p. 86); (EP) CB 1.5.6 (p. 118); (EP) CB 5.2.3 (p. 121). *Peneide* CB 2.7a.2
      (p. 119); *Dafnes* incorrectly for *Danae*, see Baudri 2a.21 n. (p. 108)
[8] (EP) Cino 4.13 (p. 318); (EP) *quella di Peneo* Cino 4.6 (p. 318). For the identification of
      Laura with Daphne see p. 336 and Petrarch 1.34 ff. (p. 321); Petrarch 2.7 f., 13 f. (pp. 321 f.);
      Petrarch 3.2, 8 (p. 322); Petrarch 5.1 (p. 323); Petrarch 6.167 (p. 324)
Darius
[5] Gauc. Faid. 3.14 (p. 159)
[6] (C) Perr. Ang. 1.40 (p. 209)
[7] *ein Persân* (emended) Sigeher 1.2 (p. 267)
Daulias see **Procne**
David
[4] (C) Theod. 1.30 (p. 101); (C) MLat. Anon. 1.7.3 (p. 106); (C) Carm. Cant. 1.4a.6 (p. 106);
      (C) Archipoeta 1.6.2 (p. 113); (C) *Daviticae . . . vitae* Venant. 1.78 (p. 98); (C) *Daviticae . . .*
      virtutis Poeta Saxo 1.661 (p. 102)
[5] (EP) Peire Vid. 1.54 (p. 160)
[6] (EP) Thib. Ch. 2.34 (p. 207)
[7] (C, hypothetical) Boppe 1.3 (p. 262); (C) Boppe 2.10 (p. 264); (I) Goldener 1.3 (p. 268);
      (EP) Dürinc 1.17 (p. 266); (EP) Frauenlob (?) 7.4 (p. 274); Marner 3.15 n. (p. 249)
[8] (C) Binduccio 1.13 (p. 319); (EP) *e 'l pastor ch'a Golia ruppe la fronte* Petrarch 16.5 ff.
      (p. 330)
Decii
[4] (C) Poeta Saxo 1.655 (p. 102)
Deionis see **Proserpina**
Deiphobus
[1] *Od.* 9.517 (p. 22)
Delius see **Apollo**
Diana see **Artemis**
[2] (C) Verg. 1.499 (p. 29); Verg. 5.652 (p. 32)
[3] (C) Ov. 5.31 (p. 65)
[4] (C) Claud. 3b.270 (p. 91); (C) Baudri 2a.115 (p. 109); (C) Ripoll 5.21, 23 (p. 117); (C) Gi-
      rald. 1.15 (p. 125); G. Vins. 2.615 (p. 127). (C) *Latonia* Stat. 1a.115 (p. 86). *Cynthia* Claud.
      3a.17 (p. 90). *Delia* Sid. 5.90 (p. 96)
[7] see (C) *Dijâne* Walther (?) 2.6 n. (p. 245)
[8] (C) Petrarch 7.1 (p. 325)
Dido
[2] Verg. 1.496, 503 (pp. 29, 30)
[4] (C) CB 8.1 (p. 124); Sid. 5.70 (p. 96). *Elisse* Benzo 1.7 (p. 107)
[6] (C) Duchesse 1.7 (p. 219)
[7] (I, hypothetical) *Tidô* Hausen 1.5 (p. 240)
[8] (EP) Dante 1.36 (p. 320)

Dijâne see under **Diana**
Diomedes
[3] (I, negated) *Tydides* Ov. **9**.5 (p. 67); (EP) Ov. **2**.31 (p. 63)
[5] *lo fil Tideus* Azalais **1**.64 (p. 178)
Dione see also **Venus**
[7] (C) *Djone* (emended) Tannhäuser **1**.II.6 (p. 260)
Dionisius
[4] (C) Primas **1**.79 (p. 112)
Donna del Lago, la
[8] (C) Donzella **1**.4 (p. 312)
Echetus
[1] *Od.* **10**.XXI.308 (p. 23)
Echo
[6] (C) Rich. Fourn. **1**.8 (p. 212); Rich. Fourn. **1**.16 (p. 213)
Eckehart
[7] (I, hypothetical) Alexander **1**.12 (p. 262)
Edonis
[3] (C) Prop. **1**.5 (p. 47)
Eëtion
[3] Ov. **20**.44 (p. 72)
Elijah
[4] (C) Venant. **2**.25 (p. 98)
Elissa see **Dido**
Emenadus
[5] (C) Raimb. Vaq. **1**.28 (p. 163)
Enêas see **Aeneas**
Engles
[5] Raimb. Vaq. **2d**.84 (p. 166)
Enide
[5] (C) Guil. R. Giron. **1**.48 (p. 182); Raimb. Vaq. **2d**.81 (p. 166)
Enipeus
[3] Prop. **4**.21 (p. 48)
Ennius
[8] (EP) Petrarch **15**.12 (p. 329)
Enyalius see **Ares**
Erec
[5] (C) Raimb. Vaq. **2d**.81 (p. 166); (C) Oc. Anon. **3**.113 (p. 186); Guil. R. Giron. **1**.49 (p. 182)
Ermenrich
[7] (I, hypothetical) Alexander **1**.11 (p. 262)
Eryx
[4] (C) Sid. **2a**.161 (p. 92)
Eschenbach, der von
[7] (C) Frauenlob **3**.1 (p. 270)
Esmena
[5] (C) Arn. Mar. **3a**.156 (p. 149)
Esther
[7] (I) *Hester* Marner **3**.8 (p. 249); (EP) Frauenlob **2**.III, 3.2 (p. 270)
Eteocles
[5] (emended) (C) Arn. Mar. **3b**.160 n. (p. 150)
Euhan see **Bacchus**
Eumenides
[2] Verg. **3**.469 (p. 31)
Euphorbus
[1] see *Il.* **3** (p. 12)

Euridice
[4] (C) Baudri 2a.24 (p. 109)
[8] (C) Petrarch 10.51 (p. 326)
Europa
[4] (C) CB 4.5.6 (p. 120); *puella* Hil. 1b.30 (p. 111); (C) *Agenore natam* G. Vins. 2.617 (p. 127)
Euryalus
[1] *Od.* 8.115 (p. 22)
[4] (C) *natus Ophelte* Sid. 2a.164 (p. 92)
Eurytion
[1] (C, implied) *Od.* 10.295 n. (p. 22)
Eusebia
[4] Venant. 4.5 (p. 99)
Evadne
[4] Sid. 5.71 (p. 96)

Fabius
[4] (C) Venant. 1.84 (p. 98); (C) *gens Fabiorum* Poeta Saxo 1.657 (p. 102); (C) *Fabios* Benzo 1.9 (p. 107)
Fabricius
[4] (C) Sid. 3d.227 (p. 94); (C) *Fabricios* Benzo 1.10 (p. 107)
Ferragutz
[5] (C) Raimb. Vaq. 3a.11 (p. 166)
Flaccus see **Horace**
Floris
[5] (C) Arn. Mar. 3b.153 (p. 149); (C) Gauc. Faid. 1.65 (p. 159); (C) Raimb. Vaq. 2c.58 (p. 165); (C) Comt. Dia 1.14 (p. 168); (C) Uc Bac. 1.14 (p. 168); (C) Falq. Rom. 1.7 (p. 174); (C) Falq. Rom. 2a.18 (p. 175); (C) Falq. Rom. 2b.17 (p. 175); (C) Falq. Rom. 3a.138 (p. 175); (C) Oc. Anon. 3.113 (p. 186); Aim. Bel. 1.51 (p. 177); Cerverí 3.13 (p. 182)
[7] (EP) Gutenburg 1b.1b.23 (p. 258)
Florissen
[5] Arn. Mar. 3b.168 (p. 150)
Folquet (de Marseille)
[8] (C) Bonagiunta 1a.5 (pp. 299 f.); Bonagiunta 1b.8 (p. 300)
Forcon (for **Folque/Fouque**)
[6] Duchesse 1.15 (p. 220)
France, queen of
[4] (C) CB 6e.2.6 and n. 9 (p. 122)
[5] Raim. Jord. 2.24 (p. 147); Gauc. Faid. 2.43 (p. 159); Raimb. Vaq. 2a.29 (p. 164); *s'amia* Falq. Rom. 3a.183 (p. 175)
Frauenlob
[7] Frauenlob 3.5 (p. 270)
Furies
[2] *Dirae* Verg. 3.473 (p. 31)

Gabriel, St.
[5] (C) Peire Vid. 6.20 (p. 162)
Gahmuret
[7] (EP) Frauenlob 5.IV, 12.8 (p. 272)
Galicia
[4] *Gallicia* Venant. 2.17 (p. 98)
Ganymede
[3] (C) *aquosa raptus ab Ida* Hor. 6.15 f. n. (p. 58)
[4] (C) Hil. 1a.22 (p. 111); see also Hil. 1b.29 ff.; 1c.17 ff. (p. 111)
[8] see Petrarch 6.165 and n. (p. 324)

Gaudile
[4] (C) CB **8**.6 (p. 124)
Gaul
[4] *Gallia* Sid. **3a**.116 (p. 93)
Gauvain/Gawan/Gawein
[5] (C) Bertr. Born **3**.38 (p. 154); (C) Peire Vid. **4**.17, 49 (p. 161); (C, hypothetical) Raimb. Vaq. **3c**.44 (p. 167); (C) Aim. Peg. **2**.14 (p. 171); (EP) Oc. Anon. **1**.6 (p. 184); Peire Card. **2**.7 (p. 179)
[7] (C) Rotenburg **2**.192 (p. 256); (C, hypothetical) Boppe **1**.14 (p. 262); (EP) Alexander **1**.1 (p. 261)
Genievre see **Guinevere**
Gerhart von der Hoye
[7] Frauenlob **4a**.17 (p. 271)
Gherardo
[8] Cino **4**.3 (p. 317)
Giano see **Janus**
Gingamur (for **Guigemar**)
[6] (EP) Gace (?) **1**.31 (p. 219)
Giove see **Jupiter**
[8] Cino **1**.1 (p. 316); Petrarch **3**.4 (p. 322); Petrarch **6**.163 (p. 324); *quel dio* Cino **1**.9 (p. 316)
Glaucus
[3] (C) *miraque quem . . . reddidit herba deum* Ov. **12**.160 n. (p. 68)
Glies see **Cliges**
Gnosia see **Ariadne**
Gnosida see **Ariadne**
God
[4] Primas **1**.74 (p. 112); CB **3**.14, 3 (p. 120). *pater* Gottsch. **1a**.29, 1 (p. 103); Baudri **1**.117, 119 (p. 108). *qui sedet super celos* Primas **1**.43 (p. 112)
[5] Rig. Berb. **1**.29 (p. 143); *Nostre Segner* Bertr. Born **3**.37 (p. 154); Peire Vid. **3**.16 (p. 160); Peire Vid. **6**.30 (p. 162); P. R. Tolosa **1**.31 (p. 169); Guir. Cal. **2**.1 (p. 174); Peire Card. **1**.3 (p. 178); Peire Card. **2**.16 (p. 179); Zorzi **2**.35 (p. 180); Daude Prad. (?) **1**.10 (p. 183)
[6] Couci **1**.18 (p. 201); Blondel **1b**.65 (p. 203); Thib. Ch. **3**.11 (p. 208); Comte Bret. **1**.28 (p. 215); Wil. Corb. **1**.42 (p. 211); OF Anon. **10g**.29 (p. 227)
[8] *l'alto Edeo* D. Maiano **1**.12 (p. 305); *Idio Mar. Am.* **1b**.323 (p. 310)
Golfier de las Tors
[5] (C) Guil. Magr. **2**.1 (p. 162)
Goliath
[7] Marner **3**.15 (p. 249)
[8] Petrarch **16**.5 (p. 330)
Gorgon see **Medusa**
[1] (C) *Il.* **2**.349 (p. 12)
[3] Prop. **6**.8 (p. 49)
[4] Sid. **5**.88 (p. 96)
[7] Marner **2**.2 (p. 249)
Gostanza see **Constance**
Graces
[1] (C) Χαρίτεσσιν *Il.* **3**.51 (p. 12)
Gradivus see **Mars**
Gralant
[7] (C) Gliers **3**.19 (p. 254)
Gregory
[4] (C) G. Vins. **1**.16 (p. 126)
Gui de Nanteuil
[5] (C) Raimb. Vaq. **2a**.13 (p. 164)

Guenelon
[6] (C) Thib. Ch. **6**.36 (p. 209); (C) OF Anon. **8**.15 (p. 224)
Guinevere
[6] Gille Vin. **1**.33 (p. 206)
[8] (C) *Ginevra* M. Torr. **1**.3 (p. 313)
Gunther
[4] Sed. **3**.7 (p. 105)
Guraz
[7] (C) Rotenburg **2**.182 (p. 256); (C, hypothetical) Boppe **1**.12 (p. 262)

Hebe
[3] Prop. **4**.23 (p. 48)
Hector
[1] *Il.* **2**.348 (p. 12); *Il.* **10a**.47 (p. 13); see also *Il.* **5** and **9** (pp. 12, 13)
[3] (I) Prop. **8**.34 (p. 51); (EP) Prop. **8**.31 (p. 51); Ov. **18**.19 (p. 71); Ov. **19**.30 (p. 71)
[4] (C) Ermold. **2**.34 (p. 104); (C) MLat. Anon. **2**.1 (p. 116). (I) *Priamidem* Serlo **1**.12 (p. 115).
    Priami filius Ermold. **2**.33 (p. 104); see also CB **2**.7c.1 and n. (p. 119)
[5] Raim. Jord. **1**.28 (p. 146); Peire Card. **2**.5 (p. 179)
[6] (C) Gaut. Darg. **1**.22 (p. 205)
[8] (C) Cino **2**.6 (p. 317)
Hecuba
[2] *Cisseis* Verg. **9b**.320 (p. 35)
[4] (C) CB **8**.4 (p. 124)
Helen
[1] *Od.* **1**.12 (p. 17); *Od.* **2**.121 (p. 17)
[3] See (C) *Ledae partu gratior, una tribus* Prop. **4**.30 and n. (p. 48); (C) *qualis ab Eurota*
    Phrygiis avecta carinis | coniugibus belli causa duobus erat Ov. **3**.1 f. n. (p. 64)
[4] (I) CB **3**.8.4, 14.4 (p. 120); (C) CB **6b**.3.3 (p. 121); (C) CB **8**.2 (p. 124); Stat. **1b**.214 (p. 87);
    (I, hypothetical) CB **6c**.3.3 (p. 122). (C) *Tindaris* CB **1**.3.6 (p. 118); (I) CB **2**.6.4 (p. 119);
    (C) CB **6a**.5.1 (p. 121); (C) CB **6d**.9.6 (p. 122). (C) *filia Ledae* Baudri **2a**.19 (p. 108); *cygno*
    Iove nata Sid. **5**.69 (p. 95)
[5] (C) Raim Jord. **1**.28 (p. 146); (C) Arn. Mar. **2**.17 (p. 148); (C) Arn. Mar. **3a**.155 (p. 149);
    see n. *senhal* (I) Bertr. Born. **2a**.9, **2b**.7 (p. 153); Arn. Mar. **3b**.151 (p. 149); Arn. Dan. **1**.48
    (p. 151); Guir. Born. **1**.30 (p. 155); Guil. Ad. **1**.66 (p. 169); Cerverí **3**.14 (p. 182): Oc. Anon.
    3.112 (p. 186)
[6] (C) OF Anon. **5**.10 (p. 223); (C) OF Anon. **6**.49 (p. 223); Thib. Bl. **1**.41 (p. 204); J. Neuv.
    1.21 (p. 206); Perr. Ang. **3**.24 (p. 210); R. Soiss. (?) **3**.31(p. 215); OF Anon. **10a**.28 (p. 225);
    OF Anon. **10b**.16 (p. 225); OF Anon. **10c**.28 (p. 225); OF Anon. **10d**.12 (p. 226); OF Anon.
    10e.8 (p. 226)
[7] (C) Walther (?) **2**.6 (p. 245); (C) Rotenburg **2**.205 (p. 256); *ein wip* Frauenlob (?) **7**.12
    (p. 274); see also Morungen (?) **3**.3 f. n. (p. 244)
[8] (C) Fil. Mess. **1**.10 (p. 294); (C) Sicil. Anon. **5c**.101 (p. 299); (C) Chiaro **1b**.21 (p. 301);
    (C) Chiaro (?) **1e**.13 (p. 302); (C) Guittone **2a**.7 (p. 306); (C) Guittone **2b**.8 (p. 307);
    (C) Alb. Mass. **1**.8 (p. 312); (C) *Leda . . . sua figlia* Petrarch **8**.43 f. (p. 325); (C, periphrasis)
    Petrarch **9**.7 f. (p. 326); Rin. Aq. **2**.3 (p. 292); D. Maiano **2**.8 (p. 306)
Helle
[3] (C) Prop. **10**.5 (p. 52)
Hercules
[3] (C) Hor. **5**.1 (p. 58); (C) Hor. **7**.31 (p. 59); (EP) Prop. **4**.23 (p. 48); Ov. **17**.253 (p. 71)
[4] (C) Claud. **3**.38 (p. 90); *Herculeo . . . dorso* Sid. **3e**.584 (p. 94). (C) *Alcides* Claud. **2**.533
    (p. 89); (C) Sid. **3b**.183 (p. 94); (C) Baudri **2a**.116 n. (p. 109); (C) CB **7b**.4a.1 (p. 123).
    (C) *Tirynthius heros* Sid. **3e**.581 (p. 94)
Hermione
[1] *Od.* **1**.14 (p. 17)

[3] (C) Prop. **3.6** (p. 48)
Hero
[4] *Sestias* Sid. **5.71** (p. 96)
[5] Raim. Jord. **1.30** (p. 146); Arn. Mar. **3b.**150 (p. 149)
Herod
[4] (C) Primas **1.78** (p. 112)
Hester see **Esther**
Hiberia
[4] Sid. **5.86** (p. 96)
Hippodamia
[4] Sid. **5.69** (p. 95)
Hippolyte
[2] see Verg. **5.661** n. (p. 32)
[4] Claud. **3a.**35 (p. 90). *Thermodontiaca . . . genetrice* Sid. **5.76** (p. 96)
Hippolytus
[4] (C) Sid. **3c.**199 (p. 94); (C) CB **7g.**4.2 (p. 124). (C) *Virbium* Claud. **3a.**17 n. (p. 90). (C) *The-side* Serlo **1.14** (p. 115). See periphrasis Sid. **5.76** f. n. (p. 96)
[7] (EP) *Ypolitus* Gliers **2.16** n. (p. 254)
Hippomenes
[3] (I) Ov. **14.**124 (p. 69)
[4] Sid. **5.87** (p. 96)
Holofernes
[7] (EP) Frauenlob (?) **7.10** (p. 274)
Homer
[3] *Maeonium vatem* Ov. **18.**21 (p. 71)
[4] (I) Petr. Gramm. **1.5.**1 (p. 100); (C) Paul. Diac. **1.4.**1 (p. 101); (C) Einh. (?) **1.**74 (p. 101); (I) Sed. **3.5** (p. 105); (I) Baudri **2b.**31 (p. 110); see also Sid. **4.**122 n. (p. 95)
[8] Petrarch **15.**1 (p. 329)
Horace
[4] (I) *Flaccus* Petr. Gramm. **1.5.**3 (p. 100); (C) Paul. Diac. **1.4.**1 (p. 101)
Horant
[7] (C, hypothetical) Boppe **1.5** (p. 262)
Hylas
[3] (C) *Theiodamanteo . . . Hylae* Prop. **5.6** (p. 49)
Hypsipyle
[4] *Lemnias* Sid. **5.66** (p. 95)
[8] (C) Petrarch **9.**11 (p. 326)

Icarius
[1] *Od.* **7.**195 (p. 21)
[3] Ov. **20.**44 (p. 72)
Icarus
[3] (C) *Daedaleo . . . Icaro* Hor. **2.13** (p. 57)
[6] (EP) *Dedalus . . . et ses fix* Ad. Halle **1.**29 ff. (p. 216)
Idomeneus
[1] *Il.* **6c.**XIII.500 (p. 13)
Ilia
[3] (C) Hor. **3.8** (p. 57)
[4] (C) *Martia Ilia* Stat. **1c.**243 (p. 87)
Inachus see **Io**
Io
[3] *Inachidos* Prop. **2.20** (p. 47)
[4] (C) Baudri **2a.**21 (p. 108); (C) G. Vins. **2.**616 (p. 127)
Iovis see **Jupiter**

Iris/Hyris
[5] (C) Arn. Mar. **3b.**169 n. (p. 150); (C) Aim. Bel. 1.46 (p. 177)
Isaac
[4] (C) Sed. **2.**56 (p. 105); Sed. **2.**54, 58 (p. 105)
Isabel
[4] (C) CB **8.**5 (p. 124)
Ischomache
[3] (C) Prop. **6.**9 (p. 49)
Iseut/Isolde/Isalde/Ysalde/Isaotta
[5] (C) Arn. Mar. **3a.**157 (p. 149); (C) Bertr. Born. **1.**38 (p. 153); Raimb. Or. **1.**29 (p. 144); Bern. Vent. **2.**48 (p. 145); Arn. Mar. **3b.**163 (p. 150); Raimb. Vaq. **2b.**56 (p. 165); Pons Capd. **1b.**15 (p. 173); Falq. Rom. **3a.**136 (p. 175); Falq. Rom. **3b.**26 (p. 176); Falq. Rom. **3c.**43 (p. 176); *la bell' a cui servi Tristans* Raim. Mir. **1.**45 (p. 170); *s'amia* Raim. Mir. **2.**34 (p. 170); *s'amia* Aim. Peg. **1.**31 (p. 171); *s'amia* Pons Capd. **1a.**43 (p. 172)
[6] (C) Moniot **1.**50 (p. 204); (C) OF Anon. **3.**50 (p. 222); (C) *celle . . . cui Tristans provait a l'essai* OF Anon. **10h.**33 f. (p. 227); (C) OF Anon. **10j.**18 (p. 227); Pr. *Trist.* **1b.**83 (p. 215); R. Soiss. (?) **3.**18 (p. 215); Comte Bret. **1.**31 (p. 215); OF Anon. **10i.**6 (p. 227)
[7] (C) Liechtenstein **2.**2 (p. 252); (C) Tannhäuser **1.II.**5 (p. 260); (EP) Marner **1.**21 (p. 248); Bernger **1.**4 (p. 242); *der küniginne* Veldeke **1.**2 (p. 241); *eines wibes* Zweter **1.**2 (p. 246)
[8] (C) Giac. Lent. **2.**46 (p. 292); (C) Sicil. Anon. **5b.**7 (p. 298); (C) Chiaro **1d.**7 (p. 302); (C) D. Maiano **1.**14 (p. 305); (C) M. Torr. **1.**3 (p. 313); (EP) Sicil. Anon. **2.**13 (p. 297); Giac. Lent. **1.**39 (p. 291); Giac. Pugl. **1.**28 (p. 294); Fil. Mess. **1.**11 (p. 294); Re Giov. **1.**53, 60 (p. 295); Bonagiunta **2b.**33 (p. 300)
Itylus
[1] *Od.* **6.**522 (p. 19)
[3] Catull. **1.**14 (p. 38)
Iwein see **Yvain**

Jacob
[4] (C) Sed. **2.**57 (p. 105); (C) *proles Isaac* Sed. **2.**54 (p. 105)
[5] (C) Peire Vid. **6.**50 (p. 162)
[7] (C) Boppe **2.**14 (p. 264)
Jael
[7] (I) Marner **3.**11 (p. 249)
James, St.
[4] (C) Venant. **2.**20 (p. 98)
Janus
[8] *Giano* ('month of January') Petrarch **3.**6 (p. 322)
Jason
[3] see Ov. **12.**158 n. (p. 68)
[6] (C) Thib. Ch. **1.**4 (p. 207)
Jehan, Maistre
[6] *Jeux-partis* **2.**41 (p. 218)
Jeroboam
[7] (C) Boppe **2.**15 (p. 264)
Jesus/Jesus Christ see **Christ**
Job
[7] (C) Boppe **2.**13 (p. 264)
John, St.
[4] (C) Venant. **2.**20 (p. 98); (C) G. Vins. **1.**11 (p. 126)
John (John of Damascus?)
[4] (C) G. Vins. **1.**15 and n. (p. 126)
Jonah
[4] (I) Archipoeta **2.**19, 21, 45 (pp. 113 f.)

Jonathan
[7] (C) *Jonatas* Boppe **2.**11 (p. 264)
Joseph
[4] (C) Theod. **1.**30 (p. 101)
Joshua
[7] (C) Boppe **2.**18 (p. 264)
Josiah
[7] (C) Boppe **2.**10 (p. 264)
Jove, Jovis see **Jupiter**
Juba
[8] Amico **1.**3 (p. 319)
Judas (Iscariot)
[8] (C) Chiaro **2b.**17 (p. 303); (C) *Mar. Am.* **1b.**321 (p. 310)
Judas (Maccabeus)
[4] (C) MLat. Anon. **1.**7.4 (p. 106)
[7] (C) Boppe **2.**11 (p. 264)
Judith
[7] (I) Marner **3.**6 (p. 249)
Julius/Julius Caesar see also **Caesar**
[4] (C) MLat. Anon. **1.**7.1 (p. 106); (I) Benzo **1.**8 (p. 107); (I) Baudri **3.**4 (p. 110)
[5] (EP) Arn. Mar. **1.**29 (p. 148)
[6] (C) Andr. Contr. **1.**40 (p. 205); (C) Thib. Ch. **2.**16 (p. 207)
[7] (C, hypothetical) Gliers **1.**2 (p. 253)
[8] (EP) Guittone **1.**37 (p. 306); (EP, periphrasis) Petrarch **16.**1 f. (p. 330)
Junia
[3] Catull. **5.**16 (p. 42)
Juno
[3] (C) *Iove digna soror* Prop. **6.**6 and n. (p. 49); see (C) *divae* Prop. **6.**13 n. (p. 49); (EP) Catull. **4.**138 f. (p. 41)
[4] (C) Baudri **2a.**20 (p. 108); Stat. **1a.**134 (p. 86); *novercae* Sid. **3e.**582 (p. 94)
[7] Frauenlob **1.**V.5 (p. 269)
Jupiter/Iup(p)iter, gen. **Jovis**
[2] Verg. **4.**567 (p. 31)
[3] (EP) Catull. **4.**140 (p. 41); (EP) Prop. **8.**25 (p. 51); Prop. **4.**29, 32 (p. 48); Prop. **6.**6 (p. 49); Ov. **3.**8 (p. 64); *plumis abditus albis callidus . . . adulter ave* Ov. **3.**3 f. n. (p. 64)
[4] (C) CB **7c.**4b.2 (p. 123); (C) CB **7d.**2.2 (p. 123); Stat. **1a.**136 (p. 87); Sid. **5.**89 (p. 96); Hil. **1a.**21, 24 (p. 111); Hil. **1b.**29 (p. 111); Hil. **1c.**24 (p. 112); Baudri **2a.**20, 22, 67, 68 (pp. 108 f.); CB **4.**5.1 (p. 120); CB **6f.**8.7 (p. 122); *Priiupiter* CB **7a.**2b.1 (p. 122); G. Vins. **2.**613 (p. 127); *aethrae rector* Stat. **1a.**135 f. (p. 87); *rector superorum* Hil. **1c.**17 (p. 111)
Justinian
[4] (C) *Iustinianos* Benzo **1.**14 (p. 107)

Kahedin
[8] (C) *Caedin Mar. Am.* **5.**333 (p. 311)
Karolus/Karl see **Charles (Charlemagne)**
Kronos see **Zeus**

Ladas
[3] (I) Catull. **7.**15 (p. 43)
Lady of the Lake see **Donzella del Lago, La**
Laertes
[1] *Od.* **7.**192 (p. 21)
[4] see (C) *vim Laertidae* 'Laus Pis.' **1.**61 (p. 86)

Lais
[3] (C) Ov. **1**.12 (p. 63)
Lancelot
[5] (EP) Uc Pena **1**.25 (p. 183)
[6] (EP) Gille Vin. **1**.34 (p. 206)
[8] (C) Sicil. Anon. **4**.57 (p. 298); (C, hypothetical) *Mar. Am.* **3**.33 (p. 311)
Landrics
[5] (C) P. R. Tolosa **1**.32 (p. 169); (C) Pons Capd. **2**.42 (p. 173); see also *Enricx* Paul. Mars. **1**.4 n. (p. 178)
Laodamia
[3] (C) Catull. **2**.74 (p. 39); see also (C) Catull. **3**.129–132 (p. 40); (C) Ov. **18**.20 (p. 71)
[4] (C) *quam fecerunt . . . maenada planctus* Stat. **2**.49 (p. 88)
Larina
[2] Verg. **5**.655 (p. 32)
Latona see **Leto**
[2] Verg. **1**.502 (p. 29)
[4] Ermold. **1**.534 (p. 103)
Latonia see **Diana**
Laura
[8] Petrarch **10**.50 (p. 326); Petrarch **12**.4 (p. 328); *quel sole* Petrarch **15**.2 (p. 329); *questo novo fior d'onestate et di bellezze* Petrarch **15**.11 (p. 329). For the identification of Laura with Daphne, see under **Daphne**
Laurence, St.
[8] *Lorenzo* (C) Cino **3**.7 (p. 317)
Lavinia
[4] (C) Stat. **1c**.244 (p. 87)
[5] Arn. Mar. **3b**.155 (p. 149)
[7] (C) Rotenburg **1**.57 (p. 255); Gutenburg **1d**.Vb.28 (p. 260)
Lazarus
[4] (I) Gottsch. **1b**.56.3 (p. 103)
Leander
[5] (C) Raim. Jord. **1**.30 (p. 146); (C) Arn. Mar. **3b**.150 (p. 149)
Leda
[3] (C) Prop. **4**.29 (p. 48); (C) Ov. **3**.3 (p. 64); (EP) Ov. **4**.42 (p. 65); Prop. **4**.30 (p. 48)
[4] (C) G. Vins. **2**.620 (p. 127); (C, implied) CB **4**.5.7 n. (p. 120); Claud. **3a**.6 (p. 90); see Stat. **1a**.135 n. (p. 87)
[5] (C) Arn. Mar. **3a**.155 (p. 149)
[8] Petrarch **8**.43 (p. 325)
Leo, Pope
[4] (C) G. Vins. **1**.15 (p. 126)
Lethaea
[3] (C) Ov. **16a**.70 (p. 70)
Leto see **Latona**
[1] *Od.* **3**.106 (p. 18)
Liber see **Bacchus**
Louis, king
[5] (C) *Lodoyc* Raimb. Vaq. **5**.74 (p. 167); Raimb. Vaq. **3b**.10 (p. 166)
Louis the Pious
[4] *Ludewicus* Sed. **2**.53, 56 (p. 105)
Lucan
[8] Amico **1**.8 (p. 319)
Lucifer
[6] (C) Ad. Halle **2**.37 (p. 216)
[7] (EP) Henneberger **2**.7 n. (p. 267)

[8] (C) Chiaro **3b**.65 (p. 304)
Lucretia
[8] (C, periphrasis) Petrarch **9**.9 f. (p. 326)
Lunete
[7] Frauenlob **1**.IV.6 (p. 269)
Lydia
[3] Hor. **3**.6, 7 (p. 57)

Machaon
[3] *inermis* Ov. **17**.256 (p. 71); *Machaoniis . . . artibus* Ov. **21**.5 (p. 72)
Maeonian
[2] Verg. **9a**.216 (p. 34)
[3] Ov. **18**.21 (p. 71)
Magi
[8] (C) Lapo **1**.1 (p. 315)
Maioranus
[4] Sid. **2a**.182 (p. 92)
Manlius
[3] Catull. **5**.16 (p. 42)
Marcus (Aurelius)
[4] (C) Prisc. **1**.46 (p. 97); (C) Einh. (?) **1**.73 (p. 101); (C) Serlo **1**.16 (p. 115); (I) Serlo **2**.13 (p. 115)
Mark (king)
[8] Re Giov. **1**.55 (p. 295)
Maro see **Virgil**
Mars see also **Ilia, Penthesilea**
[2] *Mavors* (C) Verg. **6**.332 (p. 33)
[3] Ov. **9**.6 (p. 67)
[4] (C) Claud. **2**.526 (p. 89); Stat. **1**.243 (p. 87); Baudri **2a**.20 (p. 108); (with the meaning 'war') Sid. **2b**.233 (p. 93). *Gradivus* (C) Claud. **1**.120 (p. 88)
[7] Würzburg **1**.15 (p. 253)
Martin, St. (of Tours)
[4] (C) Archipoeta **1**.6.3 (p. 113); Venant. **2**.17 (p. 98)
Martin, St. (of Galicia)
[4] (I) Venant. **2**.17 (p. 98)
Mary
[6] Thib. Ch. **6**.31 (p. 208); *fille et mere a Jhesu le Creatour* OF Anon. **11**.13 f. (p. 228)
[7] *du vil wîsen Salomônes wol gezierter küneges trôn* Marner **3**.5 (p. 249)
Mavors see **Mars**
Medea
[4] Sid. **5**.68 (p. 95)
[7] Tannhäuser **1**.II.7 (p. 261)
Medusa see **Gorgon**
[8] (C) Petrarch **5**.6 (p. 323)
Meges
[1] *Il.* **6a**.II.627 (p. 12)
Mei von Lone
[7] (C) Botenlouben **1**.61 n. (p. 247)
Meleager
[5] (C) Arn. Dan. **2**.32 (p. 152)
Meliboea
[4] (C) Stat. **2**.48 (p. 88)
Melioth
[7] (C) Rotenburg **1**.47 (p. 255)

Menelaus
[1]   *Od.* **9**.518 (p. 22)
[4]   (C) *brevitatem Atridae* 'Laus Pis.' **1**.61 (p. 86)
[6]   (C) J. Neuv. **1**.20 (p. 206)
Mercury
[3]   Prop. **6**.11 (p. 49)
Meriones
[1]   *Il.* **7**.651 (p. 13)
Merlin
[5]   (EP) Oc. Anon. **1**.7 (p. 185)
Messiah
[4]   Carm. Cant. **1**.4a.7 (p. 106)
Metabus
[4]   (C) Sid. **2a**.190 (p. 92)
Midas
[5]   See periphrasis (C) Folq. Mars. **1**.39 f. (p. 154)
Miels de dompna
[5]   Rig. Berb. **2**.8 (p. 143)
Milanion
[3]   Ov. **5**.29 (p. 65)
Minerva see **Athena**
[3]   (C) Ov. **8**.659 (p. 66); Ov. **2**.18 (p. 63)
[4]   (C) Venant. **4**.8 (p. 99)
Minne see **Amor**
[7]   Veldeke **1**.4 (p. 241); Veldeke **2**.1 (p. 242); Bernger **1**.7 (p. 242); Marner **1**.22 (p. 248); Gliers
      2.9 (p. 254); Gutenburg (?) **1a**.44 (p. 257); Frauenlob **1**.IV.1 (p. 269); MHG Anon. **1**.9
      (p. 276); =Venus, Frauenlob **1**.V.2 (p. 269)
Minotaur
[3]   (I) *custos . . . ille Cretum* Catull. **7**.14 (p. 43)
Mnemosyne
[4]   (C) G. Vins. **2**.618 (p. 127); see also Sid. **5**.90 n. (p. 96)
Morando
[8]   (C) *Mem. Bol.* **1**.26 (p. 314)
Morgana (la fata)
[8]   (C) Guid. Col. **1**.35 (p. 293); (C) Sicil. Anon. **5a**.17 (p. 298); (C) Sicil. Anon. **5b**.7 (p. 298);
      (C) Chiaro **1a**.8 (p. 301); (C) Chiaro **1b**.21 (p. 301); (C) Chiaro **1c**.4 (p. 301); (C) Chiaro (?)
      1e.12 (p. 302); (C) Donzella **1**.3 (p. 312); (C) *Mem.Bol.* **2**.55 (p. 314); Sicil. Anon. **4**.57
      (p. 298); *Mar. Am.* **3**.32 (p. 311)
Moses
[7]   (C) Boppe **2**.14 (p. 264)
Muse/Muses
[3]   *Pegasides* Ov. **11**.27 (p. 68)
[4]   (pl.) (C) Sid. **4a**.124 (p. 95); Sed. **3**.6, 9 (p. 105); Baudri **2a**.52 (p. 109)

Nadriano see **Andrieu (of France/Paris)**
Naiad
[4]   *Naïs* (C) Girald. **1**.16 (p. 125)
Napaea
[4]   (C) Venant. **3**.105 (p. 99)
Narcissus
[5]   (C) Bern. Vent. **1**.24 (p. 145); (C) Peirol **1**.20 (p. 169)
[6]   (I) Thib. Ch. **4**.36 (p. 208); (C) R. Soiss. **1**.59 (p. 214); (C, hypothetical) *Jeux-partis* **2**.42
      (p. 218); (C) OF Anon. **9**.16 (p. 224); Rich. Fourn. **1**.10, 15 (pp. 212 f.)
[7]   *ein kint* Morungen **1**.6 (p. 243)

[8] (C) Rin. Aq. **1**.32 (p. 292); (C) Sicil. Anon. **3**.1 (p. 297); (C) Chiaro **4**.1, 13 (p. 305); (EP) Petrarch **11**.12 ff. (p. 327); *Mar. Am.* **1a**.87 (p. 309)

Nathanael
[4] (C) MLat. Anon. **1**.3.4 (p. 106)

Nausicaa
[1] *Od.* **2**.VI.17 (p. 18); see also *Od.* **3** and **4** (p. 18)

Neptune
[3] (EP) *Taenarius deus* Prop. **4**.22 (p. 48)

Nereid
[4] (C) Venant. **3**.104 (p. 94); Stat. **1**.116 (p. 86)

Nereus see **Thetis**

Nero
[4] (C) Serlo **2**.25 (p. 115)

Nerva
[4] (C) Prisc. **1**.47 (p. 97)

Nessus
[3] Hor. **7**.32 (p. 59)

Nestor
[3] (I) Prop. **9**.10 (p. 52); (C) Ov. **7**.736 (p. 66)
[4] (C) *Append. Tull.* **1**.49 (p. 85); (C) *Nestorei . . . mellis* 'Laus Pis.' **1**.64 (p. 86); (C) Serlo **2**.27 (p. 115); (I) M. Vend. **1**.52.62 (p. 125)

Nicola of Bari
[5] (C) Raim. Jord. **3**.9 n. (p. 147)

Niobe
[3] (C) Prop. **7**.7 (p. 50)

Nireus
[3] (C) Hor. **6**.15 (p. 58)

Nycteus see **Antiopa**

Odysseus see **Ulysses**
[1] *Il.* **10b**.II.636 (p. 13); *Od.* **6**.XX.80 (p. 21); *Od.* **7**.192, 195 (p. 21); *Od.* **9**.517 (p. 22)

Olenos
[3] (C) Ov. **16a**.69 (p. 70)

Oliver
[5] (C) Guir. Born. **2**.40 (p. 156); (C) Gar. Apch. **1**.17 (p. 156); (C) Peire Vid. **2**.13 (p. 160); (C) Cerverí **1**.47 (p. 181)

Olympian gods
[1] 'Ολύμπια δώματ' ἔχοντες *Od.* **6**.XX.79 (p. 21)

Opheltes see **Euryalus**

Orestes
[2] (C) *Agamemnonius . . . Orestes* Verg. **3**.471 (p. 31)

Orpheus
[3] Ov. **16a**.64 (p. 70)
[4] (C) *Thrax vates* Sid. **4a**.122 (p. 95); Baudri **2a**.24 (p. 109)
[8] (C) Petrarch **10**.51 (p. 327)

Otto der Lange
[7] Goldener **1**.15 (p. 269)

Ottokar
[7] Sigeher **1**.9 (p. 268)

Paean see **Apollo**

Palaemon
[3] (C) Ov. **12**.159 (p. 68)

Pallas see **Athena**

[3] (C) Prop. **6**.7 (p. 49); see (C) *divae* Prop. **6**.13 n. (p. 49)

[4] (C) CB **8**.3 (p. 124); CB **1**.3.1, 5.8 (pp. 118 f.)

[7] (C) Rotenburg **1**.59 (p. 255); Frauenlob **1**.V.5 (p. 269); Tannhäuser **1**.II.8 (p. 261)

Pan

[4] (C) *deus Arcas* Sid. **4a**.122 (p. 95)

Pandareos

[1] *Od.* **6**.518 (p. 19); Pandareos, daughter of, see **Aëdon**; Pandareos, daughters of, (EP) *Od.* **6**.XX.66 (p. 20)

Parcae

[4] Claud. **4**.1 (p. 91)

Paris

[2] (I) Verg. **9a**.215 (p. 34); (I) Verg. **9b**.321 (p. 35)

[3] *Phrygium . . . iudicem* Catull. **5**.18 f. and n. (p. 42). *pastor* Prop. **6**.13 (p. 49)

[4] (C) Serlo **2**.26 f. (p. 115); (C) MLat. Anon. **2**.1 (p. 116); (C) CB **7e**.3.7 (p. 123); (I) CB **7f**.2.3 (p. 123); Baudri **2a**.19 (p. 108); (I) CB **6a**.5.2 (p. 121); CB **6b**.3.2 (p. 121); (I, hypothetical) CB **6c**.3.3 (p. 122). (C) *pastor* Stat. **1b**.214 (p. 87); Sid. **5**.80 (p. 96). See also CB **2**.7c.1 n. (p. 120)

[5] (C) Arn. Mar. **3b**.151 (p. 149); (C) Arn. Dan. **1**.47 (p. 151); (C) Guir. Born. **1**.30 (p. 155); (C) Guil. Ad. **1**.66 (p. 169); (C) Oc. Anon. **3**.112 (p. 186); Cerverí **3**.14 (p. 182); *al fraire Ector* Raim. Jord. **1**.28 (p. 146)

[6] (C) Blondel **1b**.61 (p. 203); (C) Thib. Bl. **1**.40 (p. 204); (C) Perr. Ang. **3**.24 (p. 210); (C) R. Soiss. **2**.60 (p. 214); (C) R. Soiss. (?) **3**.31 (p. 215); (C) OF Anon. **10a**.28 (p. 225); (C) OF Anon. **10b**.16 (p. 225); (C) OF Anon. **10c**.28 (p. 225); (C) OF Anon. **10d**.11 (p. 226); (C) OF Anon. **10e**.7 (p. 226); (C) OF Anon. **10f**.25 (p. 226); (C) *cil de Troie* OF Anon. **6**.25 (p. 223); OF Anon. **5**.10 (p. 223)

[7] (EP) Frauenlob **5**.IV, 14.11 (p. 272); Morungen (?) **3**.3 f. (p. 244); Frauenlob **1**.V.2 (p. 269)

[8] (C) Rin. Aq. **2**.3 (p. 292); (C) Bonagiunta **1a**.7 (p. 299); (C) D. Maiano **2**.7 (p. 306); Fil. Mess. **1**.10 (p. 294); Guittone **2b**.8 (p. 307); Alb. Mass. **1**.8 (p. 312)

Parthenopaeus

[4] (C) *Arcas* Sid. **2**.166 (p. 92)

Parzival see **Perceval**

pastor see **Paris**

Patroclus

[1] *Il.* **8**.783 (p. 13)

Paul, St.

[4] (C) Venant. **2**.19 (p. 98); (C) G. Vins. **1**.12 (p. 126)

Pegasides see **Muses**

Pegasus

[3] *Pegaseo . . . volatu* Catull. **7**.16 (p. 43)

Peir der mære

[7] (C) Botenlouben **1**.59 (p. 247)

Peire Vidal

[8] (C) Bonagiunta **1a**.6 (p. 299)

Peleus

[3] Tibull. **1**.45 (p. 45)

[4] (C) Stat. **1b**.215 (p. 87)

[5] (EP) *de Pelaus la lansa* Bern. Vent. **3**.46 (p. 145)

[6] (EP) *la lance Pelee* Wil. Corb. **1**.36 (p. 211)

[8] (C) *com Peleüs sua lanza* Chiaro **3b**.46 (p. 304); (C) T. Faenza **1**.39 (p. 308); (C) *la bocca . . . mi fu lancia di Pelùs* Mar. Am. **1a**.98 ff. (p. 309); (EP) Chiaro **3a**.1 (p. 304); (EP) Giov. Arezzo **1**.1 (p. 307); emended (EP) J. Mostacci **1**.48 n. (p. 295)

Pelides see **Achilles**

Pelops
[4] (C) Primas **1**.42 (p. 112); Sid. **5**.87 (p. 96)
Penelope see also **Telemachus**
[1] *Od.* **5**.36 (p. 19); *Od.* **7**.194, 198 (p. 21); see also *Od.* **6** (p. 19)
[3] (C) Prop. **11b**.38 (p. 52); (I, negated) Hor. **4**.11 n. (p. 58); (C) Ov. **18**.22 (p. 71); see
     periphrasis (C) Ov. **20**.44 and n. (p. 72); *Telemacho . . . Penelopeo* Catull. **6**.222 f. (p. 43)
[4] (C) Stat. **2**.47 (p. 88)
Peneus see **Daphne**
Penthesilea
[2] see Verg. **5**.662 n. (p. 32)
Pentheus
[2] (C) Verg. **3**.469 (p. 31)
Perceval/Parzival
[5] (C) Rig. Berb. **2**.1 (p. 143); (C) Raimb. Vaq. **1**.17 (p. 163)
[7] (C) Rotenburg **1**.45 (p. 255); (C) Frauenlob **6a**.13 (p. 273); (EP) Dürinc **1**.11 (p. 266);
     (EP) Frauenlob (?) **7**.17 (p. 274)
Perrinez
[6] Thib. Ch. **6**.38 (p. 209)
Perseus
[3] (I) Catull. **7**.15 (p. 43)
[4] Sid. **5**.88 (p. 96)
[7] (incorrectly *Antaeus* for *Perseus*) (C) Marner **2**.4 (p. 249)
Persia, king of
[3] (C) Hor. **3**.4 (p. 57)
Pertenopés
[6] (EP) Gace (?) **1**.22 f. (p. 219)
Peter, St.
[4] (C) Venant. **2**.19 (p. 98); (C) G. Vins. **1**.12 (p. 126)
Phaedra
[4] *Gnosiacae novercae* Sid. **5**.77 (p. 97)
Philo
[4] (I) Petr. Gramm. **1**.5.2 (p. 100); (C) Paul. Diac. **1**.4.2 (p. 101)
Philoctetes
[3] (C) *Poeantius Herculis heres* Ov. **17**.253 (p. 71); (C) *Poeantius . . . heros* Ov. **21**.5 (p. 72)
Phoebus see **Apollo**
Phyllis
[4] Sid. **5**.70 (p. 96)
Pilate
[7] (C) *Wartburgkrieg* **1**.6 (p. 275); (EP) *Wartburgkrieg* **1**.1 (p. 275)
Pippin
[4] (C) *Pipinos* Benzo **1**.15 (p. 107); Ermold. **2**.36 (p. 104)
Pirithous
[1] *Od.* **10**.296 (p. 22)
[4] (C) Serlo **1**.12 (p. 115)
Plato
[4] (C) CB **7c**.4b.3 (p. 123)
Podalirius
[3] (C) Ov. **7**.735 (p. 66); (I) Ov. **10**.313 (p. 67)
Poeas, Poeantius see **Philoctetes**
Poitou, lord of
[5] Bertr. Born **2b**.8 (p. 153)
Pollux
[3] See (C) *Ledae partu gratior, una tribus* Prop. **4**.30 and n. (p. 48)
[4] (C) Sid. **2a**.183 (p. 92)

Polycletus
[8] (C) *Pollicreto* Binduccio **1**.11 (p. 318)
Polyxena
[8] (C) Petrarch **9**.11 (p. 326); (C) (emended) Sicil. Anon. **5c**.102 (p. 299)
Pompey
[4] (C) Poeta Saxo **1**.657 (p. 102); MLat. Anon. **1**.8.4 (p. 106)
[6] Thib. Ch. **2**.16 (p. 207)
[8] *il marito di sua figlia* Petrarch **16**.3 (p. 330)
Porus
[6] (C) Pr. *Trist.* **1a**.40 (p. 211)
Poseidon
[1] (C) *Il.* **1**.479 (p. 11)
Postumus
[3] (I) Prop. **11a**.23 (p. 52)
Priam
[1] *Il.* **10a**.47 (p. 13)
[2] Verg. **8b**.742 (p. 34)
[4] Ermold. **2**.33 (p. 104)
Priamides see **Hector**
Primas
[4] Primas **1**.42 (p. 112)
Procne
[3] (C) *Daulias* Catull. **1**.14 (p. 38); (C) *nocturna volucris . . . Attica* Prop. **7**.5 f. (p. 50)
Prodigal Son
[4] (I) Gottsch. **1**.29.1 (p. 103); (I) *filius ille, | qui pavi porcos in longinqua regione . . .* Baudri **1**.114 f. (p. 108)
Proserpina
[4] [C] *Deionis* G. Vins. **2**.619; see **2**.613 ff. n. (p. 127)
Protesilaus
[3] *Protesilaëam . . . domum* Catull. **2**.74 (p. 39); *flavo . . . viro* Catull. **3**.130 (p. 40); *extincto . . . viro* Ov. **18**.20 (p. 71)
Pulzella Laida, la
[8] (C, hypothetical) *Mar. Am.* **2**.211 (p. 310)
Pygmalion
[8] (EP) Petrarch **13**.12 (p. 328)
Pylaemenes
[1] *Il.* **6b**.V.576 (p. 13)
Pyramus
[5] (C) Arn. Mar. **3b**.152 (p. 149); (C) Guir. Sal. **1**.27 (p. 157); (C) Raimb.Vaq. **1**.12 (p. 163)
[6] (C) Blondel **1b**.62 (p. 203); (I) Thib. Ch. **3**.12 (p. 208); (C) OF Anon. **2**.26 (p. 221); (C) OF Anon. **9**.16 (p. 224)
[7] (EP) Gliers **2**.15 (p. 254); (EP) Der j. Meissner **1**.13 (p. 265); (EP) Der j. Meissner **2**.18 (p. 265)
[8] (C) Pier Vign. **1**.15 (p. 295); R. Filippi **1**.11 (p. 307)
Pyrrhus
[4] Sid. **3d**.226 (p. 94)

Quendis
[5] Arn. Mar. **3b**.165 (p. 150)

Rachel
[5] Peire Vid. **6**.50 (p. 162)
Raoul de Cambrai
[5] (C) Falq. Rom. **1**.6 (p. 174)

Raphael, St.
[5] Peire Vid. **6**.49 (p. 162)
Reinmar
[7] *Reimar* = Reinmar von Zweter, (C) Frauenlob **3**.1 (p. 270)
Rennewart
[7] (I) Frauenlob **4a**.15 (p. 271)
Rhesus
[3] Catull. **7**.17 (p. 43)
Richard Cœur de Lion
[5] *lo reis* Gauc. Faid. **3**.10 (p. 159)
[7] (EP) *den künic von Engellant* Walther **1**.10 (p. 244)
Riwalin
[7] (EP) Würzburg **1**.20 (p. 253)
Robert
[4] Serlo **2**.11 (p. 115)
†Rodocesta†
[5] (C) Arn. Mar. **3a**.153 n. (p. 149)
Roland
[5] (C) Arn. Mar. **4**.44 (p. 151); (C) Gar. Apch. **1**.18 (p. 156); (C) Guir. Sal. **2**.16 (p. 157); (C) Peire Vid. **2**.13 (p. 160); (C) Raimb. Vaq. **4**.101 (p. 167); (C) Raimb. Vaq. **5**.76 (p. 167); (C) Cerverí **1**.47 (p. 181); (EP) Oc. Anon. **1**.2 (p. 184); Raimb. Vaq. **3a**.12 (p. 166)
[6] (C) OF Anon. **9**.15 (p. 224)
[8] (C) *Mem. Bol.* **1**.24 (p. 314)
Rôme, künic von
[7] Boppe **2**.2 f. (p. 263)
Romulus
[4] see Benzo **1**.6 (p. 107)
Roschi bîse, der vrouwen . . . de la
[7] (C) Gutenburg **1c**.IVb.17 (p. 259)
Rüedeger
[7] (C) Herger **1**.4 (p. 240)

Sabine
[4] (C) *Sabinos* Benzo **1**.16 (p. 107)
Saladin
[7] (C) Wernher **1**.11 (p. 247); (I) Goldener **1**.2 (p. 269); (EP) Walther **1**.7 (p. 244)
Salamandra
[5] Arn. Mar. **3b**.161 (p. 150)
Salmonida see **Tyro**
Samson
[4] (C) Serlo **1**.13 (p. 115); (C) CB **7c**.4b.4 (p. 123)
[5] (C) Arn. Mar. **4**.45 (p. 151); (EP) Marc. **1**.14 (p. 142); (EP) Peire Vid. **1**.55 (p. 160); (EP) Oc. Anon. **1**.4 (p. 184)
[7] (C, hypothetical) Boppe **1**.4 (p. 262); (C) Boppe **2**.16 (p. 264); (EP) Zweter **2**.4 (p. 246); (EP) Dürinc **1**.13 (p. 266); (EP) Frauenlob (?) **7**.2 (p. 274)
[8] (C, hypothetical) Lapo **2**.17 (p. 315)
Samuel
[4] (C) MLat. Anon. **1**.3.2 (p. 105)
[7] (C) Boppe **2**.12 (p. 264)
Sarah
[5] Zorzi **2**.121 (p. 180)
Saul
[8] Petrarch **16**.7 (p. 330)
Schoeneida see **Atalanta**

Scipio (Africanus)
[4] (C) Benzo **1.4** (p. 107); (C) *Scipiadę* Poeta Saxo **1.655** (p. 102)
[8] (EP) *quel fiore anticho di vertuti et d'arme* Petrarch **15.9** (p. 329)
Scylla
[4] Sid. **5.68** (p. 95)
Seguis
[5] Arn. Mar. **3b**.166 and n. (p. 150); Comt. Dia **2.11** and n. (p. 168)
Semele see **Euhan** *s.v.* **Bacchus**
Semiramis
[3] (C) Ov. **1.11** (p. 65)
[5] (C) Arn. Mar. **3a**.154 (p. 149)
Seneca
[7] (C, hypothetical) Boppe **1.15** (p. 262)
Serena (for **Seneca**?)
[5] (C) Guir. Ros. **1.22** n. (p. 158)
Sestias see **Hero**
Sibyl
[4] (I) Baudri **2a**.54 (p. 109)
[8] (I) M. Torr. **1.10** (p. 313)
Simeon
[7] (C) Boppe **2.15** (p. 264)
Sinon
[4] (I) M. Vend. **2.53.8** (p. 125)
Sipylus
[3] Prop. **7.8** (p. 50)
Sisora
[7] Marner **3.**11 (p. 249)
'Smondo, (di)
[8] (C) Bonagiunta **1a**.6 (p. 299); Bonagiunta **1b**.8 (p. 300)
Sobrepretz
[5] Cerverí **1.45** (p. 181)
Solomon
[4] (C) Venant. **1.80** (p. 98); (C) Theod. **1.29** (p. 101); (C) Sed. **2.52** (p. 104); (C) Benzo **1.11**
       (p. 107); (C) Serlo **1.15** (p. 115); (C) Serlo **2.25** (p. 115)
[5] (C) Falq. Rom. **1.43** (p. 174); (C) Zorzi **1.60** (p. 180); (EP) Peire Vid. **1.53** (p. 160); (EP) Oc.
       Anon. **1.1** (p. 184); Peire Card. **2.8** (p. 179)
[6] (EP) Couci **2.9** (p. 202); (EP) Thib. Ch. **2.34** (p. 207)
[7] (C, hypothetical) Boppe **1.1** (p. 262); (C) Boppe **2.17** (p. 264); (EP) Veldeke **2.1** (p. 242);
       (EP) Zweter **2.6** (p. 246); (EP) Dürinc **1.18** (p. 266); (EP) Frauenlob (?) **7.5** (p. 274); Marner
       3.5 (p. 249)
[8] (C, hypothetical) Lapo **2.17** (p. 315)
Soramonde
[6] (C) OF Anon. **7.150** (p. 223)
Spain
[6] Guil. Ferr. **1.18** (p. 201)
Stheneboea see **Bellerophon**

Tantalus
[5] (C) Raimb. Vaq. **1.20** (p. 163); (C) Calvo **1.55** (p. 179)
[7] (C) Liechtenstein **1a**.114 (p. 251); (C) MHG Anon. **1.1** (p. 276)
Tarpeia
[2] Verg. **5.656** (p. 32)
Telamon see **Aias/Ajax**

Telemachus
[3] (C) *Telemacho . . . Penelopeo* Catull. **6**.222 f. (p. 43)
Telephus
[3] (C) *qui bibit ubera cervae,* | *armatique tulit vulnus, inermis opem* Ov. **17**.255 f. (p. 71)
Tertullus
[4] (I) Petr. Gramm. **1**.5.2 (p. 100); (C) Paul. Diac. **1**.4.2 (p. 101)
Thebana see **Andromache**
Theodamas see **Hylas**
Theodosius
[4] (C) Poeta Saxo **1**.662 (p. 102); (C) *Theodosios* Benzo **1**.14 (p. 107)
Thersites
[4] (I) M. Vend. **2**.53.7 (p. 125)
Theseus
[3] *Thesea . . . carina* Prop. **1**.1 (p. 47); Ov. **2**.15 (p. 63)
[4] Stat. **1**.132 (p. 86). (C) *Atticus Aegides* Sid. **2a**.193 (p. 92)
[6] (EP) *la Theseü* Rich. Fourn. **2**.35 (p. 213)
Thesides see **Hippolytus**
Thetis
[3] (C) *Nereis . . . Thetis* Tibull. **1**.45 f. (p. 45); (C) Ov. **13**.60 (p. 69); Hor. **1**.14 (p. 56)
[4] Stat. **1b**.216 (p. 87); Claud. **3a**.7 (p. 90)
Thibaut
[5] (C) Raimb. Vaq. **3b**.10 (p. 166)
Thisbe
[5] (C) Arn. Mar. **3a**.155 (p. 149); Arn. Mar. **3b**.152 (p. 149); Guir. Sal. **1**.27 (p. 157); Raimb. Vaq. **1**.12 (p. 163)
[6] (I) Thib. Ch. **3**.12 (p. 208); OF Anon. **2**.28 (p. 221)
[7] (EP) Der j. Meissner **1**.13, 18 (p. 265); (EP) Der j. Meissner **2**.18 (p. 265)
[8] (C) Chiaro **1a**.8 (p. 301); (C) Chiaro **1b**.20 (p. 301); (C) Chiaro **1c**.4 (p. 301); (C) Chiaro **1d**.7 (p. 302); (C) R. Filippi **1**.11 (p. 307); Pier Vign. **1**.15 (p. 293)
Thyrsis
[4] Scd. **3**.5 (p. 105)
Tibullus
[4] (I) Petr. Gramm. **1**.5.3 (p. 100); (C) Paul. Diac. **1**.4.3 (p. 101)
Tidô see **Dido**
Tiphys
[3] (I) Ov. **6**.8 (p. 65); (EP) Ov. **6**.6 (p. 65)
[8] (I) Petrarch **14**.13 (p. 328)
Tiresias
[4] (I) M. Vend. **2**.53.8 (p. 125)
Titan
[4] *Append. Tibull.* **1**.51 (p. 85)
Tithonus
[3] (I) Prop. **9**.10 (p. 52)
[8] (C) *Titon* Petrarch **12**.5 (p. 328)
Titus
[4] (C) Prisc. **1**.48 (p. 97)
Trajan
[4] (C) Sid. **3**.116 (p. 93); (C) Prisc. **1**.49 (p. 97); (C) Venant. **1**.82 (p. 98)
[7] (EP) *Troianus* Henneberger **1**.1 (p. 266)
Tristan/Tristran/Tristram/Tristano
[5] (C) Raimb. Or. **1**.29 (p. 144); (C) Bern. Vent. **2**.46 (p. 145); (C) Arn. Mar. **3b**.163 (p. 150); (C) Raimb. Vaq. **2b**.55 (p. 165); (C) Uc Bac. **1**.14 (p. 168); (C) Raim. Mir. **1**.45 (p. 170); (C, hypothetical) Raim. Mir. **2**.34 (p. 170); (C) Aim. Peg. **1**.30 (p. 171); (C) Aim. Peg. **2**.16 (p. 171); (C) Pons Capd. **1a**.43 (p. 172); (C) Pons Capd. **1b**.15 (p. 173); (C) Falq. Rom.

3a.136 (p. 175); (C) Falq. Rom. **3b**.26 (p. 176); (C) Falq. Rom. **3c**.43 (p. 176); (C) Cerverí
2.35 (p. 182); (C) Daude Prad. (?) **1**.21 (p. 183); (C) Oc. Anon. **2**.3 (p. 185); (C) Oc. Anon.
3.113 (p. 186); (EP) Oc. Anon. **1**.5 (p. 184) Bertr. Born **1**.38 (p. 153); Peire Card. **2**.3 (p. 179)
[6] (C) Chrétien **1**.29 (p. 200); (C) Couci **1**.19 (p. 201); (C) Guiot **1**.48 (p. 202); (C) Blondel
1a.54 (p. 202); (C) Blondel **1b**.62 (p. 203); (C) Eustache **1**.33 (p. 203); (C) Moniot **1**.50
(p. 202); (C) Thib. Ch. **5**.34 (p. 208); (C, hypothetical) R. Soiss. **2**.60 (p. 214); (C) R. Soiss. (?)
3.18 (p. 204); (C) Comte Bret. **1**.30 (p. 215); (C) OF Anon. **1**.5 (p. 221); (C) OF Anon. **7**.68
(p. 223); (C) OF Anon. **9**.17 (p. 224); (C) OF Anon. **10f**.26 (p. 226); (C) OF Anon. **10g**.32
(p. 227); (C) OF Anon. **10i**.6 (p. 227); Pr. *Trist.* **1a**.28 (p. 211); OF Anon. **10h**.34 (p. 227)
[7] (C) Veldeke **1**.1 (p. 241); (C) Bernger **1**.2 (p. 242); (C) Zweter **1**.1 (p. 246); (EP) Marner
1.21 (p. 248); (EP) Gliers **2**.13 (p. 254); Liechtenstein **2**.III.2 (p. 252)
[8] (C) Giac. Lent. **1**.39 (p. 291); (C) Giac. Pugl. **1**.27 (p. 294); (C) Fil. Mess. **1**.11 (p. 294);
(C) Re Giov. **1**.52 (p. 295); (C) Sicil. Anon. **1**.60 (p. 296); (C) Bonagiunta **2a**.31 (p. 300);
(C) Bonagiunta **2b**.33 (p. 300); (C) Binduccio **1**.12 (p. 318); (EP) Sicil. Anon. **2**.13 (p. 297);
Re Giov. **1**.58 (p. 295)
Troianus see **Trajan**
Troilus (son of Priam)
[4] Sid. **2**.191 (p. 92)
Troilus (lover of Brizeida)
[5] Azalais **1**.63 (p. 177)
Tulla
[2] Verg. **5**.656 (p. 32)
Tullius see **Cicero**
Turnus
[2] Verg. **6**.324, 337 (p. 33)
[4] Stat. **1c**.245 (p. 87)
[7] (C) Gutenburg **1d**.Vb.25 (p. 260)
Tydides see **Diomedes**
Tyndareos
[1] *Od.* **7**.199 (p. 21)
Tyndaris see **Helen**
Typhoeus (?)
[3] see Hor. **7**.32 f. n. (p. 59)
Tyro
[3] (EP) *Salmonida* Prop. **4**.21 (p. 48)

Ugly Maiden, the, see **Pulzella Laida, la**
Ulysses see **Odysseus**
[3] (I) Prop. **11a**.23 (p. 52)
[4] (C) *Append. Tull.* **1**.49 (p. 85); (C) Archipoeta **1**.5.1 (p. 113); (C) MLat. Anon. **2**.1 (p. 116);
Stat. **2**.47 (p. 88). (C) *vim Laertidae* 'Laus Pis.' **1**.61 (p. 86)
[8] Petrarch **15**.6 (p. 329)

Valensa
[5] (C) Arn. Mar. **3b**.166 and n. (p. 150); (C) Comt. Dia **2**.10 and n. (p. 168)
Venus see **Aphrodite**
[2] Verg. **9b**.321 (p. 35)
[3] (C) Catull. **5**.18 (p. 42); (C) Ov. **8**.659 (p. 66); Hor. **4**.9 (p. 58); Ov. **5**.60 (p. 65); Ov. **6**.7
(p. 65). *Dione* (C) Ov. **4**.33 n. (p. 64); see (C) *divae* Prop. **6**.13 n. (p. 49).
[4] (C) Claud. **4**.3 (p. 91); (I) Venant. **3**.103 (p. 99); (C) Venant. **4**.8 (p. 99); (C) Baudri **2a**.20
(p. 108); Ripoll **1**.39 (p. 116); (C) *Veneris . . . formam* Ripoll **4**.3 (p. 117); (C) Ripoll **5**.21,
23 (p. 117); (C) CB **1**.3.7 (p. 118); (I) CB **3**.8.4, 14.4 (p. 120); see (C) *me quoque* Sid. **5**.80
(p. 96); *egomet* Stat. **1a**.116 (p. 86); Claud. **3**.16 (p. 90); Venant. **3**.49, 99 (p. 99); Ermold.
2.33 (p. 104); Ripoll **4**.3, 5 (p. 117); CB **1**.5.2 (p. 118); CB **7b**.4a.3 (p. 123); CB **7f**.2.2

(p. 123); with the meaning 'love', Sid. **2b**.233 (p. 93); *de spe Venerea* CB **7a**.2b.2 (p. 122). (C) *Cypris* Girald. **1**.15 (p. 125); CB **7e**.3.5 (p. 123). (C) *deam Cithaream* Ripoll. **3**.22 f. (p. 116); *Cytharee* CB **1**.3.2 (p. 118); *Cytharea* CB **5**.2.8 (p. 121)
[7] (I) Morungen **2**.1 (p. 244); (C) Wolfram (?) **1**.10 (p. 245); Dürinc **1**.10 (p. 266); see *Minne* Frauenlob **1**.V.2 (p. 269). See also under **Dione**
[8] (I) *dea d'amare* Mar. Am. **1a**.134 (p. 309); (C) *d'amore la dea* Alb. Mass. **1**.9 (p. 312); Bonagiunta **1a**.8 (p. 299)

Verres
[4] (I) M.Vend. **2**.53.8 (p. 125)
Virbius see **Hippolytus**
Virgil
[4] (I) Petr. Gramm. **1**.5.1 (p. 100); (C) Paul. Diac. **1**.4.1 (p. 101); (I) *Maronem* Serlo **2**.13 (p. 115)
[7] (C, hypothetical) Boppe **1**.8 (p. 262); (EP) Frauenlob (?) **7**.8 (p. 274)
[8] (EP) Chiaro **2b**.21 (p. 303); Petrarch **15**.1 (p. 329)
Vivianz
[7] (I) Frauenlob **4b**.18 (p. 272)
Vogelweide, der von
[7] (C) Frauenlob **3**.3 (p. 270)
Vrouwenlob see **Frauenlob**
Vulcan
[2] Verg. **7**.439 (p. 34)
[3] (EP) Ov. **7**.741 (p. 66)
[8] Petrarch **3**.3 (p. 322)

Waldemar
[7] Frauenlob **4b**.19 (p. 272)
Wernhart
[7] Herger **1**.1 (p. 240)
Wilhalm von Hunesburg
[7] Wernher **1**.6 (p. 247)
Wood nymph see **Napaea**

Ypolitus see **Hippolytus**
Ysalde see under **Iseut**
Yvain/Iwein
[5] (C) Aim. Peg. **2**.15 (p. 171)
[6] (EP) Perr. Ang. **2**.34 (p. 210)
[7] (C) Frauenlob **1**.IV.5 (p. 269)
[8] (C) *Ivano* Bonagiunta **2a**.30 (p. 300)

Zacheus
[4] (C) Primas **1**.76 (p. 112)
Zethus
[1] *Od.* **6**.523 (p. 19)
Zeus
[1] (C) *Il.* **1**.478 (p. 11); (C) *Il.* **10a**.47 (p. 13); (C) *Il.* **10b**.II.636 and n. (p. 13); Κρονίων 'son of Kronos' *Il.* **4**.209 (p. 12); *Od.* **3**.105 (p. 18); *Od.* **4**.151 (p. 18); *Od.* **6**.XX.61 (p. 20)

General Index

alba, influence of 321
antonomasia 2–3 and n. 3, 77 and n. 8, 78

comparison/identification attributes 4, 14, 23, 26, 72, 79, 132, 135–6, 186–7, 236, 277, 283, 284, 286, 331, 337, 345, 348, 353

Disticha Catonis 102

exemplars, types of:
  biblical 4, 84, 128, 130–1, 188–9, 228, 231, 279–80, 281, 302–3, 334, 354
  classical authors 95, 100, 101, 105, 110
  classical mythological 4, 23, 27, 36, 38, 44, 53, 77–9, 84, 127–30, 188–9, 229, 230–1, 279–80, 333–4, 345–6, 347–8, 349, 351–2, 353–4, 355
  divine beings: general comparisons 10–11, 17, 18, 27, 29; specific comparisons 14–15, 17, 23, 35, 79, 128, 197, 344–5, 355
  figures of drama 31, 37
  historical/legendary 2, 4, 5, 6, 61, 79, 84, 127 and n. 12, 128, 130, 140, 187, 189, 229, 231, 236, 280, 334, 341, 346, 348, 349, 351, 352, 354, 355
  medieval 5–6, 120, 122, 188–90, 203, 231, 280–1, 334, 349, 351–2, 354
exemplary comparison, definition 2
exemplary comparison/identification in apostrophe 2, 27, 56, 60, 64, 68, 69, 71, 74, 81 n. 11, 134, 137, 168, 177–8, 197, 236, 249, 249–50 (typological), 267, 269, 275, 286, 294, 298–9, 300–1, 302, 305–6, 306–7, 309, 312–15, 318–19, 340
exemplary parallel 2, 4–5, 26, 28, 46, 48, 51, 54–6, 60–2, 74–5, 76, 77, 82, 136–7, 346, 348
exemplum 6, 62, 74–5, 108, 118, 216, 278, 303 and n. 7, 332–3, 337, 351, 353, 354

function of examples 3, 7, 9, 19, 24, 27, 28, 34, 37, 54, 56, 62, 73, 74, 75, 76, 82–3, 84, 135, 142, 188, 196, 229, 277–9, 333, 343, 347, 348, 351, 352–3, 354

genres associated with comparison/identification 4, 6, 7, 14, 23, 26–7, 35, 44–5, 59, 62, 77, 83, 85, 127, 142 and n. 2, 178, 186, 199–200, 228, 236, 238–40, 276–7, 290, 331, 343, 346, 347, 350, 351, 353

identification, definition 2–3
identification 2–3, 4, 5, 6, 8, 34–6, 43, 46–7, 53, 58, 72, 81, 100, 128, 132, 134–5, 187, 229, 236, 278, 285, 286, 331, 336, 341, 342

Jove/Jupiter, disguises 64, 87, 96–7, 109, 111–12, 120, 127, 130, 324

names, types and placing 7–8, 15, 23–4, 36, 73, 77–9, 82, 128–32, 140, 189–91, 192–3, 198, 229–31, 232–3, 236–7, 279–81, 283–4, 331, 333–5, 342, 345, 346, 348, 349, 350, 352
narrative references 4, 5, 6, 136–7, 188, 230, 236, 282, 286, 291, 333, 352, 353, 354

Paris, judgement of 42, 49–50, 96–7, 244, 269
pastourelle, influence of 208–9, 325

senhal 143, 153, 155 and n. 4, 187 and n. 7, 241–2, 349
simile 1, 3, 5, 9–10, 14, 16, 17, 28, 29, 101, 344, 355
structure/syntax of examples 3, 15–16, 17, 25–6, 27, 36, 53–4, 56, 59, 61–2, 72–3, 79, 80, 132–3, 140, 193–6, 233–5, 282–5, 336–9

typology 3, 106, 114, 249–50

voice and person 4, 5, 6, 14, 23, 35, 38, 44, 73–4, 81, 137–9, 196–7, 235–6, 285–6, 287, 339–41, 344, 347, 348, 350, 351, 352, 354, 355
  female voice 110, 168, 177–8, 212, 219–20, 221, 222, 230, 339
  speech and dialogue 13, 14, 18, 19–20, 21, 22, 34–5, 57, 59, 67, 86–7, 92–4, 95–6, 99, 106, 112, 120, 122, 138–9, 197, 208–9, 247, 270, 314